Professional Responsibility

Professional Responsibility

Problems of Practice and the Profession

Third Edition

Nathan M. Crystal

Class of 1969
Professor of Professional Responsibility
University of South Carolina School of Law

ASPEN

PUBLISHERS

111 Eighth Avenue, New York, NY 10011
www.aspenpublishers.com

Permissions
Aspen Publishers
111 Eighth Avenue
New York, NY 10011

Printed in the United States of America.

2 3 4 5 6 7 8 9 0

ISBN 0-7355-5080-8

Library of Congress Cataloging-in-Publication Data

Crystal, Nathan M.
  Professional responsibility : problems of practice and the
profession / Nathan M. Crystal.—3rd ed.
      p. cm
  Includes index.
  ISBN (invalid) 0-7355-0625-3
  1. Legal ethics—United States. 2. Legal ethics—United States—Cases. I. Title.

  KF306.C79   2004
  174′.3′0973—dc22   2004040972

About Aspen Publishers

Aspen Publishers, headquartered in New York City, is a leading information provider for attorneys, business professionals, and law students. Written by preeminent authorities, our products consist of analytical and practical information covering both U.S. and international topics. We publish in the full range of formats, including updated manuals, books, periodicals, CDs, and online products.

Our proprietary content is complemented by 2,500 legal databases, containing over 11 million documents, available through our Loislaw division. Aspen Publishers also offers a wide range of topical legal and business databases linked to Loislaw's primary material. Our mission is to provide accurate, timely, and authoritative content in easily accessible formats, supported by unmatched customer care.

To order any Aspen Publishers title, go to *www.aspenpublishers.com* or call 1-800-638-8437.

To reinstate your manual update service, call 1-800-638-8437.

For more information on Loislaw products, go to *www.loislaw.com* or call 1-800-364-2512.

For Customer Care issues, e-mail *CustomerCare@aspenpublishers.com;* call 1-800-234-1660; or fax 1-800-901-9075.

Aspen Publishers
A Wolters Kluwer Company

To Nancy: all of my books are dedicated to you, but this one especially.

Summary of Contents

Contents

--------------------------------- Chapter 1 ---------------------------------
Introduction to Professional
Responsibility

——————————— **Chapter 2** ———————————
Defense and Prosecution of Criminal Cases

——————————— **Chapter 3** ———————————

Ethical Issues in Civil Litigation: The Client-Lawyer Relationship, Confidentiality, and Conflicts of Interest

—————————— Chapter 4 ——————————

Ethical Issues in Civil Litigation: Limitations on Zealous Representation, Alternative Dispute Resolution, and Delivery of Legal Services

——————————— PROBLEM 4-1 ———————————

FRIVOLOUS CLAIMS   338

——————————— PROBLEM 4-2 ———————————

INVESTIGATION: CONTACTS WITH EMPLOYEES   349

——————————— PROBLEM 4-3 ———————————

INVESTIGATION: SECRET TAPE RECORDING AND INADVERTENT DISCLOSURES   364

──────────── **Chapter 5** ────────────

Ethical Issues in Office Practice

—————— Chapter 6 ——————
Lawyers in Public Service: Judges, Government Attorneys, and Public Interest Lawyers

———————— **Chapter 7** ————————
Special Ethical Problems of Law Firms

Preface

The fundamental theme of this book is the necessity for lawyers to develop a philosophy of lawyering. Chapter 1 outlines three interrelated aspects of a philosophy of lawyering. At the personal level, a philosophy of lawyering deals with the relationship between lawyers' personal lives and values and their professional roles. At the practice level, a philosophy of lawyering provides guidance for lawyers on how to resolve uncertain issues of professional ethics. At the institutional level, a philosophy of lawyering involves a critical examination of the fundamental values of the legal system, such as the adversary system of dispute resolution, methods of regulating lawyers, and mechanisms for delivering legal services. Chapter 1 also provides an overview of various rules and standards of professional conduct and the regulatory structure governing lawyers.

Chapters 2 through 6, the core of the book, present difficult problems of professional responsibility in various areas of practice—criminal defense and prosecution, civil litigation, office practice, government, public interest, and the judiciary. These chapters focus on both the practice and the institutional dimensions of a theory of lawyering. The problems do not have easy answers and will require you to learn to exercise personal and professional judgment within a framework of rules of ethics.

The book is organized first by area of practice (chapters) and then by ethical concept within area of practice (chapter divisions). Thus, problems of the client-lawyer relationship, confidentiality, conflicts of interest, limitations on zealous representation, and delivery of legal services appear in several chapters. I have chosen this organization for several reasons. First, context matters; for example, confidentiality problems in the criminal defense area differ from those in office practice. The book includes frequent cross-references so that you can compare confidentiality or conflict of interest problems as they appear in different practice fields. I hope that review and comparison of issues in various types of practice will deepen your understanding of ethical dilemmas. Second, choice of area of practice is an important aspect of a person's philosophy of lawyering. Organization by area of practice should help you to obtain a feel for what it is like to be, for example, a criminal defense lawyer, a prosecutor, a civil litigator, or a business attorney. The book contains references to the literature on various areas of practice for those of you who would like to delve further into these issues.

Instructors who used the second edition will notice the following significant changes: First, I have added a modest number of cases to complement the text and problems and highlight several significant issues of professional responsibility. Second, some instructors may prefer to use a more traditional, doctrinal organization. The book can easily be adapted to this method of presenting the material. The teacher's manual provides a sample syllabus and other guidance for instructors who prefer this approach. Third, this edition incorporates significant developments since the last edition was published, particularly the final release of the Restatement (Third) of the Law Governing Lawyers, the 2002 and 2003 revisions to the Model Rules, and the Sarbanes-Oxley Act and regulations.

A number of instructors who used earlier editions offered very helpful comments that provide the foundation for this edition. My thanks especially go to Anita Bernstein (Emory), Jennifer Brown (Quinnipiac), Gerry Clark (Suffolk), David Cummins (Texas Tech), Marjorie Girth (Georgia State), Vincent Johnson (St. Mary's), Nancy Moore (Boston University), Andy Perlman (Suffolk), Roy Simon (Hofstra), and Lena Velasquez (California Western). Colleagues at South Carolina—Gregory Adams, Jane Aiken (now at Washington University), Ladson Boyle, James Flanagan, John Freeman, Alan Medlin, Dennis Nolan, Eldon Wedlock, and Robert Wilcox—reviewed portions of the manuscript and made invaluable suggestions. As always, my wife, Nancy McCormick, to whom this edition is dedicated, provided terrific support and assistance. Writing and revising this book continues to be both educational and pleasurable. I hope that students and instructors who use the book have a similar experience. Needless to say, I would appreciate receiving your comments.

Nathan Crystal

January 2004

Acknowledgments

I would like to thank the following authors and copyright holders for permission to reprint portions of their work:

American Academy of Matrimonial Lawyers, Bounds of Advocacy, Standards 1.3 and 3.2, with comments. Excerpts reprinted with consent of the American Academy of Matrimonial Lawyers.

American Bar Association, Canons of Professional Ethics, Canon 35; Formal Opinion 280, at 618. Copyright 1967. Reprinted with permission of the American Bar Association.

American Bar Association, Commission on Evaluation of Professional Standards (Kutak Commission), Discussion Draft of the Model Rules of Professional Conduct (Jan. 30, 1980), Rule 3.1. Copyright 1980. Reprinted with permission of the American Bar Association.

American Bar Association, Committee on Professional Ethics and Grievances, Formal Opinion 266. Copyright 1945. Reprinted with permission of the American Bar Association.

American Bar Association, Committee on Ethics and Professional Responsibility, the following Formal Opinions: 335 (1974), at 3; 339 (1975), at 3; 346 (1982), at 9; 85-352, at 4; 87-355, at 2; 91-359, at 6; 92-362, at 4-5; 92-363; 92-368, at 1; 93-372, at 2; 95-396; 99-413, at 11; 01-422. Reprinted with permission of the American Bar Association.

American Bar Association, Criminal Justice Mental Health Standard, §7-4.2 cmt. (1986). Copyright 1986. Reprinted with permission of the American Bar Association.

American Bar Association, Model Code of Judicial Conduct (1999), Canon 5A(3)(d); definition of "impartiality." Copyright 1999. Reprinted with permission of the American Bar Association.

American Bar Association, Model Code of Professional Responsibility, Disciplinary Rule 5-102(A) and Ethical Considerations 5-9, 7-14, and 7-21. Copyright 1983. Reprinted with permission of the American Bar Association.

American Bar Association, Model Rules of Professional Conduct and Comments as follows: 1.5(e); 1.7 cmts. 22, 23, 27; 1.8 cmt. 11; 1.8(c); 1.8(d); 1.14 cmts. 5, 6; 2.3(a) cmt. 3; 3.3 cmt. 9 (1983); 3.3 cmt. 6; 3.4(e); 3.6(b); 3.6(c); 3.8(d); 4.2; 4.2 cmt. 4 (1983); 4.3 cmts. 2, 7; 4.4(a); 4.4 cmt. 3;

Nathan M. Crystal, Ethical Problems in Marital Practice, 30 S.C. L. Rev. 321, 325-328 (1979). Reprinted with permission of the South Carolina Law Review.

Charles P. Curtis, The Ethics of Advocacy, 4 Stan. L. Rev. 3, 14-18 (1951). Copyright 1951 by the Board of Trustees of the Leland Stanford Junior University. Reprinted with permission of the Stanford Law Review and Fred B. Rothman & Co.

Developments in the Law — Conflicts of Interest in the Legal Profession, 94 Harv. L. Rev. 1244, 1428-1433 (1981). Copyright 1981 by the Harvard Law Review Association. Reprinted with permission.

Arnold N. Enker, The Rationale of the Rule That Forbids a Lawyer to Be Advocate and Witness in the Same Case, 1977 Am. Bar Found. Res. J. 455, 457 and 463. Copyright 1977. Reprinted with permission of the University of Chicago Press.

William H. Fortune et al., Modern Litigation and Professional Responsibility Handbook §4.5, at 179-180 and §14.3.1, at 507-509 (2d ed. 2001). Copyright 1996. Reprinted with permission of Aspen Publishers.

Monroe H. Freedman, Must You Be the Devil's Advocate? Legal Times of Washington (Aug. 23, 1993). Reprinted with permission of the Legal Times. Copyright 1993.

Monroe H. Freedman, The Morality of Lawyering, Legal Times of Washington (Sept. 20, 1993). Reprinted with permission of the Legal Times. Copyright 1993.

Monroe H. Freedman & Abbe Smith, Understanding Lawyers' Ethics, 13-14, 201 (2d ed. 2002). Reprinted with permission of the authors and Matthew Bender & Co., Inc., a member of the LexisNexis Group. All rights reserved.

Stephen B. Goldberg et al., Dispute Resolution: Negotiation, Mediation, and Other Processes, 212-215 (4th Ed. 2003). Reprinted with permission of Aspen Publishers.

Geoffrey C. Hazard, Jr. & W. William Hodes, The Law of Lawyering, §26.3 at 26-6, §29.11 at 17 (3d ed. 2001). Reprinted with permission of Aspen Publishers.

Oliver A. Houck, With Charity for All, 93 Yale L.J. 1415, 1439-1443 (1984). Reprinted with permission of The Yale Law Journal Company, Fred B. Rothman & Company, and the author.

Seth F. Kreimer & David Rudovsky, Double Helix, Double Bind: Factual Innocence and Postconviction DNA Testing, 151 U. Pa. L. Rev. 547, 555-557, 606-616 (2002). Reprinted with permission of the University of Pennsylvania Law Review.

Catherine J. Lanctot, The Duty of Zealous Advocacy and the Ethics of the Federal Government Lawyer: The Three Hardest Questions, 64 S. Cal. L. Rev. 951, 955-957 (1991). Reprinted with permission of the Southern California Law Review.

David Luban, Lawyers and Justice: An Ethical Study, 84, 341 (1988). Copyright 1988 by Princeton University Press. Reprinted with permission of Princeton University Press.

Gerald E. Lynch, The Lawyer as Informer, 1986 Duke L.J. 491, 537. Reprinted with permission of the Duke Law Journal.

Ronald E. Mallen & Jeffrey M. Smith, Legal Malpractice, (vol. 4) §31.6, at 664 (4th ed. 1996). Reprinted with permission of West Group.

Sara Mathias, Electing Justice: A Handbook of Judicial Election Reforms, 5 (1990). Reprinted with permission of the American Judicature Society.

Geoffrey P. Miller, Government Lawyers' Ethics in a System of Checks and Balances, 54 U. Chi. L. Rev. 1293, 1294-1295 (1987). Reprinted with permission of the University of Chicago Law Review.

Leslie A. Minkus, The Sale of a Law Practice: Toward a Professionally Responsible Approach, 12 Golden Gate U. L. Rev. 353, 356-357 (1982). Reprinted with permission of the Golden Gate University Law Review and Leslie A. Minkus.

John B. Mitchell, The Ethics of the Criminal Defense Attorney — New Answers to Old Questions, 32 Stan. L. Rev. 293, 296-303, 321-323, 326-331 (1980). Copyright 1980 by the Board of Trustees of the Leland Stanford Junior University. Reprinted with permission of the Stanford Law Review and Fred B. Rothman & Co.

Lee A. Pizzimenti, Prohibiting Lawyers from Assisting in Unconscionable Transactions: Using an Overt Tool, 72 Marq. L. Rev. 151, 174 (1989). Reprinted with permission of the Marquette Law Review.

Ted Schneyer, Moral Philosophy's Standard Misconception of Legal Ethics, 1984 Wis. L. Rev. 1529, 1532-1533. Reprinted with permission of the author.

E. Wayne Thode, Reporter's Notes to the Code of Judicial Conduct, 84-85 (1974). Copyright 1974. Reprinted with permission of the American Bar Association.

Michael Tigar, Setting the Record Straight on the Defense of John Demjanjuk, Legal Times of Washington (Sept. 6, 1993). Reprinted with permission of the Legal Times. Copyright 1993.

Rodney J. Uphoff, The Role of the Criminal Defense Lawyer in Representing the Mentally Impaired Defendant: Zealous Advocate or Officer of the Court? 1988 Wis. L. Rev. 65, 99. Reprinted with permission of the Wisconsin Law Review.

Lyle Warrick, Judicial Selection in the United States: A Compendium of Provisions, 1993, page v. Reprinted with permission of the American Judicature Society.

James J. White, Machiavelli and the Bar: Ethical Limitations on Lying in Negotiation, 1980 Am. B. Found. Res. J. 926, 927-928. Copyright 1980. Reprinted with permission of the University of Chicago Press.

Wigmore on Evidence (Vol. 8) §2292, at 554 (McNaughton ed. 1961). Reprinted with permission of Little, Brown & Co.

Barry Winston, "Stranger Than True: Why I Defend Guilty Clients," Harper's 70-71. Copyright 1986. All rights reserved. Reproduced from the December issue by special permission of Harper's Magazine.

Professional Responsibility

Chapter 1

Introduction to Professional Responsibility

A. The Foundations of Professional Responsibility

Almost all lawyers want to be professionally responsible, but what does it mean to be a professionally responsible lawyer? Issues of professional responsibility pose some of the most difficult problems that lawyers face in practice. The perplexing nature of these problems usually flows from the fact that troubling issues of professional ethics involve tensions or conflicts among three ideas that are central to the lawyer's role: the lawyer as fiduciary, the lawyer as an officer of the court functioning in an adversarial system, and the lawyer as an individual with personal values and interests. As the Preamble to the American Bar Association's Model Rules of Professional Conduct says:

> Virtually all difficult ethical problems arise from conflict between a lawyer's responsibilities to clients, to the legal system and to the lawyer's own interest in remaining an ethical person while earning a satisfactory living.

Model Rules, Preamble, ¶9.

1. The Lawyer as Fiduciary

Courts, disciplinary bodies, and scholars often state that lawyers owe fiduciary obligations to their clients. As we will see, many of the rules of professional ethics can be understood as expressing fiduciary duties of attorneys. In addition, the law of agency, which governs the client-lawyer relationship, also defines the nature of fiduciary obligations. Indeed, one leading scholar of professional ethics, Professor Charles Wolfram, has referred to lawyers as "fiduciary agents."[1]

---

1. Charles W. Wolfram, Modern Legal Ethics 145 (1986) [hereinafter Wolfram, Modern Legal Ethics]. On the relationship between agency law and professional responsibility see Deborah A. DeMott, The Lawyer as Agent, 67 Fordham L. Rev. 301 (1998).

What does it mean to say that a lawyer is a fiduciary? A fiduciary relationship is different from an arm's-length business relationship. In an arm's-length transaction the parties do not have obligations to protect the interests of the other party, although they do owe each other certain obligations, such as the duty not to engage in fraud. Instead, parties to an ordinary business transaction have the responsibility to protect their own interests. By contrast, fiduciaries have special obligations to care for and to protect the interests of their beneficiaries or clients.[2] While fiduciary relationships may have contractual aspects (for example, fee agreements between lawyers and clients), the contractual aspects of fiduciary relationships are secondary to the duties that fiduciaries owe to their clients.

The fiduciary obligations that lawyers owe their clients include three specific duties: First, attorneys owe their clients a *duty of competence*, a duty expressed in American Bar Association (ABA) Model Rule 1.1. See also Model Rule 1.3 (duty to handle matter with reasonable diligence and promptness).[3] Section B below discusses the method of adoption of rules of professional conduct and the ABA's role in the process. Note that the duty of competence goes beyond knowledge of the law to encompass skills, preparation, and diligence. Lawyers who violate the duty of competence not only commit an ethical transgression but also can be held liable to their clients for damages.[4] Indeed, courts are increasingly willing to hold attorneys liable even to third parties who are not clients.[5]

Second, attorneys owe their clients a *duty of loyalty*. The ethical rules dealing with conflicts of interest express this concept of loyalty. Conflicts of interest can arise in various forms: between current clients in a single matter or in unrelated matters (Model Rule 1.7), between a current client and a former client (Model Rule 1.9), conflicts between the interest of a client and a lawyer's personal or financial interest (Model Rule 1.8(a)).[6]

The rules dealing with conflicts of interest are rarely absolute. For example, a lawyer is not necessarily precluded under Model Rule 1.9 from undertaking representation against a former client. The lawyer may do so, even without the former client's consent, if the current and former matters are not "substantially related."[7] The fact that the rules do not adopt a per se prohibition on representation against a former client shows that the issue involves interests in addition

---

2. See Restatement (Second) of Agency §13, cmt. *a* (1958).

3. See also id. §379(1) (agent subject to duty to principal to act with standard care and with the skill that is standard in locality for kind of work that agent is employed to perform and, in addition, to exercise any special skill that agent has).

4. See generally Ronald E. Mallen & Jeffrey M. Smith, Legal Malpractice (5th ed. 2000) [hereinafter Mallen & Smith, Legal Malpractice]; Manuel R. Ramos, Legal Malpractice: The Profession's Dirty Little Secret, 47 Vand. L. Rev. 1657 (1994).

5. See Restatement (Third) of the Law Governing Lawyers §51 (2000) (Duty of Care to Certain Nonclients).

6. See also Restatement (Second) of Agency §387 (1958).

7. See id. §396 (after termination of relationship agent "has no duty not to compete with the principal").

to those of the former client. When we discuss former client conflicts of interest, we will examine those interests in more detail.

Third, attorneys owe their clients a *duty of confidentiality*. While closely related to the duty of loyalty, the obligation of confidentiality is important enough to warrant separate treatment. Attorneys have an ethical obligation to maintain confidentiality of information. Model Rule 1.6 broadly expresses this duty as follows: "A lawyer shall not reveal information relating to representation of a client unless the client gives informed consent. . . ."[8] Like the rules dealing with conflicts of interest, the duty of confidentiality is not absolute. Rule 1.6 provides a number of exceptions to the duty, exceptions that express interests thought to be sufficiently important to override the general duty of confidentiality.[9]

The scope and limitations of the duty of confidentiality have been among the most controversial issues facing the profession in recent years. Debate continues to rage over issues such as whether lawyers should be required to reveal perjury committed by criminal defendants and whether lawyers must reveal information showing that clients have committed fraud in business transactions.

2. The Lawyer as an Officer of the Court Functioning in an Adversarial System of Justice

Professional obligations would be difficult enough if lawyers simply owed fiduciary obligations to their clients. However, lawyers serve not only as fiduciaries but also as officers of the court functioning in an adversarial system of justice.

What is meant by an *adversarial system of justice?* In broad terms an adversarial system is characterized by (1) a neutral decisionmaker, (2) competent advocates zealously presenting the positions of each of the interested parties, and (3) rules of procedure fairly designed to allow the presentation of relevant evidence to the decisionmaker.[10] A number of rules of professional conduct that we will study are designed to preserve the integrity and proper functioning of the adversarial system. For example, lawyers may not make false statements of law or fact to tribunals (Model Rule 3.3); try to influence judges, jurors, or other officials by improper means (Rule 3.5); or engage in trial publicity that has a substantial likelihood of materially prejudicing a proceeding (Rule 3.6).

Like other rules of professional conduct, the rules dealing with the maintenance of the adversarial system are subject to exceptions and qualifications.

8. See also id. §395.

9. Similarly, agency law recognizes exceptions to the duty of confidentiality. The Restatement of Agency provides that an agent is privileged to reveal confidential information to protect the superior interest of the agent or of a third person, including information that the principal is committing or about to commit a crime. Id. §395, cmt. *f.*

10. Charles W. Sorenson, Jr., Disclosure Under Federal Rule of Civil Procedure 26(a)—"Much Ado about Nothing?" 46 Hastings L.J. 679, 764 (1995).

For example, consider the possibility of what could be called a "pure" adversarial system. Under such a system, lawyers would have no obligation to evaluate the merits of their clients' cases. If a client wished to bring a case in court, the lawyer could do so. Indeed, we might even go further, viewing lawyers as, in essence, common carriers, required to bring an action in court if clients wanted to employ their services. The prevailing conception of the adversarial system is not, however, this pure version. Under the standard view of the adversarial system, the lawyer may not bring an action, indeed may not file any document in court, when the claim would be frivolous. See Model Rule 3.1 and Federal Rule of Civil Procedure 11. We will consider these limitations in Problem 4-1.

Many lawyers function in capacities that do not involve litigation. Major law firms represent corporate clients in a wide range of business and financial transactions. During the savings and loan debacle in the 1990s some prominent law firms were accused of assisting their clients in fraud. Lawyer participation in corporate fraud again became a major public issue in 2002 in connection with scandals involving Enron and WorldCom. In response to these recent scandals, Congress enacted the Sarbanes-Oxley Act of 2002, which requires the Securities and Exchange Commission to adopt regulations establishing standards of professional conduct for lawyers appearing before the SEC.[11] In Problem 5-2 we will examine the ethical and legal issues that arise when a lawyer represents a corporate client that is engaging in fraud.

3. The Lawyer as a Person with Personal and Financial Interests

Our lives have many dimensions: work, family, religion, community. As a professional occupation law is or will soon be an important part of your lives, but most of us hope that the law will not become our entire life. Personal interests and professional obligations interact in various and complex ways. Since the practice of law is both a profession and a livelihood for most lawyers, the relationship between the business and professional aspects of practice is significant. The practice of law has become much more competitive in recent years. Solo practitioners, small to medium-sized firms, and mega-firms practicing throughout the country and the world face growing economic pressures. In part, the pressure flows from changes in the market for legal services, including increased advertising and solicitation by lawyers and greater scrutiny of fees by clients such as insurance companies.

The rules of professional conduct deal to a limited degree with the business aspects of legal practice. The rules contain some regulation of fee agreements and business transactions between lawyers and clients (Model Rules 1.5 and 1.8(a)), limitations on advertising and solicitation (Model Rules 7.1-7.5), and prohibitions on unauthorized practice of law (Model Rule 5.5). But the formal

---

11. 15 U.S.C. §7245.

rules only touch the ways in which business considerations shape a whole range of issues of professional ethics, such as conflicts of interest, establishment of legal fees, and marketing of legal services. Moreover, the rules barely hint at the relationship between the business pressure of practice and the personal lives of lawyers.

Professional obligations can involve personal values and interests at a level deeper than financial. For example, a lawyer who is opposed to abortion may be appointed to represent a minor who is seeking the right to have an abortion. A lawyer who strongly supports the rights of gays and lesbians may represent a testator who has decided to disinherit his gay son. Problem 5-4 considers issues involved in counseling clients in estate planning.

How should lawyers think about resolving the tensions that arise among their obligations as fiduciaries, as officers of the court, and as individuals with their own interests and values? To begin to think about these tensions, consider the following case.

In re Pautler

Supreme Court of Colorado, En Banc
47 P.3d 1175 (2002)

Justice KOURLIS delivered the Opinion of the Court.

> I will employ such means as are consistent with Truth and Honor; I will treat all persons whom I encounter through my practice of law with fairness, courtesy, respect, and honesty.

Oath of Admission—Colorado State Bar, 2002.

In this proceeding we reaffirm that members of our profession must adhere to the highest moral and ethical standards. Those standards apply regardless of motive. Purposeful deception by an attorney licensed in our state is intolerable, even when it is undertaken as a part of attempting to secure the surrender of a murder suspect. A prosecutor may not deceive an unrepresented person by impersonating a public defender. . . .

I.

The hearing board found the following facts by clear and convincing evidence: On June 8th, 1998, Chief Deputy District Attorney Mark Pautler arrived at a gruesome crime scene where three women lay murdered. All died from blows to the head with a wood splitting maul. While at the scene ("Chenango apartment"), Pautler learned that three other individuals had contacted the sheriff's department with information about the murders. Pautler drove to the location where those witnesses waited ("Belleview apartment"). Upon arrival, he learned that the killer was William Neal. Neal had apparently abducted the three murder victims one at a time, killing the first two at the Chenango apartment over a three-day period. One of the witnesses at the Belleview apartment, J.D.Y., was the third woman abducted. Neal also took her to the Chenango apartment where he tied her to a bed using eyebolts he had screwed into the floor specifically for that purpose. While J.D.Y. lay spread-eagled on the bed, Neal brought a fourth woman to the Chenango apartment. He taped her mouth shut and tied her to a chair within J.D.Y.'s view. Then, as J.D.Y. watched in horror, Neal split the fourth victim's skull with the maul. That night he raped J.D.Y. at gunpoint.

The following morning, Neal returned with J.D.Y. to the Belleview apartment. First one friend, a female, and then a second friend, a male, arrived at the apartment. Neal held J.D.Y. and her two friends in the Belleview apartment over thirty hours. He dictated the details of his crimes into a recorder. Finally, he abandoned the apartment, leaving instructions with J.D.Y. and her friends to contact police, and to page him when the police arrived.

When Pautler reached the Belleview apartment, Deputy Sheriff Cheryl Moore had already paged Neal according to the instructions Neal had left. Neal answered the page by phoning the apartment on a cell-phone. The ensuing conversation lasted three-and-a-half hours, during which Moore listened to Neal describe his crimes in detail. She took notes of the conversation and occasionally passed messages to Pautler and other officers at the scene. Sheriff Moore developed a rapport with Neal and continuously encouraged his peaceful surrender. Meanwhile, other law enforcement officers taped the conversation with a hand-held recorder set next to a second phone in the apartment. Efforts to ascertain the location of Neal's cell-phone were unsuccessful.

At one point, Neal made it clear he would not surrender without legal representation; Moore passed a message to that effect to Pautler. Neal first requested an attorney who had represented him previously, Daniel Plattner, but then also requested a public defender (PD). Pautler managed to find Plattner's office number in the apartment telephone book. When he called the number, however, Pautler received a recorded message indicating the telephone was no longer in service. Pautler believed that Plattner had left the practice of law, and he therefore made no additional attempt to contact Plattner. Upon learning that Plattner was unavailable, Sheriff Moore agreed with Neal to secure a public defender. However, no one in the apartment made any attempt to contact a PD or the PD's office.

Pautler later testified that he believed any defense lawyer would advise Neal not to talk with law enforcement. Pautler also testified that he did not trust anyone at the PD's office, although on cross-examination he admitted there was at least one PD he did trust. Law enforcement officials present at the Belleview apartment, testifying in Pautler's defense, said they would not have allowed a defense attorney to speak with Neal because they needed the conversation to continue until they could apprehend Neal. Instead of contacting the PD's office, or otherwise contacting defense counsel, Pautler offered to impersonate a PD, and those law enforcement agents at the scene agreed.

When Neal again requested to speak to an attorney, Sheriff Moore told him that "the PD has just walked in," and that the PD's name was "Mark Palmer," a pseudonym Pautler had chosen for himself. Moore proceeded to brief "Palmer" on the events thus far, with Neal listening over the telephone. Moore then introduced Pautler to Neal as a PD. Pautler took the telephone and engaged Neal in conversation. Neal communicated to Pautler that he sought three guarantees from the sheriff's office before he would surrender: 1) that he would be isolated from other detainees, 2) that he could smoke cigarettes, and 3) that "his lawyer" would be present. To the latter request, Pautler answered, "Right, I'll be present."

Neal also asked, "Now, um, at this point, I want to know, um, what my rights are—you feel my rights are right now." Pautler did not answer the question directly, but asked for clarification. Neal then indicated he sought assurance that the sheriff's office would honor the promises made. Pautler communicated to Neal that he believed the sheriff's department would keep him isolated as requested. Pautler did not explain to Neal any additional rights, nor did Neal request more information on the topic. In later conversations, it was clear that Neal believed "Mark Palmer" from the PD's office represented him.

Neal eventually surrendered to law enforcement without incident. An officer involved in the arrest approached Pautler with the news that Neal had asked whether his attorney was present. Pautler was at the scene but did not speak with Neal, although he asked the officer to tell Neal that the attorney was indeed present. Evidence at the hearing indicated that Neal was put into a holding cell by himself and received his requested cigarettes as well as a telephone call.

Pautler made no effort to correct his misrepresentations to Neal that evening, nor in the days following. James Aber, head of the Jefferson County Public Defender's office, eventually undertook Neal's defense. Aber only learned of the deception two weeks later when listening to the tapes of the conversation whereupon he recognized Pautler's voice. Aber testified at Pautler's trial that he was confused when Neal initially said that a Mark Palmer already represented him. Aber told the board that he had difficulty establishing a trusting relationship with the defendant after he told Neal that no Mark Palmer existed within the PD's office. Several months later Neal dismissed the PD's office and continued his case pro se, with advisory counsel appointed by the court. Ultimately, Neal was convicted of the murders and received the death penalty. The parties dispute whether Neal dismissed Aber out of the mistrust precipitated by Pautler's earlier deception. . . .

We take note of additional facts pertinent to our decision here. First, Neal was an unrepresented person at the time Pautler spoke with him; the parties stipulated to this fact after the PDJ's ruling but before Pautler's trial. Second, Pautler is a peace officer, level Ia, as defined in section 18-1-901(3)(l)(II)(A), 6 C.R.S. (2001), by virtue of his position in the DA's office. As such, Pautler carries a badge and is authorized to carry a weapon. He was armed during these events. He is further authorized to use lethal force, when necessary, to apprehend a dangerous felon. §18-1-707(2)(a)(I), 6 C.R.S. (2001). Also, all parties acknowledged Pautler's reputation for honesty and high ethical standards. Finally, Pautler testified that given the same circumstance, he would not act differently, apart from informing Neal's defense counsel of the ruse earlier.

II.

Lawyers, as guardians of the law, play a vital role in the preservation of society. The fulfillment of this role requires an understanding by lawyers of their relationship with and function in our legal system. A consequent obligation of lawyers is to maintain the highest standards of ethical conduct.

Colo. R.P.C. pmbl.

The jokes, cynicism, and falling public confidence related to lawyers and the legal system may signal that we are not living up to our obligation; but, they certainly do not signal that the obligation itself has eroded. For example, the profession itself is engaging in a nation-wide project designed to emphasize that "truthfulness, honesty and candor are the core of the core values of the legal profession."[2] Lawyers themselves are recognizing that the public perception that lawyers twist words to meet their own goals and pay little attention to the truth, strikes at the very heart of the profession—as well as at the heart of the system of justice. Lawyers serve our system of justice, and if lawyers are dishonest, then there is a perception that the system, too, must be dishonest. Certainly, the reality of such behavior must be abjured so that the perception of it may diminish. With due regard, then, for the gravity of the issues we confront, we turn to the facts of this case.

III.

. . . The complaint charged Pautler with violating Colo. RPC 8.4: "It is professional misconduct for a lawyer to: . . . (c) engage in conduct involving dishonesty, fraud, deceit or misrepresentation." This rule and its commentary are devoid of any exception. Nor do the Rules distinguish lawyers working in law enforcement from other lawyers, apart from additional responsibilities imposed upon prosecutors. See Colo. RPC 3.8; see also Berger v. United States, 295 U.S. 78, 88 (1935).

A. PAUTLER'S DEFENSE

We are unpersuaded by Pautler's assertion that his deception of Neal was "justified" under the circumstances, and we underscore the rationale set forth in People v. Reichman, 819 P.2d 1035 (Colo. 1991). There, a district attorney sought to bolster a police agent's undercover identity by faking the agent's arrest and then filing false charges against him. Id. at 1036. The DA failed to

---

2. Professional Reform Initiative project of the National Conference of Bar Presidents, 2001.

notify the court of the scheme. Id. We upheld a hearing board's imposition of public censure for the DA's participation in the ploy. Id. at 1039. [The court then discussed decisions from New York and Illinois in which prosecutors were disciplined for deception.]

Thus, in *Reichman*, we rejected the same defense to Rule 8.4(c) that Pautler asserts here. We ruled that even a noble motive does not warrant departure from the Rules of Professional Conduct. Moreover, we applied the prohibition against deception a fortiori to prosecutors:

> District attorneys in Colorado owe a very high duty to the public because they are governmental officials holding constitutionally created offices. This court has spoken out strongly against misconduct by public officials who are lawyers. The respondent's responsibility to enforce the laws in his judicial district grants him no license to ignore those laws or the Code of Professional Responsibility.

Reichman, 819 P.2d at 1038-39 (citations omitted).

We stress, however, that the reasons behind Pautler's conduct are not inconsequential. In *Reichman*, we also stated, "While the respondent's motives and the erroneous belief of other public prosecutors that the respondent's conduct was ethical do not excuse these violations of the Code of Professional Responsibility, they are mitigating factors to be taken into account in assessing the appropriate discipline." Id. at 1039. Hence, *Reichman* unambiguously directs that prosecutors cannot involve themselves in deception, even with selfless motives, lest they run afoul of Rule 8.4(c).

[handwritten margin note: not to be excused but account for in discipline]

B. Imminent Public Harm Exception

Pautler requests this court to craft an exception to the Rules for situations constituting a threat of "imminent public harm." In his defense, Pautler elicited the testimony of an elected district attorney from a metropolitan jurisdiction. The attorney testified that during one particularly difficult circumstance, a kidnapper had a gun to the head of a hostage. The DA allowed the kidnapper to hear over the telephone that the DA would not prosecute if the kidnapper released the hostage. The DA, along with everyone else involved, knew the DA's representation was false and that the DA fully intended to prosecute the kidnapper. Pautler analogizes his deceptive conduct to that of the DA in the hostage case and suggests that both cases give cause for an exception to Rule 8.4(c).

We first note that no complaint reached this court alleging that the DA in the kidnapper scenario violated Rule 8.4(c), and therefore, this court made no decision condoning that DA's behavior. But assuming arguendo that the DA acted in conformity with the Rules, one essential fact distinguishes the hostage scenario from Pautler's case: the DA there had no immediately feasible alternative. If the DA did not immediately state that he would not prosecute, the hostage might die. In contrast, here Neal was in the midst of negotiating his surrender to authorities. Neal did make references to his continued ability to kill, which Pautler described as threats, but nothing indicated that any specific person's safety was in imminent danger. More importantly, without second guessing crime scene tactics, we do not believe Pautler's choices were so limited. Pautler had several choices. He had telephone numbers and a telephone and could have called a PD. Indeed, he attempted to contact attorney Plattner, an indication that communicating with a defense attorney was not precluded by the circumstances. Pautler also had the option of exploring with Neal the possibility that no attorney would be called until after he surrendered. While we do not opine, in hindsight, as to which option was best, we are adamant that when presented with choices, at least one of which conforms to the Rules, an attorney must not select an option that involves deceit or misrepresentation.[6] The level of ethical standards to which our profession holds all attorneys, especially prosecutors, leaves no room for deceiving Neal in this manner. Pautler cannot compromise his integrity, and that of our profession, irrespective of the cause.

[The Court then discussed and rejected Pautler's defenses of duress, choice of evils, and permissible misrepresentation during negotiation under the comment to Model Rule 4.1. The Court also found that even though Pautler was a "peace officer" pursuant to Colorado statute by virtue of being a district attorney, his obligations as an attorney "trump" his other duties, including apprehension of criminals.]

IV.

The complaint also charges Pautler with violating Rule 4.3. . . . This rule targets precisely the conduct in which Pautler engaged. At all times relevant, Pautler represented the People of the State of Colorado. The parties stipulated that Neal was an unrepresented person. Pautler deceived Neal and then took no steps to correct the misunderstanding either at the time of arrest or in the days following. Pautler's failure in this respect was an opportunity lost. Where he could have tempered the negative consequences resulting from the deception, he instead allowed them to linger.

While it is unclear whether Pautler actually gave advice to Neal, he certainly did not inform Neal to retain counsel. In addition, Pautler went further than implying he was disinterested; he purported to represent Neal. Without doubt, Pautler's conduct violated the letter of Colo. RPC 4.3.

For reasons substantially similar to those above, we refuse to graft an exception to this rule that would justify or excuse Pautler's actions. Instead, we affirm the ruling of the hearing board finding a violation of Colo. RPC 4.3 and turn now to consider the sanction imposed.

---

6. We do not address whether, under some unique circumstances, an "imminent public harm" exception could ever apply to the Colorado Rules of Professional Conduct. We hold only that this is not such case.

V.

[In deciding the appropriate sanction, the Court used the framework set forth in the ABA Standards for Imposing Lawyer Sanctions. These standards require examination of the duty involved, the lawyer's mental state, the potential or actual injury caused by the lawyer's misconduct, and the existence of aggravating or mitigating circumstances. Under the standards, a lawyer who engages in deceit or misrepresentation typically should receive at least a suspension and in extreme cases disbarment. The Court found that the mitigating factors present in the case outweighed the aggravating factors and imposed a three-month suspension, stayed during twelve months of probation.]

Notes and Questions

1. As the introductory text points out, lawyers often face difficult decisions involving a tension between their obligations as fiduciaries, officers of the court, and human beings. Try and put yourself in Pautler's position. Why do you suppose he acted the way he did? What did he consider to be his most important obligation?

2. Now try and put yourself in the position of the judges deciding the case. What did they consider to be Pautler's most important obligation?

3. Pautler made the offer to impersonate the PD. Suppose Pautler had decided that he could not personally impersonate a PD because that would be unethical, but he suggested that one of the officers on the scene impersonate a PD. Would that have been improper? Read Model Rule 8.4(a). Suppose an officer rather than Pautler suggested that the officer impersonate the PD. What should Pautler have done then?

4. As the court points out, prosecutors and other government attorneys have heightened ethical obligations beyond those applicable to other attorneys. We will consider some of those obligations in connection with Problem 2-10.

5. Discipline of attorneys for misconduct is one of several formal mechanisms for regulating lawyer conduct. Section D of this chapter discusses the disciplinary process and other methods of regulating lawyer conduct in more detail. The conduct of lawyers, however, is often governed more by informal mechanisms, such as the culture of the institutions (law firms, corporations, or government agencies) where lawyers work. Did you learn anything from *Pautler* about informal methods of regulation?

B. Resolving Tensions in the Lawyer's Role: Complying with Rules and Standards of Professional Conduct and the Law Governing Lawyers

In re Pautler suggests an answer to the question of how lawyers should resolve tensions they face in determining their professional obligations: Follow the rules of professional conduct applicable to lawyers. We will consider later in this chapter whether this answer is sufficient. But before doing so we need to be more precise in specifying the rules applicable to lawyers. These rules can be divided into two categories: professional rules and standards and the law governing lawyers.

1. *Professional Rules and Standards: ABA Codes of Ethics, Ethics Advisory Opinions, Specialized Codes, and Practice Norms*

In almost all states, authority to regulate the practice of law in the state courts rests with the highest court in the state. New York is a notable exception. In New York, section 90 of the Judiciary Law authorizes the four appellate divisions of the New York Supreme Court to issue rules of conduct for lawyers in the state. Each federal court has its own rules of admission and practice, but these rules often follow those of the state in which the federal court sits.[12]

Pursuant to their authority to regulate the practice of law, courts issue a number of rules. The primary focus of this book is on the rules of professional conduct. Rather than writing their own rules of professional conduct, most state and federal courts base their rules on the American Bar Association's Model Rules of Professional Conduct, originally adopted in 1983.

While the ABA has no legal authority over the practice of law, it does wield considerable influence in the area of professional responsibility. The Model Rules of Professional Conduct is the third in a series of ABA recommendations regarding lawyers' ethics. The immediate predecessor to the Model Rules was the ABA's Model Code of Professional Responsibility, adopted in 1969. The 1969 Code succeeded the ABA's Canons of Ethics, issued in 1908 and amended on a number of occasions until replaced by the Code.[13]

Even though the Code of Professional Responsibility is no longer in effect in most jurisdictions, some familiarity with the Code is useful because many provisions of the Model Rules are based on provisions of the Code and because a number of important court decisions under the Code continue to be relevant under the Model Rules. This book refers to significant provisions of the Code when relevant.

The format of the Code differs significantly from that of the Model Rules. The Code has a three-part structure: canons, disciplinary rules (DRs), and

---

12. See Judith A. McMorrow and Daniel R. Coquillette, The Federal Law of Attorney Conduct (2001); Bruce A. Green, Whose Rules of Professional Conduct Should Govern Lawyers in Federal Court and How Should the Rules be Created? 64 Geo. Wash. L. Rev. 460 (1996).

13. For an overview of the history of codes of professional conduct in the United States and a comparison with developments in other countries, see Mary C. Daly, The Dichotomy Between Standards and Rules: A New Way of Understanding the Difference in Perceptions of Lawyer Codes of Conduct by U.S. and Foreign Lawyers, 32 Vand. Transnatl. L. 1117 (1999).

ethical considerations (ECs). The drafters intended for the canons to serve as axioms of lawyers' obligations. For example, Canon 4 states: "A lawyer should preserve the confidences and secrets of a client." The disciplinary rules are detailed black-letter statements of minimum standards, the violation of which could be the basis of professional discipline. By contrast, the ethical considerations serve as both commentary on the disciplinary rules and aspirational norms that lawyers should strive to achieve, but the violation of which would not be the basis of discipline.[14]

Soon after its adoption, the Code of Professional Responsibility was criticized on two grounds. First, the division into canons, ethical considerations, and disciplinary rules was complex and confusing.[15] Second, the Code concentrated on the role of lawyers as advocates, largely ignoring representation as counselors or transactional attorneys. In 1977, only eight years after adopting the Code, the ABA appointed a Commission on Evaluation of Professional Standards (the Kutak Commission) to recommend revisions to the Code. The Kutak Commission instead proposed replacement of the Code, and in 1983 the ABA adopted the Model Rules of Professional Conduct.

The Model Rules abandoned the structure of the Code and adopted a simpler framework of black-letter rules followed by comments, much like the Restatements. The Model Rules are grouped under eight sections:

1. client-lawyer relationship
2. counselor
3. advocate
4. transactions with persons other than clients
5. law firms and associations
6. public service
7. information about legal services
8. maintaining the integrity of the profession

sections of model rules

Some of the rules, such as Rule 1.8 dealing with prohibited transactions, are quite specific; others, such as Rule 1.7 dealing with conflicts of interest, set forth general standards. Some provisions of the Model Rules are not rules at all because they give lawyers discretion as to how to act. For example, Rule 1.6(b) and comment 15 state that lawyers have professional discretion to reveal confidential information in some situations. Other provisions are aspirational, as illustrated by Model Rule 6.1, which states that lawyers "should aspire" to render at least 50 hours of pro bono service per year. As to the authority of the comments, ¶21 of the Scope states: "The Comments are intended as guides to interpretation, but the text of each Rule is authoritative."

---

14. See ABA, Model Code of Professional Responsibility, Preliminary Statement.
15. Geoffrey C. Hazard, Jr., Address, Legal Ethics: Legal Rules and Professional Aspirations, 30 Clev. St. L. Rev. 571 (1981).

More than 40 states adopted the 1983 version of the Model Rules, although most states approved some variations from the ABA's Model Rules.[16] In 1997 the President of the ABA appointed an Ethics 2000 Commission to consider changes in the Model Rules.[17] In 2002 the ABA House of Delegates adopted a comprehensive revision of the Model Rules based on the report of its Ethics 2000 Commission. While the 2002 version of the Model Rules makes many important revisions, the organization, structure, approach, and numbering of the rules (except for a few additions) remain unchanged.[18] As of this writing only a handful of states have adopted the 2002 revision of the Model Rules, but it is anticipated that the level of enactment nationwide should be at least as great as with the 1983 version of the Model Rules. Model Rule sections cited or quoted in this book are to the 2002 revision of the Model Rules, unless otherwise stated.

While the vast majority of state supreme courts adopted the Model Rules, with some variations, a few important states have not done so. New York has a Code of Professional Responsibility that in form is based on the ABA's 1969 Code but actually is a medley of the Code, the Model Rules, and provisions unique to New York. California has adopted its own Rules of Professional Conduct that vary considerably from the ABA's Model Rules. The District of Columbia Rules of Professional Conduct follow the format of the Model Rules but with some significant substantive modifications.

The ABA has also been influential in the area of judicial ethics. In 1972 the ABA adopted a Model Code of Judicial Conduct that was adopted in most states. In 1990 the ABA revised the Code of Judicial Conduct. While the 1990 Code carries forward many of the provisions of the 1972 Code, it includes important changes, particularly with regard to racial bias and sexual discrimination. Chapter 6 examines ethical issues facing judges.

Some scholars of the legal profession have been extremely critical of the bar's efforts to write rules of professional conduct. They have argued that the purpose of these rules is not to control the conduct of lawyers but to serve the interests of lawyers, principally by enhancing professional prestige, controlling competition, and maintaining independence from outside regulation.[19]

---

16. For a listing of the states that have adopted the Model Rules, the dates of their adoption, and a summary of variations from the ABA's Model Rules, see Laws. Man. on Prof. Conduct (ABA/BNA) 01:3 et seq. For an argument in support of federalization of legal ethics, see Fred C. Zacharias, Federalizing Legal Ethics, 73 Tex. L. Rev. 335 (1994).

17. See Laws. Man. on Prof. Conduct (ABA/BNA), 13 Current Rep. 140, 168 (1997).

18. Comprehensive material on the 2002 revisions can be found at the Web site of the ABA Center for Professional Responsibility, http://www.abanet.org/cpr/ethics2k.html (visited May 27, 2003). For a discussion by the Chief Reporter of the Ethics 2000 Commission of the minimalist philosophy adopted by the Commission, see Nancy J. Moore, Lawyer Ethics Code Drafting in the Twenty-First Century, 20 Hofstra L. Rev. 923 (2002).

19. See Richard L. Abel, Why Does the ABA Promulgate Ethical Rules? 59 Tex. L. Rev. 639 (1981); Stephen Gillers, What We Talked About When We Talked About Ethics: A Critical View of the Model Rules, 46 Ohio St. L.J. 243 (1985); Susan P. Koniak, The Law Between the Bar and the State, 70 N.C. L. Rev. 1389 (1992); Deborah L. Rhode,

Any set of rules raises issues of interpretation. National, state, and local bar associations have established committees to offer interpretations of the Code of Professional Responsibility and the Model Rules; one of the most influential of these committees is the ABA Standing Committee on Ethics and Professional Responsibility.[20] The ABA committee issues both formal and informal opinions on issues of professional ethics. Formal opinions are those that the committee considers to be of widespread interest or unusual importance. All other opinions are informal.[21] Bar association ethics advisory opinions are not binding on courts, but good faith reliance on an opinion could be used in defense of a disciplinary or perhaps even a malpractice case.[22]

While the Rules of Professional Conduct set forth general principles applicable to all areas of practice, the practice of law is highly specialized. Because of this gap between general professional rules and specific problems that lawyers encounter in practice, various bodies, including associations of lawyers and bar-appointed study commissions, have prepared standards or codes of conduct focusing on ethical problems in particular areas of practice.[23] Although these standards or codes are of no legal effect unless adopted by a court or legislature, they may provide guidance to practitioners in those fields, be used as evidence of the appropriate standard of conduct in a malpractice case, and help support a good faith defense if a lawyer faces disciplinary charges. Some of the more important standards are the following:

Why the ABA Bothers: A Functional Perspective on Professional Codes, 59 Tex. L. Rev. 689 (1981). See also Charles W. Wolfram, Parts and Wholes: The Integrity of the Model Rules, 6 Geo. J. Legal Ethics 861 (1993) (criticizing Model Rules for failure to "interconnect well and clearly with each other").

20. ABA committee opinions are published in the ABA Journal, the ABA/BNA Lawyers' Manual on Professional Conduct, and in computerized research services. Opinions from state and local bar associations are available in the ABA/BNA Lawyers' Manual and computerized research services. Many opinions are now posted on the Internet.

21. See ABA Comm. on Ethics and Prof. Resp., Rules of Procedure, Rule 3.

22. For an overview of ethics opinions in the United States and proposals for change, see Peter A. Joy, Making Ethics Opinions Meaningful: Toward More Effective Regulation of Lawyers' Conduct, 15 Geo. J. Legal Ethics 313 (2002). Scholars have offered mixed views about the work of bar association ethics committees. In an early study Professors Finman and Schneyer criticized the work of the ABA Committee. While finding the committee's work to have substantial influence, they also concluded that "these opinions are seriously flawed, so much so that their overall influence may well be unfortunate." Ted Finman & Theodore Schneyer, The Role of Bar Association Ethics Opinions in Regulating Lawyer Conduct: A Critique of the Work of the ABA Committee on Ethics and Professional Responsibility, 29 UCLA L. Rev. 67, 72 (1981). See also Lawrence K. Hellman, When "Ethics Rules" Don't Mean What They Say: The Implications of Strained ABA Ethics Opinions, 10 Geo. J. Legal Ethics 317 (1997). For a more favorable view of state ethics opinions, see Bruce A. Green, Bar Association Ethics Committees: Are They Broken?, 30 Hofstra L. Rev. 731, 732 (2002) (ethics opinions "have been greatly undervalued by their critics and . . . they are not inherently flawed").

23. See Nathan M. Crystal, The Incompleteness of the Model Rules and the Development of Professional Standards, 52 Mercer L. Rev. 839 (2001).

- *arbitration and mediation:* Code of Ethics of the American Arbitration Association for Arbitrators in Commercial Disputes[24] and Model Standards of Conduct for Mediators[25]
- *civil litigation:* American Bar Association, Section of Litigation, Civil Discovery Standards,[26] Guidelines for Conduct,[27] and Ethical Guidelines for Settlement Negotiations[28]
- *criminal defense and prosecution:* American Bar Association, Standards for Criminal Justice: The Prosecution Function and the Defense Function
- *matrimonial practice:* American Academy of Matrimonial Lawyers, The Bounds of Advocacy[29]
- *professionalism in general:* American Bar Association, "Lawyer's Creed of Professionalism";[30] many state bar associations have also adopted standards of professionalism
- *trust and estate practice:* American College of Trust and Estate Counsel, Commentaries on the Model Rules of Professional Conduct[31]

Norms of conduct or mores of the legal institutions in which lawyers practice are also an important source of lawyers' obligations. For example, issues of professional responsibility arise in a wide range of day-to-day settings in which lawyers practice: small firms in rural communities, mega-firms practicing throughout the world, boutique firms with highly specialized practices, offices of prosecutors or public defenders, legal services programs, private corporations, and federal or state agencies, to name just a few. Every practice context will have its own norms of behavior—ways in which the lawyers in that organization handle professional problems that they encounter.[32] These norms of behavior will, of course, be heavily influenced by formal professional rules and standards, but some institutions may develop norms that conflict with established professional obligations. One of your tasks as you move into the practice of law should be to judge critically the norms of behavior of the various practices with which you come into contact: What norms of behavior has this particular practice developed? Do these norms conflict with formal professional norms? If so, what is my reaction to this conflict? If the norms are within the "range of discretion" allowed by formal rules of the profession, do I agree with how

---

24. http://www.adr.org/index2.1.jsp?JSPssid = 15718 (visited June 1, 2003).
25. Id.
26. http://www.abanet.org/litigation/taskforces/standards.html (visited June 1, 2003).
27. http://www.abanet.org/litigation/litnews/practice/guidelines.html (visited October 16, 2003).
28. http://www.abanet.org/litigation/ethics/ (visited June 1, 2003).
29. http://www.aaml.org (visited June 1, 2003).
30. Laws. Man. on Prof. Conduct (ABA/BNA) 01:401.
31. http://www.actec.org/pubInfoArk/comm/toc.html (visited June 1, 2003).
32. *Compare* John P. Heinz & Edward O. Laumann, Chicago Lawyers: The Social Structure of the Bar (rev. ed. 1994) *with* Donald D. Landon, Country Lawyers: The Impact of Context on Professional Practice (1990).

discretion is being exercised? If not, what if anything can I do to change these practice norms?

2. Law Governing Lawyers

When adopted by a court with authority to regulate the practice of law, rules of professional conduct become law, and lawyers who violate these rules are subject to professional discipline. The rules of professional conduct are not, however, the only source of law applicable to lawyers. Court decisions, statutory law, administrative rules and regulations, and procedural rules all apply to lawyers.[33]

Court decisions are an important source of obligations of professional conduct. In the field of professional responsibility, courts have rendered decisions in five major categories of cases: disciplinary, malpractice, disqualification, sanctions, and criminal. Disciplinary cases are proceedings brought against lawyers charging them with violation of the rules of professional conduct or other forms of misconduct. The ultimate punishment in a disciplinary proceeding is disbarment from the practice of law; lesser sanctions include suspensions and reprimands. Section D of this chapter examines the disciplinary system in more detail. Malpractice actions are civil lawsuits brought by clients or third parties seeking damages from lawyers. Malpractice claims may be based on a variety of legal theories, including negligence, fraud, and breach of fiduciary duty. Disqualification motions are not separate proceedings but motions filed as part of civil or criminal actions. The essence of the disqualification motion is that the attorney representing the opposing party should be disqualified from representing that party because of some ethical violation, typically a conflict of interest. Like disqualification motions, claims for sanctions are part of an underlying case rather than separate proceedings. Such motions typically seek a monetary punishment against a party or that party's lawyer for some form of litigation misconduct, such as discovery abuse. Lawyers have been prosecuted criminally or held in contempt of court for various types of misconduct.

Statutory law is somewhat less significant in the area of lawyers' obligations than in many other fields of law because the regulation of lawyers and judges is largely the constitutional province of courts. Indeed, state courts have sometimes declared legislation dealing with the practice of law unconstitutional as a violation of the doctrine of separation of powers.[34] A number of federal and state statutes, however, may be applicable to lawyers. At the federal level, statutes govern the conduct of lawyers (and nonlawyers) entering or leaving

---

33. See generally Geoffrey C. Hazard, Jr. & W. William Hodes, The Law of Lawyering (3d ed. 2000) (hereinafter Hazard & Hodes, The Law of Lawyering).

34. See Restatement (Third) of the Law Governing Lawyers §1, cmt. *c* & Reporter's Note (2000).

government service.[35] Federal statutes also govern the disqualification and discipline (short of removal) of federal judges.[36] Various statutes and rules also apply to lawyers acting in other capacities, such as members of Congress or lobbyists.

Statutory regulation of lawyers varies widely from state to state. Both California and New York have fairly extensive schemes of statutory regulation; most other states do not.[37] For example, a California statute provides that sexual relations between a lawyer and a client may subject the attorney to discipline under some circumstances.[38] California also has a statutory provision limiting the percentage of fees that attorneys may charge in contingent fee cases against health care providers.[39] Most states have ethics-in-government statutes regulating the activities of governmental officials, governmental employees, and lobbyists, many of whom are lawyers.

Many lawyers practice before federal and state agencies, such as the Internal Revenue Service (IRS), the Securities and Exchange Commission (SEC), the Patent and Trademark Office (PTO), workers' compensation boards, and zoning commissions. These agencies, particularly federal agencies, may have *administrative rules and regulations* governing admission of practitioners and rules of conduct for practitioners before such agencies.[40] (It should be noted that many administrative agencies like the IRS allow nonlawyers as well as lawyers to practice before the agency.) Agency rules often provide standards similar to the Rules of Professional Conduct, but they may specify different or additional obligations. For example, as a result of the scandals involving corporations such as Enron and WorldCom, Congress enacted the Sarbanes-Oxley Act of 2002.[41] Section 307 of the Act[42] directed the SEC to adopt standards of professional conduct for lawyers appearing and practicing before the Commission, including rules requiring lawyers to report corporate fraud or other wrongdoing to appropriate corporate officials. The SEC has promulgated regulations implementing the Act's directive.[43] Problem 5-2 examines lawyers' obligations when confronted with corporate fraud, including the effect of the

---

35. E.g., Restrictions on Former Officers, Employees, and Elected Officials of the Executive and Legislative Branches, 18 U.S.C. §207; Acts Affecting a Personal Financial Interest, 18 U.S.C. §208; Disclosure of Confidential Information Generally, 18 U.S.C. §1905.

36. Disqualification of Justice, Judge, or Magistrate, 28 U.S.C. §455; Complaints Against Judges and Judicial Discipline, 28 U.S.C. §351. Note, however, that federal judges may be removed from office only through impeachment under U.S. Const. art. II, §4.

37. Cal. Bus. & Prof. Code, Attorneys, §§6000 et seq.; N.Y. Jud. Law, Attorneys and Counselors, §§460 et seq.

38. Cal. Bus. & Prof. Code §6106.9.

39. Id. §6146.

40. E.g., SEC, 17 C.F.R. pts. 201 & 205; IRS, 31 C.F.R. pt. 10; PTO, 37 C.F.R. pt. 10.

41. Pub. L. No. 107-204, 116 Stat. 745 (codified in scattered sections of 11, 15, 18, 28, and 29 U.S.C.A.).

42. 15 U.S.C. §7245.

43. 17 C.F.R. pt. 205.

Sarbanes-Oxley regulations. Similarly, the IRS has adopted standards of conduct with respect to matters such as preparing tax returns and issuing tax shelter opinions.[44] Problem 5-5 considers ethical obligations of attorneys who specialize in tax.

In court proceedings lawyers have a duty to comply with applicable *court rules*. Indeed, the Rules of Professional Conduct incorporate by reference procedural rules as standards of conduct. Model Rule 3.4(c) states that a lawyer shall not "knowingly disobey an obligation under the rules of a tribunal except for an open refusal based on an assertion that no valid obligation exists." Lawyers who violate court rules, such as Rule 11 of the Federal Rules of Civil Procedure, may be subject to monetary sanctions.

In an effort to bring some order to the body of law dealing with lawyers' obligations, the American Law Institute has completed the preparation of the *Restatement (Third) of the Law Governing Lawyers*. The relationship between the Restatement and the Model Rules is complex. To some extent the two documents deal with different topics. For example, the Restatement contains extensive treatment of lawyer civil liability; such liability is outside the scope of the Model Rules. Often, however, the Restatement and the Model Rules both deal with the same issue. When the Restatement and the Model Rules treat the same topic, conflicts can arise. For example, both the Model Rules and the Restatement deal with the scope of the lawyer's duty of confidentiality, but until the ABA amended its rule in 2003, they adopted different positions on exceptions to the duty.[45] Since the Restatement does not constitute law, while rules of professional conduct adopted by a court are legally binding, lawyers must follow applicable rules rather than the Restatement. When the Restatement differs from rules of professional conduct, however, it may serve as the basis for revision of the rules.

3.   Research Tools

In the field of professional responsibility the following research tools are particularly useful:

- ABA, Annotated Model Rules of Professional Conduct (5th ed. 2003)
- Lawyers' Manual on Professional Conduct (ABA/BNA), a comprehensive research service covering reported decisions, ethics opinions, and current developments
- American Law Institute, Restatement (Third) of the Law Governing Lawyers (2000)
- William H. Fortune et al., Modern Litigation and Professional Responsibility Handbook: The Limits of Zealous Advocacy (2d ed. 2001)

44. 31 C.F.R. §§10.33, 10.34.
45. Compare Model Rule 1.6 with Restatement (Third) of the Law Governing Lawyers §67 (2000).

- Monroe H. Freedman & Abbe Smith, Understanding Lawyers' Ethics (2d ed. 2002), a critical view of the Model Rules, particularly in the context of criminal defense and prosecution
- Geoffrey C. Hazard, Jr. & W. William Hodes, The Law of Lawyering (3d ed. 2000), textual discussion with illustrations of the Model Rules containing citations to significant decisions and scholarship
- Ronald E. Mallen & Jeffrey M. Smith, Legal Malpractice (5th ed. 2000), the leading treatise on legal malpractice
- Charles W. Wolfram, Modern Legal Ethics (1986), a comprehensive handbook

Shortened references are made to these sources throughout this text.

4. *Limitations of Professional Rules and of the Law Governing Lawyers and the Need for a Philosophy of Lawyering*

In many situations rules of professional conduct or the law governing lawyers or both provide clear guidance to lawyers. Recall In re Pautler where the prosecutor violated Rules 4.3 and 8.4 dealing with communication with an unrepresented person and misrepresentation. As *Pautler* demonstrates, violation of the rules of professional conduct or provisions of general law exposes lawyers to serious legal consequences, such as loss of professional license, civil liability, and even criminal prosecution. Other situations in which rules of professional conduct or general law provide lawyers with clear answers are easy to find. To take one example, the Model Rules require contingent fee agreements to be in writing and signed by the client. See Model Rule 1.5(c).

Having emphasized the importance of following applicable rules, it is a mistake to reach the conclusion that professional responsibility is the equivalent of rule following. Many difficult questions of professional responsibility do not admit of black-or-white answers. Instead, lawyers must exercise sound judgment in resolving these questions. Sometimes rules of professional conduct or governing law provide almost no guidance for lawyers. For example, how much pro bono work should I assume as an associate, when my firm doesn't have any clear rules, when I want to make partner, and when I have a two-year-old at home? Should I accept this malpractice case against one of my classmates when I think the case has merit, when the client has not been able to find another lawyer to take the case, and when the statute of limitations is about to run? Other times the rules provide general standards, but lawyers must exercise judgment in applying these principles. Should I agree to handle this multimillion dollar case against a company that my firm did some work for three years ago? How should I respond to a request for production of documents in discovery when I know what the other side wants, but the request is worded in such a way that I could, arguably, deny the existence of what was requested?

Being a professionally responsible lawyer requires careful attention to the rules of ethics and applicable law, but it also demands much more: It means that lawyers must develop an approach to handling questions when the rules of professional conduct do not provide answers or offer only general principles to guide lawyers in exercising judgment. I use the term "philosophy of lawyering" to refer to a general approach for dealing with difficult questions that lawyers face in the practice of law.[46] The material in the next three sections will help you begin to think about developing your own philosophy of lawyering.

C. Going Beyond the Rules: Client-Centered Lawyering, Moral Values, Principles of Professionalism, and Other Sources of Guidance for Lawyers

If the rules of professional conduct or applicable law do not provide a clear answer to an issue of professional responsibility, lawyers must turn to other sources for guidance. You probably already have some ideas about how you would deal with such questions. Your thinking will mature as you consider issues raised in this course and as you face a myriad of ethical problems in practice. To begin developing your philosophy of lawyering, you may find it useful to think about the various approaches that have been debated by scholars of the legal profession.

The traditional approach to resolving questions of professional ethics when the rules are unclear could be labeled a *client-centered philosophy*. In articles written in 1978 and 1983, Professor Murray Schwartz set forth two principles that he argued accurately described the essence of client-centered lawyering. First, lawyers act as zealous partisans on behalf of their clients, doing everything possible to enable their clients to prevail in litigation or to obtain their clients' objectives in nonlitigation matters, except to the extent that clear rules of professional conduct or legal principles prohibit the lawyer from acting. Under a client-centered philosophy, if doubt exists about the propriety of an action, the lawyer is justified in proceeding. Only clear violations of law or rules of ethics, such as bribing witnesses, are prohibited. Schwartz referred to this idea as the "principle of professionalism." Second, when acting in this professional role, lawyers are not legally or morally accountable for their actions. Schwartz called this concept the "principle of nonaccountability."[47] Similarly, Professor

---

46. See Nathan M. Crystal, Developing a Philosophy of Lawyering, 14 Notre Dame J.L. Ethics & Pub. Pol'y 75 (2000). See also W. Bradley Wendel, Value Pluralism in Legal Ethics, 78 Washington U.L.Q. 113 (2000) (arguing that the foundational values of legal ethics are plural and often incommensurable, resulting in the need for lawyers to exercise professional judgment).

47. Murray L. Schwartz, The Zeal of the Civil Advocate, 1983 Am. Bar Found. Res. J. 543; Murray L. Schwartz, The Professionalism and Accountability of Lawyers, 66 Cal. L. Rev. 669 (1978). See also David Luban, Lawyers and Justice 7 (1988) (relying on Schwartz's principles as the basis for a normative evaluation of the adversary system).

William Simon has referred to two principles of conduct—neutrality and parti-sanship—as forming the core of what he called the "ideology of advocacy."[48] Following Simon, many writers now use the term "neutral partisanship" to refer to the standard conception of the lawyer's role. A more colloquial way of putting these ideas is that lawyers are "hired guns."

Critics of neutral partisanship have argued that the client-centered philoso-phy is morally unsound[49] because it requires lawyers in the course of representa-tion of clients to engage in conduct that violates conventional morality:

> [The critics] claim that lawyers routinely do things for clients that harm third parties and would therefore be immoral, even in the lawyers' eyes, if done for themselves or for non-clients. Such actions constitute "role-differentiated behavior" in the sense that the actors, if asked to justify themselves, would claim that their role as a lawyer required them to "put to one side [moral] considerations . . . that would otherwise be relevant if not decisive." A lawyer's role-differentiated behavior could involve helping a client pursue a morally objectionable aim, or using a hurtful or unfair tactic to give a client an advantage. Specific examples might include invoking the statute of frauds to help a client avoid paying a debt he really owes, attacking an honest person's veracity in order to discredit him as a witness, taking advantage of an opponent's misunderstanding of the applicable law in settlement negotiations, or suggesting that a corporate client lay off some of its workers until the Justice Department comes to see the merits of the company's merger proposal. Off duty, lawyers would presumably not think it appropriate to avoid repaying a debt, impugn a truthful person's honesty, take advantage of another's mistake, or exploit workers. On duty, the philosophers say, lawyers routinely do such things for their clients.[50]

The critics of neutral partisanship have offered an alternative philosophy that could be called a *philosophy of morality*.[51] Under this philosophy, lawyers

48. William H. Simon, The Ideology of Advocacy: Procedural Justice and Profes-sional Ethics, 1978 Wis. L. Rev. 29, 34-39.

49. Another thread of the critique of client-centered lawyering is that this philosophy ignores the importance of truthful resolution of legal disputes. In 1975, federal Judge Marvin Frankel noted that the litigator "is not primarily crusading after truth, but seeking to win." Marvin E. Frankel, The Search for Truth: An Umpireal View, 123 U. Pa. L. Rev. 1031, 1039 (1975). See also Marvin E. Frankel, Partisan Justice (1980). Judge Frankel went on to propose a rule of professional ethics designed to force lawyers to give greater weight to the truth. 123 U. Pa. L. Rev. at 1057-1058. For a critique of Judge Frankel's views see Freedman & Smith, Understanding Lawyers' Ethics Ch. 2, The Adversary System.

50. Ted Schneyer, Moral Philosophy's Standard Misconception of Legal Ethics, 1984 Wis. L. Rev. 1529, 1532-1533. The moral critique of the role of neutral partisanship is developed in Alan H. Goldman, The Moral Foundations of Professional Ethics 90-155 (1980); David Luban, Lawyers and Justice (1988); Gerald J. Postema, Moral Responsibility in Professional Ethics, 55 N.Y.U. L. Rev. 63 (1980); William H. Simon, The Ideology of Advocacy: Procedural Justice and Professional Ethics, 1978 Wis. L. Rev. 29; and Richard Wasserstrom, Lawyers as Professionals: Some Moral Issues, 5 Human Rights 1 (1975).

51. Probably the most comprehensive development of a philosophy of morality can be found in David Luban, Lawyers and Justice (1988). A number of other scholars have also offered their views on how moral values can be incorporated into the lawyer's role. See generally Thomas L. Shaffer & Robert F. Cochran, Jr., Lawyers, Clients, and Moral

are morally accountable for the actions that they take on behalf of their clients and must be prepared to defend the morality of what they do. Adoption of a philosophy of morality has a number of practical lawyering consequences. Lawyers would decline representation in more cases than under a client-centered philosophy, turning down cases in which the lawyers concluded that the representation was morally indefensible. Lawyers would withdraw from representation more frequently, for example in cases in which clients demanded that lawyers pursue goals or tactics that the lawyers found to be morally unsound. Lawyers would take a broader view of their obligations as counselors, at a minimum raising moral issues with their clients and often trying to convince their clients to take what the lawyer considered to be the morally correct action. In situations in which lawyers had professional discretion about how to act or in which the rules were unclear, a lawyer acting under a philosophy of morality would take the action that the lawyer believed to be indicated by principles of morality, even if this action was not necessarily in the client's interest.[52]

Other critics of the client-centered philosophy have sought to develop approaches based on social values or norms rather than principles of morality. The major advantage of a *philosophy of social value* is that it is grounded in norms expressed in social institutions. Such values are likely to be seen as more objective and justified than moral values, which are often viewed as individual, subjective, and controversial. It should be noted that the philosophies of morality and social value are not inconsistent because social values often embody moral principles. For example, Professor Robert Gordon advocates a vision of law as a public profession and describes ways in which lawyers could implement that ideal in the conditions of modern practice.[53] Professor Bradley Wendel strives to develop a set of public values of lawyering derived from the "social function of lawyers and from the traditions and practices of the legal profession."[54] Professor Timothy Terrell and Mr. James Wildman examine the factors that have caused a crisis of professionalism for lawyers.[55] They argue that the true foundation of professionalism must be found in a commitment to the rule of law.[56] Terrell and Wildman identify six values that they believe lie at the core of professionalism:

Responsibility (1994). Other commentators have focused on the relationship between religious values and lawyering styles. See Symposium: The Relevance of Religion to a Lawyer's Work: An Interfaith Conference, 66 Fordham L. Rev. 1075 (1998).

52. Luban, Lawyers and Justice at 160, 173-174. For discussion of the difficulty of incorporating a philosophy of morality into the actual practice of lawyers, where morality is often vague and uncertain, see Paul R. Tremblay, Moral Activism Manqué, 44 S. Tex. L. Rev. 127 (2002).

53. Robert W. Gordon, Corporate Law Practice as a Public Calling, 49 U. Md. L. Rev. 255 (1990).

54. W. Bradley Wendel, Public Values and Professional Responsibility, 75 Notre Dame L. Rev. 1, 7 (1999).

55. Rethinking "Professionalism," 41 Emory L.J. 403 (1992).

56. Id. at 423.

- an ethic of excellence
- an ethic of integrity: a responsibility to say "no"
- a respect for the system and rule of law: a responsibility to say "why"
- a respect for other lawyers and their work
- a commitment to accountability
- a responsibility for adequate distribution of legal services[57]

The most comprehensive statement of a philosophy of lawyering based on social values is found in Professor Simon's work. He argues for the following basic principle: "[T]he lawyer should take such actions as, considering the relevant circumstances of the particular case, seem likely to promote justice."[58] Simon uses the term "justice" not in some abstract or philosophical sense, but rather as equivalent with "legal merit" of the case.[59] In deciding the legal merit of the case, the lawyer must exercise contextual or discretionary decisionmaking.[60] Simon identifies two dimensions to this approach. First, in deciding whether to represent a client a lawyer should assess the "relative merit" of the client's claims and goals in relation to other clients that the lawyer might serve. Simon recognizes that financial considerations play a significant role in lawyers' decisions to represent clients, but he calls on lawyers to take into account relative merit in addition to financial considerations.[61] Second, in the course of representation, Simon calls on lawyers to assess the "internal merit" of their clients' claims. Simon rejects the view that lawyers should assume responsibility for determining the outcome of cases: "Responsibility to justice is not incompatible with deference to the general pronouncements or enactments of authoritative institutions such as legislatures and courts. On the contrary, justice often, perhaps usually, requires such deference."[62] When procedural defects exist, however, the lawyer's obligation to do justice requires the lawyer to assume responsibility for promoting the substantively just outcome: "[T]he more reliable the relevant procedures and institutions, the less direct responsibility the lawyer need assume for the substantive justice of the resolution; the less reliable the procedures and institutions, the more direct responsibility she needs to assume for substantive justice."[63]

---

57. Id. at 424-431. For other perspectives on the issue of professionalism, see other essays in 41 Emory L.J. no. 2 (1992).

58. William H. Simon, The Practice of Justice 9 (1998).

59. Id. at 10.

60. See id. ch. 6.

61. William H. Simon, Ethical Discretion in Lawyering, 101 Harv. L. Rev. 1083, 1092-1093 (1988).

62. Simon, The Practice of Justice at 138. See also Simon, Ethical Discretion in Lawyering, 101 Harv. L. Rev. at 1096-1097.

63. Simon, The Practice of Justice at 140. See also Simon, Ethical Discretion in Lawyering, 101 Harv. L. Rev. at 1098. While Professor Simon focuses on decisionmaking by lawyers, Professor Deborah Rhode has argued for structural change in the legal profession to promote justice. Deborah L. Rhode, In the Interests of Justice: Reforming the Legal Profession (2000).

These criticisms and suggestions for modification of the role of neutral partisanship have generated a number of responses. Some scholars have challenged the claim that neutral partisanship accurately describes the behavior of most lawyers.[64] Professors Stephen Ellmann and Ted Schneyer have made at least three major objections to the empirical validity of the concept of neutral partisanship. First, the rules of ethics already grant lawyers considerable discretion to take into account moral considerations in their representation: "Lawyers have considerable freedom to reject cases, to limit their representation so as to exclude repugnant objectives or tactics, and to urge their own moral views upon clients whether or not the clients have requested such enlightenment."[65] In particular, Model Rule 2.1 states that, in giving advice to their clients, lawyers "may refer not only to law but to other considerations such as moral, economic, social and political factors," and Rule 1.16(b)(4) allows lawyers to withdraw when "the client insists upon taking action that the lawyer considers repugnant or with which the lawyer has a fundamental disagreement."

Second, some empirical studies of the behavior of criminal defense lawyers, lawyers in small communities, lawyers in nonlitigation activities, and lawyers in large law firms, although limited in number and scope, cast doubt on the claim that neutral partisanship accurately describes the behavior of most lawyers. Indeed, some of these studies suggest that the problem of the role of lawyers is the opposite of neutral partisanship: lawyers are not sufficiently zealous in representing their clients because they are concerned about protecting their reputations; preserving relationships with other lawyers, judges, or officials; or advancing their own interests.[66]

Third, lawyers are not necessarily acting as neutral partisans simply because they agree to represent or continue representation of clients even though they believe that the client's goals are morally repugnant. Lawyers may find such representation morally justified because the representation advances some higher principle—freedom of speech or due process of law, for example. An ACLU lawyer who defends the Nazi Party's right to march in a Jewish neighborhood may do so, not because he is acting as a neutral partisan, but because he considers protecting the principle of free speech more important than restricting

---

64. See Stephen Ellmann, Lawyering for Justice in a Flawed Democracy, 90 Colum. L. Rev. 116 (1990) [reviewing Luban, Lawyers and Justice]; Ted Schneyer, Moral Philosophy's Standard Misconception of Legal Ethics, 1984 Wis. L. Rev. 1529.

65. Ellmann, Lawyering for Justice in a Flawed Democracy, 90 Colum. L. Rev. at 121. See also Schneyer, Moral Philosophy's Standard Misconception of Legal Ethics, 1984 Wis. L. Rev. at 1564-1566. Professor Fred Zacharias agrees that the Code and the Model Rules authorize lawyers to incorporate moral factors in their representation of clients, but he argues that the ethos of the practice has developed to limit the exercise of objective judgment. He proposes a number of institutional changes that can help reintroduce objectivity into the lawyer's role. Fred C. Zacharias, Reconciling Professionalism and Client Interests, 36 Wm. & Mary L. Rev. 1303 (1995).

66. Schneyer, Moral Philosophy's Standard Misconception of Legal Ethics, 1984 Wis. L. Rev. at 1544-1550. For a response to the criticism that neutral partisanship does not accurately describe lawyer behavior, see Luban, Lawyers and Justice at 393-403.

dissemination of their immoral views.[67] Further, many lawyers find moral value to the preservation of the client-lawyer relationship.

Other scholars have defended client-centered lawyering. Professor Stephen Pepper argues that the lawyer's amoral role is morally justified because the role assists clients in exercising autonomy. For lawyers to exercise moral control over their clients would undermine that autonomy.[68] Professor Norman Spaulding has offered a reinterpretation and defense of client-centered lawyering focusing on a "thin" conception of the lawyer's role and an ethic of service.[69]

Problem 1-1

The Moral Accountability of Lawyers

Write a letter to the editor commenting on the following exchange between Professor Monroe Freedman and Professor Michael Tigar regarding the moral accountability of lawyers.

Monroe Freedman, Must You Be the Devil's Advocate?

Legal Times, August 23, 1993

Item. A lawyer at New York's Sullivan & Cromwell recently turned down a court appointment to represent Mahmoud Abou-Halima, who is charged with involvement in the car-bombing of the World Trade Center. A Sullivan & Cromwell partner explained to *The Wall Street Journal* that the firm did not want to dedicate its resources to the case, because the bombing was "such a heinous crime" and because the defendant is "so personally objectionable." The partner added that Abou-Halima is "anti-Semitic in the most dangerous way." And the firm was also concerned about adverse reactions from some of its current clients.

Item. Michael Tigar, a professor at Texas Law School, recently argued in a federal appeals court that John Demjanjuk should be allowed to return to the United States when he leaves Israel. The Israeli Supreme Court has reversed

---

67. Ellmann, Lawyering for Justice in a Flawed Democracy, 90 Colum. L. Rev. at 126; Schneyer, Moral Philosophy's Standard Misconception of Legal Ethics, 1984 Wis. L. Rev. at 1562-1564.

68. See Stephen L. Pepper, The Lawyer's Amoral Ethical Role: A Defense, A Problem, and Some Possibilities, 1986 Am. Bar Found. Res. J. 613. For criticisms of this view and Professor Pepper's response, see Symposium on the Lawyer's Amoral Ethical Role, 1986 Am. Bar Found. Res. J. 613. See also Charles Fried, The Lawyer as Friend: The Moral Foundations of the Lawyer-Client Relation, 85 Yale L.J. 1060 (1976).

69. See Norman W. Spaulding, Reinterpreting Professional Identity, 74 U. Colo. L. Rev. 1 (2003).

Demjanjuk's conviction for participating in the mass murder of Jews in the gas chambers of Treblinka. The court was won over by compelling evidence that Demjanjuk has an alibi. Because he had been engaged in the mass murder of Jews at other Nazi camps, Demjanjuk couldn't possibly have been a guard at Treblinka.

Was Sullivan & Cromwell right to refuse to defend Abou-Halima? Was Tigar right to represent Demjanjuk? And what do the rules of ethics say about it?

. . . Under the traditional view, a lawyer is bound to represent a client zealously, using all reasonable means to achieve the client's lawful objectives. . . .

That does not mean that lawyers should disregard moral concerns in representing clients. On the contrary, if a lawyer believes that what the client proposes is immoral or even simply imprudent, the client is entitled to the lawyer's judgment and counsel. But "[in] the final analysis . . . the lawyer should always remember that the decision whether to forgo legally available objectives or methods because of non-legal factors is ultimately for the client and not for himself." American Bar Association Model Code of Professional Responsibility, EC 7-8. [See Model Rules 1.2(a) and 2.1.]

Thus, a lawyer's decision to represent a client may commit that lawyer to zealously furthering the interests of one whom the lawyer or others in the community believe to be morally repugnant. For that reason, the question of whether to represent a particular client can present the lawyer with an important moral decision—a decision for which the lawyer can properly be held morally accountable, in the sense of being under a burden of public justification.

FREE TO CHOOSE

[Freedman then pointed out that ethically a lawyer may generally refuse to represent a client whose character or cause the lawyer finds repugnant. Model Rule 6.2, cmt. 1]

Thus, Sullivan & Cromwell violated no ethical rule in declining to defend Mahmoud Abou-Halima. Indeed, on the facts as reported, the firm would have acted unethically if it had taken the case. Under Disciplinary Rule 5-101 of the ABA Model Code, which is controlling in New York, a lawyer has a conflict of interest if the exercise of her professional judgment on behalf of her client "reasonably may be affected" by her own personal or business interests. [See Model Rule 1.7(a)(2).]

And that is precisely the position of the lawyers at Sullivan & Cromwell who find the potential client so personally objectionable that they don't think the partnership should put its resources into the case, who find the crime so heinous that they don't want to be associated with its defense, and who are worried about how other clients and potential clients will view the representation. Certainly those powerful concerns may reasonably be expected to affect the zeal with which those lawyers would represent that client.

What then about Michael Tigar's representation of John Demjanjuk?

[Freedman then stated that at one time he did not believe that lawyers were morally accountable for their decisions to represent clients, but he changed his mind after a debate with Michael Tigar.]

And so I now ask my victorious opponent in that long-ago debate: Mike Tigar, is John Demjanjuk the kind of client to whom you want to dedicate your training, your knowledge, and your extraordinary skills as a lawyer? Did you go to law school to help a client who has committed mass murder of other human beings with poisonous gases? Of course, someone should, and will, represent him. But why you, old friend?

Michael Tigar, Setting the Record Straight on the Defense of John Demjanjuk

Legal Times, September 6, 1993

All of Monroe Freedman's statements about me in this newspaper are wrong, except two: We are—or were—old friends. And I do represent John Demjanjuk. . . .

Professor Freedman is wrong about the Israeli Supreme Court decision and about the American judicial decisions that caused Demjanjuk to linger in a death cell for years, for a crime he did not commit.

John Demjanjuk was extradited to Israel to stand trial as "Ivan the Terrible" of Treblinka, one of the worst mass murderers of the Holocaust. It turned out that crucial exculpatory evidence—that someone named Ivan Marchenko, not Demjanjuk, was Ivan the Terrible—was withheld from the defense. That evidence was not an "alibi"; it had to do with tragically mistaken identification and the U.S. government's failure to live up to its obligations of candor to its adversary and to the courts.

Freedman is wrong about what the Israeli Supreme Court did once it found doubt that Demjanjuk was Ivan. That court did not, as Freedman asserts, hold that Demjanjuk was guilty of other crimes. The Israeli court did consider whether Demjanjuk should be convicted as having served at other Nazi death camps, but found that Demjanjuk never had a fair opportunity to rebut evidence of service at other camps.

In 1981, a U.S. district judge found that Demjanjuk should be denaturalized. The judge found that Demjanjuk was Ivan the Terrible, a decision that is now universally conceded to have been wrong. There is powerful evidence that government lawyers suppressed evidence that would have shown that decision to have been wrong when made.

The U.S. judge also considered the question of whether Demjanjuk served at other camps. The judge found that, since Demjanjuk was Ivan and denied being Ivan, he probably should not be believed when he denied other culpable conduct at other camps. Thus, the judge's decision, now argued by the government as barring judicial review of Demjanjuk's right to enter the United States, was taken in the shadow of these now-discredited allegations.

Those are the facts. I represent Mr. Demjanjuk pro bono, along with the federal public defender, in an American judicial proceeding. The proceeding will, we hope, vacate earlier judgments against Demjanjuk and leave the government free—if it wishes—to bring and try fairly its allegations that John Demjanjuk served at death camps.[70] If, as Professor Freedman says, there is evidence of such service, which Mr. Demjanjuk has denied, my client is entitled to a fair trial where that evidence can be tested. . . .

We must remember the Holocaust, and we should pursue and punish its perpetrators. We dishonor that memory and besmirch the pursuit if we fail to accord those accused of Holocaust crimes the same measure of legality and due process that we would give to anyone accused of wrongdoing. Precisely because a charge of culpable participation in the Holocaust is so damning, the method of judging whether such a charge is true should be above reproach.

STANDING UP

So much for the factual difficulties in which Professor Freedman finds himself. Let us turn to his analysis of the ethical issues.

Professor Freedman begins by lauding a major law firm for refusing a court appointment to represent an unpopular indigent defendant. The firm doesn't like the client, doesn't like the fact that he is accused of a "heinous crime," and is afraid that its other clients will object. OK, says Freedman, those are good reasons for the law firm to refuse.

Let us all hurry to the library, and rewrite *To Kill a Mockingbird*. Atticus Finch is not a hero after all. He should have thought more of maintaining his law practice and refused to represent someone charged with a heinous—and possibly racially motivated—crime. Clarence Darrow should have stayed with the railroad, instead of taking on those Commie unionists as clients. The lawyers who lost their licenses for daring to represent the colonial newspaper editor John Peter Zenger for the heinous crime of seditious libel were chumps. And John Hancock, that notorious tax evader, had no right to have John Adams as his counsel.

Maybe Sullivan & Cromwell has the right to refuse a court appointment, and maybe it should have that right. I have represented plenty of unpopular folks in my 25 years at the bar and have always stood up to the task of telling my paying clients that they just have to understand a lawyer's responsibility in such matters, or they should take their business elsewhere.

ONE MAN'S CONSCIENCE

From praise of Sullivan & Cromwell, Professor Freedman then makes a giant leap. He invents a new rule of legal ethics. Based on the supposed right

---

70. The Sixth Circuit subsequently upheld Demjanjuk's appeal. Demjanjuk v. Petrovsky, 10 F.3d 338 (6th Cir. 1993), *cert. denied*, 513 U.S. 914 (1994).—Ed.

to refuse a court appointment, we are told that every lawyer must bear "a burden of public justification" for representing someone accused of odious crimes. There is no rule of professional responsibility that so provides, and several rules cut directly against his assertions.

If Atticus Finch decides to represent an indigent defendant, Freedman will require him not only to incur the obloquy of his friends and clients, but to undertake a public defense of his ethical right to accept the case.

To put lawyers under such a burden of public justification undermines the right to representation of unpopular defendants. It invites the kind of demagoguery that we are now seeing in the attacks on lawyers for defendants in capital cases. It even invites the kinds of unwarranted attacks on zealous advocacy that have often been directed—and quite unjustly—at Professor Freedman.

I undertook the pro bono representation of John Demjanjuk in the 6th Circuit after a thorough review of the facts and law. I can no more be under a duty to make a public accounting of why I took this case than I can be under a duty to open up the files of all my cases to public view.

AN INSULTING QUESTION

[Tigar went on to argue that lawyers were morally accountable to their own consciences for the clients they choose to represent and the positions they advance.]

I have answered that question for myself, and it is insulting for Professor Freedman to suggest that I am faithless to my principles. When the most powerful country on earth gangs up on an individual citizen, falsely accuses him of being the most heinous mass murderer of the Holocaust, and systematically withholds evidence that would prove him guiltless of that charge, there is something dramatically wrong. When that man is held in the most degrading conditions in a death cell based on those false accusations, the wrong is intensified. When the government that did wrong denies all accountability, the judicial branch should provide a remedy. I have spent a good many years of my professional life litigating such issues. I am proud to be doing so again.

Monroe Freedman, The Morality of Lawyering

Legal Times, September 20, 1993

. . . My question to Tigar relates to one of the most fundamental issues of lawyers' ethics and the nature of the lawyer's role. That issue is frequently posed by asking whether one can be a good person and a good lawyer at the same time. Or whether the lawyer forfeits her conscience when she represents a client. Or whether the lawyer is nothing more than a hired gun. Essentially, these questions ask whether the lawyer, in her role as a lawyer, is a moral being. There are three answers to that question:

no moral

- *The amoral lawyer.* One answer has been dubbed "the standard conception." It holds that the lawyer has no moral responsibility whatsoever for representing a particular client or for the lawful means used or the ends achieved for the client. Critics have accurately pointed out that under the standard conception, the lawyer's role is at best an amoral one and is sometimes flat-out immoral.
- *Moral control of the client.* A second answer insists that the lawyer's role is indeed a moral one. It begins by agreeing with the standard conception that the lawyer's choice of client is not subject to moral scrutiny. But it holds that the lawyer can impose his moral views on the client by controlling both the goals pursued and the means used during the representation.

According to this view, the lawyer can properly stop the client from using lawful means to achieve lawful goals. For example, the lawyer, having taken the case and having induced the client to rely upon her, can later threaten to withdraw from the representation—even where this would cause material harm to the client—if the client does not submit to what the lawyer deems to be the moral or prudent course. . . .

- *Choice of client as a moral decision.* The third answer also insists that the lawyer's role is a moral one. It begins by agreeing with the standard conception that the client is entitled to make the important decisions about the client's goals and the lawful means used to pursue those goals. But this answer recognizes that the lawyer has the broadest power—ethically and in practice—to decide which clients to represent. And it insists that the lawyer's decision to accept or to reject a particular client is a moral decision. Moreover, that decision is one for which the lawyer can properly be held morally accountable.

high moral

Although critics have erroneously, and repeatedly, identified me with the standard conception, I have consistently advocated the third answer for 17 years. It is refreshing, therefore, to be criticized at last for what I believe, rather than for what I don't believe.

A JUDGMENT OF ONE'S OWN

Some of the responses to my column suggest that a lawyer can't "know" that a potential client or cause is morally repugnant until there has been a trial by jury that has determined guilt or innocence. But this confuses a legal adjudication of guilt with the lawyer's personal decision about what is true or false and what is right or wrong based upon the available evidence.

? shouldn't matter

And we make that kind of personal decision all the time. . . .

One letter in response to my column said that the question was "impertinent." No lawyer, the writer said, should be under a burden of public moral accountability. That, indeed, is the standard conception. As I have indicated, one reason I reject that view is that I believe that the lawyer's role is neither an immoral nor an amoral one.

Moreover, we are a profession that exists for the purpose of serving the public, and we hold a government-granted monopoly to do so. As the U.S.

Supreme Court has repeatedly held, lawyers are an essential part—a constitutionally required part—of the administration of justice. It is therefore contrary to democratic principles for lawyers to contend that we owe the public no explanation of what we do and why we do it. Further, I believe that a major reason for lawyer-bashing (which is not a new phenomenon) is that our profession has failed to explain and to justify the true nature and importance of the lawyer's role in American society. . . .

A MORAL DEFENSE

It is no surprise that Tigar, in response to my question, has come through with a powerful, persuasive explanation—a moral explanation—of his decision to represent John Demjanjuk. . . .

First, he notes that the memory of the Holocaust should not be dishonored by denying even its perpetrators the fullest measure of legality. One lesson of the Holocaust is that the vast powers of government must constantly be subjected to the most exacting scrutiny in order to guard against their abuse.

Further, Tigar refers to "powerful evidence" that lawyers in the Department of Justice suppressed evidence that would have shown that Demjanjuk should not have been extradited on charges of being Ivan the Terrible. (Note that these government lawyers have not been found guilty after trial by jury, but that Tigar nevertheless—and properly—finds enough evidence of their guilt to justify his personal moral decision.) This kind of corruption of justice is an intolerable threat to American ideals, regardless of one's opinion of the accused.

And Tigar concludes: "When the government that did wrong denies all accountability, the judicial branch should provide a remedy. I have spent a good many years of my professional life litigating such issues. I am proud to be doing so again."

Thus, Tigar's moral response to my question illuminates a crucial issue of enormous public importance about what lawyers do and why they do it. And it illustrates why I am proud to call Mike Tigar my friend.

D. Issues Facing the Profession: Methods of Regulating Attorney Conduct

Rules of professional conduct and the law governing lawyers focus almost exclusively on issues lawyers encounter in practice. These rules provide lawyers with little guidance in addressing issues facing the profession as a whole. In these materials we will examine a number of significant systemic topics: methods of regulating lawyer conduct, limitations on the adversarial system of adjudication, approaches to improving the delivery of legal services, and remedies for discrimination in the profession.

Formal regulation of attorney conduct has traditionally occurred in two ways: admission of lawyers to practice and discipline of lawyers admitted to practice for misconduct.[71] While the courts have ultimate authority over both the admission and disciplinary systems, in fact the legal profession has exercised substantial control over both systems. A major theme in the history of the American legal profession has been the question of whether the legal profession can be trusted to regulate its members in the public interest or whether the profession will exercise this power for the benefit of its members.[72]

As a result of criticism of the profession's ability to regulate its members in the public interest, in recent years courts and to some extent legislatures have made a number of inroads into the self-regulatory power of the legal profession. Court decisions imposing civil liability or criminal punishment on attorneys and establishing constitutional rights of attorneys have been particularly significant developments. Some state legislatures are assuming a more active role in regulation of the legal profession. The likelihood is that these pressures on the self-regulatory authority of the profession will continue and even intensify. This section provides an overview of the traditional methods of attorney regulation—admission and discipline—along with these emerging methods of control. Professor David Wilkins has written a comprehensive analysis of the various mechanisms for regulating lawyer conduct.[73] Professor Wilkins argues against a unitary system of enforcement and in favor of a multifaceted system in which enforcement methods are matched with problems.

1. Admission to Practice

To practice law before a court, a lawyer must be admitted to the bar of that court. In state court this is normally done by admission to practice before the highest court in the state. This admission typically carries with it the right to practice law before all lower courts in that state. To practice before a federal court— whether the Supreme Court, the courts of appeal, or the district courts—an attorney must be admitted to practice by that court. The federal courts, however, normally rely heavily on the state court admission process. Federal administrative agencies have the power to establish their own rules of practice,

71. For a discussion of the advantages and disadvantages of formal and informal methods of regulation see W. Bradley Wendel, Nonlegal Regulation of the Legal Profession: Social Norms in Professional Communities, 54 Vand. L. Rev. 1955 (2001).

72. See Benjamin H. Barton, An Institutional Analysis of Lawyer Regulation: Who Should Control Lawyer Regulation—Courts, Legislatures, or the Market, 37 Ga. L. Rev. 1167 (2002) (arguing that Congress or state legislatures would be more likely to produce public-minded regulation and limit lawyer rent-seeking). See generally Symposium, The Future Structure and Regulation of Law Practice, 44 Ariz. L. Rev. 521 (2002). For a discussion of factors leading to increased regulation of lawyers, see Charles W. Wolfram, Toward a History of the Legalization of American Legal Ethics—II, The Modern Era, 15 Geo. J. Legal Ethics 205 (2002).

73. David B. Wilkins, Who Should Regulate Lawyers? 105 Harv. L. Rev. 799 (1992). See Special Issue, Institutional Choices in the Regulation of Lawyers, 65 Fordham L. Rev. No. 1 (1996) (symposium examining and developing Professor Wilkins's approach to lawyer regulation).

including rules that allow nonlawyers to practice before the agency. Under the Supremacy Clause of the United States Constitution, art. VI, cl. 2, states may not prohibit nonlawyers admitted by federal agencies from practicing before those agencies pursuant to agency rules.[74]

The rules for admission to practice vary from state to state. Typically, states have three requirements for admission. First, applicants must have graduated from law school. Most states require applicants to have graduated from a law school accredited by the ABA, but some states, including California, allow applicants to graduate from unaccredited law schools. The requirement of ABA accreditation obviously gives the ABA a powerful voice in the control of legal education and of the practice of law. In a critical study of the ABA's role in raising bar educational requirements, Professor Jerold Auerbach argues that increased educational requirements were part of an overall effort by the organized bar to reduce the impact of the rising tide of immigrants on the profession.[75] Second, most states require applicants to pass the state's bar examination. In a few states applicants who graduate from a law school within the state have a "diploma privilege" for admission to the bar without having to sit for the bar examination.[76] Third, applicants must be of "good moral character."[77]

Good moral character is a universal requirement for admission to the bar, but its precise meaning is unclear. The Supreme Court has characterized the term as "unusually ambiguous," but has indicated that the inquiry should focus on whether a "reasonable man could fairly find that there were substantial doubts about [the applicant's] 'honesty, fairness and respect for the rights of others and for the laws of the state and nation.' "[78]

In a series of cases beginning in the 1950s the Supreme Court considered constitutional limitations on inquiry by bar officials into political beliefs and activities of applicants for admission to the bar. The Court held that states could not deny bar admission simply because of past membership in organizations like the Communist Party when the applicants introduced substantial evidence of good moral character.[79] Later cases dealt with the extent to which bar officials could inquire into applicants' political affiliations in application questions. The

---

74. Sperry v. Florida ex rel. Florida Bar, 373 U.S. 379 (1963) (Florida could not prevent nonlawyer admitted to practice before United States Patent Office from representing clients pursuant to Patent Office Rules on the ground that he was engaged in the unauthorized practice of law).

75. Jerold S. Auerbach, Unequal Justice (1976).

76. E.g., Wis. Sup. Ct. R. 40.03.

77. For a state-by-state comparison of bar admission requirements, see Comprehensive Guide to Bar Admission Requirements, published annually by the American Bar Association Section of Legal Education and Admissions to the Bar and the National Conference of Bar Examiners.

78. Konigsberg v. State Bar of California, 353 U.S. 252, 263-264 (1957) (*Konigsberg I*).

79. Schware v. Board of Bar Examiners, 353 U.S. 232 (1957); *Konigsberg I*, 353 U.S. at 267-268.

Court ruled that most such inquiries were unconstitutional.[80] In Law Students Civil Rights Research Council, Inc. v. Wadmond,[81] however, the Court in a 5-4 opinion upheld several questions on the New York bar application that inquired into the applicant's *knowing* membership in organizations that advocated the violent overthrow of the government with *specific intent* to foster the aims of such organization.

Since the trilogy of 1971 cases the Supreme Court has not dealt with the constitutionality of the moral character requirement, but the issue of moral character has been before the state courts on a number of occasions. For example, in Florida Board of Bar Examiners re N.R.S.,[82] the Florida Supreme Court held that there was no rational connection between an applicant's acknowledged homosexuality and his fitness to practice law. By contrast, in In re Converse,[83] the Nebraska Supreme Court upheld the decision of its bar commission denying Converse's application to take the bar exam based on numerous instances of personal attacks against students and faculty with whom he had had disputes along with display of obscene material while in law school. While Converse's conduct may have had some degree of First Amendment protection, the court held that the commission could nonetheless consider his actions in deciding whether he possessed the moral character sufficient for admission to the bar.

In a comprehensive study of the history and implementation of the moral character requirement, Professor Deborah Rhode questions the wisdom of having this condition for bar admission. Among the criticisms she makes are the following: First, bar admission officials do not have the resources for adequate investigation into moral character, and the inquiries they do conduct are only minimally helpful in determining the moral character of applicants. Second, because of the vagueness of the moral character concept, the admission process is left to the subjective judgment of bar officials. Her study indicates a lack of consensus among these officials as to the types of conduct that warrant investigation or denial of admission. Third, review of character has First Amendment implications, inhibiting freedom of expression by some individuals and deterring others from applying for bar admission. Wide-ranging inquiry into the activities of applicants also raises privacy issues. Professor Rhode concludes that the bar would be better off abandoning the moral character requirement for bar admission and instead using its limited resources in disciplining lawyers for actual misconduct.[84]

---

80. Konigsberg v. State Bar of California, 366 U.S. 36 (1960) (*Konigsberg II*); In re Anastaplo, 366 U.S. 82 (1960); In re Stolar, 401 U.S. 23 (1971); Baird v. State Bar of Arizona, 401 U.S. 1 (1971).

81. 401 U.S. 154 (1971).

82. 403 So. 2d 1315 (Fla. 1981).

83. 602 N.W.2d 500 (Neb. 1999).

84. Deborah L. Rhode, Moral Character as a Professional Credential, 94 Yale L.J. 491 (1985). See also Michael K. McChrystal, A Structural Analysis of the Good Moral Character Requirement for Bar Admission, 60 Notre Dame L. Rev. 67 (1984).

States traditionally included some form of residency in the state as a requirement for bar admission,[85] but in a series of decisions the Supreme Court invalidated various residency requirements under the Privileges and Immunities Clause of the United States Constitution, art. IV, §2.[86] Even if a residency requirement is no longer a substantial barrier to practice across state lines, the bar examination is. As a general rule, a lawyer admitted to practice in one state cannot practice in another state unless the lawyer meets the bar admission requirements, including passage of the bar examination, in the second state. Historically, there have been two exceptions to this requirement. First, some states grant admission on motion by reciprocity to a lawyer in a second state, if the second state recognizes a similar form of admission to lawyers in the first state. Second, almost all states allow a lawyer to appear "pro hac vice" for the purpose of handling a particular matter.[87] Pro hac vice admission typically requires association of local counsel and cannot be used by a lawyer who regularly engages in practice in a state in which the lawyer is not admitted.[88] In addition, pro hac vice admission is unavailable for transactional matters. In recent years, many lawyers and scholars have argued that the barriers to multijurisdictional practice should be lowered. In August 2002, the ABA adopted the recommendations of its Commission on Multijurisdictional Practice, including revised Model Rule 5.5, which deals with the unauthorized practice of law and multijurisdictional practice.[89] We will study this rule in more detail in connection with Problem 4-8.

2. The Disciplinary System

Problem 1-2

Reporting Misconduct by Another Lawyer

You are the only associate recently hired by a solo practitioner, Norman Wilson. You were hired about a year ago after a lengthy job search. You feel extremely fortunate to have the job because the market for lawyers

---

85. Citizenship as a requirement for bar admission is unconstitutional. See In re Griffiths, 413 U.S. 717 (1973) (state failed to satisfy heavy burden of proof required to use suspect category of status as alien).

86. See Supreme Court of N.H. v. Piper, 470 U.S. 274 (1985); Supreme Court of Virginia v. Friedman, 487 U.S. 59 (1988); Barnard v. Thorstenn, 489 U.S. 546 (1989). Cf. Frazier v. Heebe, 482 U.S. 641 (1987) (invalidating Louisiana federal district court residency rule under Court's supervisory power).

87. See Leis v. Flynt, 439 U.S. 438 (1979) (no due process right to hearing on denial of pro hac vice admission).

88. See South Carolina Medical Malpractice Joint Underwriting Assn. v. Froelich, 377 S.E.2d 306 (S.C. 1989) (out-of-state attorney could not continue to use pro hac vice admission and would be enjoined from engaging in the unauthorized practice of law).

89. http://www.abanet.org/cpr/mjp-home.html (visited July 8, 2003).

in your area has been very tight; a number of your classmates still do not have a position.

One of the matters on which you have worked is Sylvia v. United Truck Lines, an automobile accident case in which the firm represented the plaintiff, Sylvia. The case settled about a month ago for $250,000, and the file was closed. You did some legal research on the case and met with the client on several occasions regarding discovery issues. You did not participate in settlement negotiations or in disbursement of settlement funds.

Recently, you came across a research memo that you did in Sylvia v. United Truck Lines that was misfiled. You pulled the file of the *Sylvia* case from the firm's closed files. As you were putting the research memo into the file, you happened to notice the closing statement in the case. The statement signed by the client showed a structured settlement in which $100,000 was paid immediately and $25,000 payable over each of the next six years. The statement also showed that the firm's one-third attorney fee was paid fully out of the initial payment. Thus, the client only received about $17,000 now. The closing statement struck you as strange because you were sure that the case had been settled for a lump sum. As you thumbed through the file, you found a letter from the insurance company stating that it was enclosing its draft in the amount of $250,000 as lump sum settlement of the case, along with its standard form general release. You are mystified about this and unsure how to proceed. What should you do?

Read Model Rules 1.6, 5.2, 8.3, and comments.

Duty to report misconduct by another lawyer

Disciplinary Rule 1-103(A) of the Code of Professional Responsibility required lawyers to report unprivileged knowledge of violations of any disciplinary rule by other lawyers. The language of the rule imposed a reporting obligation regardless of the seriousness of the violation. Thus, under the rule lawyers were equally obligated to report violations of the advertising rules and theft of client money. It was clear, however, that in fact lawyers did not comply with this broad duty of disclosure. A 1978 study conducted by the Arizona Law Review found that where the conduct involved serious harm to a client or obstruction of justice, the vast majority of attorneys would report the misconduct: 89 percent of the respondents would report misappropriation of client funds to a disciplinary body and 79 percent would report the destruction of evidence. If the conduct did not involve serious harm to a client or obstruction of justice, however, attorneys were generally unwilling to report even serious criminal conduct. More than 50 percent of the respondents would take no action on learning that another attorney had willfully evaded income tax. Similarly, 65 percent would not report improper solicitation of business.[90]

Recognizing this reluctance to report misconduct, the drafters of the Model Rules imposed a more limited but realistic obligation to report misconduct. Rule 8.3(a) of the Model Rules of Professional Conduct provides that a lawyer who knows of misconduct by another lawyer "that raises a substantial question as to that lawyer's honesty, trustworthiness or fitness as a lawyer in other respects, shall inform the appropriate professional authority."[91] Section (b) imposes a similar obligation on lawyers to report misconduct by judges.

A leading case dealing with the lawyer's obligation to report misconduct by another lawyer is Wieder v. Skala.[92] The plaintiff, Wieder, was a litigation associate in the defendant law firm. Wieder asked the law firm to represent him in the purchase of a condominium apartment. The firm agreed to do so, and assigned a fellow associate (L.L.) to handle the matter. L.L. neglected the matter and made fraudulent misrepresentations to Wieder to conceal his neglect. Wieder learned from two senior associates that the firm knew that L.L. was a "pathological liar" and that he had previously lied to other members of the firm about pending matters. When Wieder discovered the fraud, he informed the partners in the firm and asked them to report L.L.'s misconduct as required by DR 1-103(A) of the New York Code of Professional Responsibility. The partners refused to do so. In an effort to dissuade Wieder from reporting L.L.'s misconduct, the firm agreed to reimburse Wieder for his losses. In addition, the firm threatened to fire Wieder if he reported L.L.'s misconduct. Ultimately, however, at Wieder's insistence, the firm reported L.L.'s misfeasance. The firm continued to employ Wieder for several months because he was working on an important litigation matter, but two partners in the firm berated him for forcing them to report L.L. Finally, the firm fired Wieder.

Wieder brought suit for breach of contract and in tort for abusive discharge. The lower courts dismissed both causes of action, relying on prior decisions of the New York Court of Appeals holding that an at-will employee could be discharged regardless of cause, unless the employer had expressly agreed in manuals or otherwise to limit its right of discharge. The court of appeals affirmed the dismissal of the tort claim, holding that while the plaintiff's arguments were persuasive and the circumstances compelling, recognition of a tort cause of action was best left to the legislature.[93] The court, however, reversed as to the breach of contract cause of action. While reaffirming the rules that

---

90. David R. Ramage-White, Note, The Lawyer's Duty to Report Professional Misconduct, 20 Ariz. L. Rev. 509, 516-517 (1978). See also David O. Burbank & Robert S. Duboff, Ethics and the Legal Profession: A Survey of Boston Lawyers, 9 Suffolk L. Rev. 66, 100 (1974) (few respondents would contact the bar association when they learned of serious criminal conduct by a member of their firm).

91. See Douglas R. Richmond, The Duty to Report Professional Misconduct: A Practical Analysis of Lawyer Self-Regulation, 12 Geo. J. Legal Ethics 175 (1999).

92. 609 N.E.2d 105 (N.Y. 1992).

93. Id. at 110.

it had established in prior employment cases, the court of appeals held that *∅ at will?* the employment relationship between lawyers and their firms was fundamentally different from the relationship between employees and commercial enterprises:

> We agree with plaintiff that in any hiring of an attorney as an associate to practice law with a firm there is implied an understanding so fundamental to the relationship and essential to its purpose as to require no expression: that both the associate and the firm in conducting the practice will do so in accordance with the ethical standards of the profession. Erecting or countenancing disincentives to compliance with the applicable rules of professional conduct, plaintiff contends, would subvert the central professional purpose of his relationship with the firm— the lawful and ethical practice of law. . . .
>
> Moreover, as plaintiff points out, failure to comply with the reporting requirement may result in suspension or disbarment. . . . Thus, by insisting that plaintiff disregard DR 1-103(A) defendants were not only making it impossible for plaintiff to fulfill his professional obligations but placing him in the position of having to choose between continued employment and his own potential suspension and disbarment. We agree with plaintiff that these unique characteristics of the legal profession in respect to this core Disciplinary Rule make the relationship of an associate to a law firm employer intrinsically different from that of the financial managers to . . . corporate employers. . . .[94]

In Bohatch v. Butler & Binion,[95] the Texas Supreme Court decided as a matter of law a firm could not be held liable for damages to a partner who the firm expelled for alleging in good faith that another partner had violated ethical rules. The court was sensitive to the argument that its decision discouraged lawyers from reporting misconduct, but it concluded that the firm's action nonetheless did not subject it to liability because allegations of misconduct, whether true or not, undermine the trust that is essential to the partnership relationship.[96] While the majority did not mention *Wieder*, concurring Justice Hecht distinguished the case because *Wieder* did not involve a partnership relationship and because the misconduct in *Wieder* was clear.[97] Two justices dissented and would have held the firm liable for retaliating against a partner who made a good faith effort to alert other members of the firm to possible overbilling of a client.[98]

Exceptions to the duty to report misconduct by another lawyer

The duty to report misconduct by another lawyer is subject to several limitations and exceptions. First, the duty applies only if the lawyer "knows" of misconduct. The terminology section of the Model Rules draws a distinction between

94. Id. at 108-109.
95. 977 S.W.2d 543 (Tex. 1998).
96. Id. at 546-547.
97. Id. at 557.
98. Id. at 561.

"know" and "reasonably should know." Compare Model Rule 1.0(f) with Rule 1.0(j). The former requires actual knowledge while the latter is an objective standard based on what a reasonably prudent and competent lawyer would know. It should be noted, however, that since it is impossible to penetrate into a person's mind, actual knowledge can be inferred from the circumstances. See Model Rule 1.0(f). Relevant also is a well-established body of criminal law involving lawyers and other professionals holding that a person has knowledge of a fact if the person's conduct shows conscious avoidance or deliberate ignorance of facts.[99]

Second, under Rule 8.3(c) an attorney's duty to report misconduct is subject to the attorney's duty of confidentiality to the client: "This rule does not require disclosure of information otherwise protected by Rule 1.6. . . ." Rule 1.6 states: "A lawyer shall not reveal information relating to the representation of a client unless the client gives informed consent . . . [subject to certain exceptions]."[100]

In In re Himmel,[101] the Illinois Supreme Court held that the attorney-client privilege did not excuse an attorney from the duty to report misappropriation of funds by the client's former attorney. In *Himmel*, however, the client had not asked the lawyer to maintain confidentiality, and the lawyer thought that the client had reported the matter. In addition, *Himmel* was decided under DR 1-103(A) of the Code of Professional Responsibility, which states that the lawyer has a duty to report "unprivileged" knowledge of misconduct by another lawyer. The use of the word "privilege" seems to refer to the attorney-client evidentiary privilege. In fact, the Illinois Supreme Court in *Himmel* found that the attorney-client privilege did not prevent Himmel from being required to report the former lawyer's misconduct because Himmel had not received the information about the former lawyer's misconduct in a communication from his client that was protected by the evidentiary attorney-client privilege. A communication is subject to the attorney-client privilege only if the communication is made in confidence; if a third party, who is not the agent of either the lawyer or the client, is present when the communication is made, the communication usually is not in confidence.[102] When the client told Himmel of the former lawyer's misconduct, a third party was present; Himmel also obtained information about the lawyer's misappropriation from an insurance company.[103] By contrast, under Model Rule 8.3(c) the duty to report does not apply to information "protected by Rule 1.6," which encompasses information "relating to the representation of a client," regardless of whether it is subject

99. See generally John P. Freeman & Nathan M. Crystal, Scienter in Professional Liability Cases, 42 S.C. L. Rev. 783, 833-838 (1991).

100. State Bar of Mich., Comm. on Prof. and Jud. Ethics, Op. RI-220 (1994) (no duty to report under Rule 8.3 when information is covered by Rule 1.6).

101. 533 N.E.2d 790 (Ill. 1988).

102. Restatement (Third) of the Law Governing Lawyers §70 (definition of "privileged persons").

103. 533 N.E.2d at 794.

to the evidentiary attorney-client privilege.[104] Later problems in these materials explore in more detail the relationship between the ethical duty of confidentiality and the evidentiary attorney-client privilege.

Wisdom of the reporting requirement as a matter of policy

Should the rules of professional conduct impose a duty to report misconduct by another lawyer at all? Our society does not impose an obligation on citizens to report crimes of which they have knowledge.[105] Professor Gerald Lynch argues that the absence of such a general duty is justified because the decision whether to inform is a complex moral choice that requires weighing the harm to relationships that may result from informing with the harm to be avoided by reporting.[106] He goes on to argue that the ethical obligation to report that is imposed on lawyers is also unjustified:

> It is difficult to imagine that the special circumstances of the lawyer's position in society alter the balance in every case to the point that the complexity of the moral calculation disappears. In other words, it is not clear, even for lawyers, that the moral basis of informing will be so clear in so many cases that a generalized obligation to inform should be imposed.[107]

Some states, notably California, do not include an obligation to report misconduct by another lawyer.[108]

Problem 1-3

Evaluation of Your State's System of Lawyer Discipline

a. How does your state's system of lawyer discipline compare with ABA recommendations as discussed in the reading material that follows? Consider the following topics.

    1. authority to discipline: bar or court?

---

104. See In re Ethics Advisory Panel Op. No. 92-1, 627 A.2d 317 (R.I. 1993) (distinguishing *Himmel* and holding that the duty to report under Rule 8.3 is subordinate to the duty of confidentiality under Rule 1.6). Hazard and Hodes argue that Rule 8.3(c) "effectively eliminates the duty to report another lawyer's misconduct in most cases that arise in the context of client representation, which is to say most cases." 2 Hazard & Hodes, The Law of Lawyering, §64.8, 18-19.

105. See Gerald E. Lynch, The Lawyer as Informer, 1986 Duke L.J. 491, 517-521.

106. Id. at 521-535.

107. Id. at 537. See also Arthur F. Greenbaum, The Attorney's Duty to Report Professional Misconduct: A Roadmap for Reform, 16 Geo. J. Legal Ethics 259 (2003) (arguing that the case for a mandatory reporting rule is uncertain, but calling for redrafting to make a mandatory reporting rule work).

108. See Laws. Man. on Prof. Conduct (ABA/BNA) ¶101:201.

2. confidentiality
3. disciplinary effect of conviction of a crime
4. scope of public protection: To what extent does your state have the following in addition to a system of lawyer discipline?
    a. client protection fund
    b. mandatory arbitration of fee disputes
    c. voluntary arbitration of lawyer malpractice claims and other disputes
    d. mediation
    e. lawyer practice assistance
    f. lawyer substance abuse counseling
5. provisions for minor misconduct
6. degree of lay participation
7. complainants' rights
8. random audit of trust accounts

b. Your instructor will invite to class one or more individuals involved in your state's disciplinary system to speak on the current operation of the system, problems that they see with the system, and their recommendations for change. Be prepared to ask them questions about the operation of the system. Consider the areas set forth in part *a* above.

The system of lawyer discipline received little attention until 1967,[109] when the ABA appointed a special committee chaired by Justice Tom C. Clark of the United States Supreme Court to study the system and to make recommendations. In 1970 the committee issued its report finding the "existence of a scandalous situation that requires the immediate attention of the profession."[110] Among the problems found by the committee were the following:

> The Committee has found that in some instances disbarred attorneys are able to continue to practice in another locale; that lawyers convicted of federal income tax violations are not disciplined; that lawyers convicted of serious crimes are not disciplined until after appeals from their convictions have been concluded, often a matter of three or four years, so that even lawyers convicted of serious crimes, such as bribery of a governmental agency employee, are able to continue to practice before the very agency whose representative they have corrupted; that even after disbarment lawyers are reinstated as a matter of course; that lawyers fail to report violations of the Code of Professional Responsibility committed by their brethren, much less conduct that violates the criminal law; that lawyers will not appear or cooperate in proceedings against other lawyers but instead will

---

109. See generally Mary M. Devlin, The Development of Lawyer Disciplinary Procedures in the United States, 7 Geo. J. Legal Ethics 911 (1994).

110. ABA, Special Comm. on Evaluation of Disciplinary Enforcement, Problems and Recommendations in Disciplinary Enforcement 1 (1970) [hereinafter the Clark Committee].

exert their influence to stymie the proceedings; that in communities with a limited attorney population disciplinary agencies will not proceed against prominent lawyers or law firms and that, even when they do, no disciplinary action is taken, because the members of the disciplinary agency simply will not make findings against those with whom they are professionally and socially well acquainted; and that, finally, state disciplinary agencies are undermanned and underfinanced, many having no staff whatever for the investigation or prosecution of complaints.[111]

The report identified 36 major problems with the disciplinary system nationwide and made specific recommendations for change.

As a result of the Clark Committee's report, the ABA appointed a standing Committee on Professional Discipline. The committee prepared Standards for Lawyer Discipline, adopted by the ABA in 1979, which followed many of the recommendations made by the Clark Committee. Since then the ABA adopted a new set of provisions, the Model Rules for Lawyer Disciplinary Enforcement.[112] The description of the disciplinary process that follows is based on the ABA's model rules, but it is important to note that the procedures for lawyer discipline, like those for admission to the bar, vary from state to state, so lawyers should consult their local rules of court to determine the procedures in effect in that state.

The ABA Model Rules for Lawyer Disciplinary Enforcement call for the creation of a statewide board to administer the lawyer discipline and disability system. Rule 2(A). The board is appointed by "the court with the requisite authority and responsibility to administer the lawyer discipline and disability system." Rule 2(B). Typically, this will be the state supreme court. The board appoints hearing committees and the court appoints disciplinary counsel. Rules 3 and 4. When a charge of misconduct is filed against an attorney, disciplinary counsel has the responsibility of conducting an investigation. Rule 11. At the conclusion of the investigation, disciplinary counsel may (a) dismiss, (b) in a matter involving minor misconduct, refer respondent to the Alternatives to Discipline Program, or (c) recommend probation, admonition, the filing of formal charges, the petitioning for transfer to disability inactive status, or a stay. Rule 11(B)(1). The complainant may ask for review by the chair of the hearing committee of the disciplinary counsel's decision to dismiss the matter. Rule 11(B)(3). If the disciplinary counsel recommends either admonition or probation, the accused lawyer may request formal proceedings. If the lawyer does not request formal proceeding, the lawyer is deemed to have consented to the sanction recommended by disciplinary counsel. Rule 11(C).

If formal charges are instituted against an attorney, disciplinary counsel gives the attorney written notice of the charges, the attorney files an answer to the charges, and certain discovery is conducted. When the case involves material issues of fact, or when the attorney wishes to present evidence in

111. Id. at 1-2.
112. http://www.abanet.org/cpr/disenf/contents.html (visited July 8, 2003).

mitigation, the hearing committee will hold an evidentiary hearing where the accused lawyer may be represented by counsel, present evidence, and cross-examine witnesses. Rule 11(D). The hearing committee then prepares a report to the board that includes its findings of fact, conclusions of law, and recommendations. Rule 3(D). The board reviews the report of the hearing committee and issues its own report and decision, subject to review by the court. Rule 11(E), (F).

The ABA Model Rules for Lawyer Disciplinary Enforcement specify grounds for discipline, which include violation of the state's rules of professional conduct. Rule 9(A). Under the Model Rules of Professional Conduct, a lawyer engages in misconduct when a lawyer commits a criminal act that "reflects adversely on the lawyer's honesty, trustworthiness or fitness as a lawyer in other respects." Model Rule 8.4(b). Thus, criminal conduct is also a basis for professional discipline. Indeed, the Model Rules for Lawyer Disciplinary Enforcement provide for interim suspension of a lawyer who has been convicted of a serious crime. Rule 19. The Model Rules of Professional Conduct also apply to lawyers even when they are acting in a nonlegal capacity. As a result, a lawyer could be disciplined for "improper conduct in connection with business activities, individual or personal activities, and activities as a judicial, governmental or public official."[113] A lawyer may also be disciplined for willful failure to cooperate with disciplinary authorities. Rule 9(A)(3). See also Model Rule 8.1 (prohibiting misrepresentation, nondisclosure, and noncooperation in connection with admissions and disciplinary matters). If a lawyer is found guilty of misconduct, sanctions include the following: disbarment, suspension for a fixed period not to exceed three years, probation not in excess of two years, reprimand, admonition, restitution to persons financially injured by the attorney, costs of the disciplinary proceeding, and limitations on the attorney's future practice. Rule 10. The sanctions of disbarment, suspension, probation, and reprimand are made public. Rule 10(D). An admonition, which is in effect a warning to the attorney, can be issued only in cases of minor misconduct. Rule 10(A)(5).

What is the nature of the disciplinary process and to what extent are lawyers entitled to constitutional protections? The ABA Model Rules for Lawyer Disciplinary Enforcement refer to the disciplinary process as sui generis. Rule 18(A). The Supreme Court, however, has characterized the disciplinary process as "quasi criminal" and has held that certain (but not all) due process requirements apply, including the requirement of fair notice of the charges.[114] Similarly, the Court held in Spevack v. Klein,[115] that a lawyer could not be disciplined for invoking the privilege against self-incrimination in responding to a subpoena duces tecum in a disciplinary proceeding. The *Spevack* decision, however, provides lawyers only a limited degree of protection because the Supreme Court subsequently limited the scope of the privilege. The privilege against

113. ABA Comm. on Ethics and Prof. Resp., Formal Op. 336, at 2 (1974).
114. See In re Ruffalo, 390 U.S. 544 (1968).
115. 385 U.S. 511 (1967).

self-incrimination generally does not prevent lawyers from being required to produce documents and records; it does not preclude a state from disciplining lawyers for noncooperation in disciplinary cases that do not involve criminal misconduct; and it would allow a state to compel lawyers to testify in disciplinary cases that involved possible criminal liability so long as the lawyers received use immunity against any criminal prosecution resulting from their testimony.[116]

The burden of proof required to find a lawyer guilty of misconduct reflects the unique character of disciplinary proceedings. In most states, a finding of misconduct must be supported by "clear and convincing evidence," a standard higher than the civil standard of a preponderance of the evidence but lower than the criminal standard of proof beyond a reasonable doubt. See ABA Model Rules for Lawyer Disciplinary Enforcement, Rule 18(C).

Since the issuance of the Clark Committee's report in 1970, the disciplinary process has been the subject of considerable debate.[117] The overriding question in the discussion has been whether the process deals effectively with lawyer misconduct. Critics argue that a system controlled by lawyers can never properly regulate lawyers. Opponents of the present system have sought a process subject to public control. Defenders of self-regulation argue that issues of professional responsibility are too complex to be left to laypeople, that the bar has done a generally credible job in dealing with misconduct, that public control would undermine the independence of lawyers, and that defects in the system can be remedied by greater openness and some public participation in the system rather than scrapping the system in its entirety.

The ABA Model Rules for Lawyer Disciplinary Enforcement, while obviously preserving the principle of professional self-regulation, do include some modest reforms in the disciplinary system. The rules place the system under the control of the judiciary rather than the bar and call for lay membership on both the board and hearing committees, but lay membership is a minority of both of these bodies. See Rules 2(B) and 3 (three of nine members of board and one of three members of hearing committees are public members). The rules provide that proceedings are generally confidential until formal proceedings begin, at which time the proceedings become public. Rule 16. Admonitions of attorneys remain private. Rule 10(A)(5).

In 1989 the ABA appointed another commission to study the disciplinary system and to make recommendations to the ABA. In 1991 the ABA Commission on Evaluation of Disciplinary Enforcement (the McKay Commission) issued its report. The commission found "revolutionary changes" since the Clark Committee's report.[118] The commission also found that "times have

---

116. See generally Geoffrey C. Hazard, Jr. & Cameron Beard, A Lawyer's Privilege Against Self-Incrimination in Professional Disciplinary Proceedings, 96 Yale L.J. 1060 (1987).

117. See note 72 above.

118. ABA Commn. on Evaluation of Disciplinary Enforcement, Lawyer Regulation for a New Century xiv (1992), http://www.abanet.org/cpr/mckay_report.html (visited July 8, 2003).

changed" and that further improvements and modifications of disciplinary systems were required.[119] The commission's report outlined 21 recommendations for improvement of the disciplinary process. At its February 1992 meeting the ABA House of Delegates adopted the McKay Commission's report and its recommendations, with some modifications. As adopted by the ABA, the recommendations include the following:

- Professional conduct should be regulated by the judiciary rather than the bar. Recommendations 1-2.
- The scope of public protection should be expanded to include the following component agencies:
  (a)   lawyer discipline
  (b)   client protection fund
  (c)   mandatory arbitration of fee disputes
  (d)   voluntary arbitration of lawyer malpractice claims and other disputes
  (e)   mediation
  (f)   lawyer practice assistance
  (g)   lawyer substance abuse counseling. Recommendations 3-4.
- Courts should appoint disciplinary officials and disciplinary counsel to assure independence from the bar. Recommendations 5-6.
- All disciplinary proceedings should be made public after a determination has been made that probable cause exists. Recommendation 7.
- Complainants should be entitled to greater involvement in disciplinary proceedings. Recommendation 8.
- The disciplinary process should include procedures for cases involving minor misconduct. Recommendations 9-10.
- Disciplinary systems should be adequately funded. Recommendations 13-15.
- Lawyers' trust accounts should be subject to random audit. Recommendation 16.
- Improvements should be made in the National Discipline Data Bank and in interstate coordination. Recommendations 20-21.

Probably the most significant change made by the ABA to the commission's recommendations dealt with confidentiality of the disciplinary process. The commission had recommended that the disciplinary process be public from the time of the complainant's initial communication with the disciplinary agency. The ABA House of Delegates changed this proposal to make the process public after a determination has been made that probable cause exists.[120]

---

119. Id. at xv.
120. On the need for more public information about disciplined lawyers, see Sandra L. DeGraw & Bruce W. Burton, Lawyer Discipline and "Disclosure Advertising": Toward a New Ethos, 72 N.C. L. Rev. 351 (1994). See also Steven K. Berenson, Is It Time for Lawyer Profiles?, 70 Fordham L. Rev. 645 (2001).

Studies of the disciplinary process in various states have shown that lawyers in firms of fewer than ten attorneys are subject to discipline to a much greater extent than lawyers in large firms. For example, between 50 and 60 percent of the California bar practices in small firms, yet a 2001 study of the California disciplinary process found small-firm lawyers accounted for 95 percent of disciplinary investigations and 98 percent of all lawyers disciplined. Studies in New Mexico and Oregon reached similar conclusions. How can the differences between discipline of lawyers in large and small firms be explained? Some observers have charged that the disciplinary process is biased against small-firm practitioners and perhaps against minorities as well, who practice to a greater extent than nonminorities in small firms. The California study rejected that claim finding that disciplinary investigations were proportional to the number of complaints filed against lawyers with solo or small firm practices. Similarly, a 2000 Virginia study did not find any correlation about the outcome of a disciplinary proceeding and race, age, or gender. A number of factors could explain the difference between the impact of the disciplinary process on large and small firms. Large firms will normally have well-established systems in place for docket control, accounting, and prevention of conflicts of interest, while small firms are more likely to be informal in their law office management. In addition, because of financial pressures, small firm lawyers may be more inclined to accept cases, leading to excessive case loads and other ethical problems.[121]

While the disciplinary process has traditionally focused on the conduct of individual lawyers, some studies have argued that the process should be applied to law firms.[122] In 1996 New York became the first state to adopt rules for discipline of law firms.[123]

3. Civil Liability and Criminal Punishment

Three forms of civil remedies now occupy a central place in regulation of lawyer conduct: legal malpractice, disqualification, and monetary sanctions. The term *legal malpractice* is often used to refer to lawyers' civil liability, but the term is a misnomer because the law does not recognize a single cause of action for legal malpractice. Legal malpractice is a catch-all phrase that refers

---

121. Mark Hansen, Picking on the Little Guy, 89 A.B.A.J. 30 (March 2003). The California study is available on line at the bar Web site, http://www.calbar.ca.gov (visited July 19, 2003).

122. Ted Schneyer, Professional Discipline for Law Firms? 77 Cornell L. Rev. 1 (1991). But see Julie Rose O'Sullivan, Professional Discipline for Law Firms? A Response to Professor Schneyer's Proposal, 16 Geo. J. Legal Ethics 1 (2002). See also Irwin D. Miller, Preventing Misconduct by Promoting the Ethics of Attorneys' Supervisory Duties, 70 Notre Dame L. Rev. 259 (1994).

123. See Laws. Man. on Prof. Conduct (ABA/BNA), 12 Current Rep. 191 (1996). DR 1-102 of the New York Code of Professional Responsibility defines misconduct to include conduct by a lawyer or a law firm.

to a group of causes of action by which clients, and in some cases third parties, can recover damages from lawyers (or their malpractice insurers) for some form of lawyer misconduct.[124] When a client claims that a lawyer mishandled a legal matter, the client's cause of action will typically be for negligence. The duty of care that lawyers owe their clients requires them to "exercise the competence and diligence normally exercised by lawyers in similar circumstances."[125] Lawyers who practice in a specialized field, such as securities or tax, are held to the standard of care normally exercised by specialists.[126] If a lawyer in the course of representation intentionally violates a fiduciary obligation to the client—for example, by representing conflicting interests—then the client may have a cause of action for breach of fiduciary duty.[127] In some cases, clients have alleged that their lawyers misrepresented facts to them or failed to disclose material information giving rise to causes of action for fraud, misrepresentation, or nondisclosure.[128]

Causes of action by nonclients against lawyers have traditionally been much more difficult to sustain than causes of action by clients because of the "privity" rule. Under this rule, lawyers generally have not been liable to persons other than their clients. The privity rule has been justified for two reasons: First, liability to nonclients would create conflicts of interest between lawyers' duties to their clients and their duties to third persons. Second, liability to nonclients would expose lawyers to potentially vast damages of uncertain amount and scope. Despite these policies, the privity rule has been eroded in recent years, and lawyers are increasingly being held liable to third parties.[129]

What is the relationship between the rules of professional conduct and malpractice liability?[130] The Model Rules impose an obligation of competence on lawyers. See Model Rule 1.1. See also Model Rule 1.3 (diligence). The Model Rules, however, state that violation of the rules is not itself a basis for malpractice liability. Model Rules Scope ¶20. Thus, merely because a lawyer has

---

124. See generally Mallen & Smith, Legal Malpractice. See also Restatement (Third) of the Law Governing Lawyers, ch. 4.

125. Restatement (Third) of the Law Governing Lawyers §52(1).

126. See Horne v. Peckham, 158 Cal. Rptr. 714 (Ct. App. 1979); Restatement (Third) of the Law Governing Lawyers §52, cmt. *d.* See generally Buddy O. Herring, Liability of Board Certified Specialists in a Legal Malpractice Action: Is There a Higher Standard? 12 Geo. J. Legal Ethics 67 (1998) (board certification will not increase attorneys' malpractice liability because attorneys who qualify will already be subject to higher standard of care applicable to specialists).

127. Restatement (Third) of the Law Governing Lawyers §49. See, e.g., Moguls of Aspen, Inc. v. Faegre & Benson, 956 P.2d 618 (Colo. Ct. App. 1997) (negligence does not equal breach of fiduciary duty).

128. Restatement (Third) of the Law Governing Lawyers §56, cmt. f.

129. See 1 Mallen & Smith, Legal Malpractice ch. 7; Restatement (Third) of the Law Governing Lawyers §§51 (duty of care to certain nonclients), 56 (liability to client or nonclient under general law). See generally Symposium, The Lawyer's Duties and Liabilities to Third Parties, 37 S. Tex. L. Rev. 957 (1996).

130. See generally John Leubsdorf, Legal Malpractice and Professional Responsibility, 48 Rutgers L. Rev. 101 (1995).

violated the rules of professional conduct does not per se produce malpractice liability. To establish malpractice liability for negligence, it is necessary to show that the attorney's conduct fell below generally accepted standards of conduct in the profession. This standard typically requires expert testimony.[131] Most courts will allow experts to consider rules of ethics in deciding whether the attorney's conduct did not meet generally accepted standards of the profession.[132] In addition, to establish malpractice liability a plaintiff must also prove that the attorney's breach of duty caused damages to the plaintiff.[133] Potential malpractice liability can be a powerful force affecting the conduct of lawyers, just as it has been for doctors. These materials include discussion of significant malpractice cases.

Modern litigation has seen an explosive growth of *disqualification motions*— motions filed by one party seeking a court order that the other party's lawyer may not continue to represent that party because of some violation of the rules of professional responsibility, typically a conflict of interest.[134] Disqualification motions are not separate proceedings but are filed as part of civil or criminal actions. Originally, disqualification motions were used in cases in which the party filing the motion was a former client and was seeking disqualification to prevent that former lawyer from now using confidential information on behalf of a new client against the former client. This situation continues to be a major area in which disqualification motions have come before the courts. See Problem 3-5. Disqualification motions, however, are now being filed in many other situations, for example if the opposing lawyer might be called as a witness in the case or if the lawyer had used some improper investigative technique, such as contacting the employees of the moving party. Some courts have begun to register skepticism about disqualification motions because they deprive clients of the right to counsel of their choice, because they can interfere with the efficient processing of cases, and because they can be used for strategic purposes. We will consider the use of disqualification motions in a number of problems in these materials.

Monetary sanction for litigation abuse is another form of civil liability that in recent years has come to have an increasingly important impact on lawyer conduct. The principal source of this body of law is Rule 11 of the Federal Rules of Civil Procedure. Under this rule, if a lawyer files a motion or other

---

131. See Vandermay v. Clayton, 984 P.2d 272 (Or. 1999) (en banc) (while expert testimony is generally required in legal malpractice cases, court may determine whether jury is capable of deciding lawyer's negligence without expert testimony).

132. See, e.g., Allen v. Lefkoff, Duncan, Grimes & Dermer, P.C., 453 S.E.2d 719 (Ga. 1995) (ethics rules relevant on standard of care in legal malpractice case); Smith v. Haynsworth, Marion, McKay & Geurard, 472 S.E.2d 612 (S.C. 1996) (expert witness may rely on violation of rule of ethics as evidence of violation of standard of care). See generally Note, The Evidentiary Use of the Ethics Codes in Legal Malpractice: Erasing a Double Standard, 109 Harv. L. Rev. 1102 (1996).

133. See Restatement (Third) of the Law Governing Lawyers §53.

134. See generally Kenneth L. Penegar, The Loss of Innocence: A Brief History of Law Firm Disqualification in the Courts, 8 Geo. J. Legal Ethics 831 (1995).

paper in court, the lawyer certifies that the document is not "frivolous" either in law or in fact. Courts have rendered a vast body of decisional law establishing obligations of lawyers regarding frivolous lawsuits and motions under Rule 11. Courts have ordered lawyers who have violated this rule to pay monetary sanctions, such as attorney fees of the opposing party. Rule 11 applies only to actions in federal court, but many states have rules of civil procedure modeled on federal Rule 11. Problem 4-1 examines Rule 11 and other limitations on frivolous litigation conduct.

The *criminal law* plays an increasingly important role in the regulation of lawyers, both directly when lawyers engage in conduct that violates the criminal law and indirectly when criminal standards influence disciplinary standards.[135] Lawyers can also be held in *contempt of court*.

For example, 18 U.S.C. §401 provides:

> A court of the United States shall have power to punish by fine or imprisonment, or both, at its discretion, such contempt of its authority, and none other, as—
>
> (1) Misbehavior of any person in its presence or so near thereto as to obstruct the administration of justice;
>
> (2) Misbehavior of any of its officers in their official transactions;
>
> (3) Disobedience or resistance to its lawful writ, process, order, rule, decree, or command.

Contempt orders can be either criminal or civil.[136] When an order is intended to punish misconduct, vindicate the court's authority, or deter future conduct, it is criminal in nature, and various due process safeguards are necessary.[137] If the contempt order is intended to coerce compliance with a court's order rather than punish for violation, it amounts to civil contempt.[138] Thus, if a court orders a person incarcerated until the person complies with the court's order, the sanction amounts to civil contempt so long as it is still reasonably possible for the person to comply with the order.[139] Regardless of whether the contempt is criminal or civil, a hearing is generally required before issuance of an order, but when the contempt occurs in the presence of the court and immediate

---

135. See Bruce A. Green, The Criminal Regulation of Lawyers, 67 Fordham L. Rev. 327 (1998). Professor Green discusses the tensions that can arise between criminal and ethical standards and argues that the criminal law and prosecutors should sometimes show greater deference to lawyers' ethical obligations. For a somewhat different view see Charles W. Wolfram, Lawyer Crimes: Beyond the Law?, 36 Val. U.L. Rev. 73 (2001).

136. For a discussion of the distinction between civil and criminal contempt, see United States v. Lippitt, 180 F.3d 873 (7th Cir.), *cert. denied* 528 U.S. 958 (1999)).

137. See In re Air Crash at Charlotte, N.C. on July 2, 1994, 982 F. Supp. 1092 (D.S.C. 1997) (lawyer subject to criminal contempt for providing daily transcript to fact witness and for improper use of subpoena).

138. See United States v. Lippitt, 180 F.3d at 876-877.

139. Id.

action is necessary to vindicate the court's authority, courts have the power to order summary contempt.[140]

4. *Legislation and Administrative Rules*

As mentioned earlier, legislatures have not been a major force in the regulation of the legal profession because courts have been aggressive in asserting their constitutional prerogative to supervise attorneys. Courts have often struck down on separation of powers grounds legislative attempts to regulate the profession.[141]

In recent years legislatures have become somewhat more active in efforts to control the profession. Several states have statutes limiting contingent fee agreements. A few states have authorized nonlawyers to provide legal services. We will consider some of these provisions in connection with problems later in these materials.

In addition, the federal government has recently become more actively involved in the regulation of attorneys. As mentioned previously, in 2002 in the wake of corporate scandals involving the Enron and WorldCom corporations, Congress enacted the Sarbanes-Oxley Act, directing the SEC to establish rules of conduct governing attorneys admitted to practice before the Commission. We will consider this major development in more detail in connection with Problem 5-2.

E. The Concept of a Philosophy of Lawyering

The previous sections have suggested that the task of being a professionally responsible lawyer is challenging. In day-to-day practice lawyers often face difficult issues of professional responsibility that are not clearly answered by the rules of professional conduct or the law governing lawyers. In addition, issues of professional responsibility go beyond everyday practice to include the relationship between a lawyer's personal life and professional role and to encompass the lawyer's involvement in institutional issues facing the profession.

I use the term "philosophy of lawyering" to refer to a general approach to dealing with these issues of professional responsibility.[142] A philosophy of lawyering operates at three interrelated levels: the personal, the practice, and

140. See Pounders v. Watson, 521 U.S. 982 (1997) (no need to show pattern of repeated violations by attorney for court to exercise power of summary contempt when necessary to vindicate court's authority).

141. See Cleveland Bar Assn. v. Picklo, 772 N.E.2d 1187 (Ohio 2002) (statute allowing nonlawyers to appear in court for landlords violated doctrine of separation of powers). For criticisms of the "negative inherent powers doctrine," see Wolfram, Modern Legal Ethics §2.2.3, at 27-31 and Nathan M. Crystal, Core Values: False and True, 70 Fordham L. Rev. 747, 765-769 (2001).

142. For a comprehensive discussion of the concept of a philosophy of lawyering and a proposal for a bar admission requirement to implement the concept, see Nathan M.

the institutional. At the *personal level* a philosophy of lawyering focuses on how lawyers integrate their personal and professional lives.[143] For example, consider the dilemma facing lawyers who wish to advance their professional careers without sacrificing the needs of their families in the process. Or think about the problem facing lawyers who may be asked by clients or senior lawyers to engage in conduct that they find personally distasteful although not illegal.

Lawyers choose how they integrate their personal and professional lives. These choices can be made intelligently, based on thoughtful analysis of the relevant considerations, or they can be made haphazardly, by default, or even by others on the lawyer's behalf. An important aspect of how you decide to integrate the personal and the professional is your choice of type of practice.[144] Different types of practice will make distinctive demands on your time and energies and will provide disparate forms of rewards. In addition, the nature of the ethical problems and the tensions you face will vary depending on the type of practice you choose. For example, in private business or commercial practice you will usually not encounter problems of pretrial publicity, but you will certainly face issues of conflicts of interest, and you may face difficult questions of how to deal with client fraud. You cannot avoid difficult ethical problems regardless of your choice of type of practice, but you can shape the nature of the problems you face. Thus, as you begin to develop a philosophy of lawyering, you will want to consider a number of questions:

1. What type of practice do I see myself going into: plaintiff's litigation, corporate law, prosecution or defense, legal services? Large or small organization? What area of the country or the world?
2. What types of ethical problems am I likely to encounter in this type of practice?
3. What level of income do I aspire to have? Will the practice that I plan to undertake meet this goal?
4. What kind of personal life do I wish to have? Will the demands of the type of practice that I envision allow me to have the kind of personal life I desire?
5. Do I have enough information about the type of practice that I envision to answer these questions? If not, how am I going to get this information? If the type of practice that I contemplate will not allow me to meet either my income or personal desires, are there alternatives I should consider?

In the chapters that follow we will examine a variety of problems of professional responsibility arising in several areas of practice: criminal defense

---

Crystal, Developing a Philosophy of Lawyering, 14 Notre Dame J.L. Ethics & Pub. Pol'y 75 (2000).

143.   Deborah L. Rhode, Balanced Lives for Lawyers, 70 Fordham L. Rev. 2207 (2002).

144.   Andrew M. Perlman, A Career Choice Critique of Legal Ethics Theory, 31 Seton Hall L. Rev. 829 (2001).

and prosecution, civil litigation, office practice, and government and public interest practice. As you study these chapters, you may find it useful to sample some of the literature dealing with various areas of practice. The bibliography at the end of this chapter provides some suggestions for your reading.

At the *practice level* a lawyer's philosophy of lawyering provides guidance to the lawyer on how to resolve difficult issues that arise in the practice of law and that are not clearly answered by rules of conduct or the law governing lawyers. Indeed, the Scope section of the Model Rules explicitly recognizes the need for lawyers to go beyond the rules when dealing with difficult questions of professional responsibility:

> The Rules do not, however, exhaust the moral and ethical considerations that should inform a lawyer, for no worthwhile human activity can be completely defined by legal rules. The Rules simply provide a framework for the ethical practice of law. ¶16.

In section C of this chapter we considered three broad approaches for you to consider in dealing with difficult issues of professional responsibility that arise in the daily practice of law: client-centered lawyering, a philosophy of moral values, and a philosophy of social values. As we proceed to consider ethical issues in particular areas of practice you may find it useful to refer back to these approaches for guidance in answering uncertain questions.

Finally, the *institutional level* refers to the lawyer's involvement in and position regarding issues facing the profession as a whole rather than the individual lawyer.[145] As the previous section shows, the effectiveness of the attorney disciplinary system has been a significant issue for the profession for a number of years. Increasingly, the profession's effort to preserve the principle of self-regulation has come under attack from various quarters.[146] At several places in these materials we will consider a number of other issues facing the profession as a whole: the adequacy of our system for delivery of legal services to indigents and people of moderate means, criticisms of the adversarial system of dispute resolution, and the problem of discrimination within the profession. Lawyers seeking to develop a comprehensive philosophy of lawyering will strive to be knowledgeable about institutional issues facing the profession and prepare to work for institutional reform where appropriate.[147]

---

145. See Deborah L. Rhode, Ethical Perspectives on Legal Practice, 37 Stan. L. Rev. 589 (1985).

146. See Deborah L. Rhode, The Rhetoric of Professional Reform, 45 Md. L. Rev. 274 (1986).

147. Scholars have written about issues of institutional reform of the legal profession for years. See John Leubsdorf, Three Models of Professional Reform, 67 Cornell L. Rev. 1021 (1982); David B. Wilkins, Legal Realism for Lawyers, 104 Harv. L. Rev. 468 (1990). Recent significant contributions to the topic include Deborah L. Rhode, In the Interests of Justice: Reforming the Legal Profession (Oxford 2000); Conference on Legal Ethics, "What Needs Fixing?", 30 Hofstra L. Rev. 685 (2002); Colloquium: What Does It Mean to Practice Law "In the Interests of Justice" in the Twenty-First Century?, 70 Fordham L. Rev. 1543 (2002). See also Thomas D. Morgan, Real World Pressures on Professionalism,

————————— **Problem 1-4** —————————

Developing a Philosophy of Lawyering

a. Role models.   One way to begin thinking about developing a philosophy of lawyering is to look for role models. What lawyers do you admire? They may be family members, friends, or outstanding lawyers whose biographies you have read or plan to read. What is it you admire about these lawyers? How do they integrate their private and professional lives? What approach or approaches do these lawyers use in dealing with difficult questions of professional responsibility? To what institutional issues do these lawyers devote their time? What principles inform their thinking about these issues? Write an essay describing and either defending or critiquing the philosophy of lawyering of some lawyer you know well personally, or who has been the subject of a biography, or who has been depicted in literature or film. See the list of biographies contained in the bibliography at the end of this chapter.

b. Atticus Finch.   Atticus Finch, the hero of Harper Lee's Pulitzer Prize-winning novel, *To Kill a Mockingbird*, personified in Gregory Peck's Academy Award winning performance, has left a lasting impression on generations of American lawyers. Write an essay describing and critically considering the philosophy of lawyering exemplified by Atticus Finch, using either the book or the film. Do you think Finch is a useful role model for you? Why or why not?[148]

c. Articulating your own philosophy of lawyering.   Write an essay describing and defending your own philosophy of lawyering. Your essay should include discussion of the personal, the practice, and the institutional dimensions of a philosophy of lawyering. It should discuss a broad range of specific issues, such as the following:

1. choosing a type of practice
2. deciding to take or decline cases
3. counseling a client regarding exercise of the client's legal rights
4. exercising professional discretion on behalf of a client (e.g., deciding whether to cross-examine a witness)
5. withdrawing from representation because the lawyer concludes that the client is acting immorally
6. preventing the client from doing harm to others (e.g., disclosing the client's intention to commit a wrongful act)

———————————————

23 U. Ark. Little Rock L. Rev. 409 (2001) (discussing eight developments in the world in which lawyers practice that put pressure on achieving professional ideals).

148. For different perspectives on Atticus Finch, *compare* Thomas L. Shaffer, The Moral Theology of Atticus Finch, 42 U. Pitt. L. Rev. 181 (1991) *with* Monroe H. Freedman, Atticus Finch—Right and Wrong, 45 Ala. L. Rev. 473 (1994). The Freedman article is part of a symposium issue on *To Kill a Mockingbird*.

7. acting on behalf of a client in ways that will harm others
8. participating in pro bono, law reform, and other professional activities to improve the law

Bibliography on the Practice of Law and Selected Biographies of Lawyers

Generally

Richard L. Abel, American Lawyers (1989).

Jerold S. Auerbach, Unequal Justice: Lawyers and Social Change in Modern America (1976).

Gary Bellow & Martha Minow eds., Law Stories (1996).

Gerald J. Clark, American Lawyers in the Year 2000: An Introduction, 33 Suffolk U.L. Rev. 293 (2000).

Mary Ann Glendon, A Nation Under Lawyers: How the Crisis in the Legal Profession is Transforming American Society (1994).

John P. Heinz & Edward O. Laumann, Chicago Lawyers: The Social Structure of the Bar (rev. ed. 1994).

Philip B. Heymann & Lance Liebman, The Social Responsibilities of Lawyers (1988).

Michael J. Kelly, Lives of Lawyers: Journeys in the Organizations of Practice (1994).

Anthony T. Kronman, The Lost Lawyer: Failing Ideals of the Legal Profession (1993).

Sol M. Linowitz with Martin Mayer, The Betrayed Profession: Lawyering at the End of the Twentieth Century (1994).

Mark C. Miller, The High Priests of American Politics: The Role of Lawyers in American Political Institutions (1995).

Robert L. Nelson, David M. Trubek & Rayman L. Solomon, Lawyers' Ideals/ Lawyers' Practices: Transformations in the American Legal System (1992).

Rodent (Attorney), Explaining the Inexplicable: The Rodent's Guide to Lawyers (1995).

Two periodicals, The American Lawyer and the National Law Journal, contain extensive coverage of various aspects of professional life.

Biographies

Clark M. Clifford, Counsel to the President: A Memoir (1991).

Johnnie L. Cochran with Tim Rutten, Journey to Justice (1996).

Morris Dees, A Lawyer's Journey: The Morris Dees Story (2001).

William Henry Harbaugh, Lawyer's Lawyer: The Life of John W. Davis (1973).

Laura Kalman, Abe Fortas (1990).

William M. Kuntsler with Sheila Eisenberg, A Man of the Sixties: My Life as a Radical Lawyer (1994).

Arthur L. Liman with Peter Israel, Lawyer: A Life of Counsel and Controversy (1998).

Alpheus Thomas Mason, Brandeis, A Free Man's Life (1946).

Louis Nizer, Reflections Without Mirrors: An Autobiography of the Mind (1978).

Victor Rabinowitz, Unrepentant Leftist (1996).

Mary Beth Rogers, Barbara Jordan: American Hero (1998).

Gerry Spence, The Making of a Country Lawyer (1996).

Evan Thomas, The Man to See: Edward Bennett Williams (1991).

Kevin Tierney, Darrow, A Biography (1979).

Michael E. Tigar, Fighting Injustice (2002).

Lawrence E. Walsh, The Gift of Insecurity: A Lawyer's Life (2003).

Juan Williams, Thurgood Marshall: American Revolutionary (1998).

Career Choice

American Bar Association, Careers in Law Series, includes publications on admiralty and maritime law, civil litigation, entertainment law, family law, government practice, intellectual property, international law, labor law, natural resources and environmental law, nonlegal careers, public interest law, and sports law. See http://www.abanet.org/abapubs/legalprof.html (visited July 10, 2003). The ABA Journal also runs a monthly column on Law Practice.

Deborah L. Arron, What Can You Do with a Law Degree? A Lawyer's Guide to Career Alternatives Inside, Outside & Around the Law (3d ed. 1997).

Susan J. Bell, Full Disclosure: Do You *Really* Want to be a Lawyer? (1989).

Jay G. Foonberg, How to Start & Build a Law Practice (4th ed. 1999).

Hillary Jane Mantis, Alternative Careers for Lawyers (1997).

Suzanne B. O'Neill & Catherine Gerhauser Sparkman, From Law School to Law Practice: The New Associate's Guide (2d ed. 1998).

Civil Rights (See also *Biographies, Public Interest,* and *Legal Services*)

Jack Greenberg, Crusaders in the Courts: How a Dedicated Band of Lawyers Fought for the Civil Rights Revolution (1994).

Richard Kluger, Simple Justice: The History of Brown v. Board of Education and Black America's Struggle for Equality (1975).

Mark V. Tushnet, Making Civil Rights Law: Thurgood Marshall and the Supreme Court, 1936-1961 (1994).

Corporate Counsel

Symposium, The Role of General Counsel, 46 Emory L.J. 1005 (1997).

Criminal Practice (See also *Prosecutors*)

Abraham S. Blumberg, The Practice of Law as a Confidence Game: Organizational Cooption of a Profession, 1 Law & Socy. Rev. 15 (1967).

Alan M. Dershowitz, The Best Defense (1982).

James S. Kunen, "How Can You Defend Those People?": The Making of a Criminal Lawyer (1983).

Kenneth Mann, Defending White-Collar Crime: A Portrait of Attorneys at Work (1985).

Lisa J. McIntyre, The Public Defender: The Practice of Law in the Shadows of Repute (1987).

Seymour Wishman, Confessions of a Criminal Lawyer (1981).

Labor Law

Thomas Geoghegan, Which Side Are You On? Trying to Be For Labor When It's Flat on Its Back (1991).

Law Firms (See Separate Entry for *Washington Lawyers*)

Lincoln Caplan, Skadden: Power, Money, and the Rise of a Legal Empire (1993).

Marc Galanter & Thomas Palay, Tournament of Lawyers: The Transformation of the Big Law Firm (1991).

Robert W. Gordon, Corporate Law Practice as a Public Calling, 49 Md. L. Rev. 255 (1990).

Deborah Holmes, Structural Causes of Dissatisfaction Among Large-Firm Attorneys: A Feminist Perspective (1988).

William R. Keates, Proceed with Caution: A Diary of the First Year at One of America's Largest, Most Prestigous Law Firms (1997).

Nancy Lisagor, A Law Unto Itself: The Untold Story of The Law Firm of Sullivan & Cromwell (1988).

Ralph Nader & Wesley J. Smith, No Contest: Corporate Lawyers and the Perversion of Justice in America (1996).

James B. Stewart, The Partners: Inside America's Most Powerful Law Firms (1983).

Legal Services

Gary Bellow, Turning Solutions into Problems: The Legal Aid Experience, 34 Natl. Legal Aid Defender Assn. Briefcase 106 (1977).

Douglas J. Besharov, Legal Services for the Poor: Time for Reform (1990).

Melissa Fay Greene, Praying for Sheetrock (1991).

Stephen Wexler, Practicing Law for Poor People, 79 Yale L.J. 1049 (1970).

Litigation

Jonathan Harr, A Civil Action (1995).

John A. Jenkins, The Litigators: Inside the Powerful World of America's High-Stakes Trial Lawyers (1989).

Douglas E. Rosenthal, Lawyer and Client: Who's in Charge? (1974).

Stuart M. Speiser, Lawsuit (1980).

Matrimonial Practice

Lynn Mather et al., Divorce Lawyers at Work: Varieties of Professionalism in Practice (2001).

Richard Ross, A Day in Part 15: Law and Order in Family Court (1997).

Austin Sarat & William L. F. Felstiner, Divorce Lawyers and Their Clients: Power and Meaning in the Legal Process (1995).

Prosecutors

Mark Baker, D.A.: Prosecutors in Their Own Words (1999).

David Heilbroner, Rough Justice: Days and Nights of a Young D.A. (1990).

James B. Stewart, The Prosecutors: Inside the Offices of the Government's Most Powerful Lawyers (1987).

Public Interest

Nan Aron, Liberty and Justice for All: Public Interest Law in the 1980s and Beyond (1989).

Ann Fagan Ginger, The Relevant Lawyers (1972).

Gerald P. Lopez, Rebellious Lawyering: One Chicano's Vision of Progressive Law Practice (1992).

Roger V. Stover, Making It and Breaking It: The Fate of Public Interest Commitment During Law School (1989).

Small Firm/Small Town

Jerome E. Carlin, Lawyers on Their Own: The Solo Practitioner in an Urban Setting (1994).

Donald D. Landon, Country Lawyers: The Impact of Context on Professional Practice (1990). See also articles by the same author at 1985 Am. Bar Found. Res. J. 81 and at 1982 Am. Bar Found. Res. J. 459.

Philip C. Williams, From Metropolis to Mayberry: A Lawyer's Guide to Small Town Law Practice (1996).

Washington Lawyers

Joseph C. Goulden, The Super-Lawyers: The Small and Powerful World of the Great Washington Law Firms (1972).

Mark J. Green, The Other Government: The Unseen Power of Washington Lawyers (rev. ed. 1978).

Robert L. Nelson et al., Private Representation in Washington: Surveying the Structure of Influence, 1987 Am. Bar Found. Res. J. 141.

Women and Minorities

ABA Commn. on Women in the Profession, Various Reports on the Status of Women in the Profession. See http://www.abanet.org/women/ (visited July 16, 2003).

ABA, Dear Sisters, Dear Daughters: Words of Wisdom from Multicultural Women Attorneys Who Have Been There and Done That (2000).

Virginia G. Drachman, Sisters in Law: Women Lawyers in Modern American History (1998).

Cynthia Fuchs Epstein, Women in Law (2d ed. 1993).

John Hagan & Fiona Kay, Gender in Practice: A Study of Lawyers' Lives (1995).

Mona Harrington, Women Lawyers: Rewriting the Rules (1994).

Suzanne Nossel and Elizabeth Westfall, Presumed Equal: What America's Top Women Lawyers Really Think About Their Firms (1998).

Jennifer L. Pierce, Gender Trials: Emotional Lives in Contemporary Law Firms (1995).

J. Clay Smith, Jr. ed., Rebels in Law: Voices in History of Black Women Lawyers (1998).

Symposium, First Women: The Contribution of American Women to the Law, 28 Val. U. L. Rev. No.4 (1994).

Chapter 2

Defense and Prosecution of Criminal Cases

No doubt many more students will engage in civil litigation or office practice than in representation of clients in criminal cases. These materials begin with the field of criminal practice, however, because this area presents a wide range of fundamental issues of professional responsibility in a setting that illuminates the difficult decisions that lawyers often must make. Lawyers who represent criminal defendants can face gut-wrenching problems of confidentiality, zealous representation, and obligations to the system of justice. In an era of increasing public concern about criminality in general and terrorism in particular, prosecutors may face enormous pressures to publicize their activities and obtain rapid convictions. Examining tensions among the values that are at the core of professional responsibility helps to build a foundation for study of these values in other settings.[1]

Section A considers the client-lawyer relationship in criminal defense practice, focusing on justifications for defending guilty clients, the duty of competency, and payment of legal fees. The scope and limitations of the duty of confidentiality form the topics of section B. The materials examine the lawyer's duty of confidentiality when the lawyer learns that the client intends to commit a crime, when the lawyer discovers incriminating material, and when the lawyer knows that the client either has or intends to commit perjury. Section C considers conflicts of interest that can arise in criminal defense practice, while section D focuses on limitations on defense and prosecutorial conduct. Delivery of legal services to indigent criminal defendants is the topic of section E.

---

1. See generally ABA Criminal Justice Section, Ethical Problems Facing the Criminal Defense Lawyer (Rodney J. Uphoff ed., 1995); John Wesley Hall, Jr., Professional Responsibility of the Criminal Lawyer (2d ed. 1996).

A.   The Client-Lawyer Relationship

—————————————— **Problem 2-1** ——————————————

Justifications for Defending the Guilty

You have been asked to speak to a local community group on the topic, "How can lawyers defend clients they know are guilty?" What would you say? What questions would you expect to receive and how would you respond?

———

Read Model Rules 1.2(d), 3.1, and comments.

——————————————————————   —————————————————

Charles P. Curtis, The Ethics of Advocacy
4 Stan. L. Rev. 3, 14-18 (1951)

The classical solution to a lawyer taking a case he knows is bad is Dr. Johnson's. It is perfectly simple and quite specious. . . .

"What do you think," said Boswell, "of supporting a cause which you know to be bad?"

Johnson answered, "Sir, you do not know it to be good or bad till the Judge determines it. I have said that you are to state facts fairly; so that your thinking, or what you call knowing, a cause to be bad, must be from reasoning, must be from your supposing your arguments to be weak and inconclusive. But, Sir, that is not enough. An argument which does not convince yourself, may convince the Judge to whom you urge it: and if it does convince him, why, then, Sir, you are wrong, and he is right."

Dr. Johnson ignored the fact that it is the lawyer's job to know how good or how bad his case is. It is his peculiar function to find out. Dr. Johnson's answer is sound only in cases where the problem does not arise.

A lawyer knows very well whether his client is guilty. It is not the lawyer, but the law, that does not know whether his case is good or bad. The law does not know, because it is trying to find out, and so the law wants everyone defended and every debatable case tried. Therefore the law makes it easy for a lawyer to take a case, whether or not he thinks it bad and whether or not he thinks other people think it bad. It is particularly important that it be made as easy as possible for a lawyer to take a case that other people regard as bad. Otherwise, to take a current example, people who are now being charged with being Communists, who heaven knows need a lawyer, what with the capering of congressional committees, will find it hard to get counsel. . . .

No, there is nothing unethical in taking a bad case or defending the guilty or advocating what you don't believe in. It is ethically neutral. It's a free choice. There is a Daumier drawing of a lawyer arguing, a very demure young woman sitting near him, and a small boy beside her sucking a lollypop. The caption says, "He defends the widow and the orphan, unless he is attacking the orphan and the widow." And for every lawyer whose conscience may be pricked, there is another whose virtue is tickled. Every case has two sides, and for every lawyer on the wrong side, there's another on the right side.

I am not being cynical. We are not dealing with the morals which govern a man acting for himself, but with the ethics of advocacy. We are talking about the special moral code which governs a man who is acting for another. Lawyers in their practice—how they behave elsewhere does not concern us—put off more and more of our common morals the farther they go in a profession which treats right and wrong, vice and virtue, on such equal terms. Some lawyers find nothing to take its place. There are others who put on new and shining raiment.

I will give you as good an example as I know that a lawyer can make a case as noble as a cause. I want to tell you how Arthur D. Hill came into the *Sacco-Vanzetti Case*. It was through Felix Frankfurter, and it is his story. Frankfurter wrote some of it in the newspapers shortly after Arthur's death, and he told it to me in more detail just after the funeral.

When the conviction of Sacco and Vanzetti had been sustained by the Supreme Judicial Court of Massachusetts, there was left an all but hopeless appeal to the federal courts, that is, to the Supreme Court. "It was at this stage," Felix Frankfurter said, "that I was asked if I would try to enlist Arthur Hill's legal services to undertake a final effort, hopeless as it seemed, by appeal to the Federal Law."

Frankfurter called Arthur Hill up and said that he had a very serious matter to discuss with him. "In that case," said Arthur Hill, "we had better have a good lunch first. I will meet you at the Somerset Club for lunch and afterwards you will tell me about it." They lunched together at the Somerset Club, and after lunch they crossed Beacon Street and they sat on the bench in Boston Common overlooking the Frog Pond. And Frankfurter asked Arthur Hill if he would undertake this final appeal of the *Sacco-Vanzetti Case* to the Supreme Court.

Arthur Hill said, "If the president of the biggest bank in Boston came to me and said that his wife had been convicted of murder, but he wanted me to see if there was any possible relief in the Supreme Court of the United States and offered me a fee of $50,000 to make such an effort, of course I would take the retainer, as would, I suppose, everybody else at the bar. It would be a perfectly honorable thing to see whether there was anything in the record which laid a basis for an appeal to the Federal Court.

"I do not see how I can decline a similar effort on behalf of Sacco and Vanzetti simply because they are poor devils against whom the feeling of the community is strong and they have no money with which to hire me. I don't particularly enjoy the proceedings that will follow, but I don't see how I can possibly refuse to make the effort."

. . . Arthur Hill was hired. He did get a fee. Arthur Hill took it as a law case. To him it was a case, not a cause. He was not the partisan, he was the advocate. . . .

I have talked perhaps too lovingly about the practice of the law. I have spoken unsparingly, as I would to another lawyer. In a way the practice of the law is like free speech. It defends what we hate as well as what we most love. . . .

Monroe H. Freedman & Abbe Smith, Understanding Lawyers' Ethics

13-14 (2d ed. 2002)

In its simplest terms, an adversary system resolves disputes by presenting conflicting views of fact and law to an impartial and relatively passive arbiter, who decides which side wins what. In the United States, however, the phrase "adversary system" is synonymous with the American system for the administration of justice—a system that was constitutionalized by the framers and has been elaborated by the Supreme Court for two centuries. Thus, the adversary system represents far more than a simple model for resolving disputes. Rather, it consists of a *core* of basic rights that recognize, and protect, the dignity of the individual in a free society.

The rights that comprise the adversary system include personal autonomy, the effective assistance of counsel, equal protection of the laws, trial by jury, the rights to call and to confront witnesses, and the right to require the government to prove guilt beyond a reasonable doubt and without the use of compelled self-incrimination. These rights, and others, are also included in the broad and fundamental concept that no person may be deprived of life, liberty, or property without due process of law—a concept which itself has been substantially equated with the adversary system. An essential function of the adversary system, therefore, is to maintain a free society in which individual human rights are central.

Former Federal Judge Marvin E. Frankel has written that the adversary system is "cherished as an ideal of constitutional proportions," in part because it embodies "the fundamental right to be heard," and Professor Geoffrey Hazard adds that the adversary system "stands . . . as a pillar of our constitutional system." Accordingly, the Supreme Court has reiterated that the right to counsel is "the most precious" of our rights, because it affects one's ability to assert any other right. It follows, therefore, that the professional responsibilities of the lawyer, serving as counsel within our constitutionalized adversary system, must be informed by the same civil libertarian values that are expressed in the Constitution.

John B. Mitchell, The Ethics of the Criminal Defense Attorney—New Answers to Old Questions

32 Stan. L. Rev. 293, 296-303, 321-323, 326-331 (1980)

I. "MAKING THE SCREENS WORK": THE ROLE OF THE CRIMINAL DEFENSE ATTORNEY

By providing a rigorous defense for a person the attorney knows is factually guilty, an attorney fulfills two significant functions. First, the attorney ensures that the guilty defendant—entitled to the full benefit of our legal process regardless of guilt or innocence—is treated fairly and humanely while in that legal process. I will discuss this function in some detail later when I explore why I personally defend the guilty. Second, and as I will discuss in this part, the attorney performs a function which protects all members of society; I will call this function "making the screens work.". . .

Our criminal justice system is more appropriately defined as a screening system than as a truth-seeking one. This screening process is directed at accurately sorting out those whose deviancy has gone beyond what society considers tolerable and has passed into the area that substantive law labels criminal. The ultimate objective of this screening is to determine who are the proper subjects of the criminal sanction. The process goes on continually at every level of society. We all make judgments about someone's unusual behavior, a window that looks pried open, a suspicious-looking stranger. Neighbor talks to neighbor, and information filters to the police. The police comb the streets gathering information to find those whose behavior warrants special attention. Finally, prosecutors, courts, and juries constantly sift through those selected by the police to make final determinations about who is to be subjected to the criminal sanction.

In performing this screening process, however, the criminal justice system does not operate primarily as a truth-seeking process in the scientific sense. It is weighted at trial in favor of protecting the innocent, even at the cost of acquitting the guilty. It is weighted on the streets in favor of protecting the individual from intrusion by the state, at the cost of the more efficient methods of crime control that would result if police could stop, question, and search anyone they desired. In so doing, our process protects two interrelated and overlapping values (or perhaps, more accurately, two aspects of the same value, human freedom)—dignity and autonomy.

The "weighting" of the system to avoid conviction of the innocent reflects the paramount value this society places upon the dignity of the individual, as well as our concern for the value of human autonomy, a concern which makes us reticent to allow government to enter our daily lives either to restrict our freedom or to intrude into our privacy. The "weighting" against police intrusion similarly reflects these two interrelated values.

The criminal justice system is itself composed of a series of "screens," of which trial is but one. By keeping innocents out of the process and, at the same time, limiting the intrusion of the state into people's lives, each of these screens functions to protect the values of human dignity and autonomy while enforcing our criminal laws. Further, to ensure that the intrusion of the state into the individual's life will be halted at the soonest possible juncture, our system provides a separate screen at each of the several stages of the criminal process. Thus, at any screen, the individual may be taken out of the criminal process and returned to the society with as little disruption of his or her life as possible. . . .

[T]he ingenuity of our criminal justice system goes beyond the screens themselves, for the quality of the screens is no better than the performance of those who make them work. The system has built-in checks on those in charge of the various screens, and . . . the defense attorney who insists on defending the innocence of a guilty defendant plays an important role in making sure that these built-in checks operate effectively. . . .

II. WHY I DEFEND THE GUILTY

A. LESSONS BETTER NOT LEARNED

The criminal justice system provides an institution through which we as a society can demonstrate that we are just and can teach that there is a better way to live than the predatory life of crime. But somehow the noble purpose of our criminal courts, our "schools for justice," has gone awry. Our courts are not just, and they are most frequently unjust when dealing with the most powerless defendants, the poor and the minorities.

Many judges in large urban court systems, interested only in clearing their dockets, and often given to a martinet's temperament, shuttle the 20 or so new faces represented by the same public defender each day from arraignment through guilty plea. Police often lie, while prosecutors suppress evidence favorable to the defense. This governmental lawbreaking passes without the slightest notice. Under the umbrella of almost limitless discretion, judges are often guided only by their inclinations. From my experience, many of them consistently rule in favor of the prosecution and hide their biases while prejudicing any jury over which they are presiding. It is my belief that written motions filed by the defense attorney are frequently not read, while they are routinely denied with no more cogent opposition from the district attorney than the single word "submitted." If it seems that the process is rigged, it is because it is meant to appear that way. Defendants are not there to file motions, have hearings, and go to trial; they are there to plead guilty. As such, the courts have not ceased to be teachers of lessons. It is only that the lessons have changed—and they have changed in a way that approves the normative system of the criminal defendant. . . .

Our criminal courts must teach better lessons. It is to this end that I defend the guilty, for they, above all, must be taught the right lesson. It is not that I naively believe that most convicted defendants would thank a judge for being "fair" while sending them to prison. From my experience, however, the prevalent injustice in the current process does do harm by further lessening respect for the law, not just in the criminal defendants, but also in friends, family, witnesses, and spectators. The lessons are communicated to all of those who are touched by the process.

The defense of the guilty teaches new lessons. The act of defense itself teaches that the indigent defendant is not alone and worthless without money. The slow process of a rigorous defense may anger the judge by delaying the court's schedule, but it also forces the court to view the defendant as a person rather than a file. On some deeper level, the attorney's ardent defense itself communicates to the judge a sense of the defendant's human worth, and to the extent that a sincere, competent advocate earns the grudging respect of the court, some of that respect transfers to the defendant. As a result of this respect—and the knowledge that every ruling adverse to the defense will be contested—the judge rules more favorably for the defendant in order to avoid complications. Finally, police and prosecutors, aware that a defense attorney is carefully questioning and reviewing all their actions, begin to hesitate to engage with such broad abandon in illegality and misconduct for fear of getting caught. Power will thus begin to conform more to law than the other way around.

B.   THE RAVAGES OF CONVICTION

1.   The Prisons

A lengthy exposition on the nightmarish conditions in our jails and prisons would cover little new ground. Literature and reports documenting the horrors are extensive. These horrors are not isolated to some crazed southern jail or labor camp, or to a 20th century Bastille in upstate New York called Attica—they exist even in our most affluent state, California. I have seen many of California's prisons and jails and witnessed the ravages of boredom and the constant fear of violent assault. Over the past 7 years, I have seen inmates who were assaulted and tormented by guards, and others who were beaten by members of prison gangs. I have listened to a terrified young man who, sentenced to 45 days in county jail for vehicular manslaughter, sat awake his first night to the sounds of the inmate in the cell to the left of him being sexually assaulted and the old man in the cage to his right having his head slammed against the floor by some younger ones; while the guards just ignored both and busied themselves with paperwork and cups of coffee. I have seen the anger and bitterness build in some, and I have seen the total mental degeneration of others. Worst of all, I have seen the inhuman degradation of their spirit.

I will not dwell on this. Those guilty of serious crimes merit the wrath of our society. But almost no one deserves the hell holes that we call jails and prisons. There is almost no case I would not defend if that meant keeping a human being, as condemnable as he or she may be, from suffering the total, brutal inhumanity of our jails and prisons. . . .

2. *The Revolving Door*

The entire criminal system, at least for minority defendants, seems to operate like a great revolving door from which they cannot exit once they have been caught up in its momentum. . . .

Long periods of incarceration in prison mean extreme dislocation from family, friends, and work. On release, assimilation is difficult. This time the defendant is an ex-con on parole, not probation. It makes little difference. Before he can reestablish his personal or work lives, one of the dozens of prying eyes now looking at him detect something and he is returned to the system. This cycle continues.

The earlier this cycle is broken by a defense attorney's acquittal or dismissal for the defendant, the better the chances that he can get his life in order. . . .

Barry Winston, Stranger Than True: Why I Defend Guilty Clients
Harper's 70-71 (Dec. 1986)

Let me tell you a story. A true story. The court records are all there if anyone wants to check. It's three years ago. I'm sitting in my office, staring out the window, when I get a call from a lawyer I hardly know. Tax lawyer. Some kid is in trouble and would I be interested in helping him out? He's charged with manslaughter, a felony, and driving under the influence. I tell him sure, have the kid call me.

So the kid calls and makes an appointment to see me. He's a nice kid, fresh out of college, and he's come down here to spend some time with his older sister, who's in med school. One day she tells him they're invited to a cookout with some friends of hers. She's going directly from class and he's going to take her car and meet her there. It's way out in the country, but he gets there before she does, introduces himself around, and pops a beer. She shows up after a while and he pops another beer. Then he eats a hamburger and drinks a third beer. At some point his sister says, "Well, it's about time to go," and they head for the car.

And, the kid tells me, sitting there in my office, the next thing he remembers, he's waking up in a hospital room, hurting like hell, bandages and casts all over him, and somebody is telling him he's charged with manslaughter and DUI because he wrecked his sister's car, killed her in the process, and blew fourteen on the Breathalyzer. I ask him what the hell he means by "the next thing he remembers," and he looks me straight in the eye and says he can't remember anything from the time they leave the cookout until he wakes up in the hospital. He tells me the doctors say he has post-retrograde amnesia. I say of course I believe him, but I'm worried about finding a judge who'll believe him.

I agree to represent him and send somebody for a copy of the wreck report. It says there are four witnesses: a couple in a car going the other way who passed the kid and his sister just before their car ran off the road, the guy whose front yard they landed in, and the trooper who investigated. I call the guy whose yard they ended up in. He isn't home. I leave word. Then I call the couple. The wife agrees to come in the next day with her husband. While I'm talking to her, the first guy calls. I call him back, introduce myself, tell him I'm representing the kid and need to talk to him about the accident. He hems and haws and I figure he's one of those people who think it's against the law to talk to defense lawyers. I say the D.A. will tell him it's O.K. to talk to me, but he doesn't have to. I give him the name and number of the D.A. and he says he'll call me back.

Then I go out and hunt up the trooper. He tells me the whole story. The kid and his sister are coming into town on Smith Level Road, after it turns from fifty-five to forty-five. The Thornes—the couple—are heading out of town. They say this sports car passes them, going the other way, right after that bad turn just south of the new subdivision. They say it's going like a striped-ass ape, at least sixty-five or seventy. Mrs. Thorne turns around to look and Mr. Thorne watches in the rearview mirror. They both see the same thing: halfway into the curve, the car runs off the road on the right, whips back onto the road, spins, runs off on the left, and disappears. They turn around in the first driveway they come to and start back, both terrified of what they're going to find. By this time, Trooper Johnson says, the guy whose front yard the car has ended up in has pulled the kid and his sister out of the wreck and started CPR on the girl. Turns out he's an emergency medical technician. Holloway, that's his name. Johnson tells me that Holloway says he's sitting in his front room, watching television, when he hears a hell of a crash in his yard. He runs outside and finds the car flipped over, and so he pulls the kid out from the driver's side, the girl from the other side. She dies in his arms.

And that, says Trooper Johnson, is that. The kid's blood/alcohol content was fourteen, he was going way too fast, *and* the girl is dead. He had to charge him. It's a shame, he seems a nice kid, it was his own sister and all, but what the hell can he do, right?

The next day the Thornes come in, and they confirm everything Johnson said. By now things are looking not so hot for my client, and I'm thinking it's about time to have a little chat with the D.A. But Holloway still hasn't called me back, so I call him. Not home. Leave word. No call. I wait a couple of days and call again. Finally I get him on the phone. He's very agitated, and won't talk to me except to say that he doesn't have to talk to me.

I know I better look for a deal, so I go to the D.A. He's very sympathetic. But. There's only so far you can get on sympathy. A young woman is dead, promising career cut short, all because somebody has too much to drink and drives. The kid has to pay. Not, the D.A. says, with jail time. But he's got to plead guilty to two misdemeanors: death by vehicle and driving under the influence. That means probation, a big fine. Several thousand dollars. Still, it's hard for me to criticize the D.A. After all, he's probably going to have the MADD mothers all over him because of reducing the felony to a misdemeanor.

On the day of the trial, I get to court a few minutes early. There are the Thornes and Trooper Johnson, and someone I assume is Holloway. Sure enough, when this guy sees me, he comes over and introduces himself and starts right in: "I just want you to know how serious all this drinking and driving really is," he says. "If those young people hadn't been drinking and driving that night, that poor young girl would be alive today." Now, I'm trying to hold my temper when I spot the D.A. I bolt across the room, grab him by the arm, and say, "We gotta talk. Why the hell have you got all those people here? That jerk Holloway. Surely to God you're not going to call him as a witness. This is a guilty plea! My client's parents are sitting out there. You don't need to put them through a dog-and-pony show."

The D.A. looks at me and says, "Man, I'm sorry, but in a case like this, I gotta put on witnesses. Weird Wally is on the bench. If I try to go without witnesses, he might throw me out."

The D.A. calls his first witness. Trooper Johnson identifies himself, tells about being called to the scene of the accident, and describes what he found when he got there and what everybody told him. After he finishes, the judge looks at me. "No questions," I say. Then the D.A. calls Holloway. He describes the noise, running out of the house, the upside-down car in his yard, pulling my client out of the window on the left side of the car and then going around to the other side for the girl. When he gets to this part, he really hits his stride. He describes, in minute detail, the injuries he saw and what he did to try and save her life. And then he tells, breath by breath, how she died in his arms.

The D.A. says, "No further questions, your Honor." The judge looks at me. I shake my head, and he says to Holloway, "You may step down."

One of those awful silences hangs there, and nothing happens for a minute. Holloway doesn't move. Then he looks at me, and at the D.A., and then at the judge. He says, "Can I say something else, your Honor?"

All my bells are ringing at once, and my gut is screaming at me, Object! Object! I'm trying to decide in three quarters of a second whether it'll be worse to listen to a lecture on the evils of drink from this jerk Holloway or piss off the judge by objecting. But all I say is, "No objection, your Honor." The judge smiles at me, then at Holloway, and says, "Very well, Mr. Holloway. What did you wish to say?"

It all comes out in a rush, "Well, you see, your Honor," Holloway says, "it was just like I told Trooper Johnson. It all happened so fast. I heard the noise, and I came running out, and it was night, and I was excited, and the next morning, when I had a chance to think about it, I figured out what had happened, but by then I'd already told Trooper Johnson and I didn't know what to do, but you see, the car, it was upside down, and I did pull that boy out of the left-hand window, but don't you see, the car was upside down, and if you turned it over on its wheels like it's supposed to be, the left-hand side is really on the right-hand side, and your Honor, that boy wasn't driving that car at all. It was the girl that was driving, and when I had a chance to think about it the next morning, I realized that I'd told Trooper Johnson wrong, and I was scared and I didn't know what to do, and that's why"—and now he's looking right at me—"why I wouldn't talk to you."

Naturally, the defendant is allowed to withdraw his guilty plea. The charges are dismissed and the kid and his parents and I go into one of the back rooms in the courthouse and sit there looking at one another for a while. Finally, we recover enough to mumble some Oh my Gods and Thank yous and You're welcomes. And that's why I can stand to represent somebody when I know he's guilty.

The extent of erroneous convictions[2]

Winston's essay raises a larger question: How often are innocent people convicted of crimes? The question is particularly significant in death penalty cases, where the consequences of an erroneous conviction are irreversible. In 1932 Yale Law Professor Edwin M. Borchard published a study of erroneous convictions in capital and noncapital cases.[3] A study by Professors Hugo Adam Bedau and Michael Radelet, published in 1987, identified 350 cases in which defendants were convicted of capital or potentially capital crimes and were later found to have been innocent. Bedau and Radelet based their finding of "innocence" on a number of criteria, principally judicial action (no retrial or acquittal on retrial) or executive action (pardon).[4] The most recent major study of erroneous convictions in death penalty cases was conducted by a team of researchers led by Professor James Liebman of Columbia Law School.[5] Their study analyzed the outcomes on judicial review of more than 5,800 death penalty cases in states that still recognize the death penalty. It found that more than two-thirds of the cases were reversed either on direct appeal or subsequent postconviction relief proceedings.[6] Other findings indicate that "these high reversal rates reflect badly on the accuracy of most capital verdicts."[7] Doubts about the fairness of the death penalty prompted the ABA to recommend a moratorium on the death penalty until steps are taken to reduce the risk of sentencing innocent persons to death.[8]

The advent of DNA testing in the 1990s has moved the issue of erroneous convictions from social science research into courtrooms. The Innocence Project, started in 1992 at Cardozo Law School, provides representation in "cases

2. See generally Wrongful Convictions of the Innocent, 86 Judicature #2 (2002).

3. Edwin M. Borchard, Convicting the Innocent: Sixty Five Actual Errors of Criminal Justice (1932).

4. Hugo Adam Bedau & Michael L. Radelet, Miscarriages of Justice in Potentially Capital Cases, 40 Stan. L. Rev. 21 (1987). For a criticism of the Bedau/Radelet study, particularly their criteria for determining "innocence," see Stephen J. Markman & Paul G. Cassell, Protecting the Innocent: A Response to the Bedau-Radelet Study, 41 Stan. L. Rev. 121 (1988).

5. See http://justice.policy.net/jpreport/ (visited June 16, 2003).

6. See James B. Liebman, Rates of Reversible Error and the Risk of Wrongful Execution, 86 Judicature #2, at 78 (2002).

7. Id. at 81-82.

8. ABA, Resolution 107 (1997).

where postconviction DNA testing of evidence can yield conclusive proof of innocence."[9] As of June 16, 2003, the project listed 131 cases in which DNA evidence has exonerated a convicted defendant.[10]

Why do erroneous convictions occur? The Innocence Project studied the factors that appeared in the first 70 DNA exonerations:

Mistaken I.D.	61
Serology Inclusion	40
Police Misconduct	38
Prosecutorial Misconduct	34
Defective or Fraudulent Science	26
Bad Lawyering	23
Microscopic Hair Comparison Matches	21
False Witness Testimony	17
Informants/Snitches	16
False Confessions	15
Other Forensic Inclusions	6
DNA Inclusions	2[11]

On January 11, 2003, George Ryan, then the Republican Governor of Illinois, commuted all death sentences to life imprisonment because he concluded that the system of capital punishment in Illinois was fundamentally unfair.[12] Governor Ryan had previously declared a moratorium on the use of the death penalty and had appointed a commission to study the issue and make recommendations. The Commission's report contains a number of recommendations to reduce the likelihood of wrongful convictions.[13]

───────────────────── **Problem 2-2** ─────────────────────

Competency of Defense Counsel and Legal Fees in Criminal Cases

a. You have been appointed to represent Edward Donald to seek postconviction relief from his conviction in state court for armed robbery of a check-cashing service. Attorney Thomas Long represented Donald at trial. Donald first met Long a week before trial for about an hour. Donald told Long that he was innocent of the charges and that he was at a bar with a friend when the robbery occurred. Donald also asked Long about the possibility of a plea bargain. Long said he would try to locate

9. http://www.innocenceproject.org/ (visited June 16, 2003).
10. Id. See Barry Scheck et al., Actual Innocence (2000).
11. http://www.innocenceproject.org/causes/index.php (visited June 16, 2003).
12. N.Y. Times, Sun. Jan. 12, 2003.
13. See http://www.idoc.state.il.us/ccp/ccp/reports/index.html (visited June 16, 2003). For a summary of the recommendations by the Commission's cochair, see Thomas P. Sullivan, Preventing Wrongful Convictions, 86 Judicature #2, at 106 (2002).

the friend and to discuss a plea with the prosecutor. At trial the next week, Long told Donald that he had been unable to locate the friend. Long also advised Donald that the prosecutor refused to plea bargain because of Donald's criminal history. (Donald has a long record, beginning with minor crimes as a juvenile and now including burglary, assault, and drug offenses.) At trial the prosecution called the owner of the service as its only witness; the owner testified about the robbery and identified Donald as the perpetrator of the crime. <u>Long did not ask the owner any questions</u>. Donald was particularly upset about this because the owner was old and wore glasses. Donald told Long that he wanted to testify to refute the owner's testimony and to establish his alibi, but Long said that he could not call him as a witness because of his criminal record. The defense rested without calling any witnesses. Long gave a brief closing argument in which he pointed out that the case rested on the store owner's identification, that the store owner was elderly and wore glasses, and that under these circumstances the state had not proven its case beyond a reasonable doubt. The jury convicted Donald, the trial judge sentenced him to twenty years in prison (the maximum allowed by statute), and the conviction and sentence were affirmed by the state supreme court. Be prepared to argue in support of and in opposition to a motion to set aside Donald's conviction because of ineffective assistance of counsel.

b. You are an associate in a private law firm that specializes in criminal defense work. The firm would like your opinion of the propriety of the following provision in its standard engagement agreement:

> Client agrees to pay the Firm a fee of _____. This fee covers the Firm's representation of Client through the trial of this case. The fee does not cover subsequent proceedings, such as appeals, or retrials of the case should that be necessary. The Firm does not agree to represent Client in any subsequent proceedings unless Client and the Firm enter into a written engagement agreement covering such a proceeding. The fee for any subsequent proceeding shall be subject to negotiation by Client and the Firm. **THE CLIENT UNDERSTANDS AND AGREES THAT THE FEE SET FORTH ABOVE IS NONREFUNDABLE REGARDLESS OF WHEN THIS MATTER IS CONCLUDED.**
>
> This fee does not cover expenses, such as the cost of expert witnesses, travel expenses, transcription costs, and other out-of-pocket expenses incurred by the Firm. The Client has paid _____ as an advance against expenses. If this advance is exhausted, the Firm will bill Client for actual expenses incurred on a monthly basis. The Client agrees to pay such expenses within 15 days.

c. The firm has been asked to represent the defendant in a highly publicized prosecution for homicide. The state contends that the defendant murdered two infants in a day care center by brutally shaking them. The defendant and her family have only limited funds. Your partner tells you that the firm is willing to handle the case pro bono if necessary, but the possibility exists that the defendant or her family might receive revenue as a result of the publicity surrounding the case, such as fees for appearances on television shows and royalties from books, television, or movies. The partner wants to know whether the firm could take a security interest in any revenues that the defendant might receive from such sources to secure payment of its fees. What advice would you give?

Read Model Rules 1.1, 1.5(a) and (d), 1.8(d), 1.15, and comments.

The ethical duty of competency, ineffective assistance of counsel, and malpractice liability of defense counsel

Under the Model Rules of Professional Conduct, lawyers have an ethical duty to provide competent representation. The duty of competency is multidimensional, including knowledge of the law, skill, and preparation. See Model Rule 1.1. Despite this obligation, the level of representation provided by appointed counsel in criminal cases is often shockingly low, even in death penalty cases. Examples of recent cases in which lawyers have slept through substantial portions of the trial[14] or have been under the influence of alcohol or drugs[15] are easy to find. One reason for the low level of representation by appointed counsel is that the compensation paid to such counsel is woefully inadequate in most states.[16] We will return to the topic of delivery of legal services to indigents in criminal cases in Problem 2-12.

Lawyers who fail to adhere to their duty to provide competent representation may be subject to professional discipline.[17] For example, in Florida Bar v. Sandstrom[18] the respondent represented the defendant in a prosecution for the murder of his wife, who died after the defendant struck her during an

---

14. Burdine v. Johnson, 262 F.3d 336 (5th Cir. 2001) (counsel who slept through not insubstantial portions of critical guilt-innocence phase of capital murder trial was presumptively ineffective).

15. Payne v. United States, 697 A.2d 1229 (D.C. 1997) (drug use by defense counsel known by trial judge).

16. See Zarabia v. Bradshaw, 912 P.2d 5 (Ariz. 1996) (en banc) (county system for appointment of counsel in criminal cases violated defendants' constitutional right to effective assistance of counsel because, among other reasons, system provided compensation for defense counsel at amount that was significantly less than their overhead expenses with no compensation for their time). But see Sheppard & White, P.A. v. City of Jacksonville, 827 So. 2d 925 (Fla. 2002) ($40 hourly rate set by administrative order of chief judge of circuit for court appointed conflict counsel in death penalty case did not infringe defendant's right to effective assistance of counsel even though rate did not allow counsel to cover expenses or earn profit).

17. Debra T. Landis, Annotation, Negligence, Inattention, or Professional Incompetence of Attorney in Handling Client's Affairs in Criminal Matters as Ground for Disciplinary Action—Modern Cases, 69 A.L.R.4th 410 (1989).

18. 609 So. 2d 583 (Fla. 1992).

altercation. The defendant was convicted, but his conviction was set aside because of ineffective assistance of counsel. The Florida Supreme Court imposed a 60-day suspension on defense counsel based on the following findings of fact by the referee in the case about defense counsel's ineffective assistance at trial:

> Sandstrom failed to take any pretrial depositions; failed to conduct a proper investigation as related to evidence available to establish that the proximate cause of the wife's death was medical malpractice; failed to timely challenge the admission of evidence relating to a search of Arner's car trunk; failed to discover that a fence, surrounding the scene of the alleged crime and injurious to Arner's defense, was not erected until over a year after the alleged crime; failed to present a tape recording to impeach a prosecution witness; and failed to become familiar with or know the physical evidence in the case.[19]

While disciplinary proceedings charging lawyers with incompetent representation in criminal cases are not uncommon, the number of such cases is tiny compared to the frequency of proceedings in which defendants seek postconviction relief based on charges of ineffective assistance of counsel. In Strickland v. Washington[20] the Court established a two-part test for determining when ineffective representation required reversal of a conviction: First, the defendant must show that counsel's performance fell below an objective standard of "reasonably effective assistance."[21] In making this judgment, a court should consider all facts and circumstances, including prevailing norms of the profession. The Court warned that judicial scrutiny should be "highly deferential" and should engage in a "strong presumption" that counsel's conduct was reasonable.[22] Second, "any deficiencies in counsel's performance must be prejudicial to the defense in order to constitute ineffective assistance under the Constitution."[23] In defining prejudice, the Court rejected a test that would have required the defendant to show that the attorney's ineffective assistance was "outcome determinative." Instead, the Court stated: "The defendant must show that there is a reasonable probability that, but for counsel's unprofessional errors, the result of the proceeding would have been different. A reasonable probability is a probability sufficient to undermine confidence in the outcome."[24]

In thousands of cases federal and state courts have applied the *Strickland* standard to determine whether to grant postconviction relief.[25] While the *Strick-*

---

19. Id.
20. 466 U.S. 668 (1984).
21. Id. at 687.
22. Id. at 689.
23. Id. at 692.
24. Id. at 694.
25. In 1996 Congress passed the Antiterrorism and Effective Death Penalty Act of 1996, Pub. L. No. 104-132, 110 Stat. 1214. The Act included an amendment to the federal postconviction relief statute, 28 U.S.C. §2254, which limits the authority of federal courts to grant postconviction relief. The amendment provides:

land requirements are difficult to establish,[26] they are not impossible, at least in capital cases. In two recent decisions, Williams v. Taylor[27] and Wiggins v. Smith,[28] the Court found defense counsel ineffective for failure to investigate mitigating evidence to counter the state's efforts to obtain the death penalty. In *Williams* the Court described defense counsel's conduct as follows:

> Although . . . counsel competently handled the guilt phase of the trial, . . . their representation during the sentencing phase fell short of professional standards—a judgment barely disputed by the State in its brief to this Court. The record establishes that counsel did not begin to prepare for that phase of the proceeding until a week before the trial. . . . They failed to conduct an investigation that would have uncovered extensive records graphically describing Williams' nightmarish childhood, not because of any strategic calculation but because they incorrectly thought that state law barred access to such records. Had they done so, the jury would have learned that Williams' parents had been imprisoned for the criminal neglect of Williams and his siblings,[29] that Williams had been severely and repeatedly beaten by his father, that he had been committed to the custody of the social services bureau for two years during his parents' incarceration (including one stint in an abusive foster home), and then, after his parents were released from prison, had been returned to his parents' custody.
>
> Counsel failed to introduce available evidence that Williams was "borderline mentally retarded" and did not advance beyond sixth grade in school. . . . They failed to seek prison records recording Williams' commendations for helping to crack a prison drug ring and for returning a guard's missing wallet, or the testimony of prison officials who described Williams as among the inmates "least likely to act in a violent, dangerous or provocative way." . . . Counsel failed even to return the phone call of a certified public accountant who had offered to testify that he had visited Williams frequently when Williams was incarcerated as part of a prison ministry program, that Williams "seemed to thrive in a more regi-

---

(d) An application for a writ of habeas corpus on behalf of a person in custody pursuant to the judgment of a State court shall not be granted with respect to any claim that was adjudicated on the merits in State court proceedings unless the adjudication of the claim—

    (1) resulted in a decision that was contrary to, or involved an unreasonable application of, clearly established Federal law, as determined by the Supreme Court of the United States. . . .

26. See, e.g., Williams v. Henry, 185 F.3d 986 (9th Cir. 1999).

27. 529 U.S. 362 (2000).

28. 123 S. Ct. 2527 (2003).

29. Juvenile records contained the following description of his home:

The home was a complete wreck. . . . There were several places on the floor where someone had had a bowel movement. Urine was standing in several places in the bedrooms. There were dirty dishes scattered over the kitchen, and it was impossible to step any place on the kitchen floor where there was no trash. . . . The children were all dirty and none of them had on under-pants. Noah and Lula were so intoxicated, they could not find any clothes for the children, nor were they able to put the clothes on them. . . . The children had to be put in Winslow Hospital, as four of them, by that time, were definitely under the influence of whiskey. . . .

mented and structured environment," and that Williams was proud of the carpentry degree he earned while in prison. . . .

Of course, not all of the additional evidence was favorable to Williams. The juvenile records revealed that he had been thrice committed to the juvenile system—for aiding and abetting larceny when he was 11 years old, for pulling a false fire alarm when he was 12, and for breaking and entering when he was 15. . . . But as the Federal District Court correctly observed, the failure to introduce the comparatively voluminous amount of evidence that did speak in Williams' favor was not justified by a tactical decision to focus on Williams' voluntary confession. Whether or not those omissions were sufficiently prejudicial to have affected the outcome of sentencing, they clearly demonstrate that trial counsel did not fulfill their obligation to conduct a thorough investigation of the defendant's background. See 1 ABA Standards for Criminal Justice 4-4.1, commentary, p. 4-55 (2d ed. 1980).

We are also persuaded, unlike the Virginia Supreme Court, that counsel's unprofessional service prejudiced Williams within the meaning of *Strickland.* After hearing the additional evidence developed in the postconviction proceedings, the very judge who presided at Williams' trial, and who once determined that the death penalty was "just" and "appropriate," concluded that there existed "a reasonable probability that the result of the sentencing phase would have been different" if the jury had heard that evidence. . . .

The Virginia Supreme Court's own analysis of prejudice reaching the contrary conclusion was thus unreasonable in at least two respects. First, . . . the State Supreme Court mischaracterized at best the appropriate rule, made clear by this Court in *Strickland,* for determining whether counsel's assistance was effective within the meaning of the Constitution. While it may also have conducted an "outcome determinative" analysis of its own, . . . it is evident to us that the court's decision turned on its erroneous view that a "mere" difference in outcome is not sufficient to establish constitutionally ineffective assistance of counsel. . . .

Second, the State Supreme Court's prejudice determination was unreasonable insofar as it failed to evaluate the totality of the available mitigation evidence—both that adduced at trial, and the evidence adduced in the habeas proceeding in reweighing it against the evidence in aggravation. . . .[30]

In a few limited types of cases, the courts will presume that the defendant has suffered prejudice. As we shall see in connection with Problem 2-7, when defense counsel has an actual conflict of interest that affects the representation, prejudice is presumed. In addition, some cases of ineffective assistance involve structural errors that go to the accuracy and reliability of the trial process. For example, defense counsel's failure to inform the defendant of the right to a jury trial is a structural error where prejudice is presumed.[31] Finally, in some cases defense counsel's representation is so deficient that the trial did not constitute a true adversarial proceeding. In United States v. Cronic,[32] decided the same day as Strickland v. Washington, the Court held

30. 529 U.S. at 395-398.
31. White v. Johnson, 180 F.3d 648 (5th Cir. 1999).
32. 466 U.S. 648 (1984).

*no prej.
req. if
no adversarial
hearing*

that the defendant need not establish prejudice to obtain relief on the ground of ineffective assistance of counsel when counsel "entirely fails to subject the prosecution's case to meaningful adversarial testing. . . ."[33] In Bell v. Cone,[34] the Court substantially narrowed the *Cronic* exception. *Bell* was a prosecution for murder. During the sentencing phase, defense counsel cross-examined prosecution witnesses, but did not introduce any evidence on behalf of the defendant. Defense counsel waived closing argument and did not ask for mercy for the defendant. The Court held that the *Cronic* exception only applies when counsel's failure was "complete."[35] Thus, counsel's performance was judged under the *Strickland* standard. The Court also found that defense counsel's performance did not fall below reasonable professional standards because he had tactical reasons for the way he handled the sentencing phase of the case.[36]

Defendants can assert ineffective assistance of counsel claims not only as a basis for setting aside convictions but also in actions for damages for legal malpractice against defense counsel.[37] These claims are likely to be difficult to sustain, however. Many courts have erected substantive and procedural hurdles to such lawsuits. For example, in Coscia v. McKenna & Cuneo,[38] the California Supreme Court held that a criminal defendant must prove that he was actually innocent of the crime of which he was charged to recover against his lawyer for malpractice.[39] In addition, the defendant must obtain reversal of his conviction or other postconviction relief to satisfy the requirement of proof of actual innocence.[40] Finally, the defendant must file the malpractice claim within the applicable statute of limitations, even if the defendant has not yet obtained postconviction relief. The malpractice action should then be stayed pending the outcome of postconviction relief proceedings.[41] States are divided on whether public defenders and appointed counsel should be entitled to immunity from malpractice liability.[42] Actions against federal public defenders must be brought against the United States under the Federal Tort Claims Act rather

---

33. Id. at 659.

34. 535 U.S. 685 (2002).

35. Id. at 697.

36. Id. at 702.

37. On the malpractice liability of criminal defense counsel, see generally 3 Mallen & Smith, Legal Malpractice ch. 25 and Gregory G. Sarno, Annotation, Legal Malpractice in Defense of Criminal Prosecution, 4 A.L.R.5th 273 (1993).

38. 25 P.3d 670 (Cal. 2001).

39. Most courts agree. See Schreiber v. Rowe, 814 So. 2d 396 (Fla. 2002); Glenn v. Aiken, 569 N.E.2d 783 (Mass. 1991); Carmel v. Lunney, 511 N.E.2d 1126 (N.Y. 1987); and Peeler v. Hughes & Luce, 909 S.W.2d 494 (Tex. 1995). But see Krahn v. Kinney, 538 N.E.2d 1058 (Ohio 1989) (proof of innocence not required).

40. 25 P.3d at 674.

41. Id. at 680.

42. *Compare* Dziubak v. Mott, 503 N.W.2d 771 (Minn. 1993) (public defenders immune) *with* Barner v. Leeds, 13 P.3d 704 (Cal. 2000) *and* Schreiber v. Rowe, 814 So. 2d 396 (Fla. 2002) (no immunity).

than against the individual attorney.[43] Professor Susan Koniak has criticized the cases that have erected barriers to malpractice actions against defense counsel. She argues that a proper assessment of the values at stake would impose greater obligations on criminal defense counsel than those imposed on counsel in civil cases.[44]

Ethical issues regarding fees in criminal cases

Model Rule 1.5 establishes ethical standards for legal fees. Under Rule 1.5(a) a lawyer may not charge unreasonable fees. We will consider the general reasonableness standard in connection with fees in civil cases in Problem 3-1.

In criminal cases private defense lawyers often require clients to make substantial payments before undertaking representation. The ethical propriety of such fee arrangements depends on the type of payment received. Lawyers often refer to such advance payments as "retainers." It is important to distinguish, however, among general retainers (often referred to as "engagement retainers"), special retainers (often called "advance fees"), flat fees (sometimes called "lump-sum fees"), and expense deposits. A general retainer is a payment to the lawyer for agreeing to take the case, or for agreeing to be available to handle legal matters for the client during a specified period of time. A special retainer (or advanced fee), as the name indicates, is an advanced payment by the client of fees for services to be rendered in the future. A flat fee is a payment of a fixed amount for specific services.[45] An expense deposit is an amount paid to the firm to be applied to future expenses in the client's case.

General retainers differ from special retainers in two significant respects. First, the lawyer earns a general retainer when it is received, so it is part of the firm's general revenue and should not be deposited in the firm's trust account. By contrast, the firm does not earn the special retainer when received. It should be deposited in the firm's trust account, and the firm should then charge against this amount periodically as it performs services for the client. See Model Rule 1.15 on lawyers' obligations regarding trust accounts, discussed more fully below. Second, since the purpose of the general retainer is to assure the availability of the firm rather than to serve as payment for specific services rendered, the retainer is nonrefundable. By contrast, since the special retainer is an advanced fee payment, if the fee for those services is less than the advance payment, the lawyer must refund to the client any excess of the advance fee over the fee for services rendered.[46]

43. See Sullivan v. United States, 21 F.3d 198 (7th Cir.), *cert. denied*, 513 U.S. 1060 (1994).

44. Susan P. Koniak, Through the Looking Glass of Ethics and the Wrong With Rights We Find There, 9 Geo. J. Legal Ethics 1, 5 (1995).

45. On the distinction between types of payments, see Restatement (Third) of the Law Governing Lawyers §34, cmt. e.

46. Id. §38, cmt. g.

A flat fee differs from a special retainer in one crucial respect: Under a flat fee a lawyer cannot contractually charge the client any additional amounts for the services rendered, regardless of how long it takes to perform those services. Because a special retainer is simply an advance fee, however, the lawyer is not contractually limited to the amount of the retainer. The lawyer may charge the client additional amounts for services rendered if the special retainer is exhausted.

In Iowa Supreme Court Board of Professional Ethics & Conduct v. Apland,[47] the Iowa Supreme Court held that nonrefundable special retainers in criminal cases were unethical and void. The court stated:

> such agreements (1) interfere with client's right to discharge an attorney, (2) attempt to limit attorney's duty to refund promptly, upon discharge, all those fees not yet earned . . . and (3) result in an excessive fee to the extent the fee is not earned. . . .[48]

Other courts agree that nonrefundable special retainers are improper.[49]

The courts that have voided nonrefundable retainers have not, however, discussed whether the decisions apply to flat fees. In contrast to a nonrefundable retainer, a flat fee offers an advantage to the client because it imposes a limit on the amount the client must pay for the lawyer's services. In fact, the flat fee has advantages and disadvantages to both the lawyer and the client. A flat fee provides certainty to both the lawyer and client regarding the amount of the fee. In exchange for this certainty, however, both the client and the lawyer make concessions. The client gives up the right to a refund if the time value of the lawyer's services is less than the amount of the flat fee (for example, if the case is dismissed or the client pleads guilty before the case goes to trial). The lawyer gives up the right to seek additional compensation if the time value of the lawyer's services exceeds the amount of the flat fee (for example, if the case goes to trial and the trial takes substantially longer than the lawyer anticipates). Ethics opinions in North Carolina and Ohio have advised that lawyers may charge clients flat fees provided the amount of the fee is reasonable. The opinions ruled that lawyers may consider flat fees like general retainers, treating the flat fee payment as earned income to be deposited in the firm's business account rather than in its trust account. The opinions warned lawyers

---

47. 577 N.W.2d 50 (Iowa 1998).

48. Id. at 57.

49. E.g., In re Thonert, 682 N.E.2d 522 (Ind. 1997) (unethical to demand nonrefundable fee in criminal case when no evidence of any value received by the client or detriment incurred by the attorney in return for the nonrefundable provision); In re Cooperman, 633 N.E.2d 1069 (N.Y. 1994) (divorce case). See generally Lester Brickman & Lawrence A. Cunningham, Nonrefundable Retainers Revisited, 72 N.C.L. Rev. 1 (1993) (supporting the decision in *Cooperman* finding that nonrefundable retainers result in excessive fees).

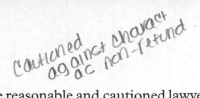

that the amount of the flat fee must be reasonable and cautioned lawyers against characterizing flat fees as nonrefundable.[50]

In addition to the prohibition on nonrefundable special retainers, fees in criminal cases are subject to several other specific restrictions. Model Rule 1.5(d) prohibits contingent fees in criminal cases,[51] although it is difficult to offer a sound rationale for the rule.[52] Indeed, the comments to Rule 1.5 offer no justification.[53] It has been argued that the purpose of the rule is to prevent corruption of justice by criminal defense counsel who would have a financial interest in the outcome through a contingent fee, but the same argument could be made against contingent fees in civil cases.[54] Some commentators have suggested that the prohibition of contingent fees in criminal cases exists to avoid a conflict of interest: If the contingent fee were earned only by an acquittal, defense counsel would have a conflict of interest because counsel would have a financial disincentive against plea bargaining.[55] This problem could be handled, however, by requiring a sliding scale of contingent fees depending on the outcome, much like the sliding scale typically used in personal injury cases.

Another rule that restricts legal fees in criminal cases is Model Rule 1.8(d), which provides as follows:

> Prior to the conclusion of representation of a client, a lawyer shall not make or negotiate an agreement giving the lawyer literary or media rights to a portrayal or account based in substantial part on information relating to the representation.

While the rule is not strictly limited to criminal cases, it comes up more frequently in criminal cases because they are more likely to be sensational than are civil cases. The rationale for the rule is to prevent lawyers from having a financial interest that would interfere with their independent professional judgment. For example, if a lawyer who is representing a client in a criminal case has acquired literary or media rights based on the representation, the lawyer might be inclined to forgo plea bargaining in order to sensationalize the

---

50. N.C. St. Bar Op. 4 (1998) (Nonrefundable Fees), 1998 WL 716663; Ohio Bd. Com. Griev. Disp., Adv. Op. 96-4, 1996 WL 362465.

51. See Winkler v. Keane, 7 F.3d 304 (2d Cir. 1993), *cert. denied*, 511 U.S. 1022 (1994) (fee agreement in which defense counsel was to receive additional $25,000 if defendant was found not guilty constituted an unethical contingency fee, but court refused to set aside conviction because defendant failed to prove that trial counsel's representation was adversely affected).

52. See Thomas D. Morgan, The Evolving Concept of Professional Responsibility, 90 Harv. L. Rev. 702, 734 (1977) (arguing that prohibition on contingent fees in criminal cases protects defense bar's practice of charging up-front fixed fees by suppressing competition through contingent fees).

53. For a criticism of the traditional justifications of the rule and an argument that contingent fees should be allowed in criminal cases in some limited circumstances, see Pamela S. Karlan, Contingent Fees and Criminal Cases, 93 Colum. L. Rev. 595 (1993).

54. 1 Hazard & Hodes, The Law of Lawyering §8.14.

55. Id.

[handwritten: lawyer may change The way The case is handled.]

case and thereby increase the value of the lawyer's interest in media or literary rights. Note that the rule applies only to agreements made "[p]rior to the conclusion of representation of a client." Presumably this means that a lawyer in a criminal case, after the conclusion of the criminal matter, could agree to represent the client in connection with literary or media rights growing out of the case, with the lawyer receiving an interest in such rights as payment for the lawyer's services.[56]

The California Supreme Court has held that in order to be able to retain counsel a criminal defendant may consent to a fee agreement in which the lawyer has an interest in literary or media rights.[57] The California Rules of Professional Conduct, however, do not have a provision like Model Rule 1.8(d). It appears that the drafters of the Model Rules intended to prohibit such fee agreements even with client consent because the drafters concluded that such fee agreements inherently involved a conflict of interest.[58]

It is also interesting to note that a number of states and the federal government have enacted statutes to prevent criminal defendants from profiting from commercial exploitation of their crimes.[59] (Such statutes are often referred to as "Son of Sam" laws, after the New York serial killer David Berkowitz.) These statutes typically require convicted criminals to pay any funds received from commercial portrayals of their crimes to a fund for victims of their crimes. In Simon & Schuster, Inc. v. Members of the New York State Crime Victims Board,[60] the Supreme Court held the New York statute invalid under the First Amendment. In 1992 the New York legislature passed a revised law.[61]

Trust accounts and client property

Lawyers often come into possession of client money or property, or money or property belonging to a third person. In criminal cases lawyers often receive special retainers, flat fees, or expense advances. In personal injury matters

---

56. Rule 1.8(d) also applies to civil cases, so a lawyer could not acquire an interest in literary or media rights that were the subject of civil litigation in which the lawyer was involved prior to the conclusion of the representation. See also Rule 1.8(i). On conclusion of the matter on which the literary or media rights would be based, the lawyer could negotiate contracts regarding those rights and could have an interest in those rights without violating Rule 1.8(d), provided the lawyer also complied with the requirements of Rule 1.8(a) dealing with business transactions between lawyer and client. See also Restatement (Third) of the Law Governing Lawyers §36, cmt. d.

57. Maxwell v. Superior Court, 639 P.2d 248 (Cal. 1982) (en banc).

58. See 1 Hazard & Hodes, The Law of Lawyering §12.10.

59. See 18 U.S.C. §§3681-3682 (special forfeiture of collateral profits of crime).

60. 502 U.S. 105 (1991).

61. See N.Y. Exec. Law §632-a. For an analysis of the Supreme Court's decision in *Simon & Schuster* and of the revised law, see Amr F. Amer, Comment, Play It Again Sam: New York's Renewed Effort to Enact a "Son of Sam" Law that Passes Constitutional Muster, 14 Loy. L.A. Ent. L.J. 115 (1993).

lawyers obtain and disburse settlement proceeds. In real estate matters lawyers hold payments for purchase of property. See Problem 5-3. In business transactions lawyers receive and disburse funds in corporate acquisitions. Model Rule 1.15,[62] dealing with lawyers' obligations regarding money and property belonging to clients and third parties, imposes several obligations:

1. *The duty not to commingle.* Lawyers must keep money and property belonging to clients and third persons separate from their personal and firm funds.

The rule against commingling acts as a prophylactic against lawyer misuse of client funds and protects such funds from being subject to the claims of lawyers' creditors.[63] Lawyers have been disciplined for commingling even when clients have not suffered any financial harm and even when the lawyer acted innocently.[64] The standard method used to prevent commingling is establishment of escrow or trust accounts, separate from lawyers' general accounts, into which money belonging to a client or third party is deposited. It is unnecessary for lawyers to have a separate account for each client or third party. Client and third-party funds may be combined with the funds of other clients and third parties in one account, so long as lawyers' records identify the share of each client or third party and so long as the account is separate from the lawyer's funds.[65] Since funds in trust accounts belong to the clients, lawyers may not receive interest on the account. If the account bears interest, the interest must be allocated to the clients. In many states, court rules allow lawyers to participate in IOLTA (interest on lawyer trust account) programs, in which interest on trust accounts is paid to a special fund to be used for a public purpose, typically delivery of legal services to indigents.[66] As noted previously, lawyers must deposit special retainers and expense advances in their trust accounts, while general retainers and flat fees are earned income deposited in the firm's business account. When fees are earned or expenses incurred, lawyers must withdraw these funds from their trust accounts, so long as there is no dispute about the lawyer's right to receive these funds.[67]

---

62. Restatement (Third) of the Law Governing Lawyers §§44 and 45 impose similar duties.

63. Id. §44, cmt. *b.*

64. See State ex rel. Oklahoma Bar Assn. v. Watson, 897 P.2d 246 (Okla. 1994).

65. Restatement (Third) of the Law Governing Lawyers §44, cmt. *d.*

66. IOLTA programs were attacked as unconstitutional on the ground that they amount to a taking of the client's property without compensation. In Brown v. Legal Foundation of Washington, 123 S. Ct. 1406 (2003), the Supreme Court held that such programs were a taking of client property for a public purpose, but that clients were not entitled to compensation because the program did not deprive the clients of any interest that they could have received.

67. Restatement (Third) of the Law Governing Lawyers §44, cmt. *f.*

2. *The duty to maintain records.* Lawyers must keep careful records of client money and property that comes into their possession. Model Rule 1.15(a) provides that records shall be kept for a period of five years after termination of representation, but prudent lawyers will keep important records indefinitely.

3. *The duty to notify promptly* clients or third parties when lawyers receive money or property in which clients or third parties have an interest.

4. *The duty to deliver promptly* to clients or third parties any funds or other property in which such person has an interest.

5. On request, *the duty to render a full accounting* regarding such money and property.

B. Confidentiality

Problem 2-3

Information About Unsolved or Contemplated Crimes

You are an attorney with the office of the public defender. You have been appointed to represent Albert Simmons, who has been accused of a series of burglaries in the community.

For several months the police have been investigating the disappearance of a teenager. The family and friends of the teenager have organized a massive public campaign in an effort to obtain information about their daughter, but with no success. According to the local newspaper, the investigation is at a dead end, without any leads. Television reports have described the emotional suffering of the teenager's family. In fact, the teenager's father has been hospitalized because of stress.

During the course of one of your interviews with Simmons, he begins crying uncontrollably and tells you that he has a terrible secret that he can't keep to himself any longer: He killed the girl that the police have been looking for. Simmons also tells you that he left her body in an abandoned mine several miles from the city. Simmons goes on to tell you that he is sure the police will find her body and that they'll trace it to him because he left "some other stuff there." Simmons says he's got to get out of jail to get the stuff and to hide the body. He asks you what his chances are of getting out on bail. Assume that Simmons has a reasonable chance of being released on bail. Be prepared to analyze your ethical obligations and to explain how you would proceed.

Suppose you tell Simmons that he doesn't qualify for bail. He tells you that "I'm dead if they find the body. I've got to get out of here." What would you do? Why?

Read Model Rules 1.2, 1.6, 1.16, and comments.

The ethical duty of confidentiality, the attorney-client privilege, and the work product doctrine

In understanding the principle of confidentiality, it is important to distinguish among three related but distinct concepts: the *ethical duty of confidentiality*, the evidentiary *attorney-client privilege*, and the *work product doctrine*. Model Rule 1.6 expresses the ethical duty of confidentiality. Subject to certain exceptions that we will discuss later, the rule requires lawyers to maintain the confidentiality of information "relating to the representation," under all circumstances, whether in connection with court proceedings or otherwise.

By contrast, the attorney-client privilege is a rule of evidence that deals with the question when a lawyer may be compelled in court or other official proceedings or investigations to reveal information received in confidence from a client. Although the scope of the attorney-client privilege depends on the rules of evidence applicable in each jurisdiction, a frequently cited formulation is the one offered by Professor Wigmore:

> (1) Where legal advice of any kind is sought (2) from a professional legal adviser in his capacity as such, (3) the communications relating to that purpose, (4) made in confidence (5) by the client, (6) are at his instance permanently protected (7) from disclosure by himself or by the legal adviser, (8) except the protection be waived.[68]

The work product doctrine, a discovery rule recognized by the Supreme Court in the leading case of Hickman v. Taylor,[69] prevents discovery of materials prepared "in anticipation of litigation" unless the party seeking discovery makes a special showing that the party has "substantial need" for the materials and cannot obtain equivalent materials without "undue hardship."[70] Although client confidences may be embodied in attorney work product, the work product doctrine is designed to preserve the proper functioning of the adversarial system—to allow attorneys to prepare their cases without fear that material prepared in anticipation of litigation will be available to the opposing side.[71] In criminal cases, where discovery is limited, the work product doctrine has little application.[72]

The duty of confidentiality, the attorney client privilege, and the work product doctrine are all subject to exceptions that we will discuss in these

---

68. 8 Wigmore on Evidence §2292, at 554 (McNaughton ed. 1961). See also Unif. R. Evid. 502, 13A U.L.A. 518 (1994). Comment 3 to Model Rule 1.6 summarizes the distinction between the evidentiary privilege and the ethical duty of confidentiality. See generally Geoffrey C. Hazard, Jr., An Historical Perspective on the Attorney-Client Privilege, 66 Cal. L. Rev. 1061 (1978).

69. 329 U.S. 495 (1947).

70. See Fed. R. Civ. P. 26(b)(3).

71. See 1 McCormick on Evidence §96 (5th ed. 1999). See generally Edna S. Epstein, The Attorney-Client Privilege and the Work Product Doctrine (4th ed. 2001).

72. See 1 McCormick on Evidence §97.

materials. We will examine the scope of the evidentiary attorney-client privilege in more detail in connection with Problems 2-11 and 3-3. An excellent case dealing with the distinction between the ethical duty of confidentiality and the evidentiary privilege is Purcell v. District Attorney for the Suffolk District.

Purcell v. District Attorney for Suffolk District

Supreme Judicial Court of Massachusetts
676 N.E. 2d 436 (Mass. 1997)

WILKINS, Chief Justice.

On June 21, 1994, Joseph Tyree, who had received a court order to vacate his apartment in the Allston section of Boston, consulted the plaintiff, Jeffrey W. Purcell, an attorney employed by Greater Boston Legal Services, which provides representation to low income individuals in civil matters. Tyree had recently been discharged as a maintenance man at the apartment building in which his apartment was located. On the day that Tyree consulted Purcell, Purcell decided, after extensive deliberation, that he should advise appropriate authorities that Tyree might engage in conduct harmful to others. He told a Boston police lieutenant that Tyree had made threats to burn the apartment building.

The next day, constables, accompanied by Boston police officers, went to evict Tyree. At the apartment building, they found incendiary materials, containers of gasoline, and several bottles with wicks attached. Smoke detectors had been disconnected, and gasoline had been poured on a hallway floor. Tyree was arrested and later indicted for attempted arson of a building.

In August, 1995, the district attorney for the Suffolk district subpoenaed Purcell to testify concerning the conversation Purcell had had with Tyree on June 21, 1994. A Superior Court judge granted Purcell's motion to quash the subpoena. The trial ended in a mistrial because the jury was unable to reach a verdict.

The Commonwealth decided to try Tyree again and once more sought Purcell's testimony. Another Superior Court judge concluded that Tyree's statements to Purcell were not protected by the attorney-client privilege, denied Purcell's motion to quash an anticipated subpoena, and ordered Purcell to testify. Purcell then commenced this action . . . .

There is no question before this court, directly or indirectly, concerning the ethical propriety of Purcell's disclosure to the police that Tyree might engage in conduct that would be harmful to others. As bar counsel agreed in a memorandum submitted to the single justice, this court's disciplinary rules regulating the practice of law authorized Purcell to reveal to the police "[t]he intention of his client to commit a crime and the information necessary to prevent the crime." S.J.C. Rule 3:07, Canon 4, DR 4-101(C)(3), as appearing in 382 Mass. 778 (1981).[1] The fact that the disciplinary code permitted Purcell

---

1. The same conclusion would be reached under Rule 1.6(b)(1) of the Proposed Massachusetts Rules of Professional Conduct, now pending before the Justices. Under

to make the disclosure tells us nothing about the admissibility of the information that Purcell disclosed. . . .

The attorney-client privilege is founded on the necessity that a client be free to reveal information to an attorney, without fear of its disclosure, in order to obtain informed legal advice. Matter of a John Doe Grand Jury Investigation, 408 Mass. 480, 481-482, 562 N.E.2d 69 (1990). It is a principle of long standing. The debate here is whether Tyree is entitled to the protection of the attorney-client privilege in the circumstances.

The district attorney announces the issue in his brief to be whether a crime-fraud exception to the testimonial privilege applies in this case. He asserts that, even if Tyree's communication with Purcell was made as part of his consultation concerning the eviction proceeding, Tyree's communication concerning his contemplated criminal conduct is not protected by the privilege. We shall first consider the case on the assumption that Tyree's statements to Purcell are protected by the attorney-client privilege unless the crime-fraud exception applies.

"It is the purpose of the crime-fraud exception to the attorney-client privilege to assure that the 'seal of secrecy,' . . . between lawyer and client does not extend to communications 'made for the purpose of getting advice for the commission of a fraud' or crime" (citation omitted). United States v. Zolin, 491 U.S. 554, 563 (1989), quoting O'Rourke v. Darbishire, [1920] App. Cas. 581, 604 (P.C.). There is no public interest in the preservation of the secrecy of that kind of communication. . . . [In] Commonwealth v. Dyer, 243 Mass. 472, 138 N.E. 296, cert. denied, 262 U.S. 751 (1923) . . . we said that "[t]here is no privilege between attorney and client where the conferences concern the proposed commission of a crime by the client." Id. at 505-506, 138 N.E. 296. The cases cited in our *Dyer* opinion and the facts of that case—the attorney was alleged to be part of the conspiracy— demonstrate that the exception asserted concerned conferences in which the attorney's advice was sought in furtherance of a crime or to obtain advice or assistance with respect to criminal activity.

We, therefore, accept the general principle of a crime-fraud exception. The Proposed Massachusetts Rules of Evidence adequately define the crime-fraud exception to the lawyer-client privilege set forth in rule 502(d)(1) as follows: "If the services of the lawyer were sought or obtained to enable or aid anyone to commit or plan to commit what the client knew or reasonably should have known to be a crime or fraud." We need not at this time consider seemingly

---

Rule 1.6(b)(1), as now proposed, a lawyer may reveal confidential information relating to a client "to prevent the commission of a criminal or fraudulent act that the lawyer reasonably believes is likely to result in death or substantial bodily harm, or in substantial injury to the financial interests or property of another." Unlike DR 4-101(C)(3), which allows disclosure of a client's intention to commit any crime, disclosure of a client's intention to commit a crime is permissible under proposed Rule 1.6(b)(1) only as to crimes threatening substantial consequences, and disclosure is permitted based on an attorney's reasonable belief of the likely existence of the threat rather than, as is the case under DR 4-101(C)(3), a known intention of the client to commit a crime.

minor variations of the exception expressed in various sources. See Restatement (Third) of the Law Governing Lawyers §132, and authorities cited in Reporter's Note at 465-466 (Proposed Final Draft No. 1 1996) [Adopted as §82—Ed.]. The applicability of the exception, like the existence of the privilege, is a question of fact for the judge.

The district attorney rightly grants that he, as the opponent of the application of the testimonial privilege, has the burden of showing that the exception applies. . . . In its *Zolin* opinion, the Supreme Court did not have to decide what level of showing the opponent of the privilege must make to establish that the exception applies. See United States v. Zolin, supra at 563-564 n.7. We conclude that facts supporting the applicability of the crime-fraud exception must be proved by a preponderance of the evidence. However, on a showing of a factual basis adequate to support a reasonable belief that an in camera review of the evidence may establish that the exception applies, the judge has discretion to conduct such an in camera review. United States v. Zolin, supra at 572. Once the judge sees the confidential information, the burden of proof normally will be unimportant.

In this case, in deciding whether to conduct a discretionary in camera review of the substance of the conversation concerning arson between Tyree and Purcell, the judge would have evidence tending to show that Tyree discussed a future crime with Purcell and that thereafter Tyree actively prepared to commit that crime. Without this evidence, the crime of arson would appear to have no apparent connection with Tyree's eviction proceeding and Purcell's representation of Tyree. With this evidence, however, a request that a judge inquire in camera into the circumstances of Tyree's apparent threat to burn the apartment building would not be a call for a "fishing expedition," and a judge might be justified in conducting such an inquiry. The evidence in this case, however, was not sufficient to warrant the judge's finding that Tyree consulted Purcell for the purpose of obtaining advice in furtherance of a crime. Therefore, the order denying the motion to quash because the crime-fraud exception applied cannot be upheld.

There is a consideration in this case that does not appear in other cases that we have seen concerning the attorney-client privilege. The testimony that the prosecution seeks from Purcell is available only because Purcell reflectively made a disclosure, relying on this court's disciplinary rule which permitted him to do so. Purcell was under no ethical duty to disclose Tyree's intention to commit a crime. He did so to protect the lives and property of others, a purpose that underlies a lawyer's discretionary right stated in the disciplinary rule. The limited facts in the record strongly suggest that Purcell's disclosures to the police served the beneficial public purpose on which the disciplinary rule was based.

We must be cautious in permitting the use of client communications that a lawyer has revealed only because of a threat to others. Lawyers will be reluctant to come forward if they know that the information that they disclose may lead to adverse consequences to their clients. A practice of the use of such disclosures might prompt a lawyer to warn a client in advance that the disclosure of certain information may not be held confidential, thereby chilling free discourse between lawyer and client and reducing the prospect that the lawyer will learn of a serious threat to the well-being of others. To best promote the purposes of the attorney-client privilege, the crime-fraud exception should apply only if the communication seeks assistance in or furtherance of future criminal conduct. When the opponent of the privilege argues that the communication itself may show that the exception applies and seeks its disclosure in camera, the judge, in the exercise of discretion on the question whether to have an in camera proceeding, should consider if the public interest is served by disclosure, even in camera, of a communication whose existence is known only because the lawyer acted against his client's interests under the authority of a disciplinary rule. The facts of each situation must be considered.

It might seem that this opinion is in a posture to conclude by stating that the order denying the motion to quash any subpoena to testify is vacated and the matter is to be remanded for further proceedings concerning the application of the crime-fraud exception. However, the district attorney's brief appears to abandon its earlier concession that all communications between Tyree and Purcell should be treated as protected by the attorney-client privilege unless the crime-fraud exception applies. The question whether the attorney-client privilege is involved at all will be open on remand. We, therefore, discuss the issue.

The attorney-client privilege applies only when the client's communication was for the purpose of facilitating the rendition of legal services. See Rule 502(b) of the Proposed Massachusetts Rules of Evidence; Restatement (Third) of the Law Governing Lawyers §118 (Proposed Final Draft No. 1, 1996) (communication "for the purpose of obtaining or providing legal assistance") [Adopted as §68—ED.]; 8 J. Wigmore, Evidence §2292, at 554 (McNaughton rev. ed. 1961) (communication relating to seeking legal advice). . . . The burden of proving that the attorney-client privilege applies to a communication rests on the party asserting the privilege. . . . The motion judge did not pass on the question whether the attorney-client privilege applied to the communication at all but rather went directly to the issue of the crime-fraud exception, although not using that phrase.

A statement of an intention to commit a crime made in the course of seeking legal advice is protected by the privilege, unless the crime-fraud exception applies. That exception applies only if the client or prospective client seeks advice or assistance in furtherance of criminal conduct. It is agreed that Tyree consulted Purcell concerning his impending eviction. Purcell is a member of the bar, and Tyree either was or sought to become Purcell's client. The serious question concerning the application of the privilege is whether Tyree informed Purcell of the fact of his intention to commit arson for the purpose of receiving legal advice or assistance in furtherance of criminal conduct. Purcell's presentation of the circumstances in which Tyree's statements were made is likely to be the only evidence presented.

This is not a case in which our traditional view that testimonial privileges should be construed strictly should be applied. . . . A strict construction of the privilege that would leave a gap between the circumstances in which the crime-fraud exception applies and the circumstances in which a communication is protected by the attorney-client privilege would make no sense. The attorney-client privilege "is founded upon the necessity, in the interest and administration of justice, of the aid of persons having knowledge of the law and skilled in its practice, which assistance can only be safely and readily availed of when free from the consequences or the apprehension of disclosure." Matter of a John Doe Grand Jury Investigation, 408 Mass. 480, 481-482, 562 N.E.2d 69 (1990), quoting Hunt v. Blackburn, 128 U.S. 464, 470 (1888). Unless the crime-fraud exception applies, the attorney-client privilege should apply to communications concerning possible future, as well as past, criminal conduct, because an informed lawyer may be able to dissuade the client from improper future conduct and, if not, under the ethical rules may elect in the public interest to make a limited disclosure of the client's threatened conduct.

A judgment should be entered in the county court ordering that the order denying the motion to quash any subpoena issued to Purcell to testify at Tyree's trial is vacated and that the matter is remanded for further proceedings consistent with this opinion.

So ordered.

Notes and Questions

1. As finally adopted, Massachusetts Rule of Professional Conduct 1.6(b)(1) provides as follows:

> (b) A lawyer may reveal, and to the extent required by Rule 3.3, Rule 4.1(b), or Rule 8.3 must reveal, such information:
> (1) to prevent the commission of a criminal or fraudulent act that the lawyer reasonably believes is likely to result in death or substantial bodily harm, or in substantial injury to the financial interests or property of another, or to prevent the wrongful execution or incarceration of another; . . .

How does this rule compare the ABA Model Rule 1.6(b)? Which rule do you think is superior? Why?

2. Like Massachusetts, many states have adopted confidentiality rules that differ from the ABA's Model Rule. For a listing of state variations, see Thomas D. Morgan & Ronald D. Rotunda, Selected Standards on Professional Responsibility 144 (2004) (Appendix A, Ethics Rules on Client Confidences). What is the confidentiality rule in your state? How does it compare to the ABA Model Rule?

3. The court rejected the district attorney's contention that the attorney-client privilege did not apply because Tyree was not seeking legal advice when he made his threat. Some other courts may disagree with this approach. See United States v. Alexander, 287 F.3d 811 (9th Cir. 2002) (attorney's testimony regarding threats by client to harm attorney and others was not subject to the

attorney-client privilege because the client was not seeking legal advice). Which view do you think is correct? Why?

4. Under *Purcell* a lawyer ethically may disclose confidential information to prevent a client from committing a crime that will harm another person, but the lawyer cannot be compelled to testify about the communication because the lawyer's testimony would violate the attorney-client privilege. Why should the law treat the ethical duty of confidentiality and the attorney-client privilege differently?

Exceptions to the duty of confidentiality: consent, prevention of harm, and past wrongful conduct

Rule 1.6(a) provides that a lawyer may reveal confidential information if the "client gives informed consent." For the definition of "informed consent" see Rule 1.0(e).

A dramatic example of the application of the consent exception is McClure v. Thompson.[73] Attorney Christopher Mecca represented Robert McClure, who was accused of the murder of Carol Jones. When McClure was arrested, two of Jones's children were missing. Mecca and McClure had several discussions about the children, but McClure did not tell Mecca whether they were dead or alive. However, McClure drew a map indicating where the children might be. Mecca had his secretary place an anonymous phone call to the authorities to inform them where the children might be found. Based on this information, the sheriff's office located the bodies of the children. Mecca then withdrew from representing McClure, who was subsequently convicted of all three murders and sentenced to life in prison. McClure filed a petition for habeas corpus relief claiming that Mecca rendered ineffective assistance of counsel. He argued that Mecca failed to obtain his informed consent before disclosing confidential information, did not make a sufficient inquiry before disclosing confidences, and suffered from a conflict of interest. While McClure did not expressly consent to Mecca's disclosure to the authorities, the court accepted the state court's finding of fact that Mecca had "inferred" that McClure had consented to disclosure, but the court ruled that the fact of consent was insufficient because Mecca had not advised his client of the potentially harmful consequences of disclosure.[74] Although the court found that Mecca was not authorized to disclose McClure's confidences under the consent exception, it still denied relief. In a 2-1 decision, the court found that Mecca was authorized to disclose the information to prevent imminent death because he had a reasonable belief that the children were still alive.[75] The majority was not completely comfortable with its decision, stating that the case was a close

---

73. 323 F.3d 1233 (9th Cir. 2003).
74. Id. at 1244-1245.
75. Id. at 1246-1247.

one.[76] A strongly worded dissent argued that a lawyer must have a firm factual basis before disclosing a client's confidences; the information Mecca had did not meet that standard and he failed to investigate further to determine whether the children were alive.[77]

One of the most hotly debated issues in the profession over the past 20 years has been the extent to which the duty of confidentiality should be limited when disclosure would either *prevent* the client from committing a wrongful act or would *rectify* the consequences of a wrongful act that the client has committed.[78] Model Rule 1.6 as originally adopted in 1983 contained a very narrow exception to the duty of confidentiality to prevent harm. Rule 1.6(b)(1) allowed a lawyer to reveal information relating to the representation of a client "to prevent the client from committing a criminal act that the lawyer believes is likely to result in imminent death or substantial bodily harm." The 2002 amendments to the Model Rules broadened the harm-prevention exception to read as follows: "to prevent reasonably certain death or substantial bodily harm." The revision to Rule 1.6 widens the exception to confidentiality by eliminating the requirement of a criminal act by the client. Thus, under the revised rule a lawyer would have discretion to reveal confidential information to prevent the execution of an innocent person.[79] The rule would not, however, allow a lawyer to reveal confidential information regarding past crimes unless the revelation could prevent reasonably certain death or substantial bodily harm. In 2003 the ABA made further amendments to Rule 1.6 dealing with revelation of confidential information to prevent or rectify financial crimes or frauds when the lawyer's services were involved. We will consider this issue in Problem 5-2 when we examine lawyers' ethical and legal obligations regarding fraud by clients in business transactions.

The California Rules of Professional Conduct do not contain a provision on confidentiality. The California Supreme Court rejected a proposed rule that would have allowed a lawyer to disclose confidential information to prevent a client from committing a "criminal act that the member believes is likely to

76. Id. at 1247.
77. Id. at 1252-1256.
78. See Nathan M. Crystal, Confidentiality Under the Model Rules of Professional Conduct, 30 Kan. L. Rev. 215 (1982).
79. Symposium, Executing the Wrong Person: The Professionals' Ethical Dilemmas, 28 Loy. L.A.L. Rev. 1543 (1996). Of course, even if a lawyer could ethically reveal confidential information to prevent an unjust conviction or incarceration, the attorney-client privilege might prevent the attorney from testifying about such communications. See State v. Macumber, 544 P.2d 1084 (Ariz. 1976) (en banc) (attorneys were properly prevented, on grounds of attorney-client privilege, from testifying that person other than defendant, which person had since died, had confessed to them of committing crime for which defendant was being tried); State v. Macumber, 582 P.2d 162 (Ariz. 1978) (en banc) (after waiver by mother of deceased son's attorney-client privilege, trial judge properly excluded testimony of former attorneys that their client had confessed to crime for which defendant was charged because testimony lacked sufficient circumstantial probability of trustworthiness). See also Purcell v. District Attorney for the Suffolk Dist., 676 N.E.2d 436 (Mass. 1997), discussed above.

result in death or substantial bodily harm."[80] For many years §6068(c) of the California Business and Professional Code set forth a duty of confidentiality without exceptions.[81] This duty, however, was in tension with California evidence law, under which a threat to commit a crime was not privileged.[82] In 2003 California amended §6068(e) to provide that an attorney may reveal confidential information to the extent reasonably necessary "to prevent a criminal act that the attorney reasonably believes is likely to result in death of, or substantial bodily harm to, an individual."

Tort or criminal liability for failure to disclose confidential information to prevent or rectify wrongful conduct

The rules of professional conduct are not the only guidelines for determining whether a lawyer is authorized or required to disclose confidential information to prevent or rectify wrongful conduct. The Model Rules recognize and incorporate a requirement that lawyers comply with "other law." Model Rule 1.6(b)(6) states that a lawyer may disclose confidential information to the extent the lawyer reasonably believes necessary "to comply with other law or a court order." See also comments 12 and 13. What does "other law" require? In particular, does either tort or statutory law require disclosure of what would otherwise be confidential information?

In Tarasoff v. Regents of the University of California,[83] a patient confided to a psychotherapist employed by the University of California his intention to kill a young woman who had rejected his advances. The doctor concluded that his patient should be committed and notified the police, who arrested the patient but released him when he appeared to be rational. The doctor did not notify the young woman or her family of the threat to her life. The patient subsequently carried out his threat and killed the young woman. The California Supreme Court held that her parents stated a cause of action against the defendants for negligent failure to warn the young woman of the threat to her life. The court held that the special relationship between doctor and patient was sufficient to create a duty of care to third parties foreseeably injured by the patient.[84] Defendants argued that liability should not be imposed because psychotherapists cannot accurately predict dangerousness. The court rejected this blanket argument, noting that doctors were required only to exercise reason-

---

80. Prop. Cal. R. Prof. Conduct 3-100(C)(2) (1993).

81. See Los Angeles County Bar. Assn., Ethics Op. #504 (2001) (attorney is ethically required to follow the instructions of a minor client to maintain confidentiality when the minor discloses that the minor has been the victim of sexual abuse, provided the attorney properly counsels the client and believes that the minor is competent to make an informed decision).

82. See People v. Dang, 113 Cal. Rptr. 2d 763 (Ct. App. 2001), *review denied* (2002); Kevin E. Mohr, California's Duty of Confidentiality: Is It Time for a Life-Threatening Criminal Act Exception?, 39 San Diego L. Rev. 307 (2002).

83. 551 P.2d 334 (Cal. 1976) (en banc).

84. Id. at 344.

able care, and in any event the argument did not apply to the case before the court since the doctor had accurately concluded that the patient was dangerous but had failed to warn the potential victim.[85] Defendants also argued that the imposition of liability interfered with "free and open communication . . . essential to psychotherapy." While recognizing that there was a public policy in favor of confidentiality between psychotherapist and patient, the court concluded that this policy must yield to the public policy in favor of preventing harm to others: "The protective privilege ends where the public peril begins."[86]

Subsequent California cases, however, have limited *Tarasoff* to situations in which the patient threatens an "identifiable" victim rather than simply posing a danger to the community as a whole.[87] Failure-to-warn claims have also been brought in other jurisdictions, but recovery has been rare.[88]

Could attorneys be held liable in tort for failure to warn third parties of threats by their clients?[89] Hawkins v. King County[90] appears to be the only case that has dealt directly with the issue. In *Hawkins* the court appointed an attorney to represent Hawkins, who was accused of possession of marijuana. The attorney learned from another lawyer employed by his client's mother that his client was mentally ill and dangerous. A psychiatrist advised the attorney that his client was dangerous to himself and to others and should not be released from custody. The attorney represented the client at a bail hearing and obtained his release on a personal surety bond. The attorney did not inform the court of the information about his client's dangerousness. Neither the judge nor the prosecutor raised any questions about the client's dangerousness. Eight days after his release, Hawkins assaulted his mother and attempted suicide. The Hawkinses then brought suit naming the attorney as one of the defendants. They alleged two theories: First, that the attorney violated a duty imposed by rules of ethics and court rules to disclose to the court information about his client's dangerousness. Second, based on *Tarasoff*, the attorney should be held liable for failure to warn of his client's dangerousness. The court rejected the first theory. It found no specific provision in either the rules of ethics or court rules that required a lawyer to reveal adverse information about a client:

---

85. Id. at 345.

86. Id. at 346-347.

87. See, e.g., Thompson v. County of Alameda, 614 P.2d 728 (Cal. 1980). But see Reisner v. Regents of the University of California, 37 Cal. Rptr. 2d 518 (Ct. App.), *review denied* (1995) (doctor who learned that patient was HIV-infected during operation had duty to warn because it was reasonably foreseeable that patient would have intimate relationships in the future, even though doctor did not know identity of future partners).

88. Cases are collected in John C. Williams, Annotation, Liability of One Treating Mentally Afflicted Patient for Failure to Warn or Protect Third Persons Threatened by Patient, 83 A.L.R.3d 1201 (1978).

89. See generally Davalene Cooper, The Ethical Rules Lack Ethics: Tort Liability When a Lawyer Fails to Warn a Third Party of a Client's Threat to Cause Serious Physical Harm or Death, 36 Idaho L. Rev. 479 (2000); Vanessa Merton, Confidentiality and the "Dangerous" Patient: Implications of *Tarasoff* for Psychiatrists and Lawyers, 31 Emory L.J. 263 (1982).

90. 602 P.2d 361 (Wash. Ct. App. 1979).

We believe that the duty of counsel to be loyal to his client and to represent zealously his client's interest overrides the nebulous and unsupported theory that our rules and ethical code mandate disclosure of information which counsel considers detrimental to his client's stated interest. Because disclosure is not "required by law," appellants' theory of liability on the basis of ethical or court rule violations fails for lack of substance.[91]

As to the *Tarasoff* theory, the court appeared to hold that on appropriate facts a cause of action could be stated against an attorney for failure to warn, but that the case before it was distinguishable from *Tarasoff*:

In the instant case Michael Hawkins' potential victims, his mother and sister, knew he might be dangerous and that he had been released from confinement, contrary to Tatiana Tarasoff's ignorance of any risk of harm. Thus, no duty befell Sanders to warn Frances Hawkins of a risk of which she was already fully cognizant. Further, it must not be overlooked that Sanders received no information that Hawkins planned to assault anyone, only that he was mentally ill and likely to be dangerous to himself and others. That Sanders received no information directly from Michael Hawkins is the final distinction between the two cases.

The common law duty to volunteer information about a client to a court considering pretrial release must be limited to situations where information gained convinces counsel that his client intends to commit a crime or inflict injury upon unknowing third persons. Such a duty cannot be extended to the facts before us.[92]

In addition to tort law, statutes may impose an obligation on lawyers to disclose confidential information to prevent or rectify harm. For example, in a few states statutes may require attorneys to reveal confidential information to prevent child abuse.[93]

If a statute *expressly* requires a lawyer to disclose information, the lawyer must comply with the statute, unless compliance would violate the client's constitutional rights, a point discussed below. The situations in which a statute expressly imposes a disclosure obligation on an attorney are rare. Far more common are statutes that apply broadly to "any person" and do not include a specific exemption for attorneys. A famous example is the *Lake Pleasant bodies* case, *People v. Belge*.[94] Two lawyers, Armani and Belge, were representing a

---

91. Id. at 365.

92. Id. at 365-366. Cf. State v. Hansen, 862 P.2d 117 (Wash. 1993) (en banc) (attorney has duty to warn judge of client's intention to attack judge; *Hawkins* distinguished because mother and sister were aware of danger while judge was not).

93. See Ellen Marrus, Please Keep My Secret: Child Abuse Reporting Statutes, Confidentiality, and Juvenile Delinquency, 11 Geo. J. Legal Ethics 509, 515-520 (1998). See also Brooke Albrandt, Note, Turning in the Client: Mandatory Child Abuse Reporting Requirements and the Criminal Defense of Battered Women, 81 Tex. L. Rev. 655 (2002).

94. 372 N.Y.S.2d 798 (County Ct.), aff'd, 376 N.Y.S.2d 771 (App. Div. 1975), aff'd, 359 N.E.2d 377 (N.Y. 1976). For a personal view of the case coauthored by one of the lawyers, see Tom Alibrandi & Frank H. Armani, Privileged Information (1984). See also Richard Zitrin & Carol M. Langford, The Moral Compass of the American Lawyer ch. 1 (1999).

defendant accused of murder when the defendant informed them that he had committed three unsolved murders. The defendant told his lawyers of the location of one victim's body. Belge went to the location and inspected the body to verify the client's story. The lawyers did not reveal the information, but their knowledge later became public during the defendant's trial as part of their insanity defense. Because of public outrage against the lawyers' conduct, the district attorney presented the matter to a grand jury, which returned an indictment against Belge, but not against Armani, for violation of two provisions of the New York Public Health Law, one requiring that the dead be given a decent burial, the other directing any person knowing of the death of a person without medical assistance to report the matter to the authorities. Neither statute expressly referred to attorneys. While the trial court dismissed the indictment and the appellate division affirmed, the victory for the duty of confidentiality was far from clear cut. The trial court did not decide that the attorneys' conduct was clearly proper. Instead, it concluded that it must balance the rights of the defendant against the interests of society. The court seemed particularly influenced by the fact that the grand jury had returned an indictment against Belge but not against Armani, characterizing the grand jury as "grasping at straws." The court went on to state that Belge's conduct amounted to obstruction of justice and that the decision of the court would have been much more difficult if he had been indicted on that ground.

The appellate court was equally lukewarm in its support of Belge. While finding that the attorney-client privilege protected Belge from responsibility under the public health law, the court stated:

> In view of the fact that the claim of absolute privilege was proffered, we note that the privilege is not all-encompassing and that in a given case there may be conflicting considerations. We believe that an attorney must protect his client's interests, but also must observe basic human standards of decency, having due regard to the need that the legal system accord justice to the interests of society and its individual members.
>
> We write to emphasize our serious concern regarding the consequences which emanate from a claim of an absolute attorney-client privilege. Because the only question presented, briefed and argued on this appeal was a legal one with respect to the sufficiency of the indictments, we limit our determination to that issue and do not reach the ethical questions underlying this case.[95]

What should be the scope of the duty of confidentiality?

Advocates of a strict view of confidentiality have typically made two arguments in support of their position. One argument rests on the "rights" of clients, either legal rights or more broadly defined moral rights. The other argument rests on the social utility of client confidentiality.

Proponents of a strong view of confidentiality have argued that clients

---

95. 376 N.Y.S.2d at 772.

have constitutional rights to confidentiality based on the Fifth Amendment privilege against self-incrimination and the Sixth Amendment right to counsel. In Fisher v. United States[96] the Supreme Court held that the privilege against self-incrimination protected information that a client had given to a lawyer (1) if the attorney-client privilege applied to the conveyance of the information from the client to the lawyer, and (2) if the information could not have been obtained directly from the client because of the privilege against self-incrimination. (We will consider *Fisher* in more detail in connection with Problems 2-4 and 2-5.) Under *Fisher* it is unlikely that a rule requiring or allowing a lawyer to reveal confidential information to prevent a criminal or wrongful act would violate the client's privilege against self-incrimination. First, the attorney-client privilege may not apply to the information. If the client does not convey the information for the purpose of seeking legal advice, the privilege does not apply.[97] Thus, if the client simply makes threats to harm others, the privilege may not apply.[98] Even if the client is seeking legal advice about his plans, then the privilege may still not apply because one of the well-recognized exceptions to the attorney-client privilege is the "crime-fraud exception." Under this exception a client's communications are not privileged when the client is seeking legal advice to enable or assist the client in committing a crime or fraud.[99] Second, the privilege against self-incrimination applies only if the information is incriminating. To the extent that the attorney's disclosure prevents a crime (or the attempt to commit a crime), there is no incrimination. Recall, however, that in *Purcell* the court held that the client's threats to burn down the apartment building were subject to the attorney-client privilege. The court rejected the district attorney's arguments that the crime-fraud exception applied and that the client had not sought legal advice. In addition, the lawyer's disclosure led to the client's prosecution for *attempted* arson. Third, disclosure of information to prevent noncriminal conduct would not implicate the privilege against self-incrimination. Finally, disclosure would not violate the privilege against self-incrimination if the client received "use immunity" against being prosecuted based on the disclosed information. The attorney could request such immunity from the authorities before revealing the client's intention to commit a crime.[100]

Similarly, the Sixth Amendment right to counsel should not prevent disclosure of information to prevent harm. First, the right to counsel does not attach in criminal cases until the initiation of adversary judicial proceedings.[101] A rule that required disclosure of information prior to that time would not implicate the Sixth Amendment. Even if the disclosure obligation attached after initiation of formal proceedings, the Sixth Amendment requires that counsel conform

96. 425 U.S. 391 (1976).
97. Restatement (Third) of the Law Governing Lawyers §72.
98. See United States v. Alexander, 287 F.3d 811 (9th Cir. 2002).
99. Restatement (Third) of the Law Governing Lawyers §82.
100. See Harry I. Subin, The Lawyer as Superego: Disclosure of Client Confidences to Prevent Harm, 70 Iowa L. Rev. 1091, 1120-1127 (1985).
101. See Moran v. Burbine, 475 U.S. 412, 428 (1986).

to reasonable professional standards. A lawyer who has a reasonable belief that another person faces imminent death or substantial bodily harm and who discloses confidential information to prevent this harm in accordance with the rules of professional conduct does not violate the defendant's Sixth Amendment right to effective assistance of counsel.[102] Finally, the Sixth Amendment does not guarantee a right to a particular counsel, only a right to effective representation. Any Sixth Amendment problem with a rule requiring lawyers to disclose information to prevent serious harm could be resolved, therefore, by appointing another lawyer to represent the client.[103]

A broader statement of the clients' rights argument focuses on moral rather than legal rights.[104] Under this view the client's moral rights to privacy and autonomy justify an obligation of confidentiality.[105] But moral philosophy recognizes that rights such as privacy and autonomy may be limited in various situations, in particular when a person intends to harm others.[106] Thus, neither constitutional nor moral rights justify a strict rule of confidentiality.

The social utility argument for confidentiality claims that if clients are encouraged to reveal confidential information, including information about wrongdoing, lawyers will be in a position to dissuade them from wrongful conduct. Thus, a rule of confidentiality is more likely to prevent harm than a rule of disclosure. The social utility argument is based on assumptions that are both unproven and of doubtful validity.[107] First, the argument assumes that clients will be deterred from seeking legal advice about wrongful conduct if lawyers have an obligation to disclose the intention of their clients to commit wrongs. In many cases, clients have no choice about seeking representation. In addition, law-abiding clients have an incentive to seek legal advice regardless of the disclosure rule in order to conform their conduct to the law. Second, the argument assumes that lawyers can be effective in dissuading clients from engaging in wrongful conduct. In many cases, however, the wrongful nature of the conduct and the possible consequences are clear. Rather, the client intends to commit the act regardless of the consequences.[108] Further, limited

---

102. McClure v. Thompson, 323 F.3d 1233 (9th Cir. 2003).

103. See Subin, The Lawyer as Superego, 70 Iowa L. Rev. at 1127-1132; see also Crystal, Confidentiality Under the Model Rules of Professional Conduct, 30 Kan. L. Rev. 215.

104. See generally Nancy J. Moore, Limits to Attorney-Client Confidentiality: A "Philosophically Informed" and Comparative Approach to Legal and Medical Ethics, 36 Case W. Res. L. Rev. 177 (1985).

105. Id. at 188-191.

106. Id. at 194.

107. See Daniel R. Fischel, Lawyers and Confidentiality, 65 U. Chi. L. Rev. 1 (1998) (confidentiality rules benefit lawyers but are of dubious value to clients and society as a whole).

108. See Crystal, Confidentiality Under the Model Rules of Professional Conduct, 30 Kan. L. Rev. at 225-226 (using a hypothetical analysis of types of clients that lawyers represent to conclude that a disclosure rule is more likely to reduce harm than a rule of confidentiality); Subin, The Lawyer as Superego, 70 Iowa L. Rev. at 1166-1172 (instrumental defense less persuasive than rights-based argument for confidentiality). See also Steven

empirical studies of attorney-client confidentiality lend little support to the need for strict confidentiality.[109]

Even if one accepts the conclusion that a rule of strict confidentiality is not justified by either clients' rights or social utility, a more difficult question remains: What should be the scope of the duty of confidentiality? In particular, how far should the "harm prevention" principle be taken? Professor Harry Subin argues that lawyers should have a duty to reveal confidential information to prevent clients from committing a felony.[110] Other scholars have argued for even broader rules of disclosure.[111]

Confidentiality problems are, of course, not unique to the area of criminal defense practice. We will also encounter confidentiality problems in the context of civil litigation and in connection with business practice.

Problem 2-4

Dealing with Physical Evidence, Fruits, and Instrumentalities of Crimes

You represent Robert Williams, a young man accused of armed robbery of a local convenience store. Your client was identified by the store clerk as the robber, but you think the identification is weak, and you may well be able to obtain an acquittal or at least negotiate a favorable plea bargain.

Your client first denied that he was involved in the robbery, but at your last meeting he admitted that he committed the crime. He said he put the money from the robbery in a bag in a closet at his girlfriend's apartment. She doesn't know that it is there, but he thinks she may find it. He wants to know what to do. What advice would you give and what steps would you take?

Suppose the girlfriend comes to your office with the bag of money that she has found and asks you what to do with it. What would you do?

Read Model Rules 1.2(d), 2.1, 3.4, 4.3, 8.4, and comments.

Shavell, Legal Advice About Contemplated Acts: The Decision to Obtain Advice, Its Social Desirability, and Protection of Confidentiality, 17 J. Legal Stud. 123 (1988) (developing model dealing with effect of advice and confidentiality on rational decisionmaking).

109. See Fred C. Zacharias, Rethinking Confidentiality, 74 Iowa L. Rev. 351 (1989). But see Leslie C. Levin, Testing the Radical Experiment: A Study of Lawyer Response to Clients Who Intend to Harm Others, 47 Rutgers L. Rev. 81 (1994) (survey of lawyer responses under New Jersey rule requiring lawyers to reveal confidential information to prevent clients from committing criminal, fraudulent, or illegal acts that would seriously harm others, casting doubt on wisdom of mandatory disclosure rule).

110. Subin, The Lawyer as Supcrego, 70 Iowa L. Rev. at 1172-1176.

111. See Crystal, Confidentiality Under the Model Rules of Professional Conduct, 30 Kan. L. Rev. 215; Moore, Limits to Attorney-Client Confidentiality, 36 Case W. Res. L. Rev. 177.

The obligations of lawyers regarding tangible criminal material in their possession

We saw in Problem 2-3 that under the Model Rules of Professional Conduct, lawyers have discretion to reveal confidential information to prevent reasonably certain death or serious bodily harm, but lawyers have an ethical obligation to maintain confidentiality of information regarding past crimes. Suppose, however, a lawyer has more than information about a past crime. Suppose a lawyer obtains possession of tangible property related to a crime. Lawyers can come into possession of fruits of criminal conduct (stolen money, for example), instrumentalities of crimes (such as weapons), contraband (material the possession of which is illegal, such as narcotics), or tangible evidence of crimes (for example, incriminating documents or tape recordings). The discussion that follows uses the term "tangible criminal material" to refer to these items collectively. Lawyers can obtain possession of tangible criminal material in a variety of ways: from clients, from third parties, or as a result of their own investigation. What are a lawyer's legal and ethical obligations if the lawyer comes into possession of tangible criminal material?

Lawyers may not assist their clients by actively concealing tangible criminal material. The leading case establishing this proposition is In re Ryder.[112] Ryder represented an individual accused of bank robbery with a sawed-off shotgun. The FBI told Ryder that his client had bills taken in the bank robbery in his possession when he was arrested. Ryder's client told him that a man whom he would not identify had paid him $500 to put a package in a safety deposit box, a story Ryder did not believe. Ryder had his client sign a power of attorney so that he could obtain possession of the client's safety deposit box. When Ryder opened his client's box, he found a sawed-off shotgun and a bag of money, among other items. Ryder transferred the contents of his client's box to a new box that he had opened in his name. The FBI later discovered Ryder's box containing the money and gun. Ryder testified that he intended to return the money to the true owner. He claimed that his purpose in transferring the money and gun to his own box was to support an argument that the money and gun were inadmissible in a prosecution against his client because of the attorney-client privilege. The court removed Ryder from the case, and later the United States attorney instituted disciplinary proceedings against him. The district court suspended Ryder from practice for 18 months. The court ruled that Ryder had gone far beyond the receipt of confidential information to become an active participant in concealment of a crime. On appeal the Fourth Circuit approved the district court's order:

> It is an abuse of a lawyer's professional responsibility knowingly to take possession of and secrete the fruits and instrumentalities of a crime. Ryder's acts bear no reasonable relation to the privilege and duty to refuse to divulge a client's confidential communication. Ryder made himself an active participant in a criminal act,

112. 263 F. Supp. 360 (E.D. Va.), *aff'd*, 381 F.2d 713 (4th Cir. 1967).

ostensibly wearing the mantle of the loyal advocate, but in reality serving as accessory after the fact.[113]

A number of courts have gone beyond the decision in *Ryder* and have held that attorneys who come into possession of tangible criminal material have an obligation to turn the material over to the authorities. In State ex rel. Sowers v. Olwell,[114] Olwell, an attorney representing a suspect in a murder, came into possession of a knife. It was unclear from the case whether Olwell obtained the knife from his client or from another source. A few days before a coroner's inquest into the death, Olwell received a subpoena duces tecum, directing him to produce "all knives in your possession" that related to the death. Olwell refused to comply with the subpoena, claiming a confidential relationship of attorney and client. The Washington Supreme Court held that Olwell must produce the knife.[115] Although Olwell was under subpoena, the court stated that he had an obligation "on his own motion" to turn the material over to the authorities after a reasonable period of time for examination.[116]

Several courts have applied the *Olwell* approach to other types of tangible criminal material and in a variety of other settings. In Morrell v. State[117] the defendant Morrell was charged with kidnapping and rape. A public defender was appointed to represent Morrell. About a month later, the lawyer received a telephone call from a friend of Morrell's who had been living in Morrell's home with his consent while Morrell was awaiting trial. The friend told the lawyer that he had found a legal pad that appeared to have a kidnapping plan written on it. The lawyer took possession of the pad and asked his client about it. Morrell denied that the plan implicated him; he said that he had written the plan in response to a television report about an earlier kidnapping. Unsure how to proceed, the lawyer sought the advice of the Ethics Advisory Committee of the Alaska Bar Association. The committee advised the lawyer to return the plan to the friend, to advise the friend about the law on concealment of evidence, and to withdraw from the case if it became obvious that a violation of rules of ethics would occur. The lawyer basically followed this advice. The friend decided to turn the pad over to the police, and it was introduced into evidence at Morrell's trial, at which he was convicted. Morrell argued on appeal that his former attorney's conduct had denied him effective assistance of counsel.

---

113. 381 F.2d at 714. *Accord* State ex rel. Oklahoma Bar Assn. v. Harlton, 669 P.2d 774, 777 (Okla. 1983) (attorney received five-year suspension after pleading guilty to charge of hindering prosecution by concealing shotgun; attorney "embraced the role of an accessory to a crime as a personal accommodation to its perpetrator").

114. 394 P.2d 681 (Wash. 1964).

115. Id. at 684-685.

116. Id. at 686. See also Quinones v. State, 766 So. 2d 1165 (Fla. Dist Ct. App. 2000) (defense attorney violated ethical obligations under Rules 3.4(a) and (c) by failing to disclose possession of knife; court indicates that the attorney's conduct may also be a crime).

117. 575 P.2d 1200 (Alaska 1978).

The Alaska Supreme Court rejected this argument, relying on *Olwell*, *Ryder*, and other cases:

> From the foregoing cases emerges the rule that a criminal defense attorney must turn over to the prosecution real evidence that the attorney obtains from his client. Further, if the evidence is obtained from a non-client third party who is not acting for the client, then the privilege to refuse to testify concerning the manner in which the evidence was obtained is inapplicable.[118]

In dictum, the court stated that the attorney's obligation would have been the same even if he had received the evidence directly from his client rather than from a third party.[119] Similarly, in State v. Carlin[120] the defendant was prosecuted for making terroristic threats. The defendant had made tape recordings of his conversations, which he had turned over to his attorney. The court ordered the attorney to produce the tapes for the prosecution, but the attorney objected, claiming that he had obtained the tapes in a privileged communication. The court of appeals affirmed: "Since the appellant's attorney had a duty to turn over the evidence under the line of cases mentioned above, there was no error in the court ordering him to do so."[121]

The Restatement of the Law Governing Lawyers incorporates the line of cases discussed above:

§119. Physical Evidence of Client Crime

With respect to physical evidence of a client crime, a lawyer:

(1) may, when reasonably necessary for purposes of the representation, take possession of the evidence and retain it for the time reasonably necessary to examine it and subject it to tests that do not alter or destroy material characteristics of the evidence; but

(2) following possession under Subsection (1), the lawyer must notify prosecuting authorities of the lawyer's possession of the evidence or turn the evidence over to them.[122]

---

118. Id. at 1210.

119. Id. at 1211.

120. 640 P.2d 324 (Kan. Ct. App. 1982).

121. Id. at 328. See also In re Original Grand Jury Investigation, 733 N.E.2d 1135 (Ohio 2000) (attorney who received possession of threatening letter written by client must relinquish the letter to law enforcement and comply with any subpoena); Henderson v. State, 962 S.W.2d 544 (Tex. Ct. Crim. App. 1997) (en banc), *cert. denied*, 525 U.S. 978 (1998) (trial court properly required production of maps in lawyers' possession showing where baby was buried because privilege must yield when possible to prevent death or serious injury).

122. The comments to the Restatement broadly define the types of material subject to the attorney's duty to produce:

> This Section applies to evidence of a client crime, contraband, weapons, and similar implements used in an offense. It also includes such material as documents and material in electronically retrievable form used by the client to plan the offense, documents used in the course of a mail-fraud violation, or transaction documents evidencing a crime.

While most of the cases have involved situations in which lawyers have been subject to subpoena or in which defendants have made claims of ineffective assistance of counsel, lawyers who keep possession of tangible criminal material run the risk of criminal prosecution for violation of statutes dealing with obstruction of justice, concealment of evidence, and similar crimes. In *Morrell* the court discussed the application of criminal statutes as follows:

> While statutes which address the concealing of evidence are generally construed to require an affirmative act of concealment in addition to the failure to disclose information to the authorities, taking possession of evidence from a non-client third party and holding the evidence in a place not accessible to investigating authorities would seem to fall within the statute's ambit.[123]

In Commonwealth v. Stenhach[124] two public defenders were prosecuted for hindering prosecution and tampering with evidence because they kept possession of a rifle stock used in a homicide committed by their client. The lawyers had learned of the existence and location of the weapon in a confidential communication from their client. The jury found the defendants guilty. The appellate court first joined the "overwhelming majority of states which hold that physical evidence of crime in the possession of a criminal defense attorney is not subject to a privilege but must be delivered to the prosecution."[125] The court, however, then went on to reverse the defendants' convictions on the ground that the statutes as applied to them were vague and overbroad.

Attorneys facing the question of how to deal with tangible criminal material, however, can take little comfort from *Stenhach*. First, the attorneys were convicted at trial and only obtained a reversal on appeal. The emotional and financial costs to them were undoubtedly great. Second, given the body of law now on the books requiring lawyers to turn over tangible criminal material to the authorities, future courts are much less likely to be sympathetic to due process claims.

Despite the widespread acceptance of the attorney's duty to turn over physical evidence as articulated by the court in *Olwell*,[126] lawyers confronted

---

> Witness statements, photographs of the scene of a crime, trial exhibits, and the like prepared by a lawyer or the lawyer's assistants constitute work product and thus are not subject to the Section, even if such material could constitute evidence of a client crime for some purposes, such as if waived. . . .

Restatement (Third) of the Law Governing Lawyers §119, cmt. *b*.

123. 575 P.2d at 1212. See also State ex rel. Oklahoma Bar Assn. v. Harlton, 669 P.2d 774 (Okla. 1983) (disciplinary proceeding based on attorney's pleading guilty to charge of hindering prosecution by concealing shotgun).

124. 514 A.2d 114 (Pa. Super. Ct. 1986).

125. Id. at 119.

126. For a criticism of the duty to turn over tangible criminal material and a recommendation that attorneys be granted, by legislation if necessary, a limited privilege to possess such material, see Jane M. Graffeo, Note, Ethics, Law, and Loyalty: The Attorney's Duty to Turn Over Incriminating Physical Evidence, 32 Stan. L. Rev. 977 (1980). A similar approach is recommended by Stephanie J. Frye, Comment, Disclosure of Incriminating

with actual or potential possession of tangible criminal material may face a number of questions regarding the application of the doctrine.

Application of the attorney-client privilege after tangible criminal material is turned over to the authorities

The line of cases discussed in the preceding section establishes the principle that lawyers have a duty on their own motion even in the absence of a subpoena to turn over to the authorities tangible criminal material that comes into their possession. After the material is turned over to the authorities, does the attorney-client evidentiary privilege have any relevance? In particular, can the prosecution introduce evidence of the source of the incriminating material? The prosecution may claim a need to prove the source of the material to establish a foundation for admission of the evidence. On the other hand, the defense will obviously be severely prejudiced if the trier of fact learns that defense counsel turned over incriminating material to the authorities.[127]

In People v. Meredith[128] one of two codefendants was accused of conspiracy to murder. A crucial fact in the case was the location of the victim's wallet. The defendant had told his lawyer that the wallet was in a trash can behind his residence. The lawyer's investigator retrieved the wallet and the attorney then turned it over to authorities. At trial the defense and prosecution agreed that the prosecution could introduce the wallet into evidence and that the conversations between the defendant and his lawyer were privileged. The issue in the case was whether the prosecution could call the investigator to testify regarding his observation of the location of the wallet. The court first held that the attorney-client privilege applied not just to communications between attorney and client but also to observations made as a consequence of protected communications. The court also held, however, that an observation by a lawyer or his agent would lose its privileged character if "the defense by altering or removing physical evidence has precluded the prosecution from making that same observation."[129]

The Court in State ex rel. Sowers v. Olwell (discussed above), however, struck a balance between the state's need for evidence and preservation of the attorney-client privilege:

> We think the attorney-client privilege should and can be preserved even though the attorney surrenders the evidence he has in his possession. The prosecution, upon receipt of such evidence from an attorney, where charge against the attorney's client is contemplated (presently or in the future), should be well aware of the

---

Physical Evidence Received from a Client: The Defense Attorney's Dilemma, 52 U. Colo. L. Rev. 419 (1981).

127. See Norman Lefstein, Incriminating Physical Evidence, The Defense Attorney's Dilemma, and the Need for Rules, 64 N.C. L. Rev. 897, 909-910 (1986).

128. 631 P.2d 46 (Cal. 1981).

129. Id. at 48.

existence of the attorney-client privilege. Therefore, the state, when attempting to introduce such evidence at the trial, should take extreme precautions to make certain that the source of the evidence is not disclosed in the presence of the jury and prejudicial error is not committed. By thus allowing the prosecution to recover such evidence, the public interest is served, and by refusing the prosecution an opportunity to disclose the source of the evidence, the client's privilege is preserved and a balance is reached between these conflicting interests.[130]

The Restatement expands on the balancing approach used in *Olwell*:

> The prosecution and defense should make appropriate arrangements for introduction and authentication of the evidence at trial. Because of the risk of prejudice to the client, that should be done without improperly revealing the source of the evidence to the finder of fact. The parties may also agree that the tribunal may instruct the jury, without revealing the lawyer's involvement, that an appropriate chain of possession links the evidence to the place where it was located before coming into the lawyer's possession. In the absence of agreement to such an instruction by the defense, the prosecutor may offer evidence of the lawyer's possession if necessary to establish the chain of possession.[131]

Application of the Fifth Amendment privilege against self-incrimination

Does the obligation imposed on lawyers to turn over to the authorities tangible criminal material that is in their possession violate the client's Fifth and Fourteenth Amendment privilege against self-incrimination? Analysis of this issue begins with the Supreme Court's decision in Fisher v. United States.[132]

In *Fisher* the Supreme Court established Fifth Amendment principles applicable to this situation. *Fisher* involved an investigation of possible civil and criminal violations of the federal income tax laws. The taxpayers obtained their accountants' work papers relating to the preparation of their tax returns and turned the documents over to their attorneys for assistance in the investigation. The Internal Revenue Service subsequently issued subpoenas to the attorneys seeking production of these documents. When the attorneys refused to comply, the government brought enforcement actions against them.

Fisher considered two major issues: Does the privilege against self-incrimination apply to documents voluntarily prepared by the defendant or third parties? Can the privilege continue to apply when a client transfers documents to his attorney? On the first issue, the Court held that the privilege protects a criminal defendant from being compelled to give incriminating testimony

---

130. 394 P.2d at 685.

131. Restatement (Third) of the Law Governing Lawyers §119, cmt. c. See also Hitch v. Pima County Superior Court, 708 P.2d 72 (Ariz. 1985) (en banc) (defendant forced to choose between having lawyer testify or stipulation regarding original location of material).

132. 425 U.S. 391 (1976).

against himself; it does not bar the use of incriminating evidence against a person. Because the accountants' work papers did not involve any testimony by the taxpayers, they were not subject to the privilege against self-incrimination.[133] In its discussion the Court confirmed that "purely evidentiary (but 'nontestimonial') materials, as well as contraband and fruits and instrumentalities of crime, may now be searched for and seized under proper circumstances."[134]

The Court qualified the proposition that nontestimonial materials may be searched and seized by recognizing the "act of production" doctrine. The Court noted that the act of production of documents voluntarily prepared (as opposed to their substantive content) could have testimonial aspects, depending on the circumstances. In some cases, production of documents or other evidence could establish their existence, possession or control by the taxpayer, or authentication.[135] In a subsequent case, United States v. Doe,[136] the Court applied the act of production doctrine and held that the government could not enforce a subpoena directed to the owner of sole proprietorships seeking the production of voluntarily prepared business records unless it granted the defendant "use immunity" from any incrimination resulting from the production of the material.[137]

On the second issue, because the Court had defined the privilege as protecting a person from being compelled to give incriminating testimony, it ruled that the privilege did not prevent enforcement of the subpoenas against the attorneys; the subpoenas did not compel the taxpayers to do anything.[138] While the privilege against self-incrimination no longer applied directly, it still continued to apply indirectly:

> Where the transfer is made for the purpose of obtaining legal advice, the purposes of the attorney-client privilege would be defeated unless the privilege is applicable. "It follows, then, that *when the client himself would be privileged* from production of the document, because of self-incrimination, the attorney having possession of the document is not bound to produce."[139]

Thus, under *Fisher* an attorney is not bound to produce information if (1) the attorney received the information from a client in a communication

---

133. Id. at 409-410.

134. Id. at 407.

135. Id. at 410.

136. 465 U.S. 605 (1984).

137. Id. at 616-617. In United States v. Hubbell, 530 U.S. 27 (2000), the Court held that the grant of use immunity must be coextensive with the scope of the privilege against self-incrimination. Therefore, the grant of use immunity prohibited the prosecution from making both direct and derivative use of the material produced under the grant of immunity. The prosecution must show that evidence arises from a legitimate source wholly independent of produced testimony. Id. at 39-40.

138. 425 U.S. at 397.

139. Id. at 404 (emphasis in original).

that is subject to the attorney-client privilege and (2) the compulsion, if directed toward the client rather than the attorney, would violate the Fifth Amendment because the client would be compelled to give incriminating testimony against himself.

It is unclear the extent to which *Fisher* and *Doe* apply to the duty of lawyers to deliver to the authorities tangible criminal material in their possession. In many cases it would appear that an attorney's production of the material would not violate the client's privilege against self-incrimination. If the attorney received the material in a communication not subject to the attorney-client privilege, there would not be a Fifth Amendment problem. Under *Fisher* the privilege against self-incrimination does not apply unless the attorney received the material in a communication that was subject to the attorney-client privilege. Thus, if the attorney received the material from a third party, not the client, the privilege would not generally apply.[140] Similarly if the attorney received the material for the purpose of hiding it from authorities, as in *Ryder,* subsequent production by the attorney, either voluntarily or pursuant to subpoena, would not violate the client's privilege against self-incrimination because the conveyance to the attorney would almost certainly be subject to the crime-fraud exception to the attorney-client privilege. However, if the attorney received the material from the client in a communication that was subject to the attorney-client privilege, and the attorney's production of the material established the existence of the material, the defendant's possession or control of the material, or the material's authenticity, then under the act of production doctrine, the defendant's privilege against self-incrimination could be infringed. The state could respond by granting the defendant use immunity, but this would prevent the state from making any direct or derivative use of the produced material. The state would need to prove the tangible criminal material through a legitimate source wholly independent of the defendant and his attorney.[141] This is likely to be very difficult to do, but not necessarily impossible. For example, in *Ryder* the authorities learned about the attorney's safety deposit box from other sources. Similarly, in *Olwell,* the authorities learned that the attorney might be in possession of a knife presumably from sources other than the attorney or the defendant.

Professor Kevin Reitz has argued that the duty to turn over material recognized by *Olwell* is fundamentally inconsistent with the privilege as recognized by *Fisher* and *Doe.* As a result he argues for a modification of both the privilege against self-incrimination and the lawyer's duty to produce tangible criminal material.[142]

---

140. See People v. Sanchez, 30 Cal. Rptr. 2d 111 (Ct. App., *review denied* (1994)) (no violation of privilege against self-incrimination when defense counsel turned over incriminating diaries that he received from defendant's sisters to court).

141. See United States v. Hubbell, 530 U.S. 27 (2000).

142. Kevin R. Reitz, Clients, Lawyers and the Fifth Amendment: The Need for a Protected Privilege, 41 Duke L.J. 572 (1991).

How should attorneys comply with an obligation to turn tangible criminal material over to the authorities?

Assuming lawyers have an obligation to turn tangible criminal material in their possession over to the authorities, usually it will not make sense for lawyers voluntarily to take possession of such material.[143] Possession of the material places lawyers in an ethical quandary in which they are required to act contrary to their clients' interests and exposes them to legal risks, including in extreme cases, criminal prosecution.

One reason for doing so would be if the material could be exculpatory. Another possible reason for a lawyer to take possession of tangible criminal material is to attempt to assert a claim to prevent the prosecution from using the material based on the client's privilege against self-incrimination. If the attorney believes the authorities are likely to locate the material in the normal course of investigation, the attorney could take possession of the material, either directly from the client or based on information received from the client, inform the authorities that the attorney has possession of certain tangible criminal material, and request use immunity for the client in connection with the delivery of the material. If the prosecution rejected the request, the attorney could either file a motion in limine seeking to prevent the prosecution from using the material based on the client's privilege against self-incrimination or hold the material awaiting a subpoena and then move to quash the subpoena based on the client's privilege against self-incrimination.

In some cases, however, the attorney may not have a choice about obtaining or keeping possession of tangible criminal material. The material may be delivered anonymously to the lawyer or the party making the delivery may refuse to keep it.

What should a lawyer do if the lawyer has received possession of such material, either voluntarily or involuntarily? One possibility would be to return the material to its original location rather than to the authorities. The ABA Standards for the Defense Function and some court decisions recognize return of the property to its original location as an option.[144] In other jurisdictions, however, return of the material to the original source may not be ethically permissible.[145] Even if case law in the jurisdiction does not absolutely foreclose the return option, the circumstances of the case may make return impossible. The Restatement states:

---

143. See Barry S. Martin, Incriminating Criminal Evidence, Practical Solutions, 15 Pacific L.J. 807 (1984).

144. ABA Standards for Criminal Justice, Defense Function Standard 4-4.6(b) (3d ed. 1993); Hitch v. Pima County Superior Court, 708 P.2d 72 (Ariz. 1985) (en banc).

145. In California the approach of returning the property to its original location finds support in the *Meredith* case (discussed above), which held that the privilege is lost if the attorney prevents the authorities from being able to obtain the material through an independent investigation. A subsequent California appellate decision, however, states that if a lawyer takes possession of physical evidence, the lawyer must immediately notify the court so that the prosecution can have access to the evidence. See People v. Superior Court (In re Fairbank), 237 Cal. Rptr. 158 (Ct. App., *review denied* (1987)).

Some decisions have alluded to an additional option—returning the evidence to the site from which it was taken, when that can be accomplished without destroying or altering material characteristics of the evidence. That will often be impossible. The option would also be unavailable when the lawyer reasonably should know that the client or another person will intentionally alter or destroy the evidence.[146]

The ABA Standards agree with this limitation.[147]

Another option would be to turn the material over to the authorities anonymously to protect client confidentiality to the maximum extent possible. Defense counsel could hire another attorney for the purpose of delivering the materials to the authorities. Normally, the identity of a client is not subject to the attorney-client privilege, but at least one court has held that the identity of a client from whom an attorney received stolen property was privileged.[148] On the other hand, an anonymous return may effectively deprive the prosecution of evidence of a crime: What is a prosecutor to do with a gun returned anonymously without any identification of the crime to which the gun is related?[149]

Finally, as discussed above, the attorney could inform the authorities that the attorney has possession of tangible criminal material and will turn the material over to the authorities if the client receives use immunity. Such a tactic is ethically troubling, however, in those cases where the attorney is taking possession of the material to prevent the prosecution from finding the material in the normal course of the investigation. In addition, the prosecution could argue that the privilege against self-incrimination does not apply in this situation because the client's primary purpose in turning over the material to the lawyer was to interfere with the investigation, not to seek legal advice.

Problem 2-5

False Testimony in Criminal Cases[150]

Melinda Lee represents Neil Denny in a prosecution for robbery of a convenience store. At the initial interview, Denny told Lee that he was

---

146. Restatement (Third) of the Law Governing Lawyers §119, cmt. *c*.

147. ABA Standards for Criminal Justice, Defense Function Standard 4-4.6(c) (3d ed. 1993) ("If defense counsel tests or examines the item, he or she should thereafter return it to the source unless there is reason to believe that the evidence might be altered or destroyed or used to harm another or return is otherwise impossible.").

148. Anderson v. State, 297 So. 2d 871 (Fla. Dist. Ct. App. 1974).

149. See Norman Lefstein, Incriminating Physical Evidence, The Defense Attorney's Dilemma, and the Need for Rules, 64 N.C. L. Rev. 897, 936-937 (1986). See also Hitch v. Pima County Superior Court, 708 P. 2d 72, 78 (Ariz. 1985) (en banc) (rejecting the anonymous return option).

150. This problem and the relevant rules generally use the term "false testimony" rather than "perjury," which is a crime. Ethical duties attach even if no crime has been committed, for example, if a client mistakenly testifies falsely. See Restatement (Third) of the Law Governing Lawyers §120, cmt. *d*.

nowhere near the convenience store and that he did not commit the robbery. When Lee asked Denny where he was, Denny was vague and hesitant, but he finally said that he was "with some friends." Lee interviewed the friends that Denny identified and learned that Denny was with them from about 8:00 P.M. until about 10:30 P.M., but that he had left them before the robbery occurred at 11:00.

At a subsequent meeting Lee informs Denny of the results of her investigation. Denny says that he now remembers that he was with his friends early in the evening, but that he spent the rest of the evening with his girlfriend, Robin Gayle, at her apartment. Lee then interviews Gayle, who says that she and Denny were together the entire evening from about 7:30 until 1:00 A.M. watching television. She doesn't remember, however, what they watched, and her recall of the evening is sketchy. Lee concludes that Gayle is lying to protect Denny.

a. What would you do if you were in Lee's position and Denny insists on taking the stand to present his alibi defense and demands that Lee call Gayle as a witness on his behalf? Why?

b. Suppose Lee counsels Denny that he must testify truthfully and informs him of the possible consequences of presenting false testimony. Nonetheless, Denny insists on taking the stand to present his alibi defense and on offering Gayle as a witness in his behalf. Suppose Lee then informs the court that Denny is planning to testify falsely and to offer the false testimony of an alibi witness. If you were the judge, what would you do?

c. Suppose Lee counsels Denny that he must testify truthfully, that false testimony has a number of adverse consequences, and that Lee will inform the court if Denny insists on offering false testimony. As a result, Denny does not take the stand and does not present Gayle as an alibi witness. The jury convicts Denny of armed robbery. Denny then files a petition seeking postconviction relief on the ground that Lee's actions violated Denny's Sixth and Fourteenth Amendment right to effective assistance of counsel. Analyze whether Denny's right to effective assistance of counsel has been violated.

d. Suppose Lee counsels Denny that he must testify truthfully and informs him of the possible consequences of presenting false testimony. Nonetheless, Denny insists on taking the stand to present his alibi defense and on offering Gayle as a witness in his behalf. Suppose Lee then informs the court that Denny is planning to testify falsely and to offer the false testimony of an alibi witness. The judge advises Denny of his obligation to testify truthfully and warns Denny that if he commits perjury, Denny may be prosecuted; the judge also advises Denny that the judge may take the perjury into account in sentencing if Denny is convicted. The judge further rules that Lee has the authority to decide whether to offer Gayle as a witness. Denny testifies in his own behalf and presents his alibi defense, but Lee refuses to offer Gayle as a witness. The jury convicts Denny of armed robbery. Denny then files a petition seeking postconviction relief on the ground that Lee's actions violated his Fifth and Fourteenth Amendment privilege against self-incrimination. Analyze whether Denny's privilege against self-incrimination has been violated.

e. Based on your analysis of the situations above, how would you as defense counsel handle an initial client interview? What, if anything, would you say about confidentiality when you first meet with the defendant? What would you say if the defendant said to you: "Everything I tell you is confidential, right?"

f. You are a member of a bar committee appointed by your state supreme court to review the rules of ethics in your state. Which approach to the problem of false testimony by a criminal defendant would you favor? Why?

Read Model Rules 1.2, 1.16, 2.1, 3.3, and comments.

Approaches to the problem of false testimony by the criminal defendant

What should defense counsel do when the defendant insists on taking the stand and testifying falsely (contemplated false testimony) or when defense counsel learns that the defendant has testified falsely (completed false testimony)?[151] Put aside for the moment the question of when a lawyer "knows" that a client will testify falsely. We will consider that point later in the discussion. Assume that, by whatever standard of knowledge is applicable, the lawyer does know that the client will testify or has testifed falsely. Five approaches have been suggested for how defense counsel should respond either to contemplated or completed false testimony by a criminal defendant.

1. Full representation. In a famous 1966 article Professor Monroe Freedman argued that if a criminal defendant insists on taking the stand and testifying falsely, defense counsel should not move to withdraw from the case and should not inform the court of the false testimony. Instead, defense counsel should allow the defendant to take the stand and to testify; defense counsel should not do anything that would either explicitly or implicitly disclose the attorney's knowledge to the judge or jury. More specifically, Freedman's approach meant that the attorney would examine the defendant in the normal fashion, even if

---

151. For an historical survey of some of the most important cases involving perjured testimony, see Richard H. Underwood, Perjury: An Anthology, 13 Ariz. J. Intl. & Comp. L. 307 (1996).

the defendant's answers were false, and that the attorney would make normal closing arguments to the finder of fact, including arguments based on false testimony.[152] In later works Professor Freedman explained the basis for his position. At its deepest level, his view of the obligations of defense counsel is founded on the value of the "dignity of the individual in a free society." Constitutional rights, such as due process of law, right to counsel, and the privilege against self-incrimination, express this basic value. Confidentiality of communications between lawyer and client is central to all of these rights, since without client trust and complete information, lawyers cannot adequately defend their clients' rights.[153] In addition, Professor Freedman has criticized the practicality and constitutionality of the alternatives that others have proposed for dealing with the issue of false testimony by criminal defendants.[154]

2.   *Disclosure to the court.*   Professor Freedman's position met with immediate criticism from then United States Circuit Judge (later Chief Justice of the United States Supreme Court) Warren Burger. Justice Burger claimed that a lawyer could never under any circumstances participate in a fraud on the court, and that for a lawyer to ask questions of a client that would elicit false testimony was clearly improper.[155] Logically, the opposite position to Freedman's position of full representation would be full disclosure by defense counsel to the court of the defendant's contemplated or completed false testimony. Although Justice Burger did not go that far in his 1966 article, he later came to endorse that position in his opinion in Nix v. Whiteside,[156] discussed in detail below.

Professor Freedman's and Justice Burger's views on the issue of false testimony by the criminal defendant represent the polar positions for dealing with the problem. Each has the advantage of being clear in its direction to counsel, but each can be criticized for ignoring an important competing value: the integrity of the adversarial system in Freedman's case and the importance of client confidentiality to individual liberty in Justice Burger's case. Not surprisingly, other courts and scholars have attempted to find a middle ground that balances or accommodates in some fashion these competing values. Three

152. Monroe H. Freedman, Professional Responsibility of the Criminal Defense Lawyer: The Three Hardest Questions, 64 Mich. L. Rev. 1469, 1475-1478 (1966).

153. Freedman & Smith, Understanding Lawyers' Ethics 13-14, 19-21. See also Jay S. Silver, Truth, Justice, and the American Way: The Case *Against* the Client Perjury Rules, 47 Vand. L. Rev. 339 (1994) (criticizing the disclosure obligations of the Model Rules because they impede the discovery of truth, subvert the rights of the accused, and undermine the adversarial process).

154. See Monroe H. Freedman, Lawyers' Ethics in an Adversary System 27-42 (1975) and Freedman & Smith, Understanding Lawyers' Ethics ch. 6.

155. Warren E. Burger, Standards of Conduct for Prosecution and Defense Personnel: A Judge's Viewpoint, 5 Am. Crim. L.Q. 11, 13 (1966). For a history of the Freedman-Burger dispute, see Lyle Denniston, When Your Client Lies, 6 Cal. Law. 55, 57 (July 1986).

156. 475 U.S. 157 (1986).

alternatives to the full representation position of Professor Freedman and the disclosure position of Justice Burger are the following: withdrawal without disclosure, narrative testimony, and avoidance of knowledge.

   3.   *Withdrawal without disclosure.*   An attorney confronted with a client who plans to take the stand and testify falsely or who has already testified falsely could move to withdraw from the case and still protect the confidentiality of client communications. The lawyer could, for example, move to withdraw because of "ethical reasons" or because of a "conflict of interest" or because of "privileged reasons."[157] Professor Freedman has criticized the withdrawal solution on a number of grounds, including the following: First, if the court grants the motion, the problem is simply passed on to successor counsel who will either face the same dilemma or who will not learn of the false testimony because the client has now been educated about what can and cannot be told to a lawyer. If the latter occurs, the withdrawal solution is no solution at all since it allows false testimony to take place, but adds cost to the operation of the judicial system. Second, if the matter occurs on the eve of or during the trial, the judge will almost certainly deny the motion. The "withdrawal approach" does not guide the attorney about how to act in that event. Third, if the attorney moves to withdraw, the court may order the lawyer to reveal the reason, so it may be impossible to maintain confidentiality.[158] In addition, if the lawyer does reveal the reason for moving to withdraw, and the client takes the stand, the judge may take the client's false testimony into account in sentencing.[159]

   4.   *Narrative testimony.*   In 1971 the American Bar Association adopted Defense Function Standard 7.7 to guide defense lawyers in dealing with perjury by the criminal defendant. In 1979 the ABA Committee on Standards for Criminal Justice proposed a revised version of 7.7, but then withdrew this proposal from consideration by the ABA on the understanding that the issue of perjury by the criminal defendant would be considered by the ABA committee working on the Model Rules of Professional Conduct. Revised Defense Func-

   157. See Manfredi & Levine v. Superior Court (Barles), 78 Cal. Rptr. 2d 494 (Ct. App. 1998) (decision to grant motion to withdraw within discretion of trial court; court should ordinarily accept representations of counsel that confidentiality precludes disclosure of specific reasons for motion when court concludes counsel is acting in good faith). See also Lawyer Disciplinary Board v. Farber, 488 S.E.2d 460 (W. Va. 1997) (lawyer received four-month suspension for disclosure of confidential information in connection with motion to withdraw in criminal case because disclosure went beyond what was necessary and was accompanied by threats to client).
   158. Freedman & Smith, Understanding Lawyers' Ethics 158-160.
   159. See United States v. Dunnigan, 507 U.S. 87 (1993) (upholding trial judge's enhancement of defendant's sentence under federal sentencing guidelines because of perjury committed at trial), abrogated on other grounds, United States v. Wells, 519 U.S. 482 (1997).; United States v. Grayson, 438 U.S. 41 (1978) (upholding sentencing increase because of defendant's perjury).

tion Standard 7.7, however, did provide a detailed statement of the narrative approach to perjury by the criminal defendant.

Revised Standard 7.7 granted lawyers discretion to move to withdraw if the issue of client perjury arose before trial. If withdrawal was not feasible or was denied by the court, the standard provided as follows:

> (c) If withdrawal from the case is not feasible or is not permitted by the court, or if the situation arises immediately preceding trial or during the trial and the defendant insists upon testifying perjuriously in his or her own behalf, it is unprofessional conduct for the lawyer to lend aid to the perjury or use the perjured testimony. Before the defendant takes the stand in these circumstances, the lawyer should make a record of the fact that the defendant is taking the stand against the advice of counsel in some appropriate manner without revealing the fact to the court. The lawyer may identify the witness as the defendant and may ask appropriate questions of the defendant when it is believed that the defendant's answers will not be perjurious. As to matters for which it is believed the defendant will offer perjurious testimony, the lawyer should seek to avoid direct examination of the defendant in the conventional manner; instead, the lawyer should ask the defendant if he or she wishes to make any additional statement concerning the case to the trier or triers of the facts. A lawyer may not later argue the defendant's known false version of the facts to the jury as worthy of belief, and may not recite or rely upon the false testimony in his or her closing argument.

Standard 7.7 represents an effort to walk a tightrope between the full representation and the disclosure approaches to perjury by the criminal defendant. Under the narrative approach defense counsel should not reveal client perjury, but at the same time defense counsel must strictly avoid any involvement in client perjury.

The principal objection to the narrative testimony approach is that it sacrifices both of the principles it seeks to protect: The solution does not prevent perjury from taking place, and it infringes confidentiality because both the judge and jury are almost certain to know that defendant's lawyer does not trust his own client's testimony.[160] Moreover, the narrative solution does not address the question of what the lawyer should do when the lawyer learns that the client has already testified perjuriously. Nevertheless, several courts have adopted the narrative solution as an ethically proper way for defense counsel to deal with the problem[161] and it has been incorporated in the District of

---

160. Freedman & Smith, Understanding Lawyers' Ethics 160-163.

161. People v. Guzman, 755 P.2d 917 (Cal. 1988) (en banc); People v. DePallo, 754 N.E.2d 751 (NY 2001). In *DePallo*, the Court of Appeals held that defense counsel did not render ineffective assistance of counsel when he presented the defendant's testimony in narrative form. The court did not specifically hold that attorneys were required to follow the narrative approach. Id. at 754. See also People v. Johnson, 72 Cal. Rptr. 2d 805 (Ct. App. 1998) (court adopts narrative solution after comprehensive review of other options; court finds, however, that even though defendant did not testify, error was harmless beyond a reasonable doubt because of other evidence).

Columbia Rules of Professional Conduct.[162] Some commentators also support the narrative approach.[163]

   5. Avoidance of knowledge. Some commentators have suggested that the most practical way for a lawyer to deal with the problem of false testimony by a criminal defendant is to make sure that the lawyer avoids knowing that the client intends to testify falsely. For example, if defense lawyers ask their clients to inform them about "what the prosecution is likely to say" and "your memory of what happened," rather than "what happened," then defense counsel can obtain all the facts without committing their clients to a particular version of what occurred. Professor Freedman characterizes this as "sophistry" and a "disingenuous evasion" designed to achieve the same result that he advocates openly and defends on the basis of fundamental values.[164] Further, this solution does not address the issue of the lawyer's obligation if the lawyer learns of false testimony despite efforts to avoid knowledge.

The approach of the Model Rules of Professional Conduct and the Restatement of the Law Governing Lawyers

The philosophy of the Model Rules and the Restatement of the Law Governing Lawyers is that a lawyer should not knowingly participate in the introduction of false testimony. A lawyer must refuse to present such testimony if the lawyer knows of its falsity before it is offered and a lawyer must take reasonable remedial measures to correct false testimony that has been offered, including, if necessary, disclosure of the falsity of the testimony to the tribunal. Under the Model Rules and the Restatement, the integrity of the tribunal is superior to any interest the client may have in loyalty and confidentiality regarding false testimony. Model Rule 3.3(a)(3) and cmt. 2.[165]

   While the general approach of the Model Rules and the Restatement is clear, the implementation of this philosophy in the 2002 revision of the Model Rules raises a number of interpretative issues, leading to some possibly surprising conclusions.[166] Analytically, it is useful to consider various steps that a lawyer can consider when confronted with false testimony by a criminal defendant: (1) remonstration, (2) withdrawal, (3) disclosure to prevent false testimony,

   162. D.C. R. Prof. Conduct 3.3(b).
   163. The most extensive defense of the narrative approach can be found in Norman Lefstein, Client Perjury in Criminal Cases: Still in Search of an Answer, 1 Geo. J. Legal Ethics 521 (1988). See also Crystal, Confidentiality Under the Model Rules of Professional Conduct, 30 Kan. L. Rev. at 236-244.
   164. Freedman & Smith, Understanding Lawyers' Ethics 163, 188.
   165. See Restatement (Third) of the Law Governing Lawyers §120.
   166. See Nathan M. Crystal, False Testimony by Criminal Defendants: Still Unanswered Ethical and Constitutional Questions, 2003 Ill. L. Rev. 1529 (hereinafter cited as Crystal, False Testimony by Criminal Defendants).

(4) refusing to call the criminal defendant as a witness, (5) narrative testimony, and (6) remedial measures after false testimony has been offered.

Remonstration.   The first step for the lawyer representing a criminal defendant who intends to testify falsely is to remonstrate with the client in an effort to dissuade the client from the testimony. While the text of Rule 3.3 does not mention remonstration, the comments do: "If a lawyer knows that the client intends to testify falsely or wants the lawyer to introduce false evidence, the lawyer should seek to persuade the client that the evidence should not be offered." Model Rule 3.3, cmt. 6. Even if a lawyer does not know that the client intends to testify falsely, a lawyer who believes that the defendant's testimony lacks credibility has an obligation to counsel the client regarding the possible ramifications of the testimony. See Model Rule 2.1. In remonstrating with a client, the lawyer could emphasize factors such as the following:[167] The client has a legal obligation to testify truthfully. False testimony by the client may be unsuccessful either because of vigorous cross-examination by the prosecutor or because the jury rejects the testimony. If the judge believes the defendant testified perjuriously, the judge may take the perjury into account in sentencing. The defendant may be prosecuted for perjury. The lawyer ethically may move to withdraw.

Withdrawal.   If the lawyer has a reasonable belief (as opposed to knowledge) that the defendant intends to testify falsely, the lawyer has discretion but is not ethically required to move to withdraw. Model Rule 1.16(b)(2). If a lawyer has actual knowledge that a defendant intends to testify falsely, some commentators have argued that the lawyer must move to withdraw.[168] Rule 3.3, however, appears to reject the proposition that lawyers have an ethical obligation to move to withdraw when they know that a criminal defendant intends to testify falsely unless the confrontation with the client has produced an extreme deterioration of the relationship so that the lawyer can no longer competently represent the client. Model Rule 3.3, cmt. 15.

Disclosure to prevent false testimony from being offered.   The 2002 revision of the Model Rules adds a new section 3.3(b) which imposes additional disclosure obligations on lawyers: "A lawyer who represents a client in an adjudicative proceeding and who knows that a person intends to engage, is engaging or has engaged in criminal or fraudulent conduct related to the proceeding shall take reasonable remedial measures, including, if necessary, disclosure to the tribunal." The new rule clearly requires a lawyer to disclose information to prevent conduct such as bribery, intimidation, or unlawful destruction of docu-

---

167. See Charles Wolfram, Client Perjury, 50 So. Cal. L. Rev. 809, 846-847 (1977) (discussing five elements of remonstration).

168. 2 Hazard & Hodes, The Law of Lawyering §29.13, at 21. For a criticism of this view see Crystal, False Testimony by Criminal Defendants, 2003 Ill. L. Rev. at 1539-1540. See also Freedman & Smith, Understanding Lawyers' Ethics at 160 (withdrawal should never be viewed as a solution to the perjury problem).

ments, whether the conduct is by the client or a third person. See comment 12. Does the rule require a lawyer to disclose the client's intention to testify falsely? The rule could certainly be read to require disclosure, treating false testimony by the criminal defendant as one type of criminal conduct. On the other hand, several reasons can be given to interpret the rule not to require disclosure to prevent false testimony by a criminal defendant. First, the rule only requires disclosure as a "remedial" measure. The common meaning of remedial is to correct or cure a problem rather than prevent one from occurring. Second, the rule only requires disclosure when "necessary." A lawyer could reason that disclosure is only necessary when the false testimony has occurred; a client who is threatening false testimony may always change his mind. Third, the comments do not mention disclosure before the false testimony occurs. Comments 10 and 11, which deal with remedial measures, including disclosure, do not mention disclosure before the client testifies, only after the fact. In particular, comment 6 indicates that rather than disclosing planned false testimony the lawyer should refrain from asking questions that would elicit false testimony. Finally, neither the text of Rule 3.3(b) nor the comment to the rule specifically mention false testimony by a criminal defendant.[169]

Refusing to call the criminal defendant as a witness. Revised Rule 3.3(a)(3) adds the following new sentence: "A lawyer may refuse to offer evidence, *other than the testimony of a defendant in a criminal matter,* that the lawyer reasonably believes is false" (emphasis added). The sentence seems intended to protect criminal defendants against a mistaken belief by defense counsel that a defendant intends to testify falsely. Comment 9 reaffirms this point, but it also indicates that the rule imposes a duty that many defense counsel may find startling—a duty not to offer the testimony of a criminal defendant when defense counsel knows the testimony will be false: "*Unless the lawyer knows the testimony will be false, the lawyer must honor the client's decision to testify.* See also Comment [7]." (Emphasis added.)

An ethical obligation to refuse to call a criminal defendant to testify even if the lawyer knows the testimony will be false raises significant constitutional questions. In Rock v. Arkansas,[170] the Supreme Court held that defendants enjoy a fundamental constitutional right to testify in their own behalf. Almost all courts of appeals have held that the right to testify is personal to the defendant and not waivable by defense counsel.[171] Addressing this precise issue, the Seventh Circuit has stated that defense counsel may not prevent the defendant from testifying, even if counsel knows the testimony will be false:

What *Rock* holds is that the accused may not be prohibited from testifying—not by a judge, not by a lawyer. So if a defendant's theory were that he told his lawyer that he wanted to testify, but that his lawyer refused to allow this (for example,

---

169. Crystal, False Testimony by Criminal Defendants, 2003 Ill. L. Rev. at 1541-1542. On the issue of whether disclosure should be discretionary, see id. at 1542-1543.

170. 483 U.S. 44 (1987).

171. See, e.g., Brown v. Artuz, 124 F.3d 73, 77 (2d Cir. 1997) (citing cases from the First, Third, Fourth, Fifth, Seventh, Eighth, Ninth, and Eleventh circuits).

flatly refused to call his client to the stand without suggesting the possibility, if he thought that his client's testimony would be perjury, that he could withdraw and allow the accused to represent himself, see *Nix v. Whiteside*, 475 U.S. 157 (1985)), this would be a sound constitutional claim.[172]

How should lawyers proceed in light of the questionable constitutionality of the "duty" set forth in Rule 3.3(a)(3) and comment 9 to refuse to honor the defendant's decision to testify if the lawyer knows the testimony will be false? One way to proceed is for the lawyer to conclude that the defendant has a constitutional right to testify in his own behalf and that this right trumps the lawyer's duty to refuse to offer testimony that the lawyer knows is false. This approach is reasonable, but it means that the lawyer is ignoring an ethical obligation based on a constitutional right that is unclear under the current state of the law.

A better approach is for the lawyer to attempt to honor both the ethical obligation and the defendant's constitutional right to testify. How can a lawyer harmonize the ethical duty and the defendant's right to testify? Reconciliation can be achieved if the attorney refrains from calling the defendant as a witness but makes it possible for the defendant to call himself. When the time comes for the defendant to testify, the attorney would not formally call the defendant as a witness but would instead make a statement like the following: "Your honor, the defendant would now like to exercise his constitutional right to testify in his own behalf." During the examination of the defendant, the attorney would not ask questions that would elicit false testimony. See Model Rule 3.3, cmt. 6.[173]

Narrative testimony.   The 1983 version of the Model Rules specifically rejected the narrative approach to false testimony by a criminal defendant. The comments stated:

> Three resolutions of this dilemma have been proposed. One is to permit the accused to testify by a narrative without guidance through the lawyer's questioning. This compromises both contending principles; it exempts the lawyer from the duty to disclose false evidence but subjects the client to an implicit disclosure of information imparted to counsel. . . . Model Rule 3.3, cmt. 9 (1983).

Revised rule 3.3, however, is much more tolerant of the narrative solution. Comment 7 provides the narrative solution is permissible in those jurisdictions

---

172. Taylor v. United States, 287 F.3d 658, 661-662 (7th Cir. 2002). On the facts of *Taylor* the court found that the defendant's constitutional rights had not been violated. The court held that defense counsel was not constitutionally required to give the defendant a *Miranda*-type warning that the decision of whether to testify was the defendant's alone. Id. at 661-663.

173. Crystal, False Testimony by Criminal Defendants, 2003 Ill. L. Rev. at 1546-1547.

where it is specifically authorized. A growing number of jurisdictions have adopted the narrative solution, including California and New York through court decision and the District of Columbia by rule.[174]

While comment 7 to revised Rule 3.3 explicitly authorizes the use of the narrative solution in those jurisdictions that have directed lawyers to follow this approach, it could be read as implicitly rejecting the use of the narrative solution in those jurisdictions that have not specifically approved of this approach. However, comment 6 appears to approve the use of what is in essence the narrative solution in other situations:

> If a lawyer knows that the client intends to testify falsely or wants the lawyer to introduce false evidence, the lawyer should seek to persuade the client that the evidence should not be offered. If the persuasion is ineffective and the lawyer continues to represent the client, the lawyer must refuse to offer the false evidence. If only a portion of a witness's testimony will be false, the lawyer may call the witness to testify but may not elicit or otherwise permit the witness to present the testimony that the lawyer knows is false.

Thus, under revised rule 3.3 it appears that lawyers should use the narrative solution in two situations: first, if the jurisdiction in which they practice requires use of the narrative solution and second, in all other jurisdictions when the lawyer remains in the case and a portion of the defendant's testimony will be false. These two situations cover almost all cases the lawyer will face. The result is that comments 6 and 7 taken together move a long way toward adoption of the narrative solution.[175]

Remedial measures after false testimony has been offered.   If false testimony has been presented to the tribunal, whether by the lawyer, the lawyer's client, or a witness called by the lawyer, the lawyer must take reasonable remedial measures, including disclosure to the tribunal if necessary. Rule 3.3(a)(3). Withdrawal will normally not be a reasonable remedial measure because it will not undo the false testimony. Model Rule 3.3, cmt. 10. However, the lawyer may be able to take remedial measures that do not involve disclosure of confidential information. The lawyer could attempt to persuade the client to take the stand and correct the client's false testimony. In some instances the lawyer may be able to move to strike or withdraw the evidence.[176]

If the testimony has been presented in narrative form, must the lawyer take any further action? The answer is unclear. Arguably not, because the duty to disclose only attaches under Rule 3.3(a)(3) when the lawyer "comes to know" that false testimony has been offered. The language of section appears to contemplate a duty to disclose when the lawyer is surprised by false testimony. It may not apply if defense counsel knows that a defendant will testify falsely but

---

174. See notes 161-162, above.
175. Crystal, False Testimony by Criminal Defendants, 2003 Ill. L. Rev. at 1548.
176. See also Restatement (Third) of the Law Governing Lawyers §120, cmt. *h.*

continues the representation in narrative form under comment 6. In addition, it can be argued that if the defendant testifies in narrative form no disclosure is necessary because the tribunal has been implicitly informed of the matter and may make such inquiry as it deems appropriate.[177]

If a lawyer informs the court that a defendant either intends to or has testified falsely, what should the court do about the matter? Comment 10 to Model Rule 3.3 provides only a small degree of guidance: "It is for the tribunal then to determine what should be done—making a statement about the matter to the trier of fact, ordering a mistrial or perhaps nothing." In United States v. Scott,[178] defendant's public defender moved to withdraw for unspecified ethical reasons. The trial judge informed the defendant that he had the choice of either proceeding pro se or with the assistance of counsel who would make the decision about whether to allow the defendant to testify. The defendant chose to continue the case pro se. The Eleventh Circuit reversed the defendant's conviction, holding that the trial judge had put the defendant to an unconstitutional choice between the constitutional rights to testify and to effective assistance of counsel. The court stated that the trial judge should have simply decided the issue of whether to grant counsel's motion to withdraw. The court also held that without more information the trial court should have denied the motion to withdraw.[179] The court conceded, however, that "a much more difficult case would have resulted had it been established on the record that defendant intended to commit perjury."[180]

Nix v. Whiteside

United States Supreme Court
475 U.S. 157 (1986)

Chief Justice BURGER delivered the opinion of the Court. . . .

I

A

Whiteside was convicted of second-degree murder by a jury verdict which was affirmed by the Iowa courts. The killing took place on February 8, 1977, in Cedar Rapids, Iowa. Whiteside and two others went to one Calvin Love's apartment late that night, seeking marihuana. Love was in bed when Whiteside and his companions arrived; an argument between Whiteside and Love over the marihuana ensued. At one point, Love directed his girlfriend to get his "piece," and at another point got up, then returned to his bed. According to

177. Crystal, False Testimony by Criminal Defendants, 2003 Ill. L. Rev. at 1549.
178. 909 F.2d 488 (11th Cir. 1990).
179. Id. at 493.
180. Id. at 493-494.

Whiteside's testimony, Love then started to reach under his pillow and moved toward Whiteside. Whiteside stabbed Love in the chest, inflicting a fatal wound.

Whiteside was charged with murder, and when counsel was appointed he objected to the lawyer initially appointed, claiming that he felt uncomfortable with a lawyer who had formerly been a prosecutor. Gary L. Robinson was then appointed and immediately began an investigation. Whiteside gave him a statement that he had stabbed Love as the latter "was pulling a pistol from underneath the pillow on the bed." Upon questioning by Robinson, however, Whiteside indicated that he had not actually seen a gun, but that he was convinced that Love had a gun. No pistol was found on the premises; shortly after the police search following the stabbing, which had revealed no weapon, the victim's family had removed all of the victim's possessions from the apartment. Robinson interviewed Whiteside's companions who were present during the stabbing, and none had seen a gun during the incident. Robinson advised Whiteside that the existence of a gun was not necessary to establish the claim of self-defense, and that only a reasonable belief that the victim had a gun nearby was necessary even though no gun was actually present.

Until shortly before trial, Whiteside consistently stated to Robinson that he had not actually seen a gun, but that he was convinced that Love had a gun in his hand. About a week before trial, during preparation for direct examination, Whiteside for the first time told Robinson and his associate Donna Paulsen that he had seen something "metallic" in Love's hand. When asked about this, Whiteside responded: "[I]n Howard Cook's case there was a gun. If I don't say I saw a gun, I'm dead." Robinson told Whiteside that such testimony would be perjury and repeated that it was not necessary to prove that a gun was available but only that Whiteside reasonably believed that he was in danger. On Whiteside's insisting that he would testify that he saw "something metallic" Robinson told him, according to Robinson's testimony:

> [W]e could not allow him to [testify falsely] because that would be perjury, and as officers of the court we would be suborning perjury if we allowed him to do it; . . . I advised him that if he did do that it would be my duty to advise the Court of what he was doing and that I felt he was committing perjury; also, that I probably would be allowed to attempt to impeach that particular testimony. App. to Pet. for Cert. A-85.

Robinson also indicated he would seek to withdraw from the representation if Whiteside insisted on committing perjury.[2]

---

2. Whiteside's version of the events at this pretrial meeting is considerably more cryptic:

> *Q.* And as you went over the questions, did the two of you come into conflict with regard to whether or not there was a weapon?
>
> *A.* I couldn't—I couldn't say a conflict. But I got the impression at one time that maybe if I didn't go along with—with what was happening, that it was no gun being involved, maybe that he will pull out of my trial.
>
> App. to Pet. for Cert. A-70.

Whiteside testified in his own defense at trial and stated that he "knew" that Love had a gun and that he believed Love was reaching for a gun and he had acted swiftly in self-defense. On cross-examination, he admitted that he had not actually seen a gun in Love's hand. Robinson presented evidence that Love had been seen with a sawed-off shotgun on other occasions, that the police search of the apartment may have been careless, and that the victim's family had removed everything from the apartment shortly after the crime. Robinson presented this evidence to show a basis for Whiteside's asserted fear that Love had a gun.

The jury returned a verdict of second-degree murder. [The trial court denied Whiteside's motion for a new trial and the Iowa Supreme Court affirmed. Whiteside then petitioned for habeas corpus relief in the federal courts, claiming a violation of his Sixth and Fourteenth Amendment rights to effective assistance of counsel. The Eight Circuit directed that the petition be granted, finding that Robinson's threat to inform the trial court of Whiteside's proposed testimony violated his duty of confidentiality and breached the standard of effective representation.]

II

A

The right of an accused to testify in his defense is of relatively recent origin. Until the latter part of the preceding century, criminal defendants in this country, as at common law, were considered to be disqualified from giving sworn testimony at their own trial by reason of their interest as a party to the case. . . .

By the end of the 19th century, however, the disqualification was finally abolished by statute in most states and in the federal courts. . . . Although this Court has never explicitly held that a criminal defendant has a due process right to testify in his own behalf, cases in several Circuits have so held, and the right has long been assumed. . . . We have also suggested that such a right exists as a corollary to the Fifth Amendment privilege against compelled testimony. . . .

B

In Strickland v. Washington [466 U.S. 668 (1984)], we held that to obtain relief by way of federal habeas corpus on a claim of a deprivation of effective assistance of counsel under the Sixth Amendment, the movant must establish both serious attorney error and prejudice. . . . To counteract the natural tendency to fault an unsuccessful defense, a court reviewing a claim of ineffective assistance must "indulge a strong presumption that counsel's conduct falls within the wide range of reasonable professional assistance." [466 U.S.] at 689. In giving shape to the perimeters of this range of reasonable professional assistance, Strickland mandates that "[p]revailing norms of practice as reflected in American Bar Association Standards and the like, . . . are guides to determining what is reasonable, but they are only guides." Id., at 688.

C

We turn next to the question presented: the definition of the range of "reasonable professional" responses to a criminal defendant client who informs counsel that he will perjure himself on the stand. We must determine whether, in this setting, Robinson's conduct fell within the wide range of professional responses to threatened client perjury acceptable under the Sixth Amendment.

. . . Although counsel must take all reasonable lawful means to attain the objectives of the client, counsel is precluded from taking steps or in any way assisting the client in presenting false evidence or otherwise violating the law. This principle has consistently been recognized in most unequivocal terms by expositors of the norms of professional conduct since the first Canons of Professional Ethics were adopted by the American Bar Association in 1908. [The Court cites DR 7-102(A)(4), (7) and Model Rule 1.2(d).] Both the Model Code of Professional Responsibility and the Model Rules of Professional Conduct also adopt the specific exception from the attorney-client privilege for disclosure of perjury that his client intends to commit or has committed. DR 4-101(C)(3) (intention of client to commit a crime); Rule 3.3 (lawyer has duty to disclose falsity of evidence even if disclosure compromises client confidences). Indeed, both the Model Code and the Model Rules do not merely authorize disclosure by counsel of client perjury; they require such disclosure. See Rule 3.3(a)(4); DR 7-102(B)(1). . . .

These standards confirm that the legal profession has accepted that an attorney's ethical duty to advance the interests of his client is limited by an equally solemn duty to comply with the law and standards of professional conduct; it specifically ensures that the client may not use false evidence. This special duty of an attorney to prevent and disclose frauds upon the court derives from the recognition that perjury is as much a crime as tampering with witnesses or jurors by way of promises and threats, and undermines the administration of justice. . . .

It is universally agreed that at a minimum the attorney's first duty when confronted with a proposal for perjurious testimony is to attempt to dissuade the client from the unlawful course of conduct. Model Rules of Professional Conduct, Rule 3.3, Comment. [See Model Rule 3.3 comment 6.] The commentary thus also suggests that an attorney's revelation of his client's perjury to the court is a professionally responsible and acceptable response to the conduct of a client who has actually given perjured testimony. Similarly, the Model Rules and the commentary, as well as the Code of Professional Responsibility adopted in Iowa, expressly permit withdrawal from representation as an appropriate response of an attorney when the client threatens to commit perjury. Model Rules of Professional Conduct, Rule 1.16(a)(1), Rule 1.6, Comment (1983); Code of Professional Responsibility, DR 2-110(B), (C) (1980). Withdrawal of counsel when this situation arises at trial gives rise to many difficult questions including possible mistrial and claims of double jeopardy. . . .

D

Considering Robinson's representation of respondent in light of these accepted norms of professional conduct, we discern no failure to adhere to reasonable professional standards that would in any sense make out a deprivation of the Sixth Amendment right to counsel. Whether Robinson's conduct is seen as a successful attempt to dissuade his client from committing the crime of perjury, or whether seen as a "threat" to withdraw from representation and disclose the illegal scheme, Robinson's representation of Whiteside falls well within accepted standards of professional conduct and the range of reasonable professional conduct acceptable under *Strickland*.

The Court of Appeals [held]:

> . . . Counsel's actions prevented [Whiteside] from testifying falsely. We hold that counsel's action deprived appellant of due process and effective assistance of counsel. . . . Counsel's actions also impermissibly compromised appellant's right to testify in his own defense by conditioning continued representation by counsel and confidentiality upon appellant's restricted testimony. 750 F.2d, at 714-715. . . .

The Court of Appeals' holding that Robinson's "action deprived [Whiteside] of due process and effective assistance of counsel" is not supported by the record since Robinson's action, at most, deprived Whiteside of his contemplated perjury. Nothing counsel did in any way undermined Whiteside's claim that he believed the victim was reaching for a gun. Similarly, the record gives no support for holding that Robinson's action "also impermissibly compromised [Whiteside's] right to testify in his own defense by conditioning continued representation . . . and confidentiality upon [Whiteside's] *restricted* testimony." The record in fact shows the contrary: (a) that Whiteside did testify, and (b) he was "restricted" or restrained only from testifying falsely and was aided by Robinson in developing the basis for the fear that Love was reaching for a gun. Robinson divulged no client communications until he was compelled to do so in response to Whiteside's post-trial challenge to the quality of his performance. We see this as a case in which the attorney successfully dissuaded the client from committing the crime of perjury.

Paradoxically, even while accepting the conclusion of the Iowa trial court that Whiteside's proposed testimony would have been a criminal act, the Court of Appeals held that Robinson's efforts to persuade Whiteside not to commit that crime were improper, *first*, as forcing an impermissible choice between the right to counsel and the right to testify; and, *second*, as compromising client confidences because of Robinson's threat to disclose the contemplated perjury.[7]

_____

7. The Court of Appeals also determined that Robinson's efforts to persuade Whiteside to testify truthfully constituted an impermissible threat to testify against his own client. We find no support for a threat to testify against Whiteside while he was acting as counsel. The record reflects testimony by Robinson that he had admonished Whiteside that if he withdrew he "probably would be allowed to attempt to impeach that particular

Whatever the scope of a constitutional right to testify, it is elementary that such a right does not extend to testifying *falsely*. In Harris v. New York, we assumed the right of an accused to testify "in his own defense, or to refuse to do so" and went on to hold: "[T]hat privilege cannot be construed to include the right to commit perjury" . . . . In *Harris* we held the defendant could be impeached by prior contrary statements which had been ruled inadmissible under Miranda v. Arizona, 384 U.S. 436 (1966). *Harris* and other cases make it crystal clear that there is no right whatever—constitutional or otherwise—for a defendant to use false evidence. . . .

The paucity of authority on the subject of any such "right" may be explained by the fact that such a notion has never been responsibly advanced; the right to counsel includes no right to have a lawyer who will cooperate with planned perjury. A lawyer who would so cooperate would be at risk of prosecution for suborning perjury, and disciplinary proceedings, including suspension or disbarment.

Robinson's admonitions to his client can in no sense be said to have forced respondent into an *impermissible* choice between his right to counsel and his right to testify as he proposed for there was no *permissible* choice to testify falsely. For defense counsel to take steps to persuade a criminal defendant to testify truthfully, or to withdraw, deprives the defendant of neither his right to counsel nor the right to testify truthfully. In United States v. Havens, [446 U.S. 620 (1980)], we made clear that "when defendants testify, they must testify truthfully or suffer the consequences." [446 U.S.] at 626. When an accused proposes to resort to perjury or to produce false evidence, one consequence is the risk of withdrawal of counsel.

On this record, the accused enjoyed continued representation within the bounds of reasonable professional conduct and did in fact exercise his right to testify; at most he was denied the right to have the assistance of counsel in the presentation of false testimony. Similarly, we can discern no breach of professional duty in Robinson's admonition to respondent that he would disclose respondent's perjury to the court. The crime of perjury in this setting is indistinguishable in substance from the crime of threatening or tampering with a witness or a juror. A defendant who informed his counsel that he was arranging to bribe or threaten witnesses or members of the jury would have no "right" to insist on counsel's assistance or silence. Counsel would not be limited to advising against that conduct. An attorney's duty of confidentiality, which totally covers the client's admission of guilt, does not extend to a client's announced plans to engage in future criminal conduct. See Clark v. United States, 289 U.S. 1, 15 (1933). In short, the responsibility of an ethical lawyer, as an officer of the court and a key component of a system of justice, dedicated to a search for truth, is essentially the same whether the client announces an intention to bribe or threaten witnesses or jurors or to commit or procure

_____

testimony," if Whiteside testified falsely. The trial court accepted this version of the conversation as true.

perjury. No system of justice worthy of the name can tolerate a lesser standard. . . .

E

We hold that, as a matter of law, counsel's conduct complained of here
cannot establish the prejudice required for relief under the second strand of the
Strickland inquiry. Although a defendant need not establish that the attorney's
deficient performance more likely than not altered the outcome in order to
establish prejudice under *Strickland*, a defendant must show that "there is a
reasonable probability that, but for counsel's unprofessional errors, the result
of the proceeding would have been different." 466 U.S., at 694. According to
Strickland, "[a] reasonable probability is a probability sufficient to undermine
confidence in the outcome." Ibid. The *Strickland* Court noted that the "bench-
mark" of an ineffective-assistance claim is the fairness of the adversary proceeding, and that in judging prejudice and the likelihood of a different outcome,
"[a] defendant has no entitlement to the luck of a lawless decisionmaker." Id.,
at 695.

Whether he was persuaded or compelled to desist from perjury, Whiteside
has no valid claim that confidence in the result of his trial has been diminished
by his desisting from the contemplated perjury. Even if we were to assume that
the jury might have believed his perjury, it does not follow that Whiteside was
prejudiced.

In his attempt to evade the prejudice requirement of *Strickland*, Whiteside
relies on cases involving conflicting loyalties of counsel. In Cuyler v. Sullivan,
446 U.S. 335 (1980), we held that a defendant could obtain relief without
pointing to a specific prejudicial default on the part of his counsel, provided
it is established that the attorney was "actively represent[ing] conflicting interests." Id., at 350.

Here, there was indeed a "conflict," but of a quite different kind; it was
one imposed on the attorney by the client's proposal to commit the crime of
fabricating testimony without which, as he put it, "I'm dead." This is not
remotely the kind of conflict of interests dealt with in Cuyler v. Sullivan. Even
in that case we did not suggest that all multiple representations necessarily
resulted in an active conflict rendering the representation constitutionally infirm. If a "conflict" between a client's proposal and counsel's ethical obligation
gives rise to a presumption that counsel's assistance was prejudicially ineffective,
every guilty criminal's conviction would be suspect if the defendant had sought
to obtain an acquittal by illegal means. Can anyone doubt what practices and
problems would be spawned by such a rule and what volumes of litigation it
would generate?

Whiteside's attorney treated Whiteside's proposed perjury in accord with
professional standards, and since Whiteside's truthful testimony could not have
prejudiced the result of his trial, the Court of Appeals was in error to direct
the issuance of a writ of habeas corpus and must be reversed.

[In a concurring opinion written by Justice Blackmun and joined by

Justices Brennan, Marshall, and Stevens, these justices agreed that Whiteside had failed to show any prejudice but they criticized the majority opinion for implicitly defining as a matter of constitutional law the appropriate standard of conduct for lawyers in dealing with perjury by criminal defendants. Justice Blackmun argued that states should be free to adopt "differing approaches" to a complex ethical problem: "The signal merit of asking first whether a defendant has shown any adverse prejudicial effect before inquiring into his attorney's performance is that it avoids unnecessary federal interference in a State's regulation of its bar." 475 U.S. at 190.]

Notes and Questions

1. In an article dealing with Nix v. Whiteside, I characterized the decision as a "Constitutional outlier" because it presents a very weak case for a Sixth Amendment violation: First, attorney Robinson knew *beyond any doubt* that Whiteside planned to testify falsely. Robinson's knowledge was based on (1) Whiteside's admissions to him (2) supported by uncontradicted independent evidence. Second, in *Nix,* Robinson's response to Whiteside's planned intention to offer false evidence was to attempt to dissuade him from doing so. Thus, *Nix* only dealt with attorney remonstration as a response to contemplated perjury, a response on which there was "universal[ ] agreement." 475 U.S. at 169. The Court did not consider the constitutional implications of any of the other possible responses to false testimony by a criminal defendant. Third, Whiteside's claim of prejudice was tenuous. Because Robinson's efforts to persuade Whiteside to testify truthfully were successful, he did not have to take any of the actions that he threatened. In particular, Robinson did not inform the court that Whiteside planned to testify falsely nor did he move to withdraw. In addition, Robinson's efforts did not prevent Whiteside from testifying. He took the stand and presented the substance of his claim for self-defense. Robinson supported this defense with the testimony of other witnesses. The judge instructed the jury on self-defense. See Crystal, False Testimony by Criminal Defendants, 2003 Ill. L. Rev. at 1551-1565.

Defendants may be able to establish Sixth Amendment violations on facts stronger than those presented to the Supreme Court in *Nix.* Suppose Robinson had acted based on his belief that his client was committing perjury rather than his client's admission, and suppose the substance of the client's claim of self-defense had not been presented to the jury. In such a case the defendant might be able to establish both prongs of the *Strickland* test for ineffective assistance of counsel. See State v. Jones, 923 P.2d 560 (Mont. 1996) (defendant's Sixth Amendment right violated when lawyer moved to withdraw on unsubstantiated belief that defendant intended to commit perjury).

2. *Nix* was a Sixth Amendment case. The Supreme Court has yet to address the question of the relationship between the Fifth Amendment privilege against self-incrimination and client perjury. See Crystal, False Testimony by Criminal Defendants, 2003 Ill. L. Rev. at 1567-1571; Monroe H. Freedman,

Client Confidences and Client Perjury: Some Unanswered Questions, 136 U. Pa. L. Rev. 1939 (1988). Could a lawyer's response to contemplated or completed false testimony by a criminal defendant infringe the defendant's Fifth Amendment privilege against self-incrimination? Consider the elements for a Fifth Amendment violation set forth in Fisher v. United States, discussed in connection with Problem 2-4.

3. *Nix* also did not deal with possible due process issues. If an attorney's actions in response to false testimony by the criminal defendant undermine the ability of the trier of fact to decide the case impartially, the defendant's right to due process has been infringed. Such a situation could occur in bench trials. See Lowery v. Cardwell, 575 F.2d 727 (9th Cir. 1978); State v. Jefferson, 615 P.2d 638 (Ariz. 1980) (en banc). If disclosure of the false testimony is necessary, defense counsel could inform a judge other than the trial judge, such as the chief administrative judge of the court in which the case is being heard. The Restatement suggests that disclosure to the prosecutor rather than the judge may be an appropriate remedial measure. Restatement (Third) of the Law Governing Lawyers § 120, cmt. *i*. In jury trials the conduct of defense counsel may demonstrate to the jury that the defendant's testimony is false, in which case a due process violation may be found. See State v. Robinson, 224 S.E.2d 174 (N.C. 1976). It has sometimes been claimed, without success, that the use of the narrative solution violates the defendant's right to due process because it informs the trier of fact that defense counsel does not believe the defendant's testimony. See Commonwealth v. Mitchell, 2000 WL 33119695, at *26 (Mass. Super. Dec. 18, 2000), *aff'd*, 781 N.E. 2d 1237 (Mass. 2003).

When does a lawyer "know" that a defendant intends to or has testified falsely?

Almost all of the duties set forth in Rule 3.3 depend on whether the lawyer has knowledge that the defendant intends to or has testified falsely.[181] The definition contained in Rule 1.0(k) states two propositions. First, knowledge means "actual knowledge." Second, knowledge may be inferred from the circumstances. Quite clearly "actual knowledge" is not the same as "personal knowledge,"[182] but what does it mean to say that a lawyer has actual knowledge that a criminal defendant will testify falsely? Some courts and commentators have suggested that attorney must be convinced beyond a reasonable doubt that the testimony will be false.[183] Most courts, however, have held that a

---

181. Rule 3.3(a)(3) is the only exception. It provides that a "lawyer may refuse to offer evidence, other than the testimony of a defendant in a criminal matter, that the lawyer *reasonably believes* is false," (emphasis added) but even this rule specifically exempts the situation of the criminal defendant.

182. Crystal, False Testimony by Criminal Defendants, 2003 Ill. L. Rev. at 1534.

183. E.g., Shockley v. State, 565 A.2d 1373, 1379 (Del. 1989). See also Harry I. Subin, The Criminal Lawyer's "Different Mission": Reflections on the "Right" to Present a False Case, 1 Geo. J. Legal Ethics 125, 142 (1987).

lawyer must have a "firm factual basis" before taking action to interdict false testimony.[184] The Restatement adopts this test.[185]

Assuming the firm factual basis test applies, when does a lawyer have a firm factual basis to know of false testimony? I have proposed the following refinement of the firm factual basis test:

> A lawyer has actual knowledge that a criminal defendant intends to testify falsely if the defendant's testimony will be inconsistent with facts that defendant has admitted (the factual admission test) or with facts known to the lawyer through independent investigation (the factual inconsistency test). If the defendant retracts an admission of facts, a lawyer still has actual knowledge if the retraction is so lacking in credibility that no reasonable person would accept it.[186]

The Restatement proposes a very similar test:

> A lawyer should not conclude that testimony is or will be false unless there is a firm factual basis for doing so. Such a basis exists when facts known to the lawyer or the client's own statements indicate to the lawyer that the testimony or other evidence is false.[187]

It may be necessary to a court to hold a hearing to determine whether the lawyer has a firm factual basis for action.[188]

False testimony by witnesses other than criminal defendants

Suppose the defendant wishes to call a witness that defense counsel reasonably believes will be testifying falsely. What should the lawyer do? While criminal defendants have the right to decide whether to testify in their own behalf, lawyers have the authority to determine which witnesses to call. See Model Rule 1.2(a). Similarly, ABA Defense Function Standard 4-5.2(b) provides as follows:

> Strategic and tactical decisions should be made by defense counsel after consultation with the client where feasible and appropriate. Such decisions include what witnesses to call, whether and how to conduct cross-examination, what jurors to accept or strike, what trial motions should be made, and what evidence should be introduced.

184. United States v. Long, 857 F.2d 436, 445 (8th Cir. 1988); United States ex rel. Wilcox v. Johnson, 555 F.2d 115, 122 (3d Cir. 1977); State v. James, 739 P.2d 1161, 1169 (Wash. Ct. App. 1987). For a discussion of the authorities, see Commonwealth v. Mitchell, 781 N.E.2d 1237 (Mass. 2003). See also State v. Hischke, 639 N.W.2d 6 (Iowa 2002) (lawyer must be convinced with good cause that client will testify falsely).

185. Restatement (Third) of the Law Governing Lawyers §120, cmt. *c.*

186. Crystal, False Testimony by Criminal Defendants, 2003 Ill. L. Rev. at 1537.

187. Restatement (Third) of the Law Governing Lawyers §120, cmt. *c.*

188. See State v. Jones, 923 P.2d 560 (Mont. 1996); Carol T. Rieger, Client Perjury: A Proposed Resolution of the Constitutional and Ethical Issues, 70 Minn. L. Rev. 121 (1985).

Further, Model Rule 3.3(a)(3) states "[a] lawyer may refuse to offer evidence, other than the testimony of a defendant in a criminal matter, that the lawyer reasonably believes is false."[189] Thus, if a lawyer knows that a witness will testify falsely, the lawyer has the authority and duty simply to refuse to call the witness.[190] As stated in Model Rule 1.2(a) and Defense Function Standard 4-5.2(b), the lawyer should take this step only after consultation with the client. If a lawyer learns that a witness has already testified falsely, the lawyer would have a duty to take reasonable remedial measures, including disclosure of the false testimony to the tribunal if necessary. See Model Rule 3.3(a)(3).[191]

The lawyer's refusal to call a witness could prompt a confrontation between lawyer and client that could in turn lead to the client's demand that the lawyer withdraw. The matter would then be brought to the attention of the court, which could take such action as it thought appropriate, including granting counsel permission to withdraw, directing counsel to call the defense witness, or allowing counsel to proceed without calling the witness. See Model Rule 1.2, cmt. 2.

The ethics of the lawyer's "lecture"

In cases like Nix v. Whiteside, the lawyer responded to a client's decision to testify falsely. In other cases, however, lawyers face decisions about how active they can be in coaching clients about their testimony. In the novel and movie *Anatomy of a Murder,* attorney Paul Biegler has been asked to represent Lieutenant Frederic Manion, who is accused of murdering Barney Quill. Quill raped Manion's wife, Laura. After considering the facts published in the newspapers, Biegler concludes that the only defense available to Manion is insanity at the time of the homicide. Before asking Manion to tell him about Quill's death, Biegler lectures Manion on the various legal defenses to homicide, leading Manion to shape his testimony to establish the defense of insanity.

Professor Monroe Freedman has argued that the ethical propriety of using the lecture depends on the circumstances. In many cases, he contends, the lawyer should inform the client of the legal significance of facts because it is necessary for the lawyer to do so to overcome various psychological barriers to a person's accurate recollection of events. The lawyer in these cases is not trying to create false testimony, but rather is simply seeking to obtain from the client accurate information necessary to represent the client competently. He discusses three potential psychological barriers to clients (or witnesses) giving accurate information:

First, memory is affected by various factors such as temperament, biases, expectations, and experience. As a result people reconstruct past events, often

---

189. See also Restatement (Third) of the Law Governing Lawyers §120(3).

190. See People v. Flores, 538 N.E.2d 481 (Ill. 1989), *cert. denied,* 497 U.S. 1031 (1990) (lawyer has discretion not to call nonclient witness in criminal case).

191. See also Restatement (Third) of the Law Governing Lawyers §120(2).

without being aware that they are doing so. Because of this "imaginative reconstruction" a person's memory may be "*subjectively* accurate but *objectively* false."[192] Second, people tend to remember in ways that are consistent with their own interests. Freedman notes that this often amounts to "wishful thinking" rather than deliberate dishonesty.[193] Third, people tend to respond confidently to questions about what they remember even when the actual circumstances should make them cautious about the accuracy of their recollections. Freedman concludes his discussion of the psychology of memory as follows:

> To sum up, remembering is not analogous to playing back a videotape or retrieving information from a computer. Rather, it is a process of active, creative reconstruction, which begins at the moment of perception. Moreover, this reconstructive process is significantly affected by the form of the questions asked and by what we understand to be in our own interest—even though, on a conscious level, we are responding as honestly as we can.[194]

Was the use of the lecture in *Anatomy of a Murder* improper? The answer is far from clear. If Biegler was attempting to shape Manion's testimony falsely, then the lecture was clearly improper. For example, if Manion was fully aware of what he was doing from the time he learned of the rape to the time he shot Quill, then Biegler would be attempting to get Manion to testify falsely that he did not actually have a memory of the events. On the other hand, it is possible that Manion did not have any memory of the events, but was unwilling to tell Biegler of his lack of memory because he believed, incorrectly, that a husband was legally justified in shooting a man who raped his wife. In fact, Manion mentions the "unwritten law" in his meeting with Biegler. If this was the situation, then Biegler would be acting properly in giving the lecture because he would be overcoming a barrier to Manion's telling him the truth.[195]

C. Conflicts of Interest

───────────── **Problem 2-6** ─────────────

Defendants with Diminished Capacity

You represent Henrietta Krindler, who is accused of murdering her husband. The state contends that Krindler killed her husband to collect substantial insurance proceeds on his life. Krindler has admitted to you

---

192. Freedman & Smith, Understanding Lawyers' Ethics 201 (quoting Gardner, The Perception and Memory of Witnesses, 18 Cornell L. Rev. 391 (1933)).
193. Id. at 204.
194. Id. at 205.
195. Id. at 206-209.

that she killed her husband. She says that he was suffering from terminal liver cancer and that she killed him to save him from a painful death. In fact, Krindler's husband was not ill at all. Krindler, who has a history of mental illness, suffered from a delusion about her husband's condition.

You have considered raising the issue of whether Krindler is competent to stand trial. Under your state statute, which is similar to section 4.04 of the Model Penal Code, a defendant is incompetent to stand trial if the defendant "lacks capacity to understand the proceedings against him or to assist in his own defense." You have concluded, however, that it is probably not in Krindler's interest to claim that she is incompetent to stand trial. First, you think that it is extremely unlikely that the court will find Krindler incompetent under this statute. Second, if Krindler is found incompetent, she will be institutionalized indefinitely and will still be subject to trial. Third, you believe that you have a good chance of being able to convince the jury that Krindler should be found guilty of manslaughter rather than murder because she lacks the mens rea required for murder. Fourth, if you raise the incompetency issue, any statements Krindler makes to doctors who examine her to determine her competency will probably not be privileged.[196] An examination could reveal information that would be helpful to the prosecution if the case goes to trial.

You have also considered whether to raise the defense that Krindler was not criminally responsible at the time she killed her husband. Your state supreme court has ruled that a defendant is not criminally responsible if "the defendant lacks substantial capacity either to appreciate the criminality of his conduct or to conform his conduct to the requirements of the law." You doubt that Krindler meets the requirements of this statute because it appears that she knew right from wrong when she killed her husband and that she was able to conform her conduct to the law. She acted on a mistaken belief about her husband's condition, but even if she had not been mistaken about his health, her action would still not have been justified under the law. In addition, if you enter a plea of not guilty by reason of insanity, Krindler will have to undergo examination by the state's doctors.

You have concluded, therefore, that the best strategy to follow is not to raise either a claim that Krindler is incompetent to stand trial or a defense of insanity, but instead to enter a plea of not guilty to murder and then to contend at trial that Krindler should be found guilty of at most manslaughter because she lacked the mens rea necessary for murder.

You have tried to discuss these considerations with Krindler, and she seems to understand the issues, but she has insisted that you not put

---

196. *Compare* Buchanan v. Kentucky, 483 U.S. 402 (1987) (state's use of psychiatric report to rebut mental status defense did not violate privilege against self-incrimination) *with* Estelle v. Smith, 451 U.S. 454 (1981) (Fifth Amendment violation for prosecutor to use statements made by defendant to court-appointed psychiatrist at sentencing hearing to establish future dangerousness when defendant had not put incompetency at issue).

up any defense on her behalf. She wants to enter a plea of guilty to murder, and she does not want you to introduce any evidence in mitigation at her sentencing hearing. Krindler says that she committed the crime and should be punished, that she does not want to be locked away in an institution for the rest of her life, and that her husband has told her that he wants her to join him. How should you proceed?

Read Model Rules 1.2(a), 1.14, 1.16, and comments.

Determining the client's competency

The rules of professional conduct generally assume that lawyers represent clients who are able to communicate with their lawyers and to make fundamental decisions about their cases based on the advice of counsel. See Model Rule 1.2(a).[197] Suppose this assumption fails: A lawyer represents a client who the lawyer believes suffers from diminished capacity and who is making decisions that may be harmful to the client, such as refusing to raise certain defenses or refusing to accept a favorable plea bargain. A client's diminished capacity could be caused by mental illness or retardation, physical disability, or addiction to drugs. In addition, lawyers who represent children also face the issue of dealing with clients who may have less than full capacity.

Model Rule 1.14 provides some general guidance to lawyers facing such problems. The rule envisions two types of clients with diminished capacity. One type of client suffers from diminished capacity but can participate in an attorney-client relationship to some degree. (The discussion that follows refers to such clients as "impaired.") With regard to impaired clients, Rule 1.14(a) instructs lawyers "as far as reasonably possible, maintain a normal client-lawyer relationship." However, if the client's diminished capacity is severe so that the client is at risk of substantial harm unless action is taken and the client "cannot adequately act in the client's own interest," the lawyer may take steps to protect the client from harm. Rule 1.14(b). (The discussion uses the term "incapacitated" when referring to such clients.) Thus, an initial issue a lawyer must resolve is whether the client is impaired or incapacitated. Model Rule 1.14 does not address this issue, but comment 6 provides guidance:

> In determining the extent of the client's diminished capacity, the lawyer should consider and balance such factors as: the client's ability to articulate reasoning leading to a decision, variability of state of mind and ability to appreciate consequences of a decision; the substantive fairness of a decision; and the consistency of a decision with the known long-term commitments and values of the client.

197. See also ABA Standards for Criminal Justice, Defense Function Standard 4-5.2 (3d ed. 1993) (distinguishing fundamental decisions that clients are entitled to make based on lawyers' advice from strategic and tactical decisions that lawyers are authorized to make after consultation with clients when feasible).

In appropriate circumstances, the lawyer may seek guidance from an appropriate diagnostician.

In Dusky v. United States,[198] the Supreme Court articulated the following standard for determining the defendant's competency to stand trial:

whether he has sufficient present ability to consult with his lawyer with a reasonable degree of rational understanding—and whether he has a rational as well as factual understanding of the proceedings against him.[199]

The Model Penal Code provision quoted in the problem adopts this test focusing on the defendant's ability to *understand the proceeding* and to *assist in the defense*.[200]

Suppose a lawyer is unsure whether a client is competent to stand trial or to make other decisions. How should the lawyer proceed? As an initial step the lawyer may want to consult with a psychiatrist or psychologist to obtain medical advice about the defendant's condition. A lawyer is impliedly authorized to do so even if the client objects and even if the lawyer will be revealing confidential information.[201] See Rule 1.14(c) and comment 6 (last sentence).

Suppose that the lawyer, based either on the lawyer's own observations or on the advice of a doctor, concludes that substantial doubt exists about the defendant's competency to stand trial. What should the lawyer do?[202] Due process requires that criminal defendants be competent to stand trial.[203] If a lawyer in a criminal case believes that the client is incompetent, the lawyer can deal with the problem by informing the court so that the court can hold a

---

198. 362 U.S. 402 (1960).

199. Id. Scholars have criticized the current formulation of the standard of competency to stand trial. *Compare* Richard J. Bonnie, The Competence of Criminal Defendants: Beyond *Dusky* and *Drope*, 47 U. Miami L. Rev. 539 (1993) *with* Bruce J. Winick, Reforming Incompetency to Stand Trial and Plead Guilty: A Restated Proposal and a Response to Professor Bonnie, 85 J. Crim. L. & Criminology 571 (1995). The standard for competency to waive the right to counsel and proceed pro se is the same as the standard for competency to stand trial, although the waiver must also be knowing and voluntary. Godinez v. Moran, 509 U.S. 389 (1993). The state may constitutionally place the burden of proving incompetency on the defendant, but a heightened burden of proof by clear and convincing evidence is unconstitutional. Cooper v. Oklahoma, 517 U.S. 348, 354 (1996).

200. See also ABA, Criminal Justice Mental Health Standard 7-4.1 (2d ed. 1986).

201. ABA Comm. on Ethics and Prof. Resp., Informal Op. 89-1530. See also Formal Op. 96-404 (discussing a variety of ethical issues facing lawyers who represent clients with disabilities).

202. For an empirical study of decisionmaking by lawyers with regard to insanity pleas, see Richard J. Bonnie et al., Decision-Making in Criminal Defense: An Empirical Study of Insanity Pleas and the Impact of Doubted Client Competence, 87 J. Crim. L. & Criminology 48 (1996).

203. Drope v. Missouri, 420 U.S. 162 (1975); Pate v. Robinson, 383 U.S. 375 (1966).

hearing on the defendant's competency to stand trial.[204] See Model Rule 1.14(c) and comment 8. In some cases, however, defense counsel may conclude that it is more advantageous for an incompetent defendant to proceed to trial than to raise an incompetency issue. The ABA's Criminal Justice Mental Health Standards summarize the reasons why defense counsel could reach this conclusion:

> An involuntary commitment for treatment to restore competence may extend well beyond the maximum sentence imposable for a relatively minor offense. A defendant could view the stigma flowing from a finding of mental illness as more opprobrious than that generated by a criminal conviction. An evaluation may force a defendant to reveal to a court-appointed expert information the defendant would prefer to keep secret. . . . A defendant might even prefer to be punished through imprisonment than to experience commitment to a mental hospital for treatment, given the marginal conditions in many public mental institutions. If the prosecution case against a defendant is weak, or if a defendant's assistance is not actually required during trial, defense counsel may believe that an acquittal is likely even though defendant is incompetent.[205]

One federal study has shown that confinement for mental illness typically exceeds that for the underlying offense. The study found that in felony cases the median length of commitment for patients found not guilty by reason of insanity was 49.2 months, while jail sentences for convicted felons was 33.4 months.[206]

May defense counsel decide as a matter of strategy not to inform the court when counsel has substantial doubts about a criminal defendant's competence to stand trial? (Of course, even if defense counsel does not raise the issue, either the prosecutor or the court on its own motion may do so.[207]) Despite the considerations noted above, the ABA Criminal Justice Mental Health Standards require defense counsel to move the court for a competency determination when "defense counsel has a good faith doubt as to the defendant's competence."[208] While recognizing that in some cases it may not be to the advantage of a defendant to raise the issue of competency, the commentary to the standards justifies imposing a duty on defense counsel to inform the court of the defendant's incompetency because of counsel's duty to the system: "Because the trial of an incompetent defendant necessarily is invalid as a violation of due process, a defense lawyer's duty to maintain the integrity of

204. See James A. Cohen, The Attorney-Client Privilege, Ethical Rules, and the Impaired Criminal Defendant, 52 U. Miami L. Rev. 529 (1998) (arguing that lawyers should be able to reveal confidential information to court to assist it in making competency determination).

205. ABA, Criminal Justice Mental Health Standard 7-4.2, cmt. (2d ed. 1986).

206. Paul A. Chernoff & William G. Schaffer, Defending the Mentally Ill: Ethical Quicksand, 10 Am. Crim. L. Rev. 505, 523-524, n.65 (1972).

207. See ABA, Criminal Justice Mental Health Standard 7-4.2 (2d ed. 1986).

208. Id. 7-4.2(c).

judicial proceedings requires that a trial court be advised of the defendant's possible incompetence."[209]

Model Rule 1.14, in contrast to the Mental Health Standards, does not impose on the lawyer a duty of disclosure. Comment 8 to Rule 1.14 states simply that the "lawyer's position in such cases is an unavoidably difficult one." The Restatement states that lawyers do not have a duty to inform a tribunal of a defendant's possible incompetency when the lawyer concludes that such disclosure would not be in the client's interest, unless law imposes such an obligation.[210]

In United States v. Boigegrain,[211] the Tenth Circuit ruled that a criminal defendant was not denied effective assistance of counsel when defense counsel raised the issue of his competency to stand trial over the defendant's objection. Relying on the ABA Criminal Justice Mental Health Standards, the court stated that defense counsel had a duty to bring the issue of the defendant's competency to the attention of the court: "Of all the actors in a trial, defense counsel has the most intimate association with the defendant. Therefore, the defendant's lawyer is not only allowed to raise the competency issue, but, because of the importance of the prohibition on trying those who cannot understand proceedings against them, she has a professional duty to do so when appropriate."[212] Similarly, in State v. Johnson,[213] the Wisconsin Supreme Court held that a defendant had been denied effective assistance of counsel in a murder case when his lawyer did not inform the court that the defendant might not be competent to stand trial. The court rejected arguments that defense counsel had acted properly because he had concluded that the defendant was competent and because he had decided that it was not strategically wise to raise the incompetency issue. The court held that when defense counsel has "reason to doubt the competency of his client to stand trial, he must raise the issue with the trial court."[214]

Professor Rodney Uphoff has criticized *Johnson* because it undercuts the defendant's right to zealous representation. He would allow lawyers to make case-by-case determinations of what their role should be:

> The decision as to whether to respect a client's questionable decision, assume a more paternalistic role, or raise competency depends on the lawyer's careful analysis of the degree of the client's mental impairment, the importance of the

209. Id. cmt.

210. Restatement (Third) of the Law Governing Lawyers §24, cmt. *d*.

211. 155 F.3d 1181 (10th Cir. 1998), *cert. denied*, 525 U.S. 1083 (1999).

212. 155 F.3d at 1188. Judge Holloway, concurring in part and dissenting in part, agreed that defense counsel did have a duty to raise the issue of the defendant's competency, but argued that this resulted in a conflict of interest when defense counsel proceeded to advocate the defendant's incompetency against the defendant's wishes. Judge Holloway argued that defense counsel should have been allowed to withdraw. The trial court should have appointed new counsel who would have advocated defendant's position that he was competent to stand trial. Id. at 1190-1193.

213. 395 N.W.2d 176 (Wis. 1986).

214. Id. at 182.

decision being considered, the type of case, and the costs and benefits to the client of the alternative courses of action.[215]

Representing competent but possibly impaired clients

Suppose counsel represents a defendant whom the court has found competent to stand trial but whose decisionmaking capacities the lawyer still questions. What, if anything, should the lawyer do if the defendant insists on entering a plea or demands that the lawyer conduct the case in a fashion that the lawyer concludes is clearly not in the client's best interest? Competent clients generally have the authority to make ultimate decisions about their cases. See Model Rule 1.2(a). ABA Defense Function Standard 4-5.2 provides as follows:

(a) Certain decisions relating to the conduct of the case are ultimately for the accused and others are ultimately for defense counsel. The decisions which are to be made by the accused after full consultation with counsel include:
(i) what pleas to enter;
(ii) whether to accept a plea agreement;
(iii) whether to waive jury trial;
(iv) whether to testify in his or her own behalf; and
(v) whether to appeal.
(b) Strategic and tactical decisions should be made by defense counsel after consultation with the client where feasible and appropriate. Such decisions include what witnesses to call, whether and how to conduct cross-examination, what jurors to accept or strike, what trial motions should be made, and what evidence should be introduced.
(c) If a disagreement on significant matters of tactics or strategy arises between defense counsel and the client, defense counsel should make a record of the circumstances, counsel's advice and reasons, and the conclusion reached. The record should be made in a manner which protects the confidentiality of the lawyer-client relationship.

Federal and state courts have held that competent defendants cannot be compelled to raise insanity defenses against their wishes.[216] This view finds support in the Supreme Court's decision in Faretta v. California,[217] in which the Court held that the Sixth Amendment guarantees criminal defendants the right to proceed without counsel when they voluntarily and intelligently elect to do so.

215. Rodney J. Uphoff, The Role of the Criminal Defense Lawyer in Representing the Mentally Impaired Defendant: Zealous Advocate or Officer of the Court? 1988 Wis. L. Rev. 65, 99-108. For a contrary view see Norma Schrock, Note, Defense Counsel's Role in Determining Competency to Stand Trial, 9 Geo. J. Legal Ethics 639 (1996) (arguing that lawyers should have duty to bring to attention of court issue of defendant's competency to stand trial).
216. United States v. Marble, 940 F.2d 1543 (D.C. Cir. 1991); People v. Bloom, 774 P.2d 698 (Cal. 1989) (en banc), cert. denied, 494 U.S. 1039 (1990) (defendant cannot be compelled to present a defense in a death penalty case).
217. 422 U.S. 806 (1975).

If a competent defendant has the right to decide whether to plead guilty or to raise an insanity defense, defense counsel who strongly disagrees with the decision has a limited number of options: attempt to persuade the defendant otherwise, enlist the assistance of family members in an effort to change the client's decision (Model Rule 1.14, cmt. 5), move to withdraw on the ground that the client "insists upon taking action that the lawyer considers repugnant or with which the lawyer has a fundamental disagreement" under Model Rule 1.16(b)(4), or follow the client's directions.[218] Even though the defendant may have the right to make ultimate decisions about the case, lawyers still retain the authority to make tactical decisions that are binding on their clients, at least until they are discharged.[219]

Probably the most dramatic example of a defendant who decided, against the advice of his lawyers, to forgo his legal rights and to accept the death penalty was Gary Gilmore.[220] Gilmore was convicted and sentenced to death for two brutal murders. Gilmore's lawyers told him that he had an excellent chance of having his sentence reversed because the Utah statute under which he was sentenced was constitutionally defective in that it failed to provide for mandatory appellate review of death sentences. In addition, at the sentencing hearing the trial judge had erroneously admitted evidence of another murder that Gilmore had committed.

Gilmore looked at his situation quite differently from his lawyers. He found life in prison intolerable. Gilmore told his lawyers that he needed to atone for a crime he had committed in eighteenth-century England, a crime for which he believed he had already been executed.

Gilmore finally decided to accept execution rather than to appeal his conviction, and he ordered his lawyers not to file an appeal on his behalf. When they refused because they doubted his competency, he fired them and hired

---

218. See Red Dog v. State, 625 A.2d 245 (Del. 1993) (defendant has right to forgo appeals and accept death penalty; defense counsel who finds client's decision repugnant should move to withdraw; defense counsel who has "reasonable and objective basis" to doubt client's competency must in a timely fashion inform trial court and request competency determination).

219. Faretta v. California, 422 U.S. at 820; Model Rule 1.2(a) and ABA Standards for Criminal Justice, Defense Function Standard 4-5.2 (3d ed. 1993). For discussions of the lawyer's role in representing criminal defendants who do not wish to assert possible defenses, see Josephine Ross, Autonomy Versus a Client's Best Interests: The Defense Lawyer's Dilemma When Mentally Ill Clients Seek to Control Their Defense, 35 Am. Crim. L. Rev. 1343 (1998); Christopher Slobogin & Amy Mashburn, The Criminal Defense Lawyer's Fiduciary Duty to Clients with Mental Disability, 68 Fordham L. Rev. 1581 (2000); H. Richard Uviller, Calling the Shots: The Allocation of Choice Between the Accused and Counsel in the Defense of a Criminal Case, 52 Rutgers L. Rev. 719 (2000).

220. Norman Mailer, The Executioner's Song (1979). For a review of the book highly critical of the conduct of the various lawyers who represented Gilmore, see Barbara A. Babcock, Book Review, 32 Stan. L. Rev. 865 (1980). For a study of decisionmaking by lawyers who represent death row volunteers, see C. Lee Harrington, A Community Divided: Defense Attorneys and the Ethics of Death Row Volunteering, 25 Law & Soc. Inquiry 849 (2000).

another lawyer, who had written to Gilmore and had volunteered to assist him in accepting his punishment.

The Utah Supreme Court accepted Gilmore's decision not to appeal his conviction and lifted a stay to allow his execution to proceed. His mother then filed a petition as "next friend" before the United States Supreme Court. The Court initially granted a stay, but lifted the order after reviewing the record and finding that Gilmore had made a knowing and intelligent waiver of his rights.[221] The State of Utah then executed Gilmore.

In the Unabomber case, the defendant, Theodore Kaczynski, was found competent to stand trial. He directed his lawyers not to raise an insanity defense to the murder charges against him. They strongly disagreed with this decision because they believed it was the only viable defense available to him. The lawyers finally reached an agreement with Kaczynski not to raise a formal defense of insanity but instead to claim that his mental illness negated his intent to murder. They would have supported this position by testimony of lay rather than expert witness, but this became unnecessary when the defense reached a plea bargain with the government.[222]

Issues involving representation of clients with diminished capacity can occur in civil litigation and in nonlitigation matters. Problem 3-10 deals with the topic in the context of family practice.

─────────────────────── **Problem 2-7** ───────────────────────

Multiple Representation of Codefendants

a. Two brothers, Andre and Ronald Martinez, have been indicted on charges of securities fraud in connection with a shopping mall that went bankrupt. They have asked you to defend them in the case. How would you decide whether you could legally and ethically represent them?

b. Suppose you decide, given the seriousness of the charges, that it would not be wise for you to represent both brothers. Andre retains you, while Ronald retains Selma Height. You and Selma believe that it would be in your clients' interests to enter into a joint defense agreement. Prepare a draft of an agreement. For a sample form see 5 West's Fed. Forms, District Courts-Criminal §7394 (4th ed. 2002) (available on Westlaw).

───

Read Model Rules 1.7 and 1.0(b), (e), (n) and comments.

221. Gilmore v. Utah, 429 U.S. 1012 (1976).
222. Ross, Autonomy Versus a Client's Best Interests, 35 Am. Crim. L. Rev. at 1344 n.2. See also Joel S. Newman, Doctors, Lawyers, and the Unabomber, 60 Mont. L. Rev. 67 (1999); H. Richard Uviller, Calling the Shots: The Allocation of Choice Between the Accused and Counsel in the Defense of a Criminal Case, 52 Rutgers L. Rev. 719 (2000).

Multiple representation in criminal cases and the Sixth Amendment right to counsel

Conflicts of interest present some of the most pervasive and difficult ethical problems that lawyers face in practice. In Chapter 3 we will examine a variety of conflicts of interest in civil litigation: adverse representation against a current client, multiple representation of clients in a single matter, representation against a former client, advocate-witness conflicts, and conflicts involving the lawyer's own personal or financial interest.

In criminal cases lawyers may also face conflicts of interest. For example, codefendants in a criminal case may ask a lawyer to represent them in the matter. Defendants may seek the representation of a single lawyer for a variety of reasons: for example, confidence in the lawyer, desire to present a united front, and the need to share expenses. Multiple representation in criminal cases involves not only issues of professional ethics but also issues of constitutional law—the defendants' Sixth Amendment right to effective assistance of counsel. Some scholars have argued that conflicts of interest are so pervasive in the representation of multiple criminal defendants that such representation should be prohibited either as a matter of constitutional law or under rules of ethics.[223]

Despite these arguments, neither the rules of ethics nor constitutional decisions create a per se prohibition on multiple representation, although multiple representation is discouraged. Model Rule 1.7 deals with multiple representation of clients in a single matter. While the text of Rule 1.7 makes no distinction between civil and criminal cases, Comment 23 states: "The potential for conflict of interest in representing multiple defendants in a criminal case is so grave that ordinarily a lawyer should decline to represent more than one codefendant." Similarly, ABA Defense Function Standard 4-3.5(c) provides as follows:

> The potential for conflict of interest in representing multiple defendants is so grave that ordinarily defense counsel should decline to act for more than one of several codefendants except in unusual situations when, after careful investigation, it is clear either that no conflict is likely to develop at trial, sentencing, or at any other time in the proceeding or that common representation will be advantageous to each of the codefendants represented and, in either case, that:
>
> (i) the several defendants give an informed consent to such multiple representation; and
> (ii) the consent of the defendants is made a matter of judicial record. In determining the presence of consent by the defendants, the trial judge should make appropriate inquiries respecting actual or potential conflicts of interest of

---

223. See John S. Geer, Representation of Multiple Criminal Defendants: Conflicts of Interest and the Professional Responsibilities of the Defense Attorney, 62 Minn. L. Rev. 119 (1978); Gary T. Lowenthal, Joint Representation in Criminal Cases: A Critical Appraisal, 64 Va. L. Rev. 939 (1978). See also Debra Lyn Bassett, Three's a Crowd: A Proposal to Abolish Joint Representation, 32 Rutgers L.J. 387 (2001).

counsel and whether the defendants fully comprehend the difficulties that defense counsel sometimes encounters in defending multiple clients.

The Restatement also warns about the dangers of multiple representation of criminal defendants.[224]

In a line of cases the Supreme Court has examined the impact of the Sixth Amendment right to counsel on the issue of multiple representation in criminal cases. The Court first dealt with situations in which the trial court had appointed counsel to represent codefendants over the objection of one of the defendants or defense counsel.[225] The Court held that trial courts had the obligation to inquire into whether a conflict of interest existed. In addition, when an actual conflict occurs, the defendant need not show prejudice resulting from the attorney's representation to establish a Sixth Amendment violation.[226]

In later cases the Court considered whether a Sixth Amendment violation occurred when the defendants had voluntarily hired counsel to represent them jointly rather than having counsel appointed over the objections of one of them.[227] The Court ruled that a different, more demanding standard applies in voluntary multiple representation cases. In these cases the defendant must show that "an actual conflict of interest adversely affected his lawyer's performance."[228]

In the most recent of its multiple representation cases, Wheat v. United States,[229] the Court held that trial courts have the authority at the pretrial stage to reject waivers of conflicts of interest by codefendants and to require separate rather than multiple representation whenever multiple representation involves either an actual or a serious potential for a conflict of interest.[230]

---

224. Restatement (Third) of the Law Governing Lawyers §129.

225. Glasser v. United States, 315 U.S. 60 (1942); Holloway v. Arkansas, 435 U.S. 475 (1978).

226. *Glasser*, 315 U.S. at 71, 76; *Holloway*, 435 U.S. at 488-489.

227. Cuyler v. Sullivan, 446 U.S. 335 (1980); Burger v. Kemp, 483 U.S. 776 (1987).

228. *Cuyler*, 446 U.S. at 350. See Burger v. Kemp, 483 U.S. 776 (1987) (counsel's failure to make "lesser culpability" argument on appeal insufficient to establish either actual conflict or prejudice). Although the Court in *Burger* failed to find a Sixth Amendment violation resulting from multiple representation, lower courts have done so in some cases. E.g., Griffin v. McVicar, 84 F.3d 880 (7th Cir. 1996), *cert. denied,* 520 U.S. 1139 (1997) (ineffective assistance of counsel shown when lawyer adopted common defense strategy for defendants with different degrees of culpability); Hoffman v. Leeke, 903 F.2d 280 (4th Cir. 1990) (ineffective assistance of counsel when lawyer represented codefendants in murder case and negotiated plea bargain in which one defendant implicated other).

229. 486 U.S. 153 (1988).

230. Id. at 163-164. For a criticism of the Court's decision in *Wheat* arguing that it fails to give proper weight to the right to counsel, see Bruce A. Green, "Through a Glass, Darkly": How the Court Sees Motions to Disqualify Criminal Defense Lawyers, 89 Colum. L. Rev. 1201 (1989). See also Bruce A. Green, Her Brother's Keeper: The Prosecutor's Responsibility When Defense Counsel Has a Potential Conflict of Interest, 16 Am. J. Crim. L. 323 (1989).

Deciding whether to undertake multiple representation

In light of this body of law, how should a lawyer proceed in deciding whether to undertake multiple representation in a criminal case? Lawyers in private defense practice face an initial personal decision: Am I willing to undertake the risk of multiple representation, even if it is ethically and constitutionally permitted? On one hand, some lawyers believe that representing multiple defendants is so likely to involve an actual conflict of interest that such representation should always be avoided. In addition, if a lawyer undertakes multiple representation, a conviction will often produce a claim of ineffective assistance of counsel, requiring the lawyer to withdraw from further representation in the matter and involving the lawyer in time-consuming postconviction relief proceedings. On the other hand, the potential clients may be financially unable to afford separate counsel, and joint representation may be strategically desirable because it facilitates a common defense.

If a lawyer is willing to undertake multiple representation, or if the lawyer is appointed to represent multiple clients, the lawyer must then decide whether such representation is ethically and constitutionally permitted. Under *Wheat* a Sixth Amendment violation can occur if the lawyer represents multiple defendants who have an actual conflict of interest or a serious potential conflict of interest. How does a lawyer determine whether either of these situations exists? Professors Fortune, Underwood, and Imwinkelried offer the following checklist of questions to consider in deciding whether multiple representation of criminal defendants is permissible:

1. Does one defendant have evidence to offer that inculpates the codefendant?
2. Is one defendant more culpable than the other? If so, conflict is almost inevitable, either because the prosecution will offer a deal to the one less culpable or because distinctions will need to be drawn during the case.
3. Are the defenses inconsistent in any way?
4. Will one testify and the other not? A defendant who testifies inevitably calls attention to the failure of the other defendant to take the stand. This problem is exacerbated by joint representation.
5. Will the prosecution's evidence strike the defendants unequally? If a prosecution witness implicates *A,* but not *B,* the attorney is put in the position of attacking the witness on behalf of *A,* but implying that he is telling the truth about *B.*
6. Should distinctions be drawn in closing argument? The attorney representing codefendants cannot do so.
7. Should distinctions be drawn at sentencing because of either the defendants' relative culpability or their different backgrounds?[231]

---

231. William H. Fortune et al., Modern Litigation and Professional Responsibility Handbook §14.3.1, at 507-509 (2d ed. 2001).

Lawyers who conclude that they may not undertake multiple representation because of an actual or serious potential conflict must decline representation and should move to have separate counsel appointed to represent the defendants. The failure of the trial court to appoint separate counsel on motion by defense counsel because of a conflict of interest would be a Sixth Amendment violation under *Holloway*.

Suppose the lawyer, after considering the facts and potential conflicts, concludes that multiple representation would be proper. The lawyer may do so, provided the clients give informed consent. Model Rule 1.7(b)(4). Informed consent "denotes the agreement by a person to a proposed course of conduct after the lawyer has communicated adequate information and explanation about the material risks of and reasonably available alternatives to the proposed course of conduct." Model Rule 1.0(e). The comment to the Model Rule elaborates on informed consent: "Ordinarily, this will require communication that includes a disclosure of the facts and circumstances giving rise to the situation, any explanation reasonably necessary to inform the client or other person of the material advantages and disadvantages of the proposed course of conduct and a discussion of the client's or other person's options and alternatives." Model Rule 1.0, cmt. 6. Advantages of multiple representation typically include pooling resources, obtaining the benefit of counsel with particular expertise or with knowledge of the case, and presenting a united defense front. Multiple representation poses several material risks to the clients. In broad terms multiple representation precludes defense counsel from advocating a position on behalf of one defendant that casts the blame on another represented defendant, whether in plea bargaining, witness selection, witness examination, argument, sentencing, or appeal. The defendants must understand that the lawyer will zealously represent their interests but will not favor one defendant at the expense of another. If the defendants foresee the possibility of an actual conflict of interest, they should not consent to multiple representation. The defendants should also be informed that communications with the lawyer by either defendant will not be privileged as to the other. The potential clients should also be advised of the alternatives to multiple representation. Of course, each defendant can retain separate counsel or even proceed pro se. In addition, if the defendants have separate counsel they can enter into a joint defense agreement (sometimes called a common-interest agreement).[232] Joint defense agreements are discussed in more detail below.

If the defendants conclude that the advantages of multiple representation outweigh any disadvantages, and if they are willing to consent to multiple representation, the lawyer may proceed. The 2002 revision of the Model Rules requires the consent to be "confirmed in writing." See Model Rules 1.7(b)(4) and 1.0(b). The consent should acknowledge a full consultation with the lawyer about the advantages, disadvantages, and alternatives to multiple representation, including their right to retain independent counsel with or without a joint defense agreement.

232. Restatement (Third) of the Law Governing Lawyers §76.

In federal court the rules of criminal procedure require trial judges to inquire into the propriety of joint representation. Federal Rule of Criminal Procedure 44(c) provides as follows:

> (c) *Inquiry Into Joint Representation.*
>   (1) *Joint Representation.* Joint representation occurs when:
>   (A) two or more defendants have been charged jointly under Rule 8(b) or have been joined for trial under Rule 13; and
>   (B) the defendants are represented by the same counsel, or counsel who are associated in law practice.
>   (2) *Court's Responsibilities in Cases of Joint Representation.* The court must promptly inquire about the propriety of joint representation and must personally advise each defendant of the right to the effective assistance of counsel, including separate representation. Unless there is good cause to believe that no conflict of interest is likely to arise, the court must take appropriate measures to protect each defendant's right to counsel.

The inquiry by the court under Rule 44 should be designed to prevent disclosure of confidential information to the prosecution. The Advisory Committee's notes state:

> Whenever it is necessary to make a more particularized inquiry into the nature of the contemplated defense, the court should "pursue the inquiry with defendants and their counsel on the record but in chambers" so as "to avoid the possibility of prejudicial disclosures to the prosecution."

In state court, lawyers must, of course, follow state rules of criminal procedure.[233] In the absence of a court rule, a lawyer who has accepted multiple representation should make the clients' consent a matter of judicial record as recommended by ABA Defense Function Standard 4-3.5(c).[234]

Joint defense agreements as an alternative to multiple representation

A joint defense agreement allows separately represented defendants to coordinate their defense and to share information without loss of the attorney-client privilege.[235] Thus, a joint defense agreement offers many of the advantages of multiple representation without the conflict-of-interest problems associated with multiple representation. In addition, particularly in complex cases, joint

233. See, e.g., People v. Mroczko, 672 P.2d 835 (Cal. 1983) (en banc) (trial court must initially appoint separate counsel with an instruction to inform the court if counsel, after investigation and consultation with their clients, conclude that the interests of justice and of their clients will best be served by multiple representation; court will then make such on-the-record disposition as is appropriate).
234. See Shongutsie v. State, 827 P.2d 361 (Wyo. 1992) (consent should preferably be in writing and should be included in the record).
235. Restatement (Third) of the Law Governing Lawyers §76, cmt. *b.*

defense agreements can reduce legal fees and expenses because the parties can allocate responsibility for fact investigation and legal research and then share their work product.

A significant issue that has arisen in connection with joint defense agreements is what happens if a party withdraws from a joint defense agreement and becomes adverse to the other parties. This could happen, for example, if a party negotiates a deal with the prosecution in exchange for testimony against other codefendants. In United States v. Stepney,[236] the government charged nearly 30 defendants with over 70 charges related to the operation of a street gang in San Francisco. The case was extremely complex both factually and legally. Various defense counsel sought to enter into joint defense agreements to share factual investigation and legal work product. Subsequently, one of the defense counsel moved to withdraw because he had come to believe that a defendant with whom he had entered into a joint defense agreement was cooperating with the prosecution. The moving attorney claimed that the joint defense agreement created a duty of loyalty to the cooperating defendant that would prevent the moving attorney from cross-examining the defendant.[237] The district court denied the motion to withdraw and issued guidelines for joint defense agreements. The court ruled that it had the authority to supervise joint defense agreements under its inherent supervisory power to protect the Sixth Amendment rights of defendants and under Federal Rule of Criminal Procedure 44(c), which imposes an obligation on federal courts to inquire into joint representation.[238] After reviewing precedent dealing with joint defense agreements, the court concluded that the existence of such an agreement did not create an attorney-client relationship or general duty of loyalty to the other defendants.[239] To the court such a duty would be unsound as a matter of policy because it would lead to wholesale disqualification of defense counsel whenever one of the defendants began cooperating with the prosecutors:

> There is good reason for the law to refrain from imposing on attorneys a duty of loyalty to their clients' co-defendants. A duty of loyalty between parties to a joint defense agreement would create a minefield of potential conflicts. Should any defendant that signed the agreement decide to cooperate with the government and testify in the prosecution's case-in-chief, an attorney for a non-cooperating defendant would be put in the position of cross-examining a witness to whom she owed a duty of loyalty on behalf of her own client, to whom she also would owe a duty of loyalty. This would create a conflict of interest which would require withdrawal.[240]

---

236. 246 F. Supp. 2d 1069 (N.D. Cal. 2003). The court cited with approval a model agreement, Joint Defense Agreement, Am. Law Institute-Am. Bar Assn., Trial Evidence in the Federal Courts: Problems and Solutions, at 35 (1999).

237. Id. at 1072.

238. Id. at 1076-1079.

239. Id. at 1082-1083.

240. Id. at 1083.

The court also discussed the tension between the withdrawing defendant's right to confidentiality and the right to counsel of the other represented defendants. It concluded that the withdrawing defendant's right to confidentiality should give way through a provision waiving confidentiality to the extent necessary to allow attorneys for the other defendants to cross-examine the withdrawing defendant:

> Under this regime, all defendants have waived any duty of confidentiality for purposes of cross-examining testifying defendants, and generally an attorney can cross-examine using any and all materials, free from any conflicts of interest. This form of waiver also places the loss of the benefits of the joint defense agreement only on the defendant who makes the choice to testify. Defendants who testify for the government under a grant of immunity lose nothing by this waiver. Those that testify on their own behalf have already made the decision to waive their Fifth Amendment right against self-incrimination and to admit evidence through their cross-examination that would otherwise be inadmissible.
>
> The conditional waiver of confidentiality also provides notice to defendants that their confidences may be used in cross-examination, so that each defendant can choose with suitable caution what to reveal to the joint defense group. Although a limitation on confidentiality between a defendant and his own attorney would pose a severe threat to the true attorney-client relationship, making each defendant somewhat more guarded about the disclosures he makes to the joint defense effort does not significantly intrude on the function of joint defense agreements. The attorney-client privilege protects "full and frank" communication because the attorney serves as the client's liaison to the legal system. Without a skilled attorney, fully apprised of her client's situation, our adversarial system could not function. Any secret a client keeps from his own counsel compromises his counsel's ability to represent him effectively and undermines the purpose of the attorney-client privilege.
>
> Joint defense agreements, however, serve a different purpose. Each defendant entering a joint defense agreement already has a representative, fully and confidentially informed of the client's situation. The joint defense privilege allows defendants to share information so as to avoid unnecessarily inconsistent defenses that undermine the credibility of the defense as a whole. . . . In criminal cases where discovery is limited, such collaboration is necessary to assure a fair trial in the face of the prosecution's informational advantage gained through the power to gather evidence by searches and seizures. Co-defendants may eliminate inconsistent defenses without the same degree of disclosure that would be required for an attorney to adequately represent her client. The legitimate value of joint defense agreements will not be significantly diminished by including a limited waiver of confidentiality by testifying defendants for purposes of cross-examination only.[241]

In conclusion, the court ordered that all joint defense agreements meet four requirements:

241. Id. at 1085-1086.

(1) Any joint defense agreement entered into by defendants must be committed to writing, signed by defendants and their attorneys, and submitted in camera to the court for review prior to going into effect.

(2) Each joint defense agreement submitted must explicitly state that it does not create an attorney-client relationship between an attorney and any defendant other than the client of that attorney. No joint defense agreement may purport to create a duty of loyalty.

(3) Each joint defense agreement must contain provisions conditionally waiving confidentiality by providing that a signatory attorney cross-examining any defendant who testifies at any proceeding, whether under a grant of immunity or otherwise, may use any material or other information contributed by such client during the joint defense.

(4) Each joint defense agreement must explicitly allow withdrawal upon notice to the other defendants.[242]

Mickens v. Taylor

United States Supreme Court
535 U.S. 162 (2002)

Justice SCALIA delivered the opinion of the Court.

The question presented in this case is what a defendant must show in order to demonstrate a Sixth Amendment violation where the trial court fails to inquire into a potential conflict of interest about which it knew or reasonably should have known.

I

In 1993, a Virginia jury convicted petitioner Mickens of the premeditated murder of Timothy Hall during or following the commission of an attempted forcible sodomy. Finding the murder outrageously and wantonly vile, it sentenced petitioner to death. In June 1998, Mickens filed a petition for writ of habeas corpus, see 28 U.S.C. §2254 (1994 ed. and Supp. V), in the United States District Court for the Eastern District of Virginia, alleging, inter alia, that he was denied effective assistance of counsel because one of his court-appointed attorneys had a conflict of interest at trial. Federal habeas counsel had discovered that petitioner's lead trial attorney, Bryan Saunders, was representing Hall (the victim) on assault and concealed-weapons charges at the time of the murder. Saunders had been appointed to represent Hall, a juvenile, on March 20, 1992, and had met with him once for 15 to 30 minutes some time the following week. Hall's body was discovered on March 30, 1992, and four days later a juvenile court judge dismissed the charges against him, noting on the docket sheet that Hall was deceased. The one-page docket sheet also listed Saunders as Hall's counsel. On April 6, 1992, the same judge appointed Saunders to represent petitioner. Saunders did not disclose to the court, his

242. Id. at 1086.

co-counsel, or petitioner that he had previously represented Hall. Under Virginia law, juvenile case files are confidential and may not generally be disclosed without a court order, see Va. Code Ann. §16.1-305 (1999), but petitioner learned about Saunders' prior representation when a clerk mistakenly produced Hall's file to federal habeas counsel.

The District Court held an evidentiary hearing and denied petitioner's habeas petition. . . . [T]he Court of Appeals [for the Fourth Circuit] assumed that the juvenile court judge had neglected a duty to inquire into a potential conflict, but rejected petitioner's argument that this failure either mandated automatic reversal of his conviction or relieved him of the burden of showing that a conflict of interest adversely affected his representation. Relying on Cuyler v. Sullivan, 446 U.S. 335 (1980), the court held that a defendant must show "both an actual conflict of interest and an adverse effect even if the trial court failed to inquire into a potential conflict about which it reasonably should have known," 240 F.3d, at 355-356. Concluding that petitioner had not demonstrated adverse effect, id., at 360, it affirmed the District Court's denial of habeas relief. We granted a stay of execution of petitioner's sentence and granted certiorari. 532 U.S. 970 (2001).

II

. . . As a general matter, a defendant alleging a Sixth Amendment violation must demonstrate "a reasonable probability that, but for counsel's unprofessional errors, the result of the proceeding would have been different." [Strickland v. Washington, 466 U.S.] at 694.

There is an exception to this general rule. We have spared the defendant the need of showing probable effect upon the outcome, and have simply presumed such effect, where assistance of counsel has been denied entirely or during a critical stage of the proceeding. When that has occurred, the likelihood that the verdict is unreliable is so high that a case-by-case inquiry is unnecessary. . . . But only in "circumstances of that magnitude" do we forgo individual inquiry into whether counsel's inadequate performance undermined the reliability of the verdict. . . .

We have held in several cases that "circumstances of that magnitude" may also arise when the defendant's attorney actively represented conflicting interests. The nub of the question before us is whether the principle established by these cases provides an exception to the general rule of *Strickland* under the circumstances of the present case. To answer that question, we must examine those cases in some detail.

In Holloway v. Arkansas, 435 U.S. 475 (1978), defense counsel had objected that he could not adequately represent the divergent interests of three codefendants. Id., at 478-480. Without inquiry, the trial court had denied counsel's motions for the appointment of separate counsel and had refused to allow counsel to cross-examine any of the defendants on behalf of the other two. . . . *Holloway* . . . creates an automatic reversal rule only where defense counsel is forced to represent codefendants over his timely objection, unless the trial court has determined that there is no conflict. Id., at 488. . . .

In Cuyler v. Sullivan, 446 U.S. 335 (1980), the respondent was one of three defendants accused of murder who were tried separately, represented by the same counsel. Neither counsel nor anyone else objected to the multiple representation, and counsel's opening argument at Sullivan's trial suggested that the interests of the defendants were aligned. Id., at 347-348. We declined to extend *Holloway*'s automatic reversal rule to this situation and held that, absent objection, a defendant must demonstrate that "a conflict of interest actually affected the adequacy of his representation." 446 U.S., at 348-349. . . .

Finally, in Wood v. Georgia, 450 U.S. 261 (1981), three indigent defendants convicted of distributing obscene materials had their probation revoked for failure to make the requisite $500 monthly payments on their $5,000 fines. We granted certiorari to consider whether this violated the Equal Protection Clause, but during the course of our consideration certain disturbing circumstances came to our attention: At the probation-revocation hearing (as at all times since their arrest) the defendants had been represented by the lawyer for their employer (the owner of the business that purveyed the obscenity), and their employer paid the attorney's fees. The employer had promised his employees he would pay their fines, and had generally kept that promise but had not done so in these defendants' case. This record suggested that the employer's interest in establishing a favorable equal-protection precedent (reducing the fines he would have to pay for his indigent employees in the future) diverged from the defendants' interest in obtaining leniency or paying lesser fines to avoid imprisonment. Moreover, the possibility that counsel was actively representing the conflicting interests of employer and defendants "was sufficiently apparent at the time of the revocation hearing to impose upon the court a duty to inquire further." Id., at 272. Because "[o]n the record before us, we [could not] be sure whether counsel was influenced in his basic strategic decisions by the interests of the employer who hired him," ibid., we remanded for the trial court "to determine whether the conflict of interest that this record strongly suggests actually existed," id., at 273.

Petitioner argues that the remand instruction in *Wood* established an "unambiguous rule" that where the trial judge neglects a duty to inquire into a potential conflict, the defendant, to obtain reversal of the judgment, need only show that his lawyer was subject to a conflict of interest, and need not show that the conflict adversely affected counsel's performance. Brief for Petitioner 21. He relies upon the language in the remand instruction directing the trial court to grant a new revocation hearing if it determines that "an actual conflict of interest existed," *Wood*, supra, at 273, without requiring a further determination that the conflict adversely affected counsel's performance. As used in the remand instruction, however, we think "an actual conflict of interest" meant precisely a conflict *that affected counsel's performance*—as opposed to a mere theoretical division of loyalties. It was shorthand for the statement in *Sullivan* that "a defendant who shows that a conflict of interest *actually affected the adequacy of his representation* need not demonstrate prejudice in order to obtain relief." 446 U.S., at 349-350. This is the only interpretation consistent with the *Wood* Court's earlier description of why it could not decide the case without a remand: "On the record before us, we cannot be sure whether counsel *was influenced in his basic strategic decisions* by the interests of the employer who hired him. *If this was the case*, the due process rights of petitioners were not respected. . . ." 450 U.S., at 272 (emphasis added). The notion that *Wood* created a new rule sub silentio—and in a case where certiorari had been granted on an entirely different question, and the parties had neither briefed nor argued the conflict-of-interest issue—is implausible.

Petitioner's proposed rule of automatic reversal when there existed a conflict that did not affect counsel's performance, but the trial judge failed to make the *Sullivan*-mandated inquiry, makes little policy sense. As discussed, the rule applied when the trial judge is not aware of the conflict (and thus not obligated to inquire) is that prejudice will be presumed only if the conflict has significantly affected counsel's performance—thereby rendering the verdict unreliable, even though *Strickland* prejudice cannot be shown. See *Sullivan*, supra, at 348-349. The trial court's awareness of a potential conflict neither renders it more likely that counsel's performance was significantly affected nor in any other way renders the verdict unreliable. . . . Nor does the trial judge's failure to make the *Sullivan*-mandated inquiry often make it harder for reviewing courts to determine conflict and effect, particularly since those courts may rely on evidence and testimony whose importance only becomes established at the trial.

Nor, finally, is automatic reversal simply an appropriate means of enforcing *Sullivan*'s mandate of inquiry. . . . [W]e do not presume that judges are as careless or as partial as those police officers who need the incentive of the exclusionary rule, see United States v. Leon, 468 U.S. 897, 916-917 (1984). And in any event, the *Sullivan* standard, which requires proof of effect upon representation but (once such effect is shown) presumes prejudice, already creates an "incentive" to inquire into a potential conflict. In those cases where the potential conflict is in fact an actual one, only inquiry will enable the judge to avoid all possibility of reversal by either seeking waiver or replacing a conflicted attorney. We doubt that the deterrence of "judicial dereliction" that would be achieved by an automatic reversal rule is significantly greater.

Since this was not a case in which (as in *Holloway*) counsel protested his inability simultaneously to represent multiple defendants; and since the trial court's failure to make the *Sullivan*-mandated inquiry does not reduce the petitioner's burden of proof; it was at least necessary, to void the conviction, for petitioner to establish that the conflict of interest adversely affected his counsel's performance. The Court of Appeals having found no such effect, see 240 F.3d, at 360, the denial of habeas relief must be affirmed.

III

Lest today's holding be misconstrued, we note that the only question presented was the effect of a trial court's failure to inquire into a potential conflict upon the *Sullivan* rule that deficient performance of counsel must be shown. The case was presented and argued on the assumption that (absent some exception for failure to inquire) *Sullivan* would be applicable—requiring a showing of defective performance, but *not* requiring in addition (as *Strickland* does in other ineffectiveness-of-counsel cases), a showing of probable effect upon the outcome of trial. That assumption was not unreasonable in light of the holdings of Courts of Appeals, which have applied *Sullivan* "unblinkingly" to "all kinds of alleged attorney ethical conflicts," Beets v. Scott, 65 F.3d 1258, 1266 (C.A.5 1995) (en banc). They have invoked the *Sullivan* standard not only when (as here) there is a conflict rooted in counsel's obligations to *former* clients, see, e.g., Perillo v. Johnson, 205 F.3d 775, 797-799 (C.A.5 2000); Freund v. Butterworth, 165 F.3d 839, 858-860 (C.A.11 1999) . . . but even when representation of the defendant somehow implicates counsel's personal or financial interests, including a book deal, United States v. Hearst, 638 F.2d 1190, 1193 (C.A.9 1980), a job with the prosecutor's office, Garcia v. Bunnell, 33 F.3d 1193, 1194-1195, 1198, n. 4 (C.A.9 1994), the teaching of classes to Internal Revenue Service agents, United States v. Michaud, 925 F.2d 37, 40-42 (C.A.1 1991), a romantic "entanglement" with the prosecutor, Summerlin v. Stewart, 267 F.3d 926, 935-941 (C.A.9 2001), or fear of antagonizing the trial judge, United States v. Sayan, 968 F.2d 55, 64-65 (C.A.D.C. 1992).

It must be said, however, that the language of *Sullivan* itself does not clearly establish, or indeed even support, such expansive application. "[U]ntil," it said, "a defendant shows that his counsel *actively represented* conflicting interests, he has not established the constitutional predicate for his claim of ineffective assistance." 446 U.S., at 350 (emphasis added). Both *Sullivan* itself, see id., at 348-349, and *Holloway*, see 435 U.S., at 490-491 stressed the high probability of prejudice arising from multiple concurrent representation, and the difficulty of proving that prejudice. . . . Not all attorney conflicts present comparable difficulties. Thus, the Federal Rules of Criminal Procedure treat concurrent representation and prior representation differently, requiring a trial court to inquire into the likelihood of conflict whenever jointly charged defendants are represented by a single attorney (Rule 44(c)), but not when counsel previously represented another defendant in a substantially related matter, even where the trial court is aware of the prior representation. See *Sullivan*, supra, at 346, n.10. . . .

This is not to suggest that one ethical duty is more or less important than another. The purpose of our *Holloway* and *Sullivan* exceptions from the ordinary requirements of *Strickland*, however, is not to enforce the Canons of Legal Ethics, but to apply needed prophylaxis in situations where *Strickland* itself is evidently inadequate to assure vindication of the defendant's Sixth Amendment right to counsel. See Nix v. Whiteside, 475 U.S. 157 (1986) ("[B]reach of an ethical standard does not necessarily make out a denial of the Sixth Amendment guarantee of assistance of counsel"). In resolving this case on the grounds on which it was presented to us, we do not rule upon the need for the *Sullivan* prophylaxis in cases of successive representation. Whether *Sullivan* should be extended to such cases remains, as far as the jurisprudence of this Court is concerned, an open question. . . .

For the reasons stated, the judgment of the Court of Appeals is *Affirmed*.

[Justices Stevens, Souter, Breyer, and Ginsburg dissented. Justice Stevens gave four reasons for setting aside the conviction: the trial judge was aware of the conflict when the judge appointed Saunders to represent Mickens; a presumption should exist that a defense counsel who represents a murder victim cannot form the kind of relationship with the accused that a conflict-free counsel could establish; historically the profession has prohibited representation of conflicting interests without full disclosure and consent; and public confidence in the fairness of procedures used in capital cases requires reversal of the conviction.

Justice Souter argued that the fundamental fact in deciding whether to apply the *Sullivan* requirement of adverse effect on counsel's performance or the *Holloway* rule of automatic reversal was whether the trial judge either knew or should have known of the attorney's conflict but failed to make an inquiry into the matter. In *Mickens* the trial judge who appointed Saunders to represent Mickens was the same judge who dismissed the case against the victim Hall, represented by Saunders, only a few days earlier; thus, the rule of automatic reversal applied.

Justices Breyer and Ginsburg stated that they did not need to reach the issue of the scope of the Court's prior conflict-of-interest cases. They found *Mickens* to involve an egregious situation warranting automatic reversal because defense counsel was representing the murder victim, the case involved the death penalty, and the state caused the problem through the actions of the trial judge.]

Notes and Questions

1. How do the ideas of prejudice, active representation of conflicting interests, and actual effect on the representation relate to each other?

2. One of the central points of disagreement between the majority and dissenting opinions is whether a lower burden of proof to establish ineffective assistance of counsel is triggered when defense counsel objects to representation because of a conflict of interest or when the trial court has notice of a conflict of interest. Which rule do you think is better as a matter of policy? Why?

3. As we will see in the civil litigation context, conflicts of interest can arise in forms other than multiple representation of defendants. For example, prior representation of a witness in a criminal case may disqualify the attorney from representing the defendant because the attorney may be placed in the position of either using confidential information to the detriment of the former client or sacrificing the current client's right to effective assistance of counsel. E.g., United States v. Moscony, 927 F.2d 742 (3d Cir.), *cert. denied*, 501 U.S. 1211 (1991). See Gary T. Lowenthal, Successive Representation by Criminal Lawyers, 93 Yale L.J. 1 (1983). In dictum the majority indicates that a presumption of prejudice may not apply to conflicts of interest that do not involve active representation of conflicting interests. Do you think the presumption of prejudice should apply in successive representation cases? Why?

4. In United States v. Schwarz, 283 F.3d 76 (2d Cir. 2002), one of the prosecutions growing out of the assault by New York police officers on Abner Louima in 1997, the Second Circuit reversed the conviction of Officer Schwarz because his lawyer suffered from a nonwaivable conflict of interest. The lawyer's firm had a $10 million retainer agreement with the police union of which Officer Schwarz was a member. At the same time the union was a defendant in a civil suit filed by Louima. The court held that an actual conflict of interest existed. Louima had consistently maintained that he was assaulted by two officers, Justin Volpe and one other. Schwarz, therefore, had an interest in implicating another officer in the assault. This defense, however, could have harmed the union in its defense of the civil action. Id. at 91-92. The court also held that the conflict affected defense counsel performance because defense counsel chose a strategy of claiming that Louima fabricated the second officer rather than attempting to show that the second officer was not Schwarz. Defense counsel continued this strategy even after Justin Volpe pled guilty and offered to testify that another officer other than Schwarz was involved in the assault. Id. 92-93. *Schwarz* was decided shortly before *Mickens*. Does the holding in *Mickens* cast doubt on the decision in *Schwarz*?

D. Limitations on Litigation Tactics by the Prosecution and by the Defense

Problem 2-8

Trial Publicity

a. You represent Nicholas Donetti, who has been under investigation in connection with the death of his wife, Myra. Myra drowned in what Donetti says was a boating accident. The police have been suspicious of Donetti's story from the beginning. This morning the prosecutor held a press conference to announce Donetti's indictment for murder. The prosecutor informed reporters that the couple's eight-year-old child, Michael, who was with them in the boat, had told the police that his father had killed his mother. The prosecutor also said that the police had uncovered a motive for the murder: only a month before Myra's death, Donetti had taken out a large insurance policy on her life.

You and your client are outraged at the prosecutor's conduct because the information given to the press was, in your opinion, grossly misleading. Donetti tells you that Michael did not see his mother fall into the water. What he saw was Donetti extending an oar for his wife to grab. Michael was confused as to what was happening and said, "Don't hurt mommy." Donetti also tells you that he did not take out a new insurance policy on his wife's life; he converted an existing term policy into a whole life policy.

You have just received a telephone call from a reporter for one of the local television stations. The reporter says that her station will be running the prosecutor's news conference on the 6:00 news. She wants to know if you have any comments. What would you say?

b.   Suppose defense counsel holds a press conference responding to the prosecutor's press conference. The trial judge, angered by the publicity, calls both lawyers to court and issues an order prohibiting both the prosecutor and defense counsel from "commenting publicly about the witnesses or evidence in the case." Be prepared to present an oral argument in support of and in opposition to the judge's order.

Read Model Rules 3.6, 3.8, 8.2 and comments.

Interests involved in trial publicity

The issue of the extent to which trial publicity should be regulated involves a tension both among and within several competing interests. First, the public and the media have a legitimate interest in obtaining information about legal proceedings. Several aspects of the "public's right to know," as it is often put, should be distinguished. The public has a legitimate interest in the just functioning of the legal system. Only to the extent that the public has information about the system can it evaluate the justice of legal proceedings. The public also has legitimate health and safety concerns that relate to matters being considered by the legal system. In addition, although some may question the legitimacy of this interest, matters occurring in court may be interesting to the public because they provide glimpses into the lives of others. The public interest regarding trial publicity does not, however, always support unrestricted publicity. As noted above, the public has an interest in the fairness of legal proceedings. To the extent that trial publicity prejudices proceedings and prevents justice from being done, the public has an interest in reasonable restrictions on publicity.

Second, the litigants themselves, particularly defendants in criminal cases, also have interests in trial publicity. As is true with the public interest, the interests of litigants do not point clearly in one direction. Criminal defendants certainly have an interest in not having their trials prejudiced by publicity. Indeed, as discussed below, this is not simply an interest of the criminal defendant, but a constitutional right. Yet in some cases criminal defendants may have an interest in promoting publicity about their cases, particularly when they feel that existing public information or perceptions are inaccurate or when they feel that vindication in the public forum is essential to their defense.

Finally, the various official participants in legal proceedings have an interest in trial publicity, although their interests may be entitled to somewhat lesser consideration than those of the public or the defendant. Judges, jurors, witnesses, and lawyers retain First Amendment rights even though they are involved in legal proceedings. They may feel strongly about issues in which they participate and may have unique perspectives or insights that they wish to share with the public.[243]

A brief history of the restrictions on lawyer participation in trial publicity

The current restrictions on lawyer participation in trial publicity can be traced to the Supreme Court's decision in Sheppard v. Maxwell.[244] Dr. Sam Sheppard was accused of bludgeoning his pregnant wife, Marilyn, to death. He claimed that he was innocent and that his wife had been killed by an unidentified intruder. The case appealed to the public's interest because of the wealth of the defendant, the mystery surrounding the case, and the fact that the defendant was having an affair. (The case later became the basis of the highly popular television show "The Fugitive" and the 1993 movie of the same name.) In describing the extent of publicity in the case, the Supreme Court referred to five volumes of clippings from the Cleveland newspapers, almost all of which were prejudicial to Sheppard; the Court also noted that this material did not include the radio and television coverage, which it assumed to be at least as extensive. The Court reversed Sheppard's conviction. Referring to the "carnival atmosphere" at trial, the Court held the trial judge had failed to protect the defendant's right to due process of law. The Court outlined various measures that the trial judge should have taken, including stricter rules governing the use of the courtroom by the media; insulation of witnesses from press contacts; and some control over the "release of leads, information, and gossip to the press by police officers, witnesses, and the counsel for both sides."[245]

As a result of the *Sheppard* case the ABA undertook a study of the fair trial–free press issue. This study led to the adoption of ABA Standards in 1968 and of DR 7-107 of the Code of Professional Responsibility in 1969.[246] Disciplinary Rule 7-107 governed all types of legal proceedings, but the bulk of the rule applied to criminal cases. Two major decisions from the Fourth and Seventh Circuits dealt with the constitutionality of DR 7-107: Hirschkop v. Snead[247] and Chicago Council of Lawyers v. Bauer.[248] Both courts held that it was constitutionally permissible for the state to adopt rules regulating extrajudicial statements by counsel in connection with criminal jury trials. Both courts also held, however, that it would be unconstitutional to apply these

243. For a discussion of the various interests involved in the issue of trial publicity, see Joel H. Swift, Restraints on Defense Publicity in Criminal Jury Cases, 1984 Utah L. Rev. 45, 67-84. See also Restatement (Third) of the Law Governing Lawyers §109, cmt. b.

244. 384 U.S. 333 (1966).

245. Id. at 359.

246. Wolfram, Modern Legal Ethics §12.2.2, at 633.

247. 594 F.2d 356 (4th Cir. 1979) (per curiam).

248. 522 F.2d 242 (7th Cir. 1975), *cert. denied sub nom.* Cunningham v. Chicago Council of Lawyers, 427 U.S. 912 (1976).

rules in a per se fashion. The *Bauer* court held that a lawyer could be disciplined for an extrajudicial statement only if the statement posed a "serious and imminent" threat to the trial process.[249] *Hirschkop* adopted a lesser standard: Discipline was proper if the statement posed a "reasonable likelihood" of prejudice to the administration of justice.[250]

The drafters of the Model Rules attempted to construct a trial publicity rule that balanced fair trial and free expression rights. See Model Rule 3.6, cmt. 1. They were, of course, aware of the *Bauer* and *Hirschkop* decisions, but they felt relatively free to adopt the rule that they thought best because these decisions differed in many respects. Rule 3.6(a), as originally adopted in 1983 (the current rule is discussed below), stated that a lawyer may not make an extrajudicial statement if the statement has a "substantial likelihood of materially prejudicing an adjudicative proceeding." This test lies somewhere between the *Bauer* test of "serious and imminent threat" and the *Hirschkop* test of "reasonable likelihood" of prejudice to a fair trial. Section 3.6(b) listed a number of statements that "ordinarily" have a substantial likelihood of materially prejudicing a proceeding. This flexible approach responded to the holdings in *Bauer* and *Hirschkop* that the rules could not be applied in a per se fashion. Rule 3.6(c) provided a "safe haven" list of statements that lawyers could make.

The constitutionality of Model Rule 3.6: Gentile v. State Bar of Nevada

In Gentile v. State Bar of Nevada[251] the Supreme Court considered the constitutionality of the 1983 version of Model Rule 3.6. On January 31, 1987, the Las Vegas Police Department reported the theft of large amounts of cocaine and travelers' checks from a safety deposit vault at Western Vault Company. The drugs and checks had been used in an undercover operation. Attorney Dominic Gentile's client, Grady Sanders, owned Western Vault. The sheriff originally named Sanders and police officers involved in the undercover operation as suspects, but the investigation quickly began to focus on Sanders rather than the police officers.

While two police officers had ready access to the safety deposit box, the sheriff stated that he had complete confidence in his officers. Media reports after the theft indicated that other customers of Western Vault had reported money missing. The police opened other boxes to search for the stolen items. The media reported that they seized $264,000 from a box that was listed as unrented. Subsequent reports identified the owner of this box and provided details of her drug-related background.

The sheriff soon informed the media that the two police officers had been "cleared" after taking polygraph tests. Press reports stated that Sanders could not be reached for comment and that he had refused to take a lie detector test.

---

249. 522 F.2d at 249.
250. 594 F.2d at 370.
251. 501 U.S. 1030 (1991).

Hours after his client was indicted, Gentile, a well-known criminal defense lawyer in the Las Vegas area and the former associate dean of the National College for Criminal Defense Lawyers and Public Defenders, called a press conference and delivered the following statement:

Mr. Gentile: I want to start this off by saying in clear terms that I think that this indictment is a significant event in the history of the evolution of sophistication of the City of Las Vegas, because things of this nature, of exactly this nature have happened in New York with the French connection case and in Miami with cases—at least two cases there—have happened in Chicago as well, but all three of those cities have been honest enough to indict the people who did it; the police department, crooked cops.

When this case goes to trial, and as it develops, you're going to see that the evidence will prove not only that Grady Sanders is an innocent person and had nothing to do with any of the charges that are being leveled against him, but that the person that was in the most direct position to have stolen the drugs and money, the American Express Travelers' checks, is Detective Steve Scholl.

There is far more evidence that will establish that Detective Scholl took these drugs and took these American Express Travelers' checks than any other living human being.

And I have to say that I feel that Grady Sanders is being used as a scapegoat to try to cover up for what has to be obvious to people at the Las Vegas Metropolitan Police Department and at the District Attorney's office.

Now, with respect to these other charges that are contained in this indictment, the so-called other victims, as I sit here today I can tell you that one, two—four of them are known drug dealers and convicted money launderers and drug dealers; three of whom didn't say a word about anything until after they were approached by Metro and after they were already in trouble and are trying to work themselves out of something.

Now, up until the moment, of course, that they started going along with what detectives from Metro wanted them to say, these people were being held out as being incredible and liars by the very same people who are going to say now that you can believe them.

Another problem that you are going to see develop here is the fact that of these other counts, at least four of them said nothing about any of this, about anything being missing until after the Las Vegas Metropolitan Police Department announced publicly last year their claim that drugs and American Express Travelers' checks were missing.

Many of the contracts that these people had show on the face of the contract that there is $100,000 in insurance for the contents of the box.

If you look at the indictment very closely, you're going to see that these claims fall under $100,000.

Finally, there were only two claims on the face of the indictment that came to our attention prior to the events of January 31 of '87, that being the date that Metro said that there was something missing from their box.

And both of these claims were dealt with by Mr. Sanders and we're dealing here essentially with people that we're not sure if they ever had anything in the box.

That's about all that I have to say.

[Questions from the floor followed.][252]

This was the first time in Gentile's professional career that he had called a formal press conference. He testified at his subsequent disciplinary hearing that he decided to call the conference because of "concern that, unless some of the weaknesses in the State's case were made public, a potential jury venire would be poisoned by repetition in the press of information being released by the police and prosecutors, in particular the repeated press reports about polygraph tests and the fact that the two police officers were no longer suspects." Gentile gave as a second reason for calling the press conference the serious toll that the investigation had taken on his client.[253]

Before calling the press conference, Gentile researched the issue of whether the press conference would be likely to prejudice the trial. Considering the length of time before the trial was scheduled to begin (six months), the size of the community and prior First Amendment cases, he concluded that his statements would not be prejudicial.[254] The case went to trial on schedule six months later. All of the evidence referred to in Gentile's press conference was admitted into evidence, and his client was acquitted.[255]

The state bar subsequently instituted disciplinary proceedings against Gentile for violation of Nevada Supreme Court Rule 177, which was practically identical to the 1983 version of ABA Model Rule 3.6. The Nevada Disciplinary Board found that Gentile had violated the rule and the Nevada Supreme Court affirmed. The United States Supreme Court reversed in a 5-4 decision.

The opinions of Justice Anthony Kennedy and Chief Justice William Rehnquist largely agreed that the standard set forth in Rule 3.6 of a "substantial likelihood of materially prejudicing an adjudicative proceeding" was constitutional.[256] The opinions differed on the constitutionality of the application of this standard, and on the significance of due process (fair notice), to the facts of the case. Four members of the Court (opinion of Justice Kennedy joined by Justices Blackmun, Marshall, and Stevens) would allow a state to impose discipline for pretrial statements by a lawyer only if there was a clear showing of the likelihood of material prejudice. They found Rule 3.6 as applied to the facts of this case to be unconstitutional because the likelihood of prejudice was small.[257] These four justices also found an independent due process basis for setting aside the decision of the Nevada Supreme Court. They found that Rule 3.6(c) "misled petitioner into thinking that he could give his press conference without fear of discipline. . . . [because the rule] provides that a lawyer 'may state without elaboration . . . the general nature of the . . . defense.' "[258]

252. Id. at 1059-1060.
253. Id. at 1042-1043.
254. Id. at 1044.
255. Id. at 1047.
256. Id. at 1036-1037 (opinion of Justice Kennedy) and 1075 (opinion of Justice Rehnquist).
257. Id. at 1037-1048.
258. Id. at 1048.

Four other members of the Court (opinion of Justice Rehnquist joined by Justices Scalia, Souter, and White) would give the states practically blanket authority to regulate pretrial speech by attorneys. Rather than requiring a clear showing of material prejudice, these justices focused on the special role of attorneys and the substantial state interest in protecting the integrity of criminal trials.[259] In light of the greater leeway that these justices would give to the states, they found no due process violation in the wording of the Nevada rule.[260]

Justice O'Connor cast the deciding vote in the case. While agreeing with the Rehnquist opinion, which gave states substantial leeway in regulating pretrial speech by lawyers, she also agreed with the Kennedy opinion that the wording of Rule 3.6 did not give Gentile fair notice that he would be subject to discipline.[261]

What conclusions can one draw from the *Gentile* case? First, it is clear that the standard of "substantial likelihood of materially prejudicing an adjudicative proceeding" is constitutional, having been accepted by all nine justices. Second, it also seems reasonably clear that a lawyer who gave a press conference like the one in *Gentile* could be subject to discipline if the applicable disciplinary rule did not have the due process infirmity that troubled Justice O'Connor.[262]

ABA amendments to Rule 3.6 in 1994

In response to the Supreme Court's decision in *Gentile*, the ABA adopted a revised version of Model Rule 3.6.[263] The 2002 revision of the Model Rules made only minor changes in the text of Rule 3.6. The new rule continues to use the standard of "substantial likelihood of materially prejudicing an adjudicative proceeding" that was approved by the Supreme Court in *Gentile*. See Model Rule 3.6(a). Revised Rule 3.6(b) creates a "safe harbor" of statements that lawyers may make; these are substantially the same as under the former rule. Among the statements that are allowed are the following:

- 3.6(b)(1): "the claim, offense or defense involved and, except when prohibited by law, the identity of the persons involved"
- 3.6(b)(2): "the information contained in a public record"

---

259. Id. at 1065-1076.
260. Id. at 1078-1079.
261. Id. at 1081-1082.
262. See In re Morrissey 168 F.3d 134 (4th Cir.), *cert. denied*, 527 U.S. 1036 (1999) (lawyer held in criminal contempt for violation of local rule prohibiting release of information by lawyer involved in criminal case if reasonable likelihood that such dissemination would interfere with a fair trial or otherwise prejudice the due administration of justice); United States v. Cutler, 58 F.3d 825 (2d Cir. 1995) (attorney found guilty of criminal contempt for violation of local rule prohibiting extrajudicial statements that have reasonable likelihood of interfering with fair trial).
263. The Restatement generally follows Model Rule 3.6. See Restatement (Third) of the Law Governing Lawyers §109.

The most significant change made in the new rule is the addition of Rule 3.6(c), which provides lawyers with a "right of reply":

Notwithstanding paragraph (a), a lawyer may make a statement that a reasonable lawyer would believe is required to protect a client from the substantial undue prejudicial effect of recent publicity not initiated by the lawyer or the lawyer's client. A statement made pursuant to this paragraph shall be limited to such information as is necessary to mitigate the recent adverse publicity.

While the provision is not limited to criminal cases, it will be particularly important to criminal defense counsel. It appears that Gentile's statements would have been protected under this rule.[264]

Former Rule 3.6(b) contained a list of statements that were ordinarily likely to result in material prejudice of an adjudicative proceeding. This list has been deleted from the text of the rule, but the list reappears in Comment 5; prudent lawyers should continue to consult this list for statements to avoid.

In connection with its amendments of Rule 3.6, the ABA also amended Rule 3.8, which deals with the ethical obligations of prosecutors. Rule 3.8(f), as amended in 2002, cautions prosecutors against making extrajudicial statements that "have a substantial likelihood of heightening public condemnation of the accused," except ones that serve a legitimate law enforcement purpose. In addition, prosecutors are directed to exercise reasonable care to prevent law enforcement personnel and others from making such statements. Comment 5 to the rule, however, makes it clear that prosecutors may ethically make statements allowed by revised Rule 3.6(b) or (c).

Several commentators have criticized Rule 3.6. Professor Erwin Chemerinsky argues that extrajudicial statements by lawyers about pending cases have important social value. Accordingly, restrictions on such statements should be subject to strict scrutiny. He recommends that courts apply the standard of New York Times v. Sullivan.[265] Lawyers should be prohibited from making statements only that they know to be false or that are made with reckless disregard of the truth.[266] Professor Thomas Dienes agrees that extrajudicial statements by trial participants, especially lawyers, should be subject to strict scrutiny, but he would apply a clear and present danger standard.[267]

---

264. For many years California did not have a trial publicity rule. In response to the extensive publicity surrounding the *O. J. Simpson* case, the California Supreme Court adopted a trial publicity rule based on ABA Model Rule 3.6 including its right of reply. Cal. R. Prof. Conduct 5-120. For a discussion of the ethics of the public statements made by counsel in the *O. J. Simpson* case, see Kevin Cole & Fred C. Zacharias, The Agony of Victory and the Ethics of Lawyer Speech, 69 S. Cal. L. Rev. 1627 (1996).

265. 376 U.S. 254 (1964).

266. Erwin Chemerinsky, Silence Is Not Golden: Protecting Lawyer Speech Under the First Amendment, 47 Emory L.J. 859 (1998).

267. C. Thomas Dienes, Trial Participants in the Newsgathering Process, 34 U. Rich. L. Rev. 1107 (2001). See also Joel H. Swift, Model Rule 3.6: An Unconstitutional Regulation of Defense Attorney Trial Publicity, 64 B.U. L. Rev. 1003 (1984).

Some jurisdictions have rejected the "substantial likelihood of material prejudice" test of Model Rule 3.6 in favor of a "clear and present danger" test.[268] This test gives lawyers more freedom to engage in extrajudicial statements. For example, given the timing of Gentile's statement and the size of the Las Vegas community, it is extremely doubtful that Gentile's press conference posed a clear and present danger to the integrity of his client's trial.

Court rules and gag orders

Gentile dealt with the constitutionality of a disciplinary action against an attorney for engaging in trial publicity. To prevent prejudicial pretrial publicity from occurring, some courts have adopted standing court rules prohibiting trial publicity. Other courts have imposed "gag" orders on counsel and parties involved in particular proceedings.[269] It is unclear what constitutional standard applies to such forms of regulation of trial publicity. Some courts have treated such regulations as prior restraints on speech. For example, in United States v. Salameh,[270] the judge in the trial of defendants accused of the bombing of the World Trade Center in New York in 1993 issued an order prohibiting defense counsel from making statements in the press or media that "may have something to do with the case." The Second Circuit ruled that prior restraints on speech carry a "heavy presumption" against their constitutionality. The court stated that limitations on speech must be "no broader than necessary to protect the integrity of the judicial system and the defendant's right to a fair trial." In addition, the court must explore other available remedies.[271] The Second Circuit vacated the trial judge's order because it failed to meet these standards.

Most courts, however, have upheld the constitutionality of court rules and gag orders regulating trial publicity without applying a stringent prior restraint doctrine. In United States v. Cutler,[272] the Second Circuit upheld a contempt conviction of an attorney who repeatedly violated district court orders to comply with New York District Court Local Criminal Rule 7, which prohibits extrajudicial statements that have a reasonable likelihood of interfering with a fair trial. The trial judge in that case had characterized the rule as "a kind of gag order."[273]

268. See Twohig v. Blackmer, 918 P.2d 332 (N.M. 1996) (relying on N.M.R. Prof. Conduct 16-306). See also Committee on Prof. Resp., Assn. of Bar of City of New York, The Need for Fair Trials Does Not Justify a Disciplinary Rule That Broadly Restricts an Attorney's Speech, 20 Fordham Urb. L.J. 881 (1993) (proposing amendment to New York Code of Professional Responsibility that would adopt "clear and present danger" test).

269. See C. Thomas Dienes, Trial Participants in the Newsgathering Process, 34 U. Rich. L. Rev. 1107 (2001).

270. 992 F.2d 445 (2d Cir. 1993).

271. Id. at 447.

272. 58 F.3d 825 (2d Cir. 1995).

273. Id. at 830. *Compare* United States v. Brown, 218 F.3d 415 (5th Cir. 2000) (gag order upheld using *Gentile* standard) *with* United States v. Scarfo, 263 F.3d 80 (3d Cir.

Other First Amendment issues involving lawyers

The constitutionality of restrictions on extrajudicial statements by lawyers is only one of a number of issues involving the interrelationship between lawyer speech and the First Amendment.[274] Another issue that has arisen from time to time deals with the constitutionality of restrictions on lawyer criticism of judges. Under Model Rule 8.2 lawyers who publicly criticize judges or other adjudicatory officials are not subject to discipline unless their statements are known to be false or made with reckless disregard of the truth. Thus, the rule incorporates the actual malice standard for public officials of New York Times v. Sullivan.[275] Another issue involving the constitutionality of lawyer speech deals with restrictions on lawyer advertising. We will examine this topic in Problem 4-7.

Problem 2-9

Limitations on Trial Tactics

The college town of Anderson was shocked when Thomas McSwaine, the son of one of Anderson's prominent business leaders, was arrested for rape of a young woman, Brenda Cain, at a fraternity party. Cain was badly bruised about the face and neck after the incident. You are a member of the defense team. McSwaine admits having intercourse with Cain. He also admits that they had "rough sex," but he denies the charge of rape. He claims that Cain consented to having intercourse with him and begged him to "do it like in *Rising Sun*."[276]

2001) (gag order directed to defendant's former attorney overturned applying *Gentile* standard).

274. See W. Bradley Wendel, Free Speech for Lawyers, 28 Hastings Const. L.Q. 305 (2001).

275. 376 U.S. 254 (1964). See In re Green, 11 P.3d 1078, 1084 n.4 (Colo. 2000) (en banc) (attorney's statements that trial judge was a "racist and bigot" with a "bent of mind" were opinions not subject to discipline under the First Amendment). See also Freedman & Smith, Understanding Lawyers' Ethics at 105-110. But see In re Wilkins, 777 N.W.2d 714 (Ind. 2003), where the Indiana Supreme Court in a 3-2 decision suspended the attorney for 30 days for violating Rule 8.2(a) by submitting a brief to the supreme court with the following footnote:

> Indeed, the Opinion is so factually and legally inaccurate that one is left to wonder whether the Court of Appeals was determined to find for Appellee Sports, Inc., and then said whatever was necessary to reach that conclusion (regardless of whether the facts or the law supported its decision). Id. at 715-716.

On rehearing of the case, the court rejected the argument that discipline for this statement violated the attorney's First Amendment rights, but the court did reduce the sanction to a public reprimand. 782 N.E.2d 985 (2003).

276. The novel by Michael Crichton and the movie based on the novel. A prominent scene in the book and movie involves sexual intercourse while the girl is being strangled, supposedly to heighten the experience.

With regard to the consent theory, you have hired investigators to inquire into Cain's sexual history. In particular, you were looking for information showing Cain had engaged in "rough sex" in the past or that she had had sex based on movies she had seen. Your investigation revealed two fraternity brothers of McSwaine, both of whom are prepared to testify that they had had sex with Cain and that "she liked it hard and rough." Your investigation also located a former boyfriend who will testify that the couple had watched pornographic movies and that she had asked to have sex the way it was done in the movies. Your defense strategy is to use this information in an aggressive cross-examination of Cain and to introduce the testimony of these three witnesses as part of your case in chief.

In preparing this strategy, you are concerned about the possible application of your state's rape shield law. That law, which is based on Rule 412 of the Federal Rules of Evidence, provides as follows:

Rule 412.   *Sex Offense Cases; Relevance of Alleged Victim's Past Sexual Behavior or Alleged Sexual Predisposition*

(a) Evidence generally inadmissible. The following evidence is not admissible in any civil or criminal proceeding involving alleged sexual misconduct except as provided in subdivisions (b) and (c):

(1) Evidence offered to prove that any alleged victim engaged in other sexual behavior.

(2) Evidence offered to prove any alleged victim's sexual predisposition.

(b) Exceptions.—

(1) In a criminal case, the following evidence is admissible, if otherwise admissible under these rules:

(A) evidence of specific instances of sexual behavior by the alleged victim offered to prove that a person other than the accused was the source of semen, injury or other physical evidence;

(B) evidence of specific instances of sexual behavior by the alleged victim with respect to the person accused of the sexual misconduct offered by the accused to prove consent or by the prosecution; and

(C) evidence the exclusion of which would violate the constitutional rights of the defendant.

(2) In a civil case, evidence offered to prove the sexual behavior or sexual predisposition of any alleged victim is admissible if it is otherwise admissible under these rules and its probative value substantially outweighs the danger of harm to any victim and of unfair prejudice to any party. Evidence of an alleged victim's reputation is admissible only if it has been placed in controversy by the alleged victim.

(c) Procedure to determine admissibility.—

(1) A party intending to offer evidence under subdivision (b) must—

(A) file a written motion at least 14 days before trial specifically describing the evidence and stating the purpose for which it is offered unless the court, for good cause requires a different time for filing or permits filing during trial; and

(B) serve the motion on all parties and notify the alleged victim or, when appropriate, the alleged victim's guardian or representative.

(2) Before admitting evidence under this rule the court must conduct a hearing in camera and afford the victim and parties a right to attend and be heard. The motion, related papers, and the record of the hearing must be sealed and remain under seal unless the court orders otherwise.

As the defense team prepares its case for trial, the following dialogue occurs between two members of the team:

L1: Let's discuss how we might handle the testimony of the boyfriend and the fraternity brothers. It seems to me that we have to file a motion under the rape shield law to offer this evidence, but our prospects don't look too good. As I read the statute, the only possible ground for admitting the evidence is under (b)(1)(C), where we have to establish a violation of Tom's constitutional rights.

L2: I think that's right. My research indicates that our confrontation clause argument is 50-50 at best. If we lose, we're in trouble, but I've come up with a backup strategy. At trial we can cross-examine Cain about whether she said anything to McSwaine about liking rough sex. We can also cross-examine her about the statement that Tom said she made: "do it like in *Rising Sun*." If she admits either or both of these matters, then I think we've got a good shot at an acquittal. If she denies either or both, we can then ask her if she ever engaged in rough sex in the past, or if she ever asked a partner to engage in sex like in a movie. If they object to this, we can argue that the questions are being asked not to obtain evidence in violation of section (a) of the statute, but rather as part of an inquiry into her credibility. Depending on her answers, we can then offer the testimony of her boyfriend and of the two fraternity brothers, also arguing that this testimony is being offered not as evidence of sexual behavior but to show prior inconsistent statements by Cain.

L1: Well, the court might not let us go into prior sexual history for the purpose of testing her credibility. It also might be a problem getting in the testimony of the boyfriend and the two fraternity brothers, because as I understand the rules, you can't generally introduce any collateral evidence to impeach a witness's credibility. [See Fed. R. Evid. 608(b).]

L2: That's true, but we can do several things. First of all I don't think the rule about collateral attacks on credibility prevents testimony about the witness's reputation for truth and veracity. We could put the boyfriend on the stand and have him testify that she has a reputation for lying; that's probably better than if he just testified that she liked to do it based on movies. Also, even if none of this gets in, just asking the questions or having the boyfriend and the fraternity brothers there at trial could affect the jury.

L1: One other idea. When we put the boyfriend and the fraternity

brothers on our witness list, the prosecutor will have to ask Cain
about them. If Cain tells the prosecutor what these guys told us,
then the prosecutor will have to make sure she admits this stuff
on cross, which is just what we want. The prosecutor may even
decide to bring it out on direct because it might be less damaging.
Also, when they know about these witnesses, Cain or the prosecu
tor might get scared and be more willing to negotiate a plea.

    L2:   I like it.

    After developing this strategy, the defense team files a motion to
allow the testimony of the boyfriend and the two fraternity brothers under
the rape shield law. You have argued in the motion that exclusion of the
evidence would violate your client's rights under the confrontation clause
of the Sixth Amendment as applied to the states through the Fourteenth
Amendment. After you filed your memorandum in support of your motion,
you learned of a recent decision from the United States Court of Appeals
for the Seventh Circuit holding that application of the Illinois rape shield
law did not violate the defendant's right to confrontation. Ironically, the
prosecution has found a case that the defense team has not uncovered,
Olden v. Kentucky.[277] In *Olden* the Supreme Court held that the trial
court's refusal to permit the defendant to cross-examine the alleged rape
victim about her cohabitation with her boyfriend violated the defendant's
Sixth Amendment right to confront witnesses when the defendant claimed
that the alleged victim had concocted the charge of rape because of fear
of her boyfriend's reaction if he knew that she had voluntarily engaged in
sexual relations with the defendant. The prosecution decided not to mention *Olden* in its memorandum because the lead prosecutor concluded
that *Olden* was "not a Rape Shield case." In *Olden* the Kentucky courts
found that the evidence regarding the alleged victim's cohabitation with
her boyfriend was not barred by the Kentucky Rape Shield statute. Instead,
the basis for not admitting the evidence was that its probative value was
outweighed by its possibility for prejudice.[278]

    Not wishing to rely solely on the consent theory, McSwaine's defense
team has come up with a second theory of defense, one that McSwaine
did not suggest but that defense counsel believe is plausible based on the
facts. The defense plans to contend that the alleged rape was a "setup"
by Cain to extort money from McSwaine's wealthy family. With regard
to the "setup" theory, you plan to cross-examine Cain to inquire into
whether Cain has hired a lawyer to represent her in a possible civil action
against McSwaine. You plan to ask questions about her finances and about
whether she has brought any other lawsuits or made any other charges of
rape or assault. You also plan to inquire about how she came to know
members of McSwaine's fraternity as well as McSwaine. The purpose of

---

277. 488 U.S. 227 (1988).
278. Id. at 230.

these questions is to try to portray Cain as an extortionist looking for a chance to get money from the family of an innocent, nice young man.

Under local rules you have received a list of potential jurors several weeks before trial. The list gives the names and addresses of the jurors, but no other information. To prepare for jury selection the defense has hired an investigator who will do the following: purchase credit reports that contain personal and financial information about each juror; drive by each juror's home and make observations that might be indicative of the juror's attitudes; and in some cases interview neighbors of the juror to determine the juror's attitudes and any possible grounds of bias or prejudice.

During the course of your investigation, you learn that one juror, Donald Spade, is employed by Anderson Supply Company. Anderson Supply is a subsidiary of McSwaine Enterprises, the company owned by Thomas McSwaine's father. During voir dire the jurors are asked: "Are you or any member of your immediate family employed by Quinton McSwaine or by McSwaine Enterprises? If so, please identify yourself." Spade does not respond.

Read Model Rules 3.3, 3.4, 3.5, 4.4, and comments.

Improper contacts with jurors and improper methods of jury selection

Neutral decisionmakers who resolve disputes based on the law and facts presented at trial rather than on extrajudicial influences are central to the concept of an adversarial system of justice.[279] The Model Rules recognize the importance of the integrity of decisionmakers in Model Rule 3.5.[280]

Model Rule 3.5 refers lawyers to "law" to determine whether attempts to influence or to communicate with judges, jurors, prospective jurors, and other officials are improper. Such law includes statutes, court decisions, or court rules regarding contact with jurors. By making lawyers' obligations dependent on "law," however, the Model Rules may leave lawyers in doubt about the scope of their obligations when other law is silent or uncertain.

In the absence of specific law on improper contacts, several principles can guide lawyers in dealings with jurors. First, any form of communication with jurors or prospective jurors, except in the course of official proceedings, or unless specifically authorized by law, is improper. This restriction obviously includes communications that relate to the merits of the case, but it also includes

---

279. 2 Hazard & Hodes, The Law of Lawyering §31.5, at 6-7.

280. See also Restatement (Third) of the Law Governing Lawyers §113 (prohibition on ex parte communication with or improper influence of judicial officers) and §115 (prohibition on improper communication with or improper influence of prospective, sitting, and excused jurors).

pleasantries that have nothing to do with substance. The rule operates as a prophylactic to prevent the possibility of improper influence.[281] Trial judges should instruct jurors of this prohibition so that a juror will not take a lawyer's failure to respond to pleasant conversation as rudeness.

Second, the prohibition on communication of improper influences does not generally prohibit lawyers from investigating the backgrounds of jurors for the purpose of jury selection so long as there is no communication with the juror and so long as the investigation does not violate other law.[282]

In some jurisdictions, it is common practice for lawyers to interview jurors after the conclusion of the case for the purpose of improving their trial skills or perhaps for the purpose of determining whether the jury may have acted improperly in reaching its decision. Model Rule 3.5(c) generally allows such post-discharge communications, subject to some restrictions.[283] The Restatement is similar.[284]

A few jurisdictions may be more restrictive of post-discharge communications with jurors. For example, the Massachusetts version of Rule 3.5 prohibits lawyers from contacting jurors after they have been discharged from the case without leave of court.

Jury selection is a growth industry. Especially in high profile cases, parties commonly hire jury consultants to assist in jury selection. Are there any ethical restrictions on such practices? The Model Rules do not have a specific provision on ethical obligations of lawyers in connection with jury selection.[285] Model Rule 3.4(c) states that a lawyer should not "knowingly disobey an obligation under the rules of a tribunal except for an open refusal based on an assertion that no valid obligation exists." Thus, it appears that ethical obligations in jury selection follow the procedural rules applicable to jury selection.

In a series of cases beginning with Batson v. Kentucky,[286] the Supreme Court has attempted to address the problem of discriminatory exercise of peremptory challenges. The *Batson* Court held that the prosecution violates the

---

281. See 2 Hazard & Hodes, The Law of Lawyering §31.4, at 5.

282. See Fortune et al., Modern Litigation and Professional Responsibility Handbook §9.3, at 354-358 (some courts have limited investigation of potential jurors or ordered use of anonymous juries).

283. Some decisions have held that vague and broad prohibitions on post-trial communications with jurors are unconstitutional. See Rapp v. Disciplinary Board of the Hawaii Supreme Court, 916 F. Supp. 1525 (D. Hawaii 1996) (Hawaii rule prohibiting communications with jurors unless "permitted by law" was unconstitutionally vague and overbroad); Commission for Lawyer Discipline v. Benton, 980 S.W.2d 425, *cert. denied*, 526 U.S. 1146 (1999) (Texas rule's prohibition of post-trial communications meant to "embarrass" jurors was unconstitutionally vague, but prohibitions on communications that attempt to "harass" or "influence" jurors were not).

284. Restatement (Third) of the Law Governing Lawyers §115(3). For a comparison of Model Rule 3.5 and the Restatement see 2 Hazard & Hodes, The Law of Lawyering §31.3.

285. See generally Fortune et al., Modern Litigation and Professional Responsibility Handbook §9.4.

286. 476 U.S. 79 (1986).

defendant's right to equal protection when it exercises peremptory challenges to remove jurors solely on the ground of race. In subsequent cases, the Court has dramatically expanded its scrutiny of the use of peremptory challenges, although the rationale for the decisions has shifted. The Court held that exercise of peremptory challenges based on race by private litigants in civil cases is unconstitutional because this use of peremptory challenges violates *the equal protection rights of jurors.*[287] Similarly, the Court held that the defendant's exercise of peremptory challenges based on race in a criminal case was unconstitutional because it also infringed the jurors' right to equal protection. The Court rejected the argument that restriction of the defendant's right to use peremptory challenges amounted to a violation of the defendant's constitutional right to due process, reasoning that the defendant does not have a constitutional right to any particular system of peremptory challenges.[288] The Court has expanded the prohibition on the discriminatory use of peremptory challenges to include strikes based on gender as well as race,[289] but the Court has refused to extend the right to cover the use of peremptory challenges based on religion.[290]

A lawyer who exercises a peremptory challenge in a discriminatory manner will not necessarily be found guilty of an ethical violation. Comment 3 to Rule 8.4 states: "A trial judge's finding that peremptory challenges were exercised on a discriminatory basis does not alone establish a violation of this Rule."[291]

Model Rule 3.5 prohibits ex parte contacts not only with jurors but also with judges and officials. We will examine ex parte communications with judges in more detail in Problem 6-1, which deals with conduct of judges in their official capacities.

Duty to disclose adverse facts and law

Under the Model Rules, lawyers do not have an obligation to disclose voluntarily either to the court or to the opposing side adverse factual information, even if the information is material and even if the information is not known by the court or the other side.[292] The absence of a duty of disclosure of adverse facts can be justified on several grounds. First, a duty to disclose would be inconsistent with the concept of an adversarial system of justice in which each side has

---

287. Edmonson v. Leesville Concrete Co., 500 U.S. 614 (1991).

288. Georgia v. McCollum, 505 U.S. 42 (1992).

289. J. E. B. v. Alabama ex rel. T.B., 511 U.S. 127 (1994).

290. Davis v. Minnesota, 511 U.S. 1115 (1994) (denial of certiorari in case involving exercise of peremptory challenge based on religion).

291. For a criticism of this comment and a call for more vigorous enforcement of *Batson* see Lonnie T. Brown, Jr., Racial Discrimination in Jury Selection: Professional Misconduct, Not Legitimate Advocacy, 22 Rev. Litig. 209 (2003). On the other hand, Professor Abbe Smith argues that it should not be unethical for defense counsel to use race and gender in jury selection, see Abbe Smith, "Nice Work If You Can Get It": "Ethical" Jury Selection in Criminal Defense, 67 Fordham L. Rev. 523 (1998).

292. See Wolfram, Modern Legal Ethics §12.3.2, at 639.

the obligation to investigate and to present its case. Second, clients often communicate adverse information in confidence to their lawyers. A duty to disclose would undermine the attorney-client privilege. Further, in criminal cases, imposing a duty to disclose on defense counsel would be inconsistent with the defendant's privilege against self-incrimination and other constitutional rights.

The proposition that lawyers do not have a duty to disclose adverse facts is qualified, however, by several obligations. First, lawyers and their clients have an obligation to comply with various discovery rules requiring production of information in response to inquiries from the opposing side. See Model Rule 3.4(d), which states that a lawyer shall not "fail to make reasonably diligent effort to comply with a legally proper discovery request by an opposing party." Problem 4-4 examines lawyers' legal and ethical obligations in connection with discovery in civil cases. Second, lawyers have a duty not to engage personally in fraud or criminal conduct. See Model Rules 8.4(b), (c).[293] Nor can the absence of a duty to disclose be used to justify assisting the client in conduct that is criminal or fraudulent. See Model Rules 1.2(d) and 4.1(b).[294] Third, lawyers are obligated to take reasonable remedial measures, including disclosure to the tribunal if necessary, when the lawyer, the lawyer's client, or a witness called by the lawyer has offered false testimony and the lawyer comes to know of its falsity. See Model Rule 3.3(a)(3). Recall Problem 2-5. Fourth, the 2002 revision of the Model Rules requires lawyers to take reasonable remedial measures, including disclosure to the tribunal if necessary, if the lawyer knows that any person has or plans to engage in criminal or fraudulent conduct related to the proceeding. Model Rule 3.3(b) and comment 12. Fifth, in ex parte proceedings (for example, if a lawyer is seeking a temporary restraining order), lawyers must disclose all material facts. See Model Rule 3.3(d).[295] Because ex parte proceedings do not involve an adversarial process, the rationale for nondisclosure does not apply. Cf. Model Rule 3.9 (duty to disclose representative capacity when lawyer appears in nonadjudicative proceeding). Finally, prosecutors have a duty to disclose to defense counsel exculpatory material. See Model Rule 3.8(d) and Problem 2-10.

Under the Code of Professional Responsibility lawyers had an obligation to disclose juror misconduct to tribunals. The Code's DR 7-108(G) stated: "A lawyer shall reveal promptly to the court improper conduct by a venireman or a juror, or by another toward a venireman or a juror or a member of his

---

293. See United States v. Thoreen, 653 F.2d 1332 (9th Cir. 1981), *cert. denied*, 455 U.S. 938 (1982) (improper for defense counsel to substitute individual for defendant at counsel table to test ability of witnesses to identify defendant).

294. See ABA Comm. on Ethics and Prof. Resp., Formal Op. 98-412 (lawyer who learns that client has violated court order in civil case prohibiting transfer of assets must disclose violation to court if necessary to correct prior representation by lawyer or to prevent assisting criminal or fraudulent conduct by client).

295. See Jill M. Dennis, Note, The Model Rules and the Search for Truth: The Origins and Applications of Model Rule 3.3(d), 8 Geo. J. Legal Ethics 157 (1994).

family, of which the lawyer has knowledge."[296] The 1983 version of the Model Rules did not include a provision equivalent to DR 7-108(G).[297] However, Model Rule 3.3(b) and comment 12 added in 2002 should restore this duty.

While the Model Rules do not generally require lawyers to disclose adverse factual information, the rules do impose a limited obligation to disclosed adverse law. Model Rule 3.3(a)(2) states that a lawyer must disclose legal authority in the controlling jurisdiction known to be directly adverse to the position of the client and not disclosed by the opposing lawyer. The Restatement is the same.[298] The duty to disclose adverse law under Rule 3.3 continues until the conclusion of the proceeding. See Model Rule 3.3(c).[299]

The duty to disclose adverse law can be distinguished from the obligation not to disclose adverse facts in at least two respects. First, because the duty applies to law, issues of attorney-client confidentiality are not implicated. Second, if a court decides a case based on an error of law, the decision affects third parties who must rely on and use the law. By contrast, an erroneous decision on the facts affects only the parties involved in the case.

Note that the duty to disclose is limited to authority in the "controlling jurisdiction" and to authority that is "directly adverse." Hazard and Hodes state:

> The "controlling" jurisdiction normally means the same state as the pending case for state law issues, and the same District or Circuit for federal law issues. In either event, of course, applicable decisions of the United States Supreme Court would be considered controlling.[300]

The meaning of the term "directly adverse" in Rule 3.3(a)(2) is unclear. Some might argue that any case that can be distinguished is not directly adverse. If so, however, the disclosure obligation of Rule 3.3(a)(2) is meaningless because a competent lawyer can always develop a plausible distinction. Hazard and Hodes argue that lawyers should use the standard articulated in ABA Formal Opinion 280:

> An attorney should advise the court of decisions adverse to his case which opposing counsel has not raised if the decision is one which the court should clearly consider in deciding the case, if the judge might consider himself misled by the attorney's silence, or if a reasonable judge would consider an attorney who ad-

---

296. See In re R, 554 P.2d 522 (Or. 1976) (en banc).

297. But cf. State v. Cady, 811 P.2d 1130 (Kan. 1991) (under Kansas version of Model Rules, prosecutor had duty to disclose to the trial court information that the prosecutor had received regarding juror misconduct during the trial).

298. Restatement (Third) of the Law Governing Lawyers §111(2).

299. See also ABA Comm. on Ethics and Prof. Resp., Informal Op. 84-1505 (lawyer must disclose appellate decision directly adverse to lawyer's position in motion to dismiss even though motion had earlier been denied by trial court if the issue raised in the motion to dismiss can be revived because not final and appealable).

300. 2 Hazard & Hodes, The Law of Lawyering §29.11, at 17.

vanced a proposition contrary to the undisclosed opinion lacking in candor and fairness to him.[301]

Query whether this standard is consistent with the history of Model Rule 3.3(a)(2). This definition comes very close to the proposed Model Rule that was withdrawn due to criticism of its breadth. That proposed rule stated:

> If a lawyer discovers that the tribunal has not been apprised of legal authority known to the lawyer that would probably have a substantial effect on the determination of a material issue, the lawyer shall advise the tribunal of that authority.[302]

However, in Tyler v. State,[303] the Alaska Court of Appeals adopted the Hazard & Hodes interpretation and held that a lawyer must disclose legal authority from the controlling jurisdiction that a court should in fairness consider in rendering its decision even if a reasonable attorney might conclude that the decision was factually distinguishable.

Professor Daisy Floyd has argued that courts are using their power to award sanctions for litigation misconduct under Rule 11 of the Federal Rules of Civil Procedure and similar rules to enforce a duty to disclose adverse authority that is broader than Model Rule 3.3. She warns lawyers that they are acting at their peril if they rely on the narrow standard of disclosure reflected in that rule.[304]

While Model Rule 3.3(a)(2) requires lawyers to disclose adverse law in some situations, lawyers also have a duty not to engage in misleading argument. For example, partial quotations that are misleading or citations of cases that have been overruled or questioned would be improper because they amount to misleading argument. See Model Rule 3.3, cmt. 4.

One special application of the duty to disclose adverse law in criminal cases involves the "*Anders* brief." In Anders v. California,[305] the Supreme Court held that appointed counsel who moves to withdraw from handling an appeal because counsel has concluded that the appeal is frivolous cannot simply file a "no-merit letter," but must instead accompany the motion with "a brief referring to anything in the record that might arguably support the appeal."[306] The Court made clear that the purpose of the *Anders* brief was not to require

301. ABA, Opinions on Prof. Ethics, Formal Op. 280, at 618 (1967).

302. ABA Commn. on Evaluation of Prof. Standards, Rule 3.1(c) (Discussion Draft January 30, 1980). See Geoffrey C. Hazard, Jr., Arguing the Law: The Advocate's Duty and Opportunity, 16 Ga. L. Rev. 821 (1982).

303. 47 P.3d 1095 (Alaska Ct. App. 2001). See also In re Thonert, 733 N.E.2d 932 (Ind. 2000) (attorney reprimanded for failing to reveal to court of appeals decision by state supreme court in which attorney was counsel of record that was directly adverse to his client's case).

304. Daisy H. Floyd, Candor Versus Advocacy: Courts' Use of Sanctions to Enforce the Duty of Candor Toward the Tribunal, 29 Ga. L. Rev. 1035 (1995).

305. 386 U.S. 738 (1967).

306. Id. at 744.

counsel to act as advocate against the client, but rather to provide information so that the appellate court could more easily assess whether to appoint counsel to handle the appeal. Further, the brief requirement served as a mechanism to assure that appointed counsel had thoroughly reviewed the record.[307] In McCoy v. Court of Appeals[308] the Supreme Court upheld the constitutionality of a Wisconsin rule requiring appointed counsel to include in the *Anders* brief a discussion of why issues that might arguably support the appeal lacked merit. Three justices dissented on the ground that the decision in *McCoy* effectively turned appointed counsel into an advocate against the client. In Smith v. Robbins,[309] the Supreme Court held that the procedure followed in *Anders* was not constitutionally required. States were free to adopt an alternative procedure "so long as it reasonably ensures that an indigent's appeal will be resolved in a way that is related to the merit of that appeal."[310] Several state supreme courts have rejected the *Anders* approach of filing a no-merit letter along with a brief on the ground that the filing of the letter makes the lawyer an advocate against the client. These courts require counsel to make the best arguments that can be made from the record without conceding that they are frivolous.[311]

Dealing with documents and witness examination

Under an adversarial system of justice, attorneys are granted wide latitude in the presentation of cases on behalf of their clients, subject to general rules of law, court rules, and court orders.[312] Nonetheless, some specific restrictions apply to attorney conduct in dealing with documents and other real evidence, examination of witnesses, and advocacy.

Destruction or falsification of evidence directly undermines the truthfulness of legal proceedings and is both unethical[313] and illegal.[314] The prosecution in 2002 of the Arthur Andersen accounting firm for obstruction of justice as a result of its destruction of documents in connection with the Enron scandal has highlighted the issue of when destruction of documents pursuant to a

---

307. Id. at 745.

308. 486 U.S. 429 (1988).

309. 528 U.S. 259 (2000) (upholding California's *Wende* procedure).

310. Id. at 276-277.

311. State v. McKenney, 568 P.2d 1213 (Idaho 1977); Ramos v. State, 944 P.2d 856 (Nev. 1997); State v. Cigic, 639 A.2d 251 (N.H. 1994). See James E. Duggan & Andrew W. Moeller, Make Way for the ABA: Smith v. Robbins Clears a Path for *Anders* Alternatives, 3 J. App. Prac. & Process 65 (2001).

312. See Model Rule 3.4(c); Restatement (Third) of the Law Governing Lawyers §105.

313. See Model Rule 3.4(a); In re Barrow, 294 S.E.2d 785 (S.C. 1982) (discipline for failure to inform court that client had removed warning label in products liability case).

314. American Law Inst., Model Penal Code §241.7 (offense of tampering with or fabricating evidence). See also Restatement (Third) of the Law Governing Lawyers §118. See State v. Romeo, 542 N.W.2d 543 (Iowa 1996) (attorney convicted of record tampering based on fabrication of two receipts to protect his client from theft charge).

document retention program is illegal. We will consider this issue in connection with Problem 5-2 dealing with fraud in business transactions. As discussed in Problem 2-4 lawyers who obtain possession of stolen property or of physical evidence of a crime have a duty to turn this material over to the authorities within a reasonable period of time.[315]

A number of ethical and legal restrictions apply when lawyers deal with or examine witnesses. See Problem 3-7 considering the ethical propriety of a lawyer appearing as both a witness and an advocate at trial. Lawyers may not unlawfully interfere with the other side's access to a witness.[316] Further, lawyers may not request a witness to refrain from voluntarily giving information to the other side unless the witness is a client or the relative, employee, or agent of a client and the lawyer reasonably believes that the person will not be materially and adversely affected by a refusal to give information.[317]

In preparing witnesses for trial, lawyers must draw a fine line between legitimate preparation and improper encouragement of false testimony. We encountered this issue in connection with the lawyer's lecture (Problem 2-5). See also the material on improper witness coaching in Problem 4-4.

In examining witnesses, lawyers are bound to follow the rules of civil procedure and evidence in the applicable jurisdiction. Model Rule 3.4(c) provides that a lawyer shall not "knowingly disobey an obligation under the rules of a tribunal except for an open refusal based on an assertion that no valid obligation exists."[318] In addition, Rule 3.4(e) provides that a lawyer shall not

> in trial, allude to any matter that the lawyer does not reasonably believe is relevant or that will not be supported by admissible evidence, assert personal knowledge of facts in issue except when testifying as a witness, or state a personal opinion as to the justness of a cause, the credibility of a witness, the culpability of a civil litigant or the guilt or innocence of an accused.

The Restatement expresses similar obligations.[319] If a lawyer anticipates that opposing counsel may attempt to engage in examination or offer evidence that is inadmissible, counsel should file a motion in limine seeking judicial determination of the issue in advance of trial.[320]

May a lawyer cross-examine a witness that the lawyer knows is telling the

---

315. Restatement (Third) of the Law Governing Lawyers. §§45, cmt. *f* (stolen property), 119 (physical evidence of crime).

316. Id. §116(2).

317. Model Rule 3.4(f); Restatement (Third) of the Law Governing Lawyers §116(4).

318. See generally Fortune et al., Modern Litigation and Professional Responsibility Handbook chs. 9-13.

319. Restatement (Third) of the Law Governing Lawyers §§105 (compliance with law, rules, and tribunal rulings), 107 (prohibition on reference to inadmissible evidence and expression of personal opinion).

320. See Fortune et al., Modern Litigation and Professional Responsibility Handbook §11.6, at 402-403.

truth for the purpose of undermining the credibility of the witness? Model Rule 4.4(a) provides:

> In representing a client, a lawyer shall not use means that have no substantial purpose other than to embarrass, delay, or burden a third person, or use methods of obtaining evidence that violate the legal rights of such a person.

The rule appears to permit cross-examination of a truthful witness because a lawyer engaging in this tactic has a "substantial purpose" other than harming the witness, namely winning the client's case.[321]

Nonetheless, some commentators have been troubled by the tactic. Professor Freedman points out that attacking the credibility of a truthful witness is worse than representing a defendant who testifies perjuriously. Cross-examination of a truthful witness, like perjury, is designed to mislead the trier of fact, but cross-examination involves the active participation of the lawyer and may seriously harm the witness emotionally or reputationally, for example, when the lawyer attacks the credibility of a rape victim who is telling the truth.[322]

If this argument is sound, can the tactic be justified? Hazard and Hodes argue that some sacrifice of truth is a price of the adversarial system, otherwise lawyers rather than triers of fact will assess the credibility of witnesses.[323] Professor Freedman finds the tactic justified for constitutional and utilitarian reasons.[324] On the other hand, Professor Harry Subin argues that both perjury and cross-examination of the truthful witness are improper. He would prohibit this tactic when the lawyer knows beyond a reasonable doubt that the witness is telling the truth.[325] Interestingly, Professor Freedman has decided not to represent defendants accused of rape because he does not want to be put in the position of cross-examining a truthful witness.[326]

Other authorities indicate that the issue may not be a simple choice between either allowing or prohibiting the tactic. The Restatement provides that lawyers may attempt to discredit a witness the lawyer knows is telling the truth, although the Restatement indicates that lawyers retain professional discretion whether to exercise this power.[327] The ABA Standards for the Prose-

---

321. 2 Hazard & Hodes, The Law of Lawyering §40.3, at 4.

322. Freedman & Smith, Understanding Lawyers' Ethics at 216.

323. 2 Hazard & Hodes, The Law of Lawyering §40.3, at 4.1.

324. Freedman & Smith, Understanding Lawyers' Ethics at 221-223.

325. Harry I. Subin, The Criminal Lawyer's "Different Mission": Reflections on the "Right" to Present a False Case, 1 Geo. J. Legal Ethics 125 (1987). For criticism of Subin's view and his response see John B. Mitchell, Reasonable Doubts Are Where You Find Them: A Response to Professor Subin's Position on the Criminal Lawyer's "Different Mission," 1 Geo. J. Legal Ethics 339 (1987); Harry I. Subin, Is This Lie Necessary? Further Reflections on the Right to Present a False Defense, 1 Geo. J. Legal Ethics 689 (1987).

326. Freedman & Smith, Understanding Lawyers' Ethics at 218. Recall the Freedman/Tigar debate in Chapter 1. Freedman's coauthor, Professor Abbe Smith, however, has chosen a different route and will represent indigent adults and juveniles accused of rape. Id.

327. Restatement (Third) of the Law Governing Lawyers §106, cmt. *c.*

cution and the Defense Functions express different positions on the issue of cross-examination of the truthful witness. ABA Prosecution Function Standard 3-5.7(b) states:

> The prosecutor's belief that the witness is telling the truth does not preclude cross-examination, but may affect the method and scope of cross-examination. A prosecutor should not use the power of cross-examination to discredit or undermine a witness if the prosecutor knows the witness is testifying truthfully.

ABA Defense Function Standard 4-7.6(b), however, states: "Defense counsel's belief or knowledge that the witness is telling the truth does not preclude cross-examination."

Improper argument

While scores of books have been written on the technique of argument, the rules of ethics regarding argument are relatively sparse. Lawyers must, of course, comply with rules of procedure in connection with their arguments.[328] For example, this prohibition makes improper any argument based on inadmissible evidence or that appeals to bias or prejudice.[329] The rules prohibit lawyers from expressing personal belief or personal opinion regarding the merits of the case, although lawyers who are unable to convey (as opposed to voicing) genuine belief in their clients' cases are unlikely to be successful advocates.[330]

May a lawyer argue for inferences that the lawyer knows are false but that are reasonably supportable by the evidence? This question is similar to the question of whether it is proper for a lawyer to cross-examine a witness the lawyer knows is telling the truth. Case law seems to support the proposition that defense counsel may do so, but that it is improper for a prosecutor to adopt this tactic. An interesting example is United States v. Latimer,[331] a prosecution for bank robbery. At trial, two tellers testified that they had activated the bank's camera system during the robbery. The government failed to introduce any pictures because the camera malfunctioned, but it also failed to offer evidence of the malfunction. In closing argument, defense counsel contended that the jury should draw the inference from the government's failure to offer the film that the film did not identify the defendant, even though defense counsel knew that the camera was not working. In rebuttal, the U.S. attorney explained to the jury that the camera was inoperative.[332] The Tenth Circuit

---

328. See Model Rule 3.4(c); Restatement (Third) of the Law Governing Lawyers §105. See generally Fortune et al., Modern Litigation and Professional Responsibility Handbook ch. 13.

329. Fortune et al., Modern Litigation and Professional Responsibility §§13.3.6., 13.6.4.

330. Model Rule 3.4(e) and Restatement (Third) of the Law Governing Lawyers §107.

331. 511 F.2d 498 (10th Cir. 1975).

332. Id. at 502 nn.5-6.

held that defense counsel properly argued for a favorable inference from the evidence. The court went on to find that the prosecutor had acted improperly. The court noted that even if defense counsel had made an improper argument, that does not open the door for an improper response by the prosecutor.[333] The court then discussed two ways in which the prosecutor's argument was improper:

> First, the argument went outside the record and made statements as to facts not proven. . . . Second, the statement put the personal knowledge and belief of the prosecuting attorney on the scales, which is also clearly improper.[334]

As a result the court remanded for a new trial.

——————————— **Problem 2-10** ———————————

Special Duties of Prosecutors

a.   You are an assistant state prosecutor who is handling the prosecution for murder of one Ramon Reyes. The police have arrested Charles "Twigs" Wilson for the homicide. The crime occurred in the parking lot of a convenience store and may be part of a gang feud. There were four witnesses to the crime: the store clerk, Mable Jones; Anton Josephson; Helen Josephson, Anton's wife; and Dante Watts. Mr. Josephson was pumping gas and his wife was in their car when the shooting occurred. Ms. Jones and Mr. Watts were in the store. Wilson had come into the store and purchased some food. When he left the store, he encountered Reyes and several of his friends in the parking lot. An altercation ensued, resulting in Reyes being shot. When the police interviewed Jones immediately after the crime, she told them that she didn't know the name of the person who was in the store, but she believed that she had seen him before and she thought that some of his friends called him "Shooter." The police investigated this information, but it turned out that "Shooter" was another young man who had nothing to do with the crime. The police subsequently arrested Wilson on a tip from one of the members of Reyes's gang. After Wilson's arrest, Jones picked him out from a lineup and, despite the mixup about "Shooter," she is firm in her identification of Wilson. Mr. Josephson also picked Wilson out of a lineup and is confident about his identification. His wife, however, was unable to identify Wilson. She told the police that she was so terrified by what happened that the crime is simply a blur in her mind. Mr. Watts was also unable, or perhaps unwilling, to identify Wilson. You believe that Watts may be a member of one of the gangs or is fearful for his safety if he identifies Wilson. The public defender who

———————————————————————

333. Id. at 503. See also United States v. Young, 470 U.S. 1 (1985).
334. 511 F.2d at 503.

is representing Wilson claims that his client is innocent and that Jones and Josephson have misidentified him. You have asked whether Wilson has an alibi, but the PD hasn't given you any information about Wilson's defense. Under state law, the prosecution must obtain an indictment from a grand jury in all capital cases. How should you proceed in presenting the case to the grand jury? In particular, should you lay out for the grand jury the weaknesses in the identification of Wilson so that it can make an informed decision on whether to indict? Assume the grand jury indicts Wilson. Under your state's rules of criminal procedure, the defense is not entitled to any information about your witness interviews. You have, however, received a request from the defense for "all *Brady* material." How would you respond to this request?

    b. You are an Assistant United States Attorney (AUSA) responsible for prosecution of white-collar crimes. Your office is involved in the investigation of a possible mail and wire fraud case involving a large travel agency, Rollison Travel LLC, which operates in several states. The agency is privately held by the Rollison family. Family members involved in the business are Thomas Rollison, Sr., his wife, Annabelle, and their two sons, Thomas Rollison, Jr. and Norwood Rollison. The fraud involves illegal kickbacks and overcharges to a number of corporations with which the agency does business. Recently, Norwood Rollison contacted you and arranged a meeting. Norwood tells you that he believes some bad things went on at the company but that he wasn't involved at all. He says he would be willing to help your office get information to prosecute his father and older brother provided he receives immunity. Norwood tells you that the Rollison family has hired noted defense attorney, Alan Deniro, to represent them in the matter. How would you proceed?

    Suppose the investigation of Rollison Travel is complete. You have met with Mr. Deniro and offered a plea bargain in which Thomas Rollison, Sr. and Jr. would plead guilty to numerous counts of mail and wire fraud. You have indicated that as part of the deal, you will not prosecute Mrs. Rollison, even though you believe that you have sufficient evidence against her to convict. You inform Mr. Deniro that if the plea bargain is not accepted, you will file charges against Mrs. Rollison as well. In addition, if the plea is not accepted you will seek authority to file RICO charges that could lead to forfeiture of substantial assets. Mr. Deniro has complained bitterly about your threats to charge Mrs. Rollison and to use the RICO statute if father and son Rollison do not plead guilty.

    c. You are an assistant district attorney. The district attorney is considering whether to adopt a policy for responding to requests from defendants who have been convicted but who claim their innocence for testing of DNA kits in the possession of authorities. Your boss has asked you to prepare a draft of a policy and to explain the reasons behind your approach. In connection with your presentation, determine whether your state has passed an "innocence-based post-conviction review statute." See Judith A. Goldberg & David M. Siegel, The Ethical Obligations of Prosecutors in Cases Involving Postconviction Claims of Innocence, 38 Cal. W. L. Rev. 389 (2002). If your state has such a statute, be prepared to explain the requirements it imposes for a convicted defendant to obtain DNA testing. Also be prepared to discuss what effect, if any, the existence or absence of such a statute should have on the development of the district attorney's policy.

Read Model Rule, 3.8, 4.2, and comments.

The prosecutor's ethical obligation to do justice

It is a well-accepted proposition that prosecutors have broader ethical obligations than defense counsel. While defense counsel are obligated to represent their clients zealously within the bounds of law, prosecutors have an obligation to seek justice. One of the most frequently cited statements of this principle is from Berger v. United States:[335]

> The United States Attorney is the representative not of an ordinary party to a controversy, but of a sovereignty whose obligation to govern impartially is as compelling as its obligation to govern at all; and whose interest, therefore, in a criminal prosecution is not that it shall win a case, but that justice shall be done. As such, he is in a peculiar and very definite sense the servant of the law, the twofold aim of which is that guilt shall not escape or innocence suffer. He may prosecute with earnestness and vigor—indeed, he should do so. But, while he may strike hard blows, he is not at liberty to strike foul ones. It is as much his duty to refrain from improper methods calculated to produce a wrongful conviction as it is to use every legitimate means to bring about a just one.[336]

The ABA Standards for the Prosecution Function and the Model Rules both incorporate the prosecutor's obligation to justice. Standard 3-1.2(c) states: "The duty of the prosecutor is to seek justice, not merely to convict." Comment 1 to Model Rule 3.8 provides: "A prosecutor has the responsibility of a minister of justice and not simply that of an advocate."

The general obligation of prosecutors to "do justice" is relatively uncontroversial. Problems arise, however, in making this general principle specific and in devising an appropriate remedial system to deal with violations of prosecutorial duties. Model Rule 3.8 provides a very limited number of special obligations that apply to prosecutors. More detail and specificity can be found in the ABA Standards for the Prosecution Function and in the National Prosecution

---

335. 295 U.S. 78 (1935).
336. Id. at 88.

Standards of the National District Attorneys Association.[337] Like private counsel, prosecutors can also encounter many and varied conflict-of-interest situations.[338] In these materials we will focus on five topics: disclosure of exculpatory material, charging and other discretionary decisions, ex parte contacts with represented defendants, obligations regarding postconviction claims of innocence based on DNA evidence, and prosecutorial trial conduct.

Disclosure of exculpatory evidence

We saw earlier in these materials that defense counsel in a criminal case does not have the obligation (or even the right) to disclose incriminating information that defense counsel receives in confidence. Recall Problem 2-3. Remember, however, that a distinction must be drawn between incriminating information and tangible criminal material (such as the instrumentality or fruits of a crime). A defense lawyer who obtains possession of tangible criminal material generally must turn this material over to the prosecution. Recall Problem 2-4. Note also that a distinction must be drawn between an attorney's knowledge of adverse facts and the attorney's knowledge of adverse law. Both prosecutors and defense counsel have an obligation, although a fairly limited one, to disclose adverse legal authority. See Model Rule 3.3(a)(2).

The duty of prosecutors regarding adverse facts contrasts sharply with that of defense counsel. Prosecutors have both a constitutional and a professional obligation to disclose "exculpatory" material. The leading case dealing with the due process effect of a prosecutor's failure to disclose exculpatory material is Brady v. Maryland,[339] a prosecution for murder in which defense counsel asked the prosecution to be allowed to examine extrajudicial statements made by defendant's companion. The prosecution showed defense counsel several statements, but did not disclose one statement in which the companion admitted committing the homicide. The Supreme Court held that "suppression by the prosecution of evidence favorable to an accused upon request violates due process where the evidence is material either to guilt or to punishment, irrespective of the good faith or bad faith of the prosecution."[340]

In subsequent cases the Court has refined the scope of the Brady rule. The duty to turn over exculpatory evidence applies even if the prosecution has

---

337. Scores of articles have been written on the ethical obligations of prosecutors. See, e.g., Bruce A. Green, Why Should Prosecutors "Seek Justice"?, 26 Fordham Urb. L.J. 607 (1999); H. Richard Uviller, The Virtuous Prosecutor in Quest of an Ethical Standard: Guidance from the ABA, 71 Mich. L. Rev. 1145 (1973). See generally Symposium, Ethics in Criminal Advocacy, 68 Fordham L. Rev. #5 (April 2000).

338. See generally Susan W. Brenner & James G. Durham, Towards Resolving Prosecutor Conflicts of Interest, 6 Geo. J. Legal Ethics 415 (1993); Richard H. Underwood, Part-Time Prosecutors and Conflicts of Interest: A Survey and Some Proposals, 81 Ky. L.J. 1 (1992-1993).

339. 373 U.S. 83 (1963).

340. Id. at 87.

not suppressed the evidence and even if the defense does not file a *Brady* motion.[341] The duty applies to evidence that can be used to impeach government witnesses as well as to exculpatory evidence.[342] However, the government does not have a constitutional duty to turn over impeachment evidence or evidence regarding the defendant's affirmative defenses if the defendant has waived these rights pursuant to a plea agreement.[343] While the scope of the duty of disclosure is broad, a conviction will be set aside only if the evidence is "material." Evidence is material when there is a "reasonable probability" that the outcome would have been different had the evidence been disclosed.[344] Given the uncertainty about whether the materiality test has been met, the Court has warned that the "prudent prosecutor will resolve doubtful questions in favor of disclosure."[345]

Note that the constitutional duty of disclosure does not turn on the bad faith of the prosecutor. The prosecutor has "a duty to learn of any favorable evidence known to the others acting on the government's behalf in the case, including the police."[346] The *Brady* rule only applies, however, if the evidence is in the possession of the government. If the government has failed to preserve the evidence, the defendant's constitutional rights have not been violated unless the defendant establishes that the prosecution acted in bad faith.[347]

Some prosecutors have decided to comply with the *Brady* rule by implementing an "open file policy." Even under an open file policy, a *Brady* violation can occur if exculpatory or impeachment evidence is not in the prosecution's files but is in the hands of the police.[348]

341. United States v. Agurs, 427 U.S. 97, 106-107 (1976).

342. United States v. Bagley, 473 U.S. 667, 676 (1985).

343. United States v. Ruiz, 536 U.S. 622 (2002). Under the "fast track" plea procedure involved in the case the government did agree, however, to disclose any information regarding the factual innocence of the defendant.

344. United States v. Bagley, 473 U.S. at 682. See also Strickler v. Greene, 527 U.S. 263 (1999); Kyles v. Whitley, 514 U.S. 419 (1995). For criticism of this standard, see *Bagley*, 473 U.S. at 696, 707 (Brennan and Marshall, J J., dissenting) (if prosecution fails to comply with duty to reveal all information that might reasonably be considered favorable to defense, conviction should be set aside unless prosecution establishes beyond reasonable doubt that new evidence, if developed by reasonably competent counsel, would not have affected outcome of trial).

345. 514 U.S. at 439 (quoting United States v. Agurs, 427 U.S. at 108).

346. Kyles v. Whitley, 514 U.S. 419, 437 (1995). See also Giglio v. United States, 405 U.S. 150 (1972) (assistant U.S. Attorney who presented case to grand jury had promised witness that he would not be prosecuted if he testified before grand jury and at trial; conviction of defendant reversed because of failure to disclose this promise even though assistant who made promise did not have authority to do so and even though promise was not known by U.S. Attorney or trial counsel).

347. Arizona v. Youngblood, 488 U.S. 51 (1988) (failure of prosecution to preserve semen samples and clothing of victim in child molestation case held not to violate defendant's right to due process absent showing of prosecutorial bad faith even though expert testimony indicated that timely performance of tests could have exonerated defendant).

348. Strickler v. Greene, 527 U.S. 263 (1999).

The prosecutor's duty to disclose exculpatory evidence does not, however, apply to grand jury proceedings because the grand jury is a separate constitutional body not subject to direct judicial supervision.[349] Whether a prosecutor will disclose exculpatory evidence to a grand jury is a matter of prosecutorial discretion. Some prosecutors' offices may have policies on this issue. For example, the Justice Department has the following policy for United States Attorneys:

> It is the policy of the Department of Justice, however, that when a prosecutor conducting a grand jury inquiry is personally aware of substantial evidence that directly negates the guilt of a subject of the investigation, the prosecutor must present or otherwise disclose such evidence to the grand jury before seeking an indictment against such a person. While a failure to follow the Department's policy should not result in dismissal of an indictment, appellate courts may refer violations of the policy to the Office of Professional Responsibility for review.[350]

The Model Rules of Professional Conduct and the ABA Standards for the Prosecution Function both include rules setting forth a prosecutorial obligation to disclose exculpatory material. Model Rule 3.8(d) provides that a prosecutor in a criminal case shall

> make timely disclosure to the defense of all evidence or information known to the prosecutor that tends to negate the guilt of the accused or mitigates the offense, and, in connection with sentencing, disclose to the defense and to the tribunal all unprivileged mitigating information known to the prosecutor, except when the prosecutor is relieved of this responsibility by a protective order of the tribunal.

ABA Prosecution Function Standard 3-3.11(a) is substantially the same. Rule 3.8(d) differs from the constitutional standard in at least two respects. First, the ethical duty applies only to evidence or information "known to the prosecutor," while the constitutional standard applies to any evidence in the hands of the government, even if not known by the prosecutor. Second, the "tends to" standard of the rule appears to require greater disclosure than the constitutional

---

349. United States v. Williams, 504 U.S. 36 (1992). See R. Michael Cassidy, Toward a More Independent Grand Jury: Recasting and Enforcing the Prosecutor's Duty to Disclose Exculpatory Evidence, 13 Geo. J. Legal Ethics 361 (2000) (criticizing *Williams*, reviewing approaches used by the states, and proposing that prosecutors have a duty not to distort the evidence and mislead the grand jury). See also John Gibeaut, Indictment of a System, 87 A.B.A. J. 34 (Jan. 2001) (description of prosecutorial abuses in using grand juries and proposals for reform, including presence of defense counsel).

350. Department of Justice, United States Attorneys' Manual. tit. 9-11.233. The United States Attorneys' Manual is available online at http://www.usdoj.gov/usao/eousa/foia_reading_room/usam (visited July 7, 2003).

standard.[351] A study of disciplinary sanctions against prosecutors for *Brady* violations, however, finds that cases are rarely brought and sanctions are light.[352]

For years knowledgeable observers of the criminal justice system have contended that police perjury ("testilying") is widespread.[353] Several highly publicized cases, including the O. J. Simpson trial and the case of Randall Adams (documented in the movie *The Thin Blue Line*), have given the issue greater publicity, but prosecutors have done little to address the issue.

Charging and other discretionary decisions

Prosecutors have broad discretionary power at almost every stage of criminal proceedings, including investigation, charging, and plea bargaining. Most of the decisions are subject to few, if any, ethical or legal restraints. For example, the Model Rules provide that prosecutors "shall refrain from prosecuting a charge that the prosecutor knows is not supported by probable cause." Model Rule 3.8(a). The requirements of knowledge[354] and probable cause are so weak as to make the obligation meaningless.[355] The ABA Standards for the Prosecution Function refer to the probable cause standard, but go further, stating that a "prosecutor should not institute, cause to be instituted, or permit the continued pendency of criminal charges in the absence of sufficient admissible evidence to support a conviction."[356] The standards set forth a number of

351. For a discussion of the elements of a disciplinary offense for failure to disclose exculpatory evidence see In re Attorney C, 47 P.3d 1167 (Colo. 2002). Despite the "tends to" language of the rule, the court adopted the constitutional test for materiality as an element of Rule 3.8(d). The court also stated that the requirement of timely disclosure meant that the prosecutor must disclose material exculpatory evidence before the next critical stage of the proceeding. While the prosecutor in the case failed to do so, the court refused to find a disciplinary violation because it concluded that the prosecutor did not have the mens rea of intent.

352. Richard A. Rosen, Disciplinary Sanctions Against Prosecutors for *Brady* Violations: A Paper Tiger, 65 N.C. L. Rev. 693 (1987) (recommending independent review of reported criminal cases by bar counsel for *Brady* violations and automatic reversal when prosecutors act in bad faith). For a recent case in which a prosecutor had his license suspended for making false statements to a court and for failing to disclose material exculpatory evidence, see Committee on Prof. Ethics & Conduct v. Ramey, 512 N.W.2d 569 (Iowa 1994).

353. Alan Dershowitz, Is Legal Ethics Asking The Right Questions? 1 J. Inst. for Study Legal Ethics 15 (1996); Richard H. Underwood, The Professional and the Liar, 87 Ky. L.J. 919, 966-999 (1998-1999).

354. See In re Lucareli, 611 N.W.2d 754 (Wis. 2000) (prosecutor must know that charges are not warranted to be subject to discipline; negligence in bringing charges is not sufficient).

355. Consider Kenneth J. Melilli, Prosecutorial Discretion in an Adversary System, 1992 B.Y.U. L. Rev. 669 (prosecutors should charge only in cases in which they are convinced of defendant's guilt beyond a reasonable doubt).

356. ABA Standards for Criminal Justice, Prosecution Standard 3-3.9(a) (3d ed. 1993).

factors that prosecutors should take into account in making the decision whether to charge:

(i) the prosecutor's reasonable doubt that the accused is in fact guilty;
(ii) the extent of the harm caused by the offense;
(iii) the disproportion of the authorized punishment in relation to the particular offense or the offender;
(iv) possible improper motives of a complainant;
(v) reluctance of the victim to testify;
(vi) cooperation of the accused in the apprehension or conviction of others; and
(vii) availability and likelihood of prosecution by another jurisdiction.[357]

The ABA Standards also state that a "prosecutor should not be compelled by his or her supervisor to prosecute a case in which he or she has a reasonable doubt about the guilt of the accused"[358] and that in "making the decision to prosecute, the prosecutor should give no weight to the personal or political advantages or disadvantages which might be involved or to a desire to enhance his or her record of convictions."[359]

Both for reasons for fairness and efficiency most prosecutors will not bring criminal charges unless they believe that they can convict. For example, the Justice Department has the following policy: "[B]oth as a matter of fundamental fairness and in the interest of the efficient administration of justice, no prosecution should be initiated against any person unless the government believes that the person probably will be found guilty by an unbiased trier of fact."[360] The Justice Department has also articulated policies regarding the exercise of discretion to prosecute.[361]

The same set of facts may often give rise to several criminal changes. Defendants sometimes complain that prosecutors overcharge or threaten to overcharge in order to induce or coerce defendants to enter into plea bargains. Under the doctrine of prosecutorial "vindictiveness," the Supreme Court has imposed some limits on a prosecutor's discretion to charge after the defendant exercises a right to appeal,[362] but the Court has also ruled that the doctrine does not apply when the prosecutor informed the defendant during plea bargaining that he would face higher charges if he did not agree to the bargain offered by the prosecutor.[363] The Court found the prosecutor's actions to be

---

357. Id. 3-3.9(b).
358. Id. 3-3.9(c).
359. Id. 3-3.9(d).
360. Department of Justice, United States Attorneys' Manual, tit. 9-27-220(B).
361. Id. 9-27-220(A) et seq.
362. Blackledge v. Perry, 417 U.S. 21 (1974) (unconstitutional for prosecutor to bring felony charges for assault with a deadly weapon after defendant exercised his statutory right to trial de novo on appeal from misdemeanor conviction for same conduct).
363. Bordenkircher v. Hayes, 434 U.S. 357 (1978).

part of the "give-and-take" of negotiation common in plea bargaining rather than evidence of vindictiveness.[364]

In commentary, the ABA Standards discuss the issue of "overcharging":

Discretion in Selecting the Number and Degree of Charges

The structure of the substantive law of crimes is such that a single criminal event will often give rise to potential criminal liability for a number of different crimes. Defense counsel often complain that prosecutors charge a number of different crimes, that is, "overcharge," in order to obtain leverage for plea negotiations. Although there are many different conceptions of what "overcharging" actually is, the heart of the criticism is the belief that prosecutors have brought charges, not in the good faith belief that they fairly reflect the gravity of the offense, but rather as a harassing and coercive device in the expectation that they will induce the defendant to plead guilty.

From the prosecutor's point of view, the charging decision is one that must be made at a stage when all the evidence is not necessarily in the form it will take at trial. The prosecutor must make a preliminary evaluation in order to proceed, knowing that at later stages dismissal of charges or an election among charges may be necessary. If the facts fairly warrant multiple charges growing out of a single episode, the prosecutor is, of course, entitled to charge broadly. A defendant accused of breaking and entering, robbery, rape, and murder committed in a single course of conduct involving one victim can hardly complain of "overcharging" if there is evidence of conduct supporting each charge. At some stage, of course, a voluntary dismissal of one or more of the lesser charges may very well be necessary, but a prosecutor cannot fairly be criticized for charging on all tenable counts initially.

The line separating overcharging from the sound exercise of prosecutorial discretion is necessarily a subjective one, but the key consideration is the prosecutor's commitment to the interests of justice, fairly bringing those charges he or she believes are supported by the facts without "piling on" charges in order to unduly leverage an accused to forgo his or her right to trial.

The general policy of the Justice Department is to charge the most serious offense arising from the defendant's conduct that is likely to result in a conviction.[365] With regard to overcharging, the department has the following policy: "As stated, a Federal prosecutor should initially charge the most serious, readily provable offense or offenses consistent with the defendant's conduct. Charges should not be filed simply to exert leverage to induce a plea, nor should charges be abandoned in an effort to arrive at a bargain that fails to reflect the seriousness of the defendant's conduct."[366]

364. Id. at 363.
365. Department of Justice, United States Attorneys' Manual, tit. 9-27-300(A).
366. Id. 9-27-300(B). See also id. 9-27-320(B) (Additional Charges): "It is important to the fair and efficient administration of justice in the Federal system that the government bring as few charges as are necessary to ensure that justice is done. The bringing of unnecessary charges not only complicates and prolongs trials, it constitutes an excessive—and potentially unfair—exercise of power."

United States v. Talao

United States Court of Appeals
222 F.3d 1133 (9th Cir. 2000)

POLITZ, Circuit Judge:

AUSA Robin Harris appeals the decision of the United States District Court for the Northern District of California that she violated Rule 2-100 of the California Rules of Professional Conduct. The United States petitions this court for a writ of mandamus to prevent the district court from giving a jury instruction intended to remedy what the trial court viewed as Harris' Rule 2-100 violation. For the reasons assigned, we hold that Harris did not commit an ethical violation. Accordingly, there is no longer any basis for a remedial jury instruction and the petition for mandamus is moot.

BACKGROUND

San Luis Gonzaga Construction, Inc. (SLGC) is a corporation wholly-owned by Virgilio Talao. In February 1996, several SLGC employees filed a complaint with the United States Department of Labor, Wage and Hour Division alleging that SLGC did not pay the prevailing wage, required them to kickback a portion of their wages, and made false statements to the government regarding the wages earned and hours worked by the employees. A similar complaint was filed with the Laborers' Contract Administration Trust Fund Board of Adjustment.

On June 27, 1996, the Asian Law Caucus initiated a qui tam action against SLGC, Virgilio Talao, and Gerardina Talao,[2] based on the same facts as alleged in the employees' complaints. On October 14, 1996, the criminal division of the United States Attorney's office, acting on a referral from the civil division, initiated a criminal investigation of SLGC and the Talaos relating to these charges. SLGC and the Talaos were represented in all of these matters by attorney Christopher Brose.

The prosecutor assigned to the criminal action was Assistant United States Attorney Robin Harris. In early 1997, Brose initiated discussions with government attorneys, including AUSA Harris, regarding the possibility of settling the pending civil and criminal investigations of SLGC and the Talaos.

On April 21, 1997, Department of Labor Special Agent Alfredo Nodal served a subpoena on SLGC's bookkeeper, Lita Ferrer, directing her to testify before the grand jury on April 30, 1997. When Virgilio Talao learned of the subpoena he instructed Brose to be present for Ferrer's testimony. On April 29, 1997, Brose telephoned Ferrer and arranged to meet with her the next day, prior to her grand jury appearance.

---

2. Gerardina Talao is the secretary/treasurer of SLGC and the wife of Virgilio Talao.

Later that same day, however, Ferrer repaired to the federal building and asked to see Harris. Because Harris was not available, Ferrer spoke to her immediate supervisor, AUSA Sandra Teters. Ferrer asked to have the date of her grand jury appearance changed because she did not want Brose to be present before or during her grand jury testimony. She explained that she would feel pressured to give false testimony if Brose were present. She said she had received a telephone call from Talao in which he told her to "stick with the story" she had told while testifying in one of the related administrative actions. Teters told Ferrer that she would have to testify the following day, but informed her that Brose would not be present during her testimony as attorneys are not permitted to accompany witnesses before a grand jury.

On April 30, Ferrer met with Brose as scheduled to discuss her impending grand jury appearance. They made plans to continue their discussion at the federal building immediately prior thereto. Before Brose arrived at the federal building later that day, however, Ferrer encountered AUSA Harris and SA Nodal in the hallway outside the grand jury courtroom. Nodal introduced Ferrer to Harris. Ferrer then told Harris and Nodal that she did not wish to be represented by Brose. Ferrer agreed to discuss the matter further, and Harris and Nodal took her to a witness room.

Ferrer told Harris and Nodal that she was not and did not want to be represented by Brose. Harris then informed Ferrer of her right to be represented by an attorney, but Ferrer declined representation. When asked why she did not want Brose to act as her attorney, Ferrer stated that she wished to tell the truth and that she did not believe she could do so if she had to testify in his presence. She also said that the Talaos had been pressuring her to testify untruthfully. Ferrer gave Harris and Nodal information about the rates paid by SLGC, her preparation of corporate payroll records, and the possible destruction of corporate documents. During the interview, Brose knocked on the door and demanded to speak with Ferrer. Ferrer was informed of Brose's presence and desire to speak with her, but she said she did not wish to speak with him.

Uncertain whether she should continue the interview, Harris sought guidance from her superiors. The chief of the criminal division, AUSA Joel Levin, opined that Brose was wrongfully tampering with a witness and instructed Harris to continue the interview outside Brose's presence. During the remainder of the interview, Ferrer gave further instances of wrongdoing by her employers and explained how they concealed the truth from investigators and Brose. She stated that Virgilio Talao had told her to tell untruths to the grand jury and that she believed Brose had been directed there by Talao to intimidate her and to keep her from telling the truth. A few minutes later she recounted these facts in her grand jury testimony.

On July 16, 1997, the grand jury returned a 20-count indictment against the Talaos and SLGC. In February 1998, the Talaos and SLGC filed a Joint Motion to Dismiss the indictment asserting that the contact between Harris and Ferrer had violated California's ethical rule against ex parte contacts with represented parties[4] and SLGC's constitutional rights. The court denied the motion, but found a violation of Rule 2-100 and stated that it would refer AUSA Harris' conduct to the State Bar of California. The court also declared that if the case went to trial it would inform the jury of Harris' misconduct and instruct them to take it into account in assessing Ferrer's credibility. Later, the court concluded that Harris had acted in good faith and determined not to refer the matter to the state bar.

Harris appeals the finding that she acted unethically and violated Rule 2-100. The government filed a petition for a writ of mandamus to prevent the district court from giving its proposed remedial instruction at trial. The two matters were consolidated for consideration.

ANALYSIS

[The court first found that it had jurisdiction over Harris' appeal.]

RULE 2-100 VIOLATION

In determining the applicability of Rule 2-100, we must be mindful of the fundamental reasons behind the venerable rule in legal ethics prohibiting ex parte contacts with represented parties. The rule exists in order to " 'preserv[e] . . . the attorney-client relationship and the proper functioning of the administration of justice.' " It is a rule governing attorney conduct and the duties of attorneys, and does not create a right in a party not to be contacted by opposing counsel. Its objective is to establish ethical standards that foster the internal integrity of and public confidence in the judicial system.

Preliminarily, we should point out that the parties dispute the applicability of Rule 2-100 to pre-indictment, non-custodial communications by federal prosecutors and investigators with represented parties. While it is true that this court has found Rule 2-100 not applicable to such communications in particular cases, we have declined to announce a categorical rule excusing all such communications from ethical inquiry. In United States v. Lopez, we held that "beginning *at the latest* upon the moment of indictment, a prosecuting attorney has a duty under ethical rules like Rule 2-100 to refrain from communicating with represented defendants."[20] We also observed that "courts have been divided

---

4. Rule 2-100 provides:

[w]hile representing a client, a member shall not communicate directly or indirectly about the subject matter of the representation with a party the member knows to be represented by another lawyer in the matter, unless the member has the consent of the other lawyer.

Notwithstanding this provision, however, "communications otherwise authorized by law" are permitted. Rule 2-100(C)(3).

20. 4 F.3d 1455, 1461 (9th Cir. 1993) (emphasis added).

over whether the rule applies even in a pre-indictment setting" and cited, among other cases, the Second Circuit's decision in United States v. Hammad.[22]

In *Hammad* the court rejected the argument that an ethical rule analogous to Rule 2-100 was "coextensive with the sixth amendment" and therefore remained "inoperative until the onset of adversarial proceedings," i.e., indictment.[23] Observing that the timing of indictment "lies substantially within the control of the prosecutor," the court explained that under an ethical rule that was dependent on indictment, "a government attorney could manipulate grand jury proceedings to avoid its encumbrances."[24] Rather than announcing a bright-line rule, the court preferred to apply the ethical rule through "case-by-case adjudication,"[25] policing clear misconduct while keeping in mind that prosecutors are "authorized by law" to employ legitimate investigative techniques in conducting or supervising criminal investigations.[26]

The district court relied on *Hammad* in concluding that ethical concerns were raised by the communications between Ferrer and the government here. While we disagree with the district judge's ultimate conclusion as to whether a violation occurred, his reliance on *Hammad* was well-founded. We find the Second Circuit's approach to be the proper one. Here, although at the time of the communications no indictments had yet been issued, the government and SLGC had clearly taken adversarial positions. The Department of Labor was conducting its civil investigation of SLGC's wage practices. The Asian Law Caucus had filed its qui tam action. On behalf of SLGC, attorney Brose had initiated settlement talks with the government regarding both its civil and criminal investigations. Under these circumstances, involving fully defined adversarial roles, impending grand jury proceedings, and awareness on the part of the responsible government actors of SLGC's ongoing legal representation, Rule 2-100 governed AUSA Harris' pre-indictment, non-custodial communications with Ferrer.

At this point a brief historical reference appears in order. During the early part of the decade of the 1990's, intense discussions were had between state judicial authorities and the Department of Justice over a position taken by the DOJ in a written communication popularly referred to as the "Thornburgh Memorandum." In essence, that memorandum created serious problems by excusing federal attorneys from compliance with state ethics rules. The conflict that developed was dissipated when the Congress adopted what is now 28 U.S.C. §530B, and made state ethics rules applicable to government attorneys.[27]

---

22. 858 F.2d 834 (2d Cir. 1988); *Lopez*, 4 F.3d at 1460 n.2.
23. 858 F.2d at 838.
24. Id. at 839.
25. Id. at 840.
26. Id. at 839.
27. 28 U.S.C. §530B(a) now provides in pertinent part that

[a]n attorney for the Government shall be subject to State laws and rules, and local Federal court rules, governing attorneys in each State where such attorney engages in that attorney's duties, to the same extent and in the same manner as other attorneys in that state.

Under the circumstances of this case, we conclude that Rule 2-100 did not prohibit Harris' conduct. Despite the apparent conundrum created by Ferrer's dual role as employee/party and witness, the interests in the internal integrity of and public confidence in the judicial system weigh heavily in favor of the conclusion that Harris' conduct was at all times ethical. We deem manifest that when an employee/party of a defendant corporation initiates communications with an attorney for the government for the purpose of disclosing that corporate officers are attempting to suborn perjury and obstruct justice, Rule 2-100 does not bar discussions between the employee and the attorney. Indeed, under these circumstances, an automatic, uncritical application of Rule 2-100 would effectively defeat its goal of protecting the administration of justice. It decidedly would not add meaningfully to the protection of the attorney-client relationship if subornation of perjury, or the attempt thereof, is imminent or probable.

Few, if any, unethical acts by counsel are more heinous than subornation of perjury. It would be an anomaly to allow the subornation of perjury to be cloaked by an ethical rule, particularly one manifestly concerned with the administration of justice. As commentators have noted with regard to the crime-fraud exception to the attorney-client privilege, "[s]ince the policy of the privilege is that of promoting the administration of justice, it would be a perversion of the privilege to extend it to the client who seeks advice to aid him in carrying out the illegal or fraudulent scheme."[29] In a similar vein, it would be a perversion of the rule against ex parte contacts to extend it to protect corporate officers who would suborn perjury by their employees.

Appellees maintain that application of Rule 2-100 is necessary here in order to protect the attorney-client relationship between the corporation and its counsel. We are keenly aware that assuring the proper functioning of the attorney-client relationship is an important rationale behind the rule. Again, however, like the attorney-client privilege, the prohibition against ex parte contacts protects that relationship at the expense of "the full and free discovery of the truth." For that reason, the attorney-client privilege "applies only where necessary to achieve its purpose." When a corporate employee/witness comes forward to disclose attempts by the corporation's officers to coerce her to give false testimony, the prohibition against ex parte contacts does little to support an appropriate attorney-client relationship. Once the employee makes known her desire to give truthful information about potential criminal activity she has witnessed, a clear conflict of interest exists between the employee and the corporation. Under these circumstances, corporate counsel cannot continue to represent both the employee and the corporation. Indeed, Brose made clear in his testimony at the evidentiary hearing before the district court that if Ferrer had approached him with information adverse to the interests of the corporation he would have advised her that she should retain her own lawyer. Under these circumstances, because the corporation and the employee cannot share an

---

29. McCormick on Evidence §95, 350 (Strong, ed. 1992).

attorney, ex parte contacts with the employee cannot be deemed to, in any way, affect the attorney-client relationship between the corporation and its counsel. In this setting, the corporation's interest, therefore, clearly does not provide the basis for application of the rule. The trial court erred in otherwise concluding.

The fact that we approve AUSA Harris' conduct does not mean that we suggest that attorney Brose in fact committed any act of subornation of perjury. Ferrer felt pressured when Virgilio Talao told her by phone to "stick to her story," and she believed that she would feel pressured to give false testimony if Talao's attorney were present. Harris acted appropriately on the basis of the representations volunteered to her office by Ferrer. We strongly emphasize, however, that a witness's assertion that she is afraid of testifying in an attorney's presence does not, without more, suggest that the attorney has engaged in any ethical or legal violation. Indeed, it is not unknown for corporate employees involved in alleged wrongdoing to attempt to gain favor with U.S. Attorneys by claiming that corporate officials or corporate counsel directed them to act unlawfully. Clients are sometimes willing to throw lawyers to the wolves when they believe that doing so will let them avoid prosecution or a longer prison sentence. Claims of lawyer misconduct made under such circumstances should be viewed with a most critical eye.

We should note that the U.S. Attorney here did the right thing in advising Ferrer that she had a right to be represented by an attorney and giving her the opportunity to contact substitute counsel. When a person who has been represented by institutional counsel perceives a conflict in that representation and approaches a prosecutor or investigator, the prosecutor or investigator should do as Harris did here: advise the person of his right to obtain substitute counsel. Furthermore, we do not mean to suggest that government officials have a license to approach an employee and initiate communications whenever there is a possible conflict of interest between the employee and the corporation for whom the employee works. In this case, Ferrer initiated the communications with the U.S. Attorney's office, and Harris responded properly by clarifying her ethical duties and advising Ferrer of her right to counsel. It is these circumstances and acts that make the district court's finding of an ethical violation improper in this case.

Notes and Questions

1. California Rule 2-100 applies to a "party" represented by counsel. The commentary states, however, that the rule is not limited to the litigation context. ABA Model Rule 4.2 uses the word "person" to make it clear that the rule is not limited to litigation. Both the California and ABA rules provide an exception when the communication is "authorized by law."

2. The controversy over the application of the no-contact rule, Model Rule 4.2, to federal prosecutors began with the Second Circuit's decision in *Hammad*, relied on by the court in *Talao*. In *Hammad* the Second Circuit held

that preindictment undercover investigative contacts with criminal suspects who were represented by counsel could in some circumstances violate the no-contact rule. The Justice Department considered this holding to be a significant impediment to its law enforcement activities because major criminals were often represented by counsel while they were under investigation. In response, then Attorney General Richard Thornburgh issued an internal memorandum purporting to exempt all Justice Department lawyers from the ethics rule on two grounds: Investigative activities of federal prosecutors were "authorized by law" within the meaning of the rule and the authority of the Justice Department to investigate federal crimes preempted state ethics rules. The actions of the Justice Department were controversial. In particular, state supreme courts did not agree with the Justice Department's attempt to claim exemption from at least some state ethics rules. A leading case rejecting the Justice Department's position was In re Howes, 940 P.2d 159 (N.M. 1997), where an assistant United States Attorney was disciplined for ex parte communications with a defendant who was represented by a public defender. In 1998 Congress resolved the issue of the power to regulate by passing the McDade Act, which overturned the Justice Department's regulations and subjected U.S. Attorneys to the full authority of state courts. 28 U.S.C. §530B and regulations adopted pursuant to the Act, 28 C.F.R. §77.1 et seq. See 2 Hazard & Hodes, The Law of Lawyering §38.9. For criticism of the McDade Act and proposals for regulatory alternatives, see Fred C. Zacharias & Bruce A. Green, The Uniqueness of Federal Prosecutors, 88 Geo. L.J. 207 (2000) and Regulating Federal Prosecutors' Ethics, 55 Vand. L. Rev. 381 (2002).

3. While the McDade Act resolves the issue of the power to regulate, it does not resolve the issue of the meaning of the "authorized by law" exception to Rule 4.2. Courts are divided on the issue. Some courts have held that preindictment investigative contacts with people who are represented by counsel are authorized by law so long as the contact does not violate the person's constitutional rights. See United States v. Grass, 239 F. Supp. 2d 535 (M.D. Pa. 2003). Other courts, like the court in *Talao*, examine the facts and circumstances to determine whether the prosecutor engaged in legitimate investigative techniques. Which rule do you think is better? In jurisdictions that apply the approach used by the courts in *Talao* and *Hammad*, what factors are relevant in deciding whether the prosecutor's investigation was proper? Note that in *Hammad* the prosecutor was found to have acted improperly because the prosecutor had drawn up a bogus grand jury subpoena directed to the informant that the informant used to help elicit information from the represented party.

4. What position does the Model Rules take on the meaning of the authorized by law exception? Consider the comments to Rule 4.2.

Seth F. Kreimer & David Rudovsky, Double Helix, Double Bind: Factual Innocence and Postconviction DNA Testing

151 U. Pa. L. Rev. 547, 555-558 (2002)

In 1996, in response to a National Institute of Justice (NIJ) report, Attorney General Janet Reno appointed a National Commission on the Future of DNA Evidence, composed of representatives of law enforcement, prosecutors, and defense attorneys, to recommend standards for postconviction DNA testing. The Commission developed five categories of cases:

Category 1. These are cases in which biological evidence was collected and still exists. If the evidence is subjected to DNA testing or retesting, exclusionary results will exonerate the petitioner.

Example [ ]: Petitioner was convicted of the rape of a sexually inactive child. Vaginal swabs were taken and preserved. DNA evidence that excludes the petitioner as the source of the sperm will be dispositive of innocence. Note that in a case such as this, the victim's DNA—also obtainable from the vaginal swab—operates as a control that confirms that the correct sample is being tested. In addition, the victim's age and sexual status guarantee that the swab contains only biological material related to the crime. . . .

Category 2. These are cases in which biological evidence was collected and still exists. If the evidence is subjected to DNA testing or retesting, exclusionary results would support the petitioner's claim of innocence, but reasonable persons might disagree as to whether the results rule out the possibility of guilt or raise a reasonable doubt about guilt.

Example [ ]: Petitioner was convicted of a homicide. The prosecution argued in closing that blood on a shirt found at petitioner's home came from the victim. Standard blood typing had shown a match between the sample and the victim's blood. DNA testing that excludes the victim as a source of the bloodstains might be helpful to petitioner's claims but does not prove that he was not guilty. . . .

Category 3. These are cases in which biological evidence was collected and still exists. If the evidence is subjected to DNA testing or retesting, the results will not be relevant to a guilt or innocence determination.

Example [ ]: Petitioner is presently incarcerated for a gang rape. The victim testified that seven persons were involved but that she is not sure that all actually engaged in sexual intercourse. If the vaginal swabs that were preserved are tested and petitioner's DNA profile is not found, the significance of the results will be minimal. It should be noted, however, that if other participants in the rape can be identified through DNA testing and petitioner can show the unlikelihood that he ever had any contact with the other participants, this case may fall into category 1 or 2. . . .

Category 4. These are cases in which biological evidence was never collected, or cannot be found despite all efforts, or was destroyed, or was preserved in such a way that it cannot be tested. In such a case, postconviction relief on the basis of DNA testing is not possible.

Category 5. These are cases in which a request for DNA testing is frivolous. . . .

Example [ ]: The trial transcript discloses the existence of other evidence that makes petitioner's claim meaningless, as in a burglary conviction where petitioner was apprehended at the scene of the crime.

The Commission recommended full access to DNA evidence without resort to the courts in Category 1 cases, court resolution of any disputes over access in Category 2 cases, and no access in Categories 3, 4, and 5.

We do not necessarily agree with this entire formulation as a matter of policy. For example, in Category 2, while the DNA evidence might not be determinative of guilt or innocence, where the prosecutor relied at trial on a theory inconsistent with this evidence it may well be extremely strong proof that the wrong result was reached. In Category 5, if the burglar had cut herself and left blood at the scene, DNA testing might be fully exonerating, even for a suspect found at that location. Moreover, the NIJ formulations were intended to provide guidelines for postconviction testing of DNA and not to establish constitutional standards. In our view, for the reasons set forth in this Article, postconviction access to DNA evidence is constitutionally mandated in any case in which DNA tests could either (1) definitively demonstrate innocence, or (2) provide substantial grounds for a claim of innocence sufficient to permit the defendant to pursue postconviction or habeas relief.

Many prosecutors, even without state legislation, have adopted standards similar to those promulgated by the NIJ's Commission. Some prosecutors have gone further in the proactive use of DNA to assure the integrity of the criminal justice system. A leader in this approach has been the District Attorney of San Diego who, in July of 2000, directed a review of the cases of all currently incarcerated prisoners prosecuted by the office in 1992 or earlier to determine whether current DNA technology could provide exonerating evidence. Where the District Attorney's case review disclosed the existence of untested biological evidence that could raise a "reasonable probability that, in light of all the evidence, the defendant's verdict or sentence would have been more favorable if the results had been available at the time of conviction," the San Diego protocol provides for testing of the evidence in a fashion mutually agreed upon by the prosecutor's office and defense counsel. George "Woody" Clark, one of the architects of the program, commented, "[W]e're hopeful that there aren't many cases. . . . [N]onetheless, we think it's so important . . . to our community that if it costs that money . . . then we're willing to spend it. . . ."

[The authors go on to argue that due process supports a constitutional right of access to exculpatory DNA evidence. Some prosecutors and courts have contended that the establishment of such a right is not justified because the burden imposed on the state by DNA production outweighs its usefulness. After analyzing arguments based on the state's interest in the finality of criminal judgments, avoidance of administrative burdens, and federalism, they conclude that these claims are unpersuasive.]

Note

1. With regard to the procedural issue raised by Kreimer & Rudovsky, a majority of states have passed "innocence-based post-conviction review statutes." For a discussion of the requirements of these statutes, see Judith A. Goldberg & David M. Siegel, The Ethical Obligations of Prosecutors in Cases Involving Postconviction Claims of Innocence, 38 Cal. W. L. Rev. 389 (2002). The authors propose that when faced with an innocence-based postconviction claim involving the application of new DNA technology to old evidence, that prosecutors should promptly seek the fullest accounting of the truth, effect the fullest possible disclosure, and use the most accurate science.

Courtroom misconduct by prosecutors

Berger v. United States, discussed above, provides a good example of prosecutorial overzealousness in the courtroom:

> That the United States prosecuting attorney overstepped the bounds of that propriety and fairness which should characterize the conduct of such an officer in the prosecution of a criminal offense is clearly shown by the record. He was guilty of misstating the facts in his cross-examination of witnesses; of putting into the mouths of such witnesses things which they had not said; of suggesting by his questions that statements had been made to him personally out of court, in respect of which no proof was offered; of pretending to understand that a witness had said something which he had not said and persistently cross-examining the witness upon that basis; of assuming prejudicial facts not in evidence; of bullying and arguing with witnesses; and, in general, of conducting himself in a thoroughly indecorous and improper manner. . . .
>
> The prosecuting attorney's argument to the jury was undignified and intemperate, containing improper insinuations and assertions calculated to mislead the jury. . . . The following is an illustration: A witness by the name of Goldie Goldstein had been called by the prosecution to identify the petitioner. She apparently had difficulty in doing so. The prosecuting attorney, in the course of his argument, said (italics added).
>
>> Mrs. Goldie Goldstein takes the stand. She says she knows Jones, *and you can bet your bottom dollar she knew Berger*. She stood right where I am now and looked at him and was afraid to go over there, and when I waved my arm everybody started to holler, "Don't point at him. You know the rules of law." Well, it is the most complicated game in the world. I was examining *a woman that I knew knew Berger and could identify him*, she was standing right here looking at him, and I couldn't say, "Isn't that the man?" Now, imagine that! But that is the rules of the game, and I have to play within those rules.
>
> The jury was thus invited to conclude that the witness Goldstein knew Berger well but pretended otherwise; and that this was within the personal knowledge of the prosecuting attorney.
>
> Again, at another point in his argument, after suggesting that defendants'

counsel had the advantage of being able to charge the district attorney with being unfair "of trying to twist a witness," he said:

> But, oh, they can twist the questions, . . . *they can sit up in their offices and devise ways to pass counterfeit money*; "but don't let the Government touch me, that is unfair; please leave my client alone."[367]

The ABA Standards for the Prosecution Function provide fairly detailed guidance to prosecutors on impermissible trial conduct.[368] Professor Fred Zacharias argues that the general prosecutorial obligation to "do justice" is too vague. He reasons that a more precise concept would require prosecutors to assure defendants that the basic elements of the adversary system exist at trial. Zacharias contends that this perspective would assist rule drafters in preparing more precise rules.[369]

The fundamental problem with prosecutorial misconduct in the courtroom may not be in defining it but in devising remedies to deal with it. One study considered a number of possible remedies for dealing with the problem, including greater use of the contempt power by courts and structural reform of the prosecutor's office to reduce the pressures that can lead to overzealous tactics.[370]

Should prosecutors be subject to greater regulation?

The investigation of President Bill Clinton by independent special prosecutor Kenneth Starr brought to the public attention the question of whether prosecutorial power is subject to abuse.[371] Even before "Starr Wars," a number of commentators had begun questioning the wisdom of prosecutors having the

---

367. 295 U.S. 78, 84-88 (1935). For a more recent example, see Williams v. State, 803 A.2d 897 (Del. 2002) (prosecutor's remarks during closing argument characterizing defendant as "lying" and stating that jury must find state's witnesses to be lying in order to acquit were "patently improper"; trial court's failure to act was plain error warranting reversal).

368. ABA Standards for Criminal Justice, Prosecution Function Standards 3-5.1 to 3-5.10 (3d ed. 1993).

369. Fred C. Zacharias, Structuring the Ethics of Prosecutorial Trial Practice: Can Prosecutors Do Justice? 44 Vand. L. Rev. 45 (1991). Zacharias expands the argument of this article to develop a general framework for code drafting in Specificity in Professional Responsibility Codes: Theory, Practice, and the Paradigm of Prosecutorial Ethics, 69 Notre Dame L. Rev. 223 (1993).

370. Albert W. Alschuler, Courtroom Misconduct by Prosecutors and Trial Judges, 50 Tex. L. Rev. 629 (1972). See also Ellen S. Podgor & Jeffrey S. Weiner, Prosecutorial Misconduct: Alive and Well, and Living in Indiana?, 3 Geo. J. Legal Ethics 657, 686-688 (1990).

371. E.g., Symposium, The Independent Counsel Investigation, the Impeachment Proceedings, and President Clinton's Defense: Inquiries Into the Role and Responsibilities of Lawyers, 68 Fordham L. Rev. 559 (1999).

broad, relatively unchecked power that they have traditionally exercised.[372] For example, Bruce Fein has argued that some prosecutors are deflected from seeking justice by a variety of motives: "a desire for fame and remembrance; the potential for book and movie royalties created by attacking publicly prominent personalities; vaulting political ambitions; ideological hostility towards the accused; or, vindictiveness."[373]

If inadequate regulation of prosecutors is considered to be a problem, a natural remedy is increased scrutiny of prosecutors by disciplinary authorities. Traditionally, however, disciplinary proceedings against prosecutors have been rare. Institutional considerations make it unlikely that this situation will change. Disciplinary officials and prosecutors are both in law enforcement. In addition, prosecutors have considerable political power while disciplinary authorities usually do not.[374]

Courts could subject prosecutors to increased civil liability, but that change in the law seems unlikely. Prosecutors enjoy absolute immunity "in initiating a prosecution and in presenting the State's case" at trial.[375] Outside of trial, however, the Supreme Court has limited prosecutorial immunity. In Buckley v. Fitzsimmons[376] the Court held that prosecutors were entitled only to qualified rather than to absolute immunity for investigative conduct and for statements made at press conferences. In Kalina v. Fletcher[377] the Court held that prosecutors were protected by absolute immunity in connection with preparation and filing of charging documents, but they were not entitled to such immunity with respect to executing certifications for determination of probable cause because such certificates were not part of the traditional functions of advocates.[378]

If formal methods of regulation are unlikely to have much impact, perhaps

---

372. See, e.g., Bennett L. Gershman, The New Prosecutors, 53 U. Pitt. L. Rev. 393 (1992); James Vorenberg, Decent Restraint of Prosecutorial Power, 94 Harv. L. Rev. 1521 (1981). But see Frank O. Bowman, III, A Bludgeon by Any Other Name: The Misuses of "Ethical Rules" Against Prosecutors to Control the Law of the State, 9 Geo. J. Legal Ethics 665 (1996).

373. Bruce Fein, Time to Rein in the Prosecution, 80-July A.B.A. J. 96 (1994).

374. See Fred C. Zacharias, The Professional Discipline of Prosecutors, 79 N.C. L. Rev. 721 (2001). After examining the empirical evidence, Professor Zacharias concludes that "traditional lamentations regarding the absence of bar discipline are somewhat overblown, but also contain a large measure of truth." He calls on disciplinary officials to engage in self-analysis. Id. at 778. But see Monroe H. Freedman, Professional Discipline of Prosecutors: A Response to Professor Zacharias, 30 Hofstra L. Rev. 121 (2001) (Zacharias's study supports the traditional view that discipline of prosecutors has been weak, but the language of his conclusions could lead to "undesirable complacency" on the part of disciplinary officials and judges).

375. Imbler v. Pachtman, 424 U.S. 409, 431 (1976).

376. 509 U.S. 259 (1993).

377. 522 U.S. 118 (1997).

378. In 1999 Congress passed the Hyde Amendment, which allows a defendant who prevails to recover attorney fees from the government if the defendant establishes that the government's position was vexations, frivolous, or in bad faith. Defendants are likely to have a difficult time meeting these requirements. See United States v. Manchester Farming Partnership, 315 F.3d 1176 (9th Cir. 2003).

informal methods would. Some commentators have stressed the importance of the ethical culture of the particular prosecutor's office[379] and the need for education of prosecutors so they exercise discretion to promote justice.[380]

Problem 2-11

Fee Forfeiture and Lawyer Subpoenas

a. Norman Schwartz has asked your firm to defend him in a prosecution for violation of federal drug felony statutes. You have told Schwartz that your firm charges $25,000 to take the case, plus $5,000 advanced expenses, plus fees determined on an hourly basis. Schwartz agrees to these financial arrangements. The next day he delivers to your office a personal check in the amount of $10,000, a cashier's check in the amount of $10,000, and $10,000 in cash. Both checks are drawn on different banks. Do you have any ethical or legal problems taking these payments?

b. During the course of investigation of the Schwartz case, an informant tells the prosecutors that Schwartz has invested the proceeds of his drug transactions in various real estate developments. The informant also says that he believes that the Fleming Law Firm has represented Schwartz in connection with these investments. The prosecutors then issue a subpoena duces tecum to the Fleming firm directing it to produce before the grand jury the following:

> all files relating to representation by any current or former lawyer in the Fleming Law Firm of Norman Schwartz or of any entity with which Schwartz is affiliated. As used in this subpoena, the term "affiliated" includes without limitation any form of affiliation including, by way of example, serving as an officer, director, employee, shareholder, general or limited partner, managing agent, or joint venturer.

What should the Fleming firm do in response to this subpoena? As defense counsel, what advice would you give Schwartz about the subpoena? Be

---

379. Bruce A. Green, Why Should Prosecutors "Seek Justice"?, 26 Fordham Urb. L.J. 607 (1999).

380. Ellen S. Podgor, The Ethics and Professionalism of Prosecutors in Discretionary Decisions, 68 Fordham L. Rev. 1511 (2000).

prepared to argue on Schwartz's behalf in support of a motion to quash
the subpoena and on behalf of the prosecution against the motion.

Read Model Rules 1.6, 3.8(e), 8.4, and comments.

Money laundering and fee forfeiture

One of a lawyer's fundamental professional obligations is the duty not to engage
in criminal misconduct. Model Rule 8.4(b). See also Model Rule 1.2(d) (lawyer
may not counsel or assist client in criminal or fraudulent conduct). For two
reasons, the area of criminal defense practice raises the issue of lawyer participation in criminal conduct perhaps more directly than other areas of practice.
First, by definition criminal defense practice involves representation of individuals who are under investigation for criminal violations or who have been charged
with criminal conduct. The closer one is to criminality, the more likely one is
to become involved. Recall Problem 2-4 in which we considered the ethical
and legal problems facing lawyers when they obtain possession of fruits, instrumentalities, or evidence of crimes. Second, in many cases defendants are
charged with crimes that involve money. The fact that the accused may have
tainted funds raises the possibility that the attorney fees may be derived from
criminal activity.

What criminal statutes apply to the payment of fees to lawyers? One type
of statute that could apply to payments of legal fees is one prohibiting "money
laundering." At the federal level, 18 U.S.C. §1957 makes it a crime if any
person "knowingly engages or attempts to engage in a monetary transaction
in criminally derived property that is of a value greater than $10,000 and is
derived from specified unlawful activity."[381] The statute is extremely broad in
two respects. First, the term "monetary transaction" refers to any deposit,
withdrawal, transfer, or exchange of funds in a financial institution.[382] A deposit
or withdrawal of a fee from a federally insured institution will do. Second, the
government need not prove that the recipient knew the specific crime from
which the funds were derived, only that the funds came from specified unlawful
activity.[383] Section 1957 provides an exception for "any transaction necessary
to preserve a person's right to representation as guaranteed by the sixth amendment to the Constitution."[384] This exception would probably be of little use
to attorneys prosecuted under the statute, however, because the Supreme Court
has held that the Sixth Amendment is not infringed when a statute prevents
defendants from using money that does not belong to them to hire attorneys.
See the cases dealing with the forfeiture statutes discussed below. Thus, if an

---

381. A related money laundering statute is 18 U.S.C. §1956.
382. 18 U.S.C. §1957(f)(1).
383. Id. §1957(c).
384. Id. §1957(f)(1).

attorney were charged with committing a federal crime by receiving as a fee funds derived from criminal activity, the only defense available to the lawyer would be that the lawyer did not "knowingly" receive property derived from illegal activity.

The Justice Department in its manual for U.S. Attorneys takes the position that there is no statutory prohibition on the application of the statute even to bona fide legal fees paid to defense counsel if defense counsel receives the fees knowing that they have been derived from illegal activity.[385] The department also takes the view that there is no constitutional barrier to prosecuting attorneys for receiving criminally derived funds.[386] The Justice Department recognizes, however, that attorneys must investigate matters that they handle and that the failure to do so would be a breach of their ethical obligations and a violation of defendants' constitutional right to effective assistance of counsel.[387] As part of an investigation, attorneys may acquire information that could be used to establish that they know that their fees have been paid from property derived from illegal activity. In order to avoid hampering lawyers in their ability to represent criminal defendants, the department as a matter of policy will not prosecute attorneys under section 1957 for receipt of bona fide attorney fees except under the following circumstances:

> (1) there is proof beyond a reasonable doubt that the attorney had actual knowledge of the illegal origin of the specific property received (prosecution is not permitted if the only proof of knowledge is evidence of willful blindness); and (2) such evidence does not consist of (a) confidential communications made by the client preliminary to and with regard to undertaking representation in the criminal matter; or (b) confidential communications made during the course of representation in the criminal matter; or (c) other information obtained by the attorney during the course of the representation and in furtherance of the obligation to effectively represent the client.[388]

Under general criminal standards a person is treated as having knowledge if the person exhibits "willful blindness," an intentional effort to avoid gaining knowledge.[389] As the policy states, however, the Justice Department will not prosecute attorneys under section 1957 unless attorneys have actual knowledge that the property was derived from criminal activity. In other words, the Government does not take the position that attorneys have a duty to investigate the source of the funds used to pay their fees, at least under this statute. The Justice Department's Criminal Resource Manual elaborates on the meaning

---

385. Department of Justice, United States Attorneys' Manual, tit. 9-105.600. The United States Attorneys' Manual is available online at http://www.usdoj.gov/usao/eousa/foia_reading_room/usam (visited July 7, 2003).

386. Id.

387. Id.

388. Id.

389. See generally John P. Freeman & Nathan M. Crystal, Scienter in Professional Liability Cases, 42 S.C. L. Rev. 783, 833-838 (1991).

of actual knowledge. It states that extensive prerepresentation publicity about the defendant and his affairs is "never sufficient by itself to establish actual knowledge."[390] As an additional protection for attorneys, U.S. Attorneys cannot prosecute attorneys for receiving fees in violation of section 1957 unless the Criminal Division in Washington approves the prosecution in accordance with the policies discussed above.[391] While the Justice Department's interpretation of the money laundering statute provides defense counsel with some comfort, the department's policy is for internal guidance and is not intended to create legal rights.[392]

Although state statutes dealing with money or property derived from illegal activity vary considerably, many states make it a crime for a person knowingly to receive or to possess stolen property.[393] State prosecutors typically do not operate under policy restrictions like those governing U.S. Attorneys, so a lawyer could be subject to state prosecution for receiving stolen property by taking a fee, with the only defense available that the lawyer did not know that the property was stolen. Prosecutors are attorneys too, however, and since many prosecutors become defense attorneys after they leave government service, they may tend to be sympathetic to the argument that defense attorneys should not be charged with committing crimes simply because they are paid to represent defendants in criminal cases. This may explain why there has been no reported prosecution of an attorney for obtaining a fee in violation of a statute prohibiting receipt of stolen property.[394]

Even though a lawyer may not be prosecuted by federal or state authorities, the true owner of any stolen money or property could bring an action against the attorney to recover any money or property conveyed to the attorney. In the case of money, the true owner would have to trace the funds into the lawyer's possession, which might be difficult to do.

A second class of statutes affecting fee payments to lawyers in criminal defense practice provides for forfeiture of property derived from certain illegal activity. Two federal statutes have been particularly important in connection with fee payments to attorneys: 18 U.S.C. §1963(c), which provides for forfeiture of property used in or derived from criminal activity in violation of RICO (Racketeer Influenced and Corrupt Organizations), and 21 U.S.C. §853(c), which provides for forfeiture of property used in or derived from violation of drug felony statutes. Section 853(c) provides as follows:

---

390. Department of Justice, Criminal Resource Manual 2104 (Evidence of Actual Knowledge).

391. Id. United States Attorneys' Manual, tit. 9-105.300.

392. Id. tit. 1-1.100.

393. E.g., Cal. Penal Code §496; N.Y. Penal Law §§165.40 et seq.; Model Penal Code §223.6.

394. Cf. Cardin v. State, 533 A.2d 928 (Md. Ct. Spec. App. 1987), *cert. denied*, 488 U.S. 827 (1988) (attorney convicted of theft when he received fees from savings and loan institution without performing services).

Third Party Transfers

All right, title, and interest in property [subject to criminal forfeiture] vests in the United States upon the commission of the act giving rise to forfeiture under this section. Any such property that is subsequently transferred to a person other than the defendant may be the subject of a special verdict of forfeiture and thereafter shall be ordered forfeited to the United States, unless the transferee establishes in a hearing . . . that he is a bona fide purchaser for value of such property who at the time of purchase was reasonably without cause to believe that the property was subject to forfeiture under this section.

Note that the statute states that title to the property vests in the United States when the crime is committed, not when the defendant is found guilty. Because of this "relation back" of the statute, fee payments to attorneys are subject to forfeiture.

The Justice Department has been much more aggressive in its use of the forfeiture statutes than it has been in using section 1957, the money laundering statute, against attorneys. In response, defense attorneys have vigorously contested efforts by the government seeking forfeiture of their fees, arguing that such efforts were inconsistent with the intent of these statutes and violated defendants' Sixth Amendment right to counsel.

In United States v. Monsanto[395] the Supreme Court rejected arguments that section 853 (the drug forfeiture statute) was not intended to reach attorney fees. Finding the statutory language to be "plain and unambiguous" in its coverage of "all property," the Court noted:

> In enacting §853, Congress decided to give force to the old adage that "crime does not pay." We find no evidence that Congress intended to modify that nostrum to read, "crime does not pay, except for attorney's fees."[396]

In a companion case to Monsanto, Caplin & Drysdale, Chartered v. United States,[397] the Court considered and rejected both Fifth and Sixth Amendment arguments against application of the forfeiture statutes to attorney fees. As to the Sixth Amendment argument, the Court ruled that nothing in the statute prevented defendants from hiring the counsel of their choice out of nonforfeitable assets.[398] The fact that the statute prevented defendants from using forfeitable assets to hire attorneys did not infringe the Sixth Amendment: "A defendant has no Sixth Amendment right to spend another person's money for services rendered by an attorney, even if those funds are the only way that that defendant will be able to retain the attorney of his choice."[399] The Court

---

395. 491 U.S. 600 (1989).
396. Id. at 614.
397. 491 U.S. 617 (1989).
398. Id. at 626.
399. Id.

also rejected the argument that the application of the statute to attorney fees violated the Due Process Clause of the Fifth Amendment because it upset the balance of forces between the prosecution and the defense.[400] The Court noted that any weapon in the war on crime was subject to prosecutorial abuse, but abuse should be judged on a case-by-case basis, not by invalidation of the statute as a whole.[401]

The Court dealt with one final constitutional question in *Monsanto*: the validity of the statutory provision allowing court orders freezing defendants' assets before the assets are finally adjudged to be forfeitable.[402] The Court found no constitutional prohibition against the issuance of a restraining order based on a finding of probable cause.[403] In *Monsanto* the Court did not address the need for or extent of a hearing required to restrain disposition of assets.[404] On remand the Second Circuit ruled that assets could be subject to an ex parte restraining order on a showing of probable cause by the prosecution, but that the Fifth and Sixth Amendments required a prompt adversary, postrestraint, pretrial hearing on the issues whether there was probable cause that the defendant committed the crime of which she was accused and whether the assets were probably subject to forfeiture.[405]

The Justice Department has also articulated policies regarding when it will bring actions against attorneys seeking forfeiture of fees. Any action seeking forfeiture of payments made to attorneys as legal fees requires approval from Washington by the assistant attorney general of the Criminal Division.[406] The department has articulated the following general policy on actions to forfeit attorney fees:

> While there are no constitutional or statutory prohibitions to application of the third party forfeiture provisions to attorney fees, the Department recognizes that attorneys, who among all third parties uniquely may be aware of the possibility of forfeiture, may not be able to meet the statutory requirements for relief for third party transferees without hampering their ability to represent their clients. In particular, requiring an attorney to bear the burden of proving lack of reasonable cause to believe that an asset was subject to forfeiture may prevent the free and open exchange of information between an attorney and a client. The Department recognizes that the proper exercise of prosecutorial discretion dictates that this be taken into consideration in applying the third party forfeiture provisions to attorney fees. See the Criminal Resource Manual at 2301 through 2303. Accordingly, it is the policy of the Department that application of the

400. Id. at 633.
401. Id. at 634-635.
402. 21 U.S.C. §853(e).
403. 491 U.S. at 616.
404. Id. at 615 n.10.
405. United States v. Monsanto, 924 F.2d 1186 (2d Cir.) (en banc), *cert. denied*, 502 U.S. 943 (1991). See also United States v. James Daniel Good Real Property, 510 U.S. 43 (1993) (government may not seize assets without preseizure hearing unless extraordinary circumstances are present).
406. Department of Justice, United States Attorneys' Manual, tit. 9-119.104.

forfeiture provisions to attorney fees be carefully reviewed and that they be uniformly and fairly applied.[407]

In addition, subject to approval in Washington, U.S. Attorneys may enter into agreements to exempt legitimate fee payments from forfeiture actions.[408]

In United States v. Moffitt, Zwerling & Kemler, P.C.,[409] the Moffitt law firm was retained to represent a defendant charged with drug trafficking and money laundering. The firm required the defendant to pay an up-front fee of $100,000. The defendant paid the fee in two installments of $17,000 and $86,800. Much of the $103,800 payment was in the form of $100 bills. The Fourth Circuit rejected the firm's argument that it was an innocent transferee entitled to take the payment free of the government's claim of forfeiture:

> The firm contends that its partners believed, based on their extensive interviews with him, that Covington had "squirreled" away substantial assets from legitimate business activity. And the firm asserts that Covington was informed that he could not pay in "funny money." The district court found, however, that Covington advised the firm's partners that he was broke, and for that reason continued to engage in illegal activity. . . . In addition, during the supposedly extensive interviews with Covington, the firm's partners tiptoed around the most pertinent questions. They did not even ask Covington what legitimate sources of income he had. And, conspicuously, they avoided asking Covington exactly where he had obtained the $103,800 in cash to pay his legal fee. . . . In their meetings with Covington the lawyers did not seek to obviate doubts that any person would have had about the source of Covington's substantial cash payment. The meetings, in fact, create the impression that the participants were engaging in some sort of wink and nod ritual whereby they agreed not to ask—or tell—too much. . . . Both what the law firm knew in August, 1991, and what it declined to inquire about, convinces us that it reasonably had cause to know that the $103,800 was subject to forfeiture. . . .[410]

The Court also held that the Government could pursue common law claims for conversion and detinue against the firm even though the forfeiture statute did not apply because the law firm no longer had possession of the specific cash received from the defendant.

Note that the Fourth Circuit did not mention the Justice Department's guidelines for seeking forfeiture of attorney fees. Arguably the proceeding was proper under the guidelines because the government had reasonable grounds

407. Id. tit. 9-119.200. The Department's Criminal Resource Manual establishes detailed guidelines to implement this policy. Id. tit. 9-119.202.

408. Id. tit. 9-119.203.

409. 83 F.3d 660 (4th Cir. 1996), *cert. denied,* 519 U.S. 1101 (1997).

410. 83 F.3d at 666. See also United States v. McCorkle, 2000 WL 133759 (M.D. Fla. 2000) (ordering forfeiture of attorney fees by noted criminal defense lawyer, F. Lee Bailey). The Florida Supreme Court and the Supreme Judicial Court of Massachusetts subsequently disbarred Mr. Bailey for misappropriation. The Florida Bar v. Bailey, 803 So. 2d 683 (Fla. 2001); In re Bailey, 786 N.E.2d 337 (Mass. 2003).

to believe that the law firm had actual knowledge that the fee payment was subject to forfeiture. The district court had cited the guidelines, stating that they are for internal guidance of the Justice Department and are not intended to create a legal standard.[411]

Even if fees are not subject to forfeiture under federal law, they may be subject to forfeiture under state law. A number of states have enacted forfeiture statutes that could also apply to attorney fees.[412]

Another federal statute, 26 U.S.C. §6050I, applies to fees paid to lawyers (principally in connection with criminal matters, although the statute could also apply to fees paid in civil cases as well). The statute requires reporting of "cash payments" in excess of $10,000.

> Any person—
> (1) who is engaged in a trade or business, and
> (2) who, in the course of such trade or business, receives more than $10,000 in cash in 1 transaction (or in 2 or more related transactions),
>
> shall make the return . . . with respect to such transaction (or related transactions) at such time as the Secretary may by regulations prescribe.

While the statute uses the word "cash," the statute defines the term more broadly than is commonly understood. "Cash" includes foreign currency and to the extent provided in Treasury regulations "any monetary instrument (whether or not in bearer form) with a face amount of not more than $10,000." Thus, cashiers' checks, travelers' checks, or money orders in the amount of $10,000, but not more, may be included within the term "cash."[413] (The statutory limitation of instruments to not more than $10,000 may appear to be odd, but the reason for this limitation is that cash payments of more than $10,000 to a financial institution must be reported by the institution so it is unnecessary to impose reporting requirements on recipients of instruments issued by the institution.) Payment by an ordinary check drawn on the writer's account in a financial institution is not, however, subject to reporting.[414] The reporting requirement applies even if the attorney does not receive any single payment of $10,000 or more if the payments are part of a series of connected transactions. Thus the reporting requirement would apply if the client paid two monthly installments, one for $7,500 in cash, the other with a $7,500 bank check.[415] The statute also prohibits structuring transactions to evade the reporting requirement.[416] In addition, the IRS form for reporting cash payments

411. In re Moffitt, Zwerling & Kemler, P.C., 846 F. Supp. 463, 475 (E.D. Va. 1994).
412. E.g., Cal. Penal Code §§186 et seq.; N.Y. Civ. Prac. Law §§1310 et seq.
413. Treas. Reg. §1.6050I-1(c).
414. 26 U.S.C. §6050I(d).
415. Treas. Reg. §1.6050I-1(b).
416. 26 U.S.C. §6050I(f)(1). See Office of Disciplinary Counsel v. Massey, 687 N.E.2d 734 (Ohio 1998) (lawyer disciplined for attempting to structure fee payments to avoid IRS disclosure requirements). But see In re Stiller, 725 A.2d 533 (D.C. 1999) (attorney who made series of cash deposits less than $10,000 of $135,000 cash fee received

provides: "Form 8300 may be filed voluntarily for any suspicious transaction . . . even if the total amount does not exceed $10,000."

Form 8300 requires the person reporting the transaction to disclose the identity of the individual from whom cash was received, the identity of the person on whose behalf the transaction was conducted, the nature of the transaction and the method of payment, and the business reporting the transaction. Some criminal defense counsel have argued that these requirements violate the attorney-client privilege and their clients' constitutional rights; they refused to complete the portions of the form requiring disclosure of the identity of their clients and the method of payment of their fees. Several appellate courts have ruled in favor of the IRS on the issue.[417] These courts applied traditional doctrine that the client's identity and the fees paid by the client are usually not subject to the attorney-client privilege because such information is generally not given in confidence or for the purpose of obtaining legal advice. The next section discusses the application of the attorney-client privilege to client identity and fee payments.

In a comprehensive analysis of the impact of the federal money laundering, forfeiture, and reporting statutes on lawyers, Professors Eugene Gaetke and Sarah Welling conclude that the laws require lawyers to act cautiously but they do not force lawyers to act unethically.[418] They point out, however, that these laws may produce a number of practical problems, including less informed defense counsel, reluctance of lawyers to take on certain cases, and increased use of disqualification motions by prosecutors. They find these practical problems to be disturbing because they may reduce the quality of representation received by defendants and may tip the balance between the prosecution and the defense unfairly in the prosecution's favor. Professor Ellen Podgor takes an even more critical view of the IRS reporting requirement, arguing that it undermines the adversarial system and places lawyers in the position of being government agents.[419] On the other hand, David Orentlicher claims that it is morally and ethically improper for lawyers to accept fee payments when there is good reason to think the fees come wholly or in part from illicit activity. Instead, such defendants should have to seek court-appointed counsel. He also argues that denying private representation for such defendants could well lead to greater support and funding for public defender systems.[420]

---

from client for purpose of making it more difficult for government to seek forfeiture of fees did not engage in dishonest conduct; IRS reporting requirements not discussed).

417. Gerald B. Lefcourt, P. C. v. United States, 125 F.3d 79 (2d Cir. 1997), *cert. denied*, 524 U.S. 397 (1998); United States v. Ritchie, 15 F.3d 592 (6th Cir.), *cert. denied*, 513 U.S. 868 (1994); United States v. Leventhal, 961 F.2d 936 (11th Cir. 1992). But see United States v. Sindel, 53 F.3d 874 (8th Cir. 1995) (upholding claim of privilege as to one client).

418. Eugene R. Gaetke & Sarah N. Welling, Money Laundering and Lawyers, 43 Syracuse L. Rev. 1165, 1242 (1992).

419. Ellen S. Podgor, Form 8300: The Demise of Law as a Profession, 5 Geo. J. Legal Ethics 485 (1992).

420. David Orentlicher, Representing Defendants on Charges of Economic Crime: Unethical When Done for a Fee, 48 Emory L.J. 1339 (1999). See also David Orentlicher,

The attorney-client privilege and subpoenas directed at lawyers

As discussed above, the Internal Revenue Code requires lawyers to report cash payments received from clients that exceed $10,000. In addition, as part of criminal investigations both federal and state prosecutors have on occasion subpoenaed information from lawyers about the identities of their clients or about payments of their fees. Such subpoenas raise issues of the application of the attorney-client privilege. Recall our discussion in connection with Problem 2-3 dealing with the distinction between the evidentiary attorney-client privilege and the ethical duty of confidentiality. On the distinction between the ethical duty and the evidentiary privilege, see Model Rule 1.6, cmt. 3.

If the government seeks information about a client from a lawyer in connection with a contemplated or pending legal proceeding, both the ethical duty and the evidentiary privilege are involved, but in different ways. Comment 13 to Rule 1.6 indicates how a lawyer should proceed in such a case. Initially, the ethical duty is involved. The ethical duty to protect confidential information requires the lawyer to invoke the evidentiary privilege and to refuse to provide information until the lawyer has an opportunity to consult with the client about the matter.[421] The client after consultation with the lawyer (or other counsel) could, of course, decide to waive the evidentiary privilege and provide the information to the government. If the client wishes to invoke the privilege, the attorney could seek to quash any subpoena that had been issued. Arguments to quash the subpoena would be based on the scope of the evidentiary privilege. What should the lawyer do if the trial court denies the motion to quash? Discovery orders are normally not immediately appealable, and a party who is subject to such an order can usually only obtain immediate appellate review by refusing to comply with the order, becoming subject to a contempt sanction, and then appealing the finding of contempt.[422] Most courts, however, have created an exception allowing immediate appeal by the client when a subpoena compels a lawyer to reveal documents or information that is subject to an arguable claim of privilege. As the First Circuit said:

> [A]llowing an appeal only if the attorney accepts a contempt citation pits lawyers against their clients in a manner that we do not believe is in the interests of justice. . . . A lawyer should not be required to choose between the interests of his or her client and his or her own interests. A rule that promotes conflicts of interest hinders the fair representation of the client and makes it less likely that clients will be well served by their attorneys.[423]

Fee Payments to Criminal Defense Lawyers From Third Parties: Revisiting United States v. Hodge and Zweig, 69 Fordham L. Rev. 1083 (2000).

421. ABA Comm. on Ethics and Prof. Resp., Formal Op. 94-385.

422. See United States v. Ryan, 402 U.S. 530 (1971); In re Grand Jury Subpoena (Horn), 976 F.2d 1314 (9th Cir. 1992).

423. In re Grand Jury Subpoenas, 123 F.3d 695, 699 (1st Cir. 1997). Not all courts agree. See United States v. Amlani, 169 F.3d 1189 (9th Cir. 1999) (client can only appeal subpoena directed to former not current counsel).

If the appellate court then rejects the claim of privilege, the attorney ethically is required to comply with the court order. See Rule 1.6, cmt. 13.

Does the attorney-client evidentiary privilege prevent disclosure of information regarding the identity of the client or payment of legal fees from the client to the lawyer? Courts have generally held that information about fee payments and client identity are not subject to the attorney-client privilege because such communications ordinarily do not reveal any confidential information. For example, in Clarke v. American Commerce National Bank, the Ninth Circuit stated:

> Our decisions have recognized that the identity of the client, the amount of the fee, the identification of payment by case file name, and the general purpose of the work performed are usually not protected from disclosure by the attorney-client privilege. . . . However, correspondence, bills, ledgers, statements, and time records which also reveal the motive of the client in seeking representation, litigation strategy, or the specific nature of the services provided, such as researching particular areas of law, fall within the privilege.[424]

Courts have recognized, however, some limited situations in which information about client identity or fee payments is protected by the privilege because revelation of such information would convey confidential information. In Baird v. Koerner,[425] the Ninth Circuit recognized a "legal advice" exception, although the term is not particularly descriptive of the scope of the exception. The case involved delinquent taxpayers who, based on the advice of their attorney, tendered past-due taxes. The government attempted to learn from the attorney the names of the taxpayers. The court upheld the claim of privilege because revealing the identities would clearly be revealing confidential information. Other courts have articulated "last link" or "communication" exceptions to the attorney-client privilege.[426]

Despite different formulations, these exceptions all have a common core of operative facts. When a court has upheld a claim of privilege regarding client

---

424.   974 F.2d 127, 129 (9th Cir. 1991). See also In re Grand Jury Subpoena, 204 F.3d 516 (4th Cir. 2000); In re Criminal Investigation No. 1/242Q, 602 A.2d 1220 (Md. 1992).

425.   279 F.2d 623 (9th Cir. 1960).

426.   For a general discussion of these exceptions, see In re Grand Jury Subpoenas (Anderson), 906 F.2d 1485 (10th Cir. 1990) (recognizing legal advice, last link, and confidential communication exceptions to general rule that attorney-client privilege does not apply to client identity or fee payments). See also Paul R. Rice, Attorney-Client Privilege in the United States (2d ed. 1999) (available in Westlaw). Compare In re Subpoena to Testify Before Grand Jury (Alexiou v. United States), 39 F.3d 973 (9th Cir. 1994), cert. denied, 514 U.S. 1097 (1995) (lawyer may be compelled to disclose to grand jury identity of client who gave him counterfeit bill because that would not establish "last link" necessary to convict client; prosecution must still prove knowledge and intent) with Dietz v. Doe, 935 P.2d 611 (Wash. 1997) (identity of client in hit-and-run accident can be subject to privilege under legal advice exception if revelation would implicate client in crime for which advice was sought).

identity or fee information, it is because disclosure of the identity of the client
or of the fees paid would reveal confidential information in addition to the
client's identity or fee payments, often the client's motive for seeking legal
advice.[427] Of course, even if the attorney-client privilege applies to either the
identity of the client or the fees that were paid, it is possible that some exception
to the privilege applies, such as waiver of the privilege or if the client sought
legal advice for the purpose of committing a crime or fraud (the "crime/fraud"
exception). We have already encountered the crime-fraud exception to the
attorney-client privilege in connection with the *Purcell* case, discussed in Problem 2-3. We will consider the scope and exceptions to the attorney-client privilege in civil cases in Problem 3-3.

Professor Steven Goode argues that the case law on when client identity
and fee payments are privileged is in disarray. He advocates a new approach
in which the client's identity and fee payments are privileged "whenever it is
the client's status as a client that is the relevant information sought."[428] Under his
status-as-client approach, Goode would hold that the attorney-client privilege
applies to a situation in which the plaintiffs in a civil suit seek the identity of
a hit-and-run driver from his lawyer, but not to completion by attorneys of
IRS Form 8300 requiring reporting of cash payments from clients.[429]

Should prosecutors be subject to special restrictions when they attempt
to subpoena information from attorneys about present or former clients? On
the one hand, prosecutors sometimes have legitimate reasons for seeking information from attorneys.[430] In addition, it can be argued that attorneys and
clients do not need any special protections over and above the attorney-client
privilege and the work product doctrine.[431] On the other hand, subpoenas
directed to attorneys can disrupt and sometimes destroy the attorney-client
relationship, prosecutorial use of subpoenas directed at attorneys has grown
dramatically in recent years, and traditional privileges do not provide adequate
protection because of numerous exceptions to their application.[432]

In 1990, at the urging of the criminal defense bar, the ABA adopted
Model Rule 3.8(f), now Rule 3.8(e). As originally adopted, the rule had two

427. See In re Grand Jury Subpoena for Attorney Representing Criminal Defendant
Reyes-Requena (DeGeurin), 926 F.2d 1423 (5th Cir. 1991); In re Grand Jury Proceeding
(Cherney), 898 F.2d 565 (7th Cir. 1990). See generally 1 Hazard & Hodes, The Law of
Lawyering §9.11, at 40.

428. Steven Goode, Identity, Fees, and the Attorney-Client Privilege, 59 Geo. Wash.
L. Rev. 307, 311 (1991).

429. Id. at 311-312.

430. 1 Hazard & Hodes, The Law of Lawyering §9.34, at 128-129.

431. State ex rel. Doe v. Troisi, 459 S.E.2d 139 (W. Va. 1995) (rejecting need for
preliminary showing by prosecutors to subpoena attorneys to testify before grand juries,
holding that attorney-client privilege provides sufficient protection to clients).

432. See Max D. Stern & David A. Hoffman, Privileged Informers: The Attorney
Subpoena Problem and a Proposal for Reform, 136 U. Pa. L. Rev. 1783 (1988). See also
Ellen Y. Suni, Subpoenas to Criminal Defense Lawyers: A Proposal for Limits, 65 Or. L.
Rev. 215 (1986).

parts. Section (1) established heightened standards before a prosecutor could issue a subpoena to an attorney regarding a past or present client. Section (2) required the prosecutor to obtain prior judicial approval before issuing the subpoena. In 1995, however, the ABA deleted section (2) requiring prior judicial approval, although it retained the heightened standards before a prosecutor could issue a subpoena. These standards continue in current Rule 3.8(e).

The question of whether Rule 3.8(f) can be applied to federal prosecutors has spawned significant litigation. The issue has been further complicated with the passage by Congress in 1998 of the McDade Act, which subjects U.S. attorneys "to State laws and rules, and local Federal court rules, governing attorneys in each State where such attorney engages in that attorney's duties, to the same extent and in the same manner as other attorneys in that State."[433] Recall our discussion of the Act in Problem 2-10. Outside of federal grand jury proceedings, it appears that federal prosecutors will be subject to state rules like Rule 3.8(f).[434] However, with regard to federal grand jury proceedings, state or federal district court rules that attempt to regulate the issuance of subpoenas by federal prosecutors are probably invalid either because they exceed the rule-making authority of the federal courts or invade the province of the grand jury.[435]

The Justice Department has established a policy for issuance of subpoenas by U.S. Attorneys to lawyers for information regarding representation of clients.[436] Under the policy, no subpoena can be issued except with the approval of the assistant attorney general for the Criminal Division in Washington.[437] The policy requires the assistant attorney general to apply a number of principles before approving issuance of a subpoena:

- The information sought shall not be protected by a valid claim of privilege.
- All reasonable attempts to obtain the information from alternative sources shall have proved to be unsuccessful.

---

433. 28 U.S.C. §530B(a).

434. In United States v. Colorado Supreme Court, 189 F.3d 1281 (10th Cir. 1999), the Tenth Circuit held that federal prosecutors were subject to Colorado Rule of Professional Conduct 3.8(f) by virtue of the McDade Act. The case did not, however, deal with grand jury proceedings. Id. at 1284.

435. See Stern v. United States District Court for District of Mass., 214 F.3d 4 (1st Cir.), cert. denied, 531 U.S. 1143 (2001). Stern went further, holding that the local district court rule was invalid even outside grand jury proceedings. Id. at 17-19. The court also held that the McDade Act did not validate the rule, because the rule went beyond matters of attorney conduct. Id. at 19-21. See also Baylson v. Disciplinary Bd., 975 F.2d 102 (3d Cir. 1992) (holding that local rule regulating practice before grand juries was invalid), cert. denied, 507 U.S. 984 (1993). But see Whitehouse v. United States District Court for the District of R.I., 53 F.3d 1349 (1st Cir. 1995) (district court has authority to adopt ethics rule requiring federal prosecutors to seek judicial approval before obtaining subpoenas against lawyers regarding grand jury proceedings).

436. Department of Justice, United States Attorneys' Manual, tit. 9-13.410.

437. Id. tit. 9-13.410(A).

- In a criminal investigation or prosecution, there must be reasonable grounds to believe that a crime has been or is being committed, and that the information sought is reasonably needed for the successful completion of the investigation or prosecution. The subpoena must not be used to obtain peripheral or speculative information.
- In a civil case, there must be reasonable grounds to believe that the information sought is reasonably necessary to the successful completion of the litigation.
- The need for the information must outweigh the potential adverse effects upon the attorney-client relationship. In particular, the need for the information must outweigh the risk that the attorney may be disqualified from representation of the client as a result of having to testify against the client.
- The subpoena shall be narrowly drawn and directed at material information regarding a limited subject matter and shall cover a reasonable, limited period of time.[438]

E. Delivery of Legal Services to Indigents in Criminal Cases

———————————————— **Problem 2-12** ————————————————

Evaluation of Delivery of Defense Services in Criminal Cases

You are a member of a task force of your state bar appointed to evaluate the delivery of criminal defense services in your state. The chairperson of your committee will assign you a topic for evaluation. Be prepared to report to the committee your evaluation of how well your state complies with ABA standards on the topic that has been assigned to you.

Methods of delivering defense services

In Gideon v. Wainwright[439] the Supreme Court held that the Sixth and Fourteenth Amendments guaranteed indigent defendants a right to appointed counsel in criminal prosecutions in state courts. *Gideon* was a felony prosecution. The Court subsequently held in Argersinger v. Hamlin[440] that the right to counsel applied to misdemeanor as well as to felony cases if the defendant was incarcerated as a result of the proceeding. Later decisions have refined the

---

438. Id. tit. 9-13.410(C).
439. 372 U.S. 335 (1963).
440. 407 U.S. 25 (1972).

scope of the right to counsel in misdemeanor cases.[441] Other cases have defined the types of proceedings to which the right to counsel is applicable.[442] The right to counsel attaches at any "critical stage" of the proceeding.[443]

States use three basic systems to implement the constitutional right to counsel in criminal cases. Each of these systems has suffered from problems. *Public defender programs* are used principally in large cities. Public defenders must often deal with excessive caseloads. In addition, the method of selection of the chief public defender may undermine the independence of the program. In *contract defense programs*, counsel receive fixed fees for agreeing to handle certain matters. Contract defense programs can be used in combination with defender programs to deal with excessive caseloads or conflict of interest situations. Contract defense is also used in smaller communities that are unable to afford a defender program. Critics of contract defense fear that contracts are awarded to the lowest bidder without regard to qualifications. Most small jurisdictions make use of *assigned counsel programs*. In some jurisdictions, assigned counsel receive no compensation; representation is treated as part of the lawyer's pro bono obligation. Even in jurisdictions where assigned counsel receive compensation, fees are typically capped or limited to very low hourly rates. Funds for expert witnesses and other litigation costs may be available but are severely limited.[444]

In 1992 the ABA released revised Standards for Providing Defense Services. The ABA concluded that full-time defender organizations were the most desirable method of providing defense services to indigents, but that participation by the organized bar through either assignment or contract system was also desirable.[445] Standard 5-1.2 provides as follows:

441. In Scott v. Illinois, 440 U.S. 367 (1979), the Court held that the conviction of a defendant in a misdemeanor case was not unconstitutional when the defendant was not afforded the right to counsel if no prison sentence was actually imposed even if the defendant was subject to incarceration for the crime. In Nichols v. United States, 511 U.S. 738 (1994), the Court held that a conviction under *Scott* in which the defendant was not provided with counsel could nonetheless be used in a subsequent criminal proceeding to enhance the defendant's sentence. However, Alabama v. Shelton, 535 U.S. 654 (2002), held that a defendant is entitled to counsel even if his sentence is immediately suspended if revocation of probation could result in incarceration.

442. See, e.g., In re Gault, 387 U.S. 1 (1967) (right to counsel applicable to juvenile delinquency proceedings). An ABA study 30 years after *Gault* concluded that a crisis of poor access and quality of legal services exists in juvenile delinquency proceedings. See Patricia Puritz et al., A Call for Justice: An Assessment of Access to Counsel and Quality of Representation in Delinquency Proceedings (1995).

443. See Wolfram, Modern Legal Ethics §14.3.2, at 795-796 (catalogue of critical stages).

444. See Stephen J. Schulhofer & David D. Friedman, Rethinking Indigent Defense: Promoting Effective Representation Through Consumer Sovereignty and Freedom of Choice for All Criminal Defendants, 31 Am. Crim. L. Rev. 73, 83-96 (1993).

445. A 1992 study of indigent defense systems in nine state courts of general jurisdiction found that indigent defenders handled their cases more expeditiously and at least as competently as private counsel. Roger Hansen et al., Indigent Defenders Get the Job Done and Done Well 103-104 (1992). For a study of constitutional and ethical problems under

(a) The legal representation plan for each jurisdiction should provide for the services of a full-time defender organization when population and caseload are sufficient to support such an organization. Multi-jurisdictional organizations may be appropriate in rural areas.

(b) Every system should include the active and substantial participation of the private bar. That participation should be through a coordinated assigned-counsel system and may also include contracts for services. No program should be precluded from representing clients in any particular type or category of case.

The comments explain the justification for a mixed system as follows:

When adequately funded and staffed, defender organizations employing full-time personnel are capable of providing excellent defense services. By devoting all of their efforts to legal representation, defender programs ordinarily are able to develop unusual expertise in handling various kinds of criminal cases. Moreover, defender offices frequently are in the best position to supply counsel soon after an accused is arrested. By virtue of their experience, full-time defenders are also able to work for changes in laws and procedures aimed at benefitting defendants and the criminal justice system.

There are also definite purposes served by retaining the presence of substantial private bar participation in the system for criminal defense. Just as private attorneys often can learn from the full-time lawyers of defender organizations, there are many private attorneys, qualified by training and experience, who can contribute substantially to the knowledge of defenders. In addition, a "mixed" system of representation consisting of both private attorneys and full-time defenders offers a "safety valve," so that the caseload pressures on each group are less likely to be burdensome.

In some cities, where a mixed system has been absent and public defenders have been required to handle all of the cases, the results have been unsatisfactory. Caseloads have increased faster than the size of staffs and necessary revenues, making quality legal representation exceedingly difficult. Furthermore, the involvement of private attorneys in defense services assures the continued interest of the bar in the welfare of the criminal justice system. Without the knowledgeable and active support of the bar as a whole, continued improvements in the nation's justice system are rendered less likely.

Finally, private attorney representation in criminal cases is essential because of new and stricter policies within defense services programs regarding conflicts of interest, primarily in representation of codefendants. In some cases, these policies can result in the declaration of conflicts of interest in more than 25 percent of all cases assigned to a public defender program.[446]

In 2002 the ABA adopted "Ten Principles of a Public Defense Delivery System," proposed by its Standing Committee on Legal Aid and Indigent

---

contract delivery systems, see Kelly A. Hardy, Comment, Contracting for Indigent Defense: Providing Another Forum for Skeptics to Question Attorneys' Ethics, 80 Marq. L. Rev. 1053 (1997).

446. ABA Standards for Criminal Justice, Providing Defense Services Standard 5-1.2, cmt. (3d ed. 1992).

Defendants (SCLAID).[447] In preparing the principles, the Committee drew on numerous studies and recommendations prepared by various organizations since the 1960s.[448] Its goal was to offer policymakers, many of whom were nonlawyers, a concise, practical, understandable guide to designing defender systems.

American Bar Association, The Ten Principles of a Public Defense Delivery System

(February 2002) (footnotes omitted)

1.   *The public defense function, including the selection, funding, and payment of defense counsel, is independent.*   The public defense function should be independent from political influence and subject to judicial supervision only in the same manner and to the same extent as retained counsel. To safeguard independence and to promote efficiency and quality of services, a nonpartisan board should oversee defender, assigned counsel, or contract systems. Removing oversight from the judiciary ensures judicial independence from undue political pressures and is an important means of furthering the independence of public defense. The selection of the chief defender and staff should be made on the basis of merit, and recruitment of attorneys should involve special efforts aimed at achieving diversity in attorney staff.

2.   *Where the caseload is sufficiently high, the public defense delivery system consists of both a defender office and the active participation of the private bar.*   The private bar participation may include part time defenders, a controlled assigned counsel plan, or contracts for services. The appointment process should never be ad hoc, but should be according to a coordinated plan directed by a full-time administrator who is also an attorney familiar with the varied requirements of practice in the jurisdiction. Since the responsibility to provide defense services rests with the state, there should be state funding and a statewide structure responsible for ensuring uniform quality statewide.

3.   *Clients are screened for eligibility, and defense counsel is assigned and notified of appointment, as soon as feasible after clients' arrest, detention, or request for counsel.*   Counsel should be furnished upon arrest, detention or request, and usually within 24 hours thereafter.

---

447. http://www.abanet.org/legalservices/downloads/sclaid/10principles.pdf (visited July 5, 2003). The ABA has adopted many other sets of standards for improving the criminal justice system. See the Web site of the National Legal Aid and Defender Association (NLADA) for a useful list and links to these standards. http://www.nlada.org/Defender/Defender__Standards/Defender__Standards__Home (visited July 5, 2003).

448. See id., Report.

   4.   Defense counsel is provided sufficient time and a confidential space with which to meet with the client.   Counsel should interview the client as soon as practicable before the preliminary examination or the trial date. Counsel should have confidential access to the client for the full exchange of legal, procedural and factual information between counsel and client. To ensure confidential communications, private meeting space should be available in jails, prisons, courthouses and other places where defendants must confer with counsel.

   5.   Defense counsel's workload is controlled to permit the rendering of quality representation.   Counsel's workload, including appointed and other work, should never be so large as to interfere with the rendering of quality representation or lead to the breach of ethical obligations, and counsel is obligated to decline appointments above such levels. National caseload standards should in no event be exceeded, but the concept of workload (i.e., caseload adjusted by factors such as case complexity, support services, and an attorney's nonrepresentational duties) is a more accurate measurement.

   6.   Defense counsel's ability, training, and experience match the complexity of the case.   Counsel should never be assigned a case that counsel lacks the experience or training to handle competently, and counsel is obligated to refuse appointment if unable to provide ethical, high quality representation.

   7.   The same attorney continuously represents the client until completion of the case.   Often referred to as "vertical representation," the same attorney should continuously represent the client from initial assignment through the trial and sentencing. The attorney assigned for the direct appeal should represent the client throughout the direct appeal.

   8.   There is parity between defense counsel and the prosecution with respect to resources and defense counsel is included as an equal partner in the justice system.   There should be parity of workload, salaries and other resources (such as benefits, technology, facilities, legal research, support staff, paralegals, investigators, and access to forensic services and experts) between prosecution and public defense. Assigned counsel should be paid a reasonable fee in addition to actual overhead and expenses. Contracts with private attorneys for public defense services should never be let primarily on the basis of cost; they should specify performance requirements and the anticipated workload, provide an overflow or funding mechanism for excess, unusual or complex cases, and separately fund expert, investigative and other litigation support services. No part of the justice system should be expanded or the workload increased without consideration of the impact that expansion will have on the balance and on the other components of the justice system. Public defense should participate as an equal partner in improving the justice system. This principle assumes that the prosecutor is adequately funded and supported in all respects, so that securing parity will mean that defense counsel is able to provide quality legal representation.

9.   Defense counsel is provided with and required to attend continuing legal education.   Counsel and staff providing defense services should have systematic and comprehensive training appropriate to their areas of practice and at least equal to that received by prosecutors.

10.   Defense counsel is supervised and systematically reviewed for quality and efficiency according to nationally and locally adopted standards.   The defender office (both professional and support staff), assigned counsel, or contract defenders should be supervised and periodically evaluated for competence and efficiency.

The principles refer to the following national maximum caseload standards per attorney:

150 felonies
400 misdemeanors
200 juvenile
200 mental health
25 appeals

The report also refers to the unique workload demands of capital cases: "the duty to investigate, prepare and try both the guilt/innocence and mitigation phases today requires an average of almost 1,900 hours, and over 1,200 hours even where a case is resolved by guilty plea."[449]

449. The ABA has conducted a number of studies showing persistent underfunding of the justice system. See ABA, Special Comm. on Funding the Justice System, Striving for Solutions: An Overview of Crisis Points in America's System of Justice (1995). For a criticism of inadequate funding of indigent defense and a call for systemic litigation to alleviate the problem, see Note, Gideon's Promise Unfulfilled: The Need for Litigated Reform of Indigent Defense, 113 Harv. L. Rev. 2062 (2000). See also Charles J. Ogletree, Jr., An Essay on the New Public Defender for the 21st Century, 58 Law & Contemp. Probs. 81, 93 (Winter, 1995) (discussing problems facing public defenders and proposing creation of Defender Services Center that "would focus on providing pervasive ongoing defense attorney training and on developing and sustaining a positive office culture").

Chapter 3

Ethical Issues in Civil Litigation: The Client-Lawyer Relationship, Confidentiality, and Conflicts of Interest

This chapter turns from criminal to civil litigation. Section A examines various aspects of the fiduciary relationship between lawyers and clients, including attorney fees, scope of representation, authority of attorneys, and withdrawal from representation. Confidentiality is the topic of section B, which includes problems on the use of the Internet, the scope of the attorney-client privilege, and the work product doctrine. Section C addresses the various types of conflicts of interest: representation against current clients, representation against former clients, and conflicts when the lawyer may be required to be a witness in a case. Further, some areas of practice, such as tort litigation, insurance defense, and marital practice, pose special conflict of interest problems.

A. The Client-Lawyer Relationship

Problem 3-1

Contingent Fees, Expenses, and Fee Splitting

Harriet Carnes, an employee of Johnson Manufacturing Company, injured her leg while working on the job. Evidence indicates that the doctor who treated her injury, Ronald Dawson, was negligent, resulting in the amputation of her leg.

Carnes retained Isabel Lopez to represent her in obtaining workers' compensation benefits for her injury. Because Lopez does not handle medical malpractice cases, she suggested that Carnes retain a medical malpractice expert. Lopez recommended Herbert Atlee and offered to contact him on Carnes's behalf. Carnes agreed, and Lopez discussed the case with Atlee. Atlee said that his standard fee for medical malpractice cases was a 45 percent contingent fee, which included a 10 percent fee to the referring lawyer, with the client being responsible for all expenses. Lopez informed Carnes of Atlee's fee arrangements, and told Carnes that she would continue to be involved in the case on a consulting basis. Carnes then met with Atlee and signed a written contingent fee agreement that included the following provisions:

Contingent Fee. Client agrees to pay attorney a fee of 45 percent of the amount recovered in the case.

Expenses. Client is responsible for all expenses associated with the case. In his discretion attorney may advance expenses on client's behalf or bill client as expenses accrue.

Atlee was able to negotiate a settlement of the medical malpractice action for $100,000, which Carnes agreed to accept. Carnes signed a general release and received a check for $40,000. When Carnes received the check, she was uncertain how Atlee had computed her $40,000 payment, but she was hesitant to ask. A few days later she was still troubled by the amount of the check, so she called Atlee's office and spoke to his secretary, who told Carnes that the amount of her check was determined as follows:

Settlement proceeds	$100,000
Less 45% fee	(45,000)
Less expert witness fee of 10%	(10,000)
Less other expenses	(5,000)
Proceeds to client	$40,000

Carnes asked about the "other expenses" and was told that these included copying, travel, and overhead. Carnes has come to you for advice about her settlement. She says that she doesn't feel that she was fairly treated and she wants to know what, if anything, she can do about it.

Read Model Rules 1.5, 1.8(e), 1.15, 3.4, and comments.

The ethical obligation to charge reasonable fees

Model Rule 1.5(a) states that a "lawyer shall not make an agreement for, charge, or collect an unreasonable fee or an unreasonable amount for expenses."[1] Courts regulate the reasonableness of lawyers' fees in three important ways.[2] First, courts can discipline lawyers for charging excessive fees.[3] Unfortunately, some studies have provided distressing documentation of lawyers' improper billing practices, such as double billing (for example, billing two clients for the time spent in preparing a research memo involving an issue applicable to both clients) and undisclosed markups on costs.[4] In response to these abuses, the ABA Committee on Ethics and Professional Responsibility issued Formal Opinion 93-379 in which it addressed a number of issues regarding fees and expenses. The ABA committee advised lawyers who bill strictly on an hourly basis that it is improper for lawyers to charge more than the actual time expended. Thus, lawyers who have agreed to charge their clients on an hourly basis could not ethically double bill for court appearances, travel time, or for work product used in more than one case. The ABA's opinion indicated, however, that lawyers could agree to alternative methods of billing that were not strictly time based, provided the method was fully disclosed to the client. Similarly, the committee reasoned that lawyers could not charge more than the actual cost of expenses, absent full disclosure to the client. Other professional organizations have also taken steps to control improper billing practices.[5]

Second, courts have the power to reduce the amount of fees charged by attorneys if the court finds the fee to be unreasonable.[6] The issue could arise in a variety of ways: in an action by the client to recover from the attorney an excessive fee retained by the attorney, in an action by the attorney to collect a fee, or in a collateral proceeding or motion incident to a matter already in

---

1. The Restatement prohibits fees that are unreasonable or that are prohibited by law. Restatement (Third) of the Law Governing Lawyers §34.

2. See generally Wolfram, Modern Legal Ethics §9.1 (discussing supervisory power that courts exercise over fee agreements).

3. E.g., Bushman v. State Bar, 522 P.2d 312 (Cal. 1974) (en banc) (exorbitant fee in divorce case); In re Teichner, 470 N.E.2d 972 (Ill. 1984) (improper to charge 25 percent contingent fee for collection of life insurance proceeds when no dispute with company), cert. denied, 470 U.S. 1053 (1985); see Dale R. Agthe, Annotation, Attorney's Charging Excessive Fee as Ground for Disciplinary Action, 11 A.L.R.4th 133 (1982).

4. The seminal work has been done by Lisa Lerman. See Lisa G. Lerman, Lying to Clients, 138 U. Pa. L. Rev. 659 (1990); Scenes from a Law Firm, 50 Rutgers L. Rev. 2153 (1998); and Lisa G. Lerman, Blue-Chip Bilking: Regulation of Billing and Expense Fraud by Lawyers, 12 Geo. J. Legal Ethics 205 (1999). See also William G. Ross, The Honest Hour: The Ethics of Time-Based Billing by Attorneys (1996); Conference on Gross Profits, 22 Hofstra L. Rev. 625 (1994). See In re Disciplinary Proceeding Against Haskell, 962 P.2d 813 (Wash. 1998) (en banc) (only attorney in firm authorized to do work for insurance company suspended for two years for having associates use his initials on their bills, for charging personal expenses to client, and for billing for unauthorized travel expenses).

5. See ABA, Task Force on Lawyer Business Ethics, Statements of Principles, 51 Bus. Law. 745 (1996) (statements on billing for legal services, billing disbursements and other charges, and marketing legal services).

6. Some courts have held that lawyers who are guilty of serious ethical misconduct may forfeit all or a portion of their fee. Restatement (Third) of the Law Governing Lawyers §37.

court.[7] In addition, fee disputes between lawyer and client can be resolved through arbitration before a fee dispute resolution board established pursuant to court rule.[8] Third, in some cases the court must determine a reasonable fee because the fee will be paid by the defendant pursuant to statute, court rule, or contract.[9] Problem 6-4 deals with determination of legal fees under statutes providing for "fee shifting."

The ethical duty to inform the client of the basis or rate of the fee

Model Rule 1.5(b) imposes obligations on lawyers to reach clear agreements with their clients about the scope of representation and the basis of fees and expenses: "The scope of the representation and the basis or rate of the fee and expenses for which the client will be responsible shall be communicated to the client, preferably in writing, before or within a reasonable time after commencing the representation, except when the lawyer will charge a regularly represented client on the same basis or rate. Any changes in the basis or rate of the fee or expenses shall also be communicated to the client." The duty to provide information about fees and expenses applies not only at the commencement of the representation but continues even after the representation has ended.[10]

Lawyers charge fees for their services in a wide variety of ways. The fee can be determined strictly on an *hourly basis*; under this method, the fee is computed by multiplying the number of hours worked on the matter by each lawyer (or paralegal) times the hourly rate for that provider. Hourly rates for lawyers and paralegals are set based on their experience and type of practice in comparison with the fees commonly charged by other lawyers and paralegals providing similar services. Hourly fees are quite common in business and tax matters; lawyers engaged in civil defense litigation also typically bill on a hourly basis.

---

7. E.g., In re A. H. Robins Co. (Bergstrom v. Dalkon Shield Claimants Trust), 86 F.3d 364 (4th Cir.), *cert. denied*, 519 U.S. 993 (1996) (courts have inherent power to determine reasonableness of contingent fees; 10 percent limit for supplementary distribution in Dalkon Shield case); McKenzie Constr., Inc. v. Maynard, 758 F.2d 97, 101 (3d Cir. 1985) (in action by client to recover portion of contingent fee retained by lawyer, court should determine reasonableness of fee based on circumstances surrounding negotiation and performance, but "courts should be reluctant to disturb contingent fee arrangements freely entered into by knowledgeable and competent parties"); Kirby v. Liska, 351 N.W.2d 421 (Neb. 1984) (in action by attorney to collect fee in quiet title action, court reduced fee from $65,340 to $6,500 based on time and difficulty of matter).

8. See ABA Model Rules for Fee Arbitration, http://www.abanet.org/cpr/clientpro/contents.html (visited July 10, 2003).

9. See, e.g., Evans v. Jeff D., 475 U.S. 717 (1986) (dealing with recovery of attorney fees under federal fee-shifting statutes).

10. See In re Cox, 813 A.2d 429 (N.H. 2002) (letter of reprimand to attorney who failed to provide complete information about bills to client 15 months after representation ended).

Contingent fees are most commonly used by plaintiffs' lawyers in personal injury matters, but are available in other types of cases as well.[11] The essence of the contingent fee is that the lawyer's right to receive compensation is contingent on the client's receiving an award, either by settlement or judgment. Typically, contingent fees are based on a percentage of the amount recovered, and normally the fee varies depending on the stage at which the matter is concluded. Thus, a common contingent fee in a personal injury action is 25 percent if the matter is settled before trial, 33 percent if the matter is settled after a jury is selected, and 50 percent if the matter is concluded after appeal.

The major justification for contingent fees is that they allow people who could not afford an attorney to obtain access to the legal system for vindication of their rights. It is interesting to note that contingent fees are considered improper in many other countries.[12] The difference in attitude toward contingency fees between the United States and other nations reflects deeper cultural factors and institutional arrangements. In many other countries, litigation is viewed as an evil, while in the United States litigation is often a mechanism for vindication of important rights. In addition, many other countries provide access to the legal system by regulating legal fees and by providing for shifting of fees to the losing party.[13] Although the United States is experiencing trends in those directions, legal fees in this country continue to be largely a matter of contract between the client and the lawyer.

While the use of contingent fees in the United States is well established, contingent fees have been criticized on the ground that in some cases they are unreasonable when compared to the risk of nonrecovery.[14] To take an extreme example, suppose a widow retained an attorney to represent her regarding administration of her husband's estate. If the attorney charged the client a contingency fee for collecting life insurance proceeds on the husband's estate when no bona fide dispute with the insurance company existed, the attorney fee would clearly be excessive.[15] As a result, some scholars have proposed limitations on contingent fees.[16]

---

11. See Gisbrecht v. Barnhart, 535 U.S. 789 (2002) (contingent fees allowed by statute in Social Security cases).

12. See Virginia G. Maurer et al., Attorney Fee Arrangements: The U.S. and Western European Perspectives, 19 Nw. J. Intl. L. & Bus. 272 (1999).

13. Restatement (Third) of the Law Governing Lawyers §35, cmt. *b.*

14. See Frederick B. MacKinnon, Contingent Fees for Legal Services 157-211 (1964). See also Restatement (Third) of the Law Governing Lawyers §35, cmt. *b.*

15. *Compare* Committee on Legal Ethics of West Virginia State Bar v. Tatterson, 352 S.E.2d 107 (W. Va. 1986) (attorney disbarred for contingency fee to recover life insurance proceeds when there was never any reasonable doubt about payment) *with* Lawyer Disciplinary Board v. Morton, 569 S.E.2d 412 (W. Va. 2002) (contingency fee of 30 percent to recover $5,000 in medical expenses in automobile accident case was not excessive based on total time devoted to entire case before representation terminated).

16. See, e.g., Lester Brickman, Contingent Fees Without Contingencies: *Hamlet Without the Prince of Denmark?* 37 UCLA L. Rev. 29 (1989) (contingent fees proper only when case involves risk and fee must be proportional to risk). But see Herbert M. Kritzer, Seven Dogged Myths Concerning Contingency Fees, 80 Wash. U. L.Q. 739

The Restatement of the Law Governing Lawyers indicates that contingent fees can be unreasonable in two situations: "those in which there was a high likelihood of substantial recovery by trial or settlement, so that the lawyer bore little risk of nonpayment; and those in which the client's recovery was likely to be so large that the lawyer's fee would clearly exceed the sum appropriate to pay for services performed and risks assumed."[17]

Fixed fees are often employed in routine estate planning and real estate matters. Thus, a lawyer might charge a fee of $500 to examine title and prepare documents to close a residential real estate transaction. A fixed fee could also be based on a percentage of the value of the transaction. Thus, in some jurisdictions lawyers charge a fixed percentage of the value of the assets in an estate to handle the legal work involved in administration of a decedent's estate. We will consider in Problem 5-4 the propriety of such a percentage fee. One point to note here is that although this fee is expressed as a percentage, it is not a contingent fee.

Some lawyers use a *value-billing* approach. Under this method the lawyer does not set the fee in advance but rather determines the fee at the conclusion of the matter, taking into account a variety of factors. A common method of setting a fee under a value-billing approach involves two steps. First, the lawyer computes the "lodestar" fee (i.e., a fee determined by multiplying the hours worked on the matter by the hourly rates of the attorneys and paralegals who performed services in the matter). Second, the lawyer adjusts the lodestar fee either upward or downward depending on various factors, such as results obtained and the time pressure for handling the matter.

Various combinations of fees are also possible. For example, in a personal injury matter, a lawyer might charge a client a fixed fee of a certain amount coupled with a percentage of the recovery. Presumably, the percentage in this case would be less than in a pure contingency matter since the lawyer would face less risk because of the fixed fee. Some lawyers have begun charging fees based on a *blended rate*, a single rate that applies to both lawyers and paralegals. This method of billing may be attractive to clients because the hourly rate for services rendered is less than that charged for lawyers, while also being desirable for lawyers because it allows lawyers to increase their profit margins by having the work done by employees who cost the least. Some firms have also experimented with fees computed on an hourly basis, coupled with a bonus for a successful outcome.[18]

(2002) (arguing that such reform proposals are misguided based on empirical study of the contingency fee system).

17. Restatement (Third) of the Law Governing Lawyers §35, cmt. *c.* For a proposal to limit contingency fees on the riskless amount of damages by promoting early settlement offers, see Michael Horowitz, Making Ethics Real, Making Ethics Work: A Proposal for Contingency Fee Reform, 44 Emory L.J. 173 (1995). In Formal Opinion 94-389 the ABA Committee on Ethics and Professional Responsibility rejected the proposal. For criticism of the ABA Committee's decision, see Lester Brickman, ABA Regulation of Contingency Fees: Money Talks, Ethics Walks, 65 Fordham L. Rev. 247 (1996).

18. For a discussion of innovative billing techniques, see the ABA Section of Business Law, Report of Ad Hoc Committee on Billable Hours, http://www.abanet.org/careercounsel/

For a number of years in many jurisdictions, bar associations established minimum *fee schedules* that lawyers were required to use in setting their fees. In 1975 the Supreme Court declared fee schedules to be invalid in violation of the antitrust laws.[19]

In some cases a prevailing party[20] may be entitled to court-awarded fees. Court-awarded attorney fees can present a number of ethical problems, particularly for civil rights lawyers: Is it permissible for the lawyer to have a fee agreement with the client that allows the attorney to receive more than the court-awarded amount? If the defendant offers to settle the case for a lump sum including both damages and attorney fees, how is the amount allocated between fees and damages? What should a lawyer do if the defendant offers a settlement that calls for the client to waive the right to recover attorney fees? We will examine these issues in Problem 6-4.

Recall that in connection with Problem 2-2 we discussed the use of retainers and lawyers' trust account obligations.

Special ethical duties regarding contingent fees

Model Rule 1.5(c) imposes special requirements with regard to contingent fees. Agreements for contingent fees must

- be in a writing signed by the client
- state the method by which the fee is computed, including the percentages if the matter is concluded by settlement, trial, or appeal
- identify litigation or other expenses that the client is responsible to pay
- state whether expenses are deducted before or after the contingent fee percentage is computed
- clearly identify any expenses the client must pay regardless of whether the client prevails

The rule also requires lawyers to provide clients with a written settlement statement at the conclusion of the matter stating the outcome and showing how the client's remittance is computed. Violation of these requirements will not necessarily result in forfeiture of the lawyer's fee. For example, if the lawyer

---

billable.html (visited July 11, 2003); Mark A. Robertson & James A. Calloway, Winning Alternatives to the Billable Hour: Strategies That Work (2d ed. 2002). For a discussion of the ethical implications of alternative billing methods for business lawyers, see Committee on Lawyer Business Ethics, Business and Ethics Implications of Alternative Billing Practices: Report on Alternative Billing Arrangements, 54-Nov. Bus. Law. 175 (1998); Ronald D. Rotunda, Innovative Legal Billing, Alternatives to Billable Hours and Ethical Hurdles, 2 J. Inst. for Study Legal Ethics 221 (1999).

19. Goldfarb v. Virginia State Bar, 421 U.S. 773 (1975).

20. See Buckhannon Board & Care Home, Inc. v. West Virginia Department of Health and Human Resources, 532 U.S. 598 (2001) (to be a prevailing party under federal fee shifting statutes, party must obtain a judgment or court-ordered consent decree, not be a mere catalyst for relief).

fails to obtain a written contingency fee agreement, but the client does not contest the amount of the fee, the lawyer will probably be able to recover at least for the reasonable value of the lawyer's services.[21] Some states, either by statute or court rule, have imposed limitations on contingent fee percentages.[22]

When a client receives a lump-sum settlement, the lawyer's contingent fee, like other expenses, is paid at the time of the settlement. But suppose the client agrees to a structured settlement. In the typical structured settlement, the client receives a lump-sum payment coupled with periodic payments either directly from the defendant or perhaps through an annuity issued by an insurance company. When is the attorney's contingent fee paid under a structured settlement? Courts have generally upheld fee agreements in which the client agrees to pay the lawyer's contingent fee out of any lump-sum payment, even if the lawyer would be receiving the bulk of the lump sum. If the fee agreement provides for payment of the lawyer's contingent fee out of the lump-sum settlement, the amount of fee would be based on the present value of the settlement or the cost of the annuity if the settlement was being funded through an annuity.[23] In the absence of an agreement allowing the lawyer to be paid out of the lump-sum payment, the lawyer's contingent fee would be paid pro rata out of each payment received by the client.[24]

In certain cases contingent fee agreements are professionally improper. We have already encountered the rule that prohibits a lawyer from receiving a contingent fee in a criminal case. Model Rule 1.5(d)(2). See Problem 2-2. Rule 1.5(d)(1) states that contingent fees are improper in domestic relations matters when the amount of the fee is "contingent upon the securing of a divorce or upon the amount of alimony or support, or property settlement in lieu thereof." Two rationales support the rule. First, public policy favors reconciliation in domestic cases. If contingent fees were permitted in divorce cases, the lawyer's financial interest would be inconsistent with that public

---

21. Restatement (Third) of the Law Governing Lawyers §34, cmt. *g*. See Mullens v. Hansel-Henderson, 65 P.3d 992 (Colo. 2002) (even though oral contingent fee agreement in worker's compensation case was unenforceable under Colorado Rules of Civil Procedure, attorney could recover on quantum meruit basis when attorney has completed services for which retained); Starkey, Kelly, Blaney & White v. Estate of Nicolaysen, 796 A.2d 238 (N.J. 2002) (while written contingency fee agreement was unenforceable because executed 33 months after representation began, attorney still entitled to recover in quantum meruit).

22. See Fla. R. Prof. Conduct 4-1.5(f)(4); N.J. Sup. Ct. R. 1:21-7. See also Cal. Bus. & Prof. Code §6146 (limitations on contingent fees in claims against health care providers).

23. See Nguyen v. Los Angeles County Harbor/UCLA Medical Center, 48 Cal. Rptr. 2d 301 (Ct. App. 1996); Restatement (Third) of the Law Governing Lawyers §35, cmt. *e*. See also In re Fox, 490 S.E.2d 265 (S.C. 1997) (lawyer disciplined for taking fee up-front on basis of full amount of structured settlement; court holds that cost method is proper approach for valuation of structured settlements).

24. In re Myers, 663 N.E.2d 771 (Ind. 1996) (in absence of agreement lawyer cannot take total fee in structured settlement out of initial payment to client). See Restatement (Third) of the Law Governing Lawyers §35, cmt. *e*.

policy. Second, contingent fees are unnecessary to secure counsel in divorce cases. A spouse with assets can afford counsel, and in most jurisdictions courts will require the spouse with assets to pay a reasonable attorney fee if the other spouse is unable to afford counsel.[25] Since the rule applies only when the fee is contingent on divorce or settlement in lieu of divorce, it should not prohibit contingent fees to collect past-due alimony and child support because the policy in favor of reconciliation is not involved in these cases.

Divorce statutes usually allow the court to award either of the parties attorney fees or "suit money." Under such statutes, courts must determine the amount of a reasonable attorney fee. Some courts have held that a judicial enhancement of the lodestar amount to take into account the results obtained in the case constitutes an improper contingent fee in a domestic case.[26]

Contingent fees are typically charged by plaintiff's counsel. May a defense attorney charge a contingent fee? In Wunschel Law Firm, P. C. v. Clabaugh,[27] the Iowa Supreme Court held that a defense contingent fee based on a percentage of the difference between the amount demanded by the plaintiff in the complaint and the amount the defendant was required to pay was void as against public policy. The court reasoned that a defense percentage contingent fee in unliquidated tort cases was likely to produce unreasonable fees because the amount demanded in the complaint does not bear a logical relationship to the amount of any recovery. The Model Rules do not address the issue, but in Formal Opinion 93-373 the ABA Committee on Ethics and Professional Responsibility ruled that defense contingent-fee contracts were not unethical per se under the Model Rules. The committee stated that "the *Wunschel* court quite properly condemned the use of the prayer for relief as the sole basis for calculating a reverse contingent fee," but the committee went on to assert that in other cases defense contingent fees could be reasonable and in the best interest of the client.

Comment 3 to the 1983 version of Rule 1.5 stated: "When there is doubt whether a contingent fee is consistent with the client's best interest, the lawyer should offer the client alternative bases for the fee and explain their implications." This comment has been deleted in the 2002 revision. The Reporter's note explains: "The Commission proposes to delete [this sentence] because the statement is merely advisory, given that the requirement of offering an alternative type of fee is not stated or implied in any textual provision. If the contingent fee is reasonable, then lawyers need not offer an alternative fee nor need they inform clients that other lawyers might offer an alternative."

25. Restatement (Third) of the Law Governing Lawyers §35, cmt. *g*.

26. State ex rel. Oklahoma Bar Assn. v. Fagin, 848 P.2d 11 (Okla. 1992); Glasscock v. Glasscock, 403 S.E.2d 313 (S.C. 1991). *Contra* Alexander v. Inman, 974 S.W.2d 689 (Tenn. 1998) (fee agreement providing that fee would be reasonable amount for services rendered subject to minimum and maximum with maximum based on percentage of amount recovered was not a contingent fee because attorney would be paid regardless of recovery, only amount was uncertain).

27. 291 N.W.2d 331 (Iowa 1980).

Ethical obligations regarding expenses

Deposition costs, expert witness fees, copying charges, and travel expenses all make litigation costly. Who is responsible for these expenses? Lawyers act as agents for their clients; since the client is the principal, the client is legally responsible for the expenses of litigation. If the lawyer has advanced the expense on behalf of the client, the client is legally obligated to indemnify the lawyer.[28] Although the client is ultimately responsible for these expenses, the lawyer may also be liable to the provider of the service. For example, in Cahn v. Fisher[29] the Arizona Court of Appeals held that while a client is responsible for litigation costs, based on "custom and usage," an attorney was also legally responsible for paying a court reporter's charges when the attorney orders a transcript.[30]

While the client is legally responsible for expenses of litigation, many clients may not be able to afford these costs. May lawyers lend or advance litigation expenses on behalf of their clients? At common law the crime of *maintenance* prohibited advances of money to pay expenses or otherwise support litigation. A related offense, *champerty,* involved the purchase of a portion of the lawsuit. The evil to be prevented in both cases was "stirring up" litigation.[31] A more modern rationale for the prohibition against lawyers' advancing expenses to their clients is that lawyers become creditors, with interests adverse to those of their clients. An adverse financial interest may cause the lawyer to conduct the litigation to protect the lawyer's rather than the client's interest. This justification is weak, however, because contingent fee agreements also give lawyers an interest in litigation that may cause them to conduct the litigation to protect their interests over those of their clients. Yet contingent fee agreements are ethically permissible. The traditional prohibitions have been gradually relaxed so that lawyers can now advance "court costs and expenses of litigation," with repayment contingent on the outcome of the case. See Model Rule 1.8(e)(1).[32] The Model Rules go even further in the case of indigent clients, allowing lawyers to agree to pay litigation expenses with no responsibility for repayment. Model Rule 1.8(e)(2). While the rules of professional conduct allow lawyers to advance litigation expenses, lawyers are not required to do so. Lawyers may demand that clients make expense deposits and may bill them periodically for expenses incurred in their cases.

Although the rules of ethics permit lawyers to advance litigation expenses on behalf of clients, the rules still prohibit general advances or loans, such as

---

28. Restatement (Third) of the Law Governing Lawyers §17(2).

29. 805 P.2d 1040 (Ariz. Ct. App. 1991, *review denied*).

30. See also Williams v. North Alabama Court Reporting Service, 833 So. 2d 622 (Ala. Civ. App. 2001) (attorney who requested transcript of hearing liable for payment to court reporting service unless attorney makes clear that client not attorney is responsible); Restatement (Third) of the Law Governing Lawyers §30(2)(b) (lawyer liable to third person who provides goods or services used by lawyer and who relies on lawyer's credit unless liability is disclaimed).

31. Wolfram, Modern Legal Ethics §8.13, at 489-490.

32. See also Restatement (Third) of the Law Governing Lawyers §36.

for living expenses. The prohibition against loans for living expenses extends to a guarantee of a loan to the client by a third party. See Model Rule 1.8, cmt. 10. The Model Rules distinguish general advances from litigation expenses because general advances "would encourage clients to pursue lawsuits that might not otherwise be brought and because such assistance gives lawyers too great a financial stake in the litigation." Id.[33] Some courts have allowed lawyers to advance living expenses to their clients for humanitarian reasons, while others continue to apply the traditional prohibition.[34]

The concepts of champerty and maintenance continue to have contemporary relevance with regard to loans or advances made by commercial lenders rather than attorneys. Since the 1990s a growing number of law-loan companies have come into existence. These companies are willing to lend money to clients secured by the future proceeds from the client's lawsuit. In Rancman v. Interim Settlement Funding Corp.,[35] the Ohio Supreme Court held that a loan by such a company to a client at a rate that amounted to 180 percent was void under the common law doctrines of champerty and maintenance.

What litigation expenses may lawyers properly charge to their clients? Expenses involved in litigation commonly include the following: filing fees, costs of transcribing depositions, fees of expert witnesses, travel expenses, photocopying, long-distance telephone or fax charges, and computer research charges. In Formal Opinion 93-379, the ABA Committee on Ethics and Professional Responsibility considered various billing practices by lawyers. The committee ruled that general office overhead (library, insurance, rent, utilities, and similar items) was not properly chargeable as an expense to clients absent disclosure to the client in advance of the engagement.[36] The committee also decided that lawyers could not ethically charge clients for expenses in excess of actual disbursements, absent disclosure to the contrary.[37] In other words, markups or surcharges on expenses are improper unless the client consents after clear disclosure from the lawyer. The committee also considered in-house provision of services, such as photocopying, in-house meals, and similar items. As to these expenses, absent agreement to the contrary, lawyers may not ethi-

---

33. Early drafts of the 1983 edition of the Model Rules and of the Restatement of the Law Governing Lawyers would have allowed lawyers to advance living expenses under some limited circumstances if necessary to prevent the client from being forced to make an unjust settlement because of the client's need for funds, but these proposals were withdrawn. See ABA Comm. on Evaluation of Prof. Standards, Model Rules of Prof. Conduct, Rule 1.8(e)(1) (P.F.D. May 30, 1981); Restatement (Third) of the Law Governing Lawyers §48(2) (P.F.D. #1 1996). For criticism of these rules, see James E. Moliterno, Broad Prohibition, Thin Rationale: The "Acquisition of an Interest and Financial Assistance in Litigation" Rules, 16 Geo. J. Legal Ethics 223 (2003).

34. See Jack P. Stahl, The Cost of Humanitarian Assistance: Ethical Rules and the First Amendment, 34 St. Mary's L.J. 795 (2003).

35. 789 N.E.2d 217 (Ohio 2003).

36. ABA Comm. on Ethics and Prof. Resp., Formal Op. 93-379, at 8. See also Restatement (Third) of the Law Governing Lawyers §38(3)(a).

37. Formal Op. 93-379, at 9.

cally charge more than "the direct cost associated with the service (i.e., the actual cost of making a copy on the photocopy machine) plus a reasonable allocation of overhead expenses directly associated with the provision of the service (e.g., the salary of a photocopy machine operator)," as determined by standard accounting methods.[38] In its opinion, the committee emphasized the lawyer's duty to disclose to clients at the beginning of the representation the basis of the fee and other charges to the client.[39]

An issue that comes up quite frequently in personal injury matters deals with a lawyer's obligation to make payments to third parties out of the proceeds of personal injury settlements. Clients often make assignments of a portion of the proceeds of their personal injury claims to providers of medical services or to businesses (for example, the client might assign proceeds to purchase a vehicle or to pay a debt). When the case is settled, however, the client may object to the lawyer honoring the assignment. Model Rule 1.15(d) provides that "a lawyer shall promptly deliver to the client or third person any funds or other property that the client or third person is entitled to receive." The rule recognizes that parties other than the client may have an interest in money that comes into the lawyer's possession. Comment 4 to Rule 1.15 provides that "under applicable law" a lawyer may have a duty to a third party that precludes the lawyer from surrendering funds to the client. When does applicable law provide such a duty? In some cases, statutes may provide for subrogation or lien rights of third-party providers. Courts have held that lawyers have a legal and ethical duty to honor any valid contractual assignment or statutory lien of which the lawyer has received notice.[40] In the event of a dispute between the client and a third party, a lawyer should hold the disputed funds in trust until the dispute is resolved. See Model Rule 1.15(e).

Witness fees are a common litigation expense. Witnesses fall into two broad categories: fact witnesses and expert witnesses. The Model Rules provide that lawyers may not pay witnesses fees that are prohibited by law. Model Rule 3.4(b). As comment 3 indicates, the rule in most jurisdictions is that fact witnesses cannot be paid a fee for testifying, but they may be paid their expenses and any lost wages because of time spent in testifying.[41] In Formal Opinion 96-402, the ABA committee decided that lawyers could ethically pay fact witnesses a reasonable amount for their time in preparing for and in attending depositions. Expert witnesses may be paid reasonable fees for testifying, but the general rule is that expert witnesses may not be paid a fee contingent on

---

38. Id.

39. Id. at 3.

40. E.g., Herzog v. Irace, 594 A.2d 1106 (Me. 1991) (lawyers liable to doctor for failure to honor assignment); Leon v. Martinez, 638 N.E.2d 511 (N.Y. 1994) (lawyer required to honor assignment of portion of personal injury proceeds made by client). But a mere promise by the client to pay the third party does not create a lien that the lawyer is required to honor. Farmers Insurance Exchange v. Zerin, 61 Cal. Rptr. 2d 707 (Cal. Ct. App. 1997).

41. See The Florida Bar v. Wohl, 842 So. 2d 811 (Fla. 2003) (lawyer disciplined for paying consulting fees to fact witness).

their testimony or on the outcome of the case. Comment 3 to Rule 3.4(b).[42] The Restatement of the Law Governing Lawyers follows the Model Rules.[43]

Fee splitting

The term *fee splitting* can refer to transactions with both nonlawyers and lawyers. Fee splitting with nonlawyers has traditionally been improper because the practice can undermine the independence of lawyers and promote the unauthorized practice of law. See Model Rule 5.4(a). We will examine the wisdom of the rules prohibiting fee splitting with nonlawyers in Chapter 7.

Fee splitting between lawyers occurs when lawyers who are not members of a firm divide a fee in a matter. Fee splitting can arise in a variety of ways, for example, referral of a matter from one lawyer to another, association of attorneys in a case to handle different aspects of the matter, completion of a case by a second lawyer after the first lawyer withdrew from representation or after the client discharged the lawyer, and continuation of compensation to a retired member by the lawyer's former firm.

The most controversial aspect of fee splitting arises when a lawyer receives a pure referral or forwarding fee without performing any services. For example, suppose a lawyer who practices business and commercial law has a client with a personal injury claim. The lawyer might refer the case to a litigation specialist and seek a referral fee, typically one-third of the personal injury lawyer's one-third contingent fee.

The argument against allowing lawyers to pay and to receive referral fees rests on two concerns: First, referral fees result in clients paying excessive legal fees. If the lawyer performing services can afford to pay the referring lawyer a fee when the referring lawyer has performed no service, then the client is being overcharged. Second, allowing referral fees could result in such unethical practices as solicitation of business.

Critics of the prohibition on referral fees respond, however, that these concerns do not justify the prohibition. First, if rules permitted referral fees, clients would not be overcharged because referral fees would give lawyers a financial incentive to turn matters over to specialists, who presumably can handle matters more efficiently and with a higher degree of competence than generalists. Second, any concern about unethical practices should be dealt with by regulating those practices directly. Critics of the prohibition on pure referral fees also point out that it creates an arbitrary discrimination against sole practitioners and small firms because it applies only to lawyers who are not members

---

42. See Swafford v. Harris, 967 S.W.2d 319 (Tenn. 1998) (contingency fee contract for services of physician acting as medico-legal expert in personal injury case is void as against public policy; physician also denied quantum meruit recovery). The District of Columbia Rules of Professional Conduct provide that an expert witness's fee may be contingent on the outcome of the case provided that the fee is not a percentage of the recovery. See D.C.R. Prof. Conduct 3.4, cmt. 8.

43. Restatement (Third) of the Law Governing Lawyers §117.

of a firm. Lawyers in large firms are free to divide fees based on their partnership or shareholder agreements.

Under the Code of Professional Responsibility a pure referral fee—one in which the referring lawyer did nothing more than make the referral and did not perform any substantial services in the matter—was unethical. The Code provided that lawyers not in the same firm could divide fees only if the "division is made in proportion to the services performed and responsibility assumed by each." DR 2-107(A)(2). (The Code also required that the client consent to the division and that the total fee be reasonable.) Despite this prohibition, the practice of referral fees appeared to be fairly widespread in the profession.[44]

The Model Rules have loosened the restriction on referral fees from that found in the Code of Professional Responsibility. Under Rule 1.5(e) a referral fee is permitted if:

> (1) The division is in proportion to the services performed by each lawyer *or* each lawyer assumes joint responsibility for the representation;
> (2) The client agrees to the arrangement, including the share each lawyer will receive, and the agreement is confirmed in writing; and
> (3) The total fee is reasonable. [Emphasis added.]

The key change from the Code is that the Model Rules allow a referral fee even in the absence of services performed by the referring lawyer if by written agreement with the client, each lawyer assumes joint responsibility for the matter. When does a referring lawyer assume joint responsibility for the matter? Comment 7 provides: "Joint responsibility for the representation entails financial and ethical responsibility for the representation as if the lawyers were associated in a partnership." This requirement should not be interpreted to mean that the referring lawyer must be involved in all aspects of the case. Partners typically handle cases without the involvement of other partners. Instead, the requirement should mean that the referring lawyer is financially responsible if the lawyer to whom the case is referred commits malpractice[45] or misappropriates client funds, just as a partner would be. Ethical responsibility of the referring lawyer is somewhat different than financial responsibility. As we have seen, a partner is liable for the ethical misconduct of another lawyer in a firm if the partner orders, ratifies, or fails to rectify the misconduct. See Model Rule 5.1(c). This same standard should apply to the referring lawyer.

Suppose lawyers enter into a fee-splitting agreement that violates Rule 1.5(e) (for example, suppose the lawyers fail to obtain a written agreement with the client regarding their joint responsibilities). Is the agreement between the lawyers unenforceable? The courts are divided on the issue of the contractual effect of a fee-splitting agreement that violates the Rules of Professional Conduct. Some courts refuse to enforce such an agreement because it violates

---

44. Wolfram, Modern Legal Ethics §9.2.4, at 510 (practice "both rife and virtually respectable in many communities").

45. See Noris v. Silver, 701 So. 2d 1238 (Fla. Dist. Ct. App. 1997).

public policy, while others will enforce the agreement under principles of estoppel to prevent unjust enrichment.[46]

━━━━━━━━━━━━━━━━ **Problem 3-2** ━━━━━━━━━━━━━━━━

Engagement and Nonengagement Agreements

MEMORANDUM

To: Associate
From: Partner
Date: —
Re: Engagement and nonengagement agreements

a.   Approximately 90 percent of our firm's practice is personal injury. For a variety of reasons, our firm declines many more cases than it accepts. At our last partnership meeting, we discussed the firm's ethical obligations and possible malpractice liability when it rejects cases. Some firms use "nonengagement" letters when they reject cases. Please advise whether the firm has any malpractice exposure when it turns down cases, and please draft a nonengagement letter for consideration by the firm. In connection with this assignment, see the *Togstad* case, a copy of which is attached.

b.   Attached also is a copy of the fee agreement that our firm is currently using in contingent fee matters. I would appreciate your reviewing the agreement and giving me your suggestions for revisions or additions.

Read Model Rules 1.2(a) and (c), 1.4, 1.5, 1.8, 1.15, 1.16, 2.1, and comments.

Togstad v. Vesely, Otto, Miller & Keefe

Supreme Court of Minnesota
291 N.W.2d 686 ('1980)

PER CURIAM.
This is an appeal by the defendants from a judgment of the Hennepin County District Court involving an action for legal malpractice. The jury found

---

46. *Compare* Chambers v. Kay, 56 P.3d 645 (Cal. 2002) (fee splitting agreement that did not comply with California Rule of Professional Conduct 2-200 was unenforceable), *and* Christensen v. Eggen, 577 N.W.2d 221 (Minn. 1998) (fee-splitting agreement that violated Rule 1.5(e) was unenforceable), *with* King v. Housel, 556 N.E.2d 501 (Ohio 1990) (attorney estopped from claiming that fee-splitting agreement was invalid).

that the defendant attorney Jerre Miller was negligent and that, as a direct result of such negligence, plaintiff John Togstad sustained damages in the amount of $610,500 and his wife, plaintiff Joan Togstad, in the amount of $39,000. Defendants (Miller and his law firm) appeal to this court from the denial of their motion for judgment notwithstanding the verdict or, alternatively, for a new trial. We affirm.

In August 1971, John Togstad began to experience severe headaches and on August 16, 1971, was admitted to Methodist Hospital where tests disclosed that the headaches were caused by a large aneurism on the left internal carotid artery. The attending physician, Dr. Paul Blake, a neurological surgeon, treated the problem by applying a Selverstone clamp to the left common carotid artery. The clamp was surgically implanted on August 27, 1971, in Togstad's neck to allow the gradual closure of the artery over a period of days.

. . . The greatest risk associated with this procedure is that the patient may become paralyzed if the brain does not receive an adequate flow of blood. . . .

In the early morning hours of August 29, 1971, a nurse observed that Togstad was unable to speak or move. At the time, the clamp was one-half (50%) closed. Upon discovering Togstad's condition, the nurse called a resident physician, who did not adjust the clamp. Dr. Blake was also immediately informed of Togstad's condition and arrived about an hour later, at which time he opened the clamp. Togstad is now severely paralyzed in his right arm and leg, and is unable to speak.

[Plaintiffs' medical expert testified that Togstad's paralysis and loss of speech was due to a lack of blood supply to his brain and that the negligence of Dr. Blake and the hospital prevented the clamp from being opened in time to avoid permanent brain damage.] Specifically, Dr. Woods claimed that Dr. Blake and the hospital were negligent for (1) failing to place the patient in the intensive care unit or to have a special nurse conduct certain neurological tests every half-hour; (2) failing to write adequate orders; (3) failing to open the clamp immediately upon discovering that the patient was unable to speak; and (4) the absence of personnel capable of opening the clamp. [Defendants' medical expert testified that Togstad's condition was caused by blood clots going to the brain through the carotid artery and that the blood clots did not result from the clamp procedure.]

About 14 months after her husband's hospitalization began, plaintiff Joan Togstad met with attorney Jerre Miller regarding her husband's condition. Neither she nor her husband was personally acquainted with Miller or his law firm prior to that time. John Togstad's former work supervisor, Ted Bucholz, made the appointment and accompanied Mrs. Togstad to Miller's office. Bucholz was present when Mrs. Togstad and Miller discussed the case.

Mrs. Togstad had become suspicious of the circumstances surrounding her husband's tragic condition due to the conduct and statements of the hospital nurses shortly after the paralysis occurred. . . .

Mrs. Togstad testified that she told Miller "everything that happened at the hospital," including the nurses' statements and conduct which had raised a question in her mind. She stated that she "believed" she had told Miller "about the procedure and what was undertaken, what was done, and what happened." She brought no records with her. Miller took notes and asked questions during the meeting, which lasted 45 minutes to an hour. At its conclusion, according to Mrs. Togstad, Miller said that "he did not think we had a legal case, however, he was going to discuss this with his partner." She understood that if Miller changed his mind after talking to his partner, he would call her. Mrs. Togstad "gave it" a few days and, since she did not hear from Miller, decided "that they had come to the conclusion that there wasn't a case." No fee arrangements were discussed, no medical authorizations were requested, nor was Mrs. Togstad billed for the interview.

Mrs. Togstad denied that Miller had told her his firm did not have expertise in the medical malpractice field, urged her to see another attorney, or related to her that the statute of limitations for medical malpractice actions was two years. She did not consult another attorney until one year after she talked to Miller. Mrs. Togstad indicated that she did not confer with another attorney earlier because of her reliance on Miller's "legal advice" that they "did not have a case." . . .

Miller's testimony was different in some respects from that of Mrs. Togstad. Like Mrs. Togstad, Miller testified that Mr. Bucholz arranged and was present at the meeting, which lasted about 45 minutes. According to Miller, Mrs. Togstad described the hospital incident, including the conduct of the nurses. He asked her questions, to which she responded. Miller testified that "(t)he only thing I told her (Mrs. Togstad) after we had pretty much finished the conversation was that there was nothing related in her factual circumstances that told me that she had a case that our firm would be interested in undertaking."

Miller also claimed he related to Mrs. Togstad "that because of the grievous nature of the injuries sustained by her husband, that this was only my opinion and she was encouraged to ask another attorney if she wished for another opinion" and "she ought to do so promptly." He testified that he informed Mrs. Togstad that his firm "was not engaged as experts" in the area of medical malpractice, and that they associated with the Charles Hvass firm in cases of that nature. Miller stated that at the end of the conference he told Mrs. Togstad that he would consult with Charles Hvass and if Hvass's opinion differed from his, Miller would so inform her. Miller recollected that he called Hvass a "couple days" later and discussed the case with him. It was Miller's impression that Hvass thought there was no liability for malpractice in the case. Consequently, Miller did not communicate with Mrs. Togstad further.

On cross-examination, Miller testified . . . "Certainly, she was seeking my opinion as an attorney in the sense of whether or not there was a case that the firm would be interested in undertaking."

[Plaintiffs' legal experts testified that when consulted about a medical malpractice case,] the "minimum" an attorney should do would be to request medical authorizations from the client, review the hospital records, and consult with an expert in the field. . . .

Hvass stated that he had no recollection of Miller's calling him in October 1972 relative to the Togstad matter. He testified that:

> . . . when a person comes in to me about a medical malpractice action, based upon what the individual has told me, I have to make a decision as to whether or not there probably is or probably is not, based upon that information, medical malpractice. And if, in my judgment, based upon what the client has told me, there is not medical malpractice, I will so inform the client.

Hvass stated, however, that he would never render a "categorical" opinion. In addition, Hvass acknowledged that if he were consulted for a "legal opinion" regarding medical malpractice and 14 months had expired since the incident in question, "ordinary care and diligence" would require him to inform the party of the two-year statute of limitations applicable to that type of action.

This case was submitted to the jury by way of a special verdict form. The jury found that Dr. Blake and the hospital were negligent and that Dr. Blake's negligence (but not the hospital's) was a direct cause of the injuries sustained by John Togstad; that there was an attorney-client contractual relationship between Mrs. Togstad and Miller; that Miller was negligent in rendering advice regarding the possible claims of Mr. and Mrs. Togstad; that, but for Miller's negligence, plaintiffs would have been successful in the prosecution of a legal action against Dr. Blake; and that neither Mr. nor Mrs. Togstad was negligent in pursuing their claims against Dr. Blake. The jury awarded damages to Mr. Togstad of $610,500 and to Mrs. Togstad of $39,000. . . .

In a legal malpractice action of the type involved here, four elements must be shown: (1) that an attorney-client relationship existed; (2) that defendant acted negligently or in breach of contract; (3) that such acts were the proximate cause of the plaintiffs' damages; (4) that but for defendant's conduct the plaintiffs would have been successful in the prosecution of their medical malpractice claim. See, Christy v. Saliterman, 288 Minn. 144, 179 N.W.2d 288 (1970).

[The court first discussed prior cases in which claims for legal malpractice were based either on tort or contract theories.] We believe it is unnecessary to decide whether a tort or contract theory is preferable for resolving the attorney-client relationship question raised by this appeal. . . . [W]e believe a jury could properly find that Mrs. Togstad sought and received legal advice from Miller under circumstances which made it reasonably foreseeable to Miller that Mrs. Togstad would be injured if the advice were negligently given. Thus, under either a tort or contract analysis, there is sufficient evidence in the record to support the existence of an attorney-client relationship.

Defendants argue that even if an attorney-client relationship was established the evidence fails to show that Miller acted negligently in assessing the merits of the Togstads' case. They appear to contend that, at most, Miller was guilty of an error in judgment which does not give rise to legal malpractice. Meagher v. Kavli, 256 Minn. 54, 97 N.W.2d 370 (1959). However, this case does not involve a mere error of judgment. The gist of plaintiffs' claim is that Miller failed to perform the minimal research that an ordinarily prudent attorney would do before rendering legal advice in a case of this nature. The record, through the testimony of [plaintiff's experts] contains sufficient evidence to support plaintiffs' position.

In a related contention, defendants assert that a new trial should be awarded on the ground that the trial court erred by refusing to instruct the jury that Miller's failure to inform Mrs. Togstad of the two-year statute of limitations for medical malpractice could not constitute negligence. . . .

The defect in defendants' reasoning is that there is adequate evidence supporting the claim that Miller was also negligent in failing to advise Mrs. Togstad of the two-year medical malpractice limitations period and thus the trial court acted properly in refusing to instruct the jury in the manner urged by defendants. One of defendants' expert witnesses, Charles Hvass, testified [that if he had been consulted about a medical malpractice action when 14 months had elapsed since the incident] "A Yes. I believe I would have advised someone of the two-year period of limitation, yes." . . .

There is also sufficient evidence in the record establishing that, but for Miller's negligence, plaintiffs would have been successful in prosecuting their medical malpractice claim. Dr. Woods, in no uncertain terms, concluded that Mr. Togstad's injuries were caused by the medical malpractice of Dr. Blake. Defendants' expert testimony to the contrary was obviously not believed by the jury. Thus, the jury reasonably found that had plaintiff's medical malpractice action been properly brought, plaintiffs would have recovered.

Based on the foregoing, we hold that the jury's findings are adequately supported by the record. Accordingly we uphold the trial court's denial of defendants' motion for judgment notwithstanding the jury verdict. [The court rejected defendants' other arguments, including a contention that the plaintiffs' damages should be reduced by the attorney fees they would have had to pay defendants if they had prosecuted the medical malpractice action. While recognizing that the courts were divided on the issue, the court concluded that "a reduction for lawyer fees is unwarranted because of the expense incurred by the plaintiff in bringing an action against the attorney."]

Notes and Questions

1. One of the essential elements of a cause of action for legal malpractice is the existence of an attorney-client relationship. As *Togstad* shows, however, lawyers have duties to prospective clients who consult them for advice even if the lawyer later does not accept the case. We will discuss other obligations to former prospective clients in connection with Problem 3-5. What should Mr. Miller have done to avoid malpractice liability?

2. *Togstad* contains a nice summary of many of the principal doctrines in legal malpractice cases: (a) the elements of the cause of action, (b) the requirement of expert testimony, (c) proof of the "case within a case" in order to establish causation in a legal malpractice case arising out of litigation, and (d) the defense of judgmental immunity. See generally Mallen & Smith, Legal Malpractice for a complete discussion of all aspects of malpractice liability.

CONTINGENT FEE AGREEMENT

_____ (Date)

Re: [Matter Description]
    C.A. No. _____

Dear _____

This letter is to acknowledge and thank you for your request that _____ represent you in the above-referenced matter. We are pleased to have this opportunity to assist you and want to acquaint you with our manner of handling your case. This letter of engagement is being sent to you pursuant to the _____ Rules of Professional Conduct.

Scope of Representation

Our representation of you is in connection with the above-captioned matter only, unless we otherwise agree in writing.

Firm Representation

While [NAME OF OTHER ATTORNEY(S) IN OFFICE WHO WILL BE ASSISTING] _____ and I will be primarily responsible for your case, other attorneys in the firm may, from time to time, be involved in the event we are out of town or otherwise unavailable. Should we be unavailable when you call, please feel free to refer any questions to our secretaries. If they are unavailable to answer any immediate concern, [NAME OF OTHER ATTORNEY(S) IN OFFICE WHO WILL BE ASSISTING] _____ or I will be in touch with you as quickly as possible.

Efforts on Your Behalf

We will strive to complete your work as expeditiously as possible and at a fair and reasonable cost to you. We do represent other clients, and there will be times when we will be giving your work priority over others. But the converse is also true, and we trust that you will understand if reasonable delays occur in completion of your work.

    (a) **Investigation.** We will investigate to the extent we deem appropriate the liability and damages aspects of this matter.

    (b) **Evaluation.** Once the available and appropriate information is assimilated, we will discuss with you our evaluation of your case. This will include an evaluation of the liability aspects of this matter, as well as that of damages. Evaluations are nothing more than our prediction, based on our experience, of what we believe a final award might be. Our evaluation of your case may change from time to time as new information becomes available, or new developments occur in the law.

(c)   **Negotiation.** Once we have discussed our evaluation of this matter with you, we will, with your permission, attempt to negotiate a settlement. We will keep you advised of all offers of settlement.

(d)   **Filing of Suit.** If we are unable to settle this matter amicably on your behalf, it will be necessary for us to file suit. At present, it is anticipated that suit will be filed in _____ court. From our experience, it is likely to take approximately _____ months before this matter will be ready for trial.

(e)   **Status.** We will keep you advised of the status of this matter and significant developments as they occur. We ask that you keep us advised of any changes or developments of which you become aware that affect this matter or our representation of you. This would include, but not be limited to, any changes in your condition, any information affecting either liability or damages, changes of address, etc. If, at any time, you have any questions, we invite you to call [NAME OF OTHER ATTORNEY(S) IN OFFICE WHO WILL BE ASSISTING]_____ or me.

(f)   **Discovery.** Our Rules of Civil Procedure provide for a procedure called "discovery." This is a process by which each side can discover the facts and claims relied upon by the other in order to expedite the settlement process or to narrow the issues to be tried. Discovery takes many forms, and may include interrogatories, requests for production, and depositions. The other side may request that your deposition be taken. In a deposition, the other side's attorney will ask you questions under oath before a court reporter. This is typically done in one of the attorney's offices. Should the other side ask to take your deposition, we will of course let you know and discuss this with you.

Billing Basis

Attorney time for handling this matter will be charged on a contingent fee basis. Our fee will be _____ percent of any recovery obtained before trial, and _____ percent of any recovery obtained after trial of the case begins. In addition to the firm's percentage of any recovery, you will be responsible for all costs such as filing fees, depositions, travel expenses, retention of experts, court costs, witness fees, etc. For example, if your case were settled for $10,000 prior to trial, our fee would be $2,500 plus any costs incurred. On the other hand, if the case were tried and we recovered $10,000, our fee would be $3,333 plus any costs and expenses incurred. If the case is tried and we receive nothing, you will not have to pay attorney fees, but you will still be responsible for paying costs.

Billing

Since we are handling this case on a contingent fee basis, we will bill you for any fees only at the end of the case. The firm, in its discretion, may advance costs associated with this matter. Though typically we will not bill you for these advances until the end of the case, we retain the right to submit an interim bill for costs should we determine it is necessary. Once the case is ended, we will prepare a bill outlining your recovery, our attorney's fees, any costs you are required to reimburse the firm, and any other expenses deducted from your recovery. You will be provided a copy of this bill.

Appeal

Should the case be tried and lost, or should any recovery not meet our and your expectations, an appeal may be available if the court committed some error during the course of the trial. Should an adverse verdict occur, we will evaluate the merits of an appeal and advise you of our evaluation. Under the terms of this agreement, we are not required to pursue an appeal on your behalf, but will do so upon mutual agreement.

Termination

You shall at all times have the right to terminate our services upon written notice to that effect. Should you terminate our representation of you, the fee and cost arrangements discussed above will continue in effect. We shall, subject to the Rules of Professional Conduct and to applicable court requirements with respect to withdrawal, have the right to terminate our services upon reasonable written notice to you. Should we terminate our services, you will still be responsible for costs incurred in your behalf, but not for any fees.

Very truly yours,

For the firm

I AGREE TO THE TERMS OF REPRESENTATION
AND ENGAGEMENT AS OUTLINED ABOVE.

[IF CLIENT A CORPORATION,
CORPORATE NAME HERE]

_____
[Name of Individual Signing]

Scope of representation

Client-lawyer agreements are contracts, subject to the rules of contract law, but are also governed by a number of special rules that apply because of the fiduciary relationship between attorney and client.[47] The agreement between the client and the lawyer determines the matters in which the lawyer represents the client. Courts are likely, however, to resolve any ambiguities and uncertainties in the agreement against the lawyer;[48] thus, lawyers must define clearly the matters for which they are agreeing to represent their clients. For example, if a lawyer agrees to represent a client in "your suit," a court is likely to conclude that the lawyer has agreed to represent the client in any appeal arising from the action.[49] Even if the agreement between the client and the lawyer provided that the lawyer agreed to represent the client only at trial, the lawyer would still be required to move to withdraw from the case after trial and to take reasonable steps to protect the client's right to appeal if the lawyer did not plan to handle the appeal.[50]

When a client comes to a lawyer with a legal problem, the problem may involve several distinct legal matters. Consider a case in which a worker is seriously injured on the job from a defective machine and then dies in the hospital as a result of medical malpractice. This one incident involves at least four different legal matters: a products liability case against the manufacturer of the defective machine, a worker's compensation claim, a medical malpractice claim against the doctors and hospital, and administration of the decedent's estate. The lawyer should reach a clear understanding with the client regarding the matters that the firm is handling, and any matters for which the client will not be retaining the firm's services. Lawyers who fail to do so face a risk of malpractice liability.[51]

While it is clearly permissible for the client and lawyer to define the matters in which the attorney is undertaking representation, may they agree to limit the extent of the lawyer's duties in handling a matter? A lawyer may not enter into an agreement with the client prospectively limiting the lawyer's liability for malpractice. Model Rule 1.8(h).[52] Such an agreement undermines the

---

47. Restatement (Third) of the Law Governing Lawyers §18, cmt. c. See Joseph M. Perillo, The Law of Lawyers' Contracts Is Different, 67 Fordham L. Rev. 443 (1998). The ABA has published recommended forms for law firms dealing with engagement and termination of representation. See ABA Section of Business Law, Documenting the Attorney-Client Relationship: Law Firm Policies on Engagement, Termination, and Declination (1999).

48. Restatement (Third) of the Law Governing Lawyers §18(2) (agreement should be construed from the standpoint of a reasonable person in the client's circumstances).

49. Id. §18, cmt. h and illus. 4.

50. See id. §33.

51. See Meighan v. Shore, 40 Cal. Rptr. 2d 744 (Ct. App. 1995, review denied) (lawyer who represents husband in medical malpractice action has duty to inform wife of possible loss of consortium claim); Keef v. Widuch, 747 N.E.2d 992 (Ill. Ct. App. 2001, review denied) (client states cause of action for malpractice against worker's compensation attorneys for failure to advise about possible third-party claims and applicable statute of limitations even though engagement agreement limited representation to worker's compensation matters).

52. The Model Rule qualifies the prohibition by stating "unless the client is independently represented in making the agreement." The Restatement (Third) of the Law Governing Lawyers, however, contains an absolute prohibition on such agreements. See §54.

lawyer's duty to represent the client competently and diligently; moreover, clients may not have sufficient information to evaluate the reasonableness of such a disclaimer.[53] Thus, it would be unethical and contractually unenforceable for an engagement agreement to disclaim liability for malpractice. It appears that a provision in an engagement agreement to submit fee disputes and malpractice claims to arbitration will not be treated as violating Model Rule 1.8(h),[54] although such arbitration provisions may be legally unenforceable depending on the jurisdiction.[55]

Suppose, however, that the agreement does not go this far. For example, may the lawyer and client agree that the lawyer will "spend no more than five hours on this matter"? On one hand, agreements that limit the scope of a lawyer's duties can be beneficial to clients because they allow clients to obtain the degree of representation that they desire. Clients, like buyers of other goods and services, should be entitled to purchase different degrees of quality. On the other hand, some clients, particularly unsophisticated ones, may not understand the level of service that they are purchasing. The 2002 revision of the Model Rules blesses limited engagement agreements with some qualifications. Model Rules 1.2(c) states: "A lawyer may limit the scope of the representation if the limitation is reasonable under the circumstances and the client gives informed consent." Comment 7 states that the limitation of time would not be reasonable if it were not sufficient to allow the lawyer to provide advice on which the client could rely. In addition, a limited engagement does not exempt lawyers from the duty of competence, although the limitation is a factor in deciding whether the duty has been met. The Restatement is similar, although the comments elaborate on the reasonableness requirement:

> When the client is sophisticated in such waivers, informed consent ordinarily permits the inference that the waiver is reasonable. For other clients, the requirement is met if, in addition to informed consent, the benefits supposedly obtained

---

53. Id. cmt. *b.*

54. In Formal Opinion #02-425 the ABA Committee on Ethics and Professional Responsibility advised that it was ethically permissible for lawyers to enter into engagement agreements in which clients agreed to binding arbitration of fee disputes and malpractice claims under the following conditions: (1) the client has been fully apprised of the advantages and disadvantages of arbitration and has been given sufficient information to permit her to make an informed decision about whether to agree to the inclusion of the arbitration provision in the retainer agreement, and (2) the arbitration provision does not insulate the lawyer from liability or limit the liability to which she would otherwise be exposed under common and/or statutory law. The committee also ruled that such agreements do not amount to a prospective agreement limiting the lawyer's liability under Rule 1.8(h).

55. *Compare* Henry v. Gonzalez, 18 S.W.3d 684 (Tex. Civ. App. 2000) (upholding agreement to arbitrate malpractice claims), *with* Alternative Sys., Inc. v. Carey, 79 Cal. Rptr. 2d 567 (Ct. App. 1998) (engagement agreement requiring arbitration of fee disputes was unenforceable because inconsistent with statutory system for mandatory fee arbitration, which provided clients with greater protections than under agreement). The Restatement supports arbitration of fee disputes and malpractice claims. See Restatement (Third) of the Law Governing Lawyers §54, cmt. *b.*

by the waiver—typically, a reduced legal fee or the ability to retain a particularly able lawyer—could reasonably be considered to outweigh the potential risk posed by the limitation.[56]

In Lerner v. Laufer,[57] the appellate division of the New Jersey Superior Court affirmed summary judgment for the attorney in a legal malpractice case. The husband and wife had participated in a mediation, which produced a proposed property settlement agreement. The mediator recommended that the parties have the agreement reviewed by an attorney and suggested several lawyers, including the defendant. The defendant agreed to review the agreement. His engagement letter stated that he had been employed to review the agreement, that he had not conducted any discovery or obtained any factual information, and that he was therefore not able to render an opinion on the fairness of the agreement. The wife later claimed the lawyer committed malpractice by not investigating the reasonableness of the agreement. The court found that the lawyer did not breach the standard of care expected of attorneys because he had properly limited the scope of his representation pursuant to Rule 1.2(c).

Allocation of authority between lawyer and client

Issues of authority between attorney and client can arise in two ways. First, as between lawyer and client, has the attorney acted with authority? Second, is the client bound to a third party by virtue of an agreement or action taken by the lawyer, even if the lawyer acted without authority?[58]

As to the allocation of authority between client and lawyer, traditionally many attorneys viewed themselves as experts entrusted to handle their clients' matters as they thought to be in the best interest of the client.[59] The Model Rules and the Restatement of the Law Governing Lawyers reject this paternalistic view of the client-lawyer relationship because it suffers from fundamental defects. The expert model subordinates the actual client to the lawyer's view of the client's interests. In addition, this approach ignores the fact that the full participation of clients can improve the quality of the lawyer's representation because clients have information and perspectives that lawyers lack. On the other hand, the Restatement and the Model Rules do not treat lawyers as mere servants of their clients because the servant model ignores the interests of lawyers as professionals and the broader social implications of the lawyer's role. Instead,

---

56. Restatement (Third) of the Law Governing Lawyers §19, cmt. *c*.

57. 819 A.2d 471 (N.J. Super. App. Div. 2003).

58. *Compare* Restatement (Third) of the Law Governing Lawyers ch. 2, topic 3 (Authority to Make Decisions) *and* topic 4 (Lawyer's Authority to Act for Client).

59. See Douglas E. Rosenthal, Lawyer and Client: Who's in Charge? 7 (1974).

the Model Rules and the Restatement attempt to define a cooperative relation-ship.[60]

Under the cooperative model, the client sets the overall objectives of representation and the attorney chooses the means for achieving those goals. Thus, Model Rule 1.2(a) states that, subject to certain limitations, "a lawyer shall abide by a client's decisions concerning the objectives of representation and, as required by Rule 1.4, shall consult with the client as to the means by which they are to be pursued."[61]

Model Rule 1.2(a) identifies the following matters as decisions for the client to make: whether to settle a matter; in criminal cases, the plea to be entered, whether to waive jury trial, and whether the client will testify.[62] While the Model Rules do not mention the determination whether to appeal as a decision for the client to make, most other authorities do so.[63]

For years some scholars have been arguing that the rules of ethics do not sufficiently recognize the autonomy of clients and that the principle of "in-formed consent," which governs the relationship between doctor and patient, should be applied to lawyers and clients.[64] The 2002 revision of the Model Rules appears to adopt this approach. The rules replace the concept of consulta-tion with the client with "informed consent." See Model Rule 1.0(e) and cmt. 6. In addition, Rule 1.4, which deals with communication with a client, provides that a lawyer must present the client with sufficient information to enable the client to give informed consent when required by the rules. See Model Rule 1.4, cmt. 2. The implications of the new requirement of informed consent are unclear. In the medical profession, it is standard procedure to have video tapes and forms explaining to patients the benefits and risks of various procedures. Will lawyers be required to develop such tools? If they do not, do they face ethical and malpractice risks?

Although clients are entitled to make decisions regarding the objectives of representation, lawyers have a duty to counsel their clients regarding these matters. See Model Rule 2.1.[65] The role of counselor gives lawyers broad authority to advise their clients on both legal and nonlegal considerations involved in a proposed course of action. Model Rule 2.1 states that in providing

---

60. See Restatement (Third) of the Law Governing Lawyers ch. 2, topic 3, Introduc-tory note.

61. See Restatement (Third) of the Law Governing Lawyers §§22-23.

62. See also id. §22.

63. See id. §22(1).

64. Susan R. Martyn, Informed Consent in the Practice of Law, 48 Geo. Wash. L. Rev. 307 (1980); Mark Spiegel, Lawyering and Client Decisionmaking: Informed Consent and the Legal Profession, 128 U. Pa. L. Rev. 41 (1979). But see Judith L. Maute, Allocation of Decisionmaking Authority Under the Model Rules of Professional Conduct, 17 U.C. Davis L. Rev. 1049 (1984) (arguing that joint venture framework adopted by Model Rules is flexible enough to accommodate attorney, client, and social interests). For an analysis of the ways in which rules of ethics limit client autonomy and an argument that drafters should be more rigorous in identifying the justifications for such limits, see Fred C. Zacha-rias, Limits on Client Autonomy in Legal Ethics Regulation, 81 B.U. L. Rev. 199 (2001).

65. See Restatement (Third) of the Law Governing Lawyers §20(3).

advice, "a lawyer may refer not only to law but to other considerations such as moral, economic, social and political factors, that may be relevant to the client's situation."[66] The client's right to make decisions regarding the objectives of representation does not mean, however, that lawyers must follow every decision that clients make. In representing clients lawyers may not counsel or assist them to engage in conduct that the lawyer knows to be criminal, fraudulent, or in violation of a court order; lawyers who do so face the possibility of professional discipline[67] and civil liability either to the client or to third persons.[68] A client may authorize a lawyer to make a decision that the client is entitled to make, such as whether to settle a case, unless the law requires the decision to be made personally by the client, for example, pleading guilty in a criminal case.[69]

A vast number of decisions in a case are strategic or tactical rather than relating to the objectives of representation. What causes of action should be included in the complaint? How many expert witnesses should the client retain? What discovery should be done? What witnesses will be called to testify at trial? Should counsel object to a question at trial? Lawyers have broad authority to make strategic and tactical decisions in connection with the representation to advance their clients' interests.[70] The lawyer's authority to make these decisions can be limited in several ways. Clients and lawyers are generally free to allocate the authority to make strategic and tactical decisions by contract.[71] The lawyer's engagement agreement could, for example, specify that the lawyer may not employ an expert witness without the client's approval, or it could authorize the lawyer to engage in such discovery as the lawyer believes necessary, subject to a budget. Further, lawyers are required to keep their clients reasonably informed about the client's matter.[72] Clients may give lawyers instructions during the course of representation regarding strategic and tactical decisions, and lawyers are generally bound to follow these instructions, unless the client directs the lawyer to act unethically or illegally.[73] Thus, a client could instruct the lawyer that the client does not want to go to the expense of taking the deposition of an expert witness. Some tactical matters require immediate action—for example, the decision whether to object to a question at trial—so that consultation with the client is impractical. In these situations, lawyers have the authority to make the decision without client consultation.[74]

Suppose a lawyer believes that the client's instructions are "tying my

66. See also id. §94(3).
67. See Model Rule 1.2(d); Restatement (Third) of the Law Governing Lawyers §94(2).
68. See Restatement (Third) of the Law Governing Lawyers §94(1).
69. Id. §22(1), (2).
70. See Model Rule 1.2(a); Restatement (Third) of the Law Governing Lawyers §21(3) and cmt. *e*.
71. Restatement (Third) of the Law Governing Lawyers §21(1) and cmt. *c*.
72. See Model Rule 1.4(a); Restatement (Third) of the Law Governing Lawyers §20(1).
73. Restatement (Third) of the Law Governing Lawyers §21(2), cmt. *d* and §23.
74. See id. §21, cmt. *e* and §23, cmt. *d*.

hands" so that the lawyer cannot effectively carry out the representation? The lawyer may counsel the client about the wisdom of the client's decision. See Model Rule 2.1. If the issue involves a litigation expense that the client is unwilling to incur, with client consent the lawyer could advance the expense. See Model Rule 1.8(e). Finally, the lawyer could move to withdraw from the matter if the client's instructions make it unreasonably difficult for the lawyer to carry out the representation.[75]

The principles discussed above govern allocation of authority between lawyer and client. Under what circumstances is a client legally bound to a third person as a result of the lawyer's actions on behalf of the client? When a lawyer proceeds with express authority, the lawyer's action binds the client.[76] In addition, agency law provides that the actions of an agent bind the principal when the agent acts with implied or apparent authority, when the principal ratifies the agent's conduct, or when the principal is estopped from denying the agent's authority. For example, normally an attorney would have apparent authority to agree to a trial date.[77]

Settlement of a lawsuit involves both authority between lawyer and client and effect on third parties. The Model Rules provide that a client has the prerogative to decide whether to settle a case. Model Rule 1.2(a). The client's right to decide whether to accept a settlement imposes a duty on a lawyer to convey information to the client about a settlement offer. See Model Rule 1.4, cmt. 2. Recall that the rights of defendants in criminal cases are somewhat broader. See Model Rule 1.2(a) and Problem 2-6.

Suppose the plaintiff authorizes a lawyer to settle a case for any amount in excess of $200,000. The client is bound if the lawyer agrees to such a settlement.[78] If the client then refuses to proceed with the settlement, the opposing party could take legal steps to enforce the settlement (for example, a motion to the tribunal before which the case is pending to compel settlement). Suppose a lawyer agrees to a settlement that the client has *not* authorized. Normally, an attorney does not have apparent authority to settle a case on behalf of a client.[79] Thus the client is not bound by the settlement.[80] A lawyer

---

75. See Model Rule 1.16(b), which allows a lawyer to withdraw if the client decides on a course of action "with which the lawyer has a fundamental disagreement" or if "good cause" exists for withdrawal. See also Restatement (Third) of the Law Governing Lawyers §32(3).

76. Restatement (Third) of the Law Governing Lawyers §26 and cmt. *d*.

77. See id. §§26, 27, and illus. 1.

78. See Pohl v. United Airlines, Inc., 213 F.3d 336 (7th Cir. 2000) (client who gave attorney actual authority to settle is bound, even though client subjectively believed he could back out of settlement until he signed agreement).

79. Restatement (Third) of the Law Governing Lawyers §27, cmt. *d*. But see Koval v. Simon Telelect, Inc., 693 N.E.2d 1299 (Ind. 1998) (lawyers generally do not have inherent authority to settle, but exception for "in court" actions, including settlements pursuant to rules for alternative dispute resolution).

80. For an argument that courts should return to traditional agency principles to determine the enforceability of settlements, see Grace M. Giesel, Enforcement of Settlement Contracts: The Problem of the Attorney Agent, 12 Geo. J. Legal Ethics 543 (1999).

who acts without authority is subject to disciplinary action, legal liability to the client, and legal liability to third persons harmed by the lawyer's unauthorized action.[81]

Termination of the client-lawyer relationship: discharge and withdrawal

Almost all jurisdictions follow the rule that a client has the absolute right to discharge an attorney, regardless of cause. Courts reason that the relationship of client and attorney is highly personal and that clients should not be limited in their right to select counsel of their choice.[82] Recognition that the client has the right to discharge an attorney at any time for any reason, however, creates a potential problem of unfairness to the attorney. How should an attorney be compensated when the client has exercised the right to discharge the attorney?

Courts typically allow discharged attorneys to recover the reasonable value of their services, i.e., on a quantum meruit basis.[83] This method of compensation protects the client's right to discharge an attorney and protects the attorney's right to compensation for services rendered. Extreme cases could justify deviation from the quantum meruit rule. For example, if the client discharged the attorney because of the attorney's serious misconduct, a court might find

81. See Restatement (Third) of the Law Governing Lawyers §30(3).

82. See Restatement (Third) of the Law Governing Lawyers §32(1) and cmt. b. Compare Cincinnati Bar Assn. v. Shultz, 643 N.E.2d 1139 (Ohio 1994) (lawyer disciplined for including in her contingent fee agreement provision for payment of hourly fees if client discharged her firm because provision was inconsistent with shared risk basis of contingent fee agreements), with Cohen v. Radio-Elecs. Officers Union, Dist. 3, NMEBA, 679 A.2d 1188 (N.J. 1996) (retainer agreement may not limit client's right to discharge lawyer but agreement may provide for compensation to attorney when sophisticated client exercises right; six months' notice of termination held to be unreasonable, but court finds one month's notice reasonable).

83. See generally George L. Blum, Annotation, Limitation to Quantum Meruit Recovery, Where Attorney Employed Under Contingent-Fee Contract Is Discharged Without Cause, 56 A.L.R.5th 1 (1998). Some of the recent cases on the rights of discharged lawyers include the following: Greer, Klosik & Daugherty v. Yetman, 496 S.E.2d 693 (Ga. 1998) (firm entitled to quantum meruit not amount of contingent fee when client discharged firm after favorable jury verdict while case on appeal); Reynolds v. Polen, 564 N.W.2d 467 (Mich. Ct. App. 1997) (discharged contingent-fee firm entitled to be compensated on quantum meruit basis when firm acted unreasonably, but not unethically or against public policy, by being dilatory in providing notice of conflict of trial date). Whether the discharged attorney may recover from successor counsel rather than the client is uncertain. Compare Cohen v. Grainger, Tesoriero & Bell, 622 N.E.2d 288 (N.Y. 1993) (discharged lawyer has statutory lien for unpaid fee; as against client, lawyer may recover on quantum meruit basis; as against successor attorney, lawyer may elect to receive either quantum meruit immediately or percentage based on proportionate share of work performed on entire case when case finally concluded), with Howard & Bowie, P.A. v. Collins, 759 A.2d 707 (Maine 2000) (successor counsel not liable to discharged firm on quantum meruit because no unjust enrichment).

that fee forfeiture was appropriate.[84] At the other extreme, if the client discharged an attorney shortly before concluding a settlement, to deprive the attorney of a contingent fee that was all but earned, a court might allow the attorney to receive the full contractual amount.[85] In this situation, the client typically has acted in bad faith to deprive the lawyer of her fee. Moreover, allowing recovery at the full contractual rate does not burden the client's right to select counsel because the matter has been completed.[86]

In deciding the amount of quantum meruit recovery, courts will not necessarily determine the amount of recovery mechanically, based simply on the number of hours that the attorney worked on the case. Instead, courts will probably examine a variety of factors, including the number of hours worked, the lawyer's hourly rate, the difficulty of the case, the stage of the case at which the lawyer was discharged, and the benefits received by the client.[87] A number of courts limit the amount of quantum meruit recovery to the ratable portion of the contract that has been performed (not always an easy task) on the theory that a discharged attorney should not receive a benefit in excess of the contract amount. In addition, allowing recovery in excess of the contract amount would burden the client's right to select new counsel. The Restatement of the Law Governing Lawyers adopts the view that a discharged attorney is entitled to recover quantum meruit, limited by the ratable portion of the contract that has been performed.[88] When awarding quantum meruit compensation under a contingent fee contract, it seems appropriate to defer the lawyer's right to recover in quantum meruit until the client receives an award, otherwise the client's right to discharge the attorney would be burdened by the immediate obligation to pay the attorney quantum meruit compensation.[89]

The rules on withdrawal by attorneys are divided into two categories: mandatory and permissive withdrawal. Under Model Rule 1.16(a), a lawyer must withdraw from representation if the representation will result in a violation

---

84. See White v. McBride, 937 S.W.2d 796 (Tenn. 1996) (charging of excessive contingent fee in probate case was improper and justifies forfeiture of all compensation, including quantum meruit) and Restatement (Third) of the Law Governing Lawyers §37.

85. See Wegner v. Arnold, 713 N.E.2d 247 (Ill. App. Ct. 1999, *appeal denied*) (where attorney is fired immediately before settlement, factors involved in determining reasonable fee would justify awarding entire contract fee as reasonable value of services rendered); Taylor v. Shigaki, 930 P.2d 340 (Wash. Ct. App.), *review denied*, 940 P.2d 654 (Wash. 1997) (under doctrine of substantial performance lawyer entitled to full contingent fee when client discharged lawyer nine days before trial date, after substantial offer of settlement had been made, and six hours before client met with claims adjuster to negotiate final settlement); Restatement (Third) of the Law Governing Lawyers §40(2).

86. See Restatement (Third) of the Law Governing Lawyers §40(2) and cmt. *c.*

87. See Searcy, Denney, Scarola, Barnhart & Shipley, P. A. v. Poletz, 652 So. 2d 366 (Fla. 1995) (quantum meruit compensation to discharged contingent-fee attorney measured by variety of factors rather than simply "lodestar," i.e. hourly rate, amount).

88. Restatement (Third) of the Law Governing Lawyers §40(1).

89. See Rosenberg v. Levin, 409 So. 2d 1016 (Fla. 1982). But see In re Estate of Callahan, 578 N.E.2d 985 (Ill. 1991) (allowing attorney's quantum meruit claim immediately).

of the Rules of Conduct (for example, if the lawyer faces a conflict of interest or if the client demands that the lawyer engage in illegal conduct). In addition, a lawyer must withdraw if the client discharges the lawyer or if the lawyer's physical or mental condition impairs the lawyer's ability to represent the client.[90]

Model Rule 1.16(b) deals with permissive withdrawal. The rule specifies seven situations in which a lawyer is allowed to withdraw. Several of the grounds for withdrawal involve some form of misconduct, breach of contract, or noncooperation by the client. See Model Rule 1.16(b)(2), (3), and (5). Other grounds, however, are based on the lawyer's interests, either personal or financial. See Model Rule 1.16(b)(1), (4), (6), and (7).[91]

A number of interpretive issues arise under the permissive withdrawal rules. When the client is abusing the professional relationship, by demanding that the lawyer engage in illegal or unethical conduct, the lawyer's duty or right to withdraw is clear. May a lawyer withdraw if the client's conduct does not rise to this level? Under Rule 1.16(b)(4), a lawyer may withdraw if the client insists on conduct that the lawyer considers to be "repugnant or with which the lawyer has a fundamental disagreement."[92] While the language is quite broad, it appears that the intent of the rule is more limited. The Reporter's note states that withdrawal is allowed "when the disagreement over objectives or means is so fundamental that the lawyer's autonomy is seriously threatened." Similarly, the Restatement takes the view that the right to withdraw on this ground is limited to cases in which the client is demanding that the lawyer engage in conduct that no reasonable lawyer should be required to do.[93]

Thus, if the lawyer simply disagrees with the client's decision, even if the disagreement is strongly held, ground for withdrawal does not exist. For example, suppose a lawyer who represents a client in a personal injury action receives an offer to settle the case that the lawyer believes is reasonable but that the client is unwilling to accept. Since the client retains the right to accept or reject settlement offers, a lawyer would not be justified in withdrawing if the client refused to accept the lawyer's recommendation regarding the settlement offer.[94] Some courts have held that lawyers who withdraw under such circumstances forfeit their right to receive any fee.[95]

90. See also Restatement (Third) of the Law Governing Lawyers §32(2).

91. Restatement (Third) of the Law Governing Lawyers §32(3) is similar to Model Rule 1.16(b), but somewhat more restrictive of permissive withdrawal. See 1 Hazard & Hodes, The Law of Lawyering §20.8.

92. The Restatement (Third) of the Law Governing Lawyers §32(3)(f) continues to use the former formulation of "repugnant or imprudent."

93. Id. §32, cmt. j.

94. See id. (client's refusal to accept settlement is imprudent "only when no reasonable person in the client's position, having regard for the hazards of litigation, would have declined the settlement"); 1 Hazard & Hodes, The Law of Lawyering illus. 20-6.

95. See Augustson v. Linea Aerea Nacional-Chile, S.A., 76 F.3d 658 (5th Cir. 1996) (when law firm withdraws from case in dispute with client over settlement, firm is not entitled to any fee). But see Kannewurf v. Johns, 632 N.E.2d 711 (Ill. App. Ct. 1994) (lawyer who withdrew over fundamental disagreement about settlement of case entitled to quantum meruit compensation).

Rule 1.16(b)(5) allows a lawyer to withdraw if "the client fails substantially to fulfill an obligation to the lawyer regarding the lawyer's services and has been given reasonable warning that the lawyer will withdraw unless the obligation is fulfilled." If the client fails to pay fees or expenses that the client is contractually obligated to pay, the lawyer may withdraw after giving the client reasonable warning of the lawyer's intent to do so. A court may deny a motion to withdraw on this ground if the lawyer engages in strategic behavior, i.e., times the motion to attempt to coerce payment, or if severe prejudice to third parties would occur.[96]

In most contingent fee cases, clients are not obligated to pay fees except out of the proceeds of a judgment or settlement. In addition, in contingent fee matters lawyers often advance or pay expenses on their clients' behalf. Thus, Rule 1.16(b)(5) rarely applies in contingency fee matters. Sometimes cases turn out to be less valuable or more expensive than the attorney anticipated when the litigation began. May an attorney withdraw due to extreme financial hardship? The Model Rules allow an attorney to withdraw in such a situation provided court approval is obtained, Rule 1.16(b)(6); but the Restatement of the Law Governing Lawyers takes the position that financial hardship alone is not sufficient to justify withdrawal, although financial hardship is a factor that along with other factors can establish good cause for withdrawal.[97] Some courts have allowed lawyers to withdraw if continued representation would constitute an extreme financial hardship to the lawyer.[98] If the attorney voluntarily withdraws without cause, however, the lawyer may forfeit all right to compensation.[99]

Both the Model Rules and the Restatement of the Law Governing Lawyers allow a lawyer to withdraw if withdrawal can be accomplished without material adverse effect on the interests of the client.[100] The most controversial application of this rule deals with situations in which a law firm attempts to withdraw from representing one client in order to take on a more favored client (often characterized as attempting to drop a client like a "hot potato").[101] For example, suppose a law firm represents corporate client *A* in a minor litigation matter that is in its early stages. Corporation *B* approaches the law firm to seek

96. Fidelity National Title Insurance Co. of New York v. Intercounty National Title Insurance Co., 310 F.3d 537 (7th Cir. 2002) (trial judge abused discretion in denying law firm's motion to withdraw when client had stopped paying bills, outstanding fees were substantial, law firm was not engaging in strategic behavior or otherwise trying to put client "over a barrel," and prejudice to third parties was not present).

97. Restatement (Third) of the Law Governing Lawyers §32, cmt. *m*.

98. *Compare* Haines v. Liggett Group, Inc., 814 F. Supp. 414 (D.N.J. 1993) (withdrawal denied; court notes absence of provision in contingent-fee agreement allowing for withdrawal in event of financial hardship), *with* Smith v. R. J. Reynolds Tobacco Co., 630 A.2d 820 (N.J. Super. Ct. App. Div. 1993) (withdrawal for financial hardship permissible but case remanded for determination of probable recovery and anticipated litigation costs).

99. See Faro v. Romani, 641 So. 2d 69 (Fla. 1994); Ryan v. State, 51 P.3d 175 (Wash. Ct. App. 2002).

100. See Model Rule 1.16(b)(1); Restatement (Third) of the Law Governing Lawyers §32(3)(a).

101. See 1 Hazard & Hodes, The Law of Lawyering §20.10, at 24.

representation against client *A* in a major matter that is unrelated to the matter the firm is handling for client *A*. The firm seeks client *A*'s consent to undertake the representation, but client *A* refuses to consent. May the firm withdraw from representation of client *A* in order to take on the more lucrative representation of Corporation *B*, provided substitute counsel can be retained to represent *A* without material adverse effect on *A*? The Model Rules and comments are silent on the application of the hot potato doctrine. The Restatement, however, indicates that a lawyer breaches the duty of loyalty to a client by attempting to withdraw from representing a client in order to take on a more favored client.[102] Professors Hazard and Hodes disagree. In their view lawyers should be allowed to withdraw from representation of an existing client to take on a more favored client (or even for personal reasons, such as too much work), provided the withdrawal can be accomplished without material harm to the client's interests.[103]

The Restatement approach rather than the Hazard and Hodes view seems correct. First, allowing a law firm to withdraw from representing one client in order to take on a more lucrative client almost certainly violates reasonable client expectations. Most clients surely believe that when a lawyer has agreed to represent them, the lawyer cannot withdraw from representation for the lawyer's own financial interest, even if the client would not be harmed. Second, it is unlikely that many cases would arise in which a lawyer could withdraw because of lack of material adverse effect. In almost any case that has gone beyond its earliest stages, withdrawal would result in material harm to the client. Further, a client can reasonably argue that it has a material interest in retaining the law firm that it originally chose, particularly if the firm will be bringing suit against the client. Finally, the rule does not serve any substantial lawyer interest. Lawyers can avoid the problem of undertaking representation during early stages by using *investigation agreements,* in which the lawyer agrees to investigate the matter before undertaking representation.

When a matter is pending before a tribunal, a lawyer must obtain court approval to withdraw from representation, even if the withdrawal is mandatory rather than permissive. Model Rule 1.16(c). In terminating representation an attorney must take reasonable steps to protect the client's interest from prejudice.[104] Model Rule 1.16(d). For example, a lawyer should be careful to protect client confidences when moving to withdraw.[105] Thus, if the time for filing an appeal is about to expire, an attorney whose representation has termi-

---

102. Restatement (Third) of the Law Governing Lawyers §132, cmt. *c.*

103. 1 Hazard & Hodes, The Law of Lawyering §20.10. Hazard and Hodes draw a distinction between withdrawal to take on a new client and withdrawal to be able to continue to represent a current client. They would allow the former but not the latter. Id. at 24.

104. Restatement (Third) of the Law Governing Lawyers §33.

105. See In re Gonzalez, 773 A.2d 1026 (D.C. 2001) (lawyer reprimanded for revealing confidential information to support motion to withdraw; lawyer should redact damaging information and reveal remainder in camera); Restatement (Third) of the Law Governing Lawyers §32, cmt. *d.*

nated should nonetheless file notice of the appeal to protect the client's interest.[106] The lawyer could then file a motion with the appellate court to withdraw from representation.

Liens

Model Rule 1.8(i) prohibits lawyers from acquiring a proprietary interest in the cause of action or subject of litigation except for reasonable contingent fees in civil cases and "a lien authorized by law to secure the lawyer's fee or expenses."[107] Courts have generally recognized two types of lawyers' liens. The *retaining lien* is the attorney's right to retain client papers or other valuable client property in the lawyer's possession as security for any unpaid amount the client owes the lawyer.[108] The lien arises as a matter of law rather than pursuant to contract and is based on equitable principles: The attorney has rendered substantial services or advanced expenses on the client's behalf and should be entitled to compensation. The lien is purely possessory; the lawyer may not sell the client's property to satisfy the client's debt to the lawyer. Because of the coercive aspects of the lien, some jurisdictions no longer recognize it, and others have cautioned lawyers against exercising the lien when the client would be prejudiced. For example, In re White was a disciplinary proceeding in which the South Carolina Supreme Court held that the exercise of a retaining lien was not per se unethical. The court, however, warned lawyers to be careful in asserting such liens and outlined factors for lawyers to weigh in making that decision.[109]

When a lawyer has been discharged, the lawyer may consider asserting a retaining lien until the lawyer has been paid. As discussed above, lawyers must be cautious in asserting such a lien to avoid prejudice to the clients. As a condition for releasing the file, some lawyers have demanded that clients sign a release of liability. Such releases are generally unethical and unenforceable, unless the client is independently represented by counsel.[110]

---

106. Restatement (Third) of the Law Governing Lawyers §33, cmt. *b.*

107. See id. §§36 & 43. Lawyers may acquire an interest in a client's venture that is not subject to litigation. Thus, a lawyer may obtain an ownership interest in a client's business while representing the client provided the lawyer complies with the stringent requirements for business transactions between lawyer and client. See Model Rule 1.8(a) and Problem 5-1.

108. On the retaining lien, see generally Wolfram, Modern Legal Ethics §9.6.3, at 559-560.

109. 492 S.E.2d 82 (S.C. 1997).

110. See Committee on Legal Ethics v. Hazlett, 367 S.E.2d 772 (W. Va. 1988) (attorney's demand for release from liability before surrendering file was improper); Model Rule 1.8(h); Restatement (Third) of the Law Governing Lawyers §54. The Restatement provides that an agreement prospectively limiting a lawyer's liability for malpractice is unethical and unenforceable even if the client is independently represented by counsel. Id. §§54(2) and 54(4)(a) (omitting reference to independent representation found in other sections).

The Restatement of the Law Governing Lawyers rejects the general concept of a retaining lien unless established by statute because of its coercive aspects, although the drafters recognize that their position represents a minority view.[111] Under the Restatement, however, a lawyer may retain a document prepared by the lawyer for which the client has not paid the lawyer, but even in this situation the lawyer cannot do so if retention of the document will unreasonably harm the client.[112] Thus, a lawyer may not refuse to record a deed because the client has not paid the lawyer's fee.[113]

The second form of lien is the *charging lien*, which is applied against the proceeds of any settlement or judgment for any unpaid fees or expenses due the attorney. Where recognized, the charging lien is generally based on statute.[114] When the lien is created by statute, lawyers must obviously comply with statutory requirements for perfection and enforcement of a charging lien.[115]

May a lawyer ethically enter into a fee agreement that provides for a contractual charging lien? Professor Wolfram argues that contractual charging liens are of doubtful validity because Model Rule 1.8(i) prohibits a lawyer from acquiring an interest in the client's cause of action, except for liens authorized by law.[116] In a few jurisdictions, however, courts recognize contractually created liens,[117] and the Restatement of the Law Governing Lawyers allows lawyers to contract with clients for charging liens, unless prohibited by statute or court rule.[118] For a lien to be effective against a third party (for example, an insurance company or a successor counsel), a lawyer must give notice of a charging lien to such party.[119]

Lawyers may also enter into contracts with their clients in which they obtain a security interest or mortgage in the clients' property to secure payment of their fees. Because security agreements between clients and lawyers are somewhat unusual, courts are likely to scrutinize such a security arrangement under fiduciary principles of fairness and full disclosure.[120] In Formal Opinion #02-427, the ABA Committee on Ethics and Professional Responsibility advised that a lawyer may obtain a contractual security interest in the client's property to secure payment of fees and expenses, provided the lawyer complies with Rule 1.8(a) and provided the security interest is authorized by law under

---

111. Restatement (Third) of the Law Governing Lawyers §43(1) and cmts *a, b*.

112. Id. §43, cmt. *c*.

113. Id.

114. Wolfram, Modern Legal Ethics §9.6.3, at 561-562. See Potter v. Schlesser Co., 63 P.3d 1172 (Or. 2003) (interpreting Oregon's attorney lien statutes).

115. See In re Marriage of Etcheverry, 921 P.2d 82 (Colo. Ct. App. 1996) (against public policy to allow statutorily created charging lien to attach to child support payments).

116. Wolfram, Modern Legal Ethics §9.6.3, at 562.

117. See Eleazer v. Hardaway Concrete Co., 315 S.E.2d 174 (S.C. Ct. App. 1984) (recognizing common law charging lien on settlement or judgment for expenses, but not for legal fees; attorney and client may agree that attorney has lien on settlement or judgment).

118. Restatement (Third) of the Law Governing Lawyers §43(2) and cmts. *d, e*.

119. Id. §43, cmt. *e*.

120. See id. §43(4) and cmt. *i*.

Rule 1.8(i) if the property is the subject of litigation. See also Model Rule 1.8, cmt. 16. Some states may prohibit or limit lawyers from obtaining security interests or mortgages to secure payment of their fees. For example, in domestic cases in New York, lawyers may obtain a mortgage or security interest to secure their fees only when the retainer agreement provides for such an interest, notice of an application for a security interest has been given to the other spouse, and the court grants approval for the application of a security interest after submission of an application for counsel fees. In addition, a lawyer in New York may not foreclose a mortgage on a primary residence while the consenting spouse remains in the residence.[121]

The client's file

The Model Rules do not speak directly to lawyers' obligations regarding the client's file, but section 46 of the Restatement of the Law Governing Lawyers does provide some specific standards. Lawyers have a duty to take reasonable steps to safeguard documents in the lawyer's possession relating to representation of a client.[122] Clients ordinarily have the right to inspect and copy documents in their files, but a lawyer may refuse to allow the client to do so when a substantial reason exists, for example if the file contains documents subject to a protective order.[123] Clients do not have a right, however, to inspect or copy internal firm memoranda (as distinguished from research memoranda) that may be in the file.[124] On termination of representation, the client is entitled to receive all documents in the file, except internal firm memoranda.[125] The firm may not charge the client for making copies of documents that the client is entitled to receive; if the firm wishes to retain copies, it may do so at its own expense.[126] As noted above, some jurisdictions recognize a retaining lien that allows lawyers to retain possession of the file until outstanding fees and expenses are paid. The Restatement rejects the general concept of a retaining lien, but the Restatement allows lawyers to retain specific documents that they have prepared when the client has not paid the fee or expenses associated with preparation of the document, provided that nondelivery would not substantially harm the client.[127]

---

121. Procedure for Attorneys in Domestic Relations Matters, N.Y. Sup. Ct. R. §1400.5.
122. Restatement (Third) of the Law Governing Lawyers §46(1).
123. Id. §46(2) and cmt. c.
124. Id.
125. Id. §46(3).
126. Id. cmt. e. See In re Admonition Issued to X. Y., 529 N.W.2d 688 (Minn. 1995) (absent specific provision in engagement agreement lawyer may not charge client for copying file on withdrawal because file belongs to client).
127. Restatement (Third) of the Law Governing Lawyers §43(1).

B. Confidentiality

────────────────── **Problem 3-3** ──────────────────

The Ethical Duty of Confidentiality, the Attorney-Client Privilege, and the Work Product Doctrine

a. You are an associate in a large law firm working in products liability defense. One of the shareholders in your firm has expressed concern that the firm's use of e-mail, cellular telephones, and perhaps even fax machines to communicate with clients may be inconsistent with the firm's ethical duty of confidentiality to its clients. You have been asked to draft a policy for the firm's consideration on the use of such technology. Prepare an outline of the central points that you believe such a policy should cover and an explanation of these principles.

b. The firm represents International Motors, Inc. (IM), a multinational manufacturer of automobiles. In a series of cases plaintiffs have alleged that IM produced vehicles with defective fuel tanks. Plaintiffs have sought to obtain various documents involved in the design of the fuel tank. IM has resisted these efforts, claiming that the documents are covered by the attorney-client privilege and the work product doctrine. All design decisions made by IM are the responsibility of its Design Review Committee (DRC), the chairman of which has always been an attorney. All documents presented to the DRC are marked "CONFIDENTIAL MATERIAL PROTECTED BY THE ATTORNEY-CLIENT PRIVILEGE AND THE WORK PRODUCT DOCTRINE." IM has refused to produce any DRC documents (except for ones that it voluntarily produced in connection with filings with regulatory bodies), claiming that such documents are privileged. What arguments would you expect plaintiffs to make in an effort to overcome claims of privilege? What responses would you make?

───

Read Model Rule 1.6 and comments.

Confidentiality and the use of e-mail, faxes, and cellular telephones

Model Rule 1.6(a) provides that a "lawyer shall not reveal information relating to the representation of a client unless the client gives informed consent, the disclosure is impliedly authorized in order to carry out the representation or the disclosure is permitted by paragraph (b)." The rule could be read literally to impose strict liability on attorneys for any revelation of client information unless the disclosure was expressly or impliedly authorized by the client or unless one of the exceptions set forth in section (b) applies. The rule is being interpreted, however, as having a negligence standard. Lawyers must take reasonable steps to preserve client confidentiality. If a lawyer uses a means of communication that has a reasonable expectation of privacy, the lawyer complies with the obligation of confidentiality even though client information might be revealed either inadvertently or through intentional interception by another person. Thus, the Restatement of the Law Governing Lawyers provides that confidential client information must be "acquired, stored, retrieved, and transmitted under systems and controls that are reasonably designed and managed to maintain confidentiality."[128]

Use of land-line telephones and fax machines is well established in the practice of law, and both enjoy a reasonable expectation of privacy, even though such communications may be intercepted or misdirected.[129] The federal wiretapping act, the Electronic Communications Privacy Act (the ECPA), supports this expectation of privacy in two ways.[130] First, the act makes interception of wire communications a crime and imposes civil liability unless one of the parties to the communication consents to the interception.[131] Second, information gained from an unlawful interception is inadmissible in evidence.[132]

The expectation of privacy associated with cordless or cellular telephones is less certain.[133] While both cordless and cellular telephones enjoy the protection of the ECPA,[134] devices for the interception of the radio waves that transmit cordless or cellular calls are available commercially, and unauthorized interception of such communications is not uncommon. Some court decisions have held that cordless telephone calls are entitled to an expectation of privacy.[135] Ethics advisory opinions have cautioned lawyers about the use of cellular or cordless telephones. Some opinions have decided that lawyers should not use such devices for confidential communications.[136] Other opinions, while concluding that lawyers may ethically use these devices, have warned lawyers about the risk of interception and have advised that at a minimum a lawyer should

---

128. See Restatement (Third) of the Law Governing Lawyers §60, cmt. *d. Accord* ABA Comm. on Ethics and Prof. Resp., Formal Op. 99-413.

129. See Katz v. United States, 389 U.S. 347 (1967) (telephone call from booth where listening device had been attached entitled to Fourth Amendment protection); State ex rel. U.S. Fidelity & Guar. Co. v. Canady, 460 S.E.2d 677 (W. Va. 1995) (facsimile transmission held subject to attorney-client privilege).

130. 18 U.S.C. §§2510 et seq.

131. Id. §2511.

132. Id. §2515.

133. See Laws. Man. on Prof. Conduct (ABA/BNA) 55:404-408.

134. Cordless telephone calls were originally not protected by the ECPA, but amendments to the act in 1994 expanded its coverage to include cordless telephone calls. See McKamey v. Roach, 55 F.3d 1236, 1238 n.1 (6th Cir. 1995).

135. See State v. McVeigh, 620 A.2d 133, 147 (Conn. 1993); State v. Faford, 910 P.2d 447, 451-452 (Wash. 1996) (en banc).

136. E.g., Massachusetts Ethics Opinion 94-5 (1994) (lawyer should not use if risk that third party will overhear confidential communication is "nontrivial").

inform the other party to the communication that the communication may not be considered to be confidential.[137]

In a comprehensive opinion, the ABA Committee on Ethics and Professional Responsibility has examined the ethical propriety of lawyers' use of e-mail.[138] The committee first discussed the characteristics of four types of e-mail transmissions: "direct" e-mail; "private system" e-mail; on-line service provider (OSP) e-mail; and Internet service provider (ISP) e-mail. All forms of e-mail have the risk of unauthorized interception. E-mail sent through on-line service providers or over the Internet is also subject to monitoring by the service provider. The committee decided that neither of these risks was sufficient to destroy the reasonable expectation of privacy. Telephone conversations can be intercepted illegally, but that risk does not mean that lawyers act unethically when using the telephone to discuss client matters. Monitoring of e-mail by OSPs and ISPs is restricted by law and does not lessen the reasonable expectation of privacy. The committee concluded that lawyers may ethically use e-mail to convey confidential information without use of encryption or other technology:

> Lawyers have a reasonable expectation of privacy in communications made by all forms of e-mail, including unencrypted e-mail sent on the Internet, despite some risk of interception and disclosure. It therefore follows that its use is consistent with the duty under Rule 1.6 to use reasonable means to maintain the confidentiality of information relating to a client's representation.[139]

Even if a method of communication is ethically permissible because a reasonable expectation of privacy exists, as a matter of prudence lawyers may need to refrain from using a method of communication or adopt additional precautions (such as the use of scrambling devices or encryption technology[140]) for particularly sensitive information.[141] While ABA Formal Opinion 99-413 and most state opinions do not require client consent, it would be prudent for lawyers to include in their engagement agreements a provision in which clients authorize use of various forms of communication with appropriate warnings

---

137. New York City Ethics Op. 1994-11. See also Minn. Lawyers Prof. Resp. Board Op. 19 (1999) (lawyers may ethically use analog cordless or cellular telephones only with client consent after consultation).

138. ABA Comm. on Ethics and Prof. Resp., Formal Op. 99-413.

139. Id. at 11. A number of state bar ethics opinions have adopted an approach similar to the ABA committee's: use of any form of e-mail is consistent with a lawyer's obligations under Rule 1.6 without the need for encryption or client consent. Opinions in Pennsylvania and Arizona recommended that lawyers obtain client consent or use encryption. Opinions in Iowa and North Carolina took the position that lawyers should not transmit sensitive client information by e-mail. Id. at 11-12 n.40.

140. On encryption technology, see David Hricik, Lawyers Worry Too Much About Transmitting Client Confidences by Internet E-mail, 11 Geo. J. Legal Ethics 459, 493-496 (1998).

141. ABA Formal Opinion 99-413, at 2.

to the client. To reinforce claims of confidentiality, communications by fax or e-mail should contain confidentiality notices.[142]

Scope and exceptions to the attorney-client privilege

The attorney-client privilege is one of the pillars on which the legal profession rests.[143] As the Supreme Court recently stated in Swidler & Berlin v. United States:[144]

> The attorney-client privilege is one of the oldest recognized privileges for confidential communications. . . . The privilege is intended to encourage "full and frank communication between attorneys and their clients and thereby promote broader public interests in the observance of law and the administration of justice."[145]

Courts and commentators have defined the attorney-client privilege in various ways. Problem 2-3 quoted Professor Wigmore's widely cited version. The Restatement of the Law Governing Lawyers contains the following formulation:

[The] attorney-client privilege may be invoked . . . with respect to:

(1) a communication
(2) made between privileged persons
(3) in confidence
(4) for the purpose of obtaining or providing legal assistance for the client.[146]

The attorney-client privilege does not apply if any of these elements is absent. Thus, if the communication is with a third person rather than with the client,[147] or if the communication is not for the purpose of giving legal advice, the communication is not privileged. For example, in United States v. Ackert[148] the Second Circuit held that corporate counsel's discussions with an investment

142. Amy M. Fulmer Stevenson, Comment, Making a Wrong Turn on the Information Superhighway: Electronic Mail, the Attorney-Client Privilege and Inadvertent Disclosure, 26 Cap. U.L. Rev. 347, 375 n.159 (1997) (example of confidentiality notice).
143. See generally Edna S. Epstein, The Attorney-Client Privilege and the Work Product Doctrine (ABA 4th ed. 2001).
144. 524 U.S. 399 (1998) (holding that the privilege survives death of client, in this case former Deputy White House counsel Vincent Foster).
145. Id. at 403 (quoting from Upjohn v. United States, 449 U.S. 383, 389 (1981)).
146. Restatement (Third) of the Law Governing Lawyers §68.
147. Section 70 of the Restatement defines "privileged persons" as follows:

Privileged persons within the meaning of §68 are the client (including a prospective client), the client's lawyer, agents of either who facilitate communications between them, and agents of the lawyer who facilitate the representation.

148. 169 F.3d 136 (2d Cir. 1999).

banker were not protected by the attorney-client privilege even though the lawyer's goal was to obtain information to help him advise his client. The court stated "the privilege protects communications between a client and an attorney, not communications that prove important to an attorney's legal advice to a client."[149]

In addition, courts have recognized several exceptions to the privilege, the two most important of which are waiver and the crime-fraud exception. The Restatement provides that the attorney-client privilege can be waived in several ways: by agreement, disclaimer, or failure to object;[150] by voluntary disclosure in a nonprivileged communication by the client, the client's lawyer, or another authorized agent of the client;[151] or by raising the lawyer's communication or assistance as an issue in the proceeding.[152]

The Restatement provides that the attorney-client privilege does not apply to a communication occurring when a client:

> (a) consults a lawyer for the purpose, later accomplished, of obtaining assistance to engage in a crime or fraud or aiding a third person to do so, or
> (b) regardless of the client's purpose at the time of consultation, uses the lawyer's advice or other services to engage in or assist a crime or fraud.[153]

We have already encountered the application of the crime-fraud exception in Problem 2-3 in connection with *Purcell*. Another highly publicized application of the exception occurred in connection with tobacco litigation. In American Tobacco Co. v. State[154] the State of Florida brought suit against various tobacco manufacturers, seeking to recover health care expenses it incurred in treating diseases of Medicaid smokers. The state subpoenaed various documents to which the tobacco companies raised claims of privilege. The state contended that the crime-fraud exception applied because the documents would show that the tobacco companies defrauded the American public about the risks of smoking. The court of appeals agreed. The opinion focused on the procedure and standard of proof necessary to establish the exception. The court held that the procedure for determining the application of the exception was an adversarial hearing in which each party could present evidence and argument, and the standard for application of the exception was the "prima facie" evidence standard:

> [T]he party opposing the privilege on the crime-fraud exception has the initial burden of producing evidence which, if unexplained, would be prima facie proof

---

149. Id. at 139.
150. Restatement (Third) of the Law Governing Lawyers §78.
151. Id. §79.
152. Id. §80. See Frontier Refining, Inc. v. Gorman-Rupp Co., 136 F.3d 695 (10th Cir. 1998) (discussing various approaches to issue of waiver of privilege by filing lawsuit to which privileged material is relevant).
153. Restatement (Third) of the Law Governing Lawyers §82.
154. 697 So. 2d 1249 (Fla. Dist. Ct. App. 1997).

of the existence of the exception. The burden of persuasion then shifts to the party asserting the privilege to give a reasonable explanation of the conduct or communication. If the court accepts the explanation as sufficient to rebut the evidence presented by the party opposing the privilege, then the privilege remains. However, if after considering and weighing the explanation the court does not accept it, then a prima facie case exists as to the exception, and the privilege is lost. Thus, the trial court must consider the evidence and argument rebutting the existence of the crime-fraud exception and must weigh its sufficiency against the case made by the proponent of the exception.[155]

Scope and exceptions to the work product doctrine

The attorney work product doctrine has its genesis in the Supreme Court's decision in Hickman v. Taylor.[156] *Hickman* was an action for wrongful death of a seaman against the owners of a tug that sank. Plaintiffs sought to obtain by discovery copies of all written statements from members of the crew taken by defendants. The Court first held that the statements were not protected by the attorney-client privilege since they did not involve confidential communications from the client.[157] The Court went on to hold, however, that the material sought by the plaintiff was still not subject to discovery:

> Historically, a lawyer is an officer of the court and is bound to work for the advancement of justice while faithfully protecting the rightful interests of his clients. In performing his various duties, however, it is essential that a lawyer work with a certain degree of privacy, free from unnecessary intrusion by opposing parties and their counsel. Proper preparation of a client's case demands that he assemble information, sift what he considers to be the relevant from the irrelevant facts, prepare his legal theories and plan his strategy without undue and needless interference. That is the historical and the necessary way in which lawyers act within the framework of our system of jurisprudence to promote justice and to protect their clients' interests. This work is reflected, of course, in interviews, statements, memoranda, correspondence, briefs, mental impressions, personal beliefs, and countless other tangible and intangible ways—aptly though roughly termed by the Circuit Court of Appeals in this case . . . as the "Work product of the lawyer." Were such materials open to opposing counsel on mere demand, much of what is now put down in writing would remain unwritten. An attorney's thoughts, heretofore inviolate, would not be his own. Inefficiency, unfairness and sharp practices would inevitably develop in the giving of legal advice and in the preparation of cases for trial. The effect on the legal profession would be demoralizing. And the interests of the clients and the cause of justice would be poorly served.[158]

---

155. Id. at 1256. See also Haines v. Liggett Group, Inc., 975 F.2d 81 (3d Cir. 1992) (adopting "prima facie" evidence standard).
156. 329 U.S. 495 (1947).
157. Id. at 508.
158. Id. at 510-511.

The Court concluded that work product material was not absolutely immune from discovery: "Where relevant and non-privileged facts remain hidden in an attorney's file and where production of those facts is essential to the preparation of one's case, discovery may properly be had."[159]

The work product doctrine is embodied in Rule 26(b)(3) of the Federal Rules of Civil Procedure:

> Trial Preparation: Materials. Subject to the provisions of subdivision (b)(4) of this rule, a party may obtain discovery of documents and tangible things otherwise discoverable under subdivision (b)(1) of this rule and prepared in anticipation of litigation or for trial by or for another party or by or for that other party's representative (including the other party's attorney, consultant, surety, indemnitor, insurer, or agent) only upon a showing that the party seeking discovery has substantial need of the materials in the preparation of the party's case and that the party is unable without undue hardship to obtain the substantial equivalent of the materials by other means. In ordering discovery of such materials when the required showing has been made, the court shall protect against disclosure of the mental impressions, conclusions, opinions, or legal theories of an attorney or other representative of a party concerning the litigation.

Two aspects of the work product doctrine should be noted. First, for the doctrine to apply, the material must be prepared "in anticipation of litigation." Second, a party may obtain discovery of work product material by showing "substantial need" coupled with "undue hardship."[160]

In applying the work product doctrine courts have developed a distinction between ordinary and opinion work product. The Restatement provides the following definition: "Opinion work product consists of the opinions or mental impressions of a lawyer; all other work product is ordinary work product."[161] Opinion work product receives greater protection than ordinary work product. While a party may obtain ordinary work product if the party can establish substantial need for the material and inability to obtain equivalent material without undue hardship, a party may obtain opinion work product only if "extraordinary circumstances justify disclosure," unless an exception exists.[162] The work product doctrine is subject to many of the same exceptions as the attorney-client privilege. The protections of the work product doctrine can be waived,[163] and most courts recognize that the crime-fraud exception applies.[164]

---

159. Id. at 511.
160. The Restatement of the Law Governing Lawyers contains an extensive discussion of the elements of the work product doctrine. See Restatement (Third) of the Law Governing Lawyers §§87-93.
161. Id. §87(2).
162. Id. §89.
163. Id. §§91 (waiver by voluntary act), 92 (waiver by use in litigation).
164. Id. §93.

Internal investigations: scope of the corporate attorney-client privilege

When allegations of serious wrongdoing are made against corporate employees, corporations will usually investigate the charges. Are the results of such internal investigations discoverable by the opposing party, or are they protected by the attorney-client privilege or the work product doctrine? In Upjohn v. United States,[165] the Supreme Court dealt with the issue of whether under the Federal Rules of Evidence the Internal Revenue Service could subpoena written questionnaires sent by the corporation's general counsel to various middle managers as part of the corporation's internal investigation into questionable foreign payments made by one of its subsidiaries. The questionnaire sought detailed factual information about the payments. The court of appeals held that the questionnaire was not privileged because the privilege applies only to members of the "control group," not to lower-level employees. The Supreme Court reversed. It held that the control group test "overlooks the fact that the privilege exists to protect not only the giving of professional advice to those who can act on it but also the giving of information to the lawyer to enable him to give sound and informed advice."[166] The Court did not specify a clear rule for the scope of the privilege, indicating that the privilege must be decided on a case-by-case basis, but the Court did hold that the privilege could apply to communications made by both middle- and lower-level employees.

While *Upjohn* appears to provide broad protection for communications by all corporate employees to corporate counsel in federal court, *Upjohn* has not been widely followed in the state courts.[167] Some courts have accepted the control group test.[168] Others follow a "subject matter test":

> [A]n employee of a corporation, though not a member of its control group, is sufficiently identified with the corporation so that his communication to the corporation's attorney is privileged where the employee makes the communication at the direction of his superiors in the corporation and where the subject matter upon which the attorney's advice is sought by the corporation and dealt with in the communication is the performance by the employee of the duties of his employment.[169]

The Restatement formulation is very close to the subject matter test. With regard to an organizational client, Restatement §73(4) provides that a

---

165. 449 U.S. 383 (1981).

166. Id. at 390.

167. See Alexander C. Black, Annotation, What Corporate Communications Are Entitled to Attorney-Client Privilege—Modern Cases, 27 A.L.R.5th 76 (1995).

168. See, e.g., Consolidation Coal Co. v. Bucyrus-Erie Co., 432 N.E.2d 250 (Ill. 1982).

169. Southern Bell Tel. & Tel. Co. v. Deason, 632 So. 2d 1377, 1383 (Fla. 1994) (quoting Harper & Row Publishers, Inc. v. Decker, 423 F.2d 487 (7th Cir. 1970), *aff'd per curiam by an equally divided court*, 400 U.S. 348 (1971)). Compare Samaritan Found. v. Goodfarb, 862 P.2d 870 (Ariz. 1993) (en banc) (adopting narrow version of subject-matter test in which communication must relate to employee's own activities).

communication that otherwise meets the requirements for privilege retains its privileged character if it

is disclosed only to: (a) privileged persons as defined in §70; and (b) other agents of the organization who reasonably need to know of the communication in order to act for the organization.

Comment d states that cases applying the subject matter test "[i]n substance . . . comport with the need-to-know formulation in this Section (see Comment g)."

C. Conflicts of Interest

──────────────── **Problem 3-4** ────────────────

Representation Against Current Clients

You are a member of the professional responsibility committee of the law firm of Knight & McLaughlin.[170] The committee's functions include making decisions on conflicts of interest and other issues of professional ethics that the firm faces. How would you decide the following issues that have been presented to the committee?

a. During the previous two years the firm has done a small amount of legal work for the Velasquez Steel Company. The work involved some tax issues and questions under the Fair Labor Standards Act. The firm has not done any work for Velasquez Steel this year. Fees paid by Velasquez during the last two years total about $25,000. Recently, General Contractors, Inc. has asked Knight & McLaughlin to represent it in a major breach of warranty action against Velasquez. The partner in the firm who would be in charge of the matter estimates that the case would generate more than $1 million in fees for the firm.

b. The firm is handling the formation of NYM Associates, a limited partnership with ten doctors as limited partners. The partnership owns and operates sophisticated equipment used in medical testing and diagnosis. Oldtown Hospital has asked the firm to defend it in a malpractice action filed against the hospital and several doctors, one of whom is a 10 percent owner in NYM Associates. The hospital will need to argue in the litigation

───────────────────

170. Mallen and Smith, the authors of the leading treatise on legal malpractice, recommend that a law firm create a committee, which they refer to as the "quality control committee," to engage in malpractice prevention. They identify 22 functions for such a committee, including analysis of potential ethical problems. 1 Mallen & Smith, Legal Malpractice §§2.4 & 2.5.

that if any malpractice occurred, it was the fault of the doctor and that the hospital bears no responsibility.

c. The firm represents the American Plumbing Contractors Association, a national association with more than 1,000 members, in connection with federal, state, and local legislative and regulatory matters. Harriet Clawson, a discharged former executive of one of the companies in the association, has asked the firm to represent her in a wrongful discharge action against her former company.

d. The firm represents Johnson Control Company, a manufacturer of electronic parts, in a products liability action. Johnson Control is a wholly owned subsidiary of National Electric, Inc. American Computer Components has asked the firm to defend it in a products liability action brought by Wilson Disk Company. Wilson Disk Company is also a wholly owned subsidiary of National Electric. Thus, Johnson Control and Wilson Disk are both subsidiaries of National Electric.

e. One of the firm's rapidly growing clients is computerservices .com, a company that provides a variety of hardware, software, and Internet services to businesses. Computerservices has asked the firm to represent it in an appeal to the United States Court of Appeals for the Sixth Circuit involving the application of the Fair Labor Standards Act. When the matter was listed in the firm's new business report, another partner raised a question about the matter, because he represents a number of business clients in Fair Labor Standards Act cases; he was concerned that the firm might be representing clients with inconsistent legal positions.

f. The committee is considering recommending to the litigation section that the firm include the following prospective waiver of conflicts of interest in its retainer agreements. The provision would be used only with sophisticated entities that have in-house counsel:

> It is understood and agreed that the firm represents [name of entity, hereinafter referred to as "Client"] and not any of its officers, directors, shareholders, employees, subsidiaries, affiliates, or members, unless the firm specifically agrees in writing to undertake representation of any such person.
>
> It is further understood and agreed that the firm reserves the right to represent existing or new clients in matters against Client, so long as such representation is not substantially related to any matter that the firm is handling for Client, and Client hereby expressly waives any claim that such representation involves a conflict of interest or disqualifies the firm from such representation. **PLEASE CONSULT WITH YOUR IN-HOUSE COUNSEL REGARDING THIS WAIVER OF CONFLICTS OF INTEREST.**

g. The committee has been struggling with articulating a principle for deciding doubtful conflict-of-interest questions. Some more traditional members of the firm believe that the firm should turn down any matter that involves even a remote possibility of a conflict of interest, absent the consent of all affected clients, in order to avoid any appearance of impropriety. Other members of the firm point to the competitive environment in which law firms function and argue that the firm should not turn down substantial matters when the risk of disqualification or other charge of unethical conduct is modest. What approach would you favor?

Read Model Rules 1.7, 1.9, 1.13, 1.16, and comments.

Representation of one client against another client in a single matter and in unrelated matters

Conflicts of interest come in a variety of forms: adverse representation against a current client, multiple representation of clients in a single matter, representation against a former client, advocate-witness conflicts, and conflicts involving the lawyer's own personal or financial interest.[171] Problem 3-4 poses several situations involving adverse representation against a "current" client.

Model Rule 1.7(a) deals with concurrent conflicts of interest. That rule provides that a lawyer may not undertake representation that is "directly adverse" to another client unless permitted by Rule 1.7(b). In applying Rule 1.7(b) a distinction is drawn between conflicts involving representation of one client against another client in a *current proceeding before a tribunal* and in *unrelated matters*. Under Rule 1.7(b)(3) a lawyer may not undertake representation that involves a claim against another current client in the same litigation or proceeding before a tribunal, even if the clients consent. The Restatement agrees.[172]

Cases in which lawyers are asked to undertake representation on behalf of one client against another client in a single contested litigation matter are rare but do occur occasionally. For example, a lawyer may be asked to represent a driver and a passenger in an automobile accident involving another driver,

---

171. See Nathan M. Crystal, An Introduction to Professional Responsibility 85-171 (1998) (examining different types of conflicts of interest); 1 Hazard & Hodes, The Law of Lawyering ch. 10 (overview of conflicts of interest). See ABA, Task Force on Conflicts of Interest, Conflict of Interest Issues, 50 Bus. Law. 1381 (1995) (discussion of principles and suggested agreements for medium and large firms in dealing with common conflict-of-interest problems).

172. Restatement (Third) of the Law Governing Lawyers §122(2)(b) & cmt. *g(iii)*. For a review of the Restatement's provisions on conflicts of interest, see Nancy J. Moore, Restating the Law of Lawyer Conflicts, 10 Geo. J. Legal Ethics 541 (1997).

when the passenger has a claim against the driver of her vehicle.[173] See Problem 3-8. Lawyers have sometimes been asked to represent both spouses in divorce cases.[174] See Problem 3-10.

Two justifications can be given for prohibiting representation of adverse clients in a single matter, even with their consent. First, the rules dealing with conflicts of interest are based on the lawyer's duty of loyalty. See Model Rule 1.7, cmt. 1. In single-matter conflicts the lawyer cannot carry out the duty of loyalty owed to both clients. Whatever the lawyer does for one client will of necessity harm the other client in the matter. In addition, for systemic reasons representation of adverse parties in a single matter is improper. Our legal system produces decisions that serve as guidance for future conduct by third parties and as means for vindication of public interests. The adversarial nature of the system is based on the assumption of zealous representation by lawyers of the interests of their clients. If a lawyer's representation of a client is infected by a conflict of interest, the adversarial nature of the representation is undermined, and the public benefits flowing from the adversarial system may be reduced.[175] As Comment 17 to Model Rule 1.7 states, conflicts in the same proceeding are not consentable "because of the institutional interest in vigorous development of each client's position when the clients are aligned directly against each other in the same litigation or other proceeding before a tribunal."

Note also that, in general, if the rules of ethics prohibit a lawyer's conduct, that prohibition extends to all members of the lawyer's firm. See Model Rule 1.10. We will discuss the rationale, scope, and limitations of this rule of "vicarious" or "imputed" disqualification in later problems in these materials.

The rule prohibiting lawyers and members of their firms from undertaking representation adverse to current clients applies not only to adverse representation in a single matter but also to adverse representation in unrelated matters. For example, if a member of a firm represents client A in one matter, a member of that firm may not generally represent client B against A in an unrelated matter even though the firm does not represent A in that second matter. See Model Rule 1.7, cmt. 6. Grievance Committee v. Rottner illustrates this type of conflict.[176] In *Rottner*, Twible retained a law firm to represent him in a minor collection matter. While this case was pending, O'Brien asked the same firm to represent him in an action for assault and battery against Twible. Although

---

173. E.g., In re Shaw, 443 A.2d 670 (N.J. 1982); Ganiev v. Nazi, 730 N.Y.S.2d 661 (App. Div. 2001). See also Chateau de Ville Prods., Inc. v. Tams-Witmark Music Library, Inc., 474 F. Supp. 223 (S.D.N.Y. 1979) (law firm could not represent plaintiff and alleged coconspirator of defendant).

174. Klemm v. Superior Court, 142 Cal. Rptr. 509 (Ct. App. 1977) (lawyer may not represent both husband and wife in contested divorce).

175. Professor Nancy Moore, however, has criticized the "public interest" justification for limiting client consent to multiple representation. She argues that the focus should be on the client's capacity for informed and voluntary consent. Nancy J. Moore, Conflicts of Interest in the Simultaneous Representation of Multiple Clients: A Proposed Solution to the Current Confusion and Controversy, 61 Tex. L. Rev. 211, 229-230 (1982).

176. 203 A.2d 82 (Conn. 1964).

the firm informed O'Brien that it had represented Twible in prior matters and was currently representing him in the collection case, the firm did not discuss O'Brien's case with Twible, nor did the firm obtain Twible's consent to representation. The firm then filed suit on O'Brien's behalf against Twible. The complaint sought both actual and punitive damages, claiming that Twible's conduct was "wilful, wanton, malicious, premeditated and vindictive."[177] Despite protests from Twible, the firm continued representing O'Brien and even proceeded to attach Twible's home in connection with the case.

In finding that the lawyers involved in the matter were guilty of misconduct, the Connecticut Supreme Court discussed how a lawyer's representation against a client in an unrelated matter violates the principle of loyalty:

> When a client engages the services of a lawyer in a given piece of business he is entitled to feel that, until that business is finally disposed of in some manner, he has the undivided loyalty of the one upon whom he looks as his advocate and his champion. If, as in this case, he is sued and his home attached by his own attorney, who is representing him in another matter, all feeling of loyalty is necessarily destroyed, and the profession is exposed to the charge that it is interested only in money.[178]

As *Rottner* shows, a lawyer's duty of loyalty precludes the lawyer from undertaking representation of one client against another client even if the matters are unrelated to one another. Conflicts involving unrelated matters differ in two respects, however, from cases of adverse representation against a client in a current proceeding before a tribunal. First, because the matters are unrelated, the impact on the duty of loyalty is decreased. Second, the adverse representation in unrelated matters does not undermine the integrity of an adversarial presentation. Because of these differences, with informed client consent confirmed in writing a lawyer may undertake representation of clients in unrelated matters, although it may be difficult to obtain consent from both clients.[179]

Determining who is a current client

Rule 1.7(a) applies only if the clients are both current clients. If the adverse client is a former client rather than a current one, a less restrictive rule applies:

---

177. Id. at 83.

178. Id. at 84. See also Committee on Legal Ethics v. Frame, 433 S.E.2d 579 (W. Va. 1993) (improper for lawyer to represent controlling shareholder of corporation in her divorce action while another lawyer in firm represented plaintiff in personal injury action against her corporation).

179. Model Rule 1.7(b)(1), (4); Restatement (Third) of the Law Governing Lawyers §128(2) and cmt. *e.* Professor Tom Morgan argues that representation of one client against another client in unrelated matters should be improper, even if the consent of both clients cannot be obtained, only if the lawyer's representation would be materially limited. Thomas D. Morgan, Suing a Current Client, 9 Geo. J. Legal Ethics 1157 (1996).

A lawyer may ethically undertake representation against a former client, even without that former client's consent, if the current and former matters are not "substantially related" to each other. Model Rule 1.9(a). We will consider the substantial relationship test in Problem 3-5.

Determining whether a client is a current or former client is not always straightforward. If a firm is currently doing work for a client, then the client is quite clearly a current client. Even if the firm is not currently doing work for a client, however, courts will treat a client as a current client when an ongoing professional relationship exists between the client and the firm such that the client reasonably expects that the firm is its lawyer. This continuous relationship is clearly present when the client hires the firm pursuant to a general retainer, a fee paid to the firm to ensure its availability to handle work for the client, but it can also occur even when the client has not paid the firm a general retainer. (Recall the discussion of general and special retainers in Problem 2-2.)

A leading case on the issue of whether a client-lawyer relationship remains current is International Business Machines Corp. v. Levin,[180] an action brought under the federal antitrust laws by the plaintiffs, Levin and Levin Computer Corporation (LCC). The plaintiffs were represented by a law firm that had represented Levin since 1965. Beginning in 1971, the firm represented Levin and LCC in negotiations with IBM to purchase certain computer equipment on credit. IBM refused to grant purchasers of equipment financing terms as favorable as those offered to lessees. As a result Levin and LCC filed suit in June 1972, claiming that IBM had committed antitrust violations. Beginning in April 1970, other lawyers in the same firm had been representing IBM in unrelated labor matters. On the date when the firm filed the antitrust action, the firm was not handling a specific matter for IBM, but it did undertake labor work for IBM after commencing the litigation.

IBM representatives were originally unaware of the firm's dual representation. When they learned of the conflict, almost five years after the antitrust action was filed, IBM moved to disqualify the firm in the antitrust action. The firm argued that the dual representation would not have an adverse effect on its independent professional judgment on behalf of IBM. The Court of Appeals for the Third Circuit disagreed: "[A] possible effect on the quality of the attorney's services on behalf of the client being sued may be a diminution in the vigor of his representation of the client in the other matter."[181]

The court also held that there was a client-lawyer relationship between the law firm and IBM even though the firm was not currently handling a matter for IBM at the time the firm filed suit on behalf of Levin and Levin Computer Corporation against IBM. The court stated:

> Although [the law firm] had no specific assignment from IBM on hand on the day the antitrust complaint was filed and even though [it] performed services for

180. 579 F.2d 271 (3d Cir. 1978).
181. Id. at 280.

IBM on a fee for service basis rather than pursuant to a retainer arrangement, the pattern of repeated retainers, both before and after the filing of the complaint, supports the finding of a continuous relationship.[182]

Determining who is a current client in "entity" representation cases

Determining whether a person is a current client can also be complex when the client is an entity such as a partnership, corporation, or association. Merely because a law firm represents an entity does not mean that the firm has a client-lawyer relationship with every member of the entity. For example, in Formal Opinion 91-361 the ABA Committee on Ethics and Professional Responsibility addressed the question whether an attorney who represents a partnership has a client-lawyer relationship with its partners. The committee first noted that the Rules of Professional Conduct adopt in Rule 1.13(a) the concept of "entity" representation, which means that a lawyer employed by an entity represents it rather than any of its members or constituents.

The committee went on to hold, however, that an attorney who represents a partnership could also have a client-lawyer relationship with a partner, depending on the facts and circumstances:

> Whether such a relationship has been created almost always will depend on an analysis of the specific facts involved. The analysis may include such factors as whether the lawyer affirmatively assumed a duty of representation to the individual partner, whether the partner was separately represented by other counsel when the partnership was created or in connection with its affairs, whether the lawyer had represented an individual partner before undertaking to represent the partnership, and whether there was evidence of reliance by the individual partner on the lawyer as his or her separate counsel, or of the partner's expectation of personal representation.[183]

Numerous cases follow the general approach reflected in Formal Opinion 91-361.[184]

A similar facts-and-circumstances analysis applies to closely held corporations and to associations. For example, in Meyer v. Mulligan[185] the Wyoming Supreme Court reversed a trial court's decision granting summary judgment for a lawyer in a claim for legal malpractice brought by a shareholder in a

---

182. Id. at 281.

183. ABA Comm. on Ethics and Prof. Resp., Formal Op. 91-361, at 4.

184. See Hopper v. Frank, 16 F.3d 92 (5th Cir. 1994) (summary judgment for law firm affirmed in legal malpractice action claiming that law firm that represented limited partnership in securities offering had client-lawyer relationship with general partners of partnership); Responsible Citizens v. Superior Court, 20 Cal. Rptr. 2d 756 (Ct. App. 1993, *review denied*) (attorney that represents partnership does not per se have client-lawyer relationship with partners; such relationship can be formed based on express or implied agreement).

185. 889 P.2d 509 (Wyo. 1995).

closely held corporation. Relying on ABA Formal Opinion 91-361, the court held that summary judgment was inappropriate because it was unclear whom the lawyer represented.[186] Similarly, in Formal Opinion 92-365, the ABA Committee on Ethics and Professional Responsibility ruled that an attorney does not automatically have a client-lawyer relationship with a member of an association simply because the attorney represents the association, but such a relationship can arise from the facts and circumstances. The committee quoted with approval the factors that it had referred to in the partnership setting. It also indicated that another factor was the size of the association.

A leading case dealing with the existence of a client-lawyer relationship in the context of representation of associations is Westinghouse Electric Corp. v. Kerr-McGee Corp.[187] In *Westinghouse* an association of petroleum producers retained the Washington office of Kirkland & Ellis as independent special counsel to prepare a report on competition in the industry. To collect information for the report, the firm sent a questionnaire to oil companies that were members of the association; the firm also interviewed representatives of some of these companies. The firm told the companies that all information divulged to the law firm would be confidential. The final report released by the firm presented facts and arguments to show that legislation to break up the oil companies was unnecessary in light of overall competitive conditions in the energy industry. Subsequently, the firm's Chicago office filed a complaint on behalf of Westinghouse against a number of defendants, several of whom were members of the petroleum association, charging violations of the federal antitrust laws. The complaint presented theories diametrically opposed to those set forth in the report that the firm had prepared for the association. The Court of Appeals for the Seventh Circuit ruled that a client-lawyer relationship existed between the law firm and the members of the association and that the firm should therefore be disqualified from handling the antitrust case. If Kirkland & Ellis had done nothing more than represent the association, it would not have had a client-lawyer relationship with the members of the association. The firm, however, held itself out as independent counsel, communicated directly with members of the association, and assured them of confidentiality, one of the hallmarks of a client-lawyer relationship.[188]

Conflict of interest issues also arise when a law firm represents a member of a corporate group and is asked to undertake representation against either

---

186. But see Brennan v. Ruffner, 640 So. 2d 143 (Fla. Dist. Ct. App. 1994) (summary judgment granted for lawyer in legal malpractice action brought by shareholder in closely held corporation on ground that lawyer represented corporation, not individual shareholders).

187. 580 F.2d 1311 (7th Cir.), *cert. denied*, 439 U.S. 955 (1978).

188. For a somewhat different approach to the issue of whether a client-lawyer relationship exists between a firm representing an association and members of the association, see Glueck v. Jonathan Logan, Inc., 653 F.2d 746 (2d Cir. 1981) ("substantial relationship" test used to determine whether law firm that represented association should be disqualified from representation of plaintiff in action against defendant member of association).

the parent corporation or a sister corporation, as illustrated by the following case.

Discotrade Ltd. v. Wyeth-Ayerst International, Inc.

200 F. Supp. 2d 355 (S.D.N.Y. 2002)

MEMORANDUM AND ORDER

BUCHWALD, District Judge.

Plaintiff Discotrade Ltd. ("Discotrade") brings this suit against defendant Wyeth-Ayerst International, Inc. ("WAII") for fraud, breach of contract, and breach of the implied covenant of good faith and fair dealing. On April 30, 2002, the same day it filed its Complaint, Discotrade moved by order to show cause for the entry of a temporary restraining order and preliminary injunction against WAII seeking to enjoin the latter from terminating a distributorship agreement on the following day, May 1, 2002. A conference was held before the Court on April 30, 2002, in order to address Discotrade's motion. At this conference, WAII moved to dismiss Discotrade's counsel, Dorsey & Whitney LLP ("Dorsey & Whitney"), on the ground that their representation of WAII created a conflict of interest due to the fact that Dorsey & Whitney currently represents Wyeth Research, a company that is related to WAII. For the reasons that follow, WAII's motion is granted and Dorsey & Whitney is hereby disqualified from representing Discotrade in this matter.

BACKGROUND

The conflict alleged arises from Dorsey & Whitney's ongoing representation of Wyeth Pharmaceuticals Inc. ("Pharmaceuticals"). Accordingly, a summary of the corporate relationship between WAII and Pharmaceuticals is essential to our analysis. . . .

Wyeth, Inc. ("Wyeth") wholly owns AHP Subsidiary Holding Corp. ("AHP") which, in turn, wholly owns, inter alia, WAII and Pharmaceuticals, both New York corporations. Wyeth Research ("Research") is an operating unit or division of Pharmaceuticals. Affidavit of M. Andrea Ryan.[2] All of the directors of Pharmaceuticals are also directors of WAII, and the two corporations share several common officers, most notably Bernard J. Poussot, who serves as President to both corporations. According to WAII, there is "substantial integration of [ ] Pharmaceuticals and [WAII]'s day-to-day activities," such as the use of the same computer network, e-mail system, travel department, and health benefit plan. Furthermore, WAII's and Pharmaceuticals's financial

---

2. Ms. Ryan is Assistant General Counsel-Patents of Wyeth, Assistant Secretary of Wyeth, and a Vice President of Research. Ryan Aff. ¶2.

reports are consolidated and Wyeth's Chief Financial Officer serves as CFO to both corporations. Finally, WAII and Pharmaceuticals are both served by Wyeth's "in-house" law department, and virtually all legal correspondence relating to WAII and Pharmaceuticals is upon Wyeth letterhead.

Since October 2001, Dorsey & Whitney has continuously represented Research in connection with certain patent applications. Declaration of Raymond Van Dyke.[3] Dorsey & Whitney sent a retainer letter to Ms. Ryan on January 16, 2002, setting forth the terms of its representation of Research. This letter, which was apparently never signed by Ms. Ryan, states, inter alia, that "while [Dorsey & Whitney] represents a client [it] will not undertake litigation in which the client is a directly adverse party." In its capacity as counsel to Research, Dorsey & Whitney has prepared two patent applications and, as recently as April 29, 2002, presented an extensive written opinion regarding an inventorship study. Until it undertook to represent Discotrade, Ms. Ryan "considered Dorsey & Whitney to have become an integral member of Wyeth's Law Department outside counsel network, and planned to rely upon Dorsey & Whitney to handle additional legal matters in the future."

On or about April 8, 2002, Mr. Van Dyke telephoned Ms. Ryan, informing her that Dorsey & Whitney was "considering taking on a potential litigation against a Wyeth company." According to Mr. Van Dyke, Ms. Ryan "indicated that these situations happen all the time in big law firms, and that there would be no problem with the waiver." Ms. Ryan, in no uncertain terms, denies ever making such a statement. Mr. Van Dyke further claims that on or about April 18, 2002, he briefly spoke with Ms. Ryan at an American Intellectual Property Law Association meeting, at which time he expressed his appreciation for her "understanding and willingness to help regarding the possible conflict."

On April 26, 2002, Mr. Van Dyke sent a letter to Ms. Ryan stating, in pertinent part, "This waiver request is to confirm that Wyeth, and its affiliates, has agreed that [Dorsey & Whitney] is not precluded by conflicts of interest from representing Discotrade in this matter." After consulting with her colleagues, Ms. Ryan faxed a brief letter on April 30, 2002, to Mr. Van Dyke stating, "I have reviewed the [instant] matter and your letter dated April 26, 2002 seeking a waiver. I am not able to waive the conflict." The present action was filed later that day.

DISCUSSION

An attorney owes his client a duty of "undivided loyalty." Cinema 5 Ltd. v. Cinerama, Inc., 528 F.2d 1384, 1386 (2d Cir.1976). Thus, the Second Circuit has instructed us that it is prima facie improper for lawyers to take on a representation that is directly adverse to a current client. Id. at 1387. . . . Accordingly, an attorney seeking to represent a party adverse to his client bears

---

3. Mr. Van Dyke is a member of Dorsey & Whitney who represents Research. Van Dyke Decl. ¶¶2-6. [Further citations to affidavits have been deleted.—Ed.]

the burden of demonstrating "at the very least, that there will be no actual or apparent conflict in loyalties or diminution in the vigor of his representation." Id. If he fails to make such a showing, disqualification is properly granted. Board of Educ. of N.Y. v. Nyquist, 590 F.2d 1241, 1246 (2d Cir. 1979). With respect to the matter presently before the Court, we must first decide whether WAII is, for purposes of this analysis, a current client of Dorsey & Whitney. If so, we must next determine whether Dorsey & Whitney has borne the burden *Cinema 5* places upon it. For the reasons that follow, we answer the first question in the affirmative and the second question in the negative.

We find that WAII is a "current client" of Dorsey & Whitney because the corporate relationship between WAII and Pharmaceuticals[7] is so close as to deem them a single entity for conflict of interest purposes.[8] WAII and Pharmaceuticals are corporate subsidiaries of a single corporate parent, AHP, which is, in turn, a wholly-owned subsidiary of Wyeth. WAII and Pharmaceuticals share the same board of directors as well as several senior officers, including their President, Mr. Poussot. The two corporations also interact intimately, for example by using the same computer network, e-mail system, travel department, and health benefit plan. In short, WAII and Pharmaceuticals do not view each other as strangers, but more like members of the Wyeth family. Our conclusion is reinforced by the practical aspects of their relationship, including their common "Wyeth" letterhead, common "Wyeth" business cards, and common "Wyeth" e-mail addresses. WAII has met their burden of demonstrating that its relationship with Pharmaceuticals is so close that a conflict exists.

Discotrade argues that, even if a conflict exists, we should give effect to the oral waiver it claims it was granted by Ms. Ryan. ("Dorsey & Whitney was wholly justified in relying upon the oral consent given by Ms. Ryan"). We disagree. First, Ms. Ryan denies ever granting such an oral waiver to Dorsey & Whitney. Second, it is clear from the documentary record that Dorsey & Whitney knew it had not secured an effective waiver before filing this lawsuit. Finally, even if Ms. Ryan had made such a statement, she (and Wyeth in general) had the power to withdraw the waiver after consulting with her colleagues, at least before Dorsey & Whitney filed a complaint on behalf of Discotrade. Accordingly, we find that Pharmaceuticals did not waive the instant conflict.

Therefore, Dorsey & Whitney's representation of Discotrade in this matter is prima facie improper, and Discotrade bears the burden of showing that "there will be no actual or apparent conflict in loyalties or diminution in the vigor of [its] representation." *Cinema 5*, 528 F.2d at 1387. While Discotrade

---

7. Dorsey & Whitney apparently represents Research, which is a division of Pharmaceuticals. Since a division of a corporation does not have separate legal status, the representation is deemed to be of Pharmaceuticals. See People of P.R. v. Russell & Co., 288 U.S. 476, 480 (1933).

8. We note that the instant inquiry is not nearly as rigorous as an "alter ego" or "piercing the corporate veil" analysis. See JP Morgan Chase Bank v. Liberty Mut. Ins. Co., 189 F. Supp. 2d 20, 21 (S.D.N.Y. 2002).

offers several arguments in an attempt to avoid disqualification, it has not met its burden.

Discotrade first asserts that "WAII was, at best, a 'vicarious' client of Dorsey & Whitney" as that term is used in Glueck v. Jonathan Logan, Inc., 653 F.2d 746, 749 (2d Cir.1981). In *Glueck*, a former employee sued his employer for breach of contract. 653 F.2d at 748. The employer promptly moved to dismiss plaintiff's law firm on the ground that it had a conflict of interest arising out of its representation of a not-for-profit trade association of which the defendant employer was a member. The disqualification motion was denied. *Glueck* however, was a fact-specific opinion that is distinguishable from the present case. That case held only that the strict standards of *Cinema 5* need not "inevitably be invoked whenever a law firm brings suit against a member of an association that the firm represents."[10] Id. at 749. Here, by contrast, plaintiff's counsel represents a sister corporation of the defendant. Notably, *Glueck* limited its holding by stating that the *Cinema 5* analysis "is properly imposed when a lawyer undertakes to represent two adverse parties, both of which are his clients in the traditional sense," as opposed to the "vicarious" sense stemming from membership in an association. Id. We find that, for present purposes, WAII was a traditional client of Dorsey & Whitney and that the *Glueck* exception to *Cinema 5* is inapplicable to this case.

Discotrade next argues that, because the subject matter of Dorsey & Whitney's representation of Pharmaceuticals is "wholly unrelated to the subject of the instant lawsuit," disqualification is improper. This "substantial relationship" test, however, has been expressly rejected with respect to conflicts among current clients, and we decline to entertain it here. *Cinema 5*, 528 F.2d at 1387. Where the representation is ongoing, "the attorney must be prepared to show, at the very least, that there will be no actual or apparent conflict in loyalties or diminution in the vigor of his representation." Id. Dorsey & Whitney has failed to meet this "heavy burden." Id.

Finally, Discotrade argues that this case is similar to Brooklyn Navy Yard Congregation Partners L.P. v. PMNC, 174 Misc. 2d 216, 663 N.Y.S.2d 499 (N.Y. Sup. Ct. 1997), *aff'd*, 254 A.D.2d 447, 679 N.Y.S.2d 312 (2d Dep't 1998), which refused to disqualify a law firm because it was not realistic or plausible that "confidential information was or would be acquired" due to the adverse representation. Id. at 500. *Brooklyn Navy Yard*, however, is distinguishable. In that case, there was apparently no significant relationship between the two corporate affiliates. Here, by contrast, WAII and Pharmaceuticals overlap and interact in the various ways enumerated above. Accordingly, this case is closer to *JPMorgan Chase*, where the two sister corporations shared "identical corporate headquarters, an identical board, and an identical general counsel," than *Brooklyn Navy Yard*. *JPMorgan Chase*, 189 F. Supp. 2d at 23 (distinguishing

---

10. The *Glueck* Court offered an example to clarify its holding: "A law firm that represents the American Bar Association need not decline to represent a client injured by an automobile driven by a member of the ABA." 653 F.2d at 749.

Brooklyn Navy Yard on this basis). In sum, Discotrade has failed to sustain its burden.[11]

CONCLUSION

As elaborated above, we find that Dorsey & Whitney suffers from a conflict of interest by representing Discotrade in this action because it presently represents a close corporate affiliate of WAII, Pharmaceuticals. As Pharmaceuticals has expressly declined to waive the conflict, we hereby disqualify the law firm of Dorsey & Whitney from representing Discotrade in the present matter.

Notes and Questions

1. Courts are divided on how to apply the conflict of interest rules to members of corporate groups. Some decisions apply a per se rule. A lawyer who represents a member of a corporate group will be treated as having an attorney-client relationship with all subsidiaries, affiliates, or other members of the group. In McCourt Co. v. FPC Properties, Inc., 434 N.E.2d 1234 (Mass. 1982), the Massachusetts Supreme Court stated the principle as follows:

> A law firm that represents client *A* in the defense of an action may not, at the same time, be counsel for a plaintiff in an action brought against client *A*, at least without the consent of both parties.
>
> Nor does it matter that client *A* is a corporation or that client *A* consists, collectively, of a parent corporation and various wholly owned subsidiaries.

Similarly, in Stratagem Development Corp. v. Heron International N.V., 756 F. Supp. 789 (S.D.N.Y. 1991), the court held that a law firm was per se ineligible to represent the plaintiff when the firm also represented a wholly

---

11. Finally, we acknowledge that the Second Circuit has "adopt[ed] a restrained approach [to disqualification motions] that focuses primarily on preserving the integrity of the trial process." Armstrong v. McAlpin, 625 F.2d 433, 444 (2d Cir. 1980) (en banc), vacated on other grounds, 449 U.S. 1106 (1981); see *Nyquist*, 590 F.2d at 1246. . . . The Circuit has adopted this restrained approach, however, primarily because "disqualification motions are often interposed for tactical reasons [and] even when made in the best of faith, such motions inevitably cause delay." *Nyquist*, 590 F.2d at 1246 (internal citations omitted); see Allegaert v. Perot, 565 F.2d 246, 251 (2d Cir. 1977) (expressing "concern . . . that disqualification motions have become common tools of the litigation process, being used . . . for purely strategic purposes") (internal citation and quotation marks omitted) (alteration in original). These concerns, however, are inapposite to the case at bar in that Dorsey & Whitney was aware that Pharmaceuticals believed there was a conflict (and refused to waive it) before a complaint was filed. Indeed, in an e-mail from Mr. Van Dyke to Ms. Ryan dated April 30, 2002, he admits that he "had a fear that there would be a problem" with Dorsey & Whitney's representation of Discotrade against WAII. Ryan Aff. Ex. H. Accordingly, even under the "restrained approach," we find it entirely proper to disqualify Dorsey & Whitney from this action.

owned subsidiary of the defendant. This was true although the litigation concerned matters unrelated to the representation of the subsidiary. A law firm's obligation to an existing client must be measured "not so much against the similarities in litigation, as against the duty of undivided loyalty," a duty that "applies with equal force where the client is a subsidiary of the entity to be sued." Id. at 792.

2. Other courts have gone to the opposite extreme, adopting an "alter ego" test, which is very similar to "piercing the corporate veil." In Brooklyn Navy Yard Cogeneration Partners, L.P. v. Superior Court, 70 Cal. Rptr. 2d 419 (Ct. App. 1997), the California Court of Appeals held that a law firm was not disqualified from representing a client against a parent corporation when the firm represented the parent's subsidiary in unrelated matters because the parent was not the alter ego of the subsidiary. The court stated:

> The standard expression of the showing one must make to prevail on an alter ego claim is that "(1) there is such a unity of interest that the separate personalities of the corporations no longer exist; and (2) inequitable results will follow if the corporate separateness is respected." Id. at 425.

See also Reuben H. Donnelley Corp. v. Sprint Publishing & Advertising, Inc., 1996 WL 99902 (N.D. Ill. 1996) (law firm that represented one of Sprint's more than 250 subsidiaries not disqualified from representing client in litigation against another subsidiary when subsidiaries were separate entities and not alter egos). See Ronald D. Rotunda, Conflict Problems When Representing Members of Corporate Families, 72 Notre Dame L. Rev. 655 (1997) (approving of the alter ego test).

3. Other courts, as illustrated by the opinion in *Discotrade*, have adopted a functional approach under which the court examines all the fact and circumstances to determine whether the entities in question are so closely related as to amount to one client. In Formal Opinion 95-390 the ABA Committee on Ethics and Professional Responsibility supported use of a facts-and-circumstances test rather than a per se rule to determine formation of client-lawyer relationships in corporate groups. Comment 34 to revised Model Rule 1.7 follows ABA Opinion 95-390. See Charles W. Wolfram, 2 J. Inst. for Study Legal Ethics 295 (1999) (criticizing the per se and alter ego approaches and arguing in favor of a functional analysis).

4. As illustrated by *Discotrade* motions to disqualify counsel are typically supported and opposed by affidavits by counsel. What factors would you consider important to cover in an affidavit seeking to disqualify counsel in a case like *Discotrade* involving representation against a corporate affiliate?

5. The court refers to the substantial relationship test applicable to former rather than current clients. Problem 3-5 examines this issue in more detail.

Positional conflicts

Sometimes a conflict of interest can arise when a lawyer takes a legal position on behalf of one client that is adverse to the interests of another client. The term *positional conflict of interest* has been coined to refer to such conflicts. Positional conflicts can arise in a variety of ways: The purest form involves a firm taking opposing legal positions on behalf of different clients in different courts. A subtler form of positional conflict occurs when a firm represents one client in a matter that can harm the economic interests of another client.[189]

The Model Rules do not have a specific provision dealing with positional conflicts, but comment 24 to Model Rule 1.7 provides that "[o]rdinarily a lawyer may take inconsistent legal positions in different tribunals at different times on behalf of different clients" and the mere fact that an adverse precedent may result does not create a conflict of interest. However, a conflict will arise if there is a significant risk that the lawyer's action in one case will materially limit the lawyer's effectiveness in a different case, for example, if the creation of a precedent for one client is likely to "seriously weaken" the position taken on behalf of the other client. Whether this situation exists depends on an analysis of all the facts and circumstances. "Factors relevant in determining whether the clients need to be advised of the risk include: where the cases are pending, whether the issue is substantive or procedural, the temporal relationship between the matters, the significance of the issue to the immediate and long-term interests of the clients involved and the clients' reasonable expectations in retaining the lawyer." If a positional conflict arises in litigation, the lawyer may not proceed without the informed consent of both clients. The Restatement is in accord.[190]

Sometimes a positional conflict of interest arises not because of adverse legal positions but because the lawyer represents competing economic interests. Comment 6 to Model Rule 1.7 states that representation of competing economic interests is generally proper without the need for client consent: "On the other hand, simultaneous representation in unrelated matters of clients whose interests are only economically adverse, such as representation of competing economic enterprises in unrelated litigation, does not ordinarily constitute a conflict of interest and thus may not require consent of the respective clients."

In Maritrans GP, Inc. v. Pepper, Hamilton & Scheetz[191] the Pennsylvania Supreme Court created substantial concern in the profession when it held that under some circumstances it was a conflict of interest and breach of fiduciary duty for a law firm to represent competitors. In *Maritrans* the defendant law firm had been Maritrans's labor counsel for a number of years, and then began representing some of Maritrans's competitors. The firm and Maritrans initially reached an understanding in which Pepper, Hamilton agreed not to represent Maritrans's chief competitor, while Maritrans consented to the firm's representation of lesser competitors, provided the firm put in place screening mechanisms to prevent confidential information from passing between the lawyers

189. See John S. Dzienkowski, Positional Conflicts of Interest, 71 Tex. L. Rev. 457 (1993); Douglas R. Richmond, Choosing Sides: Issue or Positional Conflicts of Interest, 51 Fla. L. Rev. 383 (1999).
190. Restatement (Third) of the Law Governing Lawyers §128, cmt. *f*.
191. 602 A.2d 1277 (Pa. 1992).

representing Maritrans and those representing the competitors. Pepper, Hamilton, however, reneged on the agreement by "parking" the chief competitor with a labor lawyer in another firm who soon joined the firm. Maritrans sought an injunction to prevent Pepper, Hamilton from representing its competitors. The firm argued that the case involved a "business conflict" between competitors rather than an ethical violation. The Pennsylvania Supreme Court, however, enjoined Pepper, Hamilton from representing Maritrans's competitors because the firm was using confidential information gained during its prior representation against a former client. The court stated that it was not adopting a per se rule prohibiting a lawyer from undertaking representation of competitors, but it noted that each case must be judged on its facts. While *Maritrans* has generated a good deal of discussion, the case should not be read as prohibiting representation of clients with competing economic interests. The facts of *Maritrans* were extreme, involving abuse of a fiduciary relationship, misrepresentation to a client, and misuse of confidential information. Such conduct is far more egregious than simply representing clients with competing economic interests.

Consentable conflicts

Model Rule 1.7(b) precludes representation of one client against another client when prohibited by law or when the representation involves adverse claims in the same proceeding before a tribunal. If these limitations do not apply, a lawyer may undertake adverse representation if "(1) the lawyer reasonably believes that the lawyer will be able to provide competent and diligent representation to each affected client; . . . and (4) each affected client gives informed consent, confirmed in writing." The possibility of consentable conflicts raises several questions: Why should a lawyer ever be able to undertake representation against a client even with that client's consent? Why shouldn't a lawyer always be able to undertake representation against a client provided the client is willing to consent? What steps must the lawyer take to have effective consent?[192]

Why should a lawyer ever be able to undertake representation against a client? The rationale for allowing representation against a client with the consent of that client follows from the interests of both clients. The client seeking the lawyer's services has an interest in being able to retain the lawyer of its choice. The client against whom the lawyer would be undertaking representation has an interest in the loyalty of its counsel. In some cases, however, the impact of the representation on the lawyer's duty of loyalty to that client is farfetched. If the potentially adversely affected client is willing to "waive" any objection to the representation because it does not believe that the representation will have an impact on the lawyer's duty of loyalty to it, then the interests of both clients are being advanced. Consider the following example given by the ABA

192. See generally Fred C. Zacharias, Waiving Conflicts of Interest, 108 Yale L.J. 407 (1998).

Committee on Ethics and Professional Responsibility in Formal Opinion 93-372:

> [T]he idea that . . . a corporation in Miami retaining the Florida office of a national law firm to negotiate a lease should preclude that firm's New York office from taking an adverse position in a totally unrelated commercial dispute against another division of the same corporation strikes some as placing unreasonable limitations on the opportunities of both clients and lawyers.[193]

Why shouldn't all conflicts be subject to waiver or consent? We have already seen that in cases in which a lawyer is asked to represent clients who have adverse interests in a single contested litigation matter, representation is improper even with client consent. In these situations it is impossible for the lawyer to comply with the duty of loyalty to both clients; in addition, the systemic interest in the proper functioning of the adversarial situation justifies a per se prohibition. In most conflict situations, however, including those involving unrelated-matter conflicts, representation of both clients is permissible with their consent.

Assuming then that some, but not all, conflicts are subject to waiver or consent, what must a lawyer do to obtain effective client consent? A good example of informed consent by a client to representation against it in unrelated matters is Unified Sewerage Agency v. Jelco, Inc.[194] In *Unified Sewerage* a law firm was representing Teeples & Thatcher, a client that the firm had represented for more than 10 years, in an embryonic dispute with its general contractor, Jelco, when Jelco asked the same firm to represent it in a dispute with an electrical subcontractor. The firm advised Jelco of its representation of Teeples & Thatcher and informed Jelco that it could not undertake representation unless Jelco consented to the firm's continued representation of Teeples & Thatcher. Jelco's management, with full knowledge of the firm's representation of Teeples & Thatcher and with the advice of its general counsel, consented to the law firm's representation of Teeples & Thatcher. Subsequently, the firm filed suit in the name of Unified Sewerage for the benefit of Teeples & Thatcher against Jelco. The firm again asked Jelco whether it consented to the firm's continued representation of Teeples & Thatcher and Jelco once again gave its consent. A few months later, however, Jelco discharged the firm from handling the matter with the electrical subcontractor and also moved to disqualify the firm in the pending action brought by Unified.

The Court of Appeals for the Ninth Circuit affirmed the trial court's decision denying the motion for disqualification. While recognizing the general rule precluding representation against a present client, the court held that such representation was proper because Jelco had given informed consent. The court noted that the attorney must do more than simply inform the client of the conflict and obtain approval of the representation. The lawyer must explain

193. ABA Comm. on Ethics and Prof. Resp., Formal Op. 93-372, at 2.
194. 646 F.2d 1339 (9th Cir. 1981).

the implications of the conflict to the client. On the facts of the case the court found that this requirement was satisfied. The court placed particular emphasis on the fact that Jelco's consent had been obtained after Jelco had consulted with its general counsel about the matter.

By contrast to *Unified Sewerage*, the court in International Business Machines Corp. v. Levin, discussed above, held that the firm had not effectively obtained IBM's consent. Two partners in the law firm testified that they had independently obtained IBM's consent to the firm's representation of Levin, but representatives of IBM denied that they had given their consent. The Court of Appeals for the Third Circuit rejected the consent argument because it concluded that the law firm had not carried its burden of proving a "full disclosure" to IBM as required by DR 5-105(C) (the predecessor to Model Rule 1.7). The court noted that the alleged consent occurred during a telephone call that took at most three minutes.

Consent: validity of prospective waivers

In cases like *Unified Sewerage*, the consent occurred after the conflict situation arose. May a law firm effectively obtain a prospective waiver of future conflicts? Both the Model Rules and the Restatement approve of the use of prospective waivers but indicate that the mere fact that the client signed a waiver is not conclusive with regard to the propriety of subsequent representation against the client. The fundamental issue is whether "the client reasonably understands the material risks that the waiver entails." Model Rule 1.7, cmt. 22. The comment identifies a variety of factors that are relevant to this determination:

> Thus, if the client agrees to consent to a particular type of conflict with which the client is already familiar, then the consent ordinarily will be effective with regard to that type of conflict. If the consent is general and open-ended, then the consent ordinarily will be ineffective, because it is not reasonably likely that the client will have understood the material risks involved. On the other hand, if the client is an experienced user of the legal services involved and is reasonably informed regarding the risk that a conflict may arise, such consent is more likely to be effective, particularly if, e.g., the client is independently represented by other counsel in giving consent and the consent is limited to future conflicts unrelated to the subject of the representation.[195]

---

195. See also Restatement (Third) of the Law Governing Lawyers §122, cmt. *d*. In Formal Opinion 93-372, the ABA Committee on Ethics and Professional Responsibility advised that prospective waivers were ethically permissible but they would not be enforceable as to matters not reasonably contemplated at the time the waiver was executed. *Compare* Visa U.S.A., Inc. v. First Data Corp., 241 F. Supp. 2d 1100 (N.D. Cal. 2003) (prospective waiver by sophisticated client that identified adverse client and nature of conflict being waived was enforceable), *with* Worldspan, L.P. v. Sabre Group Holdings, Inc., 5 F. Supp. 2d 1356 (N.D. Ga. 1998) (general conflicts waiver in engagement agreement ineffective when applied to conflict that arises five years later).

Consider the following analysis of the enforceability of prospective waivers:

A blanket waiver . . . should not be enforced. Central to the effectiveness of client consent is communication of information sufficient to enable the client to make an informed decision. It is difficult to believe that a client can receive sufficient information to make an informed decision when the client, at the time of the consent, knows neither the nature of the conflict nor the person or entity with whom the conflict exists.

Moreover, the argument in support of judicial recognition of a blanket waiver is weak. The argument is based on the policy in favor of selection of counsel; it posits that if such waivers are not valid, a law firm may be unwilling to undertake representation of a new client in a matter because it fears that the new representation may require the firm's disqualification in a matter on behalf of a more substantial client who has or may have an interest adverse to that of the new client. Thus, clients may be deprived of the opportunity of obtaining the services of law firms with particular expertise.

This argument in favor of the validity of a blanket waiver ignores the economic forces that drive law firms. . . . To say that the firm would refuse to undertake representation in that matter because of some unknown, future conflict is to say that firms will refuse to take on new business because a new client might some day have a conflict with an existing client. While such a conflict might develop, the client also represents new business to the firm. Therefore, the economic drive of firms will give them a powerful incentive to take on such new business. . . .

While courts should refuse to enforce blanket prospective waivers, it would be appropriate for courts to accept more limited prospective consents. A good example of such a situation is City of Cleveland v. Cleveland Elec. Illuminating Co. [440 F. Supp. 193 (N.D. Ohio 1976), *aff'd*, 573 F.2d 1310 (6th Cir. 1977), *cert. denied*, 435 U.S. 996 (1978)]. In that case the law firm of Squire, Sanders & Dempsey had represented Cleveland Electric Company for over 65 years when the City asked the firm to handle a bond matter involving the City's competing utility company. The City was well aware of the law firm's long-time representation of Cleveland Electric because of numerous prior dealings with the Electric Company; it wished to retain the firm's services, however, because it was one of the few firms in Ohio that handled sophisticated bond work. Squire, Sanders was willing to take on the bond work only if the City waived any objection to future conflicts. The City had independent advice from its law department and waived its objections to any conflict of interest. Subsequently, the City moved to disqualify the firm in an antitrust action brought by the City against Cleveland Electric. The United States District Court for the Northern District of Ohio denied the motion for disqualification. In a lengthy opinion the court held that the City had waived any conflict of interest. The court also ruled that the City failed to show that the firm was using confidential information against its interests.

In cases like *City of Cleveland* a prospective consent should be enforced. The client was a sophisticated corporate entity with independent legal advice about the waiver. The waiver itself was limited to the firm's representation of an identified long-term client rather than a blanket prospective consent. When such factors are present, it seems reasonable to conclude that the client has sufficient information to consent to the dual representation. Moreover, unless the City had agreed to the waiver it would have been unable to obtain representation in specialized bond work. Thus, the policy argument in favor of recognizing a waiver in such a case, which rests on the ability of a client to retain counsel of its choice, seems strong. Finally, the case did not involve the use of confidential information against the client.[196]

━━━━━━━━━━ Problem 3-5 ━━━━━━━━━━

Representation Against Former Clients

For eight years the law firm of Carson, Fender & Sink was local counsel for National Securities, Inc., one of the country's largest brokerage firms. The firm defended National in a variety of securities matters, principally arbitrations of claims by customers. Three years ago National had a change of management and decided to replace many of its local counsel, including the Carson firm.

Recently, Marian Enderson, the chief executive officer of one of Carson's corporate clients, has encountered problems with one of National's brokers, Ronald Benson, an employee of National for a number of years. Enderson claims that Benson gave her misleading information about a company that has since gone bankrupt. Enderson asked the Carson firm to represent her in arbitration against National. The firm advised Enderson of its prior representation of National, but Enderson stated that she wanted the firm to represent her even if there was a risk that the firm might face a disqualification motion. Carson has filed the claim in arbitration against National. The claim alleges that National is responsible for Benson's fraud, based on agency and securities theories. National denies that Benson committed any fraud. It also argues that even if Benson did engage in fraud, it maintains proper procedures for preventing fraud and therefore is not responsible for Benson's actions. When the Carson firm filed the complaint in arbitration, counsel for National objected to the firm's representation of Enderson. After the Carson firm refused to withdraw, National filed a motion to disqualify the firm. Be prepared to argue in support of the motion to disqualify on behalf of National and in opposition to the motion on behalf of the Carson firm.

Read Model Rule 1.9 and comments.

196. Nathan M. Crystal, Disqualification of Counsel for Unrelated Matter Conflicts of Interest, 4 Geo. J. Legal Ethics 273, 307-309 (1990). See also Lawrence J. Fox, All's O.K. Between Consenting Adults: Enlightened Rule on Privacy, Obscene Rule on Ethics, 29 Hofstra L. Rev. 701 (2001) (prospective waivers that do not identify the specific matter being waived should not be unenforceable). But see Richard W. Painter, Advance Waiver Conflicts, 13 Geo. J. Legal Ethics 289 (2000) (approving of advance waivers and suggesting specific criteria governing their enforceability).

Origin and justification for the substantial relationship test

Neither the Code of Professional Responsibility nor the 1908 Canons of Ethics had a specific rule dealing with representation against a former client. In T.C. Theatre Corp. v. Warner Bros. Pictures, Inc.,[197] however, Judge Weinfeld articulated a principle for deciding when a lawyer could properly undertake representation against a former client:

> I hold that the former client need show no more than that the matters embraced within the pending suit wherein his former attorney appears on behalf of his adversary are substantially related to the matters or cause of action wherein the attorney previously represented him, the former client. The court will assume that during the course of the former representation confidences were disclosed to the attorney bearing on the subject matter of the representation. It will not inquire into their nature and extent. Only in this manner can the lawyer's duty of absolute fidelity be enforced and the spirit of the rule relating to privileged communications be maintained.
>
> . . . In cases of this sort the court must ask whether it can reasonably be said that in the course of the former representation the attorney might have acquired information related to the subject of his subsequent representation. If so, then the relationship between the two matters is sufficiently close to bring the later representation within the prohibition of Canon 6 [which prohibited lawyers from representing clients with conflicting interest and from revealing confidential information].[198]

Judge Weinfeld developed what is now widely referred to as the "substantial relationship" test for deciding when representation against a former client is permissible. Several aspects of the substantial relationship test developed by Judge Weinfeld are worth noting. Implicit in this test is recognition of the principle that if the matters are not substantially related, representation against a former client is permissible, even without the consent of that former client. Why should this be the case? Shouldn't a lawyer be absolutely precluded from undertaking representation against a former client? Even putting aside the possible misuse of confidential information, isn't representation against a former client disloyal, and doesn't it create an appearance of wrongdoing that should be avoided? While these points have merit, there are competing considerations. First, a duty of absolute loyalty to a former client would mean that a lawyer could never undertake representation against a former client without that client's consent. This rule would substantially limit the ability of other clients to select counsel of their choice. Second, a per se prohibition on representation against former clients might deter lawyers from taking on representation in relatively small matters because of concern that the representation would

197. 113 F. Supp. 265 (S.D.N.Y. 1953).
198. Id. at 268-269.

disqualify the lawyer from handling all unknown future matters against that client. Third, unless some limitation were established, lawyers would owe former clients a lifetime duty of loyalty. The existence of such a duty would almost certainly increase legal fees because lawyers would be forced to take into account the preclusive effect of representation of a client in deciding how much to charge the client for the lawyer's services. Finally, lawyers serve as agents for their clients. Under agency law, an agent after termination of employment may not use confidential information against the principal, but the agent is not prevented from competing with the principal.[199]

Judge Weinfeld also stated that if the current and former matters were substantially related, a court should make no further inquiry to determine whether confidential information is actually being used. To engage in such an inquiry would defeat the very confidentiality that the rule is designed to protect. Thus, the substantial relationship test in its original form amounted to an "irrebuttable presumption" that confidential information was likely to be used if the matters were substantially related. As noted below, however, some courts have moved away from this view and will allow the attorney to offer evidence to rebut the presumption that confidential information will be used in the subsequent representation. Finally, the remedy most frequently used for violation of the substantial relationship test has been disqualification of the lawyer and the lawyer's firm from continuing the representation of the current client in the substantially related matter against the former client.[200]

Issues in applying the substantial relationship test

Model Rule 1.9(a) codifies the substantial relationship test developed by Judge Weinfeld. A number of questions have arisen regarding the application of the test. Does the substantial relationship test only protect the former client's interest in confidentiality, as Judge Weinfeld's formulation indicates, or should the test also protect the former client's interest in loyalty? Some courts have suggested that the substantial relationship test rests both on foundations of confidentiality and loyalty to the former client. The leading case adopting this view is In re American Airlines, Inc.,[201] where the Fifth Circuit disqualified a law firm from representing Northwest Airlines in a private antitrust case against American Airlines, when the law firm had previously represented American in three matters involving antitrust issues in the airline industry. The Fifth Circuit

---

199. Restatement (Second) of Agency §396 (1958).

200. A lawyer who violates the substantial relationship test may also be subject to malpractice liability to the former client. Damron v. Herzog, 67 F.3d 211 (9th Cir. 1995), *cert. denied*, 516 U.S. 1117 (1996). On rare occasions, lawyers have been disciplined for representation against a former client in a substantially related matter. See In re Carey, 89 S.W.3d 477 (Mo. 2002) (lawyers indefinitely suspended for representing plaintiffs in class action against Chrysler when lawyers previously defended Chrysler in substantially related matter; attorneys also filed false discovery responses).

201. 972 F.2d 605 (5th Cir. 1992), *cert. denied*, 507 U.S. 912 (1993).

held that disqualification was required because of the firm's duty of loyalty to American:

> A party seeking to disqualify counsel under the substantial relationship test need not prove that the past and present matters are so similar that a lawyer's continued involvement threatens to taint the trial. Rather, the former client must demonstrate that the two matters are substantially related. Second, we adhere to our precedents in refusing to reduce the concerns underlying the substantial relationship test to a client's interest in preserving his confidential information. The second fundamental concern protected by the test is not the public interest in lawyers avoiding "even the appearance of impropriety," but the client's interest in the loyalty of his attorney.[202]

American Airlines may have been correctly decided on the facts, but the court's language goes much too far in protecting the interests of former clients. Indeed, this reasoning could easily lead to de facto abolition of the substantial relationship test and creation of an almost unlimited duty of loyalty to former clients that could not be infringed without their consent. For the policy reasons discussed above, such a broad duty to former clients seems unsound. Both the Model Rules and the Restatement reject this view. Instead, the Model Rules and the Restatement provide that the fundamental justification of the substantial relationship test is protection of the former client's right to confidentiality. Comment 3 to Model Rule 1.9 states: "Matters are 'substantially related' for purposes of this Rule if they involve the same transaction or legal dispute or if there otherwise is a substantial risk that confidential factual information as would normally have been obtained in the prior representation would materially advance the client's position in the subsequent matter." Similarly, the Restatement provides that a substantial relationship between the current and former representation exists if "there is a substantial risk that representation of the present client will involve the use of information acquired in the course of representing the former client, unless that information has become generally known."[203]

The Model Rules and the Restatement recognize, however, that a former client has a limited right to the loyalty of the former attorney. This limited duty of loyalty precludes a lawyer from attacking work product that the lawyer prepared for a prior client, even if the current representation would not pose any risk of use of the prior client's confidences. Thus, a lawyer could not seek to rescind on behalf of a current client a contract that the lawyer drafted for a prior client. Model Rule 1.9, cmt. 1.[204]

---

202. Id. at 616. See also Casco Northern Bank v. JBI Associates, Ltd., 667 A.2d 856, 860 (Me. 1995).

203. Restatement (Third) of the Law Governing Lawyers §132(2) and cmt. *d(iii)*.

204. Id. §132(1). Professor Wolfram argues that a lawyer owes duties of loyalty to a former client in three situations: (1) attack on former work product, (2) representation of one jointly represented client against a former coclient, and (3) representation against a former client when the lawyer withdrew from representation of the former client to take

Assuming the substantial relationship test primarily protects the confidentiality interest of former clients, when is there a substantial relationship between the current and former matters? Courts have developed a variety of definitions of when matters are substantially related.[205] In Trone v. Smith,[206] the Ninth Circuit stated the following fact-based application of the substantial relationship test:

> The substantial relationship test does not require that the issues in the two representations be identical.
>
> The relationship is measured by the allegations in the complaint and by the nature of the evidence that would be helpful in establishing those allegations.[207]

By contrast, other courts focus on the legal issues involved in the two matters. For example, the Second Circuit has ruled that disqualification is justified only when the relationship between the issues involved in the two matters is "patently clear."[208] The Seventh Circuit has developed a three-pronged test that combines both factual and legal analysis:

> Initially, the trial judge must make a factual reconstruction of the scope of the prior legal representation. Second, it must be determined whether it is reasonable to infer that the confidential information allegedly given would have been given to a lawyer representing a client in those matters. Finally, it must be determined whether that information is relevant to the issues raised in the litigation pending against the former client.[209]

A crucial issue in applying any of these tests is the degree of importance to the current matter that must be shown for the substantial relationship test to apply. Compare *Trone* ("helpful"), with *Government of India* ("patently clear"), with *Novo* ("relevant"). Both the Model Rules and the Restatement adopt a fairly demanding standard. Model Rule 1.9, comment 3 states that the information gained in the prior representation must "materially advance the client's position in the subsequent matter."[210] If the information in question

---

on the new, more favored client ("hot potato" situations, see Problem 3-2). See Charles W. Wolfram, Former-Client Conflicts, 10 Geo. J. Legal Ethics 677 (1997). The second situation is already covered under the substantial relationship test because the current matter grows out of the prior representation. The third situation involves a breach of a duty of loyalty to a current client by improper withdrawal, rather than a duty of loyalty to a former client.

205. See Analysis & Perspective, Conflicts of Interest: Representation Adverse to Former Client, 18 Law. Man. Prof. Con. (ABA/BNA) 490, 498-504 (2002).

206. 621 F.2d 994 (9th Cir. 1980).

207. Id. at 1000.

208. Government of India v. Cook Industries, Inc., 569 F.2d 737, 740 (2d Cir. 1978).

209. Novo Terapeutisk Laboratorium A/S v. Baxter Travenol Labs., Inc., 607 F.2d 186, 190 (7th Cir. 1979).

210. Accord Restatement (Third) of the Law Governing Lawyers §132, cmt. *d(iii)*.

has become generally known, the lawyer will usually not be disqualified. Model Rule 1.9, cmt. 3.[211] In addition, passage of time may make information gained in the prior representation stale. Model Rule 1.9, cmt. 3.

Another issue that courts have faced in applying the substantial relationship test is whether a lawyer's knowledge of a client's litigation strategy, approaches to negotiation, business practices, or key personnel is sufficient to create a substantial relationship between current and prior representation. Information of this type is often referred to "playbook" information. Such situations can arise when a lawyer has had a long-standing relationship with a client that comes to an end, for example, when a corporate counsel leaves the company to enter private practice, or when a client discharges a law firm that has represented it for many years to retain new counsel. Some courts have held that playbook information is sufficient to create a substantial relationship because the lawyer has gained confidential insight and understanding of the client that is highly useful in the current matter.[212] Other courts disagree. For example, in Duncan v. Merrill Lynch, Pierce, Fenner & Smith, Inc.[213] the Fifth Circuit held that a law firm was not disqualified from representing the plaintiff in a securities fraud action arising from the sale of municipal bonds even though the firm had previously represented Merrill Lynch in ten different securities matters over a ten-year period. The court stated that the firm's representation of "Merrill Lynch, even on a variety of matters and over a relatively long period of time, is alone insufficient to establish the required nexus with the present case." The court decided that Merrill Lynch had done nothing more than offer a "catalogue of such generalities," when disqualification required a "painstaking analysis of the facts."[214] The Model Rules and the Restatement both conclude that playbook information is generally insufficient to create a substantial relationship. Model Rule 1.9, comment 3 states: "In the case of an organizational client, general knowledge of the client's policies and practices ordinarily will not preclude a subsequent representation; on the other hand, knowledge of specific facts gained in a prior representation that are relevant to the matter in question ordinarily will preclude such a representation."[215]

---

211. Id. §132(2) ("unless that information has become generally known"). See also Jamaica Public Service Co. v. AIU Insurance Co., 707 N.E.2d 414 (N.Y. 1998) (plaintiff's law firm not disqualified for disclosure of generally known information when member of firm was former in-house counsel of defendant).

212. Kaselaan & D'Angelo Assocs., Inc. v. D'Angelo, 144 F.R.D. 235, 240-241 (D.N.J. 1992). Accord Cardona v. General Motors Corp., 942 F. Supp. 968 (D.N.J. 1996) (plaintiff's law firm disqualified in lemon law suit against GM when lawyer hired by firm had previously represented GM in similar litigation even though the lawyer was screened from participation; counsel was aware of defendant's claims and litigation philosophy, as well as its methods and procedures for defending claims).

213. 646 F.2d 1020 (5th Cir.), cert. denied, 454 U.S. 895 (1981).

214. Id. at 1029.

215. Restatement (Third) of the Law Governing Lawyers §132(2) and cmt. d(iii) ("[o]nly when such information will be directly in issue or of unusual value"). See State ex rel. Ogden Newspapers, Inc. v. Wilkes, 566 S.E.2d 560 (W. Va. 2002) (playbook

In formulating the substantial relationship test, Judge Weinfeld stated that once the former client shows that the matters are substantially related, the court will assume that the attorney acquired confidential information and "will not inquire into their nature and extent." Many courts have decided that a presumption arises that the former attorney acquired confidential information in connection with the prior representation.[216] Courts often state that the presumption is irrebuttable.[217] The purpose of this presumption is to prevent forcing the former client to reveal confidential information to establish the basis of disqualification, thus defeating the very interest that the client was seeking to protect.[218] The Model Rules indicate that the former client need not reveal confidences to establish a substantial relationship between the matters: "A conclusion about the possession of such information may be based on the nature of the services the lawyer provided the former client and information that would in ordinary practice be learned by a lawyer providing such services." Model Rule 1.9, cmt. 3. To the extent that inquiry into specific confidential information is necessary, the Restatement suggests the use of in-camera proceedings or redaction of documents to protect the former client's right to confidentiality.[219]

Some courts, however, have extended the use of presumptions further, holding that when a substantial relationship exists, an irrebuttable presumption arises that the former attorney will be in a position to use confidences gained in the prior representation against the former client.[220] This use of a presumption seems inappropriate because it effectively prevents the current client and attorney from defending themselves by showing that any confidential information gained in the prior representation would not be useful or material to the current representation. In fact, such an irrebuttable presumption seems inconsistent with Model Rule 1.6(b)(5), which allows a lawyer to reveal confidential information "to respond to allegations in any proceeding concerning the lawyer's representation of the client."

Normally, the application of the substantial relationship test requires the party seeking disqualification to show that a client-lawyer relationship formerly existed. In some cases, however, disqualification may be appropriate even

---

information about former client insufficient for disqualification, citing Restatement with approval). See also Wolfram, Former-Client Conflicts, 10 Geo. J. Legal Ethics at 723-727.

216. E.g., Allegaert v. Perot, 565 F.2d 246, 250 (2d Cir. 1977).

217. Sullivan Country Regional Refuse Disposal District v. Acworth, 686 A.2d 755, 758 (N.H. 1996). See Restatement (Third) of the Law Governing Lawyers §132(2) and cmt. *d(iii)*: "When the prior matter involved litigation, it will be conclusively presumed that the lawyer obtained confidential information about the issues involved in the litigation. When the prior matter did not involve litigation, its scope is assessed by reference to the work that the lawyer undertook and the array of information that a lawyer ordinarily would have obtained to carry out that work."

218. Wolfram, Former-Client Conflicts, 10 Geo. J. Legal Ethics at 717-718.

219. Restatement (Third) of the Law Governing Lawyers §132(2) and cmt. *d(iii)*.

220. Wolfram, Former-Client Conflicts, 10 Geo. J. Legal Ethics at 719, n.172.

when a client-lawyer relationship was not formed. One such situation involves prospective clients. Suppose a lawyer is not engaged after preliminary discussions with a prospective client. The lawyer may be unable to undertake the representation because of a conflict of interest between the prospective client and another client of the lawyer's firm. Sometimes the client may decide to retain other counsel; in an increasingly competitive market for legal services, many corporate clients shop around through a series of "beauty contests" before retaining counsel.[221] The courts are divided on whether a preliminary consultation with a client is sufficient to invoke the former client disqualification rule, but the cases usually turn on the particular facts and extent of receipt of confidential information.[222] Model Rule 1.18, adopted as part of the 2002 revision of the Model Rules, addresses the issue of prospective clients. Under the rule a lawyer who is not engaged may not use or reveal confidential information gained in the consultation against the former prospective client. Model Rule 1.18(b). The lawyer who conducted the consultation is personally disqualified from undertaking representation against the former prospective client in the same or substantially related matter if the lawyer gained information that could be significantly harmful to the former prospective client in the matter, absent client consent. Model Rule 1.18(c). However, the lawyer's firm is not disqualified if the lawyer took reasonable steps to avoid being exposed to more confidential information than was necessary to determine whether to represent the prospective client, the personally disqualified lawyer is screened from any participation in the matter, and the prospective client is promptly given written notice about the matter. Model Rule 1.18(d)(2). The Restatement is similar.[223] We will examine the concept of screening in more detail in connection with the next problem.

While Rule 1.9(a) protects a former client against the risk of use of confidential information when a former attorney undertakes representation against the former client in a substantially related matter, former clients also have the protection of Rule 1.9(c), which prohibits an attorney from using, to the disadvantage of the former client, or disclosing confidential information even if the use or disclosure does not involve representation against the former client. Rule 1.9(b) deals with situations where a lawyer changes firms. We will discuss this rule in the next problem.

---

221. See Kenneth D. Agran, Note, The Treacherous Path to the Diamond-Studded Tiara: Ethical Dilemmas in Legal Beauty Contests, 9 Geo. J. Legal Ethics 1307 (1996).

222. *Compare* Metcalf v. Metcalf, 785 So. 2d 747 (Fla. Dist. Ct. App. 2001) (firm disqualified in domestic violence case from representing husband because wife had previously consulted with member of firm about intention to institute divorce action and revealed details about domestic violence), *with* State ex rel. DeFrances v. Bedell, 446 S.E.2d 906 (W. Va. 1994) (law firm was not disqualified from representing beneficiaries in estate dispute because of one-hour meeting with testator several years before his death that did not result in billing, conveyance of any confidential information, or retention of firm's services).

223. Restatement (Third) of the Law Governing Lawyers §15.

Appearance of impropriety as a basis for disqualification

Canon 9 of the Code of Professional Responsibility provided that a lawyer should avoid "even the appearance of professional impropriety." Some courts relied on this concept to disqualify lawyers from undertaking representation against former clients, even without an inquiry into whether the current and former representations were substantially related.[224]

Many commentators and courts criticized the use of the appearance of impropriety as a basis for disqualification principally because of its vagueness: From whose perspective—the public, the bar, reasonable people, the former client—is the appearance to be judged?[225] The Model Rules do not include the concept of the appearance of impropriety.[226] Similarly, the Restatement also rejects the appearance of impropriety as a basis for prohibiting representation against former clients.[227]

Despite this widespread rejection, occasional decisions still rely on the appearance of impropriety as a basis of disqualification. For example, in Crawford W. Long Memorial Hospital of Emory University v. Yerby[228] the hospital moved to disqualify plaintiff's attorney, who had previously represented the hospital in 18 medical malpractice actions. In 1984, when the attorney was representing the hospital on other medical malpractice claims, Yerby entered the hospital for back surgery and died the same day. The court found that it was unnecessary to decide if the matters were substantially related:

> In this case, we need not determine whether the medical-malpractice claim that Bennett has brought *against* the hospital is "substantially related" to any of the eighteen medical-malpractice claims that he had defended *on behalf* of the hospital. The circumstance of representing a client against a former client in an action that is of the same general subject matter, and grows out of an event that occurred *during the time* of such representation, creates an impermissible appearance of impropriety.[229]

---

224. E.g., Renshaw v. Ravert, 460 F. Supp. 1089 (E.D. Pa. 1978) (in civil rights case substantial relationship test does not require disqualification of plaintiff's attorney, but disqualification is warranted under Canon 9 because attorney represented one of defendant police officers 10 years previously).

225. Wolfram, Modern Legal Ethics §7.1.4, at 319-323.

226. Comment 5 to the 1983 version of the Model Rules specifically rejected this principle as a basis for analysis. The 2002 revision deleted this comment, but the Reporter's Note indicates that no change in substance was intended. See Schwartz v. Cortelloni, 685 N.E.2d 871 (Ill. 1997) (rejecting appearance of impropriety standard).

227. Restatement (Third) of the Law Governing Lawyers §121, cmt. *c(iv)*.

228. 373 S.E.2d 749 (Ga. 1988).

229. Id. at 751. In Clinard v. Blackwood, 46 S.W.3d 177 (Tenn. 2001), an attorney who represented a client in a property matter later withdrew from representation of his client and subsequently joined a firm that represented the adversary in the same matter. The court disqualified the firm using the concept of the appearance of impropriety even though the firm had promptly instituted screening procedures to prevent disclosure of confidential information. The case was decided under the Code of Professional Responsibil-

---

Problem 3-6

Imputation of Disqualification

For six years Anne Reynor has been an associate with Chen & Rivera, where she has worked in the insurance defense section, principally defending medical malpractice actions. Reynor has decided to leave the firm and join a plaintiff's litigation firm. Her new firm, Howe & Associates, handles a variety of plaintiff's matters including medical malpractice. The firm is now handling several cases in which Chen & Rivera represents the defendant doctor and the insurance carrier. Howe & Associates wants to avoid any problem of disqualification because of Reynor's joining the firm. What advice would you give to the firm?

Read Model Rules 1.9, 1.10, and comments.

The imputation principle

Both the Code of Professional Responsibility in DR 5-105(D) and the Model Rules of Professional Conduct in Rule 1.10(a) recognize a principle of "imputed" or "vicarious" disqualification. Under this principle, when lawyers are currently associated in a firm, and one of the lawyers is disqualified from handling a matter, that disqualification is imputed to disqualify all members of the firm. The rationale for the rule of imputed disqualification is based on the fact that lawyers practicing in a firm have access to firm files and have mutual financial interests. As a result, it is assumed that any confidential information that one member of the firm has is accessible to other members of the firm and that any conflict of interest that affects a member of the firm will also affect other members.[230] One can question the validity of these assumptions, especially in large firms, but the principle of imputed disqualification seems to be firmly established in the law of professional ethics. It should be noted that the concept of a "firm" is broader than private law firms, and can include cocounsel relationships. See Model Rule 1.10, cmt. 1. In People ex rel. Department of Corporations v. SpeeDee Oil Change Systems, Inc.[231] the California Supreme Court held that the rule of imputed disqualification

---

ity, prior to Tennessee's adoption of the Model Rules, and the court indicated that the decision might be different under the Model Rules. 46 S.W.2d at 186, n.7.

230. The 2002 revision to the Model Rules adopts a limitation on the principle of imputed disqualification if "the prohibition is based on a personal interest of the prohibited lawyer and does not present a significant risk of materially limiting the representation of the client by the remaining lawyers in the firm." Model Rule 1.10(a). The comments provide "strong political beliefs" as an illustration of conflict based on personal interest that would not normally be imputed to other members of the firm. Id. cmt. 3.

231. 980 P.2d 371 (Cal. 1999).

extends to lawyers who are "of counsel" to firms, a relationship that is "close, personal, continuous, and regular." There are, however, qualifications and limitations to the principle of imputed disqualification.

Imputed disqualification and movement between firms

One of the most important limitations on the rule of imputed disqualification deals with movement of a lawyer from one firm to another. Strictly applied, the rule of imputed disqualification could lead to extreme instances of disqualification, even when no realistic risk of use of confidential information exists. Consider this example: Lawyer works for Old Firm. Lawyer leaves Old Firm to join New Firm. Arguably, all lawyers in New Firm are precluded from undertaking representation against any client of Old Firm on a matter that is substantially related to any matter that Old Firm was handling while Lawyer was a member of the firm, *even if Lawyer was not involved in the matter.* This result could flow from a "double imputation" of disqualification: Lawyer would be disqualified vicariously because of her membership in Old Firm. Lawyer's vicarious disqualification would then be imputed to all members of New Firm when Lawyer joins the firm.

This "double imputation" (from Old Firm members to Lawyer and from Lawyer to New Firm members) is unsound as a matter of policy. First, the risk of misuse of confidential information in this situation is small because Lawyer was not directly privy to any confidential information. Second, the use of imputed disqualification could unfairly restrict the mobility of lawyers between firms and unnecessarily limit the ability of clients to select counsel.

The leading case dealing with application of the rule of imputed disqualification when lawyers move between firms is Silver Chrysler Plymouth, Inc. v. Chrysler Motors Corp.[232] Silver Chrysler Plymouth sued Chrysler Motors for breach of contract. The Kelley Drye law firm represented its long-time client, Chrysler Motors, in the action. The firm of Hammond & Schreiber, P.C. represented the plaintiff. Dale Schreiber, a member of that firm, had worked as an associate at Kelley Drye. The defendant moved to disqualify the plaintiff's firm because of Schreiber's prior employment with Kelley Drye. The Court of Appeals for the Second Circuit rejected the notion that Schreiber should be conclusively presumed to have received confidential information:

> It is . . . well known that the larger firms in the metropolitan areas have hundreds (collectively thousands) of clients. It is unquestionably true that in the course of their work at large law firms, associates are entrusted with the confidences of some of their clients. But it would be absurd to conclude that immediately upon their entry on duty they become the recipients of knowledge as to the names of all the firm's clients, the contents of all files relating to such clients, and all confidential disclosures by client officers or employees to any lawyer in the firm.

232. 518 F.2d 751 (2d Cir. 1975).

Obviously such legal osmosis does not occur. The mere recital of such a proposition should be self-refuting. And a rational interpretation of the Code of Professional Responsibility does not call for disqualification on the basis of such an unrealistic perception of the practice of law in large firms.[233]

The court ruled that Schreiber should be disqualified only if he had actually acquired confidential information. While Schreiber had worked on some Chrysler matters, his involvement was relatively minor, consisting principally of limited research.[234] Accordingly, the court found that Schreiber had rebutted any inference that he had received confidential information and would not be disqualified.

The *Silver Chrysler Plymouth* decision has been codified in Model Rule 1.9(b). If a lawyer changes firms, the lawyer is disqualified from handling a matter involving a client of the lawyer's old firm only if the new matter is the same as or substantially related to a matter involving the client of the former firm, the interests of the new client and the former client are materially adverse, and the lawyer received confidential information materially related to the matter. The lawyer is not disqualified simply based on her membership in the old firm. If the lawyer is not disqualified under Rule 1.9(b), then her new firm is also not disqualified under Rule 1.10(a).[235]

Imputed disqualification and "screening" of disqualified lawyers

Silver Chrysler Plymouth dealt with a situation in which the lawyer moving to the new firm was not personally disqualified. Suppose, however, that the lawyer is personally disqualified, either because he acquired confidential information or because the matter that he is being asked to handle is substantially related to a matter that he handled while a member of his old firm. While the lawyer cannot personally handle the matter, can another member of his new firm do so, or is the lawyer's disqualification imputed to the new firm? Strict application of the rule of imputed disqualification would disqualify all members of the new firm. It has been suggested, however, that this is an overly broad application of the rule of imputed disqualification and that the new firm should not be disqualified from handling a matter if the personally disqualified lawyer is "screened" from any involvement in the matter (the term *Chinese Wall* is also used).

The drafters of the Model Rules debated whether screening should be allowed when a disqualified lawyer moves from one firm to another. Strong arguments were made in favor of this approach. First, the argument for absolute

---

233. Id. at 753-754.
234. Id. at 756.
235. But see State ex rel. FirsTier Bank, N. A. v. Buckley, 503 N.W.2d 838 (Neb. 1993) (adopting "bright line" test disqualifying new firm in matter substantially related to matter handled by lawyer's former firm regardless of whether lawyer received confidential information).

disqualification of the new firm was based on the assumption that the lawyer joining the new firm would violate his ethical obligation to maintain confidences of the former client. Advocates of screening argued that it was not reasonable to base rules of ethics on the assumption that lawyers would generally violate such a fundamental duty. Second, a rule of absolute disqualification unfairly penalizes clients of the new firm, who are deprived of the counsel of their choice. Third, the rule is unfair to lawyers seeking a change in employment since firms may be unwilling to hire them because of the risk of disqualification of the entire firm. Such lawyers would be viewed as "typhoid Marys."[236] In addition, it was pointed out that the Model Rules did allow screening in another context, when a lawyer moved from government service to private practice, although the interests involved in that situation are somewhat different. See Model Rule 1.11(b) and Problem 6-3. Despite these arguments, the drafters of the Model Rules chose to reject the possibility of screening when a disqualified lawyer joined a firm. Apparently, the drafters concluded that clients were entitled to assurances of confidentiality, and that this was possible only by a rule that disqualified the entire firm that hired a personally disqualified lawyer.[237] The Ethics 2000 Commission recommended that Rule 1.10 be amended to allow screening of a personally disqualified lawyer who switched firms, but the ABA's House of Delegates rejected the proposal.[238] The revised Model Rules, however, do allow screening in a number of other situations: former government lawyers, Rule 1.11; former judges or neutrals, Rule 1.12; and prospective clients, Rule 1.18.

Although the Model Rules reject screening as a way of dealing with conflicts of interest when a lawyer moves from one firm to another, the issue continues to be debated and litigated. Some courts follow the Model Rules approach and reject screening.[239] Other courts hold that despite the Model Rules, screening should be permitted.[240]

If a court permits screening of a disqualified lawyer, what procedures must the firm adopt? First, appropriate measures must be taken to prevent disclosure of confidential information by the disqualified lawyer. The personally disqualified lawyer should acknowledge her obligation not to disclose confidential information; lawyers and staff working on the matter should be informed that the disqualified lawyer is being screened and that they should not communicate with the affected lawyer with respect to the matter in question. In most instances, these measures should be confirmed in writing. See Model Rule

---

236. 1 Hazard & Hodes, The Law of Lawyering §14.8, at 14-20.

237. Id.

238. http://www.abanet.org/cpr/e2k-summary_2002.html (visited June 8, 2003).

239. E.g., Roberts v. Hutchins, 572 So. 2d 1231, 1234 n.3 (Ala. 1990).

240. E.g., Manning v. Waring, Cox, James, Sklar & Allen, 849 F.2d 222 (6th Cir. 1988); Kala v. Aluminum Smelting & Ref. Co., 688 N.E.2d 258 (Ohio 1998) (screening generally available to prevent disqualification of firm that hires personally disqualified lawyer; on facts of case, however, firm disqualified despite screening because of appearance of impropriety caused by lawyer abandoning client two weeks after seeking continuance to file appeal).

1.0(k) and cmt. 9. Second, screening measures must be instituted in a timely fashion. See Model Rule 1.0, cmt. 10. Third, the disqualified lawyer should receive no portion of the fee of any matter in which the lawyer is disqualified. See Model Rules 1.11(b)(1), 1.12(c)(1), 1.18(d)(2)(i). Finally, written notice must be given to the affected client or person. See Model Rules 1.11(b)(2), 1.12(c)(2), 1.18(d)(2)(ii).[241]

The Restatement of the Law Governing Lawyers has also approved of the use of screening to avoid disqualification of a firm when a disqualified lawyer joins the firm.[242] Under the Restatement approach, however, screening may be used only when the confidential information held by the personally disqualified lawyer is "unlikely to be significant in the subsequent matter."[243] The New York Court of Appeals has adopted the Restatement approach.[244]

Both the Model Rules and the Restatement authorize an even broader use of screening when a lawyer obtained confidential information from a former *prospective client.* In that case, the lawyer's firm may undertake representation against the former prospective client even if the lawyer obtained confidential information that could be significantly harmful to the former prospective client, provided the lawyer who received the information is screened from any participation in the matter.[245] If the information would not be significantly harmful, the lawyer could personally undertake representation against the former prospective client.[246]

Disqualification of a law firm can result from hiring paralegals or other nonlawyer employees who previously worked for an adverse party in substantially related matters. Here also the courts are divided on whether screening should be permitted.[247] If the firm does not adopt adequate screening procedures, disqualification is likely to result.[248] The comments to Model Rule 1.10 state that screening is appropriate to prevent disqualification of a firm when

---

241. See Cromley v. Board of Education of Lockport Township High School District 205, 17 F.3d 1059, 1065 (7th Cir. 1994) (outlining screening procedures).

242. Restatement (Third) of the Law Governing Lawyers §124(2).

243. Id. §124(2)(a). Comment *d* outlines certain factors that can be used to determine whether the information is significant.

244. Kassis v. Teacher's Ins. & Annuity Assn., 717 N.E.2d 674 (N.Y. 1999).

245. Model Rule 1.18(d); Restatement (Third) of the Law Governing Lawyers §15(2).

246. Model Rule 1.18, cmt. 6; Restatement (Third) of the Law Governing Lawyers §15, cmt. *c*.

247. *Compare* Hayes v. Central States Orthopedic Specialists, Inc., 51 P.3d 562 (Okla. 2002), *and* ABA Comm. on Ethics and Prof. Resp., Informal Op. 88-1526 (1988) (allowing screening), *with* Koulisis v. Rivers, 730 So. 2d 289 (Fla. Dist. Ct. App. 1999) (screening not permitted).

248. See In re Complex Asbestos Litig. (Widger v. Owens-Corning Fiberglas Corp.), 283 Cal. Rptr. 732 (Ct. App. 1991, *review denied*) (law firm disqualified when it hired paralegal employed by opposing counsel without obtaining consent or establishing appropriate screening); Grant v. Thirteenth Court of Appeals, 888 S.W.2d 466 (Tex. 1994) (disqualification of firm that hired legal secretary who had done extensive work for opposing side).

it hires a nonlawyer. See Model Rule 1.10, cmt. 4. The Restatement is in accord.[249]

Imputation when a disqualified lawyer leaves a firm

Imputation of disqualification issues can also arise as to the former firm when a lawyer leaves the firm and takes cases with her. Is the former firm precluded from handling a new matter against the former client if the new matter is substantially related to work done by the former lawyer for the client while the lawyer worked for the firm? Considering the approach of the Model Rules to imputation when a lawyer joins a firm, the answer should not be surprising. The old firm is not disqualified from handling a matter against a former client when the matter was handled by a departed lawyer unless the current matter is substantially related to the prior representation *and* some lawyer still remaining with the firm actually received material confidential information regarding the former client. Model Rule 1.10(b).[250]

Problem 3-7

Advocate-Witness Conflicts of Interest

MEMORANDUM

To: Associate
From: Partner
Date: —
Re: Staley Manufacturing v. Bowers Chemical Corp.

Bowers Chemical Corporation is one of our firm's long-time clients. We have represented the company for almost 20 years in a wide variety of business and litigation matters. Five years ago Bowers entered into a long-term supply contract with Staley under which Bowers agreed to supply all of Staley's requirements of a certain chemical.

Until about a year ago both parties performed their obligations under the contract without problem, but at that time a dispute developed because

---

249. Restatement (Third) of the Law Governing Lawyers §123, cmt. *f.*

250. See Novo Terapeutisk Laboratorium A/S v. Baxter Travenol Labs., Inc., 607 F.2d 186 (7th Cir. 1979) (law firm not disqualified from representing plaintiff when former partner of firm, while member of firm, had conference with defendant but had not shared confidential information with other members of the firm); Solow v. W.R. Grace & Co., 632 N.E.2d 437 (N.Y. 1994) (law firm not disqualified from representing plaintiff in asbestos case against manufacturer when member of firm who previously represented manufacturer has departed firm and no evidence exists that confidential information was shared with other members of firm).

Staley had increased its requirements to a level that Bowers claims is unreasonable. We tried unsuccessfully to negotiate the matter, and now Staley has filed suit against Bowers, claiming that Bowers has breached the contract by failing to meet its requirements.

We just received answers to our first set of interrogatories. In response to our request for a list of witnesses that Staley plans to call, the company included me as a <u>potential witness to testify about the negotiations leading up to the execution of the contract.</u>

I participated in the negotiations along with two representatives from Bowers: Camilla Newman, Bowers's Vice President for Sales, and Chinmay Patel, Bowers's Head of Manufacturing. During the negotiations Patel expressed concern that Staley's requirements for chemicals might exceed Bowers's ability to supply chemicals consistent with its other contractual obligations. Bowers asked Staley to provide estimates of its requirements for future years, which Staley did. During the negotiations, we discussed including the estimates as part of the contract. A draft contract I prepared, which is in the file, includes the estimates. The final version does not include the estimates. I'm not sure why that happened. It may be that we thought the estimates from Staley were sufficient and that we didn't need to include them in the contract, or it may be that Staley resisted including the estimates. Frankly, I can't recall why the estimates were not included. In any event Staley's demands now exceed its estimates.

I'm concerned that this will necessitate our firm's withdrawal from the case. Please be prepared to meet with me tomorrow to advise whether we will need to withdraw from the case.

Read Model Rule 3.7 and comments.

The advocate-witness rule under the Code of Professional Responsibility

The Code of Professional Responsibility provided that it was unethical for a lawyer to accept or to continue representation of a client if the lawyer or a member of the lawyer's firm "ought to be called as a witness" on behalf of the client. DR 5-101(B), 5-102(A). If the testimony was at the request of the opposing party rather than on behalf of the client, the Code provided that the lawyer could continue representation unless the testimony was prejudicial to the client. DR 5-102(B). It is important to note that under the Code, if the lawyer would be a witness, the lawyer's entire firm would be disqualified from appearing as counsel. In addition, unlike other conflict-of-interest rules, the client could not consent to an advocate-witness conflict.

Disciplinary Rule 5-101(B) listed four exceptions to the prohibition against a lawyer serving as both advocate and witness: (1) testimony about uncontested matters, (2) testimony regarding matters of formality when the lawyer had no reason to believe that substantial evidence would be offered in opposition, (3) testimony about the nature and value of legal services, and (4) substantial hardship to the client because of distinctive value of the lawyer or the lawyer's firm as counsel.

Ethical Consideration 5-9 offered several rationales for the advocate-witness rule:

> Occasionally a lawyer is called upon to decide in a particular case whether he will be a witness or an advocate. If a lawyer is both counsel and witness, he becomes more easily impeachable for interest and thus may be a less effective witness. Conversely, the opposing counsel may be handicapped in challenging the credibility of the lawyer when the lawyer also appears as an advocate in the case. An advocate who becomes a witness is in the unseemly and ineffective position of arguing his own credibility. The roles of an advocate and of a witness are inconsistent; the function of an advocate is to advance or argue the cause of another, while that of a witness is to state facts objectively.

A leading example of the application of the Code's advocate-witness rule is Comden v. Superior Court.[251] In *Comden* the actress Doris Day entered into a contract with Doris Day Distributing Company, authorizing the company to distribute pet products bearing her name and likeness. A dispute developed over performance of the contract, and Ms. Day brought suit seeking to enjoin the company from using her name. In support of a motion for preliminary injunction, two of Ms. Day's attorneys filed declarations. One attorney stated that he had heard one of the defendant's investors state that he had acquired a 50 percent interest in the company; this transaction violated the contract between Ms. Day and the defendant. Another attorney stated that the defendant had refused to allow the inspection of its records as provided by the contract with Ms. Day. The defendant moved to disqualify the law firm in which these two lawyers were members on the ground that they were likely to be called as witnesses. The trial court granted the motion. Ms. Day sought review by way of petition for writ of mandamus. The California Supreme Court affirmed the trial court's disqualification order under Rule 2-111(A)(4) of the California Rules of Professional Conduct, which was substantially the same as the provisions of the Code of Professional Responsibility.

In its opinion the California Supreme Court rejected several arguments against disqualification. Petitioners first argued that it was premature to order disqualification because subsequent discovery might eliminate the need for testimony by the attorneys. The court ruled that the trial court was within its discretion in ordering immediate disqualification when it was uncertain whether the lawyers would testify because "delaying the decision creates the issue of hardship."[252]

The court then rejected petitioners' argument that disqualification should

251. 576 P.2d 971 (Cal.) (en banc), *cert. denied,* 439 U.S. 981 (1978).
252. 576 P.2d at 974.

be denied because of substantial hardship to Ms. Day resulting from the "distinctive value" of the services of the firm. While finding some inconvenience present, the court ruled that "impressions and rapport with the people involved" was insufficient to establish substantial hardship. The court noted that "[i]f we were to hold that interview, research, and preliminary discussion on trial strategy are sufficient to cloak a firm with such 'distinctive value' that a loss of its service results in substantial hardship within the meaning of the rule, the latter will be consumed by exception."[253]

Finally, the court considered the petitioners' argument that the disqualification motion was a tactical device and deprived Ms. Day of the counsel of her choice. Although recognizing that disqualification motions can be employed for tactical reasons, the court pointed out that the fundamental issue was a conflict between the client's right to counsel of its choice and the preservation of ethical standards of the profession. The court ruled that the client's right to select counsel must yield under these circumstances.[254] In *Comden* the disqualification applied to the entire firm and was enforced even over the objections and despite the consent of Ms. Day.

The California Rules of Professional Conduct have been amended since *Comden* was decided. Current Rule 5-210 allows a lawyer to serve as an advocate when the lawyer is a witness in the case if the client gives informed, written consent. In addition, any disqualification under the rule applies only to the lawyer personally, not to the lawyer's firm.

Rationales for the advocate-witness rule

The rationales for the advocate-witness rule have been subject to extensive scrutiny by scholars. In a leading article, Professor Arnold Enker offered the following criticism:

> Ethical Consideration 5-9 . . . asserts that the lawyer who testifies and appears as advocate in the same case "may be a less effective witness" because he is "more easily impeachable for interest." . . . But this is hardly a persuasive argument on which to ground an ethical duty for the lawyer to withdraw from the case. It is at best a tactical consideration that counsel and client should weigh together to determine how serious the risks are in the given situation and whether they are outweighed by the advantages to the client of being represented in court by this particular lawyer. The argument fails to explain why the rule is not subject to exception with the client's consent as are [other conflicts of interest].
>
> Nor is withdrawal from the trial of the case, which constitutes the specific ethical duty, likely to cure the problem in most instances. The lawyer's personal familiarity with the facts of the case will usually stem from his representation of the client in earlier stages of the same matter. Withdrawal from the trial of the

253. Id. at 975.
254. Id.

case will not significantly alter his vulnerability because of interest. It is more likely to injure the client's representation than strengthen his witness.[255]

Professor Enker then considered the rationale set forth in EC 5-9 that the opposing counsel might be "handicapped in challenging the credibility of the lawyer when the lawyer also appears as an advocate in the case." He rejected this justification because it was based on an erroneous premise: that "opposing counsel's sense of professional fraternity will overcome his partisan duty to his client and prevent him from arguing his adversary's interest."[256] Further, even if accurate, this concern was a problem for opposing counsel, not a basis for disqualification of the advocate-witness.[257]

Ethical Consideration 5-9 also stated that "[a]n advocate who becomes a witness is in the unseemly and ineffective position of arguing his own credibility." He found this "too insubstantial a basis on which to ground such a firmly held rule."[258] Enker also rejected the justification originally set forth by Professor Wigmore that the rule was designed to protect the image of the profession from public fear that lawyers might lie to advance their clients' interests. After noting that this justification was conspicuously absent from EC 5-9, Enker found it to be "at best a makeweight."

In the last sentence of EC 5-9, however, Enker found what he considered to be the best justification for the advocate-witness rule: the distinction between testimony and advocacy. A witness testifies as to his personal knowledge and belief. A lawyer, by contrast, argues based on fact and reason, not based on her personal belief. Indeed, it is ethically improper for a lawyer to state her personal belief in the merits of the client's case. See DR 7-106(C)(3) of the Code and Model Rule 3.4(e).

> This distinction between the two roles of advocate and witness is essential to enable the lawyer to maintain independence from his client while advocating his cause. Were the lawyer to combine the two roles, the assessment of his integrity and credibility in evaluating his testimony would likely affect the evaluation of his argument.[259]

Enker drew two implications from this analysis. First, since the basis of the rule was preservation of the role of the attorney, the advocate-witness rule should not be subject to client consent or waiver. Second, since the basis of the rule was the prohibition on mixing roles, the rule should not prevent a lawyer in a firm from serving as advocate when another lawyer was a witness.[260]

By contrast to Professor Enker, the author of a lengthy student note argued

255. Arnold N. Enker, The Rationale of the Rule That Forbids a Lawyer to Be Advocate and Witness in the Same Case, 1977 Am. Bar Found. Res. J. 455, 457.
256. Id. at 457-458.
257. Id. at 458.
258. Id.
259. Id. at 463.
260. Id. at 465.

that the basis of the rule was protection of the client from either diminished effectiveness of counsel or weakened credibility of the advocate-witness. Since client protection was the basis of the rule, the author argued that the rule should be subject to the client's informed consent.[261] Other commentators have argued that the rationales for the rule are so weak that it should be repealed.[262]

The advocate-witness rule under the Model Rules: scope and exceptions

Despite arguments that the rule should be repealed, the drafters of the Model Rules decided to retain it.[263] The Restatement of the Law Governing Lawyers also continues to adhere to the rule.[264] The drafters of the Model Rules focused on two justifications for the advocate-witness rule. Model Rule 3.7, cmt. 1. First, both the tribunal and the opposing party have grounds for objection when an advocate serves as a witness because it becomes unclear whether the statement of the advocate-witness "should be taken as proof or as an analysis of the proof." Model Rule 3.7, cmt. 2. Second, serving as both advocate and witness may create a conflict of interest between lawyer and client. Model Rule 3.7, cmt. 6. Sections (a) and (b) of Rule 3.7 reflect these justifications. Since section (a) is based on the policy of preventing prejudice to the interests of the tribunal or to the opposing party rather than protecting the client from harm, it is not subject to client consent. Section (b), which is based on the principle of avoiding harm to the client, may be subject to informed consent by the client confirmed in writing.[265]

Rule 3.7 applies only if the lawyer is "likely to be a necessary witness."[266] This represents a change in language from the Code of Professional Responsibility, which provided that the lawyer must withdraw if "it is obvious that he or a lawyer in his firm ought to be called as a witness." DR 5-101(B). Under the

---

261. Note, The Advocate-Witness Rule: If Z, Then X. But Why? 52 N.Y.U. L. Rev. 1365, 1394-1400 (1977).

262. Harold A. Brown & Louis M. Brown, Disqualification of the Testifying Advocate—A Firm Rule? 57 N.C. L. Rev. 596 (1979); Jeffrey A. Stonerock, The Advocate-Witness Rule: Anachronism or Necessary Restraint? 94 Dickinson L. Rev. 821 (1990).

263. For a comparison of the Code and the Model Rules, see Richard C. Wydick, Trial Counsel as Witness: The Code and the Model Rules, 15 U.C. Davis L. Rev. 651 (1982). See also Judith A. McMorrow, The Advocate as Witness: Understanding Context, Culture and Client, 70 Fordham L. Rev. 945 (2001) (comparing application of rule in labor arbitration, federal court, and Massachusetts state court and concluding that operation of rule varies depending on context, sometimes functioning as a rule of ethics, while other times serving as rule of either procedure or evidence).

264. Restatement (Third) of the Law Governing Lawyers §108. For a comparison of the Restatement and the Model Rule, see 2 Hazard & Hodes, The Law of Lawyering §33.3.

265. See generally 2 Hazard & Hodes, The Law of Lawyering §33.5.

266. The Restatement refers to the materiality of the lawyer's testimony, but the comment indicates that this test is similar to the "necessary witness" formulation of the Model Rule. See Restatement (Third) of the Law Governing Lawyers §108 and cmt. *e.*

Code some courts had ruled that the lawyer was disqualified if the lawyer's testimony could conceivably be used at trial. See Comden v. Superior Court, discussed above. The drafters of the Model Rules intended to narrow the scope of the advocate-witness rule.[267] One important application of the "necessary witness" requirement is that the lawyer is not disqualified from serving as an advocate if the lawyer's testimony would be cumulative with that of other witnesses. An example is Cannon Airways, Inc. v. Franklin Holdings Corp.,[268] which was a suit for breach of an aircraft lease agreement. The agreement provided for recovery of "reasonable attorneys' fees." Defendant moved to disqualify plaintiff's counsel because a dispute existed regarding the scope of the clause; defendant contended that plaintiff's counsel would be required to testify about the negotiations that resulted in the clause. The court denied this motion because the attorney was not the only witness available to testify about the negotiations on behalf of the plaintiff, and the defendant had failed to show that the attorney's testimony was "necessary to supplement or to corroborate" testimony of plaintiff's other witness about the negotiations.[269]

Both the Code and the Model Rules contain similar exceptions to the advocate-witness rule. Compare Code of Professional Responsibility DR5-101(B)(1)-(4) and Model Rule 3.7(a)(1)-(3). The exceptions dealing with uncontested matters and with testimony regarding legal fees have generated little litigation and should provide few problems in application. Thus, if a lawyer must testify to identify a document so that it can be offered into evidence and there is no dispute about the authenticity of the document, the lawyer is not disqualified from continuing as an advocate in the matter because of this testimony. Similarly, in a suit for breach of contract or for collection of a note in which the contract or note provides for recovery of legal fees, testimony by the trial attorney to establish these fees is permissible and does not require disqualification of the attorney as advocate in the case.

The broadest exception to the prohibition against serving as both advocate and witness occurs when disqualification involves "substantial hardship" to the client. Here there is a modest change from the Code to the Model Rules. Under the Code the substantial hardship had to result from the "distinctive value of the lawyer or his firm as counsel in the particular case." DR 5-101(B)(4). This exception was narrowly construed by the courts and the ABA to apply only in unusual circumstances. See *Comden,* discussed above. In Formal Opinion 339 the ABA Committee on Ethics and Professional Responsibility stated:

> [E]xceptional situations may arise when . . . disadvantages to the client would
> clearly be outweighed by the real hardship to the client of being compelled to

---

267. 2 Hazard & Hodes, The Law of Lawyering §33.6.
268. 669 F. Supp. 96 (D. Del. 1987).
269. Id. at 102. See also Chappell v. Cosgrove, 916 P.2d 836 (N.M. 1996) (lawyer who accompanied client to meeting not disqualified; because four other witnesses could testify about what took place at meeting, lawyer's testimony was cumulative).

retain other counsel in the particular case. For example, where a complex suit has been in preparation over a long period of time and a development which could not be anticipated makes the lawyer's testimony essential, it would be manifestly unfair to the client to be compelled to seek new trial counsel at substantial additional expense and perhaps to have to seek a delay of the trial. Similarly, a long or extensive professional relationship with a client may have afforded a lawyer, or a firm, such an extraordinary familiarity with the client's affairs that the value to the client of representation by that lawyer or firm in a trial involving those matters would clearly outweigh the disadvantages of having the lawyer, or a lawyer in the firm, testify to some disputed and significant issue.[270]

Both the Model Rules and the Restatement broaden somewhat the substantial hardship exception by deleting the requirement of "distinctive value" and focusing instead on balancing of various factors.[271]

Suppose a lawyer is disqualified from being an advocate at a trial because the lawyer is likely to be a necessary witness and none of the exceptions in Rule 3.7 applies. Is the lawyer's entire firm disqualified, or may another lawyer in the firm handle the trial? Disciplinary Rule 5-102(A) of the Code of Professional Responsibility provided that the disqualification of a lawyer from handling a case because of the advocate-witness rule was imputed to the entire firm, preventing any lawyer in the firm from continuing the representation. The rule stated:

> If, after undertaking employment in contemplated or pending litigation, a lawyer learns or it is obvious that he *or a lawyer in his firm* ought to be called as a witness on behalf of his client, he shall withdraw from the conduct of the trial *and his firm, if any, shall not continue representation in the trial.* [Emphasis added.]

Even under the Code, however, some courts had refused to disqualify a firm simply because a member of the firm would be a witness.[272]

Both the Model Rules and the Restatement reject the principle of imputation of disqualification when one lawyer will be appearing as a witness while another attorney in the lawyer's firm will serve as the client's advocate, unless a conflict of interest exists. Rule 3.7(b) provides that "[a] lawyer may act as advocate in a trial in which another lawyer in the lawyer's firm is likely to be called as a witness unless precluded from doing so by Rule 1.7 or Rule 1.9." See also comments 4 and 7. The Restatement agrees.[273]

A conflict of interest is most obvious when the lawyer's testimony would

---

270. ABA Comm. on Ethics and Prof. Resp., Formal Op. 339, at 3 (1975).

271. See Model Rule 3.7, cmt. 4; Restatement (Third) of the Law Governing Lawyers §108, cmt. *h.* See also McElroy v. Gaffney, 529 A.2d 889 (N.H. 1987) (disqualification of plaintiff's lawyer in shareholders' derivative action denied; attorney's knowledge of transactions, complexity of litigation, and expense to plaintiff to hire new counsel are factors supporting denial of motion).

272. E.g., S & S Hotel Ventures Ltd. Partnership v. 777 S.H. Corp., 508 N.E.2d 647 (N.Y. 1987).

273. Restatement (Third) of the Law Governing Lawyers §108(3) and cmts. *f, i.*

be adverse to the client's interests. See Model Rule 1.7. Such a conflict would typically occur when the opposing side calls the lawyer as a witness. Even in this case, the firm would not necessarily be disqualified if the lawyer's testimony, although adverse, plays a relatively minor role in the case and the client gives informed consent confirmed in writing.[274] If the lawyer's testimony would have a substantial effect on the case, however, the lawyer's firm should be disqualified even if the client were willing to consent. Under Rule 1.7(b) a client may consent to a conflict of interest, but only if the "lawyer reasonably believes that the lawyer will be able to provide competent and diligent representation." It is hard to imagine that this condition could ever be met if the lawyer would be testifying adversely to the interests of the client on a significant issue in the case.[275] It is also possible that a lawyer's testimony could create a conflict of interest with a former client if the lawyer's testimony would reveal confidential information gained during the prior representation. See Model Rule 1.9(c). In this case, the conflict should be waivable with the informed consent of the former client, confirmed in writing.

If an attorney is disqualified from serving as an advocate in the case because the attorney is likely to be a necessary witness, may the attorney continue to provide legal services during discovery and after trial on appeal? In Culebras Enterprises Corp. v. Rivera-Rios[276] the First Circuit ruled that disqualification applied only at trial, not to pretrial matters, because representation at pretrial did not involve any of the purposes generally served by the rule,[277] and the Restatement adopts this view.[278] Other courts, however, disagree and have disqualified counsel from participation in pretrial matters.[279]

---

274. See Model Rule 3.7, cmt. 6 (representation is improper when there is likely to be a substantial conflict between the testimony of the client and the lawyer); 2 Hazard & Hodes, The Law of Lawyering §33.8 (consent permissible if the client is adequately counseled).

275. See Klupt v. Krongard, 728 A.2d 727 (Md. Ct. Spec. App.), *cert. denied*, 735 A.2d 1107 (Md. 1999) (lawyer disqualified from representation of patent licensor when contingent licensee planned to call lawyer as witness to testify about statements made by lawyer that would conflict with testimony of licensor; conflict was not waivable by licensor).

276. 846 F.2d 94 (1st Cir. 1988).

277. Accord DiMartino v. Eighth Judicial Dist. Court ex rel. County of Clark, 66 P.3d 945 (Nev. 2003).

278. Restatement (Third) of the Law Governing Lawyers §108, cmt. *c*. See also ABA Comm. on Ethics and Prof. Resp., Informal Op. 83-1503 (lawyer who has withdrawn as trial counsel because of advocate-witness rule may prepare brief and argue case on appeal so long as lawyer's testimony is not in issue and no conflict of interest is present); Informal Op. 89-1529 (lawyer who anticipates testifying at trial may represent party in discovery and other pretrial matters if client consents after consultation).

279. World Youth Day, Inc. v. Famous Artists Merchandising Exch., Inc., 866 F. Supp. 1297 (D. Colo. 1994) (lawyer disqualified from handling depositions because of likelihood that depositions would be used at trial, revealing lawyer's dual role); Freeman v. Vicchiarelli, 827 F. Supp. 300 (D.N.J. 1993) (early application of rule is necessary for smooth operation of adversarial system).

Avoiding advocate-witness conflicts during investigation

While rejection of the rule of imputed disqualification in the Model Rules and the Restatement has substantially reduced the impact of the advocate-witness rule, the rule still applies to a lawyer who personally will be a witness. As a result, attorneys who engage in trial practice need to be aware of the possible disqualifying effect of the rule and to guard against this eventuality when participating in matters that may lead to litigation or when interviewing witnesses in matters that are in litigation.[280] Consider the following advice from Professors Fortune, Underwood, and Imwinkelried for dealing with this problem:

> In interviewing witnesses, however, it is prudent to assume that the witness will give a different version of the facts at a later time, and that the attorney may become a necessary witness to challenge the turncoat. . . .
>
> What precautions can be taken to guard against being considered a necessary impeachment witness? First, consider having someone else conduct witness interviews, either an employee or an independent investigator. Second, have someone else present when interviewing a witness who may deny or vary a statement. Third, reduce the interview to a signed statement.[281]

Problem 3-8

Representation of Multiple Plaintiffs in Tort Cases

Scene: Office of Sandra Lawson, Esq.
Others present: Nancy Downing, the driver of a vehicle involved in a collision, and Ed Partee, the passenger. Ms. Downing and Mr. Partee are sister and brother.

Lawson: Come in, Ms. Downing and Mr. Partee. Please sit down. I understand that you were involved in an automobile accident. Why don't you tell me what happened.

Downing: We were going to a friend's house on Friday afternoon. I had stopped at a red light at the corner of Barian Way and

---

280. See Jeffrey A. Van Detta, Lawyers as Investigators: How *Ellerth* and *Faragher* Reveal a Crisis of Ethics and Professionalism Through Trial Counsel Disqualification and Waivers of Privilege in Workplace Harassment Cases, 24 J. Legal Prof. 261 (2000) (reviewing application of the advocate-witness rule in sexual harassment cases and arguing that firms that have participated in the investigation of such cases should not act as counsel if the investigation will be asserted as a defense).

281. William H. Fortune et al., Modern Litigation and Professional Responsibility Handbook §4.5, at 179-180 (2d ed. 2001). See also Restatement (Third) of the Law Governing Lawyers §108, cmt. *j* (advocate-witness rule does not apply to testimony by nonlawyer employee who does not sit at counsel table or act in advocacy support role).

North Druid Street. The light turned green, and I started
to enter the intersection when a truck came barreling through
the intersection. He obviously ran the red light because my
light was already green. He slammed into the side of the car
where Ed was riding.

Lawson: *(to Mr. Partee)* Did you see what happened?

Partee: I sure did. As Nancy started into the intersection, I saw the
truck coming and I yelled at her to stop. I guess she didn't
see him because she was changing the radio station.

Lawson: Did the police charge anyone in the accident?

Downing: The driver of the truck got a ticket for running a red light.

Lawson: Were you charged?

Downing: No.

Lawson: Tell me about your injuries.

Downing: I was shaken up pretty bad and went to the emergency room.
They X-rayed me but didn't find any broken bones or other
problems. I missed a few days of work.

Lawson: And you, Mr. Partee?

Partee: I had a broken arm and a concussion. I have been out of
work for four weeks. I feel pretty good now and plan to go
back to work next week.

Lawson: You want me to represent you in this matter, is that right?

Partee: Yes.

Downing: That's right.

Lawson: Ethically, I need to talk to you about possible conflicts of
interest. It sounds like the driver of the truck was at fault
and that you both have claims against him and not each
other, but it's possible that a conflict could occur if it turns
out that Mr. Partee has a claim against Ms. Downing. If
that happens, I couldn't continue to represent you both. If
it's agreeable with you, I would represent Mr. Partee because
he has the more serious injuries. Ms. Downing, you'd need
to get your own lawyer, but that's only if a conflict arises,
which doesn't seem likely.

Partee: Well, she's my sister and I don't want to sue her, so there's
not going to be a conflict.

Lawson: You can waive any conflict if you want to, so we can handle
it that way. I will need to get your medical records and the
accident report. Would you please sign these medical and
police authorizations so that I can obtain the records?

Be prepared to evaluate how Lawson handled the interview. What would
you have done?

Read Model Rules 1.7 and 1.0(b), (e), and (n) and comments.

Representation of multiple clients in a single matter

In earlier problems in this chapter we discussed conflicts of interest involving representation against current and former clients. Problem 3-8 deals with another type of client conflict: representation of multiple clients in a single matter. Recall Problem 2-7 dealing with multiple representation of codefendants in criminal cases. This type of conflict differs from the two that we have already considered because in those situations the lawyer was clearly undertaking representation *against* a client. In the multiple representation situation, the adversity between the clients is not readily apparent. In the case of representation of the driver and passenger in an automobile accident with another driver, both the driver and passenger appear to have a harmony of interests in establishing that the other driver was at fault. Despite this apparent unity of interests, representation of coplaintiffs, such as driver and passenger, poses a number of potential conflicts of interest, ones that may well ripen into actual conflicts.

Model Rules 1.7(a)(2) and (b) govern the situation of multiple representation of potentially conflicting interests. (Note these rules also deal with situations in which the lawyer's personal interest or that of a third person may have an impact on the lawyer's representation of a client. We will consider these situations in later problems.)

Under Rule 1.7(b) a lawyer may represent potentially conflicting interests if the lawyer reasonably believes the lawyer can provide competent and diligent representation to both clients and each client gives informed consent, confirmed in writing. If an actual conflict exists so that the lawyer would be asserting a claim by one client against the other client in the same proceeding, the lawyer cannot undertake the representation. Model Rule 1.7(b)(3).

Representation of coparties in tort litigation

A number of courts and ethics opinions have addressed the possible conflict between driver and passenger arising from an automobile accident. These authorities have held that a lawyer may not undertake representation of both a driver and passenger when the passenger has a claim against the driver for negligence.[282] If such a claim is unlikely, multiple representation is permitted provided both the driver and passenger consent to the representation after the lawyer fully discloses the advantages and risks involved.[283]

---

282. E.g., In re Thornton, 421 A.2d 1 (D.C. 1980); In re Shaw, 443 A.2d 670 (N.J. 1982); Fugnitto v. Fugnitto, 452 N.Y.S.2d 976 (App. Div. 1982); Jedwabny v. Philadelphia Transp. Co., 135 A.2d 252 (Pa. 1957), *cert. denied*, 355 U.S. 966 (1958).

283. See In re Aguiluz, 3 Cal. St. Bar Ct. Rep. 41 (Bar Ct. 1994).

Figueroa-Olmo v. Westinghouse Electric Corp.[284] illustrates the application of the conflict-of-interest rules in tort litigation involving multiple plaintiffs with potential claims against each other. In *Figueroa-Olmo* four individuals were killed when the truck in which they were riding collided with one of Westinghouse's trailers at an intersection near San Juan. Consolidated actions were brought by 40 relatives of the decedents; all the plaintiffs were represented by one law firm. Westinghouse filed counterclaims claiming that the driver and passengers of the truck were contributorily negligent. Some of the plaintiffs were heirs of the decedents, while others were not. Under Puerto Rico law an heir who accepted an interest in an estate (filing of a lawsuit on behalf of the estate amounted to acceptance of an interest in the estate) also became legally responsible for any claims against the estate. Westinghouse filed a motion to disqualify the law firm from representing all of the plaintiffs because of a conflict of interest, claiming that the plaintiffs who were not heirs had potential cross-claims against the plaintiffs who were heirs and had accepted an interest in the estate.

The law firm filed written statements with the court in which each plaintiff consented to representation by the firm. Westinghouse objected to the statements on the ground that they did not show that the firm had made the full disclosure required by the rules of professional conduct. The district court ruled that the potential for a conflict of interest between the plaintiffs did not automatically prevent multiple representation and result in disqualification. The court discussed the circumstances under which multiple representation of potentially conflicting interests would be permitted:

> According to Model Rule 1.7(b), disqualification of counsel on grounds of potential conflicting interests in multiple client representation in the same lawsuit is not automatic but may depend on whether the clients agree to being so represented after having been informed of all the risks and disadvantages involved. . . . The premise behind this pragmatic approach is to safeguard a person's right to hire a particular attorney of certain expertise who may not be affordable except by the joint resources of various litigants who team up as plaintiffs or as defendants. . . . Parties also have a right to control their litigation in light of whatever interests they consider more important and worthy of litigating. . . . However, the right to be represented by a particular attorney is not an unfettered one. Even informed consent may be insufficient to prevent disqualification, if it is not obvious to the court that the attorney will be able to represent all clients adequately, . . . or if the court believes no waiver may cure the damage to the integrity of the judicial process that such joint representation will cause. . . . The court may also examine the circumstances surrounding the consent to determine if it was truly voluntary and informed. . . . It has also been held that if the conflicts of interest involve abuse of confidential information from the client rather than the mere possibility of disloyalty in advocacy during a litigation, the client's consent might be insufficient. . . . If the simultaneously represented clients' interests are or become actually opposed or directly adverse, then disqualification

284. 616 F. Supp. 1445 (D.P.R. 1985).

should be ordered. . . . Our circuit has cautioned that it is "more important that unethical conduct be prevented than that defendant have an unfettered right to counsel of its choice."[285]

The court ruled, however, that the plaintiffs' lawyers had failed to comply with the obligation of consultation required by Rule 1.7(b); it ordered plaintiffs' counsel to conduct meetings with the plaintiffs to explain their legal rights, and to file with the court written consents in a format specified by the court.

Informed consent to multiple representation

Assuming that a lawyer reasonably believes that the lawyer may permissibly represent both the driver and passenger because no actual conflict is present, the lawyer must obtain their informed consent.[286] Model Rule 1.7(b)(4) cmt. 18 amplifies the requirement of informed consent: "When representation of multiple clients in a single matter is undertaken, the information must include the *implications of the common representation*, including possible effects on loyalty, confidentiality and the attorney-client privilege and the *advantages* and *risks* involved." (Emphasis added.) In addition, the clients' consent must be confirmed in writing. See Model Rule 1.7(b)(4) and cmt. 20.

What are the implications, advantages, and risks that should be disclosed?[287] One advantage that is often mentioned in connection with simultaneous representation is the reduction of legal fees by having one lawyer involved instead of two. While this may well be an advantage in a matter in which the client pays for the lawyer's services on an hourly basis, it is questionable whether it is an advantage in plaintiff's tort matters, which are usually handled on a contingency basis. For example, if one lawyer represents both the driver and passenger, recovers $5,000 for the driver and $10,000 for the passenger, and charges a one-third fee, the legal fees will be the same as when two lawyers independently represent the driver and the passenger, obtain the same recoveries, and charge their clients the same one-third fee.

Expense sharing is another possible advantage of simultaneous representation. Lawyers normally charge their clients for expenses incurred in a matter, such as filing fees, deposition costs, and costs of expert witnesses. If one lawyer rather than several handles the case, the clients could share the expenses, rather than each being required to pay her own expenses.

In addition to expense sharing, there are other possible advantages to the clients of simultaneous representation. Dealings between opposing sides in the

---

285. Id. at 1451-1452.
286. See *Gustafson v. City of Seattle*, 941 P.2d 701 (Wash. Ct. App. 1997) (attorney must obtain informed consent before representing driver and passenger unless it reasonably appears that other parties are solely liable).
287. See *Zador Corp. v. Kwan*, 37 Cal. Rptr. 2d 754 (Ct. App. 1995) (quoting well-drafted consent form with detailed explanations of advantages and disadvantages of multiple representation of codefendants in real estate litigation).

case and particularly with the insurance carrier for the defendant may be simplified and thereby expedited if one lawyer is involved for the plaintiffs rather than two. Further, both the driver and passenger may have trust and confidence in the particular lawyer. Permitting simultaneous representation allows both to have the lawyer of their choice.

Disadvantages to multiple representation exist as well. While the matter may not seem initially to involve an actual conflict between the clients, during the progress of the case a conflict may arise. For example, discovery may produce evidence showing that the driver of the vehicle in which the passenger was riding may have been at fault and that the passenger therefore has a claim against the driver. Comment 23 to Model Rule 1.7 identifies other possible conflicts when a lawyer represents multiple parties in litigation:

> A conflict may exist by reason of substantial discrepancy in the parties' testimony, incompatibility in positions in relation to an opposing party or the fact that there are substantially different possibilities of settlement of the claims or liabilities in question.

Representation of multiple parties can produce "aggregate settlement" conflicts. Suppose the defendant offers a lump sum to settle the entire case. A lawyer representing multiple plaintiffs cannot ethically agree to an aggregate settlement unless each client gives informed consent in a signed writing. Model Rule 1.8(g). The settlement desires of one client may therefore lead to rejection of a settlement that the other client considers advantageous.

If an actual conflict develops between the driver and passenger, the lawyer will ordinarily be required to withdraw from representation. Model Rule 1.7 comments 4 and 29. On withdrawal the lawyer could not represent either party unless both consented to the representation. After withdrawal both the clients would then be former clients. As discussed previously, a lawyer may not undertake representation against a former client in the same or substantially related matter without the consent of that client. Model Rule 1.7 comments 4 and 1.9(a).[288] Both would be forced to hire new lawyers. At a minimum this would cause delay in their case and might well result in additional expenses. The lawyer must disclose to potential coclients the possible conflicts that may arise and inform them that she would be required to withdraw from representation of both of them if an actual conflict arose.

The lawyer should also advise the driver and passenger of another aspect of joint representation—the impact on the attorney-client privilege. It is well

---

288. It may be possible for the lawyer to obtain the consent of the clients in the engagement agreement to the lawyer representing one of the clients in the event a conflict develops, particularly if the clients are sophisticated. See Zador Corp. v. Kwan, 37 Cal. Rptr. 2d 754 (Ct. App. 1995) (law firm represented multiple defendants in real estate litigation; firm was allowed to represent one defendant after withdrawing from representation of other defendant due to conflict of interest because written consent to multiple representation specified which defendant law firm could continue to represent if conflict developed).

established as a matter of evidence law that no attorney-client privilege exists between joint clients as to communications made by either client to the lawyer should a dispute develop between the joint clients.[289] For example, if a driver provides a lawyer with information showing that the driver was negligent, this information would not be privileged should the passenger later file a cross claim against the driver. The parties should be advised about this limitation on the attorney-client privilege before they agree to simultaneous representation. A lawyer who fails to obtain informed consent is exposed to the risk of malpractice liability.[290]

Conflicts of interest in class actions

The contemporary legal scene has witnessed an explosive growth of mass tort litigation involving products such as asbestos, tobacco, and contraceptive devices. Procedurally, many of these cases have been brought as class actions under Rule 23 of the Federal Rules of Civil Procedure and corresponding state rules, but others involve mass consolidations of thousands of individual claims. Regardless of the procedural device used, mass torts present a host of unique ethical problems, including conflicts of interest.[291] Federal district judge Jack B. Weinstein, who has presided over a number of significant mass tort cases, has identified three major types of conflicts of interest in mass torts: between lawyer and client, among present clients, and between present and future claimants.[292]

Because of the vast sums of money involved in class-action mass torts, class counsel may have a financial interest to settle the case and thereby obtain an early payment of substantial fees, even if the settlement does not fairly compensate the members of the class for their injuries. Conflicts of interest among current clients and between current and future claimants are also significant problems in mass torts. Most mass torts involve claimants with different degrees of injury. In addition, because of the long latency period involved in discovery of injuries caused by some products, many such cases include future

289. Restatement (Third) of the Law Governing Lawyers §75(2); Model Rule 1.7, cmt 30.

290. See Woodruff v. Tomlin, 616 F.2d 924 (6th Cir.), cert. denied, 449 U.S. 888 (1980) (cause of action for legal malpractice stated against attorney who represented two sisters—one the driver and the other a passenger—in collision case without disclosure of possible claim that passenger had against driver).

291. The leading article is Jack B. Weinstein, Ethical Dilemmas in Mass Tort Litigation, 88 Nw. U. L. Rev. 469 (1994). The literature on class actions involving mass torts is voluminous. See Symposium, Mass Torts, 148 U. Pa. L. Rev. 1851 (2000); Symposium, Mass Tortes: Serving Up Just Desserts, 80 Cornell L. Rev. 811 (1995); Symposium, The Institute of Judicial Administration Research Conference on Class Actions, 71 N.Y.U. L. Rev. 1 (1996). See also Vincent R. Johnson, Ethical Limitations on Creative Financing of Mass Tort Class Actions, 54 Brooklyn L. Rev. 539 (1988).

292. Weinstein, Ethical Dilemmas in Mass Tort Litigation, 88 Nw. U. L. Rev. at 502-510.

claimants as well as those with current injuries. Even among future claimants, conflicts can develop. Some future claimants may be identifiable as having been exposed to the product causing the illness but may not exhibit disease, while other claimants may be unidentified or even unidentifiable (the unborn, for example).

Parties to mass tort litigation have argued that these conflicts can be overcome by judicial oversight of class action settlements.[293] The Supreme Court, however, has rejected this solution. The Court has refused to approve settlements of class-action mass torts unless all the requirements of Rule 23 have been met, including representation by class counsel that does not suffer from conflicts of interest.[294] The Court has ruled that when such conflicts exist, as is often the case, subclasses with independent representation must be created.[295]

Problem 3-9

Insurance Defense Practice

Scene: Office of Roberto Sanchez, defense counsel
Others present: Joseph Taylor, truck driver for Freight Lines, Inc.
and Elaine Voss, Vice President of Operations for Freight Lines

Sanchez:	Come in, Mr. Taylor and Ms. Voss. I appreciate your coming down here. Freight Lines's insurance carrier, Interstate Insurance, has sent this suit to our firm to defend you, Mr. Taylor, and Freight Lines. Please understand that even though the insurance company is paying my fee, I am your lawyer. Anything you tell me will be kept in confidence. Mr. Taylor, why don't you tell me what happened?
Taylor:	Well, I had just delivered a load to Charleston and was on the way back to the warehouse when this guy in a little car pulled out in front of me. I hit the brakes but nothing happened. . . . *(To Voss)* I told you those brakes were going bad. . . . *(To Sanchez)* Anyway, I hit him broadside and can't remember anything else. I was in the hospital for two months. Just got out last week and I still have a lot of pain.
Sanchez:	I'm sorry you've had so much trouble. Hopefully, this case will settle soon and you can put all of this behind you.
Taylor:	What about my case against that other driver? My doctor said that some of my injuries may be permanent.
Sanchez:	I've looked at the accident report and unfortunately it appears

293. Id. at 507.
294. See Ortiz v. Fibreboard Corp., 527 U.S. 815 (1999); Amchem Prods., Inc. v. Windsor, 521 U.S. 591 (1997).
295. See *Ortiz*, 527 U.S. at 856; *Amchem Prods.*, 521 U.S. at 627-628.

that the driver did not have any insurance. Freight Lines does have uninsured motorist coverage under its policy.

Voss: How would that affect our rates?

Sanchez: Well, any claim under a policy will increase your rates, but I'm not sure how much.

Voss: I don't believe the company could authorize a claim under the uninsured motorist provision if it would substantially affect our rates. . . . There is one other thing I want to mention to you. The truck that was involved in this accident had been retired from our fleet about a month ago and removed from the list of trucks covered under the policy. We just used it that day because one of our other trucks was broken down. Fortunately, the company doesn't know about this, but I wanted to let you know about it so that you wouldn't raise it as an issue if it comes up.

Sanchez: Um. I'll have to give both of these matters some thought. . . .

Mr. Sanchez asks your advice about how he should proceed. What advice would you give?

Read Model Rules 1.7, 1.8(f) and comments.

Relationship between insured, insurance company, and defense counsel

Insurance defense is a well-recognized area of practice, in which tens of thousands of lawyers have practiced for decades. Nonetheless, controversy about the ethical obligations of defense counsel continues and, if anything, has become more heated in recent years.[296] The ethical issues arise from the tripartite or triangular relationship between insured, insurance company, and defense counsel.

The first side of the triangle is the contractual relationship between the insured and the insurance company. The standard liability policy is a contract between the insurance company and the insured. For a specified premium, the insurance company agrees (a) to defend any suit against the insured within the coverage of the policy regardless of the merit of the suit (commonly called the "duty to defend") and (b) to pay any judgment against the insured up to the applicable policy limit. Under the typical policy, the insurance company reserves the right to control the defense, including the right to accept or reject any offer of settlement, and to select counsel to defend the insured. In addition to paying the premium, the insured promises to give the insurer prompt notice of any claim or occurrence within the coverage of the policy, to cooperate fully in the defense, and to subrogate the insurance company for any amount paid

---

296. See Symposium: Liability Insurance Conflicts and Professional Responsibility, 4 Conn. Ins. L.J. 1 (1997-1998).

on behalf of the insured.[297] While the relationship between the insured and the company flows from the insurance policy, the insurance company may also have various tort and statutory obligations to the insured. In particular, most jurisdictions recognize that insurance companies may be held liable to their insureds for bad faith refusal to settle claims under their policies.[298]

The second side of the triangle is the relationship between defense counsel and the insured. Pursuant to its duty to defend the insured, the insurance company selects defense counsel. It is undisputed that defense counsel has an attorney-client relationship with the insured.[299] The insured is the named party to the litigation and the company has a contractual obligation to provide the insured with a defense.

The final leg of the triangle, the relationship between defense counsel and the insurance company, has been the focus of controversy. Here the dispute is deep and broad. At a theoretical level, it remains unclear whether the insurer is a client of defense counsel, a third party who pays for the defense, or some modified position between these extremes. At the practical level, controversy rages over many issues, such as whether defense counsel must adhere to litigation guidelines established by insurance companies to control the cost of litigation.

Areas of conflict between insured and insurance company

In most cases the insurance company and the insured have a "community of interest" with respect to any claim brought by a third party within the policy coverage: Both the insurance company and the insured have an interest in defeating the claim or in minimizing the amount of the recovery.[300]

While normally a harmony of interests exists between insurer and insured, a number of situations can develop in which the harmony of interests disintegrates.[301] The most common such situations are the following:

- *Coverage disputes.* The insurer's contractual obligation is limited to amounts that the insured is legally liable to pay and that fall within the scope of the policy's coverage. Intentional torts and punitive damages

---

297. See Richard L. Neumeier, Serving Two Masters: Problems Facing Insurance Defense Counsel and Some Proposed Solutions, 77 Mass. L. Rev. 66, 67 (1992); Charles Silver & Kent Syverud, The Professional Responsibilities of Insurance Defense Lawyers, 45 Duke L.J. 255, 264-265 (1995).

298. See Douglas R. Richmond, An Overview of Insurance Bad Faith Law and Litigation, 25 Seton Hall L. Rev. 74, 80 n.33 (third-party claims) and 104 n.170 (first-party claims) (1994). See also Roger C. Henderson, The Tort of Bad Faith in First-Party Insurance Transactions After Two Decades, 37 Ariz. L. Rev. 1153, 1153-1154 (1995).

299. 1 Hazard & Hodes, The Law of Lawyering §12.14, n.6.

300. See ABA Comm. on Prof. Ethics and Griev., Formal Op. 282 (1950).

301. See generally Douglas R. Richmond, Lost in the Eternal Triangle of Insurance Defense Ethics, 9 Geo. J. Legal Ethics 475 (1996); Symposium: Liability Insurance Conflicts and Professional Responsibility, 4 Conn. Ins. L.J. 1 (1997-1998).

typically are excluded from coverage under liability policies. Sometimes the existence of a coverage issue is apparent to the insurer at the outset of the case (for example, if the policy excludes coverage for intentional torts and punitive damages and the complaint alleges a cause of action for both). In other cases, however, facts that could establish lack of coverage may come to the attorney in confidence and may not be known by the insurer.

- *Excess claims.* In an "excess" situation, the plaintiff is seeking damages that exceed the policy limits, but has made a settlement offer that is within the policy limits. The insured has an interest in having the insurer accept this settlement since the insured will not suffer any financial loss. The insurer may have an interest in rejecting the offer, however, if the insurer believes the offer is excessive, even though within the policy limits.
- *Settlement.* Differences between insurer and insured can arise even if the plaintiff is not seeking damages that exceed the policy limits. In some cases, an insurance company may be willing to settle a case because the insurer believes the settlement is less than the expected costs and risk of litigation. On the other hand, the insured may be relatively indifferent to the cost of litigation and may be unwilling to settle because of reputational or other reasons. Some professional malpractice policies protect the insured against settlements that they find unacceptable by requiring the consent of the insured to any settlement, but the standard liability policy allows the insurer to settle the case over the objections of the insured. The reverse situation can also occur. The insurance company may receive a settlement offer within the policy limits that it considers excessive. The insured, however, may prefer a settlement regardless of the cost to the insurer.
- *Litigation guidelines and audits.* To control litigation costs, in recent years insurers have begun establishing guidelines for defense counsel with regard to handling cases and have required defense counsel to provide information to independent auditors for their review. Depending on the reasonableness of the litigation guidelines, they may interfere with the ability of counsel to provide a competent defense to the insured. Compliance with requests for information from independent auditors raises confidentiality issues.
- *Uninsured or underinsured motorist claims.* Many automobile policies have uninsured or underinsured coverage. Under such a provision, if the other driver does not have insurance (or is underinsured), the insured's own company provides coverage subject to the limits in the policy. As a result the same insurance company may be defending the insured and the opposing party.
- *Counterclaims.* As noted above, the typical liability policy provides that the insurance company has a "duty to defend" the insured. Suppose the insured has a counterclaim against the opposing party. The insured has an interest in pursuing this claim, but the insurance company has

no financial interest in paying for an attorney to obtain recovery on behalf of the insured.

- *Fraud or collusion by the insured.* In some cases (if the plaintiff is a friend or relative, for example), the insured may have an interest in conceding liability or in colluding with the plaintiff.
- *Multiple insureds.* In some cases, the insurance company may have multiple insureds in a single matter. For example, an insurance company may issue medical malpractice policies that cover several doctors involved in a malpractice case. The insureds may have conflicting interests if their degrees of fault or amount of coverage differ.
- *Subrogation.* Insurance policies typically provide that the insurance company is "subrogated" to the rights of the insured. This means that if the insurance company makes a payment to the insured (for example, for property damage), the insurance company takes over any rights that the insured may have against a third party. A conflict of interest may develop between the insured and the insurer if the insured also has claims against the third party that are not covered by the policy.

The most common failing of defense counsel: protecting the interests of the insurer over the insured

Defense counsel typically has an ongoing financial relationship with the insurance company. The company will be referring matters to defense counsel on a regular basis and paying its fees. In contrast, defense counsel's relationship with the insured is usually transitory, lasting only for the one case, and the insured does not pay any fees. As a result, it is not surprising that some defense counsel have fallen into the ethical trap of protecting the interests of the insurance company over those of the insured.

For example, in Parsons v. Continental National American Group[302] the insured was a 14-year-old charged with assault and battery of his neighbors. The liability policy issued by CNA had a $25,000 limit and excluded intentional torts. The attorney retained by the insurance company obtained the child's confidential file from a boys' school were he was being kept. The attorney wrote the insurer advising it that the file showed that the boy was "fully aware of his acts" and that "the assault he committed on claimants can only be a deliberate act on his part." In preparing for trial, the attorney interviewed the child and received a narrative statement from him. In a letter to CNA, he wrote as follows: "His own story makes it obvious that his acts were willful and criminal."[303] At trial the attorney offered no evidence on the child's behalf, and a judgment was entered against the child in the amount of $50,000. The plaintiffs then brought a garnishment action against CNA seeking the amount

302. 550 P.2d 94 (Ariz. 1976) (en banc).
303. Id. at 96.

of the policy.[304] CNA defended on the ground that the policy excluded intentional torts. The Arizona Supreme Court ruled that the company was estopped from denying liability because the attorney retained by the insurance company to defend the insured had violated his duty of confidentiality by revealing information obtained from the insured to the insurer in an effort to help the insurer establish a defense of lack of coverage:

> The attorney in the present case continued to act as Michael's attorney while he was actively working against Michael's interests. When an attorney who is an insurance company's agent uses the confidential relationship between an attorney and a client to gather information so as to deny the insured coverage under the policy in the garnishment proceeding we hold that such conduct constitutes a waiver of any policy defense, and is so contrary to public policy that the insurance company is estopped as a matter of law from disclaiming liability under an exclusionary clause in the policy.[305]

The court warned that an attorney confronted with such a conflict—confidential information received from the insured showing lack of coverage—should withdraw from representation of the insurer.[306] The insurance company was held liable for the full $50,000, an amount in excess of the policy limit, because the company had rejected an opportunity to settle the case for $25,000.

The two-client model for dealing with conflicts between insured and insurance company

If deference to the interests of the company is not the ethically proper approach, how should defense counsel proceed to handle any conflicts that arise during the representation? One answer is that counsel should proceed in accordance with principles governing multiple representation, treating both the insured and the insurance company as clients. The two-client model is the traditional answer to the obligations of defense counsel and is still followed by most courts.[307]

In fact, however, general principles of multiple representation are difficult to apply to the insurance defense setting and require some modification to take into account both traditional practice and the fact of the insurer's rights under the policy. Under standard conflict-of-interest principles, a lawyer may usually

---

304. In many jurisdictions, issues of coverage are resolved by declaratory judgment action. E.g., Employers Cas. Co. v. Tilley, 496 S.W.2d 552 (Tex. 1973) (declaratory judgment action brought by insurer against insured seeking determination whether insured's failure to give timely notice as required by policy relieved insurer of obligations under policy).

305. 550 P.2d at 99.

306. Id. at 98.

307. Laura A. Foggan, The Tripartite Relationship: Insurer Issues in Selection and Supervision of Defense Counsel, 690 PLI/Lit 579 (2003) (surveying cases around the country on who defense counsel represents).

represent multiple clients with potential conflicts of interest in a single matter provided the lawyer obtains the informed consent of the clients, confirmed in writing. See Model Rule 1.7(b). Most defense counsel do not discuss with the insured and the company conflicts that can arise nor do defense counsel normally obtain their clients' informed consent to multiple representation. Instead, when suit is filed against the insured, the insurance company typically forwards the case to defense counsel selected by it. Defense counsel then contacts the insured and proceeds to defend the case with little if any explanation of the relationship between defense counsel, insured, and insurance company. Failure by defense counsel to make full disclosure of their role and to obtain consent by the insured to multiple representation has been justified on the ground that the insured has given "consent" to the representation by forwarding court papers to the insurance company,[308] but this consent is implied rather than expressed and in any event does not include a full disclosure of defense counsel's role.[309]

Under standard ethical principles governing joint representation, when a lawyer faces an actual conflict of interest between two clients in litigation, the lawyer must normally withdraw from representation of both. Model Rule 1.7(b)(3) and cmt. 29. Applied to insurance defense counsel, however, this approach is unsatisfactory. Withdrawal of defense counsel would arise too frequently, resulting in added expense as well as loss of counsel that the insurance company has specifically chosen because of the attorney's qualifications.

Thus, insurance defense practice has developed some modifications to the standard principles governing multiple representation. Probably the most complete expression of the modified two-client approach can be found in the Guiding Principles of the National Conference of Lawyers and Liability Insurers.[310] The ABA approved the principles in 1972, but then rescinded its approval in 1980 under pressure from the Justice Department because of concern about the anticompetitive effect of intraprofessional agreements, not because of substantive problems with the principles.[311] Nonetheless, the Guiding Principles provide a set of standards based on the two-client model for the most common problems that defense counsel face.[312]

In almost all of the conflict situations outlined above, the conflict between insured and insurance company does not involve confidential information that defense counsel has received from the insured. For example, excess claims, uninsured or underinsured motorist claims, counterclaims, multiple insureds, and subrogation situations rarely involve any confidential information. In addition, many coverage disputes do not involve confidential information. In these nonconfidential information situations, the standard practice for dealing with

308. See ABA Comm. on Prof. Ethics and Griev., Formal Op. 282, at 3 (1950).
309. See ABA Comm. on Ethics and Prof. Resp., Formal Op. 96-403, at 3-5 (defense counsel should communicate to insured nature and limits on representation at earliest possible opportunity; insured consents by accepting defense).
310. Reprinted in 20 Fedn. Ins. Couns. Q. 93 (#4, 1970).
311. Wolfram, Modern Legal Ethics 8.4.2, at 429 n.97.
312. The Guiding Principles begin by recognizing both the insured and the company as clients of defense counsel. Guiding Principle I. For a comparison of the two-client model

the conflict is for the insurance company to notify the insured in writing and to inform the insured that it should consider retaining independent counsel at its own expense to protect its interests. For example, when the plaintiff makes a settlement demand within the policy limits, the insurer will send the insured an *excess letter* informing the insured of its potential liability if the case is not settled and the plaintiff obtains a recovery in excess of the policy limits.[313] Similarly, when coverage is in doubt, the insurance company will send the insured a *reservation of rights letter*, informing the insured that the company is defending the claim but is reserving its right to contest coverage, typically in an independent declaratory judgment action.[314] Defense counsel will continue to handle the case on behalf of both the insurer and the insured. The insured, with its own counsel, can participate in the proceedings to the extent appropriate to protect the insured's interest that is in conflict with the insurer's. Independent counsel can, for example, advocate on behalf of the insured that the insurer accept a settlement offer within the policy limits; similarly, independent counsel may represent the insured in any declaratory judgment action to determine coverage.

Liability insurance policies typically do not provide coverage for counterclaims by the insured. If the insured defendant has a counterclaim against the plaintiff, defense counsel should notify the insured that the policy does not cover this matter and that the insured should seek independent representation for this claim.[315] On occasion, the same insurance company may insure multiple parties in the case. The company should inform the insureds of this fact, each insured should be separately represented, and the company should share with the insureds its factual investigation in the matter (except that statements by any insured or employees of an insured should not be given to parties with adverse interests to the insured).[316] The company should provide separate counsel to defend the company in claims by the insured for uninsured motorist coverage.[317]

What should defense counsel do when counsel learns of a conflict between insured and insurance company in confidence? Suppose, for example, the insured tells defense counsel of facts unknown to the insurer that would constitute a defense of lack of coverage. If the facts show that the insured is engaged in fraud or collusion, defense counsel should at a minimum withdraw from representation. Further, depending on the confidentiality rule that applies in the jurisdiction where the lawyer practices, the lawyer may be authorized to

---

as reflected in the Guiding Principles and the one-client model discussed below see Fortune et al., Modern Litigation and Professional Responsibility Handbook ch. 15.

313. Guiding Principles II and III deal with excess situations. If the insured retains separate counsel after receiving an excess letter, the insured's attorney has the right to be informed of settlement negotiations, but the insurer retains the right to decide whether to accept settlement offers and to otherwise control the defense, pursuant to the terms of the insurance policy. (Note that some insurance policies, particularly those involving professionals, provide that the insurer may not agree to settle the case without the consent of the insured.)

314. See Guiding Principles IV and V.

315. See Guiding Principle VII.

316. See Guiding Principle VIII.

317. See Guiding Principle X.

reveal the insured's confidences to prevent a crime or fraud. See Problem 2-3 on the scope of the duty of confidentiality. If the facts revealed to defense counsel simply establish a possible coverage defense but do not involve fraud by the insured, defense counsel faces a fundamental conflict between two clients. The traditional answer to such a conflict is for the lawyer to withdraw, but in insurance defense practice this solution would do nothing but increase the cost of handling the case. In this difficult situation, the Guiding Principles state that defense counsel should continue the representation without revealing the insured's confidences to the insurer.[318]

The modified two-client model as expressed in the Guiding Principles suffers from significant weaknesses.[319] First, from defense counsel's perspective, it creates a number of difficult and confusing conflict situations. Second, from the insured's perspective, the model may not provide adequate protection for the insured's interests. For financial and relational reasons, defense counsel have an incentive to protect the interests of the company over the insured when a conflict arises. The two-client model does nothing to counterbalance this incentive. Finally, from the judicial perspective, the model promotes litigation and forces courts to make modifications to standard principles to take into account the circumstances of insurance defense. For example, under the two-client model, when a conflict arises, the typical response required of defense counsel is to notify the insured and the company of the conflict and to inform the insured of the need for independent counsel. This approach leaves unanswered the question of whether the company or the insured must pay for new counsel. Some courts have held that the insurance company must do so.[320] Other courts take a different approach. When a conflict arises, the insurance company is not required to pay for separate counsel for the insured, but defense counsel can no longer represent the company. Instead, defense counsel must represent only the insured.[321]

The one-client model and other approaches

The logical alternative to the traditional approach is the one-client model in which defense counsel represents only the insured.[322] In this conception of the

---

318. The Guiding Principles recognize that cases can arise in which defense counsel learns of coverage issues through confidential communications with the insured. In this situation, the Principles state that defense counsel should not reveal the information to the company nor should counsel advise the insured regarding coverage matters. Guiding Principle VI.

319. See Fortune et al., Modern Litigation and Professional Responsibility Handbook at 566-567.

320. San Diego Navy Federal Credit Union v. Cumis Insurance Society, 208 Cal. Rptr. 494 (Ct. App. 1984). Accord CHI of Alaska, Inc. v. Employers Reinsurance Corp., 844 P.2d 1113 (Alaska 1993).

321. Finley v. Home Insurance Co., 975 P.2d 1145 (Haw. 1998).

322. See Stephen L. Pepper, Applying the Fundamentals of Lawyers' Ethics to Insurance Defense Practice, 4 Conn. Ins. L.J. 27 (1997-1998) (comparing one- and two-client models).

relationship, the insurance company becomes a third-party payor, rather than a client of defense counsel. Under Model Rule 1.8(f) an attorney may not accept compensation from a third party unless the client gives informed consent, there is no interference with the lawyer's independent professional judgment on behalf of the client, and information relating to the representation of the client is protected as required by Rule 1.6. A number of commentators have advocated[323] and several courts have adopted the one-client model.[324]

The one-client model makes the ethical obligations of defense counsel much clearer than the two-client model. Under the one-client model defense counsel acts to further the interests of the insured client, subject to ethical and legal restraints. For example, in excess situations, defense counsel should attempt to persuade the company to accept a settlement within the policy limits rather than advising the company about the advantages and disadvantages of the settlement. If the company sets litigation guidelines that defense counsel believes interfere with the attorney's ability to competently represent the insured, defense counsel should refuse to abide by the guidelines. If defense counsel learns of a coverage issue during the course of representation, defense counsel should maintain the insured's confidence and not reveal the information to the insurer. While the company is treated as a third party under the one-client model, defense counsel, of course, cannot engage in conduct that would be improper as to a third party. Thus, defense counsel could not assist an insured in defrauding a company.[325]

Given these advantages, are there any reasons against the one-client model? In a series of articles Professor Charles Silver and his coauthors have argued that the one-client model ignores the fact that the relationships between the insured and the company and between defense counsel and the company are based on contracts.[326] For example, under the one-client model, suppose the insured wants to settle a case but the insurance company finds the plaintiff's offer unacceptable. The insured cannot force the company to settle a case when the policy gives the company the right to decide whether to settle. Defining the insured as the lawyer's only client does nothing to change this reality of

323. Robert E. O'Malley, Ethics Principles for the Insurer, the Insured, and Defense Counsel: The Eternal Triangle Reformed, 66 Tul. L. Rev. 511 (1991) (proposing set of Guiding Principles II based on one-client model). See Fortune, et al., Modern Litigation and Professional Responsibility Handbook ch. 15.

324. See Atlanta International Insurance Co. v. Bell, 475 N.W.2d 294 (Mich. 1991) (insurer may not bring malpractice action against defense counsel because counsel represents only insured not insurer); In re Rules of Professional Conduct, 2 P.3d 806 (Mont. 2000) (insured is only client).

325. See Fortune, et al., Modern Litigation and Professional Responsibility Handbook at 590.

326. Ellen S. Pryor & Charles Silver, Defense Lawyers' Professional Responsibilities: Part I—Excess Exposure Cases, 78 Tex. L. Rev. 599 (2000); Ellen S. Pryor & Charles Silver, Defense Lawyers' Professional Responsibilities: Part II—Contested Coverage Cases, 15 Geo. J. Legal Ethics 29 (2001); Charles Silver & Kent Syverud, The Professional Responsibilities of Insurance Defense Lawyers, 45 Duke L.J. 255 (1995); Charles Silver, Does Insurance Defense Counsel Represent the Company or the Insured?, 72 Tex. L. Rev. 1583 (1994).

insurance law. Similarly, because the lawyer's engagement by the company is a matter of contract, there is no reason why the lawyer's engagement cannot treat the insured as a co-client.[327]

The position of the Model Rules and the Restatement

Model Rule 1.8, cmt. 11 states in part:

> Lawyers are frequently asked to represent a client under circumstances in which a third person will compensate the lawyer, in whole or in part. The third person might be a relative or friend, *an indemnitor (such as a liability insurance company) or a co-client* (such as a corporation sued along with one or more of its employees). (Emphasis added.)

This comment appears to treat the liability insurer as a third party payor rather than a client. However, the comment also recognizes that a third-party payor can be a co-client. See also Model Rule 1.7, cmt. 13.

The Restatement is clearer and more nuanced. Section 134(1) provides that a lawyer may not accept payment from a third party unless the client gives informed consent and knows of the circumstances of the payment. This section is largely the same as Model Rule 1.8(f). However, §134(2) provides that a lawyer's services may be directed by a third party if:

> (a) the direction does not interfere with the lawyer's independence of professional judgment;
> (b) the direction is reasonable in scope and character, such as by reflecting obligations borne by the person directing the lawyer; and
> (c) the client consents to the direction under the limitations and conditions provided in §122.

This section creates an exception to the normal prohibition on interference by a third party with the lawyer-client relationship, provided the direction is reasonable and the other requirements are met.[328] Comment f goes even further in providing guidance on a number of troublesome issues:

> *f. Representing an insured.* A lawyer might be designated by an insurer to represent the insured under a liability-insurance policy in which the insurer undertakes to indemnify the insured and to provide a defense. The law governing the relationship between the insured and the insurer is, as stated in Comment a, beyond the scope of the Restatement. Certain practices of designated insurance-

---

327. Charles Silver, Does Insurance Defense Counsel Represent the Company or the Insured?, 72 Tex. L. Rev. 1583, 1604 (1994).

328. See also ABA Formal Opinion 01-421 (advising that lawyers may not follow guidelines that materially impair their ability to represent the insured competently; opinion also deals with confidentiality issues involved in responding to insurance company audit requests).

defense counsel have become customary and, in any event, involve primarily standardized protection afforded by a regulated entity in recurring situations. Thus a particular practice permissible for counsel representing an insured may not be permissible under this Section for a lawyer in noninsurance arrangements with significantly different characteristics.

It is clear in an insurance situation that a lawyer designated to defend the insured has a client-lawyer relationship with the insured. The insurer is not, simply by the fact that it designates the lawyer, a client of the lawyer. *Whether a client-lawyer relationship also exists between the lawyer and the insurer is determined under §14.* Whether or not such a relationship exists, communications between the lawyer and representatives of the insurer concerning such matters as progress reports, case evaluations, and settlement should be regarded as privileged and otherwise immune from discovery by the claimant or another party to the proceeding. Similarly, communications between counsel retained by an insurer to coordinate the efforts of multiple counsel for insureds in multiple suits and such coordinating counsel are subject to the privilege. *Because and to the extent that the insurer is directly concerned in the matter financially, the insurer should be accorded standing to assert a claim for appropriate relief from the lawyer for financial loss proximately caused by professional negligence or other wrongful act of the lawyer.* Compare §51, Comment g.

The lawyer's acceptance of direction from the insurer is considered in Subsection (2) and Comment d hereto. With respect to client consent (see Comment b hereto) in insurance representations, when there appears to be no substantial risk that a claim against a client-insured will not be fully covered by an insurance policy pursuant to which the lawyer is appointed and is to be paid, consent in the form of the acquiescence of the client-insured to an informative letter to the client-insured at the outset of the representation should be all that is required. The lawyer should either withdraw or consult with the client-insured (see §122) when a substantial risk that the client-insured will not be fully covered becomes apparent (see §121, Comment c(iii)).

> **Illustration: 5.** Insurer, a liability-insurance company, has issued a policy to Policyholder under which Insurer is to provide a defense and otherwise insure Policyholder against claims covered under the insurance policy. A suit filed against Policyholder alleges that Policyholder is liable for a covered act and for an amount within the policy's monetary limits. Pursuant to the policy's terms, Insurer designates Lawyer to defend Policyholder. Lawyer believes that doubling the number of depositions taken, at a cost of $5,000, would somewhat increase Policyholder's chances of prevailing and Lawyer so informs Insurer and Policyholder. If the insurance contract confers authority on Insurer to make such decisions about expense of defense, and Lawyer reasonably believes that the additional depositions can be forgone without violating the duty of competent representation owed by Lawyer to Policyholder (see §52), Lawyer may comply with Insurer's direction that taking depositions would not be worth the cost.

Material divergence of interest might exist between a liability insurer and an insured, for example, when a claim substantially in excess of policy limits is asserted against an insured. If the lawyer knows or should be aware of such an excess claim, the lawyer may not follow directions of the insurer if doing so would put the insured at significantly increased risk of liability in excess of the policy coverage. Such occasions for conflict may exist at the outset of the representation or may be created by events that occur thereafter. The lawyer must address a conflict whenever presented. To the extent that such a conflict is subject to client consent (see §122(2)(c)), the lawyer may proceed after obtaining client consent under the limitations and conditions stated in §122.

When there is a question whether a claim against the insured is within the coverage of the policy, a lawyer designated to defend the insured may not reveal adverse confidential client information of the insured to the insurer concerning that question (see §60) without explicit informed consent of the insured (see §62). That follows whether or not the lawyer also represents the insurer as co-client and whether or not the insurer has asserted a "reservation of rights" with respect to its defense of the insured (compare §60, Comment l (confidentiality in representation of co-clients in general)).

With respect to events or information that create a conflict of interest between insured and insurer, the lawyer must proceed in the best interests of the insured, consistent with the lawyer's duty not to assist client fraud (see §94) and, if applicable, consistent with the lawyer's duties to the insurer as co-client (see §60, Comment l). If the designated lawyer finds it impossible so to proceed, the lawyer must withdraw from representation of both clients as provided in §32 (see also §60, Comment l). The designated lawyer may be precluded by duties to the insurer from providing advice and other legal services to the insured concerning such matters as coverage under the policy, claims against other persons insured by the same insurer, and the advisability of asserting other claims against the insurer. In such instances, the lawyer must inform the insured in an adequate and timely manner of the limitation on the scope of the lawyer's services and the importance of obtaining assistance of other counsel with respect to such matters. Liability of the insurer with respect to such matters is regulated under statutory and common-law rules such as those governing liability for bad-faith refusal to defend or settle. Those rules are beyond the scope of this Restatement (see Comment a hereto). (Emphasis added.)

Several aspects of the Restatement approach are worth noting and have been highlighted. While the Restatement treats the company as a third-party payor, an attorney-client relationship between the company and defense counsel can be formed either by express agreement or by the facts and circumstances under Restatement §14. Thus, the Restatement seems to follow Professor Silver's view that the engagement between defense counsel and the company determines whether an attorney-client relationship exists. In Formal Opinion 96-403 the ABA Committee accepted this contractual approach to determining the existence of an attorney-client relationship. The opinion states that by express agreement insurer, insured, and defense counsel could agree that counsel represents (1) only the insured, (2) both insured and the insurer for all purposes, (3) both insured and insurer for all purposes except settlement, in which case counsel represents the insurer.

Even if an attorney-client relationship exists only with the insured and not with the company, the Restatement incorporates modifications to a pure one-client model to recognize the contractual realities and historical development of insurance defense practice, including the right of the insurer to control the defense so long as the insurer is acting reasonably and the right of the insurer to bring suit for malpractice. Thus, the Restatement approach can be fairly characterized as a flexible one-client model, subject to agreement of the parties.

While the Restatement provides a number of default rules that apply in the absence of agreement, it is clear that both the Model Rules and the Restatement contemplate and require defense counsel to provide both the insured and insurer with greater information about the nature of their role. Recognizing that defense lawyers have historically not provided such information, Florida has adopted amendments to its rules of professional conduct requiring insurance defense lawyers to explain to companies and insureds who they represent. Florida Rule of Professional Conduct 4-1.7(e) provides:

> *Representation of insureds.* Upon undertaking the representation of an insured client at the expense of the insurer, a lawyer has a duty to ascertain whether the lawyer will be representing both the insurer and the insured as clients, or only the insured, and to inform both the insured and the insurer regarding the scope of the representation. All other Rules Regulating the Florida Bar related to conflicts of interest apply to the representation as they would in any other situation.

In addition, Florida Rule 1.8(f) directs defense counsel to provide insureds with a detailed "Statement of Insured Client's Rights." Lawyers in other jurisdictions would be well advised to review their engagements with insureds and companies to determine whether they are complying with the obligation of informed consent required by the Model Rules and the Restatement.

Problem 3-10

Family Practice

a. Ellen Andrews and her husband, Samuel, have asked you to represent them in obtaining a no-fault divorce, which is recognized in your jurisdiction. You represented the parties previously in the purchase of their home and the preparation of their wills, but you have done no other legal work for them. They tell you that they have been married for five years, that they do not have any animosity toward each other, but that the marriage has just not worked out for them. There are no children. They also tell you that financial problems have been a factor in the divorce. Samuel was in the real estate development business, but his company failed, and he has been out of work now for more than a year. Ellen works full time as a bookkeeper in a doctor's office.

Ellen and Samuel have agreed on a division of their assets. They give you the following sheet of paper:

DIVISION OF ASSETS

1. House, 711 Camellia Drive. Approximate value $250,000. Subject to mortgage to Second Union Bank in amount of $210,000. Property to be sold. Equity used to pay off credit card debt and remaining equity divided. Ellen to live in house until sold.

2. Furnishings in house to go to Ellen except that Samuel will take the following:

Lounge chair in living room
Double bed in guest room
Samuel's chest of drawers in bedroom
GE TV and VCR
Computer and printer

3. We will each keep our cars and take over payments.
4. Credit card debt to be paid when house is sold:

VISA: $2,200
MasterCard: $3,500
Various merchants: about $5,000

What would you say to them?

b.   You are an attorney practicing domestic relations law. You have an interview with a new client, Melissa Carter, who wishes to obtain a divorce from her husband, Carl. Melissa's father, Alan Frank, accompanies her to the interview. Melissa tells you that Carl has been mentally and physically abusing her. Frank expresses hostility toward Carl. He says that he wants to make sure that Carl pays financially for what he has done to his daughter. When you raise the issue of fees, Frank states that he will be responsible for the fees. Be prepared to continue the interview from this point.

c.   You are an attorney appointed by the family court to represent Susan Van Ness, age 14, in an abuse and neglect case filed by the Department of Family and Children Services against Susan's father, Harold, and also in connection with a divorce action filed by Susan's mother, Emily. Harold denies the allegations of abuse and has sought custody of Susan in the divorce case. In his answer Harold claims that his wife is a "pathological liar" who dominates and controls Susan. You have met with Susan, the parents, a social worker, and two psychiatrists; one doctor is treating Susan, while the other psychiatrist is an expert hired by Harold. The allegations of sexual abuse originally came from the mother. Susan initially denied that the abuse occurred, but she later told her psychiatrist that the allegations were true. The treating psychiatrist is prepared to testify that in his opinion the abuse occurred. The psychiatrist for the defense disagrees and will testify that the abuse has been fabricated by the mother and indoctrinated in Susan. Susan has told you very strongly that she wants to live with her mother, not her father. You are not sure whether the allegations of abuse are true, but you believe that they probably are. You are also not sure who should have custody of Susan, but you tend to believe that she would be better off not living with either parent. Two possible choices are the wife's mother or the husband's sister, both of whom you find acceptable. How would you proceed in light of your uncertainties in the case?

Read Model Rules 1.7, 1.8(f), 1.14, 4.3, and comments.

Is multiple representation of spouses per se improper?

According to some authorities, it is ethically improper for an attorney to represent both the husband and wife in a divorce or separation, regardless of the circumstances.[329] The Bounds of Advocacy, standards of conduct adopted by the American Academy of Matrimonial Lawyers, also condemns multiple representation. Standard 3.1 provides: "An attorney should not represent both husband and wife even if they do not wish to obtain independent representation." The comment offers the following rationale: "[I]t is impossible for the attorney to provide impartial advice to both parties. Even a seemingly amicable separation or divorce may result in bitter litigation over financial matters or custody."[330]

Despite these authorities, a number of leading courts have held that it is not per se improper for a lawyer to represent both spouses in a separation or divorce matter. In Klemm v. Superior Court[331] the attorney represented both the husband and wife in a divorce action. The parties had agreed to joint custody without child support. The trial judge granted an interlocutory decree and awarded custody in accordance with the agreement, but because the wife was receiving welfare payments from the county, the judge referred the case to the county's family support division. The division recommended that the court order the husband to pay $50 per month in child support to the county as reimbursement for past and present payments made by the county to the wife. The attorney filed an objection to this recommendation. At the hearing on the issue, counsel filed written consents by both spouses to joint representation and indicated to the court that she was prepared to proceed to contest the support division's recommendation on behalf of both parties. The trial court refused to allow the attorney to proceed on behalf of both parties because

---

329. See Holmes v. Holmes, 248 N.E.2d 564 (Ind. Ct. App. 1969); Hale v. Hale, 539 A.2d 247 (Md. Ct. Spec. App.), *cert. denied,* 542 A.2d 857 (Md. 1988).

330. http://www.aaml.org/Bounds%20of%20Advocacy/Bounds%20of%20Advocacy .htm (visited August 8, 2003).

331. 142 Cal. Rptr. 509 (Ct. App. 1977).

of a conflict between the husband and wife. The court ruled that at some point the wife might no longer qualify for welfare payments, in which event a support order would accrue to her benefit.[332]

The California Court of Appeals reversed. The court drew a distinction between marital cases in which an actual rather than a potential conflict of interest exists. If an actual conflict exists, multiple representation, even with client consent, is improper:

> As a matter of law a purported consent to dual representation of litigants with adverse interests at a contested hearing would be neither intelligent nor informed. Such representation would be per se inconsistent with the adversary position of an attorney in litigation, and common sense dictates that it would be unthinkable to permit an attorney to assume a position at a trial or hearing where he could not advocate the interests of one client without adversely injuring those of the other.[333]

When a potential rather than an actual conflict exists, however, multiple representation with informed client consent is permissible. On the facts of the case the court found that the conflict was potential rather than actual: "While on the face of the matter it may appear foolhardy for the wife to waive child support, other values could very well have been more important to her than such support—such as maintaining a good relationship between the husband and the children and between the husband and herself despite the marital problems—thus avoiding . . . backbiting, acrimony and ill will. . . ."[334] Several commentators have also argued that simultaneous representation of spouses should be permissible in appropriate cases.[335]

When is simultaneous representation ethically proper?

Assuming that simultaneous representation in a divorce or separation matter is not per se improper, when may an attorney undertake such representation?

332. Id. at 511 n.1.

333. Id. at 512.

334. Id. at 513. The court also noted that the parties' agreement to waive child support would not prevent the court from ordering support at a later date if necessary. Other cases finding multiple representation in marital matters to be proper include Levine v. Levine, 436 N.E.2d 476 (N.Y. 1982) (fact that same attorney represented both parties in preparation of separation agreement does not, without more, establish overreaching on part of husband) and Halvorsen v. Halvorsen, 479 P.2d 161 (Wash. Ct. App. 1970, *review denied*) (fact that both parties to divorce were represented by same attorney did not show inadequacy of representation or justify setting aside separation agreement).

335. Nathan M. Crystal, Ethical Problems in Marital Practice, 30 S.C. L. Rev. 321, 325-328 (1979); Nancy J. Moore, Conflicts of Interest in the Simultaneous Representation of Multiple Clients: A Proposed Solution to the Current Controversy, 61 Tex. L. Rev. 211, 245-258 (1982). But see 1 Hazard & Hodes, The Law of Lawyering illus. 11-1, at 10-11 (unlikely that lawyer can satisfy requirement of reasonable belief that dual representation would not adversely affect the relationship with the other client, even in an uncontested divorce).

As noted above, if an actual conflict of interest exists between husband and wife, simultaneous representation is unethical. See Model Rule 1.7(b)(3). Even in the absence of an actual conflict, the attorney may not undertake simultaneous representation unless the attorney is able to comply with the requirements of Rule 1.7(b). Under Rule 1.7(b)(1) an attorney may not undertake multiple representation unless "the lawyer reasonably believes that the lawyer will be able to provide competent and diligent representation to each affected client." Cases will arise in which a lawyer could not have the reasonable belief required by the rule:

> [An] attorney should decline dual representation because of her inability to represent adequately the interests of both spouses if it is likely that (1) advocacy will be needed, (2) independent counseling will be necessary, or (3) the lawyer will not be able to function as a neutral intermediary.

> *1. The Need for Advocacy.* If a contested issue develops in a divorce case, advocacy will be required. In deciding whether it is likely that a contested issue will develop, the attorney should consider the following:

> (a) The degree to which the parties have discussed significant issues and reached agreement on them, at least in principle. . . .

> (b) The presence of minor children, substantial debts, or substantial assets. As the divorce becomes more complex, the potential for a contest increases. While mere complexity of the case should not preclude dual representation, if complexity is coupled with lack of agreement or consideration of basic issues, dual representation should be declined because a contested issue is likely.

> *2. The Need for Independent Counsel.* If either spouse is in a dependent condition, the spouse needs the services of an independent advisor. Whether a spouse is in this condition depends on the following:

> (a) The emotional condition of the parties. If either person is severely emotionally disturbed because of the crisis of the divorce or otherwise, the lawyer should not undertake dual representation.

> (b) The relationship between the spouses. It is not uncommon for one spouse to dominate the other. If the lawyer perceives that one spouse dominates the decision making of the other, dual representation should not be accepted.

> *3. The Lawyer's Ability to Act Neutrally.* As the representative of the spouses, the lawyer has obligations of loyalty and care to both. The lawyer should not undertake dual representation if his personal relationship with either spouse is such that he cannot fulfill this role. A dangerous situation exists if the lawyer has had a close relationship with one of the parties, for example, as business counselor to the husband, and is asked to handle the divorce on behalf of both. The prior relationship, coupled with the prospects for future legal work from the husband, may undermine the lawyer's neutrality.[336]

---

336. Nathan M. Crystal, Ethical Problems in Marital Practice, 30 S.C. L. Rev. 321, 329-330 (1979).

Assuming the lawyer reasonably believes that she can competently and diligently represent both parties, the lawyer must obtain the clients' informed consent, confirmed in writing. Model Rule 1.7(b)(4). Informed consent requires the attorney to provide information about the "implications of the common representation, including possible effects on loyalty, confidentiality and the attorney-client privilege and the advantages and risks involved." Model Rule 1.7, cmts. 18, 30, and 31. Consider the following analysis of this requirement:

1. *Advantages of Dual Representation.*—Clients usually give two reasons for wanting dual representation: a desire to save legal fees, and trust and confidence in the attorney. If one lawyer handles a complex divorce, legal fees are saved in one sense: the total dollar amount paid for legal services is less than if two attorneys are employed. In another sense, however, fees are not saved. [W]hen a lawyer represents both spouses he owes duties to both. The lawyer functions like a mediator rather than an advocate or independent counselor. While clients may rationally prefer to pay X dollars for these services rather than X plus Y dollars for the services of two independent attorneys, they should be aware that it is misleading to state that fees are being saved; different services are being purchased.

Clients should be advised that their goal of obtaining a divorce for one legal fee could be achieved even if the lawyer does not represent both. The lawyer could represent one spouse, leaving the other unrepresented. This approach offers the advantage that the lawyer would not be forced to withdraw if a contested issue developed. It has disadvantages, however. While the attorney may communicate with the unrepresented party, he is ethically prohibited from giving legal advice to that party. Although this is not a major consideration in simple divorces, in complex cases the unrepresented party is probably seriously disadvantaged by lack of counsel. Moreover, regardless of the complexity of the divorce, the unrepresented party may be troubled by his lack of representation. This may cause the divorce to proceed less smoothly than if the attorney represented both parties.

Trust and confidence of both spouses in a specific lawyer is the second reason usually given by clients who want dual representation. For some clients this reason actually represents an underlying fear that if two lawyers are participating the divorce will become formalized and adversarial. The parties should be informed that the question whether the participation of two lawyers makes a divorce more or less adversarial is problematic. Evidence indicates that some lawyers fail to consider that divorces can be resolved in a cooperative rather than adversarial spirit. On the other hand, lawyers often help promote agreements that clients could not have reached on their own.

2. *Disadvantages of Dual Representation.*—The clients should be informed of three possible detrimental effects of dual representation. First, although the parties intend a friendly divorce, a dispute may arise. If this should occur, the lawyer would be required to withdraw from the case. Each of the parties would then be forced to hire new counsel. As a result, total legal fees would probably exceed the fees that would have been paid if separate counsel had been hired initially. Second, several court decisions have overturned separation agreements when one lawyer handled the divorce on the ground that the lawyer did not adequately protect the interests of both parties. While having one lawyer handle

the case does not automatically make the agreement invalid, the parties should be aware that dual representation makes it more likely that a court will not enforce the agreement if one of the parties subsequently becomes dissatisfied with it. Third, by asking the lawyer to represent both, the parties waive their attorney-client privilege for communications made to the attorney by either of them. The attorney might be forced to testify to damaging information if the divorce becomes contested.

3. *Consent.*—If the clients decide that they want the lawyer to represent both of them after the lawyer has fully discussed the advantages and disadvantages of dual representation, the lawyer should obtain their written consent at the time representation is undertaken. The consent should state that the lawyer has explained the advantages and risks of dual representation. A clause evincing consent to the representation should also be included in the separation agreement, and the lawyer should disclose the dual representation to the court at the time of the final decree.[337]

The Restatement of the Law Governing Lawyers partially approves of a lawyer's representation of both spouses in an uncontested divorce. Section 130 offers the following illustration:

> Husband and Wife have agreed to obtain an uncontested dissolution of their marriage. They have consulted Lawyer to help them reach an agreement on disposition of their property. A conflict of interest clearly exists between the prospective clients. . . . If reasonable prospects of an agreement exist, Lawyer may accept the joint representation with the effective consent of both. . . . However, in the later dissolution proceeding, Lawyer may represent only one of the parties . . . and Lawyer must withdraw from representing both clients if their efforts to reach an agreement fail.[338]

The Restatement approach is a creative compromise between absolute prohibition and blanket endorsement of representation of spouses in domestic cases. Under the Restatement view, a lawyer may jointly represent a husband and wife who seek an uncontested divorce in negotiating an agreement to resolve differences between them, but the lawyer avoids representing opposite sides in proceedings before a tribunal.

An alternative to simultaneous representation: representation of one party with the other party being unrepresented

Even if simultaneous representation is ethically permissible, many lawyers may not be willing to run the risks that such representation entails. Indeed, even courts that have permitted simultaneous representation have warned lawyers of the potential risks of this course of action, including malpractice liability,

337. Id. at 330-332.
338. Restatement (Third) of the Law Governing Lawyers §130, illus. 6. See also §122, illus. 8.

disciplinary proceedings, and invalidation of any agreement entered into between the jointly represented parties.[339]

Because of these risks, one approach that many attorneys have used is to refuse to represent both spouses, advising the unrepresented spouse to obtain independent counsel. If the unrepresented spouse refuses to obtain counsel, the attorney proceeds with the matter on behalf of the client, dealing with the other spouse as an unrepresented party. Ethically, an attorney may represent one client and deal with an unrepresented party, provided the attorney complies with Model Rule 4.3 (dealing with unrepresented persons).

Model Rule 4.3 provides that a lawyer shall not give legal advice to an unrepresented person, other than the advice to secure counsel, if there is a reasonable possibility that the third party's interests conflict with those of the client. In light of this prohibition, may a lawyer negotiate with an unrepresented party? May a lawyer prepare a separation agreement or other documents and present them to the unrepresented party for that party's signature? May the lawyer answer questions that the unrepresented party has about the documents? While there is a danger that the unrepresented party may misunderstand the lawyer's role and rely on the lawyer for legal advice, the 2002 revision to the Model Rules makes it clear that a lawyer may do so. Comment 2 to Rule 4.3 states:

> This Rule does not prohibit a lawyer from negotiating the terms of a transaction or settling a dispute with an unrepresented person. So long as the lawyer has explained that the lawyer represents an adverse party and is not representing the person, the lawyer may inform the person of the terms on which the lawyer's client will enter into an agreement or settle a matter, prepare documents that require the person's signature and explain the lawyer's own view of the meaning of the document or the lawyer's view of the underlying legal obligations.[340]

As discussed above, the Bounds of Advocacy of the American Academy of Matrimonial Lawyers state that a lawyer should not represent both spouses in a domestic matter. These standards also deal with the situation in which the lawyer represents one spouse, while the other is unrepresented:

---

339. See Klemm v. Superior Court, 142 Cal. Rptr. 509, 514 (Ct. App. 1977). See also Ishmael v. Millington, 50 Cal. Rptr. 592 (Dist. Ct. App. 1966) (summary judgment for attorney reversed in malpractice action brought by wife claiming that attorney favored interests of husband in preparation of agreement); Columbus Bar Assn. v. Grelle, 237 N.E.2d 298 (1968) (attorney reprimanded because of misunderstandings resulting from multiple representation). But see In re Marriage of Bonds, 5 P.3d 815 (Cal. 2000) (prenuptial agreement enforceable when evidence shows that it was entered into voluntarily even though wife was not separately represented by counsel).

340. See Dolan v. Hickey, 431 N.E.2d 229, 231 (Mass. 1982) ("acts of drafting documents and presenting them for execution, without more, do not amount to 'advice,' and are proper as long as the attorney does not engage in misrepresentation or overreaching"). But see Lawyer Disciplinary Board v. Frame, 479 S.E.2d 676 (W. Va. 1996) (lawyer publicly reprimanded for preparing answer for defendant wife in divorce case).

3.2 An Attorney Should Not Advise an Unrepresented Party

COMMENT

Once it becomes apparent that another party intends to proceed without a lawyer, the attorney should, at the earliest opportunity, inform the other party in writing as follows:

1. I am your spouse's lawyer.

2. I do not and will not represent you.

3. I will at all times look out for your spouse's interests, not yours.

4. Any statements I make to you about this case should be taken by you as negotiation or argument on behalf of your spouse and not as advice to you as to your best interest.

5. I urge you to obtain your own lawyer.

While the "one client only" approach is an option for attorneys who do not want to run the risks of dual representation, some commentators have questioned whether the unrepresented client will fully understand the situation.[341]

Third-party control

Normally, the client who retains a lawyer will also pay the lawyer's fee. Situations arise, however, in which attorney fees are paid by a third party rather than by the client. For example, in Chapter 4 we will consider group legal services plans, in which a sponsor organizes a plan that provides for designated legal services to be rendered by lawyers to members of the plan.

The presence of third-party payors can raise ethical problems if the third party attempts to control the client-lawyer relationship or seeks confidential information. Recall our discussion of insurance defense practice in Problem 3-9. Model Rule 1.8(f) provides some guidance to lawyers for dealing with these issues. Under that rule a lawyer may ethically receive payment of legal fees from someone other than the client so long as the client gives informed consent to the arrangement, the third party does not interfere with the lawyer's independent professional judgment on behalf of the client, and the third person recognizes that the lawyer is bound by rules of confidentiality. When a third-party payor is involved, it would be prudent for the lawyer to obtain in writing the client's consent to payment of fees by the third party. In addition, the lawyer should notify the payor in writing of the lawyer's ethical obligations under Rule 1.8(f).

---

341. James C. Hagy, Note, Simultaneous Representation: Transaction Resolution in the Adversary System, 28 Case W. Res. L. Rev. 86, 97 (1977).

Representation of clients with diminished capacity

We saw in connection with Problem 2-6 that lawyers in criminal defense practice may face problems of representing clients with diminished capacity. The issue also arises in civil litigation. Typical situations in which lawyers can face such problems are domestic cases involving custody of minor children,[342] abuse and neglect cases,[343] representation of clients who have dementia,[344] and civil commitment proceedings.[345] In civil cases, unlike criminal cases, the Constitution does not require deferral of the trial until a party is competent to stand trial. Instead, if a party to a civil matter is incompetent, the court may appoint a guardian ad litem to protect the interests of that party.

In civil cases it is helpful to distinguish four roles that lawyers may perform. First, in some cases a court may appoint a lawyer to serve as guardian ad litem for an incompetent client. When appointed as a guardian, the lawyer is no longer acting in a legal capacity. The guardian's role is to determine what is in the best interest of the ward and to report those findings to the court.[346] Second, in some cases a court may appoint both a guardian ad litem and an attorney to represent the guardian in court. The appointment of a separate guardian and lawyer clarifies the lawyer's responsibilities. In this situation the lawyer is acting in a legal capacity as attorney for the guardian. Generally, the lawyer should look to the guardian to make recommendations to the court that affect the ward. After all, the court has appointed the guardian to make recommendations. See Model Rule 1.14, cmt. 4.[347] Occasions will arise, however, when lawyers may need to take action to protect the interests of the ward against misconduct by the guardian. The clearest case occurs when the guardian is improperly using the ward's money or property. See Model Rule 1.14, cmt. 4.

---

342. Representing Children: Standards for Attorneys and Guardians ad Litem in Custody or Visitation Proceedings (with Commentary), 13 J. Am. Acad. Matrimonial Law. 1 (1995).

343. See generally Special Issue, Ethical Issues in the Legal Representation of Children, 64 Fordham L. Rev. 1281 (1996). Both the ABA and the National Association of Counsel for Children have adopted standards for representation of children in abuse and neglect cases. For comparison of these standards, see http://naccchildlaw.org/training/standards.html (visited Aug. 8, 2003).

344. See Joint Conference on Legal/Ethical Issues in the Progression of Dementia, 35 Ga. L. Rev. 391 (2001).

345. Joshua Cook, Note, Good Lawyering and Bad Role Models: The Role of Respondent's Counsel in a Civil Commitment Hearing, 14 Geo. J. Legal Ethics 179 (2000).

346. See Paige K. B. v. Molepske, 580 N.W.2d 289 (Wis. 1998) (lawyer who serves as guardian ad litem for children in divorce case enjoys absolute immunity because lawyer serves as arm of court to advocate best interests of children). Accord Bluntt v. O'Connor, 737 N.Y.S.2d 471 (App. Div. 2002). See also Roy T. Stuckey, Guardians ad Litem as Surrogate Parents: Implications for Role Definition and Confidentiality, 64 Fordham L. Rev. 1785 (1996).

347. See also 1 Hazard & Hodes, The Law of Lawyering §18.7; Restatement (Third) of the Law Governing Lawyers §24(3).

Third, sometimes a court may appoint three representatives: a guardian for the ward, an attorney for the guardian, and an attorney for the ward. The court may find it necessary to appoint an attorney for the ward when the ward strongly disagrees with the guardian's recommendations. In this situation the attorney for the ward has the duty to advocate the ward's position, even if the lawyer disagrees with that position, so that the court can decide between the recommendation of the guardian and the ward's desires.

Finally, the most difficult role for an attorney occurs when the court appoints an attorney to represent the client but does not appoint a guardian ad litem for the client. Such cases are troublesome because the lawyer has not been appointed as guardian for the client and is therefore not authorized to make recommendations on the client's behalf, yet at the same time the client is not fully competent to make decisions.

As a general proposition lawyers should maintain a normal client-lawyer relationship with an impaired client to the maximum extent possible. Model Rule 1.14(a).[348] Thus, the lawyer is required to communicate information to the client and to assist the client in making decisions regarding the representation. This view is based on two propositions, one empirical, the other normative. Empirically, clients suffer from different degrees of impairment, from the relatively mild to the incapacitating. Many clients with some degree of impairment can participate in decisions affecting their lives. Normatively, even when a client suffers from an impairment, the client is still entitled to exercise personal liberty to the maximum extent possible.[349] In In re M.R.,[350] the New Jersey Supreme Court described the role of an attorney appointed to represent the interests of a developmentally disabled client:

> [A] declaration of incompetency does not deprive a developmentally-disabled person of the right to make all decisions. The primary duty of the attorney for such a person is to protect that person's rights, including the right to make decisions on specific matters. Generally, the attorney should advocate any decision made by the developmentally-disabled person. On perceiving a conflict between that person's preferences and best interests, the attorney may inform the court of the possible need for a guardian ad litem. . . . Our endeavor is to respect everyone's right of self-determination, including the right of the developmentally disabled.[351]

If a lawyer concludes that the client is unable to make decisions regarding the representation and is at risk of substantial harm, the lawyer has several choices on how to proceed. The lawyer could seek the appointment of a general guardian for the client's property (referred to as a conservator in many jurisdictions) or a guardian ad litem to determine the client's interest in litigation. See

---

348. See also Restatement (Third) of the Law Governing Lawyers §24(1).

349. See Model Rule 1.14, cmt. 2; Restatement (Third) of the Law Governing Lawyers §24, cmt. *c*.

350. 638 A.2d 1274 (N.J. 1994).

351. Id. at 1285.

Model Rule 1.14(b).[352] When a guardian has been appointed, the guardian is then legally authorized to make decisions on behalf of the client. The lawyer should generally follow the decisions of the guardian unless the guardian is engaged in conduct that amounts to a breach of fiduciary duty.[353]

Appointment of a guardian is a serious step that deprives the client of a substantial degree of personal liberty. Comment 7 to Model Rule 1.14 notes that appointment of a guardian may be "expensive or traumatic for the client." Thus, lawyers must exercise professional discretion in deciding whether to seek the appointment of a guardian, considering the costs and benefits to the client, along with the other possible options for dealing with the client's incompetency.[354]

What options other than appointment of a guardian ad litem should a lawyer consider? Comment 5 to Model Rule 1.14 outlines a number of possibilities:

> Such measures could include: consulting with family members, using a reconsideration period to permit clarification or improvement of circumstances, using voluntary surrogate decisionmaking tools such as durable powers of attorney or consulting with support groups, professional services, adult-protective agencies or other individuals or entities that have the ability to protect the client. In taking any protective action, the lawyer should be guided by such factors as the wishes and values of the client to the extent known, the client's best interests and the goals of intruding into the client's decisionmaking autonomy to the least extent feasible, maximizing client capacities and respecting the client's family and social connections.[355]

In Formal Opinion 96-404, the ABA Committee on Ethics and Professional Responsibility advised lawyers that the "action taken should be the least restrictive of the client's autonomy that will yet adequately protect the client in connection with the representation."[356]

May a lawyer assume decision-making authority on behalf of a client? Prior to the 2002 revision of the Model Rules, comment 2 provided: "If the person has no guardian or legal representative, the lawyer often must act as a de facto guardian." The 2002 revision deleted this comment. The Reporter's Explanation of Changes states: "The Commission views as unclear, not only what it means to act as a 'de facto guardian,' but also when it is appropriate for a lawyer to take such action and what limits exist on the lawyer's ability to act for an incapacitated client." Restatement §24(2), however, authorizes lawyers to assume such decision-making authority:

---

352. See also Restatement (Third) of the Law Governing Lawyers §24(4).
353. See id. §24(3) and cmt. *f*.
354. See Model Rule 1.14(b) and cmts. 5-7.
355. See also Restatement (Third) of the Law Governing Lawyers §24, cmt. *e*.
356. ABA Comm. on Ethics and Prof. Resp., Formal Op. 96-404, at 9.

A lawyer representing a client with diminished capacity as described in Subsection (1) and for whom no guardian or other representative is available to act, must, with respect to a matter within the scope of the representation, pursue the lawyer's reasonable view of the client's objectives or interests as the client would define them if able to make adequately considered decisions on the matter, even if the client expresses no wishes or gives contrary instructions.

Comment d explains that this authority is limited: "A lawyer should act only on a reasonable belief, based on appropriate investigation, that the client is unable to make an adequately considered decision rather than simply being confused or misguided. Because a disability might vary from time to time, the lawyer must reasonably believe that the client is unable to make an adequately considered decision without prejudicial delay."[357]

Other ethical problems in family practice

In addition to the topics discussed above, family practitioners face many other ethical problems.[358] Issues covered in other problems in these materials include the following: May a lawyer reveal confidential information received from a client to prevent child abuse? Problem 2-3. Are nonrefundable retainers and contingent fees proper in domestic relations cases? Problems 2-2 and 3-1. What are the limitations on negotiation tactics in divorce cases? Problem 4-5. When are sexual relations between a lawyer and client improper? Problem 7-1.

357. See also Paul R. Tremblay, On Persuasion and Paternalism: Lawyer Decisionmaking and the Questionably Competent Client, 1987 Utah L. Rev. 515. Working from a premise of informed consent by clients, Tremblay argues that all the choices available to lawyers who represent questionably competent clients are troublesome, but that some of the choices are ethically more defensible than others. He would prohibit lawyers from acting as de facto guardians except in emergencies and would allow lawyers to seek the appointment of guardians only in extreme cases. He favors enlisting the support of family members and persuasion for dealing with clients who have diminished capacity.

358. See generally Symposium, The Pursuit of Professionalism, 9 J. Am. Acad. Matrimonial Law. (Fall 1992). New York has adopted special rules that closely regulate professional and personal relationships between matrimonial lawyers and their clients. See Sup. Ct. App. Div. R., pt. 1400.

Chapter 4

Ethical Issues in Civil Litigation: Limitations on Zealous Representation, Alternative Dispute Resolution, and Delivery of Legal Services

In Chapter 3 we focused on the client-lawyer relationship, confidentiality, and conflicts of interest in civil litigation. In this chapter we turn to issues involving limitations on zealous representation and delivery of legal services in civil cases. While client obligations are an important element of these issues, these topics also implicate duties to third parties and the system of justice. Section A examines limitations on lawyers' conduct in connection with commencement, investigation, and discovery in civil matters. Section B considers ethical problems in dispute settlement, including negotiation, mediation, and arbitration. Section C focuses on issues of delivery of legal services, including advertising and solicitation, group legal services, and pro bono obligations.

An important point to keep in mind is that while lawyers must represent their clients with loyalty and zealousness, limitations nonetheless exist on what lawyers can do on behalf of their clients. Lawyers function in an adversarial system, but they must "play by the rules." Professors Hazard and Hodes offer the following justifications for rules that limit zealous representation:

> The justification for imposing limitations on advocacy—which concededly can work to the disadvantage even of clients who have engaged in no wrongdoing—is twofold. First, society at large has an interest in maintaining the efficiency of its tribunals. Second, society has an interest in assuring that its most coercive processes are, and are perceived to be, fair. The notion that lawyers have an

enforceable duty to be "fair" to non-clients contradicts the simplistic conception of the lawyer as hired gladiator, but it has always been a fundamental theme of the law of lawyering, as opposed to professional mythology.[1]

As we examine the rules that limit lawyers' conduct, ask yourself whether the rules limiting zealous representation draw the line at the appropriate place. If not, are the rules insufficiently sensitive to the interests of society and third parties or, on the contrary, do they excessively limit zealous representation?[2]

A. Commencement of Actions, Investigation, and Discovery

=============================== Problem 4-1 ===============================

Frivolous Claims

   a.   Erin Mueller has asked you to represent her in a medical malprac-tice action arising from back surgery. Potential defendants in the case are Dr. Nancy Seiquera, the surgeon; Dr. Robert Smith, the anesthesiologist; and Metropolitan Hospital.

   (1)   What investigation should you conduct before taking the case and before filing suit?
   (2)   Would it be proper for you to try to arrange an interview with the doctors about the surgery before filing suit?

   b.   You represent Ronald LeBanc, the defendant in a divorce action brought by his wife, Helen. After Helen told Ronald she wanted a divorce, Ronald learned that Helen had been having an affair with another man. Ronald is outraged by the affair, and he has told you that he wants to do everything he can to get back at his wife. He wants to bring an action against his wife's lover, Charles Wenrow, for "alienation of affections." How would you handle Ronald's desire that you bring suit against Wenrow?

Read Model Rules 2.1, 3.1, 3.2, 4.2, 4.3, and comments.

----

1. 1 Hazard & Hodes, The Law of Lawyering §26.3, at 26-6.
2. See Eugene R. Gaetke, Lawyers as Officers of the Court, 42 Vand. L. Rev. 39 (1989) (arguing that rules of professional conduct give insufficient substantive content to principle that lawyers are officers of courts).

Frivolous actions and delay: ethical duties and discovery sanctions

The duty of lawyers not to engage in frivolous legal proceedings represents one of the most important limitations on adversarial representation. Rule 3.1 of the Model Rules expresses the ethical obligation of lawyers not to engage in frivolous legal proceedings. Rule 3.2 sets forth a related obligation: lawyers shall exercise reasonable efforts to expedite litigation.

Several points about Model Rule 3.1 are worth noting. First, the concept of frivolousness applies not only to complaints but also to answers, motions, and other steps in a legal proceeding. Thus, counsel for both plaintiffs and defendants are subject to the obligation not to engage in frivolous representation. Second, the rule contains an exception for defense of criminal proceedings. Presumably this exception reflects the criminal defendant's constitutional right to a presumption of innocence.[3] Third, the rule does not define a frivolous action, although the comments to the rule provide some guidance. Comment 2 states that lawyers are required to make reasonable efforts to inform themselves of the facts of their clients' cases and the applicable law and to determine whether they can make good faith arguments to support their clients' positions. Under comment 2 an action is not frivolous simply because the facts have not been fully developed or because the lawyer expects to develop evidence in support of the contention during discovery. Further, an action is not frivolous "even though the lawyer believes that the client's position ultimately will not prevail." A claim is not frivolous even if the claim is not warranted under existing law if the lawyer can make a "good faith argument for an extension, modification or reversal of existing law." While the rule alludes to the concept of good faith, the standard is objective.[4]

The 1983 version of the Model Rules provided that a claim may be frivolous if it is brought for an improper purpose, even if the claim has legal and factual merit. Comment 2 to Model Rule 3.1 stated: "The action is frivolous, however, if the client desires to have the action taken primarily for the purpose of harassing or maliciously injuring a person. . . ." However, the 2002 amendments to the Model Rules deleted this language. The Reporter's notes state: "The reference to a client's purpose to harass has been dropped because the client's purpose is not relevant to the objective merits of the client's claim."

The bulk of litigation dealing with frivolous actions by lawyers has developed under Rule 11 of the Federal Rules of Civil Procedure, rather than under Model Rules 3.1 and 3.2. Rule 11 applies only to actions in federal court, but

---

3. The exception for criminal defense does not give criminal defense lawyers a license to ignore the rules of professional conduct. For example, a defense lawyer cannot assist a client in committing perjury, nor could a defense lawyer file a frivolous motion in a criminal case. See 2 Hazard & Hodes, The Law of Lawyering §27.14. The exception simply allows defense counsel to put the prosecution to its proof and vigorously to contest that proof even though the defendant is guilty and has no viable defense against the charges.

4. See 2 Hazard & Hodes, The Law of Lawyering §27.12.

many states have rules of civil procedure modeled on federal Rule 11, and state courts have usually relied on federal court decisions in interpreting their rules.[5] The reason that Rule 11 has been the vehicle for development of the law dealing with frivolous actions is that unlike Rules 3.1 and 3.2, which are enforced through the disciplinary process, Rule 11 provides for monetary sanctions. Thus, lawyers and their clients who have felt that they have been the victims of frivolous proceedings have had a financial incentive to seek relief under Rule 11. The incentive for lawyers and their clients to seek sanctions may diminish as a result of amendments to the rule in 1993, discussed below.

The amount of case law applying Rule 11 is staggering, and an introductory course on professional ethics cannot possibly cover the entire range of issues raised by the rule.[6] Rule 11 contains four specific obligations that lawyers have when they present a matter to a court, by filing documents or otherwise:

- First, "after an inquiry reasonable under the circumstances," the lawyer believes that the document "is not being presented for any improper purpose, such as to harass or to cause unnecessary delay or needless increase in the cost of litigation."
- Second, "after an inquiry reasonable under the circumstances," the lawyer believes that the legal contentions "are warranted by existing law or by a nonfrivolous argument for the extension, modification, or reversal of existing law or the establishment of new law."
- Third, "after an inquiry reasonable under the circumstances," the lawyer believes "the allegations and other factual contentions have evidentiary support or, if specifically so identified, are likely to have evidentiary support after a reasonable opportunity for further investigation or discovery."
- Fourth, "after an inquiry reasonable under the circumstances," the lawyer believes "the denials of factual contentions are warranted on the evidence or, if specifically so identified, are reasonably based on a lack of information or belief."

A lawyer's obligations under Rule 11 are governed by an objective rather than a subjective standard. The Advisory Committee notes to the 1993 amendments to Rule 11 state that the purpose of the amendment was to eliminate the "empty-head pure-heart" justification for a frivolous argument.

---

5. E.g., Bryson v. Sullivan, 412 S.E.2d 327 (N.C. 1992); Jandrt v. Jerome Foods, Inc., 597 N.W.2d 744 (Wis. 1999). See also Van Christo Advertising, Inc. v. M/A-COM/LCS, 688 N.E.2d 985 (Mass. 1998) (under Massachusetts version of Rule 11, which is based on pre-1983 federal rule, subjective rather than objective standard applies).

6. For comprehensive treatments of the rule, see Jerold S. Solovy et al., Sanctions Under Rule 11, 691 PLI/Lit 235 (2003) (on Westlaw); Georgene M. Vairo, Rule 11 Sanctions: Case Law Perspectives & Preventive Measures (3d ed. 2004) (with bibliography). See also Gregory P. Joseph, Sanctions: The Federal Law of Litigation Abuse (3d ed. 2000).

The Restatement of the Law Governing Lawyers also provides some guidance on the meaning of frivolousness. Comment *d* to section 110 states: "A frivolous position is one that a lawyer of ordinary competence would recognize as so lacking in merit that there is no substantial possibility that the tribunal would accept it."

A good example of the application of Rule 11 is White v. General Motors Corp.[7] *White* involved a suit by two former employees of General Motors Corp. (GM). The employees had terminated their employment with GM under its Special Incentive Separation Program. They received $60,000 in cash and signed general releases in which they gave up all claims, both known and unknown, based on their cessation of employment, whether arising under common law, statute, or administrative rule or regulation. Both employees subsequently filed suit claiming that they were discharged because they had complained to management about defective brake work in their plant. White also alleged that GM had slandered him by referring to him as a "troublemaker" when he gave GM as a reference for a job application at another company, Westlake Hardware.

The court of appeals affirmed the district court's decision finding that plaintiffs' attorney had violated Rule 11 in several ways. First, the attorney had failed to conduct a reasonable investigation into the facts forming the basis for the slander claim against GM. Under Kansas law, which governed the case, a slander claim must state the words spoken, the name of the person to whom they were spoken, and the time and place of publication. White's attorney failed to contact anyone at Westlake Hardware to determine whether a GM employee had made the statement that White was a troublemaker.[8] The attorney also continued to assert the slander claim even after GM's lawyers presented an affidavit from a Westlake Hardware employee that she had made no inquiry at GM and even though the attorney had no evidence to support her allegations.[9]

Second, the attorney had filed claims for wrongful discharge that were unwarranted under existing law because such claims were barred by the general releases signed by the plaintiffs. The court addressed the issue of the attorney's duty regarding affirmative defenses as follows:

> Part of a reasonable attorney's prefiling investigation must include determining whether any obvious affirmative defenses bar the case. . . . An attorney need not forbear to file her action if she has a colorable argument as to why an otherwise applicable affirmative defense is inapplicable in a given situation. For instance, an otherwise time-barred claim may be filed, with no mention of the statute of limitations if the attorney has a nonfrivolous argument that the limitation was tolled for part of the period. The attorney's argument must be nonfrivolous, however; she runs the risk of sanctions if her only response to an affirmative defense is unreasonable. . . .

7. 908 F.2d 675 (10th Cir. 1990), *cert. denied*, 498 U.S. 1069 (1991).
8. 908 F.2d at 681.
9. Id.

The court rejected plaintiffs' arguments that they had executed the releases under duress and found their arguments regarding Kansas law on duress so poorly framed and so negligently made as to be sanctionable. We agree. Among the arguments made to the district court was that the Kansas Supreme Court case of Hastain v. Greenbaum, 205 Kan. 475, 470 P.2d 741 (1970), which is binding on this court, was distinguishable because the West Publishing Company classified it as a "Bills and Notes" case in formulating its Headnotes. . . .

The district court also sanctioned plaintiffs for alleging that the releases were void due to ambiguity. Plaintiffs point out that the exact duties of GM are not set out in the releases. But the releases clearly state that all present and future claims, known and unknown, were released by White and Staponski. Further, plaintiffs failed to allege any real confusion caused by any ambiguities in the releases. There is no substantial disagreement between the parties on the terms of the contract.

[T]here were arguments to set aside the releases that could have been made that would not have warranted sanctions. A reasonably competent attorney could have filed a colorable, nonfrivolous ADEA [Age Discrimination in Employment Act] case against GM. Although it would be more difficult, a nonfrivolous common law whistleblowing claim also might have been brought. Thus, we have the tragedy of inept lawyers who failed to investigate their claims, and who compounded the court's and the defendant's problems in dealing with the case by adopting an extremely aggressive approach. Rule 11 should not be used to discourage advocacy, including that which challenges existing law. Nevertheless, the court is entitled to expect a reasonable level of competence and care on the part of the attorneys who appear before it, and to expect that claims submitted for adjudication by those attorneys will have a rational basis. We cannot find the district court's decision to award sanctions an abuse of discretion.[10]

Third, the attorney filed the action for an improper purpose. The court found evidence to support the district court's finding of improper purpose in the fact that the attorney threatened to utilize the media to create adverse publicity against GM and in the fact of unwarranted discovery requests filed by the attorney. The lack of prefiling investigation and the unwarranted nature of the claims also supported the finding of improper purpose.[11] The attorney in *White* was later ordered to pay $50,000 for violation of Rule 11,[12] and she was subsequently disbarred for misconduct in several cases, including *White*.[13]

While Rule 11 is the best-known provision regulating improper litigation tactics, it is only one of an arsenal of weapons that federal courts (or state courts whose procedural systems are based on the Federal Rules) can use to

10. Id. at 682-683.
11. Id. at 683. But see Sussman v. Bank of Israel, 56 F.3d 450 (2d Cir.), *cert. denied*, 516 U.S. 916 (1995) (district court erred in awarding sanctions for improper purpose in filing complaint—threatening negative publicity to force settlement of related litigation—when complaint was not substantively frivolous).
12. White v. General Motors Corp., 977 F.2d 499 (10th Cir. 1992).
13. In re Caranchini, 956 S.W.2d 910 (Mo. 1997) (en banc), *cert. denied*, 524 U.S. 940 (1998).

punish litigation abuse, either through the award of attorney fees or other sanctions: Rule 16(f) (failure to abide by pretrial order), 26(g) (improper discovery requests or objections), 30(g) (failure to attend a deposition or serve a subpoena on a witness to be deposed), 37 (improper failure to respond to discovery), 41(b) (dismissal of action or claim when a party fails to comply with the Federal Rules or court order), 45(e) (contempt for failure to obey subpoena), and 56(g) (presentation of affidavit in summary judgment motion in bad faith or for the purpose of delay); see also Federal Rule of Appellate Procedure 38 (power to award damages and costs for a frivolous appeal). In addition, a federal statute, 28 U.S.C. §1927, provides as follows:

> Any attorney or other person admitted to conduct cases in any court of the United States or any Territory thereof who so multiplies the proceedings in any case unreasonably and vexatiously may be required by the court to satisfy personally the excess costs, expenses, and attorneys' fees reasonably incurred because of such conduct.[14]

Finally, in Chambers v. Nasco, Inc.[15] the Supreme Court in a 5-4 decision ruled that federal courts have inherent power to impose sanctions for bad faith conduct even when the conduct is not specifically covered by rules of procedure or statutory provisions, including fraud that occurs outside court.[16]

Criticism of Rule 11, the 1993 amendment, and the Private Securities Litigation Reform Act of 1995

Rule 11 has been extensively studied and frequently criticized. Some opponents of the rule argue that it grants judges too much discretion, with the result that the application of the rule varies widely.[17] Other critics challenge the efficiency of the rule. Since the rule spawns ancillary proceedings at the trial court level and appeals to determine both violations and sanctions, these commentators question whether the benefits of the rule in deterring frivolous conduct outweigh the costs of administration.[18] Finally, other scholars charge that the rule has a

---

14. For a comparison of Rule 11 and 28 U.S.C. §1927, see Ridder v. City of Springfield, 109 F.3d 288 (6th Cir. 1997), *cert. denied*, 522 U.S. 1046 (1998).

15. 501 U.S. 32 (1991).

16. A circuit-by-circuit comparison of sanctions under Rule 11 and under these other sources of law can be found in American Bar Association Section of Litigation, Sanctions: Rule 11 & Other Powers (Melissa L. Nelken ed., 3d ed. 1992).

17. For a study supporting this conclusion, see Saul M. Kassin, An Empirical Study of Rule 11 Sanctions (1985).

18. For an analysis of whether the costs of the rule exceed its benefits, with a conclusion that they do not, at least in the Third Circuit, see Third Circuit Task Force on Federal Rule of Civil Procedure 11, Rule 11 in Transition (Stephen B. Burbank Rep. 1989).

deterrent effect on innovative advocacy, and that this impact may be especially significant in new and evolving areas of law.[19]

In 1993 the Supreme Court approved a revised Rule 11 based on recommendations of the Judicial Conference of the United States. While the substantive standards of the new rule are quite similar to those under previous Rule 11, the new rule makes a number of important changes in application. The rule provides that a motion seeking sanctions under the rule cannot be filed in court until the other party has been served with the motion and given 21 days to correct any violation.[20] Second, sanctions under the rule may be imposed not only on individual attorneys but also on their law firms.[21] This change overrules the Supreme Court decision in Pavelic & LeFlore v. Marvel Entertainment Group.[22] Third, the new rule makes explicit that the purpose of sanctions is deterrence rather than compensation. Prior to the 1993 amendments the normal sanction for violation of Rule 11 was an award of the attorney fees incurred by the moving party in responding to the frivolous conduct. The 1993 amendments deemphasize monetary awards and authorize courts to issue orders for nonmonetary sanctions to deter misconduct.[23] Fourth, under the new rule sanctions are discretionary with the court. Fifth, the rule requires specificity in court orders imposing sanctions.[24] These changes have substantially reduced the amount of Rule 11 litigation.[25]

In 1995 Congress moved to toughen the application of Rule 11 to securities cases by enacting the Private Securities Litigation Reform Act of 1995.[26] The act responded to what Congress determined to be abuses in securities litigation, including routine filing of securities fraud cases whenever a company's stock price changed, targeting of deep-pocket defendants, use of the discovery system to impose costs on defendants and thereby induce settlement, and improper control of class actions by class counsel. The act changed the procedure for

19. Melissa L. Nelken, Sanctions Under Amended Federal Rule 11—Some "Chilling" Problems in the Struggle Between Compensation and Punishment, 74 Geo. L.J. 1313 (1986). See also Jeffrey A. Parness, More Stringent Sanctions Under Federal Civil Rule 11: A Reply to Professor Nelken, 75 Geo. L.J. 1937 (1987). See generally Byron C. Keeling, Toward a Balanced Approach to "Frivolous" Litigation: A Critical Review of Federal Rule 11 and State Sanctions Provisions, 21 Pepp. L. Rev. 1067 (1994).

20. Fed. R. Civ. P. 11(c)(1)(A). See Hadges v. Yonkers Racing Corp. (In re Kuntsler), 48 F.3d 1320 (2d Cir. 1995) (district court improperly imposed sanctions when moving party failed to comply with 21-day safe harbor provision of Rule 11).

21. Fed. R. Civ. P. 11(c).

22. 493 U.S. 120 (1989).

23. Fed. R. Civ. P. 11(c)(2).

24. Id. 11(c)(3).

25. See Georgene Vairo, Rule 11 and the Profession, 67 Fordham L. Rev. 589, 626 (1998). See also Lonnie T. Brown, Jr., Ending Illegitimate Advocacy: Reinvigorating Rule 11 Through Enhancement of the Ethical Duty to Report, 62 Ohio St. L.J. 1555 (2001) (noting that the 1993 amendments have substantially reduced the impact of Rule 11 and proposing an enhanced duty to report through the creation of "litigation misconduct databases").

26. Pub. L. No. 104-67, 109 Stat. 737 (1995).

imposing Rule 11 sanctions and made sanctions mandatory rather than discretionary. Further, the act presumes that the opposing party's attorney fees and costs will be the sanction if the complaint substantially fails to comply with Rule 11.[27]

Tort liability of attorneys for frivolous actions

Not only are attorneys subject to disciplinary action under Model Rule 3.1 and to sanctions under federal Rule 11 for asserting frivolous positions, the possibility of tort liability also exists. Section 674 of the Restatement (Second) of Torts defines malicious prosecution as follows:

> ### §674. General Principle
>
> One who takes an active part in the initiation, continuation or procurement of civil proceedings against another is subject to liability to the other for wrongful civil proceedings if
>
> (a) he acts without probable cause, and primarily for a purpose other than that of securing the proper adjudication of the claim in which the proceedings are based, and
>
> (b) except when they are ex parte, the proceedings have terminated in favor of the person against whom they are brought.

Comment *d* to that section amplifies its application to attorneys, making clear that attorneys are not liable for malicious prosecution simply because they act in their professional capacity:

> d. *Attorneys.* An attorney who initiates a civil proceeding on behalf of his client or one who takes any steps in the proceeding is not liable if he has probable cause for his action (see §675); and even if he has no probable cause and is convinced that his client's claim is unfounded, he is still not liable if he acts primarily for the purpose of aiding his client in obtaining a proper adjudication of his claim. (See §676.) An attorney is not required or expected to prejudge his client's claim, and although he is fully aware that its chances of success are comparatively slight, it is his responsibility to present it to the court for adjudication if his client so insists after he has explained to the client the nature of the chances.
>
> If, however, the attorney acts without probable cause for belief in the possibility that the claim will succeed, and for an improper purpose, as, for example, to put pressure upon the person proceeded against in order to compel payment of another claim of his own or solely to harass the person proceeded against by

---

27. 15 U.S.C. §78u-4(c). See Gurary v. Nu-Tech Bio-Med, Inc., 303 F.3d 212 (2d Cir. 2002), *cert. denied*, 123 S. Ct. 1583 (2003) (complaint may amount to a substantial violation even if it contains some nonfrivolous claims).

bringing a claim known to be invalid, he is subject to the same liability as any other person. . . . [28]

Related to malicious prosecution is the tort of abuse of process. The Restatement defines abuse of process as follows:

§682. General Principle

One who uses a legal process, whether criminal or civil, against another primarily to accomplish a purpose for which it is not designed, is subject to liability to the other for harm caused by the abuse of process.

Comparison of the elements of the two torts indicates that it should be easier to establish a claim for abuse of process than a claim for malicious prosecution. Both malicious prosecution and abuse of process call for an improper purpose. Malicious prosecution, however, requires termination of the proceeding in favor of the plaintiff, while abuse of process does not. In addition, malicious prosecution requires that the proceeding be brought without probable cause. Abuse of process does not have this requirement; the tort occurs when process is used for a purpose other than that for which it was intended.

With increasing frequency, disgruntled defendants have brought claims for malicious prosecution and abuse of process against attorneys for opposing parties.[29] Such claims involve a tension between two important public policies. On one hand, the public has an interest in open access to courts. If courts hold attorneys liable for actions that they bring on behalf of clients, a "chilling effect" on the use of the judicial process may result. On the other hand, the judicial process should be used to resolve bona fide disputes rather than as a weapon to coerce defendants into paying money or for other improper purposes. Not surprisingly, the courts have struck a balance between these two policies, recognizing the possibility of attorney liability for malicious prosecution or abuse of process but indicating that liability will be imposed only in extreme cases. While such claims have rarely been successful, on occasion courts have found liability. For example, in Crowley v. Katleman[30] the California Supreme Court held that the plaintiff, an attorney, stated a cause of action for malicious prosecution against the defendant and her attorneys for challenging a will that left the defendant's husband's estate to the plaintiff attorney. The plaintiff

---

28. The Restatement of Torts focuses on malicious prosecution of claims, but one court has recognized a cause of action for malicious defense. See Aranson v. Schroeder, 671 A.2d 1023 (N.H. 1995). But see Wilkinson v. Shoney's, Inc., 4 P.3d 1149 (Kan. 2000) (rejecting cause of action for malicious defense).

29. On attorney liability for malicious prosecution and abuse of process, see Debra E. Wax, Annotation, Liability of Attorney, Acting for Client, for Malicious Prosecution, 46 A.L.R.4th 249 (1986); Debra T. Landis, Annotation, Civil Liability of Attorney for Abuse of Process, 97 A.L.R.3d 688 (1980). See also 1 Mallen & Smith, Legal Malpractice §6.6-6.22.

30. 881 P.2d 1083 (Cal. 1994) (en banc).

attorney and the decedent had been good friends; the plaintiff had not drafted the will; the decedent executed the will before he married the defendant; and the decedent did not revoke or revise the will during their marriage. The defendant wife had challenged the will on multiple grounds, including fraud, undue influence, and lack of mental capacity. The California Supreme Court found that a malicious prosecution claim could still be brought even though not all of the grounds were without probable cause. In addition, the court rejected the defendant's arguments that the appropriate remedy for frivolous claims was through court-imposed sanctions rather than by a tort action.[31]

By contrast, in Detenbeck v. Koester[32] the Texas Court of Appeals held that the plaintiff doctor failed to state a cause of action for abuse of process against the defendant and his attorneys for bringing a medical malpractice action against the plaintiff. The court ruled that bringing suit was not using process other than the purpose for which it was intended. The court also stated that if the suit were groundless the defendant could seek appropriate sanctions.[33]

Investigative contacts with potential witnesses or potential defendants prior to filing suit

We will see in the next problem that the rules of professional conduct prohibit a lawyer from communicating with a person the lawyer knows is represented by counsel in the matter without the consent of the person's attorney, unless the communication is authorized by law. Model Rule 4.2. Further, when an entity is involved in the matter, the no-communication rule applies to some current employees of the entity, even if the employee is not personally involved in the matter or personally represented by counsel.

Does the no-communication rule apply prior to the filing of a lawsuit? If not, plaintiffs' counsel could avoid the rule by conducting extensive interviews before bringing suit. Yet as we have seen, plaintiffs' counsel have an ethical and legal obligation to investigate the facts of the case before filing suit to determine if the action is meritorious. Courts have accommodated these conflicting considerations by allowing plaintiffs' counsel to engage in investigation prior to filing suit so long as they do not have actual knowledge that the person contacted is represented by counsel. For example, in Jorgensen v. Taco Bell Corp.,[34] a sexual harassment case, plaintiff's counsel hired a private investigator who interviewed the alleged harasser and two of Taco Bell's employees before plaintiff filed suit. Taco Bell subsequently moved to disqualify plaintiff's counsel. The court of appeals recognized that the anticontract rule might apply before suit was filed if the attorney had actual knowledge that the person

31. See also Mazzio's Corp. v. Bright, 46 P.3d 201 (Okla. Civ. App. 2002) (attorney held liable for malicious prosecution in handling employment discrimination claim).
32. 886 S.W.2d 477 (Tex. Ct. App. 1994, no writ).
33. Id. at 482.
34. 58 Cal. Rptr. 2d 178 (Ct. App. 1996).

contacted was represented by counsel.[35] The court concluded, however, that plaintiff's counsel did not have actual knowledge that the employees were represented by counsel; it rejected on policy grounds Taco Bell's argument that counsel "should have known" that the employees would be represented by counsel for Taco Bell:

> Frivolous litigation is frequently avoided by a careful lawyer's investigation of a client's claims before filing suit. Rule 2-100 [the California version of the no-communication rule] should not be applied to require that investigation of such claims not be undertaken before suit is filed because the party or employee investigated may be expected to obtain counsel at a future time. This file-first investigate-later result which appellant would generate through its application of rule 2-100 is practically capable of compulsorily producing the type of frivolous litigation for which the Legislature has authorized the imposition of sanctions.[36]

The court in *Jorgensen* also mentioned ways that employers could protect themselves against communications with their employees before suit was filed. The rules of ethics allow an employer to request that its employees not discuss the matter with plaintiff's counsel. See Model Rule 3.4(f)(1). An employer could also have its attorney send the other party a warning letter stating that its employees were represented by counsel in the matter and that any communications should be made through employer's counsel.[37] On receipt of such a letter, counsel would have actual knowledge that the employees were represented by counsel.

When a lawyer has actual knowledge that an employee is represented by counsel, communications prior to filing suit are improper. In Shoney's, Inc. v. Lewis[38] the Kentucky Supreme Court ordered disqualification of the lawyer for the plaintiff in a sexual harassment case for taking precomplaint statements from two of defendant's managers. The plaintiff's lawyer knew that the employer would be represented by counsel in the matter and had even had discussions with the employer's lawyer about the case before taking the statements.[39] The

---

35. Id. at 180.

36. Id. at 181. Other courts have agreed that the anticontact rule requires the lawyer to have actual knowledge that the person contacted is represented by counsel. See Gaylard v. Homemakers of Montgomery, Inc., 675 So. 2d 363 (Ala. 1996) and the Kentucky cases cited in note 39 below. Like the court in *Jorgensen* these courts have emphasized the attorney's obligation to investigate the facts before filing suit.

37. 58 Cal. Rptr. 2d at 181.

38. 875 S.W.2d 514 (Ky. 1994).

39. In K-Mart Corp. v. Helton, 894 S.W.2d 630 (Ky. 1995), plaintiff's attorney took a statement from a managerial employee of K-Mart in connection with a false imprisonment case prior to filing suit. The Kentucky Supreme Court distinguished *Shoney's* and refused to disqualify plaintiff's counsel. The court stated that in *Shoney's* the attorney knew that the employees were represented by corporate counsel. By contrast, in *K-Mart* the company had done nothing to indicate to plaintiff's counsel that its employees were represented by counsel; in fact, K-Mart had asked the employee to contact the plaintiff to try to "smooth over" the situation. Id. at 631. See also Humco, Inc. v. Noble, 31 S.W.3d 916 (Ky. 2000) (copy of letter by employee to in-house counsel did not establish that attorney knew that

court also ordered suppression of the statements because of counsel's unethical conduct.[40]

Even if the anticontact rule does not apply, a lawyer contacting a witness or a potential defendant must keep in mind the obligations with regard to unrepresented people set forth in Rule 4.3. "The lawyer shall not give legal advice to an unrepresented person, other than the advice to secure counsel, if the lawyer knows or reasonably should know that the interests of such a person are or have a reasonable possibility of being in conflict with the interests of the client." Thus, under the rule it is proper for the attorney to communicate with a witness or even with a potential defendant, but the attorney must use care in doing so. The attorney may not mislead the person about the attorney's role nor may the attorney give the other party legal advice.[41] Indeed, some attorneys may feel that some form of "*Miranda* warning" is called for whenever meeting with a witness or potential defendant.

──────────── Problem 4-2 ────────────

Investigation: Contacts with Employees

A massive fire at the International Hotel killed 15 guests and injured many more. The estate of one of the deceased guests has retained you to represent its interests. You have sent your investigator to the scene of the fire, and he learned the names of a number of the hotel's employees. Some of them worked in the kitchen where the fire began, while others worked in other parts of the hotel.

When your investigator tried to arrange an interview with one of the employees, he was told by the employee that "the hotel's lawyers told us not to talk to anyone about the case." You have learned that International has retained Steve Fairey of Wilson & Farr to represent it in the fire litigation. You called Fairey to complain about his attempts to silence International's employees.

During the course of your investigation of the fire, you learned that three months ago the hotel fired its manager, Anita Allen. You contacted Allen, who told you that the hotel fired her after she complained about the hotel's unwillingness to spend money on maintenance. Allen said that the hotel had experienced some electrical problems in the kitchen, and she suspected that this may have caused the accident. She gave you a copy of a memorandum that she sent to the home office of International

---

company employees were represented by in-house counsel). Knowledge may, however, be inferred from the circumstances. Cf. Featherstone v. Schaerrer, 34 P.3d 194 (Utah 2001).

40. 875 S.W.2d at 516.

41. See W. T. Grant Co. v. Haines, 531 F.2d 671, 675-676 (2d Cir. 1976) (outside counsel did not violate rule prohibiting advice and misrepresentation to unrepresented person, but methods used were "at least inappropriate and certainly not to be encouraged").

complaining about the lack of maintenance and raising safety concerns. Wilson & Farr has learned that you have interviewed Allen and has filed a motion to disqualify you from handling this case because of your ex parte contact with Allen.

Read Model Rules 3.4(f), 4.2, 4.4, and comments.

Prohibition of communication with a person represented by counsel: purpose and scope

An established rule of professional conduct is that a lawyer may not communicate with a person who is represented by counsel in a matter without the consent of that person's lawyer. Model Rule 4.2 as revised in 2002 provides as follows:

> In representing a client, a lawyer shall not communicate about the subject of the representation with a person the lawyer knows to be represented by another lawyer in the matter, unless the lawyer has the consent of the other lawyer or is authorized to do so by law or a court order.[42]

While the no-communication rule (often labeled the "anti-contract" rule) is well established, its rationale remains somewhat hazy.[43] Comment 1 states: "This Rule contributes to the proper functioning of the legal system by protecting a person who has chosen to be represented by a lawyer in a matter against possible overreaching by other lawyers who are participating in the matter, interference by those lawyers with the client-lawyer relationship and the uncounseled disclosure of information relating to the representation." The Restatement offers a similar rationale, although it does not refer to the proper functioning of the legal system.[44] The core idea behind the rule seems to be protection of the integrity of the attorney-client relationship from interference by a lawyer representing another person in the matter.[45]

---

42. See also Restatement (Third) of the Law Governing Lawyers §99.

43. See John Leubsdorf, Communicating with Another Lawyer's Client: The Lawyer's Veto and the Client's Interests, 127 U. Pa. L. Rev. 683 (1979).

44. Restatement (Third) of the Law Governing Lawyers §99, cmt. *b*.

45. Carl A. Pierce, Variations on a Basic Theme: Revisiting the ABA's Revision of Model Rule 4.2 (Part I), 70 Tenn. L. Rev. 121, 140-147 (2002). Professor Pierce, in his extensive study of the rule, criticizes the vagueness of some aspects of comment 1. He points out that the comment fails to make clear how the rule contributes to the proper functioning of the legal system nor does it explain what is meant by overreaching. He suggests a more precise rationale that focuses on protecting the integrity of the client-attorney relationship. Professor Pierce was Associate Reporter to the Ethics 2000 Commission and was extensively involved in the Commission's discussions regarding revision of Rule 4.2.

The 1983 version of Rule 4.2 used the term "party" rather than "person" in the text of the rule, perhaps implying that the rule was limited to situations in which litigation had begun. Courts in a few jurisdictions where the local version of the rule uses the term "party" have limited the rule to named parties represented by counsel after litigation has been filed.[46] The ABA amended the rule in 1995, substituting the word "person" for "party," to make it clear that the rule was not so limited,[47] and the 2002 revision of the rules reaffirms this position in the text and comment 2.[48] If the general purpose of the rule is to protect the integrity of the client-lawyer relationship, it should apply in all matters in which a person is represented by counsel, including transactional matters, litigation before suit is filed, and litigation after formal proceedings are begun.[49] The Restatement agrees.[50]

May a client waive the protections of the rule and communicate with a lawyer who represents another person in the matter?[51] Clients, of course, have the right not to hire lawyers and are generally free to discharge their lawyers at any time, so it would seem that a client could waive the rule. Comment 3 to the 2002 revision, however, provides that the rule applies even if the represented person "initiates or consents to the communication." The comment states that when a lawyer learns that the client is represented, the lawyer must immediately terminate the communication. If the rule provides benefits to the legal system and not just to represented clients, the prohibition on waivers can be justified. The rationale would be similar to that given for prohibiting clients from waiving a conflict of interest when the conflict involves adverse positions before the same tribunal. Cf. Model Rule 1.7(b)(3). In addition, the prohibition on waivers has a history to it. In discussions about the revision of Rule 4.2, the Commission rejected a proposal from the Conference of Chief Justices that grew out of discussions with the Department of Justice. One of the provisions of the Chief Justices' proposal would have allowed people who were represented by counsel to waive the protections of the rule and communicate directly with the government. The Commission rejected this view, although it did provide a new excep-

---

46. See Grievance Comm. for the S. Dist. of N.Y. v. Simels, 48 F.3d 640 (2d Cir. 1995) (no violation of DR 7-104(A)(1), the Code equivalent of Model Rule 4.2, to interview represented witness and potential codefendant in drug case because rule uses term *party* and should be narrowly construed); Gaylard v. Homemakers of Montgomery, Inc., 675 So. 2d 363 (Ala. 1996) (not improper under Rule 4.2 to contact employee of defendant prior to filing suit because defendant not a "party" and lawyer did not know that employer was represented by counsel in matter).

47. Pierce, Variations on a Basic Theme, 70 Tenn. L. Rev. at 147.

48. Comment 2 is intended to express the broad scope of the rule. Professor Pierce suggests that the comment is somewhat sparse and recommends a more elaborate version with some noncontroversial examples. Id. at 150.

49. Id. at 149.

50. Restatement (Third) of the Law Governing Lawyers §99, cmt. *c*.

51. See Leubsdorf, Communicating with Another Lawyer's Client (arguing that rule should be changed to allow clients to consent to communication with opposing counsel).

tion when the communication is authorized by court order.[52] The Restatement agrees that the rule is not subject to waiver by the client.[53]

The no-communication rule applies in a wide variety of settings. For example, in a divorce case, it is unethical for a lawyer representing one spouse to meet with the other spouse in an effort to negotiate a settlement without the consent of the other spouse's attorney.[54] Similarly, in a personal injury case, a lawyer representing the plaintiff may not meet with an adjuster from an insurance company without consent of the insurer's counsel.[55] Controversy has raged between the criminal defense bar and prosecutors over the issue of whether federal prosecutors and their agents may contact individuals who are represented by counsel during the course of criminal investigations without the consent of their attorneys. See Problem 2-10.

The no-communication rule is subject to some exceptions. Communication is permitted when authorized by law, for example, a communication pursuant to court rule or court order.[56] The rule applies only to lawyers, not to their clients. Thus, in a divorce case one spouse is free to negotiate directly with the other spouse. Lawyers may advise clients of their right to communicate directly with the opposing party.[57] See Model Rule 4.2, cmt. 4. Communication in an emergency is also permissible.[58]

The application of the no-communication rule to government officials has been controversial. On the one hand, people have a First Amendment right to communicate with the government. On the other hand, government employees and officials are frequently involved in litigation in which they are represented by counsel. The Model Rule does not take a position on this issue. Comment 5 states: "Communications authorized by law may include communications by a lawyer on behalf of a client who is exercising a constitutional or other legal right to communicate with the government." The Restatement is more specific. It first provides that the no-communication rule generally does not apply to "employees of a represented governmental agency or with a governmental officer being represented in the officer's official capacity."[59] The Restatement then goes on to state that the no-communication rule does apply in limited circumstances:

> In negotiation or litigation by a lawyer of a specific claim of a client against a governmental agency or against a governmental officer in the officer's official

52. Pierce, Variations on a Basic Theme, 70 Tenn. L. Rev. at 141.
53. Restatement (Third) of the Law Governing Lawyers §99, cmt. *j*.
54. E.g., In re Wehringer, 525 N.Y.S.2d 604 (App. Div.), *cert. denied*, 488 U.S. 988 (1988).
55. In re Illuzzi, 616 A.2d 233 (Vt. 1992) (lawyer violated DR 7-104(A)(1) by meeting with insurance adjuster after company had retained counsel, even though such contacts were an "accepted practice" in state).
56. Restatement (Third) of the Law Governing Lawyers §99, cmts. *g, m*.
57. Id. §99(2) and cmt. *k*. Illustration 6 indicates that a lawyer may redraft a letter that the client plans to send to the opposing party.
58. Id. cmt. *i*.
59. Id. §101(1).

capacity, the prohibition stated in §99 applies, except that the lawyer may contact any officer of the government if permitted by the agency or with respect to an issue of general policy.[60]

One of the most controversial issues involving Rule 4.2 deals with its application to employees of corporations or other entities when the entity is represented by counsel. Consider the following case.

Niesig v. Team I

New York Court of Appeals
558 N.E.2d 1030 (N.Y. 1990)

KAYE, Judge.

Plaintiff in this personal injury litigation, wishing to have his counsel privately interview a corporate defendant's employees who witnessed the accident, puts before us a question that has generated wide interest: are the employees of a corporate party also considered "parties" under Disciplinary Rule 7-104(A)(1) of the Code of Professional Responsibility, which prohibits a lawyer from communicating directly with a "party" known to have counsel in the matter?[1] The trial court and the Appellate Division both answered that an employee of a counseled corporate party in litigation is by definition also a "party" within the rule, and prohibited the interviews. For reasons of policy, we disagree.

As alleged in the complaint, plaintiff was injured when he fell from scaffolding at a building construction site. At the time of the accident he was employed by DeTrae Enterprises, Inc.; defendant J.M. Frederick was the general contractor, and defendant Team I the property owner. Plaintiff thereafter commenced a damages action against defendants, asserting two causes of action centering on Labor Law §240, and defendants brought a third-party action against DeTrae.

Plaintiff moved for permission to have his counsel conduct ex parte interviews of all DeTrae employees who were on the site at the time of the accident, arguing that these witnesses to the event were neither managerial nor controlling employees and could not therefore be considered "personal synonyms for DeTrae." DeTrae opposed the application, asserting that the disciplinary rule

---

60. Id. §101(2). For discussion of this issue and recommendation for a more specific comment to Rule 4.2, see Pierce, Variations on a Basic Theme, 70 Tenn. L. Rev. at 190-199.

1. DR 7-104(A)(1) reads, "During the course of [the] representation of a client a lawyer shall not . . . [c]ommunicate or cause another to communicate with a party [the lawyer] knows to be represented by a lawyer in that matter unless [the lawyer] has the prior consent of the lawyer representing such other party or is authorized by law to do so." Employees individually named as parties in the litigation, and employees individually represented by counsel, are not within the ambit of the question presented by this appeal. Nor, obviously, are direct interviews on consent of counsel, or those authorized by law, or communications by the client himself (unless instigated by counsel).

barred unapproved contact by plaintiff's lawyer with any of its employees. Supreme Court denied plaintiff's request, and the Appellate Division modified by limiting the ban to DeTrae's current employees.

The Appellate Division concluded, for theoretical as well as practical reasons, that current employees of a corporate defendant in litigation "are presumptively within the scope of the representation afforded by the attorneys who appeared [in the litigation] on behalf of that corporation." Citing Upjohn Co. v. United States, 449 U.S. 383, the court held that DeTrae's attorneys have an attorney-client relationship with every DeTrae employee connected with the subject of the litigation, and that the prohibition is necessitated by the practical difficulties of distinguishing between a corporation's control group and its other employees. The court further noted that the information sought from employee witnesses could instead be obtained through their depositions.

In the main we disagree with the Appellate Division's conclusions. However, because we agree with the holding that DR 7-104(A)(1) applies only to current employees, not to former employees, we modify rather than reverse its order, and grant plaintiff's motion to allow the interviews.

We begin our analysis by noting that what is at issue is a disciplinary rule, not a statute. In interpreting statutes, which are the enactments of a coequal branch of government and an expression of the public policy of this State, we are of course bound to implement the will of the Legislature; statutes are to be applied as they are written or interpreted to effectuate the legislative intention. The disciplinary rules have a different provenance and purpose. Approved by the New York State Bar Association and then enacted by the Appellate Divisions, the Code of Professional Responsibility is essentially the legal profession's document of self-governance, embodying principles of ethical conduct for attorneys as well as rules for professional discipline (see, Code of Professional Responsibility, Preliminary Statement, McKinney's Cons. Law of N.Y., Book 29, at 355). While unquestionably important, and respected by the courts, the code does not have the force of law. . . .

That distinction is particularly significant when a disciplinary rule is invoked in litigation, which in addition to matters of professional conduct by attorneys, implicates the interests of nonlawyers. . . . In such instances, we are not constrained to read the rules literally or effectuate the intent of the drafters, but look to the rules as guidelines to be applied with due regard for the broad range of interests at stake. . . .

DR 7-104(A)(1), which can be traced to the American Bar Association Canons of 1908, fundamentally embodies principles of fairness. "The general thrust of the rule is to prevent situations in which a represented party may be taken advantage of by adverse counsel; the presence of the party's attorney theoretically neutralizes the contact." (Wright v. Group Health Hosp., 103 Wash. 2d 192, 197, 691 P.2d 564, 567.) By preventing lawyers from deliberately dodging adversary counsel to reach—and exploit—the client alone, DR 7-104(A)(1) safeguards against clients making improvident settlements, ill-advised disclosures and unwarranted concessions. . . .

There is little problem applying DR 7-104(A)(1) to individuals in civil cases. In that context, the meaning of "party" is ordinarily plain enough: it refers to the individuals, not to their agents and employees. . . . The question, however, becomes more difficult when the parties are corporations—as evidenced by a wealth of commentary, and controversy, on the issue. . . .

The difficulty is not in whether DR 7-104(A)(1) applies to corporations. It unquestionably covers corporate parties, who are as much served by the rule's fundamental principles of fairness as individual parties. But the rule does not define "party," and its reach in this context is unclear. In litigation only the entity, not its employee, is the actual named party; on the other hand, corporations act solely through natural persons, and unless some employees are also considered parties, corporations are effectively read out of the rule. The issue therefore distills to *which* corporate employees should be deemed parties for purposes of DR 7-104(A)(1), and that choice is one of policy. The broader the definition of "party" in the interests of fairness to the corporation, the greater the cost in terms of foreclosing vital informal access to facts.

The many courts, bar associations and commentators that have balanced the competing considerations have evolved various tests, each claiming some adherents, each with some imperfection. . . . At one extreme is the blanket rule adopted by the Appellate Division and urged by defendants, and at the other is the "control group" test—both of which we reject. The first is too broad and the second too narrow.

Defendants' principal argument for the blanket rule—correlating the corporate "party" and all of its employees—rests on Upjohn v. United States, 449 U.S. 383, supra. As the Supreme Court recognized, a corporation's attorney-client privilege includes communications with low- and mid-level employees; defendants argue that the existence of an attorney-client *privilege* also signifies an attorney-client *relationship* for purposes of DR 7-104(A)(1).

Upjohn, however, addresses an entirely different subject, with policy objectives that have little relation to the question whether a corporate employee should be considered a "party" for purposes of the disciplinary rule. First, the privilege applies only to *confidential communications* with counsel (see, CPLR 4503), it does not immunize the underlying factual information—which is in issue here—from disclosure to an adversary (see also, Upjohn v. United States, 449 U.S. at 395-396, supra). Second, the attorney-client privilege serves the societal objective of encouraging open communication between client and counsel . . . , a benefit not present in denying informal access to factual information. Thus, a corporate employee who may be a "client" for purposes of the attorney-client privilege is not necessarily a "party" for purposes of DR 7-104(A)(1).

The single indisputable advantage of a blanket preclusion—as with every absolute rule—is that it is clear. No lawyer need ever risk disqualification or discipline because of uncertainty as to which employees are covered by the rule and which not. The problem, however, is that a ban of this nature exacts a high price in terms of other values, and is unnecessary to achieve the objectives of DR 7-104(A)(1).

Most significantly, the Appellate Division's blanket rule closes off avenues of informal discovery of information that may serve both the litigants and the entire justice system by uncovering relevant facts, thus promoting the expeditious resolution of disputes. Foreclosing all direct, informal interviews of employees of the corporate party unnecessarily sacrifices the long-recognized potential value of such sessions. "A lawyer talks to a witness to ascertain what, if any, information the witness may have relevant to his theory of the case, and to explore the witness' knowledge, memory and opinion—frequently in light of information counsel may have developed from other sources. This is part of an attorney's so-called work product." (International Business Machs. Corp. v. Edelstein, 526 F.2d 37, 41 [citing Hickman v. Taylor, 329 U.S. 495].) Costly formal depositions that may deter litigants with limited resources, or even somewhat less formal and costly interviews attended by adversary counsel, are no substitute for such off-the-record private efforts to learn and assemble, rather than perpetuate, information.

Nor, in our view, is it necessary to shield all employees from informal interviews in order to safeguard the corporation's interest. Informal encounters between a lawyer and an employee-witness are not—as a blanket ban assumes—invariably calculated to elicit unwitting admissions; they serve long-recognized values in the litigation process. Moreover, the corporate party has significant protection at hand. It has possession of its own information and unique access to its documents and employees; the corporation's lawyer thus has the earliest and best opportunity to gather the facts, to elicit information from employees, and to counsel and prepare them so that they will not make the feared improvident disclosures that engendered the rule.

We fully recognize that, as the Appellate Division observed, every rule short of the absolute poses practical difficulties as to where to draw the line, and leaves some uncertainty as to which employees fall on either side of it. Nonetheless, we conclude that the values served by permitting access to relevant information require that an effort be made to strike a balance, and that uncertainty can be minimized if not eliminated by a clear test that will become even clearer in practice.

We are not persuaded, however, that the "control group" test—defining "party" to include only the most senior management exercising substantial control over the corporation—achieves that goal. Unquestionably, that narrow (though still uncertain) definition of corporate "party" better serves the policy of promoting open access to relevant information. But that test gives insufficient regard to the principles motivating DR 7-104(A)(1), and wholly overlooks the fact that corporate employees other than senior management also can bind the corporation. The "control group" test all but "nullifies the benefits of the disciplinary rule to corporations." . . . Given the practical and theoretical problems posed by the "control group" test, it is hardly surprising that few courts or bar associations have ever embraced it.[4]

4. A "control group" test was adopted in Fair Automotive Repair v. Car-X Serv. Sys., 128 Ill. App. 3d 763, 84 Ill. Dec. 25, 471 N.E.2d 554, Maxwell v. Southwestern Bell Tel. Co. (No. 80-4239 [D. Kan., Oct. 28, 1980]), and three bar association opinions. . . .

By the same token, we find unsatisfactory several of the proposed intermediate tests, because they give too little guidance, or otherwise seem unworkable. In this category are the case-by-case balancing test . . . and a test that defines "party" to mean corporate employees only when they are interviewed about matters within the scope of their employment.

The test that best balances the competing interests, and incorporates the most desirable elements of the other approaches, is one that defines "party" to include corporate employees whose acts or omissions in the matter under inquiry are binding on the corporation (in effect, the corporation's "alter egos") or imputed to the corporation for purposes of its liability, or employees implementing the advice of counsel. All other employees may be interviewed informally.

Unlike a blanket ban or a "control group" test, this solution is specifically targeted at the problem addressed by DR 7-104(A)(1). The potential unfair advantage of extracting concessions and admissions from those who will bind the corporation is negated when employees with "speaking authority" for the corporation, and employees who are so closely identified with the interests of the corporate party as to be indistinguishable from it, are deemed "parties" for purposes of DR 7-104(A)(1). Concern for the protection of the attorney-client privilege prompts us also to include in the definition of "party" the corporate employees responsible for actually effectuating the advice of counsel in the matter (see, Polycast Technology Corp. v. Uniroyal, Inc., 129 F.R.D. 621, 625, 628, 629 [S.D.N.Y.] . . .).

In practical application, the test we adopt thus would prohibit direct communication by adversary counsel "with those officials, but only those, who have the legal power to bind the corporation in the matter or who are responsible for implementing the advice of the corporation's lawyer, or any member of the organization whose own interests are directly at stake in a representation." (Wolfram, [Modern Legal Ethics] §11.6, at 613.) This test would permit direct access to all other employees, and specifically—as in the present case—it would clearly permit direct access to employees who were merely witnesses to an event for which the corporate employer is sued.

. . . Defendants' assertions that ex parte interviews should not be permitted because of the dangers of overreaching, moreover, impel us to add the cautionary note that, while we have not been called upon to consider questions relating to the actual conduct of such interviews, it is of course assumed that attorneys would make their identity and interest known to interviewees and comport themselves ethically.

Accordingly, the order of the Appellate Division should be modified, without costs, by reversing so much of the Appellate Division order as denied plaintiff's motion to permit ex parte interviews of current DeTrae employees and, as so modified, the Appellate Division order should be affirmed and the certified question answered in the negative.

BELLACOSA, Judge (concurring).

I agree that the Appellate Division blanket test too broadly precluded ex parte interviews by defining the term "parties" as used in Disciplinary Rule 7-104(A)(1) to include all current employees of a corporate defendant. The court instead adopts an "alter ego" definition which, as I see it, will function almost identically with the rejected test. Also, it sacrifices an unnecessarily disproportionate amount of the truth-discovering desideratum of the litigation process. Lastly, circularity in the identification of and application to the "alter ego" test group may occur, which could prolong pretrial discovery and allow the shield of DR 7-104(A)(1) to be fashioned into a sword.

These concerns could be avoided by limiting "parties," for the purposes of this professional responsibility rule, only to those who are in the "control group" of the corporate defendant; that is, only those among "the most senior management who exercise substantial control over the corporation."

To be sure, that test is far from perfect itself. But the "control group" definition better balances the respective interests by allowing the maximum number of informal interviews among persons with potentially relevant information, while safeguarding the attorney protections afforded the men and women whose protection may well be of paramount concern—those at the corporate helm and the fictional entity itself, the corporation. Also, this approach is more consistent with the ordinary understanding and meaning of "party," and more reasonably fits the purpose for which the disciplinary rule exists; a professional responsibility purpose quite distinct from enactments in public law prescribing the rights and protections of parties to litigation. . . .

WACHTLER, C.J., and SIMONS, ALEXANDER, TITONE and HANCOCK, JJ., concur with KAYE, J.

Notes and Questions

1. New York continues to use the format of the old Code of Professional Responsibility. Disciplinary Rule 7-104(A)(1) of New York's Code of Professional Responsibility is substantially the same as Model Rule 4.2, except that 7-104(A)(1) uses the term "party," while Model Rule 4.2 uses the word "person." As discussed above, courts in some jurisdictions have limited the rule to formal parties to litigation, but the Model Rules clearly reject that view.

2. As the court indicates in footnote 1 of its opinion, it is important to distinguish situations in which corporate employees are named parties to litigation or are personally represented by counsel from the situation presented in the case. If the employee is a named party and is unrepresented, a lawyer for the adverse party may communicate with the employee subject to Rule 4.3. If the employee is named and is personally represented, a lawyer for the adverse party must obtain the consent of the employee's attorney, not the corporation's attorney, to communicate with the employee. *Niesig* deals with cases where only the corporation is a party and the attorney for the opposing side wishes to communicate with one of its employees.

3. As the court points out, the issue of the scope of permissible informal contacts that an investigating lawyer may make with employees of corporate parties involves a tension between competing policies. On one hand, lawyers representing clients against corporations need to be able to investigate the facts

fully to properly represent their clients. Indeed, Rule 11 of the Federal Rules of Civil Procedure and ABA Model Rule 3.1 require adequate investigation. A rule that prohibits communication with employees of a corporate party who may have been witnesses to an accident or who may otherwise have relevant information interferes with the opposing counsel's ability to investigate the facts. While an attorney could always take the deposition of an employee after a suit has been filed, depositions are more expensive than interviews and may be impractical when large numbers of employees are involved. Also, in most jurisdictions an attorney cannot take a deposition or use other discovery devices prior to filing suit. On the other hand, corporations, like individuals, have a right to be represented by counsel. Ex parte contacts between lawyers for opposing parties and corporate employees can interfere with the corporation's right to have legal assistance. To strike a balance between these competing policies, it is necessary to define the employees of organizations who are treated as represented for the purpose of the rule. Do you think the definition established by the court in *Niesig* strikes the proper balance? Consider the concurring opinion of Justice Bellacosa.

4. Comment 4 to the 1983 version of the Model Rules defined the class of employees who were treated as represented by counsel for an organization as follows:

> In the case of an organization, this Rule prohibits communications by a lawyer for another person or entity concerning the matter in representation with persons having managerial responsibility on behalf of the organization, and with any other person whose act or omission in connection with that matter may be imputed to the organization for purposes of civil or criminal liability or whose statement may constitute an admission on the part of the organization.

This test cast a broad net over almost all employees. It covered all management-level employees and employees who were involved in the matter (that is, ones whose act or omission may be imputed to the organization). Further, even employees who were not involved in the matter but who were mere witnesses were also covered by the rule if any statement by such an employee would "constitute an admission on the part of the organization." Under the federal rules of evidence (and state rules of evidence based on the federal rules), a statement by an employee within the scope of the employee's employment was admissible against the organization as an admission. See Fed. R. Evid. 801(d)(2)(D); Wilkinson v. Carnival Cruise Lines, Inc., 920 F.2d 1560 (11th Cir. 1991).

5. The 2002 revision of the Model Rules reduces the class of employees subject to the no-communication rule to the following:

> In the case of a represented organization, this Rule prohibits communications with a constituent of the organization who supervises, directs or regularly consults with the organization's lawyer concerning the matter or has authority to obligate the organization with respect to the matter or whose act or omission in connection

with the matter may be imputed to the organization for purposes of civil or criminal liability.

Model Rule 4.2, cmt. 7. The revised comment narrows the class of managerial employees subject to the no-communication rule and it eliminates the "admissions test" for determining employees subject to the rule. For discussion of the various issues involved in defining the categories of employees subject to the rule, see Pierce, Variations on a Basic Theme, 70 Tenn. L. Rev. at 152-187. How does this test compare to the one developed by the court in *Niesig*?

6. Restatement (Third) of the Law Governing Lawyers §100 provides as follows:

> A represented non-client includes
>
> (2) a representative of an organization represented by a lawyer:
> (a) who supervises, directs or regularly consults with the lawyer concerning the matter or who has power to compromise or settle the matter
> (b) whose acts or omissions may be imputed to the organization for purposes of civil or criminal liability in the matter; or
> (c) whose statements, under applicable rules of evidence, would have the effect of binding the organization with respect to proof of the matter.

Like the 2002 revision of the Model Rules, the Restatement rejects a broad anticontact rule because there is "no justification for permitting one party thus to control entirely the flow of information to opposing parties." Id. cmt. *b*. Under section (a) not all managers are subject to the rule. Id. cmt. *c* and illus. 1, 2. Employees who make statements are covered by the Restatement rule only if the statement would be binding on the organization (in the sense that the organization could not introduce evidence to refute the statement) rather than simply being admissible against the entity. The Restatement explains that a "contrary rule would essentially mean that most employees with relevant information would be within the anticontact rule, contrary to the policies described in Comment *b*." Id. cmt. *e*.

7. In *Niesig* the court reversed the decisions of the lower courts and allowed plaintiff's counsel to conduct ex parte interviews with all DeTrae employees who were on the site at the time of the accident. Did the court correctly apply its own test?

8. In narrowing the scope of the no-communication rule, the court in *Niesig* points out that a corporate party has "significant protection at hand," including possession of its own information, access to documents and employees, and the ability to counsel and prepare employees so they won't make "improvident disclosures." In addition, the Model Rules provide additional protection. Model Rule 3.4(f) states that it is improper for a lawyer to request that a person "refrain from voluntarily giving relevant information to another party," but it goes on to provide an exception if the person is "a relative or an employee or other agent of a client." Therefore, an attorney for a corporation could ask all of its employees, whether covered by Rule 4.2 or not, to voluntarily

refrain from giving information to opposing counsel except through formal discovery.

9. In *Niesig* the court warns that during the course of ex parte interviews "it is of course assumed that attorneys would make their identity and interest known to interviewees and comport themselves ethically." During the course of an otherwise permissible communication with a current employee, a lawyer may not seek to obtain privileged information. Restatement (Third) of the Law Governing Lawyers §102. Further, even if an attorney may properly communicate with an employee, it may be improper for the attorney to seek documents from the employee because such a request circumvents the discovery process and prevents opposing counsel from raising objections to the discoverability of documents. See In re Shell Oil Refinery (Adams v. Shell Oil Co.), 143 F.R.D. 105 (E.D. La. 1992) (protective order entered requiring disclosure of documents obtained through ex parte contact with employee and prohibiting their use in case). Model Rule 4.2, comment 7 also cautions lawyers not to engage in improper conduct during an otherwise proper ex parte interview with an employee: "In communicating with a current or former constituent of an organization, a lawyer must not use methods of obtaining evidence that violate the legal rights of the organization. See Rule 4.4."

Application of the prohibition on communications with an opposing person to former corporate employees

Does Rule 4.2 apply to former rather than current employees? The argument against applying the rule to former employees is that they are no longer in a position to make a decision or admission on behalf of the corporation. Yet if the former employee was involved in the matter in controversy, his conduct is still attributed to the corporation even though he has left employment. Further, an attorney communicating with a former employee could learn confidential information or could obtain privileged documents. A number of cases have considered the issue, and the vast majority have ruled that an attorney may communicate with a former employee so long as the attorney does not try to obtain confidential or privileged information.[61]

In Formal Opinion 91-359, the ABA Committee on Ethics and Professional Responsibility adopted this majority view and ruled that lawyers were not prohibited from communicating with former employees under Model Rule

---

61. Recent cases include FleetBoston Robertson Stephens, Inc. v. Innovex, Inc., 172 F. Supp. 2d 1190 (D. Minn. 2001); H.B.A. Management, Inc. v. Estate of Schwartz, 693 So. 2d 541 (Fla. 1997) (no prohibition on communication with former employees because employee cannot bind entity). See generally Benjamin J. Vernia, Annotation, Right of Attorney to Conduct Ex Parte Interviews with Former Corporate Employees, 57 A.L.R.5th 633 (1998). For an argument that contact with former employees should be regulated by amendment to the rules of civil procedure, see John E. Iole & John D. Goetz, Ethics or Procedure? A Discovery-Based Approach to Ex Parte Contacts with Former Employees of a Corporate Adversary, 68 Notre Dame L. Rev. 81 (1992).

4.2, but the committee cautioned attorneys about the possible application of other rules:

> With respect to *any* unrepresented former employee, of course, the potentially communicating adversary attorney must be careful not to seek to induce the former employee to violate the privilege attaching to attorney-client communications. . . . Such an attempt could violate Rule 4.4 (requiring respect for the rights of third persons).
>
> The lawyer should also punctiliously comply with the requirements of Rule 4.3, which addresses a lawyer's dealings with unrepresented persons. That rule, insofar as pertinent here, requires that the lawyer contacting a former employee of an opposing corporate party make clear the nature of the lawyer's role in the matter giving occasion for the contact, including the identity of the lawyer's client and the fact that the witness's former employer is an adverse party.[62]

Comment 7 to revised Model Rule 4.2 adopts this view: "Consent of the organization's lawyer is not required for communication with a former constituent." The comment also warns lawyers not to use methods of obtaining evidence that violate the legal rights of the organization. See Model Rule 4.4.

A few cases have gone somewhat further than the majority of cases and ABA Formal Opinion 91-359 in prohibiting communications with former employees. A leading example is Camden v. Maryland,[63] an employment discrimination case. The former employee contacted by plaintiff's counsel had been the affirmative action coordinator for the defendant and was responsible for handling the Camden case while employed by defendant. He prepared reports on the case for defendant's top management and met regularly with defendant's counsel, engaging in strategy sessions about the strengths and weaknesses of Camden's claims. He also signed defendant's response to the complaint filed by Camden with the EEOC. The court in *Camden* accepted the proposition that communications with former employees were generally permissible without consent of the attorney for the former employer, but the court held that such contacts were improper when the employee had been "extensively exposed" to confidential information.[64] Further, in *Camden* plaintiff's counsel intentionally sought and obtained confidential information, including documents that were marked as confidential.[65]

The Restatement of the Law Governing Lawyers provides that communication with former employees is generally proper except under limited circumstances, for example, if the former employee continues to consult with counsel for the entity.[66] The Restatement also seems to adopt the view of the court in

---

62. ABA Comm. on Ethics and Prof. Resp., Formal Op. 91-359, at 6.
63. 910 F. Supp. 1115 (D. Md. 1996).
64. Id. at 1116.
65. Id. at 1118 n.5, 1123.
66. Restatement (Third) of the Law Governing Lawyers §100, cmt. g.

Camden v. Maryland that a lawyer may not communicate with a former employee who has been "extensively exposed" to privileged information.[67]

Other applications of Rule 4.2: settlement offers, expert witnesses, and treating physicians

As we saw previously, attorneys have an ethical obligation to convey settlement offers to their clients. Model Rule 1.4(a)(1) and cmt. 2. Suppose a lawyer believes that opposing counsel has not conveyed a settlement offer to his client. May the attorney communicate the offer directly to the opposing party? In Formal Opinion 92-362 the ABA Committee on Ethics and Professional Responsibility dealt with the application of Rule 4.2 in the context of settlement offers. The committee first concluded that Rule 4.2 does not allow an attorney to make a direct communication of a settlement offer to the opposing party. The committee also reaffirmed Informal Opinion 1348 (1975), which held that it was improper for an attorney to send to the opposing party copies of settlement offers made to opposing counsel.[68] The committee did note several options available to an attorney who believes that opposing counsel is not conveying settlement offers to his client. First, the attorney could serve an "offer of judgment" on the opposing party, with copy to opposing counsel, if authorized by rules of civil procedure.[69] An offer of judgment sent to the opposing party does not violate Rule 4.2 because it is a communication "authorized by law."[70] Second, the attorney may file a copy of the settlement offer with the court.[71] Finally, the attorney could advise his client that the client has the right to convey a settlement offer directly to the opposing party. In reaching this conclusion the committee pointed out that while Rule 4.2 prohibits a lawyer from communicating with the opposing party, the rule does not apply to clients. Comment 4 states: "Parties to a matter may communicate directly with each other." The committee also referred to various rules of ethics that require lawyers to counsel clients about their rights. As a result, the committee concluded as follows:

> In the Committee's view, fulfillment of the duties imposed by these Rules requires that the lawyer for the offeror-party advise that party with respect to the lawyer's belief as to whether the offers are in fact being communicated to the offeree-party. Likewise, the offeror-party's lawyer has a duty to that party to discuss not only the limits on the lawyer's ability to communicate with the offeree-

---

67. Id. §102, cmt. *d.*
68. See Id. §99, cmt. *f.*
69. See Fed. R. Civ. P. 68.
70. ABA Comm. on Prof. Ethics, Informal Op. 985 (1967).
71. ABA Comm. on Ethics and Prof. Resp., Informal Op. 1348 (1975).

party, but also the freedom of the offeror-party to communicate with the opposing offeree-party.[72]

Although the committee recognized that Rule 8.4(a) prohibits a lawyer from violating the rules of professional conduct "through the acts of another," it decided that Rule 8.4 did not apply in the context of advising a client about the client's right to convey a settlement offer to the opposing party when the lawyer has good reason to believe that the opposing counsel has not done so.

Discovery of opinions of expert witnesses is subject to specific limitations under discovery rules,[73] so a lawyer may not informally interview an expert for the opposing party without consent of opposing counsel.[74]

In cases involving personal injuries, a common issue is whether defense counsel may informally interview the injured party's treating physician. The jurisdictions are fairly evenly divided on whether such interviews are proper.[75] When courts have found such contacts to be improper, they have generally emphasized the physician-patient privilege and the physician's ethical duty of confidentiality. Courts that have permitted such interviews have usually found that the patient waived confidentiality by bringing the lawsuit and thereby putting his physical condition in issue. On April 14, 2003, regulations under the Health Insurance Portability and Accountability Act of 1996 (HIPAA Privacy Regulations) became effective and will affect the ability of lawyers to obtain medical information either informally or through formal discovery.[76]

Problem 4-3

Investigation: Secret Tape Recording and Inadvertent Disclosures

a. Sally Pender works in the underwriting division of DAC Insurance Company. For over a year Pender's supervisor, Herbert Foster, has been making sexual advances toward her that she has rebuffed. With each

---

72. ABA Comm. on Ethics and Prof. Resp., Formal Op. 92-362, at 5. Accord Restatement (Third) of the Law Governing Lawyers §99(2).

73. See Fed. R. Civ. P. 26(b)(4).

74. See Erickson v. Newmar Corp., 87 F.3d 298 (9th Cir. 1996); In re Firestorm 1991, 916 P.2d 411 (Wash. 1996) (en banc); ABA Comm. on Ethics and Prof. Resp., Formal Op. 93-378. For a criticism of this prohibition, see Stephen D. Easton, Can We Talk?: Removing Counterproductive Ethical Restraints Upon Ex Parte Communication Between Attorneys and Adverse Expert Witnesses, 76 Ind. L.J. 647 (2001).

75. J. Christopher Smith, Comment, Recognizing the Split: The Jurisdictional Treatment of Defense Counsel's Ex Parte Contact with Plaintiff's Treating Physician, 23 J. Legal Prof. 247 (1999). See Daniel P. Jones, Annotation, Discovery: Right to Ex Parte Interview with Injured Party's Treating Physician, 50 A.L.R.4th 714 (1986).

76. See Lori G. Baer & Christiana P. Callahan, The Impact of HIPAA Privacy Regulations on Discovery of Plaintiffs' Medical Records, 21 No. 12 LJN's Prod. Liab. L. & Strategy 1 (June 2003).

of Pender's refusals, Foster has become increasingly belligerent. Pender fears for her job and even her safety. Uncertain what to do, Pender has consulted with Roberta Slinger, a local attorney who handles discrimination cases.

Slinger and Pender discuss the possibility of reporting Foster's conduct to higher officials in the company, but Pender says that she is reluctant to do that because "it's her word against his," and Foster is very well respected in the company. As they mull over how they might get concrete evidence of Foster's conduct, it occurs to Slinger that one possibility would be for Pender secretly to tape record an encounter in which Foster makes sexual advances. If you were Slinger, how would you handle this situation? Why?

    b.   Suppose Slinger has filed suit on Pender's behalf against Foster and DAC Insurance. DAC and Foster are represented by Daniel R. Chin, of the firm Chin & Rivera. One morning, Slinger's secretary, Ronald Best, comes into her office.

> *Best:*   Roberta, I reviewed your morning e-mail. I printed out one from
>   Dan Chin addressed to Milton Rodriguez, president of DAC In-
>   surance. It indicates a copy to you. I think Chin must have listed
>   you to receive a copy by mistake.
> *Slinger:* Let's see . . .

Re: Pender v. Foster and DAC Insurance

Dear Milton:

    I met with Melinda Dasher's attorney today. I think we can settle her claim against DAC and Foster on the terms we discussed, and they are agreeable to a confidentiality agreement. I'll keep you advised.

If you were Slinger, how would you proceed? Why?

Read Model Rules 1.1, 1.2(d), 4.4, 8.4, and comments.

Legality of secret tape recording

Model Rule 8.4(b) provides that it is professional misconduct for a lawyer to "commit a criminal act that reflects adversely on the lawyer's honesty, truthworthiness or fitness as a lawyer in other respects." Model Rule 1.2(d) provides that a lawyer "shall not counsel a client to engage, or assist a client, in conduct that the lawyer knows is criminal or fraudulent." Does secret tape recording amount to criminal conduct?

    The federal wiretapping statute, 18 U.S.C. §2511, prohibits interception and disclosure of wire, oral, or electronic communications. Among the statutory exceptions, however, is a section allowing recording by a party to the conversation:

> It shall not be unlawful under this chapter for a person not acting under color of law to intercept a wire, oral, or electronic communication where such person is a party to the communication or where one of the parties to the communication has given prior consent to such interception unless such communication is intercepted for the purpose of committing any criminal or tortious act in violation of the Constitution or laws of the United States or of any State.[77]

Thus, recording of a conversation with "one-party consent" is not a violation of the federal statute. A lawyer who personally records a conversation with a client or other person, or who assists a client in doing so, would not, therefore, be committing a federal crime.

Some states, however, have more restrictive statutes prohibiting recording without "two-party consent." For example, the Illinois law on electronic eavesdropping provides as follows:

> (a) A person commits eavesdropping when he: (1) Knowingly and intentionally uses an eavesdropping device for the purpose of hearing or recording all or any part of any conversation or intercepts, retains, or transcribes electronic communication unless he does so (A) with the consent of all of the parties to such conversation or electronic communication or (B) in accordance [with certain statutory procedures for use of eavesdropping devices by law enforcement officials].[78]

In states with two-party consent laws, a lawyer could not record a conversation without the consent of all parties to the conversation, and could not assist a client in doing so.

The ethical propriety of participation by lawyers in secret tape recording that is not illegal

Model Rule 8.4(c) provides that it is professional misconduct for a lawyer to "engage in conduct involving dishonesty, fraud, deceit or misrepresentation." Does secret tape recording amount to dishonesty or deceit even if the recording would not be illegal under federal or state law? In Formal Opinion 337 (1974), the ABA Committee on Ethics and Professional Responsibility ruled that it was unethical for a lawyer to record a conversation with a client or third person without that person's consent even though the recording was not a crime. The

---

77. 18 U.S.C. §2511(2)(d).
78. Ill. Ann. Stat. ch. 720, para. 5/14-2. California also requires the consent of all parties to the conversation. See Cal. Penal Code §§631, 632. See ABA Formal Opinion 01-422 n.30 (listing 12 states as of 1998 that required consent of all parties to the conversation).

committee reasoned that "conduct which involves dishonesty, fraud, deceit or misrepresentation . . . clearly encompasses the making of recordings without the consent of all parties."[79]

However, in Formal Opinion 01-422, the ABA Committee withdrew Opinion 337 and took a more generous view of recording by lawyers:

> A lawyer who electronically records a conversation without the knowledge of the other party or parties to the conversation does not necessarily violate the Model Rules. Formal Opinion 337 (1974) accordingly is withdrawn. A lawyer may not, however, record conversations in violation of the law in a jurisdiction that forbids such conduct without the consent of all parties, nor falsely represent that a conversation is not being recorded. The Committee is divided as to whether a lawyer may record a client-lawyer conversation without the knowledge of the client, but agrees that it is inadvisable to do so.

The Committee gave several reasons for its reversal of Opinion 337: First, courts and bar ethics committees had had mixed reactions to the per se rule of that opinion. Many had criticized the view that recording by a lawyer without the consent of the other party is inherently deceitful given that such conduct is lawful in the great majority of states and recording devices are now widely used. Second, recording often serves legitimate purposes; for example, when a lawyer records threats of criminal conduct or witness statements to prevent possible perjury. Third, the Code of Professional Responsibility applied when the Committee issued Opinion 337. Under the Code lawyers had an obligation to avoid even the appearance of impropriety. The Model Rules have eliminated this vague standard. With regard to the rights of third parties, Rule 4.4 governs; lawful recording for legitimate purposes without the consent of the other person does not violate that rule.

Opinion 01-422 drew a distinction between secret recording itself, which it found not to be inherently misleading, and misrepresentations by an attorney about whether a conversation was being recorded, which the committee found to be improper. Even prior to the opinion some courts had recognized this distinction.

In Attorney M v. Mississippi Bar[80] an attorney was charged with misconduct because he secretly tape recorded a telephone conversation with a doctor who was a potential defendant in a malpractice case. In finding that the attorney had not engaged in misconduct, the Mississippi Supreme Court rejected the per se prohibition on secret recording by lawyers expressed in Formal Opinion 337. Instead, the court adopted a facts-and-circumstances test to determine whether the lawyer's conduct amounted to dishonesty, fraud, deceit, or misrepresentation. The court concluded:

---

79. ABA Comm. on Ethics and Prof. Resp., Formal Op. 337, at 3 (1974). The committee noted a possible exception for lawyers involved in law enforcement activities.
80. 621 So. 2d 220 (Miss. 1992).

[W]e find that Attorney M's conduct did not rise to the level of "dishonesty, fraud, deceit, or misrepresentation." First, the express purpose of each telephone call was to obtain a statement from Dr. C concerning the physical condition of Attorney M's client upon leaving Dr. C's care. Such information is indisputably "of such a nature as reasonably to import to the person called the probability, if not certainty, that it would be taken down in some manner for future use." Further, the circumstances surrounding the incident do not suggest dishonesty, fraud, deceit, or misrepresentation. In fact, the circumstances were such that Dr. C admittedly assumed that he was being taped. During one of the telephone conversations, Attorney M expressly stated that he wished to record Dr. C's statement. In addition, there is no indication that Attorney M planned to use the recordings for any improper purpose. Contrary to the finding of the Complaint Tribunal, Attorney M did not violate MRPC Rule 8.4.[81]

In a companion case, however, the Mississippi Supreme Court ruled that an attorney was guilty of misconduct when he lied to a police chief about secretly recording their discussion of his client's prosecution. The court rejected the lawyer's argument that it was necessary for him to misrepresent the taping because that was the only way in which he could gain evidence to protect his client.[82]

While the issuance of Opinion 01-422 may prompt some courts and state ethics committees that had followed Opinion 337 to change their decisions, lawyers who practice in states where prevailing case law adheres to Opinion 337 cannot safely rely on Opinion 01-422.[83] In fact, even after the issuance of Opinion 01-422, some courts continue to find the practice of secret recording inherently deceptive. For example, in Nissan Motor Co., Ltd. v. Nissan Computer Corp.,[84] the court stated:

The Court finds that the recordation of conversations between counsel in the normal course of litigation, without consent, is a violation of California Penal Code §632. In addition to being illegal, the Court finds that it is inherently unethical for an attorney to record a conversation with another attorney regarding the routine progression of litigation without the other party's knowledge or consent. "Inherent in the undisclosed use of a recording device is an element of deception, artifice, and trickery which does not comport with the high standards of candor and fairness by which all attorneys are bound."[85]

---

81. Id. at 224-225.
82. Mississippi Bar v. Attorney ST, 621 So. 2d 229 (Miss. 1993).
83. See People v. Selby, 606 P.2d 45 (Colo. 1979) (en banc); Iowa Supreme Court Bd. of Professional Ethics & Conduct v. Plumb, 546 N.W.2d 215 (Iowa 1996); In re Anonymous Member of the S.C. Bar, 404 S.E.2d 513 (S.C. 1991), modified in In re Attorney General's Petition, 417 S.E.2d 526 (S.C. 1992) (holding that "it is not unethical for an attorney to surreptitiously record any conversation when that recording is made with the prior consent of, or at the request of, an appropriate law enforcement agency in the course of a legitimate criminal investigation").
84. 180 F. Supp. 2d 1089 (C.D. Cal. 2002).
85. Id. at 1097.

Counseling or assisting a client in secret tape recording

As discussed above, in some cases secret recording by a lawyer or client would be illegal under either federal or state law. In these situations a lawyer must not counsel or assist a client in such illegal conduct. By contrast, a few jurisdictions permit lawyers to engage in secret recording. In those jurisdictions, then, it follows that it would be ethically permissible for the lawyer to counsel or assist a client to engage in such recording.

Suppose, however, that a client suggests the possibility of making a secret recording that would be legal for the client to do, but unethical for the lawyer to do. On one hand, a lawyer cannot engage indirectly through the actions of another in conduct that it would be unethical for the lawyer to do directly. For example, in Gunter v. Virginia State Bar[86] the Virginia Supreme Court suspended a lawyer for 30 days for hiring an investigator to install a recording device on the telephone of the home of his client, the husband in a divorce case. The court stated:

> The surreptitious recordation of conversations authorized by Mr. Gunter in this case was an "underhand practice" designed to "ensnare" an opponent. It was more than a departure from the standards of fairness and candor which character- ize the traditions of professionalism. We hold that it was deceitful conduct pro- scribed by DR 1-102(A)(4) [the provision of the Code of Professional Responsibility corresponding to Model Rule 8.4(c)].[87]

On the other hand, a lawyer has the right and obligation to counsel a client about the client's legal rights. For example, in Miano v. AC & R Advertis- ing, Inc.,[88] an age discrimination suit, plaintiffs had secretly recorded some conversations they had with certain of defendant's key employees. The court held that the tapes were admissible in evidence and that the plaintiffs' lawyer had not engaged in unethical conduct in connection with the taping. In its opinion the court discussed the lawyer's obligations when a client suggests secret recording of a conversation with the defendant:

> [I]t is not improper for an attorney to advise his client of the legality of taping activity by the client. . . . The lawyer need not discourage or deter such activity, but he also may not assist, direct or otherwise participate in it so that, in effect, he is using the client as a vehicle to do what he cannot do.[89]

The 2002 revision to the Model Rules adds the following comment to Rule 8.4: "Paragraph (a), however, does not prohibit a lawyer from advising a client concerning action that the client is lawfully entitled to take."

---

86. 385 S.E.2d 597 (Va. 1989).
87. 385 S.E.2d at 600.
88. 148 F.R.D. 68 (S.D.N.Y. 1993).
89. Id. at 83.

Inadvertent disclosures of confidential information

The complexity of modern litigation coupled with liberal discovery rules some-times results in parties mistakenly producing material that is arguably subject to claims of attorney-client or work product privilege. Inadvertent disclosures raises two issues, one legal and the other ethical. Legally, does a mistaken disclosure constitute a waiver of the privilege? Courts apply three approaches to waiver of the privilege.[90] The traditional approach was that any disclosure results in a loss of the privilege because the purpose of the privilege was to protect confidential communications; by definition, a communication that has been disclosed is no longer confidential.[91] Other courts have held that the purpose of the privilege is to protect the client's reasonable expectations. Under this limited waiver approach, the privilege is lost only if the client intends to waive the privilege.[92] Finally, the modern approach looks at the facts and circumstances, especially the precautions taken, to determine whether the privilege should apply.[93]

What are a lawyer's ethical obligations if an attorney receives documents that appear on their face to be subject to a legitimate claim of privilege? In Formal Opinion 92-368, the ABA Committee on Ethics and Professional Responsibility gave this advice:

> A lawyer who receives materials that on their face appear to be subject to the attorney-client privilege or otherwise confidential, under circumstances where it is clear they were not intended for the receiving lawyer, should refrain from examining the materials, notify the sending lawyer and abide [by] the instructions of the lawyer who sent them.[94]

While recognizing that the issue could not be answered by a "literalistic reading of the black letter of the Model Rules," the committee based its decision on

---

90. For a discussion of the case law on these three approaches, see Harry M. Gruber, Note, E-Mail: The Attorney-Client Privilege Applied, 66 Geo. Wash. L. Rev. 624, 646-656 (1998).

91. 8 Wigmore on Evidence §2325, at 633 (McNaughton ed. 1961).

92. See Berg Elecs., Inc. v. Molex, Inc., 875 F. Supp. 261 (D. Del. 1995) (after discussing rationales for three approaches, court adopts limited waiver principle).

93. See Elkton Care Ctr. Assocs. LP v. Quality Care Mgmt., Inc., 805 A.2d 1177 (Md. Ct. App. 2002). In *Elkton* the court considered the following factors and found that the privilege had been waived:

> (1) the reasonableness of the precautions taken to prevent inadvertent disclosure in view of the extent of the document production; (2) the number of inadvertent disclosures; (3) the extent of the disclosure; (4) any delay and measures taken to rectify the disclosure; and (5) whether the overriding interests of justice would or would not be served by relieving a party of its error. Id. at 1184.

The Restatement adopts the factor approach. See Restatement (Third) of the Law Governing Lawyers §79, cmt. *h.*

94. ABA Comm. on Ethics and Prof. Resp., Formal Op. 92-368, at 1.

a variety of factors: the importance the Model Rules give to confidentiality, the law governing waiver of the attorney-client privilege, the law governing missent property, the similarity between the behavior in this situation and "other conduct the profession universally condemns," and the receiving lawyer's obligations to the client.[95] Several courts have followed the approach recommended in ABA Formal Opinion 92-368.[96]

The 2002 revision of the Model Rules does not go as far as Formal Opinion 92-368. Rule 4.4(b) states: "A lawyer who receives a document relating to the representation of the lawyer's client and knows or reasonably should know that the document was inadvertently sent shall promptly notify the sender." Notification allows the inadvertently producing lawyer to take protective measures. See comment 2. Comment 2 goes on to state that "[w]hether the lawyer is required to take additional steps, such as returning the original document, is a matter of law beyond the scope of these Rules, as is the question of whether the privileged status of a document has been waived." However, comment 3 provides that lawyers have professional discretion to take other steps including return of the document unread:

> Some lawyers may choose to return a document unread, for example, when the lawyer learns before receiving the document that it was inadvertently sent to the wrong address. Where a lawyer is not required by applicable law to do so, the decision to voluntarily return such a document is a matter of professional judgment ordinarily reserved to the lawyer. See Rules 1.2 and 1.4.

The Restatement also rejects Formal Opinion 92-368. Comment *m* to section 60 indicates that the receiving lawyer's ability to use the inadvertently disclosed material turns on whether the disclosure ends the legal protection for the material:

> [If the disclosure of the material was not authorized], the receiving lawyer's responsibilities depend on the circumstances. If the disclosure operates to end legal protection for the information, the lawyer may use it for the benefit of the lawyer's own client and may be required to do so if that would advance the client's lawful objectives. . . . The . . . result may follow when divulgence occurs inadvertently outside of court. . . . The receiving lawyer may be required to consult with that lawyer's client . . . about whether to take advantage of the lapse.
>
> If the person whose information was disclosed is entitled to have it suppressed or excluded . . . the receiving lawyer must either return the information or hold it for disposition after appropriate notification to the opposing person or

---

95. Id. at 2.

96. American Express v. Accu-Weather, Inc., 1996 WL 346388 (S.D.N.Y. 1996); State Compensation Ins. Fund v. WPS, Inc., 82 Cal. Rptr. 2d 799 (Ct. App. 1999); In re Meador, 968 S.W.2d 346 (Tex. 1998).

that person's counsel. A court may suppress material after an inadvertent disclosure that did not amount to a waiver of the attorney-client privilege. . . .[97]

<hr>

Problem 4-4

Discovery: Interrogatories, Document Production, and Depositions

a. You are an associate in a firm that represents the parents of a four-year-old child, Tina Small, in a products liability case alleging that Tina suffered serious injuries from using a toy manufactured by All the Best, Inc. Your boss has asked you to serve a set of interrogatories seeking as much information as possible in preparation for requests for production of documents and depositions. He suggests that you rely on standard form interrogatories that the firm has used in other products liability cases. One of the 25 standard form interrogatories requests that the manufacturer identify tests or inspections done on the product:

> 3. Please IDENTIFY all tests or inspections used by the defendant for the manufacture of the product. As used in this interrogatory, the term IDENTIFY means to state the manner in which each such test or inspection was performed and the stage of the product process at which the test or inspection was performed, the purpose of the tests or inspections, the names and last known addresses of the persons in charge of the tests or inspections at the time the product was manufactured or assembled by the defendant, whether any records of any tests or inspections performed by the defendant exist, attaching a copy to the answers to these interrogatories of all such records or stating where and when such records may be examined by counsel, and a description of each change made in the product or any part thereof as a result of any test or inspection performed on the product.

Is it proper to use this interrogatory? Consider Federal Rule of Civil Procedure 33.

b. Your firm represents All the Best in the products liability action brought by Tina Small's parents. You have received a set of 25 interrogatories from the plaintiff including the interrogatory set forth in part *a.* The partner in charge of the case tells you that All the Best has a policy of vigorously contesting all litigation using all procedural devices available to it. He directs you to object to any interrogatory on any ground that is

<hr>

97. See Aerojet-General Corp. v. Transport Indemnity Ins., 22 Cal. Rptr. 2d 862 (Ct. App. 1993) (lawyer did not act improperly in failing to disclose receipt of memorandum revealing identity of witness because such information was not privileged).

arguably permissible. What objections, if any, would you make to the interrogatory requesting identification of tests or inspections?

c. The law firm of Taylor & Peeples represents Evelyn and Andrew Purvis in a medical malpractice action against Dr. Jane Golden and Midlands Hospital. The action arises out of the death of the Purvises' baby during delivery. The plaintiffs contend that Dr. Golden failed to recognize that the baby was in distress during delivery until it was too late to take corrective action. Taylor & Peeples has filed a request for production of documents. One of the requests seeks "any documents related to disciplinary proceedings by Midlands Hospital against Dr. Jane Golden." You are counsel for Midlands Hospital. The hospital informs you that no disciplinary action has been taken against Dr. Golden. However, about two years ago the hospital investigated Dr. Golden based on complaints about the quality of her professional services but decided not to institute formal proceedings to revoke her staff privileges. How would you respond to plaintiffs' request for production of documents?

d. You represent the estate of an individual killed in an explosion at a plant. You have noticed the deposition of the defendant's supervisor, who was on duty at the time the explosion occurred. The firm that represents the defendant has a reputation for "hard ball" litigation tactics. You want to be prepared to deal with such tactics if they arise during the deposition. What types of problems can you anticipate? How would you plan to respond to these problems?

Read Model Rules 3.4, 4.4, 5.2, and comments.

The problem of discovery abuse

The philosophy of litigation underwent a radical transformation with the adoption of the Federal Rules of Civil Procedure in 1938. Prior to the approval of the Federal Rules, the pleadings served the function of defining and narrowing the issues in a case; pretrial discovery was extremely limited. The Federal Rules changed the role of pleadings to that of providing notice to the opposing side of claims and defenses, and the Rules broadly expanded the scope of pretrial discovery.[98] Since 1938 the discovery rules have been amended on many occasions, most recently in 2000. The trend recently has been to narrow the scope of discovery and restrict judicial discretion, but whether these changes are

---

98. See William A. Glaser, Pretrial Discovery and the Adversary System 15-25 (1968).

necessary is debatable.[99] The 2000 amendments also require mandatory disclosure of certain information without a discovery request.[100]

Liberal discovery and the adversary system, however, are in tension with each other. On one hand, the discovery rules require lawyers to reveal information that is often damaging to their clients' cases. On the other hand, an adversarial mentality may lead some lawyers to engage in "discovery abuse." While discovery abuse is difficult to define, the term refers to "behavior motivated by goals other than the exchange of information fairly related to the issues in dispute."[101] Discovery abuse generally falls into two categories: "(1) propounding unnecessarily broad discovery requests; and (2) withholding information from the propounding party to which that party is entitled."[102]

Civil discovery has been studied extensively.[103] The conclusions of these studies are remarkably uniform. In routine cases, discovery produces few problems, probably because little discovery takes place in such cases.[104] Discovery problems do exist, however, in high-stakes, high-conflict cases.[105]

The most frequently used discovery tools are written interrogatories under Rule 33 of the Federal Rules of Civil Procedure, requests for production of documents under Rule 34, and oral depositions under Rule 30. What types of problems can lawyers anticipate in using these discovery tools? What steps can lawyers take when they encounter what they believe to be discovery abuse?

99. See Jeffrey W. Stempel, Ulysses Tied to the Generic Whipping Post: The Continuing Odyssey of Discovery "Reform," 64-SUM Law & Contemp. Probs. 197 (2001). Professor John Beckerman argues that "discovery is riven to the core with irreconcilable theoretical and practical conflicts and will remain so despite recurring reform efforts." John S. Beckerman, Confronting Civil Discovery's Fatal Flaws, 84 Minn. L. Rev. 505, 512 (2000).

100. See Fed. R. Civ. P. 26(a)(1).

101. Earl C. Dudley, Jr., Discovery Abuse Revisited: Some Specific Proposals to Amend the Federal Rules of Civil Procedure, 26 U.S.F. L. Rev. 189, 193 (1992).

102. Id. at 194.

103. Recent studies were conducted by the RAND Institute and by the Federal Judicial Center. See James S. Kakalik et al., Rand Inst. for Civil Justice, Discovery Management: Further Analysis of the Civil Justice Reform Act Evaluation Data, 39 B.C. L. Rev. 613 (1998); Thomas E. Willging et al., Federal Judicial Center, An Empirical Study of Discovery and Disclosure Practice Under the 1993 Federal Rule Amendments, 39 B.C. L. Rev. 525 (1998). Earlier studies include the following: Paul R. Connolly et al., Federal Judicial Center, Judicial Controls and the Civil Litigative Process: Discovery (1978); Wayne D. Brazil, Views from the Front Lines: Observations by Chicago Lawyers About the System of Civil Discovery, 1980 Am. Bar Found. Res. J. 217; Wayne D. Brazil, Civil Discovery: Lawyers' Views of Its Effectiveness, Its Principal Problems and Abuses, 1980 Am. Bar Found. Res. J. 787; Wayne D. Brazil, Improving Judicial Controls over the Pretrial Development of Civil Actions: Model Rules for Case Management and Sanctions, 1981 Am. Bar Found. Res. J. 875. See also Louis Harris & Assocs., Judges' Opinions on Procedural Issues: A Survey of State and Federal Trial Judges Who Spend at Least Half Their Time on General Civil Cases, 69 B.U. L. Rev. 731 (1989).

104. See Linda S. Mullenix, The Pervasive Myth of Pervasive Discovery Abuse: The Sequel, 39 B.C. L. Rev. 683 (1998).

105. See Bryant G. Garth, Two Worlds of Civil Discovery: From Studies of Cost and Delay to the Markets in Legal Services and Legal Reform, 39 B.C. L. Rev. 597 (1998).

Discovery abuse in connection with interrogatories and requests for production of documents

The problem of discovery abuse in response to interrogatories and requests for production of documents is illustrated in Washington State Physicians Insurance Exchange & Assn. v. Fisons Corp.[106] In 1986 two-year-old Jennifer Pollock suffered seizures and permanent brain damage caused by excessive amounts of the drug theophylline in her system. Jennifer's parents brought suit against her pediatrician, Dr. Klicpera, who had prescribed Somophyllin, a theophylline-based medication, for her, and against the drug's manufacturer, Fisons Corporation. Dr. Klicpera cross-claimed for contribution and damages from Fisons. In January 1989, the Pollocks settled with Dr. Klicpera. More than a year later, an attorney for the Pollocks supplied Dr. Klicpera with a copy of a letter received from an anonymous source. The letter dated June 30, 1981, indicated that Fisons knew in 1981 of "life-threatening theophylline toxicity" in children who received the drug while suffering from viral infections. Fisons had sent the letter to a small number of what the company considered to be "influential physicians."[107] The Pollocks and Dr. Klicpera claimed that their discovery requests should have resulted in production of the letter, and they moved for sanctions against Fisons and its attorneys. The trial court denied the motion, but the Washington Supreme Court reversed. In its opinion the court cited numerous examples of discovery abuse by Fisons and its attorneys:

> In November 1986 the doctor served his first requests for production on the drug company. Four requests were made. Three asked for documents concerning Somophyllin. Request 3 stated:
>
> 3. Produce genuine copies of any letters sent by your company to physicians concerning theophylline toxicity in children.
>
> The drug company's response was:
>
> Such letters, *if any*, regarding Somophyllin Oral Liquid will be produced at a reasonable time and place convenient to Fisons and its counsel of record. . . .
>
> Had the request, as written, been complied with, the first smoking gun letter . . . would have been disclosed early in the litigation. That June 30, 1981 letter concerned theophylline toxicity in children; it was sent by the drug company to physicians.
>
> The child's first requests for production, and the responses thereto, included the following: . . .
>
> REQUEST FOR PRODUCTION NO. 13: All documents of any clinical investigators who at any time stated or recommended to the defendant that the use of the drug Somophyllin Oral Liquid might prove dangerous.

---

106. 858 P.2d 1054 (Wash. 1993) (en banc).
107. Id. at 1058.

RESPONSE: Fisons objects to this request as overbroad in time and scope for the reasons identified in response to request number 2 hereby incorporated by reference. Fisons further objects to this request as calling for materials not within Fisons' possession, custody or control. Fisons further objects to this request to the extent it calls for expert disclosures beyond the scope of [Rule] 26(b)(4) or which may be protected by the work-product and/or attorney-client privilege. *Without waiver of these objections and subject to these limitations, Fisons will produce documents responsive to this interrogatory* at plaintiffs' expense at a mutually agreeable time at Fisons' headquarters. (Italics ours.) . . .

It appears clear that no conceivable discovery request could have been made by the doctor that would have uncovered the relevant documents, given the above and other responses of the drug company. The objections did not specify that certain documents were not being produced. Instead the general objections were followed by a promise to produce requested documents. These responses did not comply with either the spirit or letter of the discovery rules and thus were signed in violation of the certification requirement.

The drug company does not claim that its inquiry into the records did not uncover the smoking gun documents. Instead, the drug company attempts to justify its responses by arguing as follows: (1) The plaintiffs themselves limited the scope of discovery to documents contained in Somophyllin Oral Liquid *files*. (2) The smoking gun documents were not intended to relate to Somophyllin Oral Liquid, but rather were intended to promote another product of the drug company. (3) The drug company produced all of the documents it agreed to produce or was ordered to produce. (4) The drug company's failure to produce the smoking gun documents resulted from the plaintiffs' failure to specifically ask for those documents or from their failure to move to compel production of those documents. (5) Discovery is an adversarial process and good lawyering required the responses made in this case.[108]

Court sanctions for discovery abuse can include fines against the offending lawyers,[109] permission for the opposing party to engage in liberal cross-examination of witnesses on issues related to the abuse,[110] disqualification of counsel who engaged in discovery abuse,[111] and in extreme cases dismissal of

---

108. Id. at 1081-1083.

109. See United States v. Shaffer Equip. Co., 158 F.R.D. 80 (S.D. W. Va. 1994), *on remand from* 11 F.3d 450 (4th Cir. 1993) (two U.S. attorneys were required to pay sanctions of $2,000 and $2,500 each, without reimbursement from government, for failing to comply with their ethical duty of candor under Model Rule 3.3 by continuing litigation even though they knew that their expert witness had lied about his credentials).

110. Berkey Photo, Inc. v. Eastman Kodak Co., 603 F.2d 263 (2d Cir. 1979), *cert. denied,* 444 U.S. 1093 (1980) (trial judge did not abuse his discretion in allowing plaintiff's lawyer to cross-examine defendant's expert regarding concealment and destruction of documents that defendant failed to reveal in response to discovery requests).

111. Briggs v. McWeeny, 796 A.2d 516 (Conn. 2002) (lawyer disqualified for unsuccessful effort to keep damaging engineering report from opponent, in violation of Rule 3.4).

the action.[112] Some cases have gone further than imposing sanctions and have found that lawyers may be held liable in tort[113] or subject to professional discipline for improper discovery conduct.[114] The term *spoliation* is used to refer to one form of discovery abuse, in which a party tampers with or conceals relevant evidence. Courts have devised a variety of remedies for spoliation, including an adverse inference instruction and tort liability.[115] Professor Bradley Wendel has argued that nonlegal sanctions, including shame, honor, and reputation play a more important role than legal sanctions in regulating lawyer behavior in discovery and other aspects of practice.[116]

Discovery abuse in deposition practice

Deposition practice is another area where problems of discovery abuse exist.[117] A leading case exemplifying problems that can develop in depositions is Eggleston v. Chicago Journeymen Plumbers' Local Union No. 130,[118] a civil rights class action brought by five named plaintiffs seeking to represent African Americans and Latinos alleging employment discrimination in their attempts to gain entry to the plumbing trade. Discovery in the case became confrontational and ultimately collapsed. One type of abuse involved the manner in which defense counsel conducted depositions of the named plaintiffs:

> *Q* Is any ancestor of yours Caucasian?
> *A* I rather not answer.
> *Q* I think it is a proper question. I believe you should answer the question, Mr. Eggleston.
> *Mr. Miner:* If you know. If you have first-hand knowledge.
> *By the Witness: A* I can only go by what my grandmother tells me, you know. I don't know if it is true or not.

112. Lipin v. Bender, 644 N.E.2d 1300 (N.Y. 1994) (dismissal of action because plaintiff took copies of privileged documents from defendant during deposition).

113. See Cresswell v. Sullivan & Cromwell, 668 F. Supp. 166 (S.D.N.Y. 1987).

114. Crowe v. Smith, 151 F.3d 217 (5th Cir 1998), *cert. denied*, 526 U.S. 1158 (1999); Mississippi Bar v. Land, 653 So. 2d 899 (Miss. 1994); Cincinnati Bar Assn. v. Wallace, 700 N.E.2d 1238 (Ohio 1998). See also In re Anonymous Member of South Carolina Bar, 552 S.E. 2d 10 (S.C. 2001) (discussing obligations of partners and supervisory lawyers regarding discovery conducted by members of firm).

115. See, e.g., Margaret M. Koesel et al., Spoliation of Evidence: Sanctions and Remedies for Destruction of Evidence in Civil Litigation (Daniel F. Gourush ed., 2000); Drew D. Dropkin, Note, Linking the Culpability and Circumstantial Evidence Requirements for the Spoliation Inference, 51 Duke L.J. 1803 (2002).

116. W. Bradley Wendel, Regulation of Lawyers Without the Code, the Rules, or the Restatement: Or, What Do Honor and Shame Have to Do with Civil Discovery Practice?, 71 Fordham L. Rev. 1567 (2003).

117. See generally A. Darby Dickerson, The Law and Ethics of Civil Depositions, 57 Md. L. Rev. 273 (1998). For a discussion of the problem, existing remedies, and proposed solutions, see Jean M. Cary, Rambo Depositions: Controlling an Ethical Cancer in Civil Litigation, 25 Hofstra L. Rev. 561 (1996).

118. 657 F.2d 890 (7th Cir. 1981), *cert. denied*, 455 U.S. 1017 (1982).

By Mr. Barron: Q   What did your grandmother tell you, sir?
             A   Well, she said our—she said yes.
             Q   That some of your ancestors were Caucasian?
             A   Yes.
             Q   And is this your mother's mother or your father's mother who told you that?
             A   My father's mother.
             Q   Is she still living?
             A   Yes.
             Q   What is her name?
             A   Berta Eggleston. Berta or Bertie.
             Q   Would you tell us what she said to you about your ancestors?
Mr. Miner: Listen. I am going to cut this off right now, and I will just instruct him not to answer any further questions. If you want to raise some doubt as to whether or not Mr. Eggleston is a black man, Howard, you are free to do so; but you have established that both his mother and father are members of the Negro race, and whether some hundred years ago he had some white blood introduced into his system is, I think, irrelevant, and I will instruct him not to answer any more questions.
By Mr. Barron: Q   Would you answer the question, please, Mr. Eggleston?
Mr. Miner: I have instructed him not to answer. You can tell him that you are not going to answer the questions when I instruct you not to.
By the Witness: A   I rather not answer.
By Mr. Barron: Q   What is your grandfather's name, Mr. Eggleston?
             A   Josef Eggleston.
             Q   Do you know your great grandfather, Mr. Eggleston, on your father's side?
Mr. Miner: Listen, Howard. This is getting bizarre. I am going to instruct him not to answer any more questions about anything beyond his grandparents just so that we might finish this in less than the time it took us to get through Mr. Plummer's deposition.
Mr. Barron: We are not through with Mr. Plummer's deposition, Mr. Miner.

Apart from the racial probing, other avenues of defendants' inquiry deserve examination. Although the deposition was not scheduled as a bar examination, Eggleston and Rose were asked questions some members of the bar might have difficulty answering correctly.

Religion also got some attention. Eggleston was asked if he purported to represent Jews as well as Buddhists. We find no issue of religion in the case.[119]

119. Id. at 897-898 n.12.

The court concluded, however, that the collapse of discovery could not be attributed solely to the defendants. Plaintiffs refused to answer a large number of deposition questions, engaged in private off-the-record conferences, and aborted many depositions unilaterally.[120]

Other cases have shown even more outrageous forms of misconduct during depositions. In *Paramount Communications Inc. v. QVC Network Inc.*[121] the Delaware Supreme Court strongly condemned the deposition conduct of well-known Texas attorney Joseph Jamail. Jamail referred to opposing counsel as an "asshole" and told him that he could "gag a maggot off a meat wagon."[122] While the court was unable to impose sanctions on Jamail because he was not admitted to practice in Delaware either by regular or pro hac vice admission, the court expressed its strong opposition to such tactics and warned Delaware lawyers against participating in such misconduct.[123]

As *Eggleston* points out, one form of improper deposition conduct involves inappropriate coaching of a witness during breaks in a deposition after a question has been posed. Improper witness coaching can also take place before the deposition (or before trial) when lawyers prepare witnesses for their appearances. But what is improper witness-coaching? Lawyers generally have substantial leeway in helping prepare witnesses to testify so long as they do not attempt to have a witness testify falsely. The Restatement of the Law Governing Lawyers provides the following helpful comment:

> In preparing a witness to testify, a lawyer may invite the witness to provide truthful testimony favorable to the lawyer's client. Preparation consistent with the rule of this Section may include the following: discussing the role of the witness and effective courtroom demeanor; discussing the witness's recollection and probable testimony; revealing to the witness other testimony or evidence that will be presented and asking the witness to reconsider the witness's recollection or recounting of events in that light; discussing the applicability of law to the events in issue; reviewing the factual context into which the witness's observations or opinions will fit; reviewing documents or other physical evidence that may be introduced; and discussing probable lines of hostile cross-examination that the witness should be prepared to meet. Witness preparation may include rehearsal of testimony. A lawyer may suggest choice of words that might be employed to make the witness's meaning clear. However, a lawyer may not assist the witness to testify falsely as to a material fact.[124]

120. Id. at 901-902.

121. 637 A.2d 34 (Del. 1994).

122. Id. at 54. See also Mullaney v. Aude, 730 A.2d 759 (Md. Ct. Spec. App.), *cert. denied*, 736 A.2d 1065 (1999) (male lawyer sanctioned for referring to female lawyer as "babe" at deposition); In re Golden, 496 S.E.2d 619 (S.C. 1998) (gratuitously insulting, threatening, and demeaning comments in the course of two depositions held to constitute misconduct warranting public reprimand for violating South Carolina Rules of Professional Conduct 4.4 and 8.4).

123. 637 A. 2d at 53-56.

124. Restatement (Third) of the Law Governing Lawyers §116, cmt. *b*. See Richard C. Wydick, The Ethics of Witness Coaching, 17 Cardozo L. Rev. 1 (1995).

If a lawyer directs a client to lie, the lawyer's misconduct is clear, but lawyers can suggest false testimony in more subtle ways. Although such conduct is difficult to detect or to police, it is nonetheless improper.[125] In 1998 the Texas law firm of Baron & Budd became involved in controversy over a memorandum entitled, "Preparing for Your Deposition," which it used to prepare clients to testify in asbestos cases. The memorandum advised clients that it was important for them to testify that they never saw any warning labels on asbestos products and cautioned them against saying that they saw more than one brand name.[126]

In Problem 2-5 we examined the issue of lawyers' ethical obligations when a defendant in a criminal case threatens to or does in fact testify perjuriously. Perjury can, of course, occur in civil cases. In Formal Opinion 93-376, the ABA Committee on Ethics and Professional Responsibility discussed a lawyer's obligations when a client commits perjury during a deposition. The committee concluded that under Model Rule 3.3, the lawyer has an obligation to advise the client to correct the perjury and to disclose the perjury if the client refuses to do so. The 2002 revision to the Model Rules makes clear that lawyers have an obligation to take reasonable remedial measures, including disclosure if necessary, to correct false testimony given at a deposition by the lawyer's client. Model Rule 3.3, cmt. 1.

Professional standards for conducting discovery and techniques for dealing with discovery abuse

As is true with so many areas of practice, the Model Rules provide almost no detail on how lawyers should conduct discovery. However, several sets of standards exist to guide lawyers who want to conduct discovery in a professionally proper manner. The ABA Section of Litigation has prepared "Civil Discovery Standards," a detailed set of standards to guide lawyers in seeking and responding to discovery.[127] The United States Court of Appeals for the Seventh Circuit has issued "Standards for Professional Conduct Within the Seventh Federal Judicial Circuit."[128] While the Seventh Circuit's Standards go beyond discovery, they include several principles that deal with discovery. The ABA Section of Litigation has also prepared "Guidelines for Conduct," a set of standards modeled on the Seventh Circuit's approach.[129]

---

125. See Liisa Renee Salmi, Note, Don't Walk the Line: Ethical Considerations in Preparing Witnesses for Deposition and Trial, 18 Rev. Litig. 135 (1999).

126. The full text of the memo is available on the Internet at ⟨http://www.dallasobserver.com/1998/081398/feature1-1.html⟩. For a defense of Baron & Budd's conduct by an expert retained on their behalf, see W. William Hodes, The Professional Duty to Horseshed Witnesses—Zealously, Within the Bounds of the Law, 30 Tex. Tech L. Rev. 1343 (1999).

127. ⟨http://www.abanet.org/litigation/taskforces/civil.pdf⟩ (visited Aug. 22, 2003).

128. ⟨http://www.ca7.uscourts.gov/Rules/rules.htm#standards⟩ (visited Aug. 22, 2003).

129. ⟨http://www.abanet.org/litigation/litnews/practice/guidelines.html⟩ (visited Aug. 22, 2003).

Unfortunately, lawyers who strive to conduct discovery in accordance with professional principles and the spirit of the rules will encounter lawyers who do not share these standards. How can lawyers deal with discovery abuse? Possible responses fall into two broad categories: formal and informal. The most obvious formal response is a motion for sanctions, typically under Federal Rule 37. A motion for sanctions is always a possibility, but attorneys should be aware of problems with this approach. First, given the demands on the judiciary, it may be difficult to obtain judicial time to consider a motion for sanctions. Second, even when the matter comes before a court, many judges are likely to be impatient with "discovery spats" because they consume judicial time, are collateral to the merits of the case, and force judges to deal with issues that they think lawyers should handle on their own. Third, except in extreme cases courts are usually unwilling to impose harsh sanctions on lawyers.[130] A court is far more likely simply to order the offending party to comply with the discovery request.

Aside from sanctions, attorneys can resort to various other formal devices to avoid or deal with discovery abuse. For example, in some cases courts may be willing to issue orders defining the scope of discovery or to appoint special masters to oversee discovery and resolve discovery disputes. The administrative judge of a court may be available by telephone to resolve immediately disputes that arise during depositions.

Often, however, lawyers must use informal methods for dealing with discovery problems. The most effective informal method for dealing with discovery issues is mutual agreement of counsel. An early meeting with opposing counsel to discuss discovery before formal discovery requests are filed may eliminate many problems. Indeed, the Federal Rules of Civil Procedure require counsel to have a discovery conference.[131] If discovery disputes develop, a frank meeting with opposing counsel to discuss the scope and objections to discovery may produce a compromise that both parties can accept. Prudent lawyers should reduce all agreements to writing either immediately or by confirming letter to avoid misunderstandings, to encourage compliance, and to provide a foundation for a motion for sanctions if the other attorney fails to live up to the agreement.

In some jurisdictions bar associations have established committees to deal with discovery disputes. Resort to such a committee may be an option for dealing with some discovery problems.

Responding in kind is rarely an effective device for dealing with discovery abuse by the opposing party.[132] Attorneys who engage in retaliation commit ethical misconduct themselves. In addition, they help poison the atmosphere of the case, often to the disadvantage of their clients. Moreover, they weaken

130. See Charles Yablon, Stupid Lawyer Tricks: An Essay on Discovery Abuse, 96 Colum. L. Rev. 1618 (1996) (arguing that judges should consider less extreme sanctions to control discovery abuse).

131. Fed. R. Civ. P. 26(f).

132. Robert K. Jenner, How to Attack Discovery Abuse, 38-Feb. Trial 28, 29 (2002).

their legal position should they wish to seek sanctions against the offending lawyer.

One possible response to discovery abuse is to look for opportunities to use the discovery abuse against the opposing party. Answers to interrogatories, responses to requests for production of documents, and oral depositions are all admissible in evidence against the party providing the answers. Unreasonable responses or answers that are obvious attempts to avoid supplying information may be used in cross-examination to undermine the credibility of the party making those answers before the trier of fact.

As the material above illustrates, deposition practice can be a troubling and unpleasant experience, particularly for young lawyers, because of the face-to-face encounter with opposing counsel in a forum without a neutral decisionmaker. Knowledge of proper objections and improper deposition conduct is essential to dealing with these problems.[133] A number of federal district courts have adopted guidelines for conducting depositions to deal with some of the problems that have arisen.[134] In Hall v. Clifton Precision[135] the court adopted the following guidelines:

1. At the beginning of the deposition, deposing counsel shall instruct the witness to ask deposing counsel, rather than the witness's own counsel, for clarifications, definitions, or explanations of any words, questions, or documents presented during the course of the deposition. The witness shall abide by these instructions.

2. All objections, except those which would be waived if not made at the deposition under Federal Rules of Civil Procedure 32(d)(3)(B), and those necessary to assert a privilege, to enforce a limitation on evidence directed by the court, or to present a motion pursuant to Federal Rules of Civil Procedure 30(d), shall be preserved. Therefore, those objections need not and shall not be made during the course of depositions.

3. Counsel shall not direct or request that a witness not answer a question, unless that counsel has objected to the question on the ground that the answer is protected by a privilege or a limitation on evidence directed by the court.

4. Counsel shall not make objections or statements which might suggest an answer to a witness. Counsels' statements when making objections should be succinct and verbally economical, stating the basis of the objection and nothing more.

5. Counsel and their witness-clients shall not engage in private, off-the-record conferences during depositions or during breaks or recesses, except for the purpose of deciding whether to assert a privilege.

6. Any conferences which occur pursuant to, or in violation of, guideline (5) are a proper subject for inquiry by deposing counsel to ascertain whether there has been any witness-coaching and, if so, what.

---

133. See William J. Snipes et al., Successful Techniques for Dealing with the Difficult Adversary, 659 PLI/Lit 151 (2001) (on Westlaw).

134. See Standing Orders of the Court on Effective Discovery in Civil Cases, 102 F.R.D. 339 (E.D.N.Y. 1984).

135. 150 F.R.D. 525 (E.D. Pa. 1993).

7. Any conferences which occur pursuant to, or in violation of, guideline (5) shall be noted on the record by the counsel who participated in the conference. The purpose and outcome of the conference shall also be noted on the record.

8. Deposing counsel shall provide to the witness's counsel a copy of all documents shown to the witness during the deposition. The copies shall be provided either before the deposition begins or contemporaneously with the showing of each document to the witness. The witness and the witness's counsel do not have the right to discuss documents privately before the witness answers questions about them.[136]

Not all courts agree with the strict requirements set down by the court in *Hall*. For example, in In re Stratosphere Corp. Securities Litigation[137] the court disagreed with the prohibition on all private off-the-record conferences during breaks in depositions. The court ruled that neither a lawyer nor a client could demand a break in a deposition while a question was pending except to discuss a possible claim of privilege, but concluded that otherwise the right to counsel allowed lawyers to discuss testimony with their clients.[138]

B.   Alternative Dispute Resolution

━━━━━━━━━━━━━━━━━━━━ **Problem 4-5** ━━━━━━━━━━━━━━━━━━━━

Negotiation

Analyze and be prepared to discuss the ethical issues raised by the following negotiation situations:

a.   In a personal injury case, the insurance company has authorized defense counsel, Dorn, to settle the case for a maximum of $100,000. At a negotiation session with plaintiff's counsel, Phillips, Dorn states, "I am authorized to settle this case for $50,000." Later in the session, Phillips states, "My client won't accept less than $75,000." In fact, Phillips has discussed settlement with the client, and the client is willing to accept $60,000 to settle the case.

136. Id. at 531-532.
137. 182 F.R.D. 614 (D. Nev. 1998).
138. Id. at 619-621. *Compare* State ex rel. Means v. King, 520 S.E.2d 875 (W. Va. 1999) (attorney may confer with client during recess or break in discovery deposition so long as attorney does not request break in questions or request a conference between question and answer for improper purpose; such a right does not apply, however, to evidence deposition or to testimony at trial), *with* In re PSE & G Shareholder Litig., 726 A.2d 994 (N.J. Super. Ct. Ch. Div. 1998) (counsel and client may not discuss testimony during deposition breaks but may confer at end of each day to prepare for witness's testimony the following day).

b.   In a wrongful discharge case, may Phillips, counsel for the plaintiff, make a claim in negotiation for plaintiff's reinstatement to his job even though the plaintiff does not want his job back, using this demand as a bargaining chip for increased damages? May Phillips claim that the discharge has caused the plaintiff "emotional distress" when in fact the plaintiff has taken the loss of his job in stride?

c.   An automobile accident occurred between two vehicles driven by Adams and Waring. Benson was a passenger in Adams's vehicle. Benson's attorney, Phillips, is negotiating with Dorn, counsel for defendant Waring. During the course of negotiation, Dorn states that Waring's insurer is willing to tender its policy limits of $300,000 to settle the case in exchange for a covenant not to sue. Dorn tells Phillips that "you should also be able to get Adams's policy limits of $100,000 to settle your claim against him." Dorn is mistaken about the limits of Adams's policy. In fact, Phillips knows that Adams has a $1,000,000 umbrella policy in addition to a basic $100,000 policy.

d.   Emerson is president and chief executive officer of More for Less, Inc., a national retail chain. The audit committee of the company's board of directors learned recently that Emerson has been embezzling substantial sums of money for several years. Matthews, an attorney retained by More for Less, has been meeting with Emerson's lawyers. Matthews says that the company would be willing not to file criminal charges against Emerson if Emerson resigns as president and transfers to the company all stock that Emerson owns in the company.

e.   Dorn, counsel retained by the defendant's insurance company in an automobile accident case, has a meeting with plaintiff's counsel, Phillips. When Phillips enters the room, Dorn smells alcohol on Philips's breath and observes that Phillips is extremely disheveled. Before Dorn can say much, Phillips expresses a willingness to settle the case for $10,000 if Dorn gets Phillips a check "right away." While outwardly calm, Dorn is shocked by this offer. Dorn and the insurance company had evaluated the case as having a settlement value of $25,000 to $50,000. Dorn suspects that Phillips is looking for a quick fee.

f.   Dorn represents defendant Harrison in a divorce proceeding brought by Harrison's wife. Dorn is about to meet with opposing counsel to see if they can work out a settlement. Harrison is extremely angry with his wife, and he has evidence of an affair. He tells Dorn, "I want her to get as little as possible out of this divorce. Use all the dirt we've got and anything else you can come up with to make them settle on our terms. Don't pull any punches."

    g. Phillips represents the plaintiff in a products liability action against National Tire Company, represented by Dorn. The complaint alleges that the plaintiff suffered permanent injuries resulting from an accident caused by defective tires manufactured by National. National has offered to settle the case for an amount that Phillips has recommended to the plaintiff and the plaintiff is willing to accept. As part of the settlement National Tire will require that the plaintiff sign a confidentiality agreement in which the plaintiff agrees not to disclose the terms of the settlement or any information obtained during discovery without the consent of National except pursuant to court order. The confidentiality agreement will be incorporated in the court order dismissing the case and the order will state that violation of the confidentiality agreement constitutes contempt of court. The settlement agreement will also require the parties to ask the court to seal all records and discovery. Finally, National requires Phillips to return all discovery material received during the case and to abide by the provisions of the confidentiality agreement.

Read Model Rules 1.2, 3.3, 4.1, 4.3, 4.4, 5.6, 8.4, and comments.

    Regardless of the type of practice—civil litigation,[139] criminal defense or prosecution, business, or labor—negotiation is an extremely important part of the work of lawyers.[140] Ethical issues in negotiation fall into two broad categories: honesty and fairness.[141]

    139. See ABA Section of Litigation, Ethical Guidelines for Settlement Negotiations, ⟨http://www.abanet.org/litigation/ethics/settlementnegotiations.pdf⟩ (visited Aug. 23, 2003). See also Symposium, Ethical Issues in Settlement Negotiations, 52 Mercer L. Rev. 807 (2001).

    140. Empirical evidence indicates that the presence of lawyers tends to promote settlement. Professors Ronald Gilson and Robert Mnookin have developed a model for analyzing whether lawyers contribute to cooperation or conflict in resolving disputes. They conclude that lawyers can promote cooperation and thereby reduce the transaction costs involved in disputes. They also identify a number of institutional factors that are more conducive to cooperation. Ronald J. Gilson & Robert H. Mnookin, Disputing Through Agents: Cooperation and Conflict Between Lawyers in Litigation, 94 Colum. L. Rev. 509 (1994). See also Jason Scott Johnson & Joel Waldfogel, Does Repeat Play Elicit Cooperation? Evidence from Federal Civil Procedure, 31 J. Legal Stud. 39 (2002) (cases that involve attorneys who interact repeatedly are resolved more quickly and are more likely to settle) and Russell Korobkin & Chris Guthrie, Psychology, Economics, and Settlement: A New Look at the Role of the Lawyer, 76 Tex. L. Rev. 77 (1997) (experimental evidence showing that lawyers share analytical approach that tends to promote higher rate of settlement than clients would achieve on their own).

    141. For an empirical study of lawyer practices in negotiation, see Scott S. Dahl, Ethics on the Table: Stretching the Truth in Negotiations, 8 Rev. Litig. 173 (1989).

Honesty in negotiation: the duty not to engage in misrepresentation

To what extent must lawyers be honest in negotiations? The question can be refined into two questions: To what extent are lawyers prohibited from making false representations in negotiations? When must a lawyer disclose material information to the opposing party in negotiation?

A plausible answer to the question of when lawyers are allowed to make false representations (or, more bluntly, to lie in negotiations) is "never." In an influential article on negotiation, however, Professor James White argues that while lawyers do have a general obligation not to engage in fraud or deceit in negotiation, it is erroneous to claim that lawyers should never engage in misrepresentation in negotiation. According to White, misrepresentation of one's position is essential to negotiation, just as it is to a game like poker:

> Like the poker player, a negotiator hopes that his opponent will overestimate the value of his hand. Like the poker player, in a variety of ways he must facilitate his opponent's inaccurate assessment. The critical difference between those who are successful negotiators and those who are not lies in this capacity both to mislead and not to be misled.
>
>   Some experienced negotiators will deny the accuracy of this assertion, but they will be wrong. I submit that a careful examination of the behavior of even the most forthright, honest, and trustworthy negotiators will show them actively engaged in misleading their opponents about their true positions. That is true of both the plaintiff and the defendant in a lawsuit. It is true of both labor and management in a collective bargaining agreement. It is true as well of both the buyer and the seller in a wide variety of sales transactions. To conceal one's true position, to mislead an opponent about one's true settling point, is the essence of negotiation.[142]

Some scholars have criticized White's view that negotiation inherently involves a degree of misrepresentation. These scholars have argued that White has an adversarial conception of negotiation; they contend that negotiation can and should be cooperative rather than adversarial. In cooperative negotiations, the effectiveness of misrepresentation is substantially diminished.[143] Other

142. James J. White, Machiavelli and the Bar: Ethical Limitations on Lying in Negotiation, 1980 Am. Bar Found. Res. J. 926, 927-928. See also Eleanor Holmes Norton, Bargaining and the Ethic of Process, 64 N.Y.U. L. Rev. 493 (1989) (necessities of bargaining process produce ethical functionalism with minimal truthfulness and fairness).

143. See generally Robert H. Mnookin et al., Beyond Winning: Negotiating to Create Value in Deals and Disputes (2000); Carrie Menkel-Meadow, Toward Another View of Legal Negotiation: The Structure of Problem Solving, 31 UCLA L. Rev. 754 (1984). For an interesting discussion of this issue, see the exchange between Professor White and Professor Roger Fisher, coauthor with William Ury of Getting to Yes (1981), a leading work on cooperative negotiation, in James J. White, Essay Review, The Pros and Cons of "Getting to Yes," 34 J. Legal Educ. 115 (1984). Professor Robert Condlin argues that there is a tension between the practical norms of negotiation, which tend to support cooperation, and the ethical norms, which direct lawyers to maximize their clients' interests.

scholars have argued that it is simply wrong for lawyers to lie in negotiation, and to the extent that current practice or rules allow misrepresentation and deceit, these rules should be changed. The leading article expressing this view is Alvin B. Rubin, A Causerie on Lawyers' Ethics in Negotiation.[144]

The Model Rules seem to adopt White's view that lawyers have a general obligation of honesty in negotiation but that deceit and misrepresentation are to some degree part of the rules of the game. Model Rule 4.1(a) states that in representing a client a lawyer shall not knowingly "make a false statement of material fact or law to a third person."[145] The comment to Rule 4.1, however, makes clear that some false statements are permissible because they do not amount to statements of material fact. Comment 2 states that "[u]nder generally accepted conventions in negotiation, certain types of statements ordinarily are not taken as statements of material fact."

How does a lawyer decide what misrepresentations under "accepted conventions" do not amount to statements of fact? Comment 2 to Rule 4.1 gives a few examples but does not provide a definition or any criteria for distinguishing permissible from prohibited misrepresentations. Case law, however, does offer some guidance. Improper misrepresentation clearly occurs when a lawyer makes a false statement about the material facts of the case—the testimony of a witness or the existence or contents of a document, for example.[146] Improper misrepresentation also occurs when a lawyer makes false statements about the effect of provisions of an agreement, about procedural aspects of the case, or about insurance coverage.[147] Such a

---

He contends that the often stylized adversarial approach to negotiation adopted by many lawyers is caused in part by the conflicting obligations these sets of norms impose on lawyers. Condlin discusses several ways in which these norms could be reconciled. Robert J. Condlin, Bargaining in the Dark: The Normative Incoherence of Lawyer Dispute Bargaining Role, 51 Md. L. Rev. 1 (1992).

144. 35 La. L. Rev. 577 (1975). See also Reed E. Loder, Moral Truthseeking and the Virtuous Negotiator, 8 Geo. J. Legal Ethics 45 (1994); Gary T. Lowenthal, The Bar's Failure to Require Truthful Bargaining by Lawyers, 2 Geo. J. Legal Ethics 411 (1988); Walter W. Steele, Jr., Deceptive Negotiating and High-Toned Morality, 39 Vand. L. Rev. 1387 (1986); Gerald B. Wetlaufer, The Ethics of Lying in Negotiations, 75 Iowa L. Rev. 1219 (1990).

145. See Restatement (Third) of the Law Governing Lawyers §98(1). See also ABA Comm. on Ethics and Prof. Resp., Formal Op. 94-387 (lawyer may negotiate regarding claim that is barred by statute of limitations and may file suit of time-barred claim so long as lawyer does not make any false representations; same rules apply to government lawyers).

146. See Ausherman v. Bank of America Corp., 212 F. Supp. 2d 435 (D. Md. 2002) (referring to disciplinary authorities and imposing sanction of attorney fees for misrepresentations by plaintiff's counsel during negotiations about identity of "kingpin" of scheme to unlawfully obtain and sell credit reports).

147. See Shafer v. Berger, Kahn, Shafton, Moss, Figler, Simon & Gladstone, 131 Cal. Rptr. 2d 777 (Ct. App., *review denied* 2003) (holding that insured's judgment creditors stated cause of action against insurer's coverage counsel for misrepresentation about lack of coverage for willful acts).

misrepresentation can result in rescission of the agreement,[148] subject the lawyer to disciplinary action,[149] or produce civil liability.[150] Note also that a lawyer's duty not to engage in misrepresentation in negotiations generally parallels a lawyer's duty not to engage in misrepresentation in court proceedings.[151]

Lawyers do not act improperly, however, when they misrepresent their true *opinions* about the relative strengths of each side of a case. Lawyers may permissibly say to their opponents that they believe they have very strong cases even though they actually believe that there are serious problems with their positions. Further, in negotiations lawyers may argue for interpretations of relevant law that are most favorable to their clients, even when lawyers believe that their opponents' positions are correct.[152]

Representations regarding settlement authority could arise in two ways. First, a lawyer could make a representation regarding settlement authority for the purpose of inducing agreement by the opposing side. Second, the opposing party may ask a question about the lawyer's settlement authority. In either situation, is it improper for a lawyer to make misrepresentations about settlement authority? Comment 2 to Rule 4.1 states that a lawyer may ordinarily make misrepresentations about a "party's intentions as to an acceptable settlement of a claim." Yet while misrepresentations of opinions about the merits of the case are essential to the negotiation process, misrepresentations of settlement authority are not. Further, settlement authority is a matter of fact, not opinion.

Responses to requests by the other side for information about settlement authority pose a more subtle problem. A lawyer's settlement authority will come from discussions with the client. These discussions will often involve

148. See Carlson v. Carlson, 832 P.2d 380 (Nev. 1992) (wife entitled to relief from property settlement agreement based on representations by husband and his attorney that division was essentially equal).

149. See In re Broome, 615 So. 2d 1333 (La. 1993) (lawyer disciplined for obtaining personal injury settlement based on false representation that suit had been timely filed).

150. See Fire Ins. Exch. v. Bell, 643 N.E.2d 310 (Ind. 1994) (lawyer subject to liability for misrepresenting limits of insurance policy; as matter of law lawyers have right to rely on representations made by opposing counsel about amount of insurance).

151. See Model Rule 3.3(a)(1); In re Neitlich, 597 N.E.2d 425 (Mass. 1992) (one-year suspension administered to lawyer who misrepresented terms of client's pending real estate transaction to court in postdivorce proceeding); ABA Formal Opinion 98-412 (dealing with disclosure obligations of lawyer who discovers that client has violated court order during litigation). Rule 3.3(a)(1) as amended in 2002 is somewhat stronger than Rule 4.1(a) because the misrepresentation to a tribunal need not be material. Rule 3.3(a)(1) as amended in 2002 also makes it improper for a lawyer to "fail to correct a false statement of material fact or law previously made to the tribunal by the lawyer." While this duty of disclosure is not explicit under Rule 4.1, the failure to make such a corrective disclosure will often amount to a misrepresentation under that rule as well. See the discussion below.

152. See White, Machiavelli and the Bar, 1980 Am. Bar Found. Res. J. at 931-932. See also Restatement (Second) of Contracts §§168, 169 (1981); Restatement (Second) of Torts §542 (1977) (reliance on statements of opinion not justified except in limited situations).

confidential information—information received from the client that is subject to either the attorney-client privilege or the work product doctrine, or both. Thus, a question about settlement authority inquires into privileged matters and seeks information that the other party is not entitled to know.[153] In addition, if lawyers and clients know that lawyers must respond truthfully to questions about authority, they can easily devise ways to avoid having to answer the question. Thus, good reasons exist why lawyers should not be required to answer truthfully questions about their settlement authority. At the same time, it is probably unnecessary for the rules to permit lawyers to lie in response to inquiries about settlement authority because such questions can easily be deflected.

Another misrepresentation that is problematic involves a "false demand," a contention injected into the negotiation process, not because it expresses a serious position by the side making the demand but because a false demand can be used as a bargaining chip to improve the overall settlement. Professor White argues that the false demand is a misrepresentation in the broadest sense because a person making a demand "implicitly or explicitly states his interest in the demand and his estimation of it," but he goes on to conclude that such demands are "not thought to be inappropriate," at least in labor negotiations.[154]

Honesty in negotiation: the duty of disclosure

So far we have discussed the question of when misrepresentation by lawyers in negotiation is improper. The issue of honesty in negotiation also raises a question of disclosure. When are lawyers required to disclose information to the opposing party in connection with negotiation? Model Rule 4.1(b) states that a lawyer may not knowingly "fail to disclose a material fact when disclosure is necessary to avoid assisting a criminal or fraudulent act by a client, unless disclosure is prohibited by Rule 1.6." The "unless" clause was added to the rule during the floor debate before the House of Delegates on adoption of the Model Rules in 1983; the result was both confusing and contradictory. The 1983 version of Rule 1.6 contained a broad confidentiality rule with only limited exceptions. As a result the "unless" clause effectively prohibited lawyers from making the disclosures that Rule 4.1(b) seemed to require.[155] Scholars attempted to reconcile the two parts of Rule 4.1(b) by arguing that lawyers must disclose information when required by "other law," which includes the law of civil procedure and tort law dealing with actionable nondisclosure.[156]

153. Cf. ABA Comm. on Ethics and Prof. Resp., Formal Op. 93-370 (judge does not have right to require lawyer to reveal settlement authority absent client's consent).

154. White, Machiavelli and the Bar, 1980 Am. Bar Found. Res. J. at 932.

155. Wolfram, Modern Legal Ethics §13.5.8, at 724. See also 2 Hazard & Hodes, The Law of Lawyering §37.2.

156. Wolfram, Modern Legal Ethics §13.5.8, at 724. See also 2 Hazard & Hodes, The Law of Lawyering §37.6. See also Restatement (Third) of the Law Governing Lawyers §98(2), (3).

In 2002 and 2003 the ABA broadened the exceptions to the duty of confidentiality in Rule 1.6. As a result of these amendments, the duty of disclosure under Rule 4.1(b) is now broader. If a client is engaging in a criminal or fraudulent act, under Rule 4.1(b) the lawyer must disclose the client's conduct if disclosure is necessary to avoid assisting the act and disclosure is permitted under Rule 1.6. Of course, in many situations a lawyer could avoid assistance of the client's crime or fraud by withdrawing from representation. See Model Rule 1.16(a).

It is a mistake to conclude, however, that Rule 4.1(b) is the only basis for a lawyer's duty of disclosure. The author of this casebook has argued that the lawyer's duty not to engage in misrepresentation under Model Rule 4.1(a) will sometimes require disclosure of material information. Such a duty of disclosure arises when nondisclosure is equivalent to misrepresentation.[157] Comment 1 to Model Rule 4.1 as amended in 2002 states: "Misrepresentations can also occur by partially true but misleading statements or *omissions that are the equivalent of affirmative false statements.*" (emphasis added). Similarly, Comment 3 to Model Rule 3.3 states: "There are circumstances where failure to make a disclosure is the equivalent of an affirmative misrepresentation." Note that when the duty of disclosure is based on the obligation not to engage in misrepresentation under either Rule 4.1(a) or 3.3(a)(1), the duty is not qualified by the obligation of confidentiality.

Case law supports this analysis. As a general proposition, lawyers do not have an obligation to disclose material information to the opposing side.[158] Numerous cases have held, however, that under some circumstances lawyers have an ethical duty to disclose information in connection with contract or settlement negotiations.[159] When does a lawyer have a duty of disclosure? The author of this casebook argues that the duty to disclose arises in four situations:[160]

A duty of *corrective disclosure* arises when a lawyer made a representation that the lawyer now learns was either false when made or has become false because of changed circumstances.[161]

If a lawyer knows that the other party is operating under a fundamental *mistake about the contents of a writing*, the lawyer has a duty to disclose the mistake to the other party. The mistake will typically arise as a result of a

---

157. Nathan M. Crystal, The Lawyer's Duty to Disclose Material Facts in Contract or Settlement Negotiations, 87 Ky. L.J. 1055, 1058 (1998–1999).

158. See Restatement (Second) of Torts §551(1) (1977) and Restatement (Second) of Contracts §161 (1981).

159. For a review of the case law, see Crystal, The Lawyer's Duty to Disclose Material Facts in Contract or Settlement Negotiations, 87 Ky. L.J. at 1059-1074.

160. Id. at 1076-1082.

161. See In re Williams, 840 P.2d 1280 (Or. 1992) (lawyer represented to landlord that he would hold tenant's rent payments in escrow pending resolution of dispute; lawyer disciplined for failing to inform landlord that statement was no longer correct). See also Restatement (Third) of the Law Governing Lawyers §98, cmt. *d* (recognizing duty of corrective disclosure). Cf. Fed. R. Civ. P. 26(e) (duty to supplement responses in discovery).

"scrivener's error."[162] The duty to disclose known mistakes in a writing also extends to situations in which a lawyer changes provisions in an agreement but fails to notify the other side of such modifications.[163]

Situations in which lawyers will have a *fiduciary duty to the opposing party to disclose material information* in negotiation will rarely occur. When the opposing party is represented by counsel, a lawyer does not have a fiduciary duty to the opposing party. If the lawyer is dealing with an unrepresented opposing party, the lawyer has an obligation to correct any misunderstanding that the other party may have about the lawyer's role in the negotiations.[164] See Model Rule 4.3. A lawyer may not give any advice to an unrepresented person, other than the advice to seek counsel.[165] Model Rule 4.3. In some limited circumstances, a lawyer may properly act to create or adjust a contractual relationship between jointly represented clients on a mutually advantageous basis. See Model Rule 1.7 and cmts. 26-33[166] and Problem 5-1. Because lawyers who undertake common representation have an attorney-client relationship with both parties, they have a fiduciary duty to disclose material information to both of them. Model Rule 1.7, cmt. 31.

The broadest and vaguest category of cases in which lawyers have a duty of disclosure occurs when disclosure is necessary to correct a mistake by the other party about basic aspects of the transaction and the *failure to disclose violates standards of good faith and fair dealing.*[167] Probably the most blatant case

162. See ABA Comm. on Ethics and Prof. Resp., Informal Op. 86-1518 (lawyer who receives contract containing scrivener's error should immediately notify other lawyer and need not consult with client because client does not have reasonable expectation of receiving erroneous provision); Stare v. Tate, 98 Cal. Rptr. 264 (Ct. App. 1971) (property settlement agreement set aside because of lawyer's failure to disclose mathematical mistake made by opposing party in its settlement offer).

163. Wright v. Pennamped, 657 N.E.2d 1223, *as modified on reh'g*, 664 N.E.2d 394 (Ind. Ct. App. 1996); In re Rothwell, 296 S.E.2d 870 (S.C. 1982).

164. Cf. Hotz v. Minyard, 403 S.E.2d 634 (S.C. 1991) (summary judgment for lawyer reversed because material issues of fact exist on whether lawyer had fiduciary duty to daughter not to misrepresent terms of her father's will, which the lawyer had drafted, when the daughter consulted the lawyer about the terms of the will, the lawyer had an ongoing professional relationship with the daughter, and the lawyer failed to disclose that he was representing the father and not the daughter with regard to the will).

165. See Russell Engler, Out of Sight and Out of Line: The Need for Regulation of Lawyers' Negotiations with Unrepresented Poor Persons, 85 Cal. L. Rev. 79 (1997) (arguing that prohibition on giving advice is widely ignored and calling for a number of possible responses to deal with the problem).

166. The 1983 version of the Model Rules dealt with such situations in Rule 2.2, defining when a lawyer could act as an intermediary between clients. The 2002 revision of the Model Rules deleted Rule 2.2 because of confusion about its scope and application, but incorporated many of the principles found in Rule 2.2 in the general conflict of interest provision, Rule 1.7, and its comments.

167. See Restatement (Second) of Torts §551(2)(e) (1977) and Restatement (Second) of Contracts §161(b) (1981). See Davin, L.L.C. v. Daham, 746 A.2d 1034 (N.J. Super., App. Div. 2000) (recognizing that landlord's attorney had duty to recommend landlord disclose to prospective tenant property was subject to foreclosure and requiring attorney to withdraw if landlord refuses to do so).

of nondisclosure that violates the duty of good faith occurs when the lawyer's client dies, but the lawyer fails to reveal this information to the other side while negotiating a settlement agreement.[168] The duty of good faith disclosure extends further, however, to encompass failure to disclose major procedural developments,[169] mistakes about the amount of insurance coverage,[170] and recantation of testimony by a significant witness.[171]

In all the cases discussed in this section, the lawyers who failed to disclose information knew that the other party was operating under a mistake, and the mistake related to fundamental information. When these factors are absent, a duty to disclose does not arise. For example, in Brown v. County of Genesee[172] the Sixth Circuit held that a settlement agreement in an employment discrimination case should not be set aside because defense counsel and his client failed to reveal to the plaintiff and her attorney that they were mistaken about the highest pay level that plaintiff would have been entitled to had she been hired immediately. Defense counsel believed that it was "probable" that the plaintiff was mistaken about pay levels, but there was no way for counsel to know that a mistake had occurred. In addition, it was unclear to the court that the highest level of pay was fundamental to the agreement because there was no such condition in the settlement.[173]

One of the most extreme reported cases of nondisclosure is Spaulding v. Zimmerman.[174] In *Spaulding* the Minnesota Supreme Court held that a minor settlement in an accident case should be set aside because the lawyer for the defendant failed to disclose to the plaintiff a doctor's report showing that, unknown to the plaintiff, he was suffering from a life-threatening aneurysm that was probably caused by the accident. While the court set aside the settlement,[175] it held that defense counsel did not have an ethical duty to disclose plaintiff's condition.[176] The author of this casebook contends that the court in *Spaulding* incorrectly decided the ethical issue. Under this analysis, contempo-

---

168. See Virzi v. Grand Trunk Warehouse & Cold Storage Co., 571 F. Supp. 507 (E.D. Mich. 1983); Kentucky Bar Assn. v. Geisler, 938 S.W.2d 578 (Ky. 1997); ABA Formal Opinion 95-397.

169. See Hamilton v. Harper, 404 S.E.2d 540 (W. Va. 1991) (lawyer failed to reveal that summary judgment had just been granted to insurer in federal court declaratory judgment action on issue of insurance coverage when lawyer accepted outstanding offer from insurance company).

170. See State ex rel. Neb. State Bar Assn. v. Addison, 412 N.W.2d 855 (Neb. 1987) (lawyer suspended for six months after failing to reveal to hospital administrator the existence of insurance policy in connection with negotiation of release of hospital's lien).

171. See Kath v. Western Media, Inc., 684 P.2d 98 (Wyo. 1984) (settlement invalidated because plaintiff's attorney failed to disclose existence of letter in which witness who was previously a lawyer for all parties to action contradicted testimony he had given in deposition).

172. 872 F.2d 169 (6th Cir. 1989).

173. Id. at 174-175.

174. 116 N.W.2d 704 (Minn. 1962).

175. Id. at 709-710.

176. Id. at 710.

rary defense lawyers who encountered a situation like *Spaulding* would have a duty to disclose under Model Rule 4.1(a) because their failure to disclose would amount to misrepresentation:

> [T]he court was wrong in its characterization of the lawyers' conduct. Under the facts of the case, defense counsel's failure to disclose was the equivalent of a misrepresentation. Defense counsel had a duty to disclose because plaintiff's physical condition was a basic fact about which plaintiff was mistaken, and the failure to disclose violated principles of good faith and fair dealing. Indeed, *Spaulding* is probably the clearest case for disclosure that can be imagined because of the threat to the plaintiff's life.[177]

Fairness of the settlement

The original draft of the Model Rules stated: "In conducting negotiations a lawyer shall be fair in dealing with other participants."[178] Whether the drafters truly intended to include a general obligation of fairness is doubtful since the comment stated that fairness in negotiations implies that representations shall be truthful. In any event, the idea of an obligation of fairness was quickly abandoned in favor of narrower rules focusing on misrepresentation and nondisclosure.[179]

Why shouldn't rules of ethics impose an obligation on lawyers to refuse to participate in agreements that are unfair? Three reasons could be given. First, there are no objective criteria of fairness that a lawyer or a disciplinary board could use to determine whether an agreement was fair. Thus, an ethical duty not to participate in an unfair outcome would be unworkable. Second, to the extent that rules of ethics prohibit lawyers from participating in settlement agreements that the lawyers know are invalid because of fraud, mistake, or other such cause, the rules already impose a substantial obligation of fairness.

177. See Crystal, The Lawyer's Duty to Disclose Material Facts in Contract or Settlement Negotiations, 87 Ky. L.J. at 1097. In a comprehensive examination of the case, Professor Roger Cramton and Lori Knowles contend the court was correct that rules of ethics and discovery rules did not then and did not in 1998 require disclosure. They argue this result shows that the confidentiality rules are unsound and should be changed. Roger C. Cramton & Lori P. Knowles, Professional Secrecy and Its Exceptions: Spaulding v. Zimmerman Revisited, 83 Minn. L. Rev. 63 (1998). In 2002 the ABA amended Rule 1.6 to provide lawyers with discretion to reveal confidential information to prevent "reasonably certain death or substantial bodily harm." Under this revised rule the lawyers in *Spaulding* would have been permitted but not required to reveal plaintiff's condition. Under the analysis suggested by the author of this casebook, the lawyers would have been required to reveal the information under Rule 4.1(a).

178. ABA, Model Rules of Professional Conduct, Rule 4.2(a) (Discussion Draft 1980).

179. See Geoffrey C. Hazard, Jr., The Lawyer's Obligation to Be Trustworthy When Dealing with Opposing Parties, 33 S.C. L. Rev. 181 (1981) (legal regulation of trustworthiness cannot go further than to proscribe fraud because of substantial difference in technical sophistication among lawyers).

Third, a duty of fairness would be inconsistent with the adversarial system, under which the fairness of the outcome is judged by the fairness of the adjudication process. Rules of ethics do not prohibit lawyers from participating in adjudication that produces an outcome that some might consider substantively unfair so long as the process is a fair one. Similarly, the rules should not prohibit lawyers from engaging in negotiations that result in an agreement that some observers might consider unfair.

Some scholars, while agreeing that lawyers should not have an ethical duty to ensure the overall fairness of negotiations, have argued for a narrower proposition: Lawyers should have an obligation not to participate in an agreement that is unconscionable. Professor Lee Pizzimenti has proposed the adoption of the following rule of ethics:

> A lawyer shall not assist in the preparation of a written instrument containing terms which are unconscionable. A lawyer may assist in such preparation where there is a basis for concluding the terms are not unconscionable that is not frivolous, including a good faith argument for an extension, modification or reversal of existing law.[180]

Improper threats

Even though the Model Rules do not impose a general obligation of fairness in connection with negotiation, there are some limitations on negotiation tactics. One limitation deals with improper threats during negotiation. Disciplinary Rule 7-105(A) of the Code of Professional Responsibility prohibited lawyers from threatening to use the criminal process solely to obtain an advantage in a civil matter. Ethical Consideration 7-21 offered the following rationale for the prohibition:

> The civil adjudicative process is primarily designed for the settlement of disputes between parties, while the criminal process is designed for the protection of society as a whole. Threatening to use, or using, the criminal process to coerce adjustment of private civil claims or controversies is a subversion of that process; further, the person against whom the criminal process is so misused may be deterred from asserting his legal rights and thus the usefulness of the civil process in settling private disputes is impaired. As in all cases of abuse of judicial process, the improper use of criminal process tends to diminish public confidence in our legal system.

The drafters of the Model Rules intentionally omitted the ban on threats of criminal prosecution.[181] They believed that the prohibition found in the Code was unwise in two respects. First, the restriction was redundant because

---

180. See Lee A. Pizzimenti, Prohibiting Lawyers from Assisting in Unconscionable Transactions: Using an Overt Tool, 72 Marq. L. Rev. 151, 174 (1989).
181. 2 Hazard & Hodes, The Law of Lawyering §40.4, at 7.

it was already covered by other rules, particularly by Model Rule 8.4(b), prohibiting lawyers from engaging in criminal conduct that reflects on their honesty, trustworthiness, or fitness to practice law, and by Model Rule 4.4, dealing with respect for the rights of third persons.[182] Second, the drafters concluded that the limitation was overbroad because some threats of criminal prosecution were proper tactics that lawyers should be allowed to use to protect clients' legitimate interests.[183]

In Formal Opinion 92-363, the ABA Committee on Ethics and Professional Responsibility discussed when a threat of criminal prosecution would be permissible under the Model Rules:

> Model Rule 8.4(b) provides that it is professional misconduct for a lawyer to "commit a criminal act that reflects adversely on the lawyer's honesty, trustworthiness or fitness as a lawyer in other respects." If a lawyer's conduct is extortionate or compounds a crime under the criminal law of a given jurisdiction, that conduct also violates Rule 8.4(b). It is beyond the scope of the Committee's jurisdiction to define extortionate conduct, but we note that the Model Penal Code does not criminalize threats of prosecution where the "property obtained by threat of accusation, exposure, lawsuit or other invocation of official action was *honestly claimed as restitution for harm done in the circumstances to which such accusation, exposure, lawsuit or other official action relates, or as compensation for property or lawful services.*" Model Penal Code, §223.4 (emphasis added). . . . [The committee then went on to discuss other provisions of the Model Rules that a threat of criminal prosecution might violate, depending on the circumstances.]
>
> Rule 4.4 (Respect for Rights of Third Persons) prohibits a lawyer from using means that "have no substantial purpose other than to embarrass, delay, or burden a third person. . . ." A lawyer who uses even a well-founded threat of criminal charges merely to harass a third person violates Rule 4.4. . . .
>
> Rule 4.1 (Truthfulness in Statements to Others) imposes a duty on lawyers to be truthful when dealing with others on a client's behalf. A lawyer who threatens criminal prosecution, without any actual intent to so proceed, violates Rule 4.1.
>
> Finally, Rule 3.1 (Meritorious Claims and Contentions) prohibits an advocate from asserting frivolous claims. A lawyer who threatens criminal prosecution that is not well founded in fact and in law, or threatens such prosecution in furtherance of a civil claim that is not well founded, violates Rule 3.1.[184]

The committee concluded that if a lawyer did not violate any of these rules, a threat of criminal prosecution to settle a civil matter was proper if the crime was *related* to the civil matter. The committee also decided that a lawyer could agree not to report a criminal offense provided such an agreement did not amount to compounding a crime. The opinion refers to rules of ethics and

---

182. See Wolfram, Modern Legal Ethics §13.5.5, at 718. See also ABA Comm. on Ethics and Prof. Resp., Formal Op. 94-383 (use of threat to file disciplinary charge against opposing lawyer to obtain advantage in civil matter is constrained by various provisions of Model Rules although not directly prohibited).

183. 2 Hazard & Hodes, The Law of Lawyering §40.4, at 7-8.

184. ABA Comm. on Ethics and Prof. Resp., Formal Op. 92-363, at 4-5.

criminal statutes in force in the jurisdiction in which the lawyer practices. The West Virginia Supreme Court largely adopted the approach of ABA Formal Opinion 92-363 in Committee on Legal Ethics v. Printz,[185] which held that an attorney may ethically threaten criminal prosecution to obtain restitution of embezzled funds.[186]

It should be noted that under the Model Rules a threat may sometimes be improper even if it does not involve a threat of criminal prosecution: for example, a threat that constitutes a tort or that is made for an improper purpose. Thus, courts have held that threats to give undue publicity to the other party's private matters in order to induce settlement are improper. In State v. Harrington[187] the Vermont Supreme Court held that a threat made by the wife's divorce lawyer to publicize her husband's adultery, a crime, in order to coerce settlement amounted to criminal extortion. Similarly, in In re Dienes[188] a lawyer received a public reprimand for making a veiled threat to inform the newspapers about his former employer's business unless the employer withdrew a motion seeking attorney fees from the lawyer.

Approaches to negotiation

Scholars who have studied lawyer negotiations have developed a typology of approaches to negotiation.[189] Fundamental to lawyer negotiation is a distinction between *style* and *strategy*.

Negotiating style refers to the personality traits that the lawyer presents in negotiation.[190] Professor Gerald Williams has identified two basic negotiating styles: competitive (or adversarial) and cooperative (or problem solving). Williams listed the following as personality traits of effective competitive negotiators:

> dominating, forceful, attacking, aggressive, ambitious, clever, honest, perceptive, analytical, convincing, and self-controlled.[191]

He identified the following as personality traits of successful cooperative negotiators:

185. 416 S.E.2d 720 (W. Va. 1992).

186. See also Ruberton v. Gabage, 654 A.2d 1002 (N.J. Super. Ct. App. Div.), *cert. denied*, 663 A.2d 1358 (N.J. 1995) (in wrongful discharge case, threat by defense counsel to institute criminal charges unless plaintiff accepted settlement not actionable as abuse of process because process not used and because statements made in course of judicial proceeding are absolutely privileged).

187. 260 A.2d 692 (Vt. 1969). See generally Joseph M. Livermore, Lawyer Extortion, 20 Ariz. L. Rev. 403 (1978).

188. 571 A.2d 1303 (N.J. 1990).

189. See Robert M. Bastress & Joseph D. Harbaugh, Interviewing, Counseling, and Negotiating 390-397 (1990).

190. Id. at 390.

191. Id. at 391.

trustworthy, fair, honest, courteous, personable, tactful, sincere, perceptive, reasonable, convincing, and self-controlled.[192]

Negotiation strategy refers to the goals of the negotiation. Building on Professor Williams's work, Professor Carrie Menkel-Meadow identified two negotiating strategies: adversarial and problem solving.[193] While the strategies appear to be identical to the styles of negotiating, a fundamental difference exists between technique of negotiation (style) and goals of negotiation (strategy). Professor Menkel-Meadow went on to discuss four possible approaches to negotiation that lawyers could adopt; these four approaches represent the logical combinations of the two styles and two strategies:

	Style	*Strategy*
(1)	Competitive	adversarial;
(2)	Cooperative	adversarial;
(3)	Competitive	problem solvers;
(4)	Cooperative	problem solvers.[194]

For example, lawyers who approach negotiations with friendly, courteous, caring attitudes but use these techniques to achieve the highest possible settlements for their clients are employing cooperative adversarial negotiation methods.

How does a lawyer make a choice of negotiating style and strategy?[195] Professors Bastress and Harbaugh argue that the choice of approach to a negotiation should be made carefully by the lawyer and client after considering the relevant factors, including the following:

1.   The goals of the client and the needs of the opposing party. For example, if the client's only goal is to obtain as much of the only fungible commodity at issue as is possible, then an adversarial strategy is likely to produce the greater gain. On the other hand, if a continuing relationship between the parties is their primary aim, problem-solving may be more appropriate.

2.   The configuration of shared, independent, and conflicting needs of the parties. For example, if the needs of the parties do not conflict but are shared or independent, it suggests that a cooperative problem-solving strategy could be very successful.

3.   The resources, including money, personnel, time, and the like, available to your client and to the opposing party.

4.   The ability of the parties to creatively generate additional issues and

192. Id.

193. Id. at 393.

194. Id. at 395.

195. For a recent study supporting the view that a problem-solving approach to negotiation is more effective than an adversarial style, see Andrea Kupfer Schneider, Shattering Negotiation Myths: Empirical Evidence on the Effectiveness of Negotiation Style, 7 Harv. Negot. L. Rev. 143 (2002).

resources to expand the subject matter of the negotiation. The greater the number of issues and the amount of resources involved in the negotiation, the easier it is to move from adversarial to problem-solving.

5. The comfort or discomfort you (and your client) experience when you behave as a competitive versus cooperative bargainer. While we encourage you to experiment with the four unions of style and strategy, we acknowledge it is difficult to successfully use a negotiation model with which you are uncomfortable. Your client's needs must also be considered. The angry client in a wrongful death case, for instance, may not be satisfied with a cooperative problem-solving approach.

6. The style and strategy combination selected by your opponent. Professor Williams, for example, found that effective competitive negotiators were quite successful when matched with cooperative bargainers.[196]

Bastress and Harbaugh go on to argue that the choice of approach to negotiation can change during the course of negotiation: Lawyers must plan for negotiation but should also remain flexible.

Model Rule 1.2(a) states that a lawyer must abide by the "client's decisions concerning the objectives of representation and, as required by Rule 1.4, shall consult with the client as to the means by which they are to be pursued." Thus, under the Model Rules lawyers have broad discretion regarding tactical matters.

The Bounds of Advocacy adopted by the American Academy of Matrimonial Lawyers embody a modification of the traditional, adversarial role for attorneys: "These AAML Bounds of Advocacy reflect a shift toward the role of constructive advocacy, a counseling, problem-solving approach for a family member in need of assistance in resolving difficult issues and conflicts within the family."[197] The following provisions on tactics illustrate this changed conception of the lawyer's role:

1.3 *An attorney should refuse to assist in vindictive conduct and should strive to lower the emotional level of a family dispute by treating all other participants with respect.*

COMMENT

Some clients expect and want the matrimonial lawyer to reflect the highly emotional, vengeful personal relationship between spouses. The attorney should counsel the client that discourteous and retaliatory conduct is inappropriate and counterproductive, that measures of respect are consistent with competent and ethical representation of the client, and that it is unprofessional for the attorney to act otherwise.

---

196. Bastress & Harbaugh, Interviewing, Counseling, and Negotiating at 402.

197. See American Academy of Matrimonial Lawyers, The Bounds of Advocacy, Attorney as Counselor and Advocate, ⟨http://www.aaml.org/Bounds%20of%20Advocacy/Bounds%20of%20Advocacy.htm⟩ (visited Aug. 24, 2003). Similarly, some attorneys advocate a new approach, which they call "collaborative lawyering." See James K.L. Lawrence, Collaborative Lawyering: A New Development in Conflict Resolution, 17 Ohio St. J. on Disp. Resol. 431 (2002).

Although the client has the right to determine the "objectives of representation," after consulting with the client the attorney may limit the objectives and the means by which the objectives are to be pursued. [Model Rule 1.2(c).—Ed.] The matrimonial lawyer should make every effort to lower the emotional level of the interaction among parties and counsel. Some dissension and bad feelings can be avoided by a frank discussion with the client at the outset of how the attorney handles cases, including what the attorney will and will not do regarding vindictive conduct or actions likely to adversely affect the children's interests. If the client is unwilling to accept the attorney's limitations on objectives or means, the attorney should decline the representation.

Similarly, Rule 6.2 of the Bounds of Advocacy provides as follows: "An attorney should not permit a client to contest child custody, contact or access for either financial leverage or vindictiveness."

Confidentiality or noncooperation agreements and judicial orders sealing court records

In contemporary litigation, parties often negotiate for confidentiality provisions in connection with settlement agreements.[198] A wide range of motivations can prompt one or both parties to seek such arrangements. Some cases—sexual harassment matters, for example—may involve information about the private lives of the parties. Other cases may deal with trade secrets, the release of which can be commercially damaging. In some matters, a party may be concerned about adverse publicity resulting from the case. Defendants in product liability cases may be worried that publicity about the existence or settlement of litigation could prompt other cases or could increase settlement values.

Confidentiality arrangements can take various forms, but in broad terms they fall into two categories: private confidentiality or noncooperation agreements and court-ordered confidentiality. In the typical confidentiality or noncooperation agreement, the plaintiff agrees not to disclose either the terms of the settlement or any information related to the case without the consent of the defendant. Such agreements usually provide that the plaintiff may reveal such information if required by court order.[199]

Defendants may not be satisfied with the protections of private confidentiality agreements and may seek court-ordered protections as well. Court-ordered confidentiality usually comes in two forms. First, as part of the court's order either dismissing the case or approving the settlement, the court can incorporate the terms of the parties' confidentiality agreement and provide that a violation of the agreement constitutes contempt of court. Second, a court can seal all or part of the record in the case.

---

198. See generally Richard Zitrin & Carol M. Langford, The Moral Compass of the American Lawyer, ch. 9 (1999).

199. See Stephen Gillers, Speak No Evil: Settlement Agreements Conditioned on Noncooperation Are Illegal and Unethical, 31 Hofstra L. Rev. 1, 4 (2002).

In most jurisdictions confidentiality agreements are enforceable and court-ordered confidentiality is permissible.[200] Some jurisdictions allow private confidentiality agreements but prohibit or limit sealing of court records, presumably based on the policy that courts are public institutions.[201] The Florida Sunshine in Litigation Act goes further, prohibiting both court orders and private confidentiality agreements dealing with a "public hazard."[202]

Scholars have increasingly criticized confidentiality arrangements. Professor Susan Koniak argues that such provisions should be unenforceable on grounds of public policy.[203] Professor Stephen Gillers contends that noncooperation agreements violate obstruction of justice statutes and are unethical under Model Rule 3.4(f), which prohibits a lawyer from requesting "a person other than a client to refrain from voluntarily giving relevant information to another party," subject to limited exceptions.[204]

Defendants may be concerned about release of information, not only by the plaintiff but by the plaintiff's lawyer. As a result defendants sometimes ask as part of the settlement that plaintiff's attorney agree not to bring any other litigation against the defendant based on the same product defect or occurrence. Such an agreement is clearly unethical and therefore unenforceable under Model Rule 5.6(b), which provides that a "lawyer shall not participate in offering or making an agreement in which a restriction on the lawyer's right to practice is part of the settlement of a client controversy." In Formal Opinion 00-417 the ABA Committee also ruled that an agreement by counsel not to use information was also improper because it would as a practical matter prevent the lawyer from representing future clients in violation of Rule 5.6(b). Oddly, however, the Committee also held that a provision in which a lawyer agreed not to disclose (rather than use) information related to the representation was permissible because such a provision is nothing more than what is required by the Model Rules absent client consent. The Committee did not explain how a lawyer could use information in litigation without disclosing it. While broad prohibitions that attempt to limit counsel from handling future cases are almost certainly invalid, some narrower restrictions may be enforceable. For example, a defendant could probably require plaintiff's counsel to agree not to disclose the terms of the settlement (for example, by sharing this information with other plaintiffs' lawyers who are handling similar cases). A defendant could also require plaintiff's counsel to turn over any discovery materials produced during the litigation. While counsel could then request such materials

200. See Arthur R. Miller, Confidentiality, Protective Orders, and Public Access to the Courts, 105 Harv. L. Rev. 427 (1991).

201. S.C. R. Civ. Proc. 41.1; Tex. R. Civ. P. 76a.

202. Fla. Stat. Ann. §69.081.

203. Susan P. Koniak, Are Agreements to Keep Secret Information Learned in Discovery Legal, Illegal, or Something in Between?, 30 Hofstra L. Rev. 783 (2002).

204. See Stephen Gillers, Speak No Evil: Settlement Agreements Conditioned on Noncooperation are Illegal and Unethical, 31 Hofstra L. Rev. 1, 4 (2002).

in future litigation, the defendant would have control of the materials in the interim.

=================== **Problem 4-6** ===================

Mediation and Arbitration

a. You represent Martinez Data Systems, Inc. (MDS), a closely held corporation that provides computer consulting services to a wide variety of clients. Raymond Martinez, the president of the company, has asked you to prepare a basic consulting contract that MDS can use when it enters into agreements with customers. In addition to reviewing MDS's current contract, you have researched various form books and checklists for ideas regarding the agreement. One issue raised in the form books is whether the agreement should include some form of alternative dispute resolution provision. Would you suggest that MDS consider including such a provision? If so, what advice would you give if Martinez asked for your recommendation regarding alternative dispute resolution?

b. A partner in your firm has been appointed as a mediator in a divorce case pursuant to court rules that call for court-annexed mediation in domestic cases. Court rules require the mediator to hold an orientation session in which the mediator explains the nature of the process to the parties and their lawyers. The partner has asked you to prepare a draft statement that he will use as the basis of his opening remarks.

Read Model Rules 1.1, 1.2, 1.4, 1.12, 2.1, 2.4, and comments.

Alternative dispute resolution in general

While *alternative dispute resolution* (ADR) is a rapidly growing field, most students still have little exposure to the area. We begin, then, with some basic ideas about ADR as an introduction to and background for discussion of several ethical issues. As you study this material, keep in mind that negotiation is one of the most important forms of ADR. We have already studied some of the major ethical problems in negotiation in Problem 4-5.

Alternative dispute resolution refers to various procedures other than litigation for resolving disputes.[205] The interest in and use of ADR has grown

---

205. See Stephen B. Goldberg et al., Dispute Resolution: Negotiation, Mediation, and Other Processes (3d ed. 1999) (with bibliography); Thomas H. Oehmke, Oehmke Commercial Arbitration (2003); Nancy H. Rogers & Craig A. McEwen, Mediation: Law, Policy & Practice (2d ed. 1994).

rapidly in recent years as public and professional dissatisfaction with delay, expense, and inflexibility of the judicial system has increased. ADR comes in a wide variety of forms and procedures.

The most common forms of ADR are *arbitration* and *mediation*. In arbitration a dispute is presented to a neutral decisionmaker (or to a panel of decisionmakers) who has the authority to render a decision that is binding on the parties. Many controversies are submitted to arbitration pursuant to agreement of the parties. Agreements to arbitrate fall into two categories: predispute and postdispute. In predispute agreements, the parties contractually agree to submit to arbitration any disputes (or perhaps a defined category of disputes) that may arise in their relationship in the future. For example, the parties to a long-term supply contract could agree that if a dispute arises regarding performance of the agreement, the dispute will be submitted to arbitration. In postdispute arbitration agreements, the parties agree to submit to arbitration a controversy that has already arisen. For example, parties involved in a minor automobile accident could agree to submit their dispute to arbitration.

Controversies can also be submitted to arbitration by court rule rather than by agreement of the parties. A growing number of state and federal courts have adopted rules for court-annexed arbitration under which disputes that meet certain requirements are sent to arbitration.

Arbitration procedures and methods of selection of the arbitrators vary depending on how the arbitration arises. In court-annexed arbitration, court rules determine the procedure to be employed and the method of selection of the arbitrators. In predispute and postdispute agreements to arbitrate, the parties must specify the procedures to be used and the method of selection of the arbitrators. The disputants can, however, adopt rules of procedure prepared by private providers of arbitration services, such as the American Arbitration Association.

The fundamental difference between mediation and arbitration is that mediators do not have the power to render decisions that are binding on the parties. Instead, mediators attempt to assist the parties in reaching an agreement. This one difference, however, affects the entire process. Mediation tends to be more informal, with the mediator meeting both individually and collectively with the parties to gather information, gain understanding of the positions of the parties, and explore ideas for settlement. Arbitration, although less formal than adjudication, still usually involves adversarial presentations by the parties, often in the format of a traditional trial or hearing.

While arbitration and mediation are the most common forms of ADR, many other hybrid forms have been developed. For example, in *med-arb* the parties agree to mediation, but also agree that if mediation is unsuccessful for a certain period of time, the matter is then submitted to binding arbitration. Parties have used *summary jury trials* and *minitrials* to gain information about the likely result if their dispute were submitted to trial, but without the delay and expense involved in a full-fledged trial. The information gained from these mock trials often leads to a negotiated settlement. Indeed, parties have virtually unlimited flexibility to create dispute resolution mechanisms tailored to their particular needs.[206]

Ethical obligations of lawyers to advise clients regarding ADR

Do lawyers have an ethical obligation to advise clients of the availability of ADR? Prior to the 2002 amendments, the Model Rules did not specifically require lawyers to advise clients of ADR options, although a number of commentators argued that such a requirement was implicit in the lawyer's general duty to counsel, reflected in Rules 1.2(a), 1.4(b), and 2.1.[207] See also Rule 3.2 requiring lawyers to make reasonable efforts to expedite litigation consistent with the client's interests. Comment 5 to Model Rule 2.1, as amended in 2002, provides as follows: "[W]hen a matter is likely to involve litigation, it may be necessary under Rule 1.4 to inform the client of forms of dispute resolution that might constitute reasonable alternatives to litigation." While the comment does not mandate that lawyers advise clients about ADR alternatives, the language is more than precatory.[208] It should encourage lawyers who are not already familiar with ADR to begin to educate themselves so that they can properly advise their clients.

Model Rule 1.1 requires lawyers to provide competent representation to their clients. In advising clients regarding ADR, competent lawyers must be aware of and must be able to explain to their clients the advantages and disadvantages of ADR. Consider the following exchange on the advantages and disadvantages of arbitration:

> The scene is the law offices of Howland and Smith, a firm with 200 lawyers, including a large litigation section. Jane Garrity, a litigator, and Jim Smith, the firm's alternative dispute resolution specialist, are discussing how to handle a pending case involving one of Howland and Smith's clients, Bramson Ball Bearing Company. Bramson had sold 50,000 ball bearings to Jones Machine Company,

---

206. See A Guide to Dispute Resolution Processes in ABA Section of Dispute Resolution, Dispute Resolution Ethics 445-449 (Phyllis Bernard & Bryant Garth, eds. 2002). For principles for organizations that provide ADR services, see CPR-Georgetown Principles for ADR Provider Organizations (2002) in *Dispute Resolution Ethics*, above, Appendix G.

207. See, e.g., Marshall J. Breger, Should an Attorney Be Required to Advise a Client of ADR Options?, 13 Geo. J. Legal Ethics 427 (2000). Some commentators have argued that lawyers could be subject to professional discipline or malpractice liability for failure to advise their clients about ADR. See Robert F. Cochran, Jr., Legal Representation and the Next Steps Toward Client Control: Attorney Malpractice for the Failure to Allow the Client to Control Negotiation and Pursue Alternatives to Litigation, 47 Wash. & Lee L. Rev. 819 (1990).

208. Douglas H. Yarn, Lawyer Ethics in ADR and the Recommendations of Ethics 2000 to Revise the Model Rules of Professional Conduct: Considerations for Adoption and State Application, 54 Ark. L. Rev. 207, 251 (2001).

a long-time customer, which Jones refused to pay for, claiming they were defective. Bramson denies any defects in the ball bearings and has asked Howland and Smith to bring suit against Jones for $75,000, the amount Jones had agreed to pay.

Smith: Jane, it seems to me this case would be ideal for arbitration. As you know we've got a three- or four-year delay before trial, and Bramson really wants to get its money. If we go to arbitration, we could wind this case up in six or seven months instead of waiting three or four years and then getting a settlement on the courthouse steps or going through litigation and a lengthy appeal. Moreover, there are likely to be difficult technical issues in connection with Jones's claim that the ball bearings were defective. If we go to court, we might have trouble explaining those issues to a judge or jury, but if we go to arbitration, we can choose an arbitrator with technical expertise.

Garrity: You ADR people are always singing the same tune: anything is better than the courts. My experience is that arbitration leaves a lot to be desired. First, it's not that easy to find a competent arbitrator. A lot of them really don't know what they're doing, and in the end they just split the difference.

Smith: I think you're too cynical about our ability to find a good arbitrator. For example, if you contact the American Arbitration Association or the Center for Public Resources they will send both parties a list of proposed arbitrators, with background material on each. Each party can strike one name from the list and rank the others in order of preference. The AAA or CPR will appoint the highest mutual choice. Other dispute resolution organizations follow similar procedures to assist disputing parties in selecting a high-quality arbitrator.

Garrity: That's fine *if* the list of arbitrators they send you has high-quality people on it, but I've heard that's not always so. Then there's no appeal; if you get a bum award, one that's based on a misapplication of the law or is contrary to the weight of the evidence, you're just stuck with it.

Smith: But how important, as a practical matter, is a right of appeal in a case like this? Not only would an appeal add to our costs, but this is a straight breach of contract case with no novel legal issues. The likelihood that an appellate court would reverse the trial court in a case like this is surely not very substantial. From that perspective, it really doesn't matter much whether we're in court or before an arbitrator.

Garrity: Maybe you're right about that, but I think that the knowledge that an appellate court may be reviewing what he does motivates the trial judge to perform to the best of his ability. That's largely missing in arbitration, where there is no meaningful judicial review.

Smith: But if we're careful in selecting the arbitrator, that's much less of a concern. Besides, what we give up in terms of a right to appeal, we gain in finality. You've told me that we have a strong case here, and if we win we won't have to worry about Jones dragging things out by taking an appeal. They could, but the likelihood of success would be so low that it's not probable that they would.

Garrity: Well, I do think that we have a winner, but you never know what an arbitrator or judge, much less a jury, will do to you. That brings me to my next concern about going to arbitration. If I lose a case in court, I can blame the judge. But if we go to arbitration, and I've participated in selecting the arbitrator, I'm likely to get the blame if we lose. So while you praise arbitration because you can pick the arbitrator, that doesn't have much appeal to me.

Smith: Well, if you don't want to select the arbitrator, turn the entire selection procedure over to AAA or CPR. That way you can't be held responsible for who the arbitrator is.

Garrity: That's a possible approach, but I'm not comfortable with turning the selection process completely over to someone else.

Smith: But that's exactly what you do when you go to court! Still, I do have another approach for you. You could pick one arbitrator, the other side could pick one, and those two could agree on a third arbitrator. That would increase costs somewhat, but it would give you some input in selecting the crucial member of the panel. It would also ensure that at least one of the arbitrators is sympathetic to your arguments.

Garrity: No, that's even worse than a single arbitrator. In addition to tripling the costs, a three-person panel more than triples the delays associated with arbitration. It's hard enough to find mutually agreeable hearing dates when you have to work with the schedules of two busy lawyers and one arbitrator: it's almost impossible if you add two more arbitrators. And, speaking of delay, I've heard of cases in which the defendant has tied up an arbitration almost indefinitely by running to court whenever there is some procedural dispute.

Smith: I'm aware of cases like that, too, but they tend to be limited to situations in which arbitration takes place under a preexisting contractual commitment to arbitrate. Those commitments are usually honored, but sometimes when a dispute actually arises, one party sees an advantage in litigation rather than arbitration. In that situation, the reluctant party may resist arbitration in every way it can, including going to court to complain of alleged procedural irregularities in the arbitration. If, however, both parties voluntarily agree to arbitration at the time the dispute arises, neither of them is likely to go to court to block arbitration. In that situation, which is what we will have here if Bramson and Jones agree to arbitrate, a skilled arbitrator can dispose of the case quickly and effectively.

Garrity: That's another problem. Those buzz words "quickly" and "effectively" mean something different to me—namely, that there's no attention paid to the rules of evidence. In arbitration they use the "kitchen sink" approach: everything goes in.

Smith: Well, that's probably an overstatement. There are some arbitrators, particularly those who are lawyers, who are quite strict about what evidence they will admit. If you want an arbitrator like that, you can select one. Alternatively, you can provide that the arbitrator must abide by whatever evidentiary rules you adopt. I just can't emphasize strongly enough that the arbitration format is entirely within the control of the parties. You can make the arbitration as formal or informal, as much or as little like a federal court procedure as you wish. Just because you contact some arbitration agency to select the arbitrator and administer the proceedings doesn't mean you must adopt their rules. That's one of the virtues of arbitration, and I wish that more people would take advantage of it.

Still, I would not advise altering standard arbitration practice in this case. You are right in assuming that the general tendency of arbitrators is not to apply the rules of evidence strictly. As I see it, though, that's a plus for arbitration, not a minus. I've long found the rules of evidence to be a major cause of unnecessarily lengthy trials. Some trial lawyers even say that the rules don't always keep evidence out: they just ensure that it takes longer to get it in, particularly in a jury trial. Surely there are simpler ways of establishing the facts, and that's just what arbitration or a properly run bench trial does: it makes it possible to get to the heart of the matter quickly and without a lot of procedural folderol.

There's one other argument in favor of arbitration that we haven't talked about yet, and that is its privacy. This case involves Jones's complaints about the quality of Bramson's ball bearings, and I doubt that Bramson is very happy at the prospect of Jones spreading those complaints all over the court records, so any newspaper reporter who is interested can write about them. If we go to arbitration, the proceedings will be entirely private, and so will the arbitrator's decision.

Garrity: That's a nice point, but I have still another concern. There's a lot we don't know about this case yet. If we go to arbitration, won't we lose the discovery opportunities we'd have in court?

Smith: Once again, that depends on you and the other party. If you want some discovery, it's important to provide for it in your agreement to arbitrate. If you don't, you may not get any more than the other side will agree to, since many arbitrators will not compel discovery to which either party objects.

My advice on this point would be to provide for only as much discovery as you absolutely need to prepare for trial. One of the things that makes arbitration attractive is that discovery has gotten completely out of hand in court. If we were to go through normal court discovery in this case, say four or five depositions, plus the five or so days you've told me it should take to try it, that could cost Jones as much as $50,000. That just doesn't make sense in a case with a maximum recovery of $75,000. I'm sure that in arbitration, if we could agree on limited discovery—say, two depositions each—and then a skilled arbitrator who didn't waste time by strictly applying the rules of evidence and following formal court room procedures, we could try this case in a maximum of two days at a cost of approximately $20,000. Even adding the arbitrator's fee and an administrative fee for the organization supplying the arbitrator, which together would probably be less than $2,500, we'd still come out way ahead, and we wouldn't have to worry about the costs of an appeal. That's why I think it makes sense to arbitrate this case, not to litigate it. Indeed, I almost think that an attorney who doesn't at least advise his client about the alternatives to litigation for resolving disputes might be guilty of malpractice. So I think you should raise this possibility with Bramson, and if they are interested, discuss it with Jones's lawyer. You might even be surprised to find him receptive to this idea.[209]

The advantages and disadvantages of ADR depend, of course, on the type of ADR under consideration.[210] Some scholars have criticized the growing use of ADR.[211] In particular, the fairness of mediation, especially in divorce cases involving an imbalance of power between husband and wife, has been questioned.[212]

Ethical obligations of lawyers serving as mediators and arbitrators

With the growth of ADR it appears likely that lawyers will increasingly be called on to serve as mediators or arbitrators of disputes. What are the ethical obligations governing lawyers serving as "neutrals"?[213] The 1983 version of the Model Rules barely mentioned the role of lawyers in ADR. The Ethics 2000 Commission received proposals for an extensive rule regulating and providing

209. Stephen B. Goldberg et al., Dispute Resolution: Negotiation, Mediation, and Other Processes 212-215 (4th ed. 2003), adapted from 75-June A.B.A. J. 70 (1989).

210. On the advantages and disadvantages of mediation, see Rogers & McEwen, Mediation: Law, Policy & Practice ch. 3. See also Special Issue, The Mediation Alternative, 49 Disp. Resol. J. 1 (March 1994).

211. See, e.g., Lisa Bernstein, Understanding the Limits of Court-Annexed ADR: A Critique of Federal Court-Annexed Arbitration Programs, 141 U. Pa. L. Rev. 2169 (1993); Carrie Menkel-Meadow, Do the "Haves" Come out Ahead in Alternative Judicial Systems?: Repeat Players in ADR, 15 Ohio St. J. on Disp. Resol. 19 (1999).

212. See Trina Grillo, The Mediation Alternative: Process Dangers for Women, 100 Yale L.J. 1545 (1991); Scott H. Hughes, Elizabeth's Story: Exploring Power Imbalances in Divorce Mediation, 8 Geo. J. Legal Ethics 553 (1995). But see Craig A. McEwen et al., Bring in the Lawyers: Challenging the Dominant Approaches to Ensuring Fairness in Divorce Mediation, 79 Minn. L. Rev. 1317 (1995) (arguing that lawyer-participant mandatory mediation in divorce cases properly balances fairness and efficiency considerations).

213. See ABA Section of Dispute Resolution, Dispute Resolution Ethics (Phyllis Bernard & Bryant Garth, eds. 2002). See also Symposium, The Lawyer's Duties and Responsibilities in Dispute Resolution, 38 S. Tex. L. Rev. 375 (1997).

guidance to lawyers who serve as neutrals.[214] The Commission rejected this approach, principally for two reasons. First, the Commission had adopted a "minimalist" philosophy for its revision project. Second, many nonlawyers serve as neutrals. A new model rule would only apply to lawyers, leading to possibly different or inconsistent standards between lawyer and nonlawyer neutrals.[215] The 2002 amendments to the Model Rules do, however, contain several provisions dealing with the role of lawyers as neutrals. The Preamble to the Model Rules explicitly recognizes that many lawyers provide services in the capacity of neutrals. Preamble ¶3. See also Model Rule 2.4(a) and comment 1. New Model Rule 2.4 imposes minimal obligations when a lawyer serves in the role of a neutral. Rule 2.4(a) defines the role without imposing any ethical obligations. Rule 2.4(b) requires the lawyer neutral to inform unrepresented parties that the neutral does not represent them. When the lawyer neutral knows or reasonably should know that a party to ADR does not understand the difference between the lawyer's role as a neutral and the lawyer's role as an attorney, the lawyer is required to explain the differences, including the inapplicability of the attorney-client privilege. See comment 3.

Comment 4 to Rule 2.4 refers to Model Rule 1.12 for conflicts of interest involving former neutrals. Under Rule 1.12(a) a former neutral, whether an arbitrator, mediator, or some other capacity, cannot personally represent anyone in connection with the same matter in which the attorney participated personally and substantially as a neutral unless all parties give their informed consent, confirmed in writing.[216] However, other members of the neutral's firm may undertake such representation without the necessity of consent provided the neutral is appropriately screened from any participation in the matter. See Model Rule 1.12(c).

The revised Model Rules also contain provisions dealing with the ethical obligations of attorneys who represent clients in ADR proceedings (as opposed to the ethical obligations of the neutral, who does not represent a client). As already mentioned, comment 5 to Model Rule 2.1 states that it may be necessary

214. See CPR-Georgetown Commission on Ethics and Standards in ADR, Proposed Model Rule of Professional Conduct for the Lawyer as Third Party Neutral (1999). See also Judith L. Maute, Public Values and Private Justice: A Case for Mediator Accountability, 4 Geo. J. Legal Ethics 503 (1991) (proposing rule for lawyers serving as mediators).

215. For a discussion of the 2002 amendments to the Model Rules dealing with ADR see Douglas H. Yarn, Lawyer Ethics in ADR and the Recommendations of Ethics 2000 to Revise the Model Rules of Professional Conduct: Considerations for Adoption and State Application, 54 Ark. L. Rev. 207 (2001). For criticism of the minimalist approach adopted by the Ethics 2000 Commission and discussion of many ethical issues that the Commission has left unresolved, see Carrie Menkel-Meadow, The Lawyer as Consensus Builder: Ethics for a New Practice, 70 Tenn. L. Rev. 63 (2002). The Restatement provides even more limited treatment than the revised Model Rules of ADR. See Carrie Menkel-Meadow, The Silences of the Restatement of the Law Governing Lawyers: Lawyering as Only Adversary Practice, 10 Geo. J. Legal Ethics 631 (1997).

216. See Poly Software International, Inc. v. Su, 880 F. Supp. 1487 (D. Utah 1995) (disqualifying lawyer who had served as mediator in intellectual property matter from representing one party against another party in subsequent substantially related proceeding).

for lawyers to counsel clients about ADR options. Comment 5 to Rule 2.4 states that the rules of professional conduct applicable to attorneys control in ADR proceedings, although it draws an interesting and somewhat controversial distinction. If the ADR proceeding is before a "tribunal" the duty of candor set forth in Model Rule 3.3 applies. If the proceeding is not before a tribunal, Rule 4.1 applies. The definition of tribunal in Model Rule 1.0(m) includes arbitration proceedings but excludes mediation. Thus, Rule 4.1 rather than Rule 3.3 applies to mediations. The duty of candor in Rule 3.3 is broader than the duty of candor in Rule 4.1 in several respects. Rule 3.3 prohibits a lawyer from knowingly making any misrepresentation. In Rule 4.1, the prohibition is only as to a material misrepresentation. Rule 4.1 allows lawyers to engage in a certain amount of puffing, while puffing before a tribunal is improper. Rule 3.3 imposes disclosure obligations on lawyers in certain situations, for example, when the lawyer or the lawyer's client has offered false testimony and the lawyer comes to know of the falsity. Disclosure obligations in Rule 4.1 are more limited.

The Model Rules do not exhaust the ethical obligations of lawyers serving as neutrals. Some courts have promulgated rules of ethics for neutrals who serve in court-annexed ADR.[217] Both lawyers and nonlawyers serving as neutrals pursuant to such rules are obviously bound to comply with these provisions. Several private organizations that sponsor or support ADR have issued codes of ethics for lawyers and nonlawyers serving as neutrals. While not legally binding unless adopted by a law-making body, they provide guidance to neutrals, and compliance with these standards is usually a condition of membership in the organization. Some of the more important codes of ethics issued by private organizations are the following:

> Association of Family and Concilliation Courts et al., Standards of Practice for Family and Divorce Mediation (2000)[218]
> American Arbitration Association, American Bar Association, and Society of Professionals in Dispute Resolution, Standards of Conduct for Mediators (1995)[219]
> American Arbitration Association and American Bar Association, Code of Ethics for Arbitrators in Commercial Disputes (2003)[220]

---

217. See Robert B. Moberly, Ethical Standards for Court-Appointed Mediators and Florida's Mandatory Mediation Experiment, 21 Fla. St. U. L. Rev. 701 (1994). On the legal liability of court-appointed mediators, see Wagshal v. Foster, 28 F.3d 1249 (D.C. Cir. 1994) *cert. denied*, 514 U.S. 1004 (1995) (quasi-judicial absolute immunity for court-appointed mediators and neutral case evaluators).

218. See ⟨http://www.mediate.com/articles/afccstds.cfm⟩ (visited Aug. 26, 2003). For the history of the drafting of the standards, see ⟨http://www.mediate.com/articles/afccstds1.cfm⟩ (visited Aug. 26, 2003).

219. ⟨http://www.abanet.org/dispute/webpolicy.html#8⟩ (visited Aug. 26, 2003).

220. ⟨http://www.abanet.org/dispute/commercial_disputes.pdf⟩ (visited Aug. 26, 2003).

Society of Professionals in Dispute Resolution (SPIDR), Ethical Standards of Professional Responsibility (1986)[221]

The Standards of Practice for Family and Divorce Mediation provide as follows (Detailed Standards are included for Standard III but are omitted for other standards.):

Standard I

A family mediator shall recognize that mediation is based on the principle of self-determination by the participants.

Standard II

A family mediator shall be qualified by education and training to undertake the mediation.

Standard III

A family mediator shall facilitate the participants' understanding of what mediation is and assess their capacity to mediate before the participants reach an agreement to mediate.

A. Before family mediation begins a mediator should provide the participants with an overview of the process and its purposes, including:

1. informing the participants that reaching an agreement in family mediation is consensual in nature, that a mediator is an impartial facilitator, and that a mediator may not impose or force any settlement on the parties;
2. distinguishing family mediation from other processes designed to address family issues and disputes;
3. informing the participants that any agreements reached will be reviewed by the court when court approval is required;
4. informing the participants that they may obtain independent advice from attorneys, counsel, advocates, accountants, therapists or other professionals during the mediation process;
5. advising the participants, in appropriate cases, that they can seek the advice of religious figures, elders or other significant persons in their community whose opinions they value;
6. discussing, if applicable, the issue of separate sessions with the participants, a description of the circumstances in which the mediator may meet alone with any of the participants, or with any third party and the conditions of confidentiality concerning these separate sessions;

---

221. The SPIDR has merged into the Association for Conflict Resolution. The Ethical Standards are under revisions. ⟨http://www.acresolution.org/research.nsf/articles/6CC4296D791D451485256C1C00657E59⟩ (visited Aug. 26, 2003).

7. informing the participants that the presence or absence of other persons at a mediation, including attorneys, counselors or advocates, depends on the agreement of the participants and the mediator, unless a statute or regulation otherwise requires or the mediator believes that the presence of another person is required or may be beneficial because of a history or threat of violence or other serious coercive activity by a participant;

8. describing the obligations of the mediator to maintain the confidentiality of the mediation process and its results as well as any exceptions to confidentiality;

9. advising the participants of the circumstances under which the mediator may suspend or terminate the mediation process and that a participant has a right to suspend or terminate mediation at any time.

B. The participants should sign a written agreement to mediate their dispute and the terms and conditions thereof within a reasonable time after first consulting the family mediator.

C. The family mediator should be alert to the capacity and willingness of the participants to mediate before proceeding with the mediation and throughout the process. A mediator should not agree to conduct the mediation if the mediator reasonably believes one or more of the participants is unable or unwilling to participate.

D. Family mediators should not accept a dispute for mediation if they cannot satisfy the expectations of the participants concerning the timing of the process.

Standard IV

A family mediator shall conduct the mediation process in an impartial manner. A family mediator shall disclose all actual and potential grounds of bias and conflicts of interest reasonably known to the mediator. The participants shall be free to retain the mediator by an informed, written waiver of the conflict of interest. However, if a bias or conflict of interest clearly impairs a mediator's impartiality, the mediator shall withdraw regardless of the express agreement of the participants.

Standard V

A family mediator shall fully disclose and explain the basis of any compensation, fees and charges to the participants.

Standard VI

A family mediator shall structure the mediation process so that the participants make decisions based on sufficient information and knowledge.

Standard VII

A family mediator shall maintain the confidentiality of all information acquired in the mediation process, unless the mediator is permitted or required to reveal the information by law or agreement of the participant.

Standard VIII

A family mediator shall assist participants in determining how to promote the best interests of children.

Standard IX

A family mediator shall recognize a family situation involving child abuse or neglect and take appropriate steps to shape the mediation process accordingly.

Standard X

A family mediator shall recognize a family situation involving domestic abuse and take appropriate steps to shape the mediation process accordingly.

Standard XI

A family mediator shall suspend or terminate the mediation process when the mediator reasonably believes that a participant is unable to effectively participate or for other compelling reasons.

Standard XII

A family mediator shall be truthful in the advertisement and solicitation for mediation.

Standard XIII

A family mediator shall acquire and maintain professional competence in mediation.

Because arbitrators, unlike mediators, have the power to render binding decisions, concerns about impartiality or conflicts of interest may be more worrisome in arbitration proceedings than in mediations. Canon II of the Code of Ethics for Arbitrators in Commercial Disputes of the American Arbitration Association and the American Bar Association (2003) provides as follows: "An arbitrator should disclose any interest or relationship likely to affect impartiality or which might create an appearance of partiality." Disclosure is required for the following:

(1) Any known direct or indirect financial or personal interest in the outcome of the arbitration; (2) Any known existing or past financial, business, professional or personal relationships which might reasonably affect impartiality or lack of independence in the eyes of any of the parties . . . ; (3) The nature and extent of any prior knowledge they may have of the dispute; and (4) Any other matters, relationships, or interests which they are obligated to disclose by the agreement of the parties, the rules or practices of an institution, or applicable law regulating arbitrator disclosure.[222]

222. For the text of the Code see the URL cited in note 220 above.

An arbitrator's failure to disclose facts that could affect the arbitrator's impartiality will not necessarily invalidate an award. In Commonwealth Coatings Corp. v. Continental Casualty Co.[223] the Supreme Court invalidated an arbitration award under section 10 of the United States Arbitration Act, 9 U.S.C. §10, which provides that a court may vacate an award "[w]here there was evident partiality or corruption in the arbitrators, or either of them."[224] In that case the neutral arbitrator (the one selected by the arbitrators chosen by each of the parties) was an engineering consultant who had substantial business ties with one of the parties. The arbitrator failed to disclose the relationship. The Court vacated the award, but the basis for its decision is obscure. Four Justices held that the award should be set aside because arbitrators, like judges, should disclose even the "slightest pecuniary interest."[225] Two concurring Justices disagreed with the plurality opinion that arbitrators should be treated like judges, but they agreed that the award should be set aside when the arbitrator failed to disclose a substantial interest.[226] Three dissenting Justices would have upheld the award because there was no evidence of "evident partiality" as required by the act. The award was unanimous and the nondisclosure was innocent.

By contrast, in Merit Insurance Co. v. Leatherby Insurance Co.[227] the Seventh Circuit refused to set aside an arbitration award in which the arbitrator failed to disclose that he had worked under the president and principal stockholder of one of the parties. The employment ended more than 10 years before the arbitration; both the president and the arbitrator testified that they had had little professional contact and no social contact.[228] The arbitrator had failed, however, to list the employment on forms required by the American Arbitration Association and he did not mention the relationship when the arbitration began even though he recognized the president.[229] Writing for the court, Judge Posner rejected Leatherby's argument that an arbitrator should be disqualified if his relationship with one of the parties was more than "trivial." Judge Posner noted that there were substantial differences between arbitration and litigation involving a trade-off between expertise and neutrality. In arbitration proceedings, parties select arbitrators because of their expertise; this necessitates a lessened expectation of impartiality. Accordingly, Posner adopted the following test for disqualification of arbitrators:

---

223. 393 U.S. 145 (1968).
224. In addition to the federal arbitration act, most states have enacted arbitration statutes. Some state statutes and case law are more restrictive of arbitration than the federal act. The Supreme Court has broadly construed the federal act to preempt state law and to apply to the full extent of the Commerce Clause whenever a transaction affects interstate commerce, regardless of whether the parties contemplated an interstate transaction. See Allied-Bruce Terminix Cos. v. Dodson, 513 U.S. 265 (1995).
225. 393 U.S. at 148.
226. Id. at 150-152.
227. 714 F.2d 673 (7th Cir.), *cert. denied*, 464 U.S. 1009 (1983).
228. 714 F.2d at 677.
229. Id. at 678.

[T]he test in this case is not whether the relationship was trivial; it is whether, having due regard for the different expectations regarding impartiality that parties bring to arbitration than to litigation, the relationship . . . was so intimate— personally, socially, professionally, or financially—as to cast serious doubt on [the arbitrator's] impartiality.[230]

Considering all the facts involved, particularly the passage of time, the court found no basis for disqualification of the arbitrator.

Moreover, the court went on to hold that even if the arbitrator had violated applicable ethical standards, that would not necessarily result in judicial nullification of the award. Citing section 10 of the United States Arbitration Act, the court ruled that the standard of "evident partiality or corruption" was more demanding than the ethical standard and required either proof of actual bias or at least that the "circumstances must be powerfully suggestive of bias."[231]

C. Delivery of Legal Services in Civil Cases

1. *Advertising and Solicitation*

—————————— Problem 4-7 ——————————
Law Firm Marketing Practices

a. You are a member of a small, aggressive plaintiff's firm, Minelli & O'Hara, that wants to expand its personal injury and products liability practice. The firm plans to run a series of television advertisements. Each ad will begin with a lawyer sitting on the side of his desk (in shirt-sleeves to convey the image of being hardworking), saying the following:

If you have been injured in an accident or while at work, we at Minelli & O'Hara are available to meet with you to discuss your legal rights. There is no charge for an initial visit and no fees are due unless we secure a recovery on your behalf.

After the introduction, the ad will have a "How we're different" segment. The following are four of the segments that the firm plans to run:

(1) "How we're different: We have a proven record of success. Unlike other firms, we survey our clients on completion of our services. More than

_____

230. Id. at 680.
231. Id. at 681. See also Montez v. Prudential Securities, Inc., 260 F.3d 980 (8th Cir. 2001) (holding that a federal court cannot vacate an arbitration award under the Federal Arbitration Act for violation of NASD disclosure rules and discussing different standards adopted by circuit courts as to meaning of "evident partiality").

95 percent of our clients are extremely satisfied or very satisfied with our work."

(2)   "How we're different: We offer discount fees. Most firms charge one-third or more to handle your case. At Minelli & O'Hara we will represent you for a 25 percent fee."

(3)   "How we're different: With most other firms, you must wait until settlement or judgment to get any money. At Minelli & O'Hara, if your case is one of clear liability, we can help you get money within 60 days."

(4)   "How we're different: Unmatched experience. Members of our firm have clerked for state court judges, served in the legislature, and worked for the Worker's Compensation Commission."

Each ad concludes: "Minelli and O'Hara, The Different Law Firm, call us at 1-800-MONEYNOW."

In addition to the television advertising, the firm will acquire names and addresses of victims from police department accident reports, which are a matter of public record. It will then send letters to individuals involved in accidents informing them that the firm is available for consultation about their legal rights arising out of the accident.

The firm would like your opinion about the ethical propriety of these plans.

b.   Because of the increased competitive environment for the practice of law, many law firms have begun aggressive marketing programs. The following is a list of some of the ways in which law firms are now marketing their services. Be prepared to discuss the ethical propriety or risks involved in these activities.

1.   News releases highlighting activities of members of the firm, including recent litigation successes.
2.   Client surveys to determine client needs and degree of satisfaction with the firm.
3.   Cross-marketing, which involves contacting existing clients to advise them of services offered by the firm that the client is not currently using.
4.   Client audits, in which the firm volunteers to audit the client's legal affairs searching for potential problems, at no cost or reduced cost to the client.
5.   Offering to conduct a "mock trial" of a client's troublesome case to assist the client and current outside counsel to appraise the case.
6.   Preparation of law firm brochures showing the backgrounds and areas of practice of the members of the firm along with a list of clients regularly represented.
7.   Newsletters to current and potential clients advising them of recent developments of interest.

8. Sponsorship of seminars, to which potential clients are personally invited, on various legal topics presented by members of the firm.

9. Hiring public relations firms and marketing directors to develop the firm's marketing program.

10. Aggressive entertainment policies in which members of the firm invite officials of existing clients to accompany them on expense-paid trips.

11. Development of strategic alliances with other firms to refer and accept referrals in areas of expertise.

12. Creation of sophisticated Web pages that provide information about members of the firm and material about areas of law in which the firm practices (both directly and through links to other sites). Many Web pages are interactive, allowing potential clients to make inquiries, to send information by completing forms on the Web page, and to arrange for electronic appointments. In addition, lawyers are participating in chat rooms and other real-time methods of communication with potential clients.

   c. Reginald Nason is the owner of the Nason Law Firm, which principally handles plaintiffs' cases arising out of mass disasters, such as hotel fires and plant explosions. The firm has created several television advertisements that it has available to run whenever a mass disaster occurs. Each of the ads begins with a dramatization and is followed by a client testimonial, like the following:

> I'm Helen Andrews, and in 1999 I was almost killed in an explosion at the plant where I worked. I was in the hospital for more than three months. You wouldn't believe what the insurance company offered me. It was ridiculous. I went to Reginald Nason. He and the lawyers in his firm took my case to trial and I got twice as much as the insurance company offered me. The lawyers at the Nason Law Firm were there when I needed them.

   In addition to television advertising, Nason takes other steps to obtain business whenever a mass disaster occurs. Shortly after a disaster takes place, Nason rents space at a hotel and conducts a seminar entitled, for example, "The Henderson Plant Explosion—Your Legal Rights." Nason advertises the seminar extensively on radio and television. At the seminar Nason and other members of his firm make presentations and provide materials to attendees. Nason and other members of his firm do not approach attendees personally, but Nason states publicly that he invites attendees to call his office for an appointment. The firm's business cards are readily available at the seminar.

   A disciplinary proceeding has been filed against Nason for violation of the jurisdiction's rules regulating advertising and solicitation. Nason denies that he has violated the rules, but he also contends that, even if he did, his television advertising and seminars are constitutionally protected. Be prepared to discuss the issues involved in this proceeding.

Read Model Rules 7.1, 7.2, 7.3, 7.4, 7.5, and comments.

Model Rules 7.1 through 7.5 regulate information about legal services.[232] Rule 7.1 prohibits false and misleading communications, regardless of form. Rule 7.2 deals with advertising, communications directed to the public at large rather than specific people. Solicitation is the subject of Rule 7.3. Solicitation differs from advertising in that it is directed to specific people. The rule distinguishes between solicitation involving personal contact, Rule 7.3(a), and "direct mail" solicitation, Rule 7.3(c). Rule 7.4 deals with communications regarding fields of practice or specialization, while Rule 7.5 deals with firm names and letterheads. Supreme Court decisions dealing with the constitutionality of rules of ethics that restrict lawyers from communicating information about their services have shaped the content of the Model Rules; review of these decisions is essential to understanding the Model Rules.

Basic constitutional principles governing regulation of lawyer advertising

Lawyers have long recognized that the practice of law is both a business and a profession and that success in the practice requires lawyers to be able to attract clients. The traditional view expressed by the profession, however, has been that commercial advertising or solicitation is unprofessional. Under this view, lawyers should attract clients through reputation rather than through marketing. Canon 27 of the original Canon of Ethics, adopted by the American Bar Association in 1908, provided as follows: "[S]olicitation of business by circulars or advertisements, or by personal communications, or interviews, not warranted by personal relations, is unprofessional."

During the last 30 years, however, the Supreme Court has established and expanded the constitutional right of lawyers to market their legal services. The genesis of this protection was the Court's decision in Virginia State Board of Pharmacy v. Virginia Citizens Consumer Council, Inc.[233] In *Virginia Pharmacy* the Court rejected the commercial speech exception to the First Amendment and held that commercial speech was entitled to some measure of First Amendment protection. The Court in *Virginia Pharmacy* reserved judgment, however, on whether its decision applied to other professions.

---

232. For discussion of the lack of enforcement of the advertising rules, the effect this has on the profession, and the lessons that rule drafters and disciplinary officials can learn, see Fred C. Zacharias, What Lawyers Do When Nobody's Watching: Legal Advertising as a Case Study of the Impact of Underenforced Professional Rules, 87 Iowa L. Rev. 971 (2002).

233. 425 U.S. 748 (1976).

One year later, in Bates v. State Bar of Arizona,[234] the Court applied its holding in *Virginia Pharmacy* to lawyer advertising. In March 1974 two Arizona lawyers left their positions with the legal services program in Phoenix and opened a "legal clinic" through which they offered legal services at modest fees to people of moderate income. After two years, they decided that their practice could not survive unless they attracted a larger clientele. To do so, they began advertising in one of the Phoenix newspapers, offering to provide various services for specified fees, including uncontested divorce, adoption, nonbusiness bankruptcy, and change of name. The Arizona Supreme Court censured the lawyers for conduct in violation of its code of professional responsibility. The United States Supreme Court reversed.

The question in *Bates* was whether the Arizona Supreme Court could constitutionally discipline lawyers for violating its code of professional responsibility by making *truthful* newspaper advertisements about the *price* and *availability* of certain routine legal services. The Court noted that the consumer's interest in commercial speech is substantial and "often may be far keener than his concern for urgent political dialogue."[235] Further, commercial speech serves important societal interests by informing the public of the availability, nature, and prices of products and services.[236] The Court held that such advertising was constitutionally protected under the First Amendment and could not be prohibited by the state.[237] In its opinion, the Court considered and rejected six justifications offered by the state of Arizona to support its ban on advertising of legal services: the adverse effect on professionalism, the inherently misleading nature of attorney advertising, the adverse effect on the administration of justice, the undesirable economic effects of advertising, the adverse effect of advertising on the quality of service, and the difficulties of enforcement.[238]

The Court in *Bates* was careful, however, to indicate the limitations of its opinion. First, the decision did not prevent state regulation of false, deceptive, or misleading advertising.[239] The Court reserved judgment on claims about

234. 433 U.S. 350 (1977).
235. Id. at 364.
236. Id.
237. Id. at 383.
238. Id. at 368-379. For articles discussing the policy issues involved in lawyer advertising, see Geoffrey C. Hazard, Jr. et al., Why Lawyers Should Be Allowed to Advertise: A Market Analysis of Legal Services, 58 N.Y.U. L. Rev. 1084 (1983); see also Richard J. Cebula, Does Lawyer Advertising Adversely Influence the Image of Lawyers in the United States? An Alternative Perspective and New Empirical Evidence, 27 J. Legal Stud. 503 (1998) (multiple regression study used to show that lawyer advertising enhances public image of profession); William E. Hornsby, Jr., Ad Rules Infinitum: The Need for Alternatives to State-Based Ethics Governing Legal Services Marketing, 36 U. Rich. L. Rev. 49 (2002). In 1995 the ABA issued a comprehensive report on lawyer advertising, ABA Commission on Advertising, Lawyer Advertising at the Crossroads (1995). The report outlines 18 considerations and 40 strategies to guide policymakers in dealing with the complex array of issues involved in lawyer advertising and solicitation.
239. 433 U.S. at 383. See, e.g., In re Zang, 741 P.2d 267 (Ariz. 1987) (en banc), *cert. denied*, 484 U.S. 1067 (1988) (lawyers disciplined for misrepresentation in advertisements

the quality of legal services: "[A]dvertising claims as to the quality of services—a matter we do not address today—are not susceptible of measurement or verification; accordingly, such claims may be so likely to be misleading as to warrant restriction."[240] Second, in-person solicitation posed unique problems that might warrant restriction. Third, the Court left open the possibility that warning or supplementation might be required, even as to advertising like that involved in *Bates*, to prevent consumers from being misled. Fourth, like other forms of speech, a state may impose reasonable "time, place, and manner" restrictions. Fifth, advertising concerning illegal transactions could be prohibited. Finally, "the special problems of advertising on the electronic broadcast media will warrant special consideration."[241]

In In re R. M. J.,[242] the Court broadened its holding in *Bates*, setting forth general principles for determining the constitutionality of restrictions on lawyer advertising. After the Supreme Court's decision in *Bates*, the Missouri Supreme Court amended its Code of Professional Responsibility to allow some lawyer advertising, but the rules continued to limit advertising to a significant degree. The rules allowed lawyers to publish in the print media 10 categories of information: name, address, and telephone number; areas of practice; date and place of birth; schools attended; foreign language ability; office hours; fee for an initial consultation; availability of a schedule of fees; credit arrangements; and the fixed fee to be charged for certain specified "routine" legal services. The state supreme court and the advisory committee charged with enforcing the rules interpreted them to mean that these 10 categories were exclusive; lawyers could not advertise information beyond these categories. The Missouri rules also placed specific restrictions on the ways in which lawyers could advertise the areas in which they practiced.

Relying on its decision in Central Hudson Gas & Electric Corp. v. Public Service Commission,[243] the Court articulated three principles to be used in determining the constitutionality of restrictions on legal advertising:

- A state may constitutionally prohibit lawyers from engaging in false or inherently misleading advertising or "when experience has proven that in fact such advertising is subject to abuse."
- A state may not prohibit advertising that is potentially misleading, but may regulate such advertising by a method "no broader than reasonably

---

regarding ability and willingness to take cases to trial); Musselwhite v. State Bar of Tex., 786 S.W.2d 437 (Tex. Ct. App. 1990, writ denied), *cert. denied*, 501 U.S. 1251 (1991) (letters and advertisement soliciting claims of foreign tort victims were false and misleading in various respects, including suggestion that lawyer already had clients arising out of incident in question and prediction of high recoveries in American courts). For a survey of cases see Jason B. Lutz, Comment, Attorney Advertising and Disciplinary Action: Some Do's and Dont's of Advertising, 25 J. Legal Prof. 183 (2001).

240. 433 U.S. at 383-384.
241. Id.
242. 455 U.S. 191 (1982).
243. 447 U.S. 557 (1980).

necessary to prevent the deception," such as by explanation or disclaimer.

• States retain the right to regulate truthful advertising in some limited circumstances if the state establishes "a substantial interest and the interference with speech must be in proportion to the interest served."[244]

The Court then considered three charges against R. M. J. in light of these principles: listing the areas of his practice in language or in terms other than those provided by the rule; listing the courts and states in which he had been admitted to practice; and mailing announcement cards to persons other than "lawyers, clients, former clients, personal friends, and relatives." (R. M. J. conceded the constitutionality of the disclaimer requirement.) The Court found that none of the charges could be upheld constitutionally. None of the advertisements were false or inherently misleading, and the state failed to present any substantial state interest to justify the restrictions.[245]

In *Bates* and *R.M.J.*, the Court had indicated that states remained free to prohibit lawyers from engaging in false or misleading advertising, but the Court did not address what types of advertisements fell within those categories. In Peel v. Attorney Registration & Disciplinary Commission[246] the Court considered whether a lawyer's identification as a "certified civil trial specialist" was false and misleading when the state did not recognize certification of civil trial specialists, but the certification was issued by a bona fide organization with demanding standards, the National Board of Trial Advocacy. The State of Illinois contended that the use of the term "certified specialist" was inherently misleading and could therefore be prohibited, but the Supreme Court in a 5-4 decision disagreed. The Court agreed that if certifications were issued for a fee by organizations that did not enforce standards, a state could prohibit their use because they would be misleading, but the Court found that the NBTA certification was not misleading.[247] The Court considered the state's argument that the statement was, if not actually misleading, at least potentially misleading. The Court then referred to its earlier decisions holding that when statements are potentially misleading, the remedy is not outright ban but required disclaimer or disclosure.

Basic constitutional principles governing regulation of in-person solicitation by lawyers

Bates and *R. M. J.* dealt with the constitutionality of restrictions on lawyer advertising. In companion cases—Ohralik v. Ohio State Bar Assn.[248] and In re

---

244. 455 U.S. at 203.
245. Id. at 205-207.
246. 496 U.S. 91 (1990).
247. Id. at 101-102.
248. 436 U.S. 447 (1978).

Primus[249]—the Court established constitutional principles governing in-person solicitation. *Ohralik* involved a classic case of "ambulance chasing." In casual conversation at a post office, attorney Ohralik heard about an automobile accident involving two young women. He telephoned the parents of the driver, learned that she was in the hospital, visited with the parents, and then met with their daughter in the hospital, where he offered to represent her on a contingency fee basis. Ohralik also contacted the passenger and volunteered to represent her as well. During these meetings, Ohralik secretly tape recorded the conversations. After both girls had signed contingency fee agreements, they decided that they did not want Ohralik to represent them, but he insisted that they were bound by their agreements with him.

The Supreme Court of Ohio indefinitely suspended Ohralik for solicitation of professional employment in violation of the Ohio Code of Professional Responsibility. The Supreme Court affirmed. The Court rejected Ohralik's argument that under the First Amendment in-person solicitation was entitled to the same degree of protection as advertising. Instead, the Court found that in-person solicitation was distinguishable from advertising because it involved conduct as well as speech:

> In-person solicitation by a lawyer of remunerative employment is a business transaction in which speech is an essential but subordinate component. While this does not remove the speech from the protection of the First Amendment, as was held in *Bates* and *Virginia Pharmacy*, it lowers the level of appropriate judicial scrutiny.[250]

As a result, the state could constitutionally prevent solicitation in furtherance of important state interests. The Court found—indeed Ohralik conceded—that the state had an important interest in preventing those aspects of solicitation that involve fraud, undue influence, intimidation, overreaching, and other forms of "vexatious conduct."[251]

In re Primus[252] involved a radically different situation from *Ohralik*. Primus practiced with a public interest law firm that was affiliated with the American Civil Liberties Union; she also served as a lawyer for the South Carolina Council on Human Relations, a nonprofit organization. During the summer of 1973, local and national newspapers had reported that pregnant women in Aiken, South Carolina, were being sterilized as a condition for receiving continued medical benefits under the Medicaid program. Primus spoke at a meeting arranged by the Council on Human Relations to women who had been steril-

---

249. 436 U.S. 412 (1978).

250. 436 U.S. at 457.

251. Id. at 462. A recent example of improper solicitation is In re Ravich, Koster, Tobin, Oleckna, Reitman & Greenstein, 715 A.2d 216 (N.J. 1998) (lawyers and law firm disciplined for solicitation after gas line explosion by setting up RV with signs across from emergency shelter, for conducting seminar in shelter, and for personal offers to provide legal services).

252. 436 U.S. 412 (1978).

ized, including Mary Etta Williams. Ms. Primus informed the attendees of their legal rights, including the right to sue any doctor who had engaged in sterilization. Subsequently, the ACLU advised Ms. Primus that it was willing to provide representation to mothers in Aiken who had been sterilized. A representative of the Council on Human Relations told Ms. Primus that Ms. Williams wanted to bring suit. After Primus received this information, she wrote Williams a letter informing her of the ACLU's willingness to represent her in a suit against the doctor who had performed the sterilization.

The South Carolina Supreme Court publicly reprimanded Primus for solicitation in violation of the Code of Professional Responsibility. The Supreme Court reversed. The Court distinguished *Ohralik*. While *Ohralik* had involved solicitation for pecuniary gain, *Primus* involved solicitation for political purposes. In NAACP v. Button[253] and subsequent cases, the Court had held that under the associational freedom guaranteed by the First Amendment, organizations such as the NAACP could solicit clients as part of "collective activity undertaken to obtain meaningful access to the courts." The Court found that there was not a "meaningful distinction" between the ACLU and the NAACP.[254] In particular, the Court rejected the argument that the ACLU should be treated differently from the NAACP under the First Amendment because the ACLU has as one of its primary purposes the rendering of legal services and because the ACLU has a policy of seeking the award of attorney fees.[255] Since Primus's solicitation came within the core of First Amendment protection, the Court ruled that she could be disciplined only if South Carolina established a compelling state interest and only if the means used were "closely drawn to avoid unnecessary abridgment of associational freedoms."[256] While the state could apply a prophylactic rule in commercial solicitation cases like *Ohralik,* in political solicitation cases like *Primus* the state must show actual injury.[257] The Court found that the state had failed to establish that any such injury occurred.[258]

The Court has not addressed the constitutionality of restrictions on in-person solicitation since the *Ohralik* and *Primus* cases, but several questions remain unanswered. In *Ohralik* the Court held that a state could adopt a per se rule prohibiting in-person commercial solicitation. By contrast, in *Primus* the Court held that solicitation by letter by a lawyer affiliated with a bona fide organization devoted to civil liberties (the ACLU) for the purpose of providing access to legal services rather than for commercial gain could not be prohibited unless the state showed actual harm resulting from the solicitation. It is unclear whether solicitation lacking some of the elements of *Primus* would be subject to the actual harm standard or to a per se rule. Suppose Primus had engaged

---

253. 371 U.S. 415 (1963).
254. 436 U.S. at 426-427.
255. Id. at 427-429.
256. Id. at 432.
257. Id. at 434-435.
258. Id.

in solicitation in person rather than by letter? Or suppose Primus had been a member of a public interest law firm that was not affiliated with an organization like the ACLU?

Another issue dealing with the scope of the constitutional protection afforded in-person solicitation deals with what Justice Marshall in *Ohralik* called "benign" solicitation:

> By "benign" commercial solicitation, I mean solicitation by advice and informa-
> tion that is truthful and that is presented in a noncoercive, nondeceitful, and
> dignified manner to a potential client who is emotionally and physically capable
> of making a rational decision either to accept or reject the representation with
> respect to a legal claim or matter that is not frivolous.[259]

The Court in *Ohralik* was not required to address the constitutionality of benign solicitation because the case dealt with in-person solicitation under circumstances where actual overreaching was likely to occur and did in fact take place.

In Edenfield v. Fane[260] the Court considered the constitutionality of a Florida Board of Accountancy rule prohibiting in-person solicitation by accoun-tants. In holding the rule unconstitutional, the Court pointed out that *Ohralik* did not hold that a state may constitutionally prohibit all in-person solicitation, but only in-person solicitation in situations "inherently conducive to overreach-ing and other forms of misconduct."[261] The Court struck down the Accountancy rule, but it distinguished accountants from lawyers on two grounds. First, "[u]nlike a lawyer, a CPA is not 'a professional trained in the art of persuasion.' " Second, the "typical client of a CPA is far less susceptible to manipulation than the young accident victim in *Ohralik*."[262] The Court, however, might apply the *Edenfield* approach if a lawyer solicited a sophisticated client rather than someone like the accident victim in *Ohralik*.[263]

Application and development: targeted and direct mail advertising

In subsequent cases, the Court has refined the application of the principles established in *Bates, R. M. J., Ohralik,* and *Primus.* The type of advertising that came before the Court in *Bates* and in *R.M.J.* was relatively bland. In a series of cases, however, a sharply divided Supreme Court has considered the

---

259. 436 U.S. at 472 n.3.
260. 507 U.S. 761 (1993).
261. Id. at 774.
262. Id. at 775. For a criticism of the Court's distinction between lawyers and accountants, see Jeffrey M. Brandt, Note, Attorney In-Person Solicitation: Hope for a New Direction and Supreme Court Protection after Edenfield v. Fane, 25 U. Tol. L. Rev. 783 (1994).
263. Rule 7.1(b) of the District of Columbia Rules of Professional Conduct allows lawyers to engage in benign solicitation. For an argument in support of this approach, see Kristina N. Bailey, Note, "Rainmaking" and D.C. Rule of Professional Conduct 7.1: The In-Person Solicitation of Clients, 9 Geo. J. Legal Ethics 1335 (1996).

issue of the constitutionality of restrictions on targeted advertising, that is, advertising that deals with particular types of litigation, and direct mail advertising.

Zauderer v. Office of Disciplinary Counsel[264] involved the constitutionality of restrictions on targeted advertising. Zauderer ran advertisements in Ohio newspapers publicizing his availability to represent, on a contingent fee basis, women who had been injured from using the Dalkon Shield contraceptive device. The advertisement included a drawing of the device with the question "DID YOU USE THIS IUD?"[265]

Before the Supreme Court, the State of Ohio conceded that Zauderer's Dalkon Shield advertisement was not false or misleading. Instead, it tried to justify discipline on three grounds. First, the state argued that Zauderer's advertisement should be treated the same as the in-person solicitation in *Ohralik,* subject to a prophylactic rule. The Court rejected this argument. The Court found that the concerns that supported the Court's decision in *Ohralik*— the possibility of overreaching coupled with the difficulty of enforcement—were not present when the lawyer used targeted advertising.[266] Second, the state argued that it could constitutionally prohibit the advertisement because it had a substantial interest in preventing lawyers from "stirring up litigation." In words that are sure to resonate with plaintiffs' lawyers, the Court stated: "[W]e cannot endorse the proposition that a lawsuit, as such, is an evil."[267] Finally, the Court found the state's claim of regulatory difficulties to be unpersuasive as a justification for prohibiting Zauderer's advertisement.[268]

The Court also held that illustrations were entitled to the same constitutional protection afforded textual communications, rejecting the argument that the state had a substantial interest in prohibiting the use of illustrations in order to uphold the dignity of the profession. After noting that there was no suggestion that Zauderer's illustration was undignified, the Court's opinion swept more broadly:

> [A]lthough the State undoubtedly has a substantial interest in ensuring that its attorneys behave with dignity and decorum in the courtroom, we are unsure that the State's desire that attorneys maintain their dignity in their communications with the public is an interest substantial enough to justify the abridgment of their First Amendment rights. Even if that were the case, we are unpersuaded that undignified behavior would tend to recur so often as to warrant a prophylactic rule.[269]

The Court also rejected Ohio's argument that the prohibition on illustrations was justified in that illustrations were misleading because they operate on an emotional or subconscious level:

264. 471 U.S. 626 (1985).
265. Id. at 630.
266. Id. at 641-642.
267. Id. at 643.
268. Id. at 645-646.
269. Id. at 647-648.

We are not convinced. The State's arguments amount to little more than unsupported assertions: nowhere does the State cite any evidence or authority of any kind for its contention that the potential abuses associated with the use of illustrations in attorneys' advertising cannot be combated by any means short of a blanket ban.[270]

In one respect, however, the Court found that Zauderer was subject to discipline. The Ohio Supreme Court had found that Zauderer violated its Code of Professional Responsibility by failing to disclose to potential clients that they would be liable for the expenses of litigation, even though they would not be liable for legal fees unless they obtained a recovery. The Court noted that "unjustified or unduly burdensome disclosure requirements might offend the First Amendment by chilling protected commercial speech." The Court ruled, however, that disclosure requirements, unlike prohibitions, were subject to less scrutiny and would be upheld "as long as [the] requirements are reasonably related to the State's interest in preventing deception of consumers."[271] The Court found that "the requirement that an attorney advertising his availability on a contingent-fee basis disclose that clients will have to pay costs even if their lawsuits are unsuccessful (assuming that to be the case) easily passes muster under this standard."[272]

In Shapero v. Kentucky Bar Assn.[273] the Court considered the constitutionality of restrictions on "direct mail advertising" by lawyers. Shapero applied to the Kentucky Attorneys Advertising Commission for permission to send the following letter to individuals against whom foreclosure proceedings had been instituted:

> It has come to my attention that your home is being foreclosed on. If this is true, you may be about to lose your home. Federal law may allow you to keep your home by ORDERING your creditor [*sic*] to STOP and give you more time to pay them.
>
> You may call my office anytime from 8:30 A.M. to 5:00 P.M. for FREE information on how you can keep your home.
>
> Call NOW, don't wait. It may surprise you what I may be able to do for you. Just call and tell me that you got this letter. Remember it is FREE, there is NO charge for calling.[274]

The matter ultimately went to the Kentucky Supreme Court. The Court found that Shapero's letter violated its Rule 7.3, which prohibited lawyers from engaging in solicitation and defined solicitation to include a "letter . . . directed to a specific recipient."[275]

---

270. Id. at 648.
271. Id. at 651.
272. Id. at 652.
273. 486 U.S. 466 (1988).
274. Id. at 469.
275. Id. at 471.

The Supreme Court granted certiorari and reversed. Characterizing the case as nothing more than "*Ohralik* in writing," the State of Kentucky contended that Shapero's letter could be prohibited without a showing of actual harm because of the serious potential for abuse involved in solicitation. Finding that this suggestion "misses the mark," the Court pointed out that the ban on solicitation approved in *Ohralik* rested on two fundamental differences between advertising and solicitation. First, the in-person character of solicitation creates a situation "rife with possibilities for overreaching, invasion of privacy, the exercise of undue influence, and outright fraud." Second, solicitation poses unique enforcement difficulties because it is "not visible or otherwise open to public scrutiny." The Court found that targeted direct mail advertising was different from in-person solicitation in both respects.[276]

The Court recognized that direct mail advertising could be subject to abuse: Recipients might overestimate the lawyer's familiarity with their problem or mistakenly assume that they have a legal problem (or a more serious legal problem) when this is not the case. The Court concluded, however, that these possibilities justified regulation, not prohibition; it suggested that states consider requiring lawyers to file their direct mail advertisements with a state agency to provide time and opportunity to review such mailings and consider forcing lawyers to identify direct mailings as "advertising material."[277] The Court also pointed out that states could discipline lawyers for false or deceptive statements in direct mail advertising just as in media or print advertising, but it found nothing in the record to support the conclusion that Shapero's advertisement was overreaching or deceptive.[278]

In a dissenting opinion in *Shapero*, Justice O'Connor criticized the line of decisions beginning with *Bates* because they failed to take into account fundamental differences between professional services and standardized consumer products. She also argued that the Court's decisions had failed to give sufficient weight to the substantial state interest in maintaining professional standards. She concluded: "In one way or another, time will uncover the folly of this approach. I can only hope that the Court will recognize the danger before it is too late to effect a worthwhile cure."[279]

Justice O'Connor's call in *Shapero* for a change in direction by the Supreme Court may have become a reality in the Court's decision in Florida Bar v. Went For It, Inc.

276. Id. at 475.
277. Id. at 476-477.
278. Id. at 478-480.
279. Id. at 491.

Florida Bar v. Went for It, Inc.

United States Supreme Court
515 U.S. 618 (1995)

JUSTICE O'CONNOR delivered the opinion of the Court.

Rules of the Florida Bar prohibit personal injury lawyers from sending targeted direct-mail solicitations to victims and their relatives for 30 days following an accident or disaster. This case asks us to consider whether such Rules violate the First and Fourteenth Amendments of the Constitution. We hold that in the circumstances presented here, they do not.

I

In 1989, the Florida Bar (Bar) completed a 2-year study of the effects of lawyer advertising on public opinion. After conducting hearings, commissioning surveys, and reviewing extensive public commentary, the Bar determined that several changes to its advertising rules were in order. In late 1990, the Florida Supreme Court adopted the Bar's proposed amendments with some modifications. . . . Two of these amendments are at issue in this case. Rule 4-7.4(b)(1) provides that "[a] lawyer shall not send, or knowingly permit to be sent, . . . a written communication to a prospective client for the purpose of obtaining professional employment if: (A) the written communication concerns an action for personal injury or wrongful death or otherwise relates to an accident or disaster involving the person to whom the communication is addressed or a relative of that person, unless the accident or disaster occurred more than 30 days prior to the mailing of the communication." Rule 4-7.8(a) states that "[a] lawyer shall not accept referrals from a lawyer referral service unless the service: (1) engages in no communication with the public and in no direct contact with prospective clients in a manner that would violate the Rules of Professional Conduct if the communication or contact were made by the lawyer." Together, these Rules create a brief 30-day blackout period after an accident during which lawyers may not, directly or indirectly, single out accident victims or their relatives in order to solicit their business.

In March 1992, G. Stewart McHenry and his wholly owned lawyer referral service, Went For It, Inc., filed this action for declaratory and injunctive relief in the United States District Court for the Middle District of Florida challenging Rules 4-7.4(b)(1) and 4-7.8(a) as violative of the First and Fourteenth Amendments to the Constitution. McHenry alleged that he routinely sent targeted solicitations to accident victims or their survivors within 30 days after accidents and that he wished to continue doing so in the future. Went For It, Inc., represented that it wished to contact accident victims or their survivors within 30 days of accidents and to refer potential clients to participating Florida lawyers. In October 1992, McHenry was disbarred for reasons unrelated to this suit, . . . Another Florida lawyer, John T. Blakely, was substituted in his stead. . . .

II

A

Constitutional protection for attorney advertising, and for commercial speech generally, is of recent vintage. Until the mid-1970's, we adhered to the broad rule laid out in Valentine v. Chrestensen, 316 U.S. 52 (1942), that, while the First Amendment guards against government restriction of speech in most contexts, "the Constitution imposes no such restraint on government as respects purely commercial advertising." In 1976, the Court changed course. In Virginia Bd. of Pharmacy v. Virginia Citizens Consumer Council, Inc., 425 U.S. 748, we invalidated a state statute barring pharmacists from advertising prescription drug prices. At issue was speech that involved the idea that " 'I will sell you the X prescription drug at the Y price.' " Id., at 761. Striking the ban as unconstitutional, we rejected the argument that such speech "is so removed from 'any exposition of ideas,' and from 'truth, science, morality, and arts in general, in its diffusion of liberal sentiments on the administration of Government,' that it lacks all protection." Id., at 762 (citations omitted).

In *Virginia Bd.*, the Court limited its holding to advertising by pharmacists, noting that "[p]hysicians and lawyers . . . do not dispense standardized products; they render professional *services* of almost infinite variety and nature, with the consequent enhanced possibility for confusion and deception if they were to undertake certain kinds of advertising." Id., at 773, n. 25. (emphasis in original). One year later, however, the Court applied the *Virginia Bd.* principles to invalidate a state rule prohibiting lawyers from advertising in newspapers and other media. In Bates v. State Bar of Arizona [433 U.S. 350 (1977)], the Court struck a ban on price advertising for what it deemed "routine" legal services: "the uncontested divorce, the simple adoption, the uncontested personal bankruptcy, the change of name, and the like." 433 U.S., at 372. Expressing confidence that legal advertising would only be practicable for such simple, standardized services, the Court rejected the State's proffered justifications for regulation.

Nearly two decades of cases have built upon the foundation laid by *Bates*. It is now well established that lawyer advertising is commercial speech and, as such, is accorded a measure of First Amendment protection. See, e.g., Shapero v. Kentucky Bar Assn., 486 U.S. 466, 472 (1988); Zauderer v. Office of Disciplinary Counsel of Supreme Court of Ohio, 471 U.S. 626, 637 (1985); In re R.M.J., 455 U.S. 191, 199 (1982). Such First Amendment protection, of course, is not absolute. We have always been careful to distinguish commercial speech from speech at the First Amendment's core. " '[C]ommercial speech [enjoys] a limited measure of protection, commensurate with its subordinate position in the scale of First Amendment values,' and is subject to 'modes of regulation that might be impermissible in the realm of noncommercial expression.' " Board of Trustees of State Univ. of N.Y. v. Fox, 492 U.S. 469, 477 (1989), quoting Ohralik v. Ohio State Bar Assn., 436 U.S. 447, 456 (1978). . . .

Mindful of these concerns, we engage in "intermediate" scrutiny of restrictions on commercial speech, analyzing them under the framework set forth in Central Hudson Gas & Elec. Corp. v. Public Serv. Comm'n of N.Y., 447 U.S. 557 (1980). Under *Central Hudson*, the government may freely regulate commercial speech that concerns unlawful activity or is misleading. Id., at 563-564. Commercial speech that falls into neither of those categories, like the advertising at issue here, may be regulated if the government satisfies a test consisting of three related prongs: First, the government must assert a substantial interest in support of its regulation; second, the government must demonstrate that the restriction on commercial speech directly and materially advances that interest; and third, the regulation must be " 'narrowly drawn.' " Id., at 564-565.

B

"Unlike rational basis review, the *Central Hudson* standard does not permit us to supplant the precise interests put forward by the State with other suppositions," Edenfield v. Fane, 507 U.S. 761, 768 (1993). The Bar asserts that it has a substantial interest in protecting the privacy and tranquility of personal injury victims and their loved ones against intrusive, unsolicited contact by lawyers. . . . This interest obviously factors into the Bar's paramount (and repeatedly professed) objective of curbing activities that "negatively affec[t] the administration of justice." . . . Because direct-mail solicitations in the wake of accidents are perceived by the public as intrusive, the Bar argues, the reputation of the legal profession in the eyes of Floridians has suffered commensurately. See Pet. for Cert. 14-15; Brief for Petitioner 28-29. The regulation, then, is an effort to protect the flagging reputations of Florida lawyers by preventing them from engaging in conduct that, the Bar maintains, " 'is universally regarded as deplorable and beneath common decency because of its intrusion upon the special vulnerability and private grief of victims or their families.' " Brief for Petitioner 28, quoting In re Anis, 126 N.J. 448, 458, 599 A.2d 1265, 1270 (1992).

We have little trouble crediting the Bar's interest as substantial. On various occasions we have accepted the proposition that "States have a compelling interest in the practice of professions within their boundaries, and . . . as part of their power to protect the public health, safety, and other valid interests they have broad power to establish standards for licensing practitioners and regulating the practice of professions." Goldfarb v. Virginia State Bar, 421 U.S. 773, 792 (1975). . . . Our precedents also leave no room for doubt that "the protection of potential clients' privacy is a substantial state interest." See *Edenfield*, supra, 507 U.S., at 769.

Under *Central Hudson*'s second prong, the State must demonstrate that the challenged regulation "advances the Government's interest 'in a direct and material way.' " Rubin v. Coors Brewing Co., 514 U.S. 476, 487 (1995), quoting *Edenfield*, supra, 507 U.S., at 767. That burden, we have explained, " 'is not satisfied by mere speculation or conjecture; rather, a governmental body seeking to sustain a restriction on commercial speech must demonstrate that the harms it recites are real and that its restriction will in fact alleviate them to a material degree.' " 514 U.S., at 487, quoting *Edenfield*, supra, 507 U.S., at 770-771. In *Edenfield*, the Court invalidated a Florida ban on in-person solicitation by certified public accountants (CPA's). We observed that the State Board of Accountancy had "present[ed] no studies that suggest personal solicitation of prospective business clients by CPA's creates the dangers of fraud, overreaching, or compromised independence that the Board claims to fear." 507 U.S. at 771. Moreover, "[t]he record [did] not disclose any anecdotal evidence, either from Florida or another State, that validate[d] the Board's suppositions." Ibid. In fact, we concluded that the only evidence in the record tended to "contradic[t], rather than strengthe[n], the Board's submissions." Id. at 772. Finding nothing in the record to substantiate the State's allegations of harm, we invalidated the regulation.

The direct-mail solicitation regulation before us does not suffer from such infirmities. The Bar submitted a 106-page summary of its 2-year study of lawyer advertising and solicitation to the District Court. That summary contains data—both statistical and anecdotal—supporting the Bar's contentions that the Florida public views direct-mail solicitations in the immediate wake of accidents as an intrusion on privacy that reflects poorly upon the profession. As of June 1989, lawyers mailed 700,000 direct solicitations in Florida annually, 40% of which were aimed at accident victims or their survivors. . . . A survey of Florida adults commissioned by the Bar indicated that Floridians "have negative feelings about those attorneys who use direct mail advertising." Magid Associates, Attitudes & Opinions Toward Direct Mail Advertising by Attorneys (Dec. 1987), Summary of Record, App. C(4), p. 6. Fifty-four percent of the general population surveyed said that contacting persons concerning accidents or similar events is a violation of privacy. Id. at 7. A random sampling of persons who received direct-mail advertising from lawyers in 1987 revealed that 45% believed that direct-mail solicitation is "designed to take advantage of gullible or unstable people"; 34% found such tactics "annoying or irritating"; 26% found it "an invasion of your privacy"; and 24% reported that it "made you angry." Ibid. Significantly, 27% of direct-mail recipients reported that their regard for the legal profession and for the judicial process as a whole was "lower" as a result of receiving the direct mail. Ibid.

The anecdotal record mustered by the Bar is noteworthy for its breadth and detail. With titles like "Scavenger Lawyers" (The Miami Herald, Sept. 29, 1987) and "Solicitors Out of Bounds" (St. Petersburg Times, Oct. 26, 1987), newspaper editorial pages in Florida have burgeoned with criticism of Florida lawyers who send targeted direct mail to victims shortly after accidents. . . . see also Peltz, Legal Advertising—Opening Pandora's Box, 19 Stetson L. Rev. 43, 116 (1989) (listing Florida editorials critical of direct-mail solicitation of accident victims in 1987, several of which are referenced in the record). The study summary also includes page upon page of excerpts from complaints of direct-mail recipients. For example, a Florida citizen described how he was " 'appalled and angered by the brazen attempt' " of a law firm to solicit him by letter shortly after he was injured and his fiancee was killed in an auto accident. Summary of Record, App. I(1), p. 2. Another found it " 'despicable and inexcusable' " that a Pensacola lawyer wrote to his mother three days after his father's funeral. Ibid. Another described how she was " 'astounded' " and then " 'very angry' " when she received a solicitation following a minor accident. Id. at 3. Still another described as " 'beyond comprehension' " a letter his nephew's family received the day of the nephew's funeral. Ibid. One citizen wrote, " 'I consider the unsolicited contact from you after my child's accident to be of the rankest form of ambulance chasing and in incredibly poor taste. . . . I cannot begin to express with my limited vocabulary the utter contempt in which I hold you and your kind.' " Ibid.

In light of this showing—which respondents at no time refuted, save by the conclusory assertion that the Rule lacked "any factual basis," . . . we conclude that the Bar has satisfied the second prong of the *Central Hudson* test. In dissent, Justice Kennedy complains that we have before us few indications of the sample size or selection procedures employed by Magid Associates (a nationally renowned consulting firm) and no copies of the actual surveys employed. . . . As stated, we believe the evidence adduced by the Bar is sufficient to meet the standard elaborated in Edenfield v. Fane, 507 U.S. 761 (1993). In any event, we do not read our case law to require that empirical data come to us accompanied by a surfeit of background information. Indeed, in other First Amendment contexts, we have permitted litigants to justify speech restrictions by reference to studies and anecdotes pertaining to different locales altogether, . . . Nothing in *Edenfield*, a case in which the State offered *no* evidence or anecdotes in support of its restriction, requires more. After scouring the record, we are satisfied that the ban on direct-mail solicitation in the immediate aftermath of accidents, unlike the rule at issue in *Edenfield*, targets a concrete, nonspeculative harm.

In reaching a contrary conclusion, the Court of Appeals determined that this case was governed squarely by Shapero v. Kentucky Bar Assn., 486 U.S. 466 (1988). Making no mention of the Bar's study, the court concluded that " 'a targeted letter [does not] invade the recipient's privacy any more than does a substantively identical letter mailed at large. The invasion, if any, occurs when the lawyer discovers the recipient's legal affairs, not when he confronts the recipient with the discovery.' " 21 F.3d, at 1044, quoting *Shapero*, supra 486 U.S. at 476. In many cases, the Court of Appeals explained, "this invasion of privacy will involve no more than reading the newspaper." 21 F.3d, at 1044.

While some of *Shapero*'s language might be read to support the Court of Appeals' interpretation, *Shapero* differs in several fundamental respects from the case before us. First and foremost, *Shapero*'s treatment of privacy was casual. Contrary to the dissent's suggestions, . . . the State in *Shapero* did not seek to justify its regulation as a measure undertaken to prevent lawyers' invasions of privacy interests. . . . Rather, the State focused exclusively on the special dangers of overreaching inhering in targeted solicitations. . . . Second, in contrast to this case, *Shapero* dealt with a broad ban on *all* direct-mail solicitations, whatever the time frame and whoever the recipient. Finally, the

State in *Shapero* assembled no evidence attempting to demonstrate any actual harm caused by targeted direct mail. The Court rejected the State's effort to justify a prophylactic ban on the basis of blanket, untested assertions of undue influence and overreaching. 486 U.S., at 475. Because the State did not make a privacy-based argument at all, its empirical showing on that issue was similarly infirm.

We find the Court's perfunctory treatment of privacy in *Shapero* to be of little utility in assessing this ban on targeted solicitation of victims in the immediate aftermath of accidents. While it is undoubtedly true that many people find the image of lawyers sifting through accident and police reports in pursuit of prospective clients unpalatable and invasive, this case targets a different kind of intrusion. The Bar has argued, and the record reflects, that a principal purpose of the ban is "protecting the personal privacy and tranquility of [Florida's] citizens from crass commercial intrusion by attorneys upon their personal grief in times of trauma." Brief for Petitioner 8; cf. Summary of Record, App. I(1) (citizen commentary describing outrage at lawyers' timing in sending solicitation letters). The intrusion targeted by the Bar's regulation stems not from the fact that a lawyer has learned about an accident or disaster (as the Court of Appeals notes, in many instances a lawyer need only read the newspaper to glean this information), but from the lawyer's confrontation of victims or relatives with such information, while wounds are still open, in order to solicit their business. In this respect, an untargeted letter mailed to society at large is different in kind from a targeted solicitation; the untargeted letter involves no willful or knowing affront to or invasion of the tranquility of bereaved or injured individuals and simply does not cause the same kind of reputational harm to the profession unearthed by the Bar's study.

[The Court then distinguished Bolger v. Youngs Drug Products Corp., 463 U.S. 60 (1983), which held that direct mail advertisements for contraceptives were constitutionally protected in part because the recipient could simply throw the advertisement away.] Here, in contrast, the harm targeted by the Bar cannot be eliminated by a brief journey to the trash can. The purpose of the 30-day targeted direct-mail ban is to forestall the outrage and irritation with the state-licensed legal profession that the practice of direct solicitation only days after accidents has engendered. The Bar is concerned not with citizens' "offense" in the abstract, . . . but with the demonstrable detrimental effects that such "offense" has on the profession it regulates. See Brief for Petitioner 7, 14, 24, 28. Moreover, the harm posited by the Bar is as much a function of simple receipt of targeted solicitations within days of accidents as it is a function of the letters' contents. Throwing the letter away shortly after opening it may minimize the latter intrusion, but it does little to combat the former. . . .

Passing to *Central Hudson*'s third prong, we examine the relationship between the Bar's interests and the means chosen to serve them. See Board of Trustees of State Univ. of N.Y. v. Fox, 492 U.S., at 480. With respect to this prong, the differences between commercial speech and noncommercial speech are manifest. In *Fox,* we made clear that the "least restrictive means" test has no role in the commercial speech context. Ibid. "What our decisions require," instead, "is a 'fit' between the legislature's ends and the means chosen to accomplish those ends," a fit that is not necessarily perfect, but reasonable; that represents not necessarily the single best disposition but one whose scope is 'in proportion to the interest served,' that employs not necessarily the least restrictive means but . . . a means narrowly tailored to achieve the desired objective." Ibid. (citations omitted). Of course, we do not equate this test with the less rigorous obstacles of rational basis review. . . .

Respondents levy a great deal of criticism, echoed in the dissent, . . . at the scope of the Bar's restriction on targeted mail. "[B]y prohibiting written communications to all people, whatever their state of mind," respondents charge, the Rule "keeps useful information from those accident victims who are ready, willing and able to utilize a lawyer's advice." Brief for Respondents 14. This criticism may be parsed into two components. First, the Rule does not distinguish between victims in terms of the severity of their injuries. According to respondents, the Rule is unconstitutionally overinclusive insofar as it bans targeted mailings even to citizens whose injuries or grief are relatively minor. Id. at 15. Second, the Rule may prevent citizens from learning about their legal options, particularly at a time when other actors—opposing counsel and insurance adjusters—may be clamoring for victims' attentions. Any benefit arising from the Bar's regulation, respondents implicitly contend, is outweighed by these costs.

We are not persuaded by respondents' allegations of constitutional infirmity. We find little deficiency in the ban's failure to distinguish among injured Floridians by the severity of their pain or the intensity of their grief. Indeed, it is hard to imagine the contours of a regulation that might satisfy respondents on this score. Rather than drawing difficult lines on the basis that some injuries are "severe" and some situations appropriate (and others, presumably, inappropriate) for grief, anger, or emotion, the Bar has crafted a ban applicable to all postaccident or disaster solicitations for a brief 30-day period. Unlike respondents, we do not see "numerous and obvious less-burdensome alternatives" to Florida's short temporal ban. . . . The Bar's rule is reasonably well tailored to its stated objective of eliminating targeted mailings whose type and timing are a source of distress to Floridians, distress that has caused many of them to lose respect for the legal profession.

Respondents' second point would have force if the Bar's Rule were not limited to a brief period and if there were not many other ways for injured Floridians to learn about the availability of legal representation during that time. Our lawyer advertising cases have afforded lawyers a great deal of leeway to devise innovative ways to attract new business. Florida permits lawyers to advertise on prime-time television and radio as well as in newspapers and other media. They may rent space on billboards. They may send untargeted letters to the general population, or to discrete segments thereof. There are, of course, pages upon pages devoted to lawyers in the Yellow Pages of Florida telephone directories. These listings are organized alphabetically and by area of specialty. . . . These ample alternative channels for receipt of information about

the availability of legal representation during the 30-day period following accidents may explain why, despite the ample evidence, testimony, and commentary
submitted by those favoring (as well as opposing) unrestricted direct-mail
solicitation, respondents have not pointed to—and we have not independently
found— a single example of an individual case in which immediate solicitation
helped to avoid, or failure to solicit within 30 days brought about, the harms
that concern the dissent, ... In fact, the record contains considerable
empirical survey information suggesting that Floridians have little difficulty
finding a lawyer when they need one. . . . Finding no basis to question the
commonsense conclusion that the many alternative channels for communicating necessary information about attorneys are sufficient, we see no defect in
Florida's regulation.

III

Speech by professionals obviously has many dimensions. There are circumstances in which we will accord speech by attorneys on public issues and
matters of legal representation the strongest protection our Constitution has
to offer. See, e.g., Gentile v. State Bar of Nevada, 501 U.S. 1030 (1991); In
re Primus, 436 U.S. 412 (1978). This case, however, concerns pure commercial
advertising, for which we have always reserved a lesser degree of protection
under the First Amendment. Particularly because the standards and conduct
of state-licensed lawyers have traditionally been subject to extensive regulation
by the States, it is all the more appropriate that we limit our scrutiny of state
regulations to a level commensurate with the " 'subordinate position' " of
commercial speech in the scale of First Amendment values. *Fox*, 492 U.S., at
477, quoting *Ohralik*, 436 U.S., at 456.

We believe that the Bar's 30-day restriction on targeted direct-mail solicitation of accident victims and their relatives withstands scrutiny under the three-
pronged *Central Hudson* test that we have devised for this context. The Bar
has substantial interest both in protecting injured Floridians from invasive
conduct by lawyers and in preventing the erosion of confidence in the profession
that such repeated invasions have engendered. The Bar's proffered study, unre-
butted by respondents below, provides evidence indicating that the harms it
targets are far from illusory. The palliative devised by the Bar to address these
harms is narrow both in scope and in duration. The Constitution, in our view,
requires nothing more.

The judgment of the Court of Appeals, accordingly, is reversed.

JUSTICE KENNEDY, with whom JUSTICE STEVENS, JUSTICE SOUTER, and
JUSTICE GINSBURG join, dissenting.

[Justice Kennedy's dissenting opinion agreed with the majority that the
Central Hudson test should be used to evaluate the constitutionality of the
Florida rule, but it disagreed with the majority on the application of every
prong of the test. He found that protection of the privacy of recipients was
not a substantial state interest because the state may not restrict speech that

might offend the listener. He pointed out that direct mail advertising provides important information to recipients. He criticized the "studies" on which the bar based its rule. Finally, Justice Kennedy argued that prohibition of direct mail advertising for 30 days was wildly disproportionate to any harm that might flow from such advertising. In conclusion, the dissenting Justices saw the Court's decision as a major retreat from First Amendment protection for commercial speech in general and lawyer advertising in particular.]

Notes and Questions

1. After the Court upheld Florida's 30-day waiting period on direct mail advertising, Congress enacted legislation prohibiting communications with victims or their families for 30 days after an airplane crash involving an interstate or foreign carrier. 49 U.S.C.A. 1136(g)(2) provides as follows:

> In the event of an accident involving an air carrier providing interstate or foreign air transportation, no unsolicited communication concerning a potential action for personal injury or wrongful death may be made by an attorney or any potential party to the litigation to an individual injured in the accident, or to a relative of an individual involved in the accident, before the 30th day following the date of the accident.

The federal statute applies to any "potential party," so it would appear to prohibit efforts by defendants and their insurance carriers to settle cases during the 30-day period after an accident.

2. In Revo v. New Mexico Supreme Court Disciplinary Bd., 106 F.3d 929 (10th Cir.), *cert. denied*, 521 U.S. 1121 (1997), the Court of Appeals held that New Mexico's ban on direct mail advertising to personal injury victims without time limit was unconstitutional. Cf. Ficker v. Curran, 119 F.3d 1150 (4th Cir. 1997) (finding unconstitutional statute prohibiting direct mail advertising to traffic and criminal court defendants within 30 days because the privacy interests of recipients were reduced and their need for services was substantial).

3. In 1999 the Florida Supreme Court revised its ethics rules to impose significant restrictions on advertising in the electronic media. Under the rules, information in the electronic media "shall be articulated by a single human voice, or on-screen text, with no background sound other than instrumental music." The rules prohibit use of a "person's voice or image, other than that of a lawyer who is a member of the firm whose services are advertised." Fla. R. Prof. Conduct 4-7.5 (amended 1999). The comments justify these special restrictions as follows:

> The unique characteristics of electronic media, including the pervasiveness of television and radio, the ease with which these media are abused, and the passiveness of the viewer or listener, make the electronic media especially subject to regulation in the public interest. Therefore, greater restrictions on the manner

of television and radio advertising are justified than might be appropriate for advertisements in the other media. To prevent abuses, including potential interferences with the fair and proper administration of justice and the creation of incorrect public perceptions or assumptions about the manner in which our legal system works, and to promote the public's confidence in the legal profession and this country's system of justice while not interfering with the free flow of useful information to prospective users of legal services, it is necessary also to restrict the techniques used in television and radio advertising.

On the wisdom of the Florida rules as a matter of policy, see William E. Hornsby, Jr. & Kurt Schimmel, Regulating Lawyer Advertising: Public Images and the Irresistible Aristotelian Impulse, 9 Geo. J. Legal Ethics 325 (1996) (empirical study of lawyer advertising shows that public image of lawyers who use stylish advertisements is greater than those lawyers who use purely informational advertising). Are the Florida Rules constitutional? Consider the application of the Florida Rules to the television advertisement in Problem 4-7(c) above.

Marketing on the Internet

Lawyers are using the Internet in a wide variety of ways to market their services, including passive Web pages, interactive Web pages, responses to e-mail inquiries, participation in chat rooms, and distribution of information to potential clients on commercially obtained lists.[280] It now seems widely accepted that the general rules governing advertising and solicitation apply to Internet communications. The revised Model Rules recognize marketing through Internet and adopt this approach. Rule 7.2(a) states that lawyers may advertise their services through electronic communications, subject to the restrictions of Rules 7.1 and 7.3. See also Model Rule 7.2, comment 3. Thus, law firm Web pages and other Internet communications must not be false or misleading in violation of Rule 7.1.[281]

Prior to the 2002 revisions Model Rule 7.2(b) provided: "A copy or recording of an advertisement or communication shall be kept for two years after its last dissemination along with a record of when and where it was used." This requirement is cumbersome for Web sites because they consist of many pages, which are revised frequently. The 2002 revision of the Model Rules deletes this provision, but it may remain applicable in many states. For example,

---

280. See Louise L. Hill, Lawyer Communications on the Internet: Beginning the Millennium with Disparate Standards, 75 Wash. L. Rev. 785 (2000).

281. See, e.g., California State Bar Standing Comm. on Prof. Resp. & Conduct, Formal Op. 2001-155, 2001 WL 34029609; N.Y. State Bar Assn., Comm. on Prof. Ethics, Op. No. 709, 1998 WL 957924. A law firm may use a domain name that differs from the actual name of the firm but the domain name must not be false or misleading. See Supreme Court of Ohio, Board of Commissioners on Grievances & Discipline, Op. No. 99-4 (1999).

in 2001 the California Ethics Committee issued a comprehensive opinion on Internet advertising.[282] The Committee stated: "Rule 1-400(F) adds the requirements that the attorney retain for two years copies or recordings of any communications by written or electronic media and that these copies or recordings be made available to the State Bar if requested. These requirements apply to each page of every version and revision of the web site."[283]

The accessibility of a lawyer's Web page or other advertising outside the jurisdiction in which the lawyer practices creates a number of intertwined problems. First, such an advertisement could be viewed as false or misleading to the extent that it implies that the lawyer can render services in jurisdictions where the lawyer is not admitted to practice. Lawyers should indicate the geographical limitations on their practice to avoid misleading potential viewers.[284] Second, lawyers who obtain clients in jurisdictions in which they are not admitted to practice may run afoul of the state's prohibitions on the unauthorized practice of law.[285] Third, states are likely to claim the right to exercise jurisdiction over lawyers admitted elsewhere who target their advertisements to residents of the state. Model Rule 8.5(a), as revised in August 2002, states: "A lawyer not admitted in this jurisdiction is also subject to the disciplinary authority of this jurisdiction if the lawyer provides or offers to provide any legal services in this jurisdiction." South Carolina has amended its rules of professional conduct to provide that lawyers who are admitted in another jurisdiction must comply with the South Carolina rules if they use various specific forms of advertising directed to South Carolinians or "[a]ny other form of advertising or solicitation which is specifically targeted at potential clients in South Carolina."[286]

When is a communication targeted to residents of a state? The Web site may itself indicate the states to which it is directed. If not, disciplinary authorities may be able to infer the targeting of the site from review of the residence of clients obtained by the firm through the site. Prudent lawyers will take steps to limit the states to which they wish their sites to apply. For example, the home page could state: "This Web site is for residents of the following states only." Firms that wish to have their Web pages effective in states with more restrictive advertising rules than their home states may need to prepare separate Web pages for those states. For example: "Florida residents should click here."

Lawyers can also violate the solicitation rules when they use the Internet. An offer to provide legal services in a chat room or other real-time method of

282. California State Bar Standing Comm. on Prof. Resp. & Conduct, Formal Opinion 2001-155, 2001 WL 34029609.

283. Id. at 2.

284. N.Y. State Bar Assn., Comm. on Prof. Ethics, Op. No. 709, 1998 WL 957924.

285. See Birbrower, Montalbano, Condon & Frank, P.C. v. Superior Court (ESQ Business Services, Inc.), 949 P.2d 1 (Cal. 1998). Problem 4-8 discusses the *Birbrower* case in more detail.

286. S. C. App. Ct. R. 418(b)(6). On the jurisdictional issues, see Pa. Bar Assn., Comm. on Legal Ethics & Prof. Resp., Op. No. 98-85, 1998 WL 988187.

communication is subject to the solicitation rules.[287] See Model Rule 7.3(a). If a lawyer simply participates in a chat room without offering to provide services, however, the lawyer probably has not crossed the line of improper solicitation.

One of the leading cases involving professional discipline of a lawyer for Internet marketing is In re Canter.[288] In *Canter* the Tennessee Supreme Court imposed a one-year suspension on a lawyer who posted an advertisement about the green card lottery program on thousands of Internet newsgroups, including ones that were unrelated to the subject matter of the message. The court found that the respondent's advertisement was an improper intrusion into the privacy of the recipients because it was unsolicited and imposed a cost on recipients without their consent (cost of time of on-line use in reading or downloading the message). In addition, respondent had failed to identify the message as an advertisement (as required by Tennessee rules) and had failed to provide the Tennessee Board of Professional Responsibility with a copy of the advertisement within three days.

2. Legal Services Plans

Legal services plans refer to contractual arrangements in which the sponsor of the plan contracts with a lawyer or law firm to provide designated legal services to the members of the plan.[289] These plans have often been referred to as "group legal services" or "pre-paid legal services" plans, but neither of these terms is completely accurate because plans come in a wide variety of forms, depending on sponsor, cost/level of benefits, and choice of attorney. Sponsors of legal services plans fall into three major categories: employers, membership groups, and prepaid providers. Some employers provide legal services plans to their employees as a fringe benefit, like health insurance.[290] Some membership organizations, like the AARP, offer legal services plans to individuals who join the organization.[291] Finally, some companies, like Pre-Paid Legal Services, Inc.,[292] market legal services plans either directly to individuals or to their employers.

287. See Florida State Bar Assn. Comm. on Prof. Ethics, Op. No. 00-1, 2000 WL 1897342.

288. No. 95-831-O-H, Tenn. 6/5/97, Laws. Man. on Prof. Conduct (ABA/BNA), 13 Current Rep. 13 (July 23, 1997).

289. Judith L. Maute, Pre-Paid and Group Legal Services: Thirty Years after the Storm, 70 Fordham L. Rev. 915 (2001); Brian Heid & Eitan Misulovin, Note, The Group Legal Plan Revolution: Bright Horizon or Dark Future?, 18 Hofstra Lab. & Emp. L.J. 335 (2000). See also the Web site of the American Prepaid Legal Services Institute, ⟨http://www.aplsi.org/legal_plans/index.htm⟩ (visited Sept. 6, 2003).

290. ⟨http://www.legalclout.com⟩ (visited Sept. 7, 2003).

291. ⟨http://www.aarp.org/lsn/overview.html⟩ (visited Sept. 7, 2003). See Wayne Moore & Monica Kolasa, AARP's Legal Services Network: Expanding Legal Services to the Middle Class, 32 Wake Forest L. Rev. 503 (1997).

292. ⟨http://www.prepaidlegal.com/⟩ (visited Sept. 7, 2003).

The cost and level of benefits of the plans also vary. Employers and membership groups often provide a basic plan to their employees or members without additional charge. These basic plans, usually referred to as "access or discount" plans, give the employee or member certain services and provide access to attorneys who agree to provide other services at discount rates. For example, the AARP plan gives members a free 30-minute initial consultation with an attorney who is part of the AARP Legal Services Network; preparation of a simple will for $75 ($100 for couples with similar distribution plans); preparation of a durable financial power of attorney for $35; and preparation of a durable health care power of attorney, also for $35. For other matters, members receive a 20 percent discount from the attorney's normal fees.[293] Other plans, usually referred to as "comprehensive" plans, provide an increased level of benefits in exchange for a monthly premium. For example, Pre-Paid Legal Services, Inc. offers a comprehensive plan to New York residents for $24 per month plus a one-time $10 enrollment fee that provides a wide range of preventive services. In addition, the plan enables subscribers to receive discounts on fees for litigation matters: $49 for defense services and 25 percent for contingency fee representation.[294]

Finally, plans differ on choice of attorney. Many plans are "closed panel," which means that the consumer must choose an attorney from a list of attorneys selected by the plan sponsor. Some plans are "open panel," under which the consumer is free to select either from a list developed by the sponsor or any other attorney of the consumer's choice. Finally, "mixed plans" are closed panel for some services, while open panel for others.[295]

The essence of a legal services plan is the tripartite relationship between sponsor, member, and lawyer. The injection of the sponsor into the attorney-client relationship, however, has made legal services plans controversial within the profession. On one hand, a sponsor can provide valuable services to its members, such as negotiating lower attorney fees and overseeing the quality of legal services. On the other hand, because the sponsor pays the lawyers for the services that the lawyers render to their clients, this financial relationship may have an impact on the lawyers' independent professional judgment. Further, the presence of the third-party sponsor poses possible confidentiality and conflict-of-interest problems.[296]

Legal services plans are well accepted today and provide benefits to millions of Americans,[297] but for most of the twentieth century the organized bar was hostile to such plans. Canon 35 of the ABA's Canons of Professional Ethics, entitled "Intermediaries," provided as follows:

293. ⟨http://www.aarp.org/lsn/overview.html⟩ (visited Sept. 7, 2003).
294. ⟨http://wserver0.prepaidlegal.com/Multisite/JSP/corp/corpregsel.jsp⟩ (visited Sept. 7, 2003).
295. See Maute, supra note 289, at 943 and Heid & Misulovin, supra note 289, at 341, n. 42.
296. For a discussion of the strengths and weaknesses of legal services plans, see Wolfram, Modern Legal Ethics §16.5.4, at 904-910.
297. See authorities cited in note 289 above.

The professional services of a lawyer should not be controlled or exploited by any lay agency, personal or corporate, which intervenes between client and lawyer. A lawyer's responsibilities and qualifications are individual. He should avoid all relations which direct the performance of his duties by or in the interest of such intermediary.

In a series of decisions beginning in 1963, the Supreme Court considered the impact of the First Amendment on the bar's prohibition on cooperation with intermediaries. In NAACP v. Button[298] the NAACP provided attorneys to assist parents in challenging racial segregation in public schools. Typically, parents learned of the availability of legal assistance through meetings sponsored by the NAACP at which staff attorneys appeared and spoke. Virginia argued that such activities amounted to improper solicitation, but the Supreme Court disagreed, holding that the NAACP's litigation activities were entitled to First Amendment protection:

> In the context of NAACP objectives, litigation is not a technique of resolving private differences; it is a means for achieving the lawful objectives of equality of treatment by all government, federal, state and local, for the members of the Negro community in this country. It is thus a form of political expression.[299]

In later cases the Court expanded the holding in *Button* to apply to labor unions, providing counsel either by referral or on salary, to assist their members in ordinary (rather than civil rights) litigation.[300] The Court summarized its holdings in these cases as follows: "The common thread running through our decisions . . . is that collective activity undertaken to obtain meaningful access to the courts is a fundamental right within the protection of the First Amendment."[301]

In light of these decisions, the ABA was forced to change its rules of professional conduct, but the change represented only a grudging acceptance of legal services plans. The Model Code of Professional Responsibility adopted by the ABA in 1969 allowed lawyers to participate with legal services plans provided that the plans met certain requirements, one of which was that cooperation was permissible "only in those instances and to the extent that controlling constitutional interpretation at the time of the rendition of the services requires the allowance of such legal service activities." DR 2-103(D)(5).[302]

During the next few years, the ABA faced continued pressure both from some ranks of the profession and from the Antitrust Division of the Justice Department to change its restrictive stance on legal services plans. In response

298. 371 U.S. 415 (1963).
299. Id. at 429.
300. See United Transp. Union v. State Bar of Mich., 401 U.S. 576 (1971); United Mine Workers of America, Dist. 12 v. Illinois State Bar Assn., 389 U.S. 217 (1967); Brotherhood of R.R. Trainmen v. Virginia ex rel. Va. State Bar, 377 U.S. 1 (1964).
301. 401 U.S. at 585.
302. See generally Wolfram, Modern Legal Ethics §16.5.5, at 912.

to these pressures, the ABA adopted amendments to the Model Code in 1974 and 1975, but even with these changes lawyer participation in legal services plans was severely restricted.[303]

The Model Rules of Professional Conduct reflect a substantial shift in attitude toward legal services plans from the bar's traditional hostility. The proposed final draft of Model Rule 5.4 included a provision allowing lawyers to participate with legal services plans provided four relatively mild conditions were met. This section was deleted, however, from the final version of the Model Rules.[304] Given the historical controversy surrounding legal services plans, it is surprising that such plans are barely mentioned in the Model Rules of Professional Conduct. (The one specific mention is in Rule 7.3(d).)[305]

The absence of a Model Rule provision dealing with legal services plans does not mean that lawyer involvement in such plans is unrestricted. Lawyers participating in legal services plans must still comply with all rules of professional conduct, including those dealing with confidentiality and conflicts of interest. In Formal Opinion 87-355, the ABA's Committee on Ethics and Professional Responsibility dealt with the status of for-profit legal services plans under the Model Rules of Professional Conduct and issued an opinion broadly endorsing such plans, provided certain ethical requirements were met:

> The plan must allow the participating lawyer to exercise independent professional judgment on behalf of the client, to maintain client confidences, to avoid conflicts of interest, and to practice competently. The operation of the plan must not involve improper advertising or solicitation or improper fee sharing and must be in compliance with other applicable law. It is incumbent upon the lawyer to investigate and ensure that the arrangement under the plan fully complies with the Rules before the lawyer participates in the plan. Where the plan or the plan sponsor is in violation of the Rules, the lawyer who participates in the plan may violate Rule 8.4(a) by assisting the plan sponsor or by violating the Rules through the acts of the plan sponsor.[306]

Rather than participating in a legal services plan sponsored by a commercial or nonprofit organization, lawyers may organize their own plans so long as they comply with the rules of professional conduct, including Rule 5.4, which prohibits a lay person from having an ownership or other interest in the plan.[307] Lawyers who are considering forming such plans should be aware that they may be subject to state or federal regulation.[308]

---

303. See id. at 912-915.
304. See id. at 915-916.
305. For a discussion of the application of Model Rule 7.3(d) to legal services plans, see 2 Hazard & Hodes, The Law of Lawyering §57.12.
306. ABA Comm. on Ethics and Prof. Resp., Formal Op. 87-355, at 2.
307. See 2 Hazard & Hodes, The Law of Lawyering §45.10 and illus. 45-3.
308. See Maute, supra note 289, at 937 n.142.

3. *Restrictions on the Unauthorized Practice of Law*

———————————— **Problem 4-8** ————————————

Regulation of the Unauthorized Practice of Law

a. You are a member of your state bar's unauthorized practice committee. The ABA Commission on Nonlawyer Practice has recommended that states reconsider their restrictions on the unauthorized practice of law. Your state supreme court has asked the committee to consider the issue and make recommendations to the court. Your committee is considering several possibilities: (1) Define the practice of law narrowly to include only appearances before courts of record. Nonlawyers would be allowed to provide legal services in transactional or administrative matters but could not hold themselves out as lawyers. Utah, by legislation, has adopted this approach. See Utah Code §78-9-102 (effective May 3, 2004). (2) Define the practice of law broadly to include court appearance, appearances before administrative bodies, preparation of documents, legal advice, and negotiation, but develop a list of specific exceptions. Arizona has adopted this approach by court rule. See Arizona Supreme Court Rule 31. (3) Allow the definition of and exceptions to the unauthorized practice doctrine to develop on a case-by-case basis. This is the approach traditionally followed in most jurisdictions. (4) Provide a procedure by which a person or entity may petition the state supreme court for an exception to the restriction on the unauthorized practice of law based on a showing that the benefits to the public from the exception are likely to exceed the costs. Be prepared to participate in a committee meeting on the issue.

b. Your state has recently adopted ABA revised Model Rule 5.5, which deals with multijurisdictional practice by lawyers. How would the rule apply to the following situations?: (1) A lawyer who is admitted to practice in another state represents a national health care provider that owns hospitals throughout the country. The provider has agreed in principle to purchase a hospital located in your state. The lawyer will be responsible for negotiation and preparation of the documents involved in purchasing the local hospital and will provide advice to the hospital on various legal issues that arise after the sale is completed, particularly issues involving federal law. (2) The children of an elderly individual residing in a nursing home in your state claim that the home abused their parent. A few attorneys throughout the country specialize in this type of litigation. The children have contacted one of these attorneys, who is admitted to practice in another state, and have arranged for him to come to your state to meet with them and advise them about their rights. (3) A technology company does business throughout the country. The company has a substantial in-house legal staff. One of its major offices is located in your state. The company has decided to transfer one of its staff attorneys to the office in your state. The company plans for the attorney to handle contract and administrative matters. If a matter requires a court appearance, the company will retain outside counsel.

Read Model Rule 5.5 and comments.

History and policy of restrictions on the unauthorized practice of law

Nonlawyers have not always been prohibited from practicing law. From the colonial period through the nineteenth century, many states allowed nonlawyers to represent clients, even in court.[309] The modern concept of unauthorized practice did not develop until the early part of this century, particularly during the Depression. Beginning in the 1930s, the ABA and many state and local bar associations appointed unauthorized practice committees. These committees engaged in a variety of activities, including bringing lawsuits, to prevent the unauthorized practice of law. During this period, many states enacted or greatly expanded statutes prohibiting the unauthorized practice of law.[310] While bar officials claimed that their aggressive enforcement efforts originated because of public demand about improper activities by nonlawyers, evidence indicates that the bar was attempting to protect its economic position, which had deteriorated during the Depression.[311]

Rules prohibiting the unauthorized practice of law can be enforced in a variety of ways.[312] Traditionally, courts have held that they have the inherent power to determine who is admitted to practice law.[313] Pursuant to this power courts have enjoined or held in contempt nonlawyers who practiced law.[314] Bar committees are typical plaintiffs in such proceedings. In the vast majority of states, legislatures have enacted statutes making the unauthorized practice of

---

309. Wolfram, Modern Legal Ethics §15.1.1, at 824-825.

310. See generally Barlow F. Christensen, The Unauthorized Practice of Law: Do Good Fences Really Make Good Neighbors—or Even Good Sense? 1980 Am. Bar Found. Res. J. 159, 161-197; Deborah L. Rhode, Policing the Professional Monopoly: A Constitutional and Empirical Analysis of Unauthorized Practice Prohibitions, 34 Stan. L. Rev. 1, 6-10 (1981).

311. Rhode, Policing the Professional Monopoly, 34 Stan. L. Rev. at 8-9.

312. For a comprehensive study of enforcement efforts, see id.

313. See Charles W. Wolfram, Lawyer Turf and Lawyer Regulation—The Role of the Inherent-Powers Doctrine, 12 U. Ark. Little Rock L.J. 1 (1989). See also Quintin Johnstone, Unauthorized Practice of Law and the Power of State Courts: Difficult Problems and Their Resolution, 39 Willamette L. Rev. 795 (2003).

314. See Florida Bar v. Furman, 451 So. 2d 808 (Fla. 1984) (respondent held in criminal contempt for violating injunction against engaging in unauthorized practice of law in divorce cases); Florida Bar v. Hughes, 824 So. 2d 154 (Fla. 2002) (nonlawyer enjoined from counseling, advising, and preparing documents for individuals to create and transfer land trusts).

law a crime.[315] Finally, the Model Rules of Professional Conduct indirectly prohibit the unauthorized practice of law because the rules forbid lawyers from assisting nonlawyers in the unauthorized practice of law. Model Rule 5.5(a).[316]

While the doctrine of the unauthorized practice of law and the judicial power to enforce the doctrine are well established, controversy regarding the unauthorized practice of law has intensified in recent years. The fundamental issue is whether broad restrictions on the unauthorized practice of law serve the public interest.[317] The basic argument in favor of prohibitions on the unauthorized practice of law rests on protection of the public. The argument runs as follows: Legal services are complicated. Because of this complexity, lay people are unable to evaluate the competency of nonlawyers who might offer to render such services. Therefore, the state is justified in prohibiting nonlawyers from engaging in the practice of law.

This argument in favor of prohibitions on the unauthorized practice of law is suspect. First, although some legal services are complex, many types of legal services are relatively uncomplicated and are routinely performed by paralegals, almost all of whom are nonlawyers. The usual response to this argument is that paralegals operate under the supervision of lawyers. But this response begs the question: It admits that nonlawyers can perform legal services, but argues that the proper form of regulation for such services is by direct lawyer supervision. Whether direct lawyer supervision should be the only means for regulating nonlawyer practice is open to question. Moreover, experienced well-trained paralegals typically require little supervision, and at least some states authorize lawyers to employ independent paralegals whom they do not directly supervise.[318]

Second, while lay people may be unable to evaluate the quality of legal services provided by nonlawyers, this does not justify the conclusion that such services should be prohibited. Lay people buy many products and services whose quality they lack the ability to evaluate. Automobiles and insurance are two examples. A variety of solutions to lack of consumer information are possible. The market will often provide a response to lack of information. *Consumer Reports* and other publications provide information to consumers about the quality of most consumer products. It is not difficult to imagine

---

315. Rhode, Policing the Professional Monopoly, 34 Stan. L. Rev. at 11-12.

316. See People v. Laden, 893 P.2d 771 (Colo. 1995) (en banc) (lawyer guilty of aiding in unauthorized practice of law by cooperating with nonlawyer who counseled and sold living trust packages).

317. For an empirical study of the unauthorized practice rules in the area of pro se divorce, see Project, The Unauthorized Practice of Law and Pro Se Divorce: An Empirical Analysis, 86 Yale L.J. 104 (1976) (study casts substantial doubt on wisdom of restrictions on unauthorized practice for nonlitigation matters, especially for indigents or individuals of modest means; benefits to clients of unauthorized practice restrictions have been exaggerated and costs are substantial).

318. In re Opinion No. 24 of Comm. on Unauthorized Practice of Law, 607 A.2d 962 (N.J. 1992). But see Carl M. Selinger, The Retention of Limitations on the Out-of-Court Practice of Law by Independent Paralegals, 9 Geo. J. Legal Ethics 879 (1996).

similar publications developing for legal services. Further, regulatory solutions short of prohibition, such as disclosure or limited licensing, can be considered.

Policy considerations and constitutional principles also raise questions about the wisdom of the prohibition on the unauthorized practice of law.[319] Low- and moderate-income individuals have a vast unmet need for legal services. Seventy-five percent of the legal needs of low-income individuals are unmet.[320] Almost two-thirds of moderate-income Americans with legal problems are not receiving professional assistance.[321] Indeed, one consequence of the continued application of rules on the unauthorized practice of law is that individuals of modest means may increasingly turn to pro se representation.[322]

The prohibitions on the unauthorized practice of law also raise constitutional issues. In Lassiter v. Department of Social Services[323] the Supreme Court held that indigents do not have an absolute right to appointed counsel in civil cases, but quite clearly access to counsel in civil cases has due process implications. Moreover, the Court has not yet addressed the question of the constitutionality under the First Amendment of prohibitions on advice by nonlawyers.[324]

Approaches to regulation of nonlawyer practice

The ABA Commission on Nonlawyer Practice has issued reports and recommendations on the extent of nonlawyer practice in the United States. In 1994 the commission issued a discussion draft that contains a wealth of factual detail on the subject.[325] The report describes practice by "legal technicians" (nonlawyers providing legal services without supervision by lawyers) in the following areas: federal and state administrative agency practice, immigration practice, federal and state taxation, specially authorized practice in certain courts, housing disputes, family law, real estate, independent claim adjusters, debt collection, debt counseling, and general practice.[326] The report also in-

---

319. Deborah L. Rhode, The Delivery of Legal Services by Non-lawyers, 4 Geo. J. Legal Ethics 209, 228-233 (1990).

320. George C. Harris & Derek F. Foran, The Ethics of Middle-Class Access to Legal Services and What We Can Learn from the Medical Profession's Shift to a Corporate Paradigm, 70 Fordham L. Rev. 775, 794 (2001) (reviewing various national and state surveys of legal needs).

321. Id. at 792.

322. Ronald W. Staudt & Paula L. Hannaford, Access to Justice for the Self-Represented Litigant: An Interdisciplinary Investigation by Designers and Lawyers, 52 Syracuse L. Rev. 1017 (2002). For a study of this issue, see Bruce D. Sales et al., Self-Representation in Divorce Cases (1993).

323. 452 U.S. 18 (1981). See Problem 4-9.

324. Robert Kry, The "Watchman for Truth": Professional Licensing and the First Amendment, 23 Seattle U. L. Rev. 885 (2000).

325. ABA Commn. on Nonlawyer Practice, Nonlawyer Practice in the United States: Summary of the Factual Record (1994).

326. Id. at 17-22.

446   4. Civil Litigation: Limitations on Zealous Representation

cludes a summary of the current rules on nonlawyer practice in many jurisdictions.

In August 1995 the commission issued a report, "Nonlawyer Activities in Law-Related Situations," finding that with adequate protection for the public, nonlawyers had an important role to play in delivery of legal services to the public. The commission recommended that the ABA reconsider its ethics rules and policies in a variety of areas, including those governing the unauthorized practice of law. The commission proposed an analytical framework that could be used by states to determine whether a particular activity should be regulated, unregulated, or prohibited:

- Does the activity if performed by nonlawyers present a serious risk to life, health, safety, or economic well-being of members of the public?
- Do potential consumers have sufficient knowledge to evaluate the qualifications of nonlawyers offering the services?
- Do the benefits to the public likely to accrue from regulation outweigh any likely negative consequences of regulation?

If the activity poses a serious risk of harm and consumers lack information to evaluate the quality of service, the commission indicated that the activity should be regulated; the form that the regulation takes would depend on a weighing of the costs and benefits of the regulation. The commission outlined a wide range of regulatory options that states might consider, including registration, licensing, or disclosure. The commission also summarized various areas in which states might consider regulation, including age, experience, education, training, recordkeeping, continuing education, and admission examinations.[327] Problem 5-3 considers various approaches to regulation of nonlawyer practice in real estate transactions.

A central issue in connection with reevaluation of restrictions on the unauthorized practice of law is bar control. The bar obviously has a financial interest in limiting competition by nonlawyers. To the extent that the bar controls such restrictions, reform is unlikely to be great.[328] The experience in California is illustrative. In July 1990, a Commission on Legal Technicians created by the California Bar issued a report recommending that the state supreme court adopt a rule allowing nonlawyers to practice law, initially in the areas of bankruptcy, family, and landlord-tenant, under a licensing and

---

327. For criticism of the commission's proposals, see Deborah L. Rhode, Professionalism in Perspective: Alternative Approaches to Nonlawyer Practice, 22 N.Y.U. Rev. L. & Soc. Change 701 (1996).

328. The ABA has largely ignored the work of its Commission on Nonlawyer Practice and has in fact gone in the opposite direction, urging jurisdictions to retain and enforce their prohibitions on the unauthorized practice of law. See Nathan M. Crystal, Core Values: False and True, 70 Fordham L. Rev. 747, 764-765 (2001).

regulatory system.[329] Unsurprisingly, the report caused considerable controversy within the bar. In August 1991 the Board of Governors of the California Bar defeated a more limited proposal for a bar-controlled board that would license legal technicians only in the area of landlord-tenant.[330] Meaningful reform of the rules on the unauthorized practice of law is likely to require reduction in bar control of the process.[331]

Application of restrictions on unauthorized practice to out-of-state lawyers

The practice of law is increasingly becoming national and even international. As a result lawyers admitted in one jurisdiction often must deal with legal problems in or the law of other jurisdictions where they are not admitted to practice. Such transactions pose unauthorized practice problems for lawyers.

One way in which such a problem can arise is if a lawyer represents a client in a legal matter that involves litigation in another jurisdiction. In this situation an out-of-state lawyer may associate local counsel and with court permission appear pro hac vice to represent the client in the matter. Often, however, an out-of-state lawyer may be called on to represent a client in connection with a matter that does not necessarily involve litigation, such as negotiating a dispute or drafting a contract.

Does a lawyer engage in the unauthorized practice of law if the lawyer handles a nonlitigation matter in a jurisdiction in which the lawyer is not admitted? The California Supreme Court addressed this issue in Birbrower, Montalbano, Condon & Frank, P.C. v. Superior Court (ESQ Business Services, Inc.).[332] Birbrower was a New York law firm without any members licensed to practice law in California. ESQ, a California corporation, retained Birbrower to represent it in a dispute with Tandem Computers regarding a software development and marketing contract. The contract stated that California law governed. Birbrower attorneys traveled to California on several occasions to meet with representatives of ESQ and its accountants, to interview potential arbitrators, and to negotiate with Tandem on ESQ's behalf. The parties ultimately agreed to a settlement of the matter before it went to arbitration. ESQ

329. See Kathleen E. Justice, Note, There Goes the Monopoly: The California Proposal to Allow Nonlawyers to Practice Law, 44 Vand. L. Rev. 179 (1991). See also Ryan J. Talamante, Note, We Can't All Be Lawyers . . . Or Can We? Regulating the Unauthorized Practice of Law in Arizona, 34 Ariz. L. Rev. 873 (1992).

330. Don J. DeBenedictis, California Bar Drops Technician Plan, 77-Nov. A.B.A. J. 36 (1991).

331. See Rhode, The Delivery of Legal Services by Non-lawyers, 4 Geo. J. Legal Ethics at 232-233. See also Alan Morrison, Defining the Unauthorized Practice of Law: Some New Ways of Looking at an Old Question, 4 Nova L.J. 363 (1980) (calling for creation of body consisting of lawyers, consumers, and competitors of lawyers to set standards for performance of legal services by nonlawyers).

332. 949 P.2d 1 (Cal. 1998).

subsequently brought a legal malpractice claim against Birbrower, and the firm counterclaimed for unpaid legal fees.

The California Supreme Court held that the firm's fee agreement was unenforceable as to work performed in California (but not necessarily for work performed in New York to the extent that it could be severed from the California work) because the firm had engaged in the unauthorized practice of law in violation of section 6125 of the California Business and Professional Code. The court stated that a lawyer admitted to practice in another state but not in California engages in the unauthorized practice of law "in California" when the lawyer has sufficient contacts with a California client to amount to a clear legal representation:

> In our view, the practice of law "in California" entails sufficient contact with the California client to render the nature of the legal service a clear legal representation. In addition to a quantitative analysis, we must consider the nature of the unlicensed lawyer's activities in the state. Mere fortuitous or attenuated contacts will not sustain a finding that the unlicensed lawyer practiced law "in California." The primary inquiry is whether the unlicensed lawyer engaged in sufficient activities in the state, or created a continuing relationship with the California client that included legal duties and obligations.[333]

Physical presence in California is a factor, but does not determine whether an out-of-state lawyer is practicing law in California. The court, however, rejected the notion a person automatically practices law in California by giving advice on California law or by entering the state virtually:

> Our definition does not necessarily depend on or require the unlicensed lawyer's physical presence in the state. Physical presence here is one factor we may consider in deciding whether the unlicensed lawyer has violated section 6125, but it is by no means exclusive. For example, one may practice law in the state in violation of section 6125 although not physically present here by advising a California client on California law in connection with a California legal dispute by telephone, fax, computer, or other modern technological means. Conversely, although we decline to provide a comprehensive list of what activities constitute sufficient contact with the state, we do reject the notion that a person automatically practices law "in California" whenever that person practices California law anywhere, or "virtually" enters the state by telephone, fax, e-mail, or satellite.[334]

The court rejected Birbrower's arguments that the California statute prohibiting the unauthorized practice of law was intended to apply only to nonlaw-

333. Id. at 5.
334. Id. at 5-6.

yers, not to out-of-state lawyers, and that the statute did not apply to representation incident to arbitration proceedings.[335]

As the court in *Birbrower* indicates, unauthorized practice problems can arise even if the lawyer does not physically enter the jurisdiction. Sometimes a lawyer admitted in one jurisdiction is asked to advise a client or represent a client in a matter involving the law of another jurisdiction. Does a lawyer engage in the unauthorized practice of law by providing advice about the law of a jurisdiction in which the lawyer is not admitted? Cases subsequent to *Birbrower* indicate that the determination of whether a lawyer is engaged in the un-authorized practice of law depends on whether the client is a "California client." For example, in Estate of Condon (Condon v. McHenry)[336] the California Court of Appeals held that a Colorado lawyer did not engage in the un-authorized practice of law when the lawyer gave advice to a Colorado resident who was co-executor of the estate of a California decedent about the application of California law, even though the lawyer entered the state physically or virtually, because the client was not a "California client."[337]

The *Birbrower* case sent shock waves through the profession as many lawyers recognized that practice across state lines could violate the rules on unauthorized practice. In 2000 the President of the ABA appointed a Commis-sion on Multijurisdictional Practice (MJP).[338] In 2002 the ABA's House of Delegates approved the recommendations of the Commission, including adop-tion of revised Model Rule 5.5, which lessens but does not eliminate the restrictions on unauthorized practice by out-of-state lawyers.[339] Revised Rule 5.5(b) establishes two general rules. First, a lawyer not admitted to practice in a jurisdiction may not establish an office or have systematic and continuous presence in the jurisdiction for the practice of law. Second, a lawyer not admitted in a jurisdiction may not hold out to the public or represent that the lawyer is admitted to practice in the jurisdiction.

Rule 5.5(c) provides four exceptions allowing out-of-state lawyers to pro-vide services in a jurisdiction in which they are not admitted on a temporary basis. As comment 6 indicates, however, temporary services may be recurring

---

335. Id. at 7-10. See also Florida Bar v. Rapoport, 845 So. 2d 874 (Fla. 2003) (enjoining District of Columbia lawyer from representing clients in securities arbitration proceedings in Florida without being admitted to practice; court rejects claim that Federal Arbitration Act preempts state unauthorized practice rules).

336. 76 Cal. Rptr. 2d 922 (Ct. App. 1998) (on reconsideration after *Birbrower*).

337. See also Fought & Co. v. Steel Eng. & Erection, Inc., 951 P.2d 487 (Haw. 1998) (supplier's Oregon general counsel did not practice law "within the jurisdiction" of Hawaii when it rendered legal services in role of consultant to supplier and supplier's Hawaii counsel, and thus statutes did not bar supplier's recovery of appellate attorney fees for general counsel's services).

338. ⟨http://www.abanet.org/cpr/mjp-home.html⟩ (visited September 8, 2003).

339. For discussion of the issues confronted by the Commission in developing Rule 5.5 by a member of the Commission, see Stephen Gillers, Lessons from the Multijurisdic-tional Practice Commission: The Art of Making Change, 44 Ariz. L. Rev. 685 (2002). For a review of the case law and a proposal for a federal solution, see Gerald J. Clark, The Two Faces of Multi-Jurisdictional Practice, 29 N. Ky. L. Rev. 251 (2002).

and may continue over a long period of time. The first three exceptions are quite specific: in association with a lawyer who is admitted in the jurisdiction; in connection with a proceeding in which the lawyer reasonably anticipates to be admitted pro hac vice; and in connection with an ADR proceeding for which the jurisdiction does not require pro hac vice admission. The fourth exception is broad and somewhat vague covering legal services that "arise out of or are reasonably related to the lawyer's practice in a jurisdiction in which the lawyer is admitted to practice."[340] See comments 13 and 14.

Rule 5.5(d) provides two situations in which a lawyer not admitted in the jurisdiction may nonetheless have an office or continuous presence in the jurisdiction. Thus, Rule 5.5(d) operates as an exception to Rule 5.5(b). Rule 5.5(d)(1) applies to the typical in-house counsel who provides legal services to an organization or its affiliates. Rule 5.5(d)(2) permits a lawyer not admitted to practice in a jurisdiction to provide legal services in the jurisdiction when permitted by federal law or by other law of the jurisdiction. For example, Rule 5.5(d)(2) would allow a lawyer who is not admitted in a jurisdiction to move to that jurisdiction and open an office for practice before the Social Security Administration.

4. *Delivery of Legal Services to Indigents in Civil Cases*

────────────── **Problem 4-9** ──────────────

Mandatory Pro Bono and Delivery of Legal Services
to Indigents

a. You have been chosen to participate in a debate on the following proposition:

> RESOLVED, that the State Bar of Your State should adopt a mandatory pro bono plan.

Be prepared to debate the affirmative or negative of that proposition at the next class.

b. Your instructor will assign members of the class to make short reports on ways in which delivery of legal services to indigents can be improved. For a bibliography of materials from which to choose a topic for a report, see Bibliography to the Conference on the Delivery of Legal Services to Low-Income Persons: Professional and Ethical Issues, 67 Fordham L. Rev. 2731 (1999). See also Roger C. Cramton, Delivery of Legal Services to Ordinary Americans, 44 Case W. Res. L. Rev. 531 (1994).

---

340. The Restatement adopts a similar exception. See Restatement (Third) of the Law Governing Lawyers §3(3).

     c.   Be prepared to articulate and justify the portion of your philoso-
phy of lawyering (recall Chapter 1 and Problem 1-4) regarding the nature
and extent of your obligation to assist in providing pro bono legal services.

Read Model Rules 6.1, 6.2, 6.3, 6.4 and comments.

Constitutional right to appointed counsel in civil cases

While indigent criminal defendants have a broad constitutional right to appointed counsel under the Sixth and Fourteenth Amendments, the Supreme
Court has refused to recognize a general right to appointed counsel in civil
cases. The leading case is Lassiter v. Department of Social Services,[341] an action
for termination of parental rights. In *Lassiter* the Supreme Court stated that a
presumption exists that appointed counsel was constitutionally required only
in cases involving a risk of incarceration.[342] The Court went on to decide,
however, that due process may require appointment of counsel in cases in
which the defendant does not face a deprivation of physical liberty:

> The case of Mathews v. Eldridge, 424 U.S. 319, 335 [(1976)], propounds
> three elements to be evaluated in deciding what due process requires, viz., the
> private interests at stake, the government's interest, and the risk that the proce-
> dures used will lead to erroneous decisions. We must balance these elements
> against each other, and then set their net weight in the scales against the presump-
> tion that there is a right to appointed counsel only where the indigent, if he is
> unsuccessful, may lose his personal freedom.[343]

The Court found that the private and governmental interests involved in cases
seeking termination of parental rights were great and the risk of error in such
cases significant. Nonetheless, the Court held that the application of the *Eldridge*
factors was not rigid and would "be answered in the first instance by the trial
court, subject . . . to appellate review."[344] The Court went on to hold that the
trial court did not commit error in failing to appoint counsel for Ms. Lassiter
because on the facts of the case these factors did not outweigh the presumption
against appointed counsel.[345]

    Justice Blackmun's dissenting opinion criticized the Court's case-by-case
approach. He concluded that this framework undermines the concept of general
fairness on which due process is based, makes it difficult for a reviewing court
to determine from the record whether the proceedings were fair since the
absence of evidence in the record may be the source of unfairness, and is

---

341. 452 U.S. 18 (1981).
342. Id. at 26-27.
343. Id. at 27.
344. Id. at 32.
345. Id. at 32-33.

cumbersome and costly.[346] In Justice Stevens's view, due process required appointed counsel in cases involving termination of parental rights, which he viewed as more serious than most criminal cases.[347]

The framework for analysis set by the Supreme Court in *Lassiter* continues to be the approach used by federal and state courts in deciding right-to-counsel issues in civil cases.[348]

Legal services programs

The Supreme Court in *Lassiter* noted that its decision was based on the minimal requirements of the Constitution: "A wise public policy, however, may require that higher standards be adopted than those minimally tolerable under the Constitution."[349] Both the federal and state governments have to varying degrees been willing to provide for appointed counsel in some civil cases as a matter of public policy; such programs are commonly referred to as *legal aid.*

The legal aid movement began in the latter part of the nineteenth and early twentieth centuries in New York, Chicago, and other large cities. Individuals and charities formed legal aid societies and other organizations to provide legal services to the poor, particularly to the large number of immigrants coming into the cities. The focus of legal aid at that time was charitable: to provide legal services to individuals who could not afford to hire lawyers.[350]

The legal aid movement showed little growth and change until the 1960s, when it underwent a fundamental transformation. One of the principal vehicles for change was the Ford Foundation, which began funding various experiments in providing legal services to the poor, including support for law reform efforts. The philosophy of law reform differs fundamentally from that of service. Under a law reform strategy, legal aid attorneys seek to use the legal system to make fundamental institutional and systemic changes that will remove discrimination against or provide benefits to the poor. Class actions and lobbying for legislative change became major tools of law reform efforts.[351]

In 1963 President Lyndon Johnson called for a "War on Poverty." Among the programs passed by Congress in response to this initiative was the Office of Economic Opportunity (OEO), which included the Legal Services Program. Thus, for the first time, the federal government became involved in the funding of legal services for the poor.[352] During the next 10 years, however, the Legal

346. Id. at 49-52.

347. Id. at 59-60.

348. See, e.g., Iraheta v. Superior Court, 83 Cal. Rptr. 2d 471 (Ct. App. 1999, *review denied*) (alleged street gang members named as defendants in action seeking injunction to abate public nuisance not entitled to counsel under *Lassiter*); Joni B. v. State, 549 N.W.2d 411 (Wis. 1996) (state statute erecting per se bar to appointment of counsel in protective services cases unconstitutional because it deprived courts of discretion under *Lassiter*).

349. 452 U.S. at 33.

350. Wolfram, Modern Legal Ethics §16.7.2, at 933.

351. Id. at 934-935.

352. Id. at 936-937.

Services Program became embroiled in political controversy, particularly its funding of law reform activities. Federal funding for legal services still continued to enjoy substantial support in the bar, particularly in the ABA.

In 1974, with the support of the president and the ABA, Congress created the Legal Services Corporation (LSC). The LSC represented a political compromise between the proponents and opponents of government-funded legal services. Its creation showed a continued commitment by the federal government to fund legal services. Indeed, legal services were now "upgraded" from a program to the status of a separate federal corporation. In addition, by creating a separate federal corporation with its own board of directors, supporters of the LSC hoped to take legal services "out of politics." At the same time, however, the statute creating the LSC put strict limits on various types of law reform activities.[353]

The hope that the creation of the LSC would remove federal funding of legal services from politics has not been realized. When the Reagan administration came to power in 1981, it targeted the LSC for abolition. Backers in Congress with the support of the ABA were able to save the LSC from extinction, but its appropriation lagged substantially behind inflation, and the number of attorneys funded by the LSC diminished.[354] In 1995 the Republican Congress again called for abolition of the LSC. In 1996 Congress reauthorized funding for legal services but placed substantial new restrictions on the activities of legal services lawyers, including limitations on the use of funds received from nonfederal sources.[355] In Legal Services Corp. v. Velazquez,[356] the Supreme Court held that the restriction prohibiting recipients of LSC funds from engaging in representation of individual clients to amend or challenge the validity of welfare laws violated the First Amendment. Lower courts, however, have upheld other LSC restrictions against constitutional challenge.[357] In recent years

353. On the history of the LSC, see id. §16.7.3, at 937-939. For articles tracing the history of legal services and discussing many of the problems confronting the effort to provide legal representation to the poor, see Marc Feldman, Political Lessons: Legal Services for the Poor, 83 Geo. L.J. 1529 (1995). For commentary on Professor Feldman's article, see Gary Bellow & Jeanne Charn, Paths Not Yet Taken: Some Comments on Feldman's Critique of Legal Services Practice, 83 Geo. L.J. 1633 (1995); Alan W. Houseman, Political Lessons: Legal Services for the Poor—A Commentary, 83 Geo. L.J. 1669 (1995).

354. Wolfram, Modern Legal Ethics §16.7.3, at 938. For a description of the impact of cuts in federal funding on legal services programs, see David Barringer, Downsized Justice, 82-Jul. A.B.A. J. 60 (1996).

355. Omnibus Consolidated Rescissions and Appropriations Act of 1996, Pub. L. No. 104-134, §504, 110 Stat. 1321 (1996) (restricting right to use federal funds to engage in activities such as class actions, to initiate rulemaking proceedings, or to claim attorney fees; restrictions also prohibit recipients of federal funds from using private, state, or local donations for these purposes or from transferring nonfederal funds to anyone who does not follow same restrictions). On the ethical obligations of legal services lawyers in light of these restrictions, see ABA Comm. on Ethics and Prof. Resp., Formal Op. 96-399.

356. 531 U.S. 533 (2001).

357. Velazquez v. Legal Servs. Corp., 164 F.3d 757 (2d Cir. 1999); Legal Aid Socy. of Haw. v. Legal Servs. Corp., 145 F.3d 1017 (9th Cir. 1998). See David Luban, Taking Out the Adversary: The Assault on Progressive Public-Interest Lawyers, 91 Cal. L. Rev.

the political controversy surrounding the LSC has subsided, largely because the LSC has changed its focus away from reform litigation toward delivery of services.[358]

Today most local legal services programs receive funding not only from the LSC but also from state and local sources as well. A major source of funding for legal services in many communities is IOLTA (Interest on Lawyer Trust Account) grants. Various charities also provide support for legal services. Nonetheless, the bulk of financing for legal services programs still comes from the LSC.[359]

Legal services programs have woefully inadequate resources to meet the needs of low- and moderate-income individuals. Forty-five million Americans qualify for civil legal aid. They are served by 4,000 legal aid lawyers and perhaps 2,000 other lawyers who provide representation to indigents. Thus, one lawyer is available to provide services for every 9,000 qualifying individuals.[360] Because of these unmet needs, proposals for imposing an obligation on lawyers to assist in providing legal services have been made from a variety of quarters.

The Marrero Committee Report

Since funded legal services programs do not have sufficient resources to come even close to satisfying the need for legal services of the poor, the bar has in recent years considered ways in which this need could be met, at least in part. One idea that has stirred considerable controversy within the profession is that lawyers be required to devote a certain amount of time periodically to providing legal services to persons of limited means.

Mandatory pro bono proposals must deal with a number of issues. Probably the most detailed mandatory pro bono proposal to date was offered in New York by the Marrero Committee;[361] the proposal has the following major elements:

1. *Quantity of required service:* 40 hours every two years.
2. *Coverage and exemptions:* All attorneys admitted to practice law in

---

209 (2003) (discussing "silencing doctrines," including LSC restrictions, that prevent public-interest lawyers and their clients from having their claims heard).

358. See John McKay, Federally Funded Legal Services: A New Vision of Equal Justice Under Law, 68 Tenn. L. Rev. 101 (2000); Mauricio Vivero, From "Renegade" Agency to Institution of Justice: The Transformation of Legal Services Corporation, 29 Fordham Urb. L.J. 1323 (2002). See also Alan W. Houseman, Civil Legal Assistance for the Twenty-First Century: Achieving Equal Justice for All, 17 Yale L. & Pol'y Rev. 369 (1998).

359. Luban, supra note 357, at 211, n.5 (discussing sources of funding for legal services).

360. Id. at 211-213, ns. 5-10.

361. Committee to Improve the Availability of Legal Services, Final Report to the Chief Judge of the State of New York (April 1990), reprinted in 19 Hofstra L. Rev. 755 (1991).

New York and currently practicing. The committee provided for exemptions for cause on a case-by-case basis. The committee also recognized that some practical difficulties could arise in applying the proposal to government lawyers and other classes of attorneys, but it concluded that universal coverage was extremely important.

3. *Qualifying services:* Services must be rendered to the poor or to organizations that serve the poor. The committee rejected two broader definitions of pro bono services—uncompensated legal service and public interest legal service—because the underlying rationale for its proposal was the special needs of the poor to have access to the legal system.

4. *Compliance:* Generally compliance must be personal, but the proposal recognizes two exceptions: First, attorneys who are members of groups such as law firms can satisfy their pro bono obligation collectively. This means that partners in firms can assign associates to handle pro bono work and obtain credit for their services. It also means that firms could hire full-time pro bono lawyers and receive credit for their services. Second, the proposal provides for a financial contribution in lieu of service at the rate of $1,000 for 20 hours ($50 per hour). The buyout option only applies, however, to lawyers practicing in firms of 10 or fewer lawyers. The committee felt that the group practice concept gave larger firms sufficient flexibility, but that smaller firms needed the additional buyout option because the group alternative would not be as useful for smaller firms.

5. *Excess time:* Excess time may be carried forward for no more than four years.

6. *Disbursements:* Reasonable expenses incurred in handling pro bono matters are reimbursable. The proposal does not specify the source of reimbursement but suggests two possibilities: funds generated by contributions in lieu of service and IOLTA funds.

7. *Professional liability insurance:* The committee concluded that no special provision for insurance was necessary because most lawyers would already have insurance that would apply or such insurance could be obtained by sponsoring organizations.

8. *Incompetence:* The committee concluded that the flexibility built in to its proposal was adequate to deal with concerns about competency of representation.

Justifications and criticisms of mandatory pro bono

What are the arguments in favor of and in opposition to mandatory pro bono? The Marrero Committee focused on several points to justify its proposal. First, numerous studies show a vast, unmet need for legal services by low-income households. Second, the failure to receive adequate legal services has inflicted an "intolerable toll" on both the poor and society as a whole. Lack of representation in eviction proceedings increases homelessness; absence of representation in domestic matters leads to violence; want of legal assistance in federal benefit cases increases the burden on the states. Further, lack of counsel undermines the legitimacy of the legal system itself.[362] The committee considered the possibility that various alternatives other than mandatory pro bono could solve or reduce the problem, but it concluded that this was unrealistic. The committee noted that the decline in federal funding for legal services and the increased economic pressures on law firms made it less likely that voluntary efforts would be successful.[363]

Given the documented need and the likelihood that the need would not be met through either federal funding or voluntary efforts, the committee turned to the role of the lawyer in providing legal services to the poor. While the committee agreed with the proposition that society as a whole bore responsibility for redressing the problem, it concluded that "lawyers, independent of their ordinary duty as citizens, have a professional responsibility to mobilize their own resources in order to meet these needs."[364] The special duty of lawyers to provide legal services to the poor flows from the unique training and skills of lawyers, their exclusive license to practice law, and the lawyers' responsibility to promote the legitimacy and proper functioning of the legal system.[365]

The principal arguments against mandatory pro bono fall into four categories: quality of service, unfairness to lawyers, administrative and practical difficulties, and lack of benefit to the poor. Some critics have questioned whether lawyers who are forced to provide legal services would do so competently. In addition, many legal problems facing the poor (welfare, housing, and employment, for example) involve complicated bodies of law in which private practitioners may have little knowledge or experience.[366] Quality-of-service issues could be addressed in several ways. While some legal problems facing the poor involve specialized bodies of law, many legal problems (divorce, wills, transfer of real estate) are fairly routine. In addition, for areas that require specialized knowledge, back-up facilities could assist lawyers in providing these services.[367] Further, the buyout provision found in the Marrero proposal could generate funds sufficient to hire lawyers with expertise to provide specialized services.

Some opponents of mandatory pro bono argue that such proposals are unconstitutional because they involve violations of individual liberty and taking

362. Id. at 774-775.
363. Id. at 776.
364. Id. at 780.
365. Id. For other arguments for pro bono service, see Robert A. Katzman ed., The Law Firm and the Public Good (1995) (essays on pro bono); Steven Lubet & Cathryn Stewart, A "Public Assets" Theory of Lawyers' Pro Bono Obligations, 145 U. Pa. L. Rev. 1245 (1997).
366. Roger C. Cramton, Mandatory Pro Bono, 19 Hofstra L. Rev. 1113, 1127 (1991).
367. See ABA, Standards for Programs Providing Civil Pro Bono Legal Services to Persons of Limited Means (1996); ABA Center for Pro Bono, Pro Bono Support and Delivery: A Directory of Statewide Models (1998).

of lawyers' property without just compensation. Such constitutional arguments have generally been rejected by the courts, however, on the ground that the legal profession is a regulated industry and requiring lawyers to devote a limited amount of time or money to provide legal services for the poor falls within the scope of reasonable regulation.[368] Even if mandatory pro bono is not unconstitutional, some adversaries argue that it is unfair to impose this burden on lawyers when society as a whole should provide for legal services to the poor. As noted above, the Marrero Report addressed this point; it concluded that lawyers have a special duty to provide legal services to the poor flowing from the unique training and skills of lawyers, their exclusive license to practice law, and the lawyers' responsibility to promote the legitimacy and proper functioning of the legal system. However, some critics, noting the increased competitiveness of the legal profession, question whether this justification is adequate.[369] Moreover, the program can generate other fairness issues. Mandatory pro bono tends to be regressive. The Marrero proposal suffers from this problem. Senior partners in large firms can satisfy their pro bono obligations by assigning associates to perform the work or by funding full-time poverty lawyers. These options are unavailable or less attractive for solo practitioners or lawyers in small firms. In addition, if the program has a fixed-dollar buyout provision, this option also operates regressively, falling more heavily on lawyers with lower incomes.[370] To the extent that the obligation is imposed only on the lawyers of certain states (New York, for example), it places those lawyers at a competitive disadvantage with lawyers in other states who do not bear this "tax."[371]

Critics of mandatory pro bono refer to significant practical and administrative difficulties with any such program. The program must address whether the requirement applies to lawyers engaged in teaching, politics, business, or government practice.[372] The definition of qualifying services must be carefully

---

368. Cramton, Mandatory Pro Bono, 19 Hofstra L. Rev. at 1131-1132.

369. Id. at 1134-1136. Professor Timothy Terrell and James Wildman also reject the monopoly argument for imposing a duty on lawyers to deliver legal services because they find that the existence of free entry, full competition, and lack of anticompetitive behavior in the legal profession means that lawyers no longer collect "monopoly rents." Timothy P. Terrell & James H. Wildman, Rethinking "Professionalism," 41 Emory L.J. 403, 421 (1992). Terrell and Wildman believe, however, that lawyers have a duty as professionals to enable those members of the profession who want to assist in delivering legal services to do so. Id. at 430. While rejecting any personal obligation to deliver legal services, Terrell and Wildman suggest that the bar could impose a tax on its members to assist other lawyers in their efforts. Id. at 431. For a contrary view arguing that a duty to provide public service is justified because lawyers receive the benefits of a state monopoly, see Tigran W. Eldred & Thomas Schoenherr, The Lawyer's Duty of Public Service: More Than Charity?, 96 W. Va. L. Rev. 367 (1993-1994). See also Steven Lubet, Professionalism Revisited, 42 Emory L.J. 197 (1993) (arguing that personal involvement of prestigious members of the profession can have a transformative impact on ways in which courts handle cases).

370. Cramton, Mandatory Pro Bono, 19 Hofstra L. Rev. at 1133-1134.

371. Id. at 1130-1131.

372. Id. at 1128.

considered. If charitable or bar work counts, then the goal of delivering legal services to the poor will be eroded, but if bar and charitable work does not qualify, the availability and willingness of lawyers to perform these services will diminish. A question exists as to whether reduced-fee work will qualify in part as pro bono work. In addition, the range of service options must be broad to avoid forcing lawyers into service that conflicts with their political or religious values.[373] Additional administrative personnel will be required to review reports to determine whether lawyers are in compliance with their pro bono obligations and to institute proceedings against lawyers who fail to do so. Finally, increasing the supply of legal services for the poor may harm rather than help the poor because more litigation may increase the cost of basic services provided to the poor, such as housing.[374]

The concept of mandatory pro bono has not been received with much enthusiasm by the bar. No state has adopted a mandatory pro bono requirement, although there has been some movement to place greater emphasis on voluntary pro bono service. In 1993 the ABA amended Model Rule 6.1 to provide for a voluntary pro bono standard of 50 hours per year, a substantial majority of which should be directed to "persons of limited means." Prior to the amendment, the rule provided:

> A lawyer should render public interest legal service. A lawyer may discharge this responsibility by providing professional services at no fee or a reduced fee to persons of limited means or to public service or charitable groups or organizations, by service in activities for improving the law, the legal system or the legal profession, and by financial support for organizations that provide legal services to persons of limited means.

The older version of Rule 6.1 did not specify an hourly standard, nor did it direct lawyers to focus their pro bono efforts on the poor.

The drafters of the 2002 revision to the Model Rules considered but finally rejected a proposal for a mandatory pro bono obligation. They did, however, add provisions strengthening the aspirational standard. Rule 6.1 now provides: "Every lawyer has a professional responsibility to provide legal services to those unable to pay." Comment 11 states that law firms should encourage all lawyers in the firm to provide pro bono services as set forth in the rule.

---

373. Id. at 1129-1130.
374. Jonathan R. Macey, Mandatory Pro Bono: Comfort for the Poor or Welfare for the Rich? 77 Cornell L. Rev. 1115 (1992). But see Ronald H. Silverman, Conceiving a Lawyer's Legal Duty to the Poor, 19 Hofstra L. Rev. 885 (1991). Professor Silverman's article is part of a symposium on mandatory pro bono, which includes the Marrero Report and the Cramton article cited earlier. See Symposium on Mandatory Pro Bono, 19 Hofstra L. Rev. No. 4 (1991). For another perspective, see Rob Atkinson, A Social-Democratic Critique of Pro Bono Publico Representation of the Poor: The Good as the Enemy of the Best, 9 Am. U.J. Gender Soc. Pol'y & L. 129 (2001) (arguing that pro bono representation is "good," but that publicly subsidized legal services is the "best" method of providing legal services to the poor because it is more efficient and fairer).

Several states, including Arizona, Florida, and Kentucky, have changed their rules of professional conduct to include more substantial provisions on voluntary pro bono representation.[375] The Florida rule provides an aspirational standard of either 20 hours of pro bono service or a contribution of $350 to a legal services organization per year.[376] Under the Florida rule lawyers must report whether they have complied with the rule's aspirational standard:[377] "The reporting requirement is designed to provide a sound basis for evaluating the results achieved by this rule, reveal the strengths and weaknesses of the pro bono plan, and to remind lawyers of their professional responsibility under this rule."[378] The majority of states, however, continue to adhere to the ABA's older version of Rule 6.1.

Despite much talk and rule changes to support pro bono services, the results are not encouraging. During 1990s pro bono hours of the most successful law firms declined by one-third.[379]

375. Ariz. R. Prof. Conduct 6.1; Fla. R. Prof. Conduct 4-6.1; Kentucky Sup. Ct. R. 3.130 (6.1).
376. Fla. R. Prof. Conduct 4-6.1(b).
377. Id. 4-6.1(d).
378. Id. cmt. Judith L. Maute, Changing Conceptions of Lawyers' Pro Bono Responsibilities: From Chance Noblesse Oblige to Stated Expectations, 77 Tul. L. Rev. 91 (2002); Kellie Isbell & Sarah Sawle, Current Developments, Pro Bono Publico: Voluntary Service and Mandatory Reporting, 15 Geo. J. Legal Ethics 845 (2002) (calling for mandatory reporting requirements).
379. Deborah L. Rhode, Access to Justice, 69 Fordham L. Rev. 1785, 1811 n.148 (2001). See also Isbell & Sawle, supra note 378, at 853.

Chapter 5

Ethical Issues in Office Practice

In previous chapters we have examined the application of fundamental ethical obligations, such as the duty of confidentiality, the obligation to avoid conflicts of interest, and limitations on zealous representation in the context of criminal practice and civil litigation. The world of office practitioners, whether they are involved in general business practice, securities, real estate, estate planning, tax, or other specialized fields, poses ethical problems that also require application of these fundamental ethical concepts. Indeed, in some respects the ethical and related legal issues facing office practitioners are more acute than in litigation practice because the amounts of money (and therefore the potential liability) involved in office practice can be staggering.

Section A of this chapter considers ethical problems of office practitioners engaged in business and securities practice. The problems focus on conflicts of interest in business formations and lawyers' obligations when they learn of fraud by their clients. Section B examines ethical issues in real estate, estate planning, and tax practice. These areas do not, of course, exhaust the specialized areas in which lawyers may practice. For example, bankruptcy practice involves a complex interrelationship between rules of professional conduct and provisions of the bankruptcy code.[1] The practice areas covered in these materials do illustrate, however, the most common ethical dilemmas faced by office practitioners.

A. Business and Securities Practice

Problem 5-1

Lawyers as Representatives of Multiple Clients, Investors, and Board Members

Nancy McDow, one of your long-time clients, has called you to arrange a meeting. McDow tells you that she and Vulkan Bronowski, a person

---

1. See generally 1 Norton Bankruptcy Law & Practice ch. 27 (2d ed.). See, e.g., In re Granite Partners, 219 B.R. 22 (Bankr. S.D.N.Y. 1998) (law firm representing Chapter

whom you have never met, wish to establish a small business to develop
and market computer programs that will assist American companies doing
business in Eastern Europe. McDow, an entrepreneur, will supply the
capital for the venture. Bronowski, an expert in computer programming
who recently emigrated to the United States, will lead the development
of software. McDow says that she and Bronowski will bring in a third
individual in the near future to take charge of marketing. McDow wants
you to handle the legal work for formation of the business. Given the
uncertain prospects for the business, McDow wants to limit cash expendi-
tures. She asks whether you would be willing to receive a 10 percent
ownership interest in the business in payment for your services. She says
that it might turn out to be "lucrative." McDow also wants you to serve
on the new company's board of directors. How would you handle the
initial meeting with McDow and Bronowski?

Read Model Rules 1.7, 1.8(a), 4.3, and comments.

Louis D. Brandeis: "lawyer for the situation"

In 1916 President Woodrow Wilson nominated a prominent Boston lawyer,
Louis D. Brandeis, to the Supreme Court. Brandeis's distinguished career had
involved him in many of the day's most important public issues.[2] The Brandeis
nomination was controversial, however, for a number of reasons. Wilson had
been elected as a minority president in a three-way election in 1912, and it
was not at all clear that he would be reelected in a direct confrontation with
a Republican. In addition, Brandeis had been a central figure in the downfall
of the Taft administration though his representation of Louis Glavis, a subordinate in the Department of the Interior, who resigned in a conservation scandal
involving the secretary of the interior. Brandeis had brought to light documents
showing that the president and the attorney general had made public misrepresentations in an effort to protect the secretary of the interior. Taft opposed the
Brandeis nomination not only because of this incident but also because he
personally wanted an appointment to the Court. Moreover, some powerful
business interests fought against the Brandeis appointment because he had
opposed them in various legal matters. Finally, Brandeis was the first Jew
nominated to the Court.[3]

Brandeis's opponents reviewed his entire legal career in an effort to find

---

11 trustee denied compensation of more than $2 million for failure to disclose conflict of
interest).

2. Biographies of Brandeis include Alpheus T. Mason, Brandeis, A Free Man's Life
(1946); Philippa Strum, Brandeis: Beyond Progressivism (1993); and Philippa Strum,
Louis D. Brandeis: Justice for the People (1984).

3. John P. Frank, The Legal Ethics of Louis D. Brandeis, 17 Stan. L. Rev. 683, 683-
685 (1965).

ammunition to scuttle the nomination. As a result, the Republican minority on the Senate Judiciary Committee issued a report charging Brandeis with 12 instances of ethical misconduct. In a study of these 12 cases, John Frank concluded that the charges against Brandeis were not meritorious and that "[o]ne's main impression is surprise that the powers of wealth and political position, which had been hitting at Brandeis for years and searching for every possible ground of complaint, should have found so little to work with."[4] One of the cases, the Lennox matter, is of particular interest to our study, because it relates to the issue of the propriety of lawyers' representing multiple clients in business transactions.

The Lennox matter involved a company that was in financial difficulty. The son of the owner of the company and an attorney for one of its creditors sought Brandeis's advice about the matter. Brandeis never specifically agreed to represent the company in the matter. Instead, he recommended an assignment for the benefit of creditors. A trust was established for the benefit of creditors, with one of Brandeis's partners as trustee. Ultimately, the company was forced into bankruptcy because the Lennox partners failed to convey assets to the trust. Brandeis represented petitioning creditors in the bankruptcy. The Lennox partners felt that Brandeis had turned against their interests, and they hired a lawyer to investigate Brandeis's conduct. Brandeis denied that he had ever agreed to represent the Lennoxes. He described his role as "counsel for the situation."[5]

Scholars have had mixed reactions to Brandeis's view of his role. Professor Thomas Shaffer praises Brandeis for a moral vision that recognizes groups as prior to individuals, and group harmony as a worthy moral goal.[6] In contrast, Clyde Spillenger criticizes Brandeis's commitment to his own independence and to autonomy from his clients.[7] John Frank, while vindicating Brandeis against charges of ethical misconduct, finds his conception of the lawyer for the situation as "too vague to be intelligible."[8]

Representation of multiple parties in business transactions under the Model Rules of Professional Conduct

Brandeis's view that a lawyer may act for multiple parties with potentially conflicting interests in an effort to produce a plan that serves all of their interests was problematic under the Code of Professional Responsibility. Disciplinary

4. Id. at 707.
5. Id. at 698-703. See also John S. Dzienkowski, Lawyers as Intermediaries: The Representation of Multiple Clients in the Modern Legal Profession, 1992 U. Ill. L. Rev. 741, 748-757.
6. Thomas L. Shaffer, The Legal Ethics of Radical Individualism, 65 Tex. L. Rev. 963, 981 (1987).
7. Clyde Spillenger, Elusive Advocate: Reconsidering Brandeis as People's Lawyer, 105 Yale L.J. 1445, 1502-1511 (1996).
8. Frank, The Legal Ethics of Louis D. Brandeis, 17 Stan. L. Rev. at 702.

Rule 5-105(C) provided that "a lawyer may represent multiple clients if it is obvious that he can adequately represent the interest of each and if each consents to the representation after full disclosure of the possible effect of such representation on the exercise of his independent professional judgment on behalf of cach." The use of the word "obvious" made it questionable whether a lawyer should represent multiple parties with different interests in a business transaction.[9]

The drafters of the Model Rules were well aware of Brandeis's concept of the "lawyer for the situation." Professor Geoffrey Hazard, the chief reporter for the Kutak Commission, devoted a chapter of his book *Ethics in the Practice of Law* to the concept. Hazard criticized the Code for recognizing only a "fragment of this kind of lawyering."[10] He suggested that it ought to be possible "to define the role of intercessor."[11] The 1983 version of the Model Rules included Rule 2.2, lawyer as intermediary, which was intended to provide standards under which a lawyer could represent multiple parties who, "though adverse in their respective positions, share a more compelling interest in reaching agreement as a group."[12]

The concept of intermediation has not fared well for several reasons. While the comments to Rule 2.2 stated that a lawyer who served as an intermediary was not serving as a mediator, the similarity in terminology caused misunderstanding. In addition, the relationship between Rule 2.2 and the general conflict of interest standard, Rule 1.7, was unclear. As a result the Restatement does not use the concept of intermediation. Instead, Restatement §130 provides standards for multiple representation in nonlitigation matters. Similarly, the 2002 revision to the Model Rules deletes Rule 2.2 and treats multiple representation in transactional matters under Rule 1.7.[13] Comments 8, 28, and 29-33 are particularly relevant to this issue.

Revised Model Rule 1.7 directs lawyers to a four-step process: (1) identification of the client or clients, (2) determination of whether a conflict exists, (3) analysis of whether any conflict is consentable, and (4) consultation with the clients to obtain their informed consent confirmed in writing. See comment 2.

Identification of the clients in business formations is very tricky. When multiple individuals are involved in the formation, it is possible for the lawyer to structure the relationship so that all of them are clients, only one of them is a client, or some group less than all of the promoters are clients. If the lawyer does not make it clear whom she represents, then all of the promoters are likely

---

9. Legal Ethics Forum, Representation of Multiple Clients, 62 A.B.A. J. 648 (1976).

10. Geoffrey C. Hazard, Jr., Ethics in the Practice of Law 62 (1978).

11. Id. at 67.

12. See 1 Hazard & Hodes, The Law of Lawyering §24.2, at 4.1.

13. It is unclear whether the states will follow the recommendation of the ABA to delete Rule 2.2. For lawyers who practice in jurisdictions that retain Rule 2.2, Professor Dzienkowski's article cited in note 5 is an excellent source for understanding the rule. See also 1 Hazard & Hodes ch. 24.

to be treated as clients.[14] If the lawyer does make it clear that the lawyer is representing only some of the promoters, then the lawyer should inform the unrepresented promoters to seek the advice of their own attorney. If they choose to be unrepresented, the lawyer must comply with Rule 4.3. Another aspect of the client identification process is the relationship between the lawyer and the entity to be formed.[15] For relatively small businesses, the assumption probably is that the lawyer will do the legal work for the entity once it is formed. Thus, unless the lawyer makes it clear that she is not representing the entity, the lawyer will also have a client-lawyer relationship with it. In summary, if a lawyer meets with a group of promoters, advises them about business formation issues, forms an entity, and then proceeds to do legal work for the entity, the lawyer very likely has a client-attorney relationship with all the promoters and with the entity. To achieve a different result, the lawyer must make clear, preferably in writing, the identity of represented parties and must comply with Rule 4.3 as to any unrepresented person.

The comments to revised Model Rule 1.7 are clear that when a lawyer represents promoters in forming a business a conflict of interest almost certainly exists under Rule 1.7(a)(2) dealing with a significant risk that the lawyer's representation will be materially limited. Comment 8 states: "For example, a lawyer asked to represent several individuals seeking to form a joint venture is likely to be materially limited in the lawyer's ability to recommend or advocate all possible positions that each might take because of the lawyer's duty of loyalty to the others." On the entire range of financial and control issues involved in a business formation the lawyer who represents multiple clients cannot advocate one client's interest over the others. The lawyer must treat the clients equally and must be neutral among them.

Assuming that a conflict exists, as is likely in any business formation, the third step in the analysis requires the lawyer to determine whether the conflict is consentable. Most conflicts are consentable, with the notable exception of adverse claims before a tribunal under Rule 1.7(b)(3); this rule would not apply to business formations. To decide whether the conflict is consentable, the lawyer must "reasonably believe[ ] that the lawyer will be able to provide competent and diligent representation to each affected client." Model Rule 1.7(b)(1). What factors should the lawyer consider in making this determination in the context of a business formation? First, the lawyer must determine whether there is a fundamental antagonism between the parties or whether they appear to have a common interest even though some differences exist. In most business ventures, the latter should be the case; if it is not, the lawyer should not proceed

14. See Restatement (Third) of the Law Governing Lawyers §14(1)(b) (providing that a client-attorney relationship is formed when the lawyer fails to inform a person that that lawyer is not representing the person and the lawyer knows or reasonably should know that the person reasonably relies on the lawyer to provide services).

15. For an excellent discussion of the client identification issues in business formations, including the lawyer's relationship with the entity, see Arizona St. Bar. Comm. on Rules of Prof. Cond., Op. 02-06 (2002).

with multiple representation. Comment 28 discusses this factor. Second, a lawyer who represents multiple clients in a business formation must be impartial. If the lawyer does not believe that she can be impartial, she should not undertake multiple representation. See comment 29. When a lawyer has a long-standing professional relationship with one of the parties to the business formation, the likelihood that the lawyer can be impartial is diminished. Third, generally in multiple representation, the lawyer must share any information received from one client that is material to the representation with the other clients. See comment 31. If one of the parties has a substantial interest in maintaining confidentiality of information from the others, the lawyer probably should not undertake multiple representation. Fourth, in multiple representation all of the clients must assume a greater role for decision making than when they are separately represented. See comment 32. If one of the parties is less capable of assuming this responsibility because of lack of experience or sophistication, multiple representation becomes questionable. On the other hand, multiple representation may provide better protection for an unsophisticated person's interests if that person would choose not to be represented should the lawyer decline multiple representation.

If the lawyer reasonably believes the conflict is consentable, then the lawyer must obtain the informed consent of each client confirmed in writing. Model Rule 1.7(b)(4). In broad terms informed consent requires the lawyer to provide the client with sufficient information for the client to understand the implications of common representation, the advantages and disadvantages of multiple representation, and the alternatives available to the clients. See comment 18. See also Model Rule 1.0(e) and comment 6. The attorney should discuss at least the following points:

Neutrality.   If one lawyer represents all of the parties, the lawyer has duties to all of them. The lawyer cannot favor one party at the expense of any other or act as a partisan or advocate for any party. See comment 32. The lawyer has a duty to raise any issue that may be material to any of the parties. The use of a single lawyer may increase the likelihood that any differences between the clients will be resolved because one lawyer can focus on common interests and agreement rather than on possible points of disagreement. While a lawyer who represents multiple parties has a duty to treat all of them evenhandedly, the lawyer may intentionally or unconsciously favor one party over the others. This risk exists particularly when the lawyer has a long-standing relationship with one of the parties.

Full disclosure/No confidentiality.   The lawyer has an obligation to provide all parties with any information that the lawyer received from any other party that is material to the representation. The parties must understand that multiple representation means that there will be no confidentiality among the clients. If a party insists on confidentiality, the lawyer will be forced to withdraw. See comment 31.

Withdrawal in the event of a dispute. If the clients fail to reach agreement or if a dispute develops that cannot be resolved, the lawyer will be forced to withdraw from representation of all the parties and cannot represent any of them without the consent of the others. See comments 29 and 33. The lawyer's withdrawal would force the parties to hire new counsel, unfamiliar with the matter, at added expense.

Attorney-client privilege in the event of litigation between the clients. The rule followed in most jurisdictions is that the attorney-client privilege does not apply to any dispute between jointly represented clients. See comment 30. Thus, the lawyer may be required to testify as to any communications received from any other party. The lawyer's files would also be available to any party to the dispute.

Fees and expenses. Multiple representation can save legal fees if the parties are able to resolve any differences they have because the parties are only hiring one lawyer rather than multiple lawyers. However, if the parties are unable to resolve their differences, the lawyer will be forced to withdraw and the clients may need to hire separate lawyers, unfamiliar with the business. In this event the clients are likely to incur greater legal expense than would have been the case if they had hired separate lawyers initially.

Alternatives to multiple representation. As part of informed consent the lawyer must also discuss with the potential clients the alternatives to multiple representation. The two obvious alternatives are separate representation with each person having his or her own counsel or separate representation with one or more people being unrepresented. Separate counsel for all parties has the advantage that each person receives the benefit of consultation and advocacy by a lawyer devoted to that person's own interests. Separate representation has the disadvantage of additional expense. In addition, separate representation may lead to an emphasis on different rather than common interests, making consensus more difficult or more time consuming, especially if several attorneys are involved. If a party chooses not to be represented, that party will not receive the advice of counsel and will be at a disadvantage in negotiations regarding issues involved in the formation of the business. The attorney who represents another party cannot give the unrepresented person any legal advice. See Model Rule 4.3.

If the clients are willing to consent to multiple representation, the lawyer must confirm their consent in writing. While the rule does not require the clients to sign a consent document, prudent lawyers will attempt to obtain a signed consent if possible. One way to do this is to send letters to each client confirming each client's oral consent. The letter could ask the clients to sign and return the consent but could also specify that the client's oral consent is nonetheless effective unless the client informs the lawyer otherwise within a specified period of time.

The Restatement, like the Model Rules, provides that lawyers may generally represent multiple clients in business formations provided the clients give informed consent.[16] The Restatement also goes somewhat further. If a dispute arises after the business has been formed, the lawyer may, with informed consent, represent the parties in an effort to resolve the dispute amicably.[17]

Conflicts of interest resulting from lawyers' ownership of interests in their clients' businesses

Ordinary commercial contracts may be rescinded because of fraud, duress, mistake, impossibility, unconscionability, illegality, and other invalidating events.[18] Contracts between fiduciaries and their clients, however, are subject to special restrictions in addition to those limitations that apply to ordinary business transactions. Clients may rescind contracts with their fiduciaries if the contract is unfair to the client or if the fiduciary fails to disclose all material facts to the client regarding the transaction. These special rules are justified because of the high degree of trust and confidence that clients repose in fiduciaries.[19]

Model Rule 1.8(a) embodies these general restrictions on business transactions between fiduciaries and their clients, but goes somewhat further as the following case illustrates:

Petit-Clair v. Nelson

New Jersey Superior Court, Appellate Division 782 A.2d 960 (2001)

HAVEY, P.J.A.D.

Defendants Christian and Phyllis Nelson retained plaintiff Edward F. Petit-Clair, Esquire, to represent their two corporations, Poseidon Associates, Inc. and Paulson Engineering, Inc. The corporations were plaintiffs in proceedings entitled Poseidon Assocs., Inc. and Paulson Eng., Inc. v. Industrial Crating and Rigging (*Paulson* litigation). During the litigation, defendants agreed to give plaintiff a mortgage on their personal residence to secure payment of legal fees incurred during the proceedings. At the conclusion of the litigation, defendants executed and delivered to plaintiff a mortgage in the amount of $41,299, securing payment of the legal fees.

When defendants defaulted, plaintiff filed a foreclosure complaint in the Chancery Division. After a bench trial, the trial court concluded that the mortgage was invalid. It held that since the mortgage was a "business transac-

---

16. Restatement (Third) of the Law Governing Lawyers §130 and cmt. *a.* and illus. 4.

17. Id. illus. 5.

18. See Charles L. Knapp, Nathan M. Crystal, and Harry G. Prince, Problems in Contract Law chs. 7 and 8 (5th ed. 2003).

19. See Restatement (Third) of the Law Governing Lawyers §126 and cmt. *b.*

tion," plaintiff had an affirmative duty to advise defendants of the desirability to seek independent counsel, but failed to do so. See RPC 1.8(a). The trial court further concluded that there was no consideration to support the giving of the mortgage. We affirm.

On March 10, 1988, plaintiff was retained by Poseidon Associates, Inc. and Paulson Engineering, Inc., to institute an action against Industrial Crating and Rigging, Inc. Defendants, Christian and Phyllis Nelson, are president and secretary of the corporations respectively. Christian executed a retainer agreement with plaintiff solely in his capacity as president of the two corporations.

A total of $8,000 was paid to plaintiff for services rendered. However, during the course of the *Paulson* litigation Christian and Phyllis, in their capacities as president and secretary of Paulson Engineering, executed a letter agreement with plaintiff dated June 17, 1989, in which they agreed to give plaintiff a security interest in Poseidon's equipment and in equipment owned by them personally. Further, both Christian and Phyllis agreed to give plaintiff a mortgage on their Kinnelon residence securing the amount of the legal fees due plaintiff. On September 27, 1989, the Nelsons executed and delivered the mortgage to plaintiff securing the legal fee debt.

The Nelsons failed to make payment on the mortgage. As a result, on August 15, 1997, eight years after execution of the mortgage, plaintiff filed a foreclosure action in the Chancery Division, Morris County. As noted, the trial court concluded that the mortgage was invalid because of plaintiff's failure to comply with RPC 1.8(a) by not advising defendants to seek independent counsel.

"[A]n attorney's freedom to contract with a client is subject to the constraints of ethical considerations" and the Supreme Court's supervision. Cohen v. Radio-Elec. Officers Union, 146 N.J. 140, 155, 679 A.2d 1188 (1996). Any transaction between an attorney and client is "subject to close scrutiny and the burden of establishing fairness and equity of the transaction rests upon the attorney." In re Gallop, 85 N.J. 317, 322, 426 A.2d 509 (1981); In re Nichols, 95 N.J. 126, 131, 469 A.2d 494 (1984). This is because " '[a]n attorney in his relations with a client is bound to the highest degree of fidelity and good faith. The strongest influences of public policy require strict adherence to such a role of conduct.' " In re Nichols, supra, 95 N.J. at 131, 469 A.2d 494 (quoting In re Gavel, 22 N.J. 248, 262, 125 A.2d 696 (1956)). Consequently, an otherwise enforceable agreement between an attorney and client is invalid "if it runs afoul of ethical rules governing that relationship." Cohen, supra, 146 N.J. at 156, 679 A.2d 1188. In that situation, the lawyer is duty-bound to "make sure that the client understands that the lawyer's ability to give undivided loyalty may be affected and must explain carefully, clearly, and cogently why independent legal advice is required." P & M Enter. v. Murray., 293 N.J.Super. 310, 314, 680 A.2d 790 (App. Div. 1996) (holding that a "transaction between a lawyer and client is presumptively invalid").

RPC 1.8(a) provides: [The court quotes NJ Rule of Professional Conduct 1.8(a)]. By its very terms, the rule is mandatory; it provides that a lawyer "shall not" knowingly acquire a security or pecuniary interest adverse to the client unless the client is advised of the desirability of seeking independent counsel. Thus, the Supreme Court has found a violation of RPC 1.8(a) where the attorney loaned his client $40,000 to purchase a house and took back a mortgage without advising her to seek advice from an independent attorney. In re Humen, 123 N.J. 289, 297-99, 586 A.2d 237 (1991). Further, in In re Loring, 62 N.J. 336, 341-42, 301 A.2d 721 (1973), the Court did not hesitate to find a conflict when an attorney representing a client in a real estate sale asserted a fee lien on the closing proceedings and took back a mortgage on the client's new residence to secure payment of the fee, noting that the client received no independent legal advice in connection with the consequence of imposition of the lien.

Here, it is clear that defendants' mortgage on their personal residence given to plaintiff was a "security. . . interest adverse to [the defendants]. . . ." Consequently, plaintiff had the burden of demonstrating both that the terms of the mortgage were fair and reasonable and that he advised defendants of the desirability of retaining independent counsel. Plaintiff admitted that he never gave such advice. Had he done so, independent counsel may have convinced defendants not to execute the mortgage since, as the trial court aptly pointed out, on its face the retainer agreement provides that the legal fee debt was owed by the corporations, not by defendants personally. Implicit in the court's determination invalidating the mortgage was that, because of plaintiff's failure to comply with the mandatory dictate of RPC 1.8(a), the making of the mortgage in plaintiff's favor was unreasonable and unfair to defendants. We agree.

Plaintiff's argument that RPC 1.8(a) is inapplicable here because he represented the corporations, and not the defendants individually, is unavailing. All that is necessary is that the parties relate "to each other generally as attorney and client. It is also clear that it is the substance of the relationship, involving as it does a heightened aspect of reliance, that triggers the need for the rule's prescriptions of full disclosure and informed consent." In re Silverman, 113 N.J. 193, 214, 549 A.2d 1225 (1988). It is undisputed that defendants and plaintiff related to each other as attorney and client. Defendants relied on plaintiff's guidance and advice. Indeed, plaintiff had previously represented Mrs. Nelson in an unrelated matter. Although Christian signed the retainer agreement only in his corporate capacity, the corporation themselves were creatures of the law which did not rely on the confidences which arose from the attorney/client relationship. . . . Obviously, it was defendants personally who consulted with plaintiff and relied on his legal representation during the *Paulson* litigation, not the corporations. Moreover, every confidential communication from plaintiff to the corporations was in fact to defendants as individuals. Finally, it was defendants, not the corporations, whom plaintiff persuaded to pledge the equity in their personal residence to secure payment of the legal fee balance.

Affirmed.

Notes and Questions

1. The 2002 revisions to Model Rule 1.8(a) strengthen the requirements of the rule. As revised, the rule imposes three requirements on lawyers who enter into business transactions with clients. First, the terms of the transaction must be fair and reasonable to the client and must be fully disclosed in a writing that can be reasonably understood by the client. Second, the lawyer must advise the client in writing of the desirability of seeking independent legal advice about the transaction and the client must have a reasonable opportunity to seek such advice. Finally, the client must give informed consent in writing signed by the client to the essential terms of the transaction including an explanation of whether the lawyer is representing the client in the transaction.

2. Comment 1 explains that Rule 1.8(a) does not apply to ordinary fee contracts, which are governed by Rule 1.5. However, as *Petit-Clair* shows, fee contracts in which the lawyer obtains an interest in the client's property as security for the fee are subject to Rule 1.8(a). If the client agrees to give the lawyer an ownership interest in the client's business in lieu of a cash fee, the rule applies. See ABA, Formal Op. 00-418 (no per se bar to lawyers taking an ownership interest in client start-ups; lawyers must comply with Rules 1.8(a) and with 1.5, when applicable; in providing legal services lawyers must take care to avoid conflicts resulting from their personal financial interest under Rule 1.7(b) and must provide independent advice under Rule 2.1). Investments are subject to the rule. Cf. Passante v. McWilliams, 62 Cal. Rptr. 2d 298 (Ct. App. 1997) (oral agreement providing for lawyer's equity interest in corporation unenforceable because of violation of California Rule 3-300, resulting in loss to lawyer estimated at $30 million). For a comprehensive discussion of lawyer equity investments in clients, see John S. Dzienkowski & Robert J. Peroni, The Decline in Lawyer Independence: Lawyer Equity Investments in Clients, 81 Tex. L. Rev. 405 (2002). The rule also applies when the lawyer sells goods or services related to the practice of law, such as title insurance or investment services. See comment 1. Chapter 7 discusses ancillary business activities by law firms. Probably the most dangerous form of transaction occurs when a lawyer borrows money from a client without adequate security. See, e.g., Lawyer Disciplinary Board v. Barber, 566 S.E.2d 245 (W.Va. 2002) (suspending lawyer for obtaining large unsecured loan from client).

3. *Petit-Clair* was a civil case in which the court invalidated the mortgage. See also Miller v. Sears, 636 P.2d 1183 (Alaska 1981) (clients able to rescind contract for sale of property by lawyer to them because of lawyer's failure to disclose personal liability of clients on note). Lawyers who violate Rule 1.8(a) may also be subject to professional discipline. See, e.g., In re James, 452 A.2d 163 (D.C. 1982), *cert. denied*, 460 U.S. 1038 (1983) (lawyer disciplined for failure to make full disclosure to clients of risks and advantages of sale of building from clients to lawyer) and the *Barber* case in note 2.

4. In *Petit-Clair* the clients agreed to the mortgage after the original engagement. Post-engagement fee modifications are subject to special scrutiny. Not only has a fiduciary relationship been formed, but the situation has a risk

of coercion because the client may be dependent on the lawyer's services and unable to easily obtain substitute counsel. See Restatement (Third) of the Law Governing Lawyers §18 and cmt. *e.*

Conflicts of interest resulting from service on the boards of directors of clients

The issue of whether lawyers should be allowed to serve as members of the boards of directors of their clients has been controversial in the profession for a number of years.[20] The Model Rules do not prohibit lawyers from serving on the boards of directors of their clients, but Comment 35 to Rule 1.7 cautions lawyers about the possible conflicts of interest that can arise and advises lawyers that if "there is material risk that the dual role will compromise the lawyer's independence of professional judgment, the lawyer should not serve as a director or should cease to act as the corporation's lawyer when conflicts of interest arise." Comment 35 further provides that a lawyer who serves as director should inform the board that in some situations communications in which the attorney is present may not be subject to the attorney-client privilege and that the lawyer's service may give rise to conflicts of interest requiring either the lawyer's recusal as a director or the firm's refusal to accept representation in a matter."[21]

Why would a lawyer agree to serve on the board of directors of a client? Prestige is one reason; service on the board of a major corporate client brings a measure of prominence to the lawyer. Service on the board can also strengthen the business relationship between the lawyer's firm and the client. In addition, service on the board can facilitate the lawyer's role as counselor because the lawyer is more familiar with the activities of the client. At the same time, any lawyer who contemplates serving on the board of directors of a client should be aware of the substantial risks involved, including the following:[22]

---

20. *Compare* David S. Ruder, The Case Against the Lawyer-Director, 30 Bus. Law. 51 (Special Issue, March 1975), *with* Sam Harris, The Case for the Lawyer-Director, 30 Bus. Law. 58 (Special Issue, March 1975).

21. See ABA Comm. on Ethics and Prof. Resp., Formal Op. 98-410 (Model Rules do not prohibit lawyer from serving as director of corporation while simultaneously serving as its legal counsel, but there are ethical concerns that lawyer occupying dual role should consider); Restatement (Third) of the Law Governing Lawyers §135, cmt. *d* (duties of director and lawyer are generally consistent; when obligations as director are materially adverse to those of lawyer as corporate counsel, lawyer may not continue to serve as corporate counsel without informed consent of corporate client). See also ABA Section of Litigation, The Lawyer-Director: Implications for Independence (1998).

22. See Craig C. Albert, The Lawyer-Director: An Oxymoron? 9 Geo. J. Legal Ethics 413 (1996) (examining the benefits and risks of dual role and arguing against rule prohibiting lawyers from serving as directors). See also James D. Cox, The Paradoxical Corporate and Securities Law Implications of Counsel Serving on the Client's Board, 80 Wash. U. L.Q. 541 (2002) (arguing that dual service leads to the paradoxical results of greater scrutiny of corporate managers and loss of business for the firm of the lawyer that serves on the board).

- *Risk of loss of the attorney-client privilege.* The privilege applies only to communications between lawyer and client for the purpose of seeking legal advice. To the extent that communications were with the lawyer in the lawyer's capacity as director or to the extent they involved business rather than legal matters, the privilege is lost. In addition, the privilege applies only if the communications were made in confidence, a condition that may not be met when the communications occur in board meetings.

- *Disqualification of the lawyer's firm.* If the corporation is a party to litigation, the lawyer's firm may be disqualified from handling the matter because the lawyer may be a witness in the matter. Similarly, if the lawyer is a party to the litigation, the firm may be disqualified because of a conflict of interest between it and the client. If the corporation is forced into bankruptcy, the firm may be disqualified from representing the corporation in bankruptcy because of the lawyer's service on the board.

- *Increased exposure to liability.* Service on the board exposes the lawyer to increased liability. Not only is the lawyer subject to liability for malpractice, but the lawyer also becomes subject to liability as a director on various theories, including violation of federal and state securities laws. Law firms may also face increased liability when one of their members serves on the board of a client. The law firm could be held vicariously liable for the lawyer's conduct.

- *Inadequate insurance.* Many malpractice policies exclude from coverage service on a board of directors or other nonlegal activities.

In Formal Opinion 98-410 the ABA Committee on Ethics and Professional Responsibility opined that lawyers may properly serve in the dual capacity of corporate director and counsel for the corporation, but the committee cautioned lawyers about the ethical difficulties involved. The committee offered lawyers a number of suggestions for performing these dual roles to avoid disciplinary violations.[23]

Problem 5-2

Fraud by Clients in Business Transactions

a. Your firm represents National Computer, Inc., a large manufacturer of computer equipment. Ellen Lee is National's vice president for procurement. Recently, Lee called you about negotiating a renewal of a supply contact between National and Microchip International. Your firm

---

23. ABA Section of Business Law, Committee on Lawyer Business Ethics, The Lawyer as Director of a Client, 57 Bus. Law. 387 (2001) (discussion of risks and how to approach issue).

prepared the original contract three years ago. Lee has told you that the contract expires in six months and that National wishes to renew the contract for as long as possible. Lee also has informed you that microchips have been in short supply and that renewal of the contract is essential to National's business. During the conversation Lee mentions that it was difficult to obtain the first contract and that she found it necessary to give Microchip's vice president of sales "something on the side" to finalize the contract. How would you proceed? How would you proceed if National Computer was a publicly held company that was required to file quarterly and annual reports with the SEC? Would it matter if you had significant involvement in preparing those reports?

b. The firm is also defending a breach of warranty action brought by one of National's customers. As far as Ms. Lee knows, there does not appear to be any relationship between this matter and the contract with Microchip, but it is a little hard to tell at this point because the firm has just submitted an answer on National's behalf. Discovery has not begun.

In addition, National Computer has a line of credit with Interstate Bank. In connection with the line of credit, your firm has given an opinion letter to Interstate regarding the Microchip agreement. The letter included the following opinions regarding the Microchip agreement:

1.   The agreement is legally enforceable against National.
2.   Execution, delivery, and performance by National of the provisions of the agreement do not breach or result in a default under any other agreements that are material to National's business.
3.   Execution, delivery, and performance by National of the provisions of the agreement do not violate applicable provisions of statutory law or regulations.
4.   There are no actions or proceedings against National, pending or overtly threatened in writing, before any court, governmental agency or arbitrator, that seek to affect the enforceability of the agreement.

In light of what Ms. Lee has told you, what actions, if any, would you take regarding the breach of warranty action and the Interstate Bank loan?

c. You have been appointed by the president of your state bar to a committee formed to study and make recommendations for revisions of your state's rules of professional conduct. To what extent does your state's current rule on confidentiality permit or require disclosure of confidential information to prevent or rectify a client's fraud in a business transaction? What changes would you recommend making in your state's rule? Why?

If you believe the current rule should not be changed, be prepared to explain why the current rule is sound as a matter of policy.

Read Model Rules 1.2(d), 1.6, 1.13, 1.16, and comments.

Controversy over lawyers' ethical and legal obligations when they encounter criminal or fraudulent conduct by their clients

For over a quarter century, the issue of how a lawyer should respond if the lawyer learns that a client plans to or has engaged in a financial crime or fraud has been the topic of heated debate within the legal profession and the subject of lawsuits, administrative proceedings, and, recently, Congressional action. The issue involves tension between two values: client confidentiality and prevention or rectification of harm resulting from client wrongdoing. Where to draw the line accommodating these two values, however, has been very controversial. The legal profession has generally favored broader protection of confidentiality while courts, administrative agencies, and Congress have tended to give greater weight to harm prevention or rectification.[24] The materials that follow discuss the following topics: (1) the ethical prohibition against lawyers counseling or assisting clients in criminal or fraudulent conduct, (2) the scope of the ethical duty of confidentiality with regard to criminal or fraudulent conduct by clients under the Model Rules, (3) the scope of the duty of confidentiality under regulations adopted by the SEC pursuant to the Sarbanes-Oxley Act, and (4) legal liability of lawyers with regard to crimes or frauds committed by their clients.

The ethical obligation not to counsel or assist clients in criminal or fraudulent conduct

Ethically, lawyers have an obligation not to counsel or assist their clients in business transactions that they know are criminal or fraudulent.[25] See Model Rule 1.2(d). Note that this obligation parallels the duty of criminal defense lawyers not to assist their clients in criminal or fraudulent activity. Recall Problem 2-4 and in particular In re Ryder.[26]

---

24. Susan P. Koniak, When the Hurlyburly's Done: The Bar's Struggle with the SEC, 103 Colum. L. Rev. 1236 (2003) (reviewing the history of lawyer involvement in major corporate scandals and the tension between the bar's ethics rules and the SEC's enforcement of the securities laws).

25. See Florida Bar v. Calvo, 630 So. 2d 548 (Fla. 1993), *cert. denied*, 513 U.S. 809 (1994) (lawyer disbarred for participation in fraudulent securities offering); Iowa Supreme Court Bd. of Professional Ethics & Conduct v. Vinyard, 656 N.W.2d 127 (Iowa 2003) (lawyer disbarred after criminal convictions for money laundering and mail fraud).

26. 263 F. Supp. 360 (E.D. Va.), *aff'd*, 381 F.2d 713 (4th Cir. 1967).

Although the principle that lawyers may not counsel or assist clients in illegal or fraudulent conduct is well established, the scope of this obligation is imprecise. First, it should be clear that a lawyer does not counsel or assist a client in committing a crime or fraud if the lawyer does nothing more than advise a client that the client's planned course of action would be illegal or fraudulent. Model Rule 1.2(d) states that a lawyer "may discuss the legal consequences of any proposed course of conduct with a client." See also Comment 9.[27]

Second, a lawyer may not counsel or assist a client in conduct that the lawyer *knows* is illegal or fraudulent, but when does the lawyer know of a crime or fraud? We encountered this issue in Problem 2-5, which addressed the lawyer's ethical obligations when a client commits perjury in a criminal case. As we saw, courts and commentators have suggested several possible standards for knowledge, including a "firm factual basis" or "beyond a reasonable doubt." Other commentators have argued that "willful blindness" or "conscious avoidance" should be treated as the equivalent of knowledge.[28]

Third, what are the consequences of the duty not to counsel or assist a client in criminal or fraudulent conduct with regard to the lawyer's ability to continue to represent the client? The lawyer obviously cannot continue to handle the legal work for illegal or fraudulent transactions (such as preparing opinions or other documents or participating in closings) since such conduct would amount to direct assistance of the client's wrongdoing. Must the lawyer formally resign from representation in connection with any wrongful transactions? For example, the client might retain other counsel, who is unaware of the wrongdoing, to handle the transaction, but might ask the first lawyer to refrain from formally resigning to avoid raising a "red flag." If the purpose of withholding the lawyer's resignation is to mislead new counsel into believing that the lawyer is still associated with the client and that the client is not engaged in misconduct, isn't the lawyer providing indirect assistance of fraud?

Is a lawyer who knows that a client is engaged in an illegal or fraudulent transaction prohibited from having any involvement whatsoever with the transaction? Suppose, for example, that a lawyer knows that a client is engaging in a fraudulent financial transaction, but the lawyer is not representing the client in the transaction. May the lawyer respond to a letter from the client's accountant asking the lawyer to state the amount of outstanding legal fees that the client owes the lawyer, or does even providing factual information constitute assistance of the fraud? In civil cases involving claims of aider and abetter liability against attorneys (discussed later in this problem), the courts have held

27. See also Geoffrey C. Hazard, Jr., Rectification of Client Fraud: Death and Revival of a Professional Norm, 33 Emory L.J. 271, 281-282 (1984).

28. Cf. John P. Freeman & Nathan M. Crystal, Scienter in Professional Liability Cases, 42 S.C. L. Rev. 783, 833-838 (1991); Hazard, Rectification of Client Fraud, 33 Emory L.J. at 282-283.

that lawyers were liable only if they provided "substantial" assistance to client fraud.[29]

A related aspect of the question as to how far the prohibition on counseling or assisting a crime or fraud extends deals with representation in unrelated matters. Does the obligation mean that the lawyer can have no involvement in transactions that are unrelated to the crime or fraud? For example, suppose a law firm knows that a client is engaging in a fraudulent securities transaction. Must the firm refuse to represent the client in unrelated civil litigation? Must it refuse to represent the client in unrelated business matters? In essence, must the firm resign from all employment by the client?

In Formal Opinion 92-366, the ABA Committee on Ethics and Professional Responsibility examined the ethical aspects of a lawyer's continued representation of a client who was engaged in fraud in matters that were both related and unrelated to the fraud. The committee opined that a lawyer was ethically required to withdraw from representation in matters directly involving fraud. As to unrelated matters, the committee concluded that withdrawal was more likely to be permissive under Model Rule 1.16. The committee also advised, however, that "complete severance may be the preferred course in these circumstances, in order to avoid any possibility of the lawyer's continued association with the client's fraud."[30]

Lawyer advice with regard to corporate document retention programs can raise issues of counseling or assisting clients in criminal or fraudulent conduct. Corporations may legally establish policies and procedures for retention and destruction of physical and electronic documents, and lawyers may ethically and legally advise their clients about the creation and implementation of such programs.[31] However, federal law, and the law of almost all states, makes obstruction of justice a crime.[32] Destruction of documents or electronic information relevant to a pending court proceeding, administrative investigation, or legislative hearing can amount to obstruction of justice.[33] It is important for lawyers to understand that obstruction of justice can occur even though a subpoena has not been issued and even before a proceeding is filed if a proceeding is likely.[34] Accordingly, a corporation's lawyer should advise the company

---

29. See SEC v. National Student Marketing Corp., 457 F. Supp. 682, 713-715 (D.D.C. 1978); see also Restatement (Second) of Torts §876(b).

30. ABA Formal Op. 92-366, at 6. See also Geoffrey C. Hazard, Jr., Lawyers and Client Fraud: They Still Don't Get It, 6 Geo. J. Legal Ethics 701, 728-729 (1993) (arguing that duty not to counsel or assist in fraud does not preclude defense of litigation arising from fraud or representation in unrelated matters).

31. Christopher R. Chase, To Shred or Not to Shred: Document Retention Policies and Federal Obstruction of Justice Statutes, 8 Fordham J. Corp. & Fin. L. 721 (2003).

32. Id. at 729-745.

33. Id.

34. Id. at 734-735, 737-738. Cf. United States v. Perlstein, 126 F.2d 789 (3d Cir.), cert. denied, 316 U.S. 678 (1942) (two lawyers convicted of conspiracy to obstruct future judicial proceeding based on their advice to a client to destroy documents if a judicial proceeding was initiated).

to suspend document destruction activities as soon as a company receives notice that a proceeding or investigation is likely.[35] In 2002 the Arthur Andersen accounting firm was convicted of obstruction of justice for destroying documents relating to its representation of the Enron corporation. The conviction led to the firm's demise. In an infamous e-mail, Andersen's in-house counsel suggested that Andersen employees continue to implement the firm's document destruction policy even though Andersen knew about an SEC investigation into the Enron scandal.[36]

The scope of the duty of confidentiality with regard to criminal or fraudulent client conduct under the Model Rules: "Reporting Up" and "Reporting Out"

The duty not to counsel or assist a client in a crime or fraud is not the only obligation applicable to lawyers when they confront such conduct. Under the Model Rules, a lawyer may also have the obligation or discretion to disclose the crime or fraud. In considering the issue of disclosure of a client crime or fraud, a distinction is drawn between "reporting up" and "reporting out," although those terms are not used in the rules. Reporting up refers to the lawyer informing higher authority *within the organization* of the crime or fraud. Model Rule 1.13 governs reporting up. Reporting out involves disclosure by the lawyer *outside the organization*. Reporting out is sometimes appropriate to prevent harm to people other than the client. Model Rule 1.6 deals with this form of reporting out. In addition, Rule 1.13(c) provides for a different form of reporting out, to prevent substantial injury to the organization.[37] The ABA adopted major amendments to Rules 1.6 and 1.13 in August 2003 based on the report of its Task Force on Corporate Responsibility. These changes occurred in response to corporate scandals involving Enron and WorldCom and Congressional enactment of the Sarbanes-Oxley Act as a result of these scandals.[38]

Model Rule 1.13(a) adopts an "entity representation" principle, providing that a lawyer retained by an organization represents the entity rather than any of its "constituents." For a corporation, the term *constituents* means officers, directors, employees, and shareholders. For other entities, the equivalent categories are treated as constituents. Model Rule 1.13, cmt. 1. The principle means that a lawyer does not have a client-lawyer relationship with any of the constituents of an entity merely because the lawyer represents the entity.[39] Even

---

35. See Chase, supra note 31, at 757-758.

36. Id. at 746-755.

37. The discussion that follows assumes that there is no proceeding pending before a tribunal. If so, Model Rule 3.3 would impose additional, more demanding disclosure obligations.

38. The report is available online at http://www.abanet.org/buslaw/corporateresponsibility/ (visited Sept. 14, 2003).

39. It is, of course, possible for a lawyer who represents an entity to also have a client-lawyer relationship with one of the entity's constituents. Such a relationship, however, arises expressly rather than by virtue of the lawyer's representation of the entity. For example,

though a lawyer does not represent a constituent of an entity, information received from any constituent of the entity may still be subject to the attorney-client evidentiary privilege, depending on how broadly a court interprets the privilege.[40]

The entity representation principle has important implications if a lawyer learns about wrongdoing by a constituent or other person associated with the organization. The lawyer cannot follow the directions or seek to protect the interests of the person who is involved in wrongdoing because the lawyer represents the entity, not that person. How should the lawyer proceed? Model Rule 1.13(b) provides that a lawyer must take action to protect the entity when the lawyer knows that a constituent or other person associated with the organization[41] acts or fails to act "in a matter related to the representation that is a violation of a legal obligation to the organization, or a violation of law that reasonably might be imputed to the organization, and that is likely to result in substantial injury to the organization." The section apparently envisions two types of cases. In the first, the person is engaged in some type of breach of fiduciary duty, such as misappropriation of the entity's funds. In the second, the person is involved in illegal conduct as to third parties, such as securities fraud.

The application of Rule 1.13(b) raises a number of issues and uncertainties. First, under the rule the lawyer must "know" of the misconduct before the duty to act applies. We have already encountered this issue in the context of false testimony by criminal defendants. Recall Problem 2-5. In some cases, the lawyer's knowledge may be clear; for example, if the lawyer has direct evidence that an officer has converted corporate funds. In many cases, particu-

---

if the lawyer for a corporation performs estate planning or real estate services for an officer of the corporation, the lawyer has a client-lawyer relationship with both the corporation and the officer. In some cases, it is permissible for a lawyer to represent both the corporation and its constituents in litigation. See Model Rule 1.13(g). In other situations, multiple representation of the corporation and its constituents may be improper. See Model Rule 1.13, cmts. 13 and 14, and Hicks v. Edwards, 876 P.2d 953 (Wash. Ct. App. 1994), *rev. denied*, 890 P.2d 20 (Wash. 1995) (discussing conflicts of interest involved in derivative actions).

40. *Compare* Upjohn Co. v. United States, 449 U.S. 383 (1981) (under federal law attorney-client privilege extends to communications between lawyers and lower-level employees and is not limited to corporate officials in "control group"), *with* Consolidation Coal Co. v. Bucyrus-Erie Co., 432 N.E.2d 250 (Ill. 1982) (control group test applies under Illinois law). See also the discussion in connection with Problem 3-3. For a criticism of the corporate attorney-client privilege, see Elizabeth G. Thornburg, Sanctifying Secrecy: The Mythology of the Corporate Attorney-Client Privilege, 69 Notre Dame L. Rev. 157 (1993). See also Garner v. Wolfinbarger, 430 F.2d 1093 (5th Cir. 1970), *cert. denied*, 401 U.S. 974 (1971) (in shareholder derivative litigation corporate attorney-client privilege does not apply if shareholders establish good cause).

41. The duty to protect the organization from substantial harm under Rule 1.13(b) is not limited to harm caused by constituents but includes any "person associated with the organization." Thus, if an independent contractor hired by the organization was engaged in such misconduct the lawyer would have the duty to act under Rule 1.13(b) even though the independent contractor is not a constituent.

larly complex corporate transactions, the lawyer may have incomplete factual information and may be unclear about the legal consequences of the constituent's conduct. How should a lawyer proceed when the lawyer has strong suspicions of misconduct but the factual and legal basis of that assessment is uncertain? Comment 3 indicates that in such cases of uncertainty the lawyer does not have an obligation to act, but lawyers should be cautious about relying on comment 3. While the comment may be helpful in defending a lawyer who decided not to report possible misconduct, prudent lawyers will err on the side of reporting up when they have strong suspicion of serious wrongdoing. A lawyer who does not report has deprived duly authorized corporate officials of the information and the ability to make decisions about possible wrongdoing that is likely to seriously harm the organization. The determination of whether wrongdoing has occurred and the nature of the response if it has happened is more properly made by those officials than by the lawyer. In addition, in the post-Enron climate, it seems more appropriate for a lawyer to act rather than to remain silent when the lawyer has strong suspicion of serious wrongdoing.

Second, the misconduct must be "in a matter related to the representation." Suppose a coworker tells a corporate lawyer of serious wrongdoing in her department that is unrelated to any work the lawyer does. If the coworker has decided not to take any action with regard to the matter, does the lawyer have a duty to act?[42] Third, the conduct must involve a substantial injury to the organization. Minor violations of the law do not require the lawyer to act.[43] The line between minor and substantial, however, may be difficult to draw. Suppose a lawyer learns that a corporate officer has sought reimbursements for a relatively small amount of personal expenses. In itself the misconduct may be minor but the failure to stop the misappropriation now could lead to more serious violations. It should also be noted that comment 4 provides that a lawyer may report up matters that the lawyer reasonably believes to be of sufficient importance in the best interest of the organization even if the lawyer is not required to do so under Rule 1.13(b).

Assuming the lawyer has a duty to act under Rule 1.13(b), what must the lawyer do? In most instances the lawyer should discuss the matter with the person whose conduct is in question, particularly if the lawyer may be mistaken about whether wrongdoing has occurred. Rule 1.13 does not specifically mention discussion with the person, but in most cases common courtesy, respect for the person's role in the organization, and minimization of reports based on mistake all justify discussion of the matter with the person before the lawyer takes any further action. In addition, discussion with the person might lead that person to self-report the matter to higher authority, eliminating the need for the lawyer to do so. Comment 4 implies that such a discussion is ordinarily appropriate while indicating that in some situations discussion with the person may not be necessary: "If the matter is of sufficient seriousness and importance

---

42. See 1 Hazard & Hodes, The Law of Lawyering illus. 17-5.
43. Id. illus. 17-6.

or urgency to the organization, referral to higher authority in the organization may be necessary even if the lawyer has not communicated with the constituent." The lawyer must exercise care in any discussions with the person the lawyer believes is involved in wrongdoing. Under Rule 1.13(f) the lawyer must "explain the identity of the client when the lawyer knows or reasonably should know that the organization's interests are adverse to those of the constituents with whom the lawyer is dealing." The purpose of Rule 1.13(f) is similar to Rule 4.3: protection of an unrepresented person from being misled about the lawyer's role. Several issues exist with regard to application of Rule 1.13(f): When does the duty to warn attach? Must the lawyer warn at the first moment the lawyer believes adversity exists, in which case the lawyer may be unable to obtain information from the person about harm to the corporation? Or can the lawyer wait to warn until the adversity is clear, seeking to obtain information from the person before warning? How extensive must the warning be? The text of the rule states that the lawyer must only inform the person that the lawyer represents the entity, but comment 10 indicates that a much more extensive warning is necessary.[44]

What should the lawyer do after discussing the matter with the constituent or other person, or after deciding that the matter is of sufficient importance for the lawyer to act without a meeting? Rule 1.13(b) and the comments state that the lawyer normally should report the matter to higher authority in the organization: "Unless the lawyer reasonably believes that it is not necessary in the best interest of the organization to do so, the lawyer shall refer the matter to higher authority in the organization, including, if warranted by the circumstances, to the highest authority that can act on behalf of the organization as determined by applicable law." Comment 4 indicates that in some instances the best interests of the organization may not require reporting up, for example, in the case of a "constituent's innocent misunderstanding of law and subsequent acceptance of the lawyer's advice." Here again lawyers should be cautious about relying on this qualification to reporting up. The strongest case for not reporting up would involve prospective conduct by a constituent who is acting in good faith and who accepts the lawyer's advice to refrain from such conduct. The case for reporting up becomes much stronger if any of these elements is missing. For example, if the conduct has already occurred but can be rectified in whole or in part, reporting up still may be necessary. The constituent's mistake in judgment is a piece of information that higher authority may consider important in evaluating the constituent's performance in the company. In addition, if the mistake has already occurred, there may be various methods of rectification. Higher officials are likely to prefer to make their own decisions about how to correct a problem that has arisen rather than allow the wrongdoer and a lawyer to make the decision.

If reporting up is required under paragraph (b), the lawyer should choose

---

44. Id. §17.13. For a discussion of the necessity, content, and timing of the warning, see Restatement (Third) of the Law Governing Lawyers §103, cmt. *e*.

the appropriate authority to whom to make the report depending on a variety of circumstances, including the entity's structure, the lawyer's role in the organization, the person's position in the organization, and the seriousness of the matter. For example, if the misconduct involves a subordinate corporate officer, reporting to the officer's immediate superior or perhaps the CEO would probably be appropriate. Whether the lawyer is required to make further reports after the initial one depends on the response to the initial report, the seriousness of the matter, and the lawyer's evaluation of whether further reporting is necessary in the best interests of the organization. As section (b) indicates, in very serious cases, the lawyer should report the matter to the highest authority that can act on behalf of the organization under applicable law. Comment 5 indicates that this will ordinarily be the board of directors or similar governing body. This comment is somewhat strange because for business corporations the shareholders in a duty constituted meeting, not the board of directors, are the highest authority that can act on behalf of the organization. (For nonprofit corporations which do not have shareholders, the board of directors may be the highest authority that can act for the organization.) Shareholders are, of course, not an ongoing body like the board, but shareholders do meet on an annual basis and can be convened for special meetings. It may be difficult, however, for a lawyer to report to a shareholders' meeting either because of the timing of the meeting or because of problems in placing the matter on the agenda. Another possibility would be to report to a shareholder or group of shareholders holding a majority interest or controlling interest in the corporation, if such a group is readily identifiable.[45]

Suppose the lawyer has reported the matter to the highest authority that can act on behalf of the organization, but that authority has refused to act or has taken action that the lawyer reasonably believes is not in the best interest of the organization. As comment 6 states, the lawyer may be required to withdraw from the representation, at least in the matter that involves criminal or fraudulent conduct: "Rule 1.2(d) may also be applicable, in which event, withdrawal from the representation under Rule 1.16(a)(1) may be required." If the lawyer has issued an opinion or other document, it may be necessary for the lawyer to disaffirm or withdraw the document to prevent continued reliance by third parties on the document. Model Rule 4.1, cmt. 3 authorizes this "noisy notice" of withdrawal. If the lawyer is required to withdraw, or if the lawyer is discharged, the lawyer nonetheless has continuing duties to act under Rule 1.13. See Model Rule 1.13(e).

45. See Restatement (Third) of the Law Governing Lawyers §96, cmt. *f* (suggesting the possibility of reporting to the owner of a majority of the stock in the corporation). Hazard and Hodes, however, treat reporting to shareholders, at least in the absence of a shareholders' meeting, as reporting outside the corporation rather than reporting to the highest authority within the corporation. See 1 Hazard & Hodes, The Law of Lawyering §17.12. Even if reporting to shareholders is treated as reporting out, under revised Model Rule 1.13(c), a lawyer would have discretion to do so in serious cases of substantial harm to the corporation when the board fails to act.

In addition to withdrawal, a lawyer may have the discretion to report the misconduct outside the corporation. Reporting out is permissible in three situations: self-defense, to prevent or rectify harm under Rule 1.6, and to prevent harm to the corporation under Rule 1.13(c). The first situation in which a lawyer may report out is in self-defense under Model Rule 1.6(b)(5). The leading decision dealing with the "self-defense" exception to the duty of confidentiality is Meyerhofer v. Empire Fire & Marine Insurance Co.[46] While the case was decided under the Code of Professional Responsibility, it remains applicable under the Model Rules. The case involved a securities fraud action alleging that Empire had marketed securities using a registration statement and prospectus that were materially false and misleading. The complaint named Empire's law firm and several of its partners as defendants. In addition, the complaint included as a defendant Stuart Goldberg, an attorney who had worked on the Empire matter but who had resigned from the firm in a dispute with the firm over the adequacy of disclosures being made in the Empire offering. On the same day that he resigned from the firm, Goldberg informed the SEC of his concerns about the offering; he subsequently filed an affidavit with the SEC about the matter. When Goldberg was named as a defendant in the securities fraud litigation, he contacted plaintiffs' counsel, informed them of his noninvolvement in the offering, and supplied them with a copy of the affidavit he filed with the SEC. As a result the plaintiffs dismissed Goldberg from the suit. Defendants then moved to disqualify plaintiffs' counsel from continuing in the case on the ground that they had received confidential information from Goldberg. The district court granted the disqualification motion but the Second Circuit Court of Appeals reversed:

> DR 4-101(C) recognizes that a lawyer may reveal confidences or secrets necessary to defend himself against "an accusation of wrongful conduct." This is exactly what Goldberg had to face when, in their original complaint, plaintiffs named him as a defendant who wilfully violated the securities laws.
>
> The charge, of knowing participation in the filing of a false and misleading registration statement, was a serious one. The complaint alleged violation of criminal statutes and civil liability computable at over four million dollars. The cost in money of simply defending such an action might be very substantial. The damage to his professional reputation which might be occasioned by the mere pendency of such a charge was an even greater cause for concern.
>
> Under these circumstances Goldberg had the right to make an appropriate disclosure with respect to his role in the public offering. Concomitantly, he had the right to support his version of the facts with suitable evidence.[47]

Although the court expressed some concern with Goldberg's method of disclosure—turning over to plaintiffs' counsel a 30-page affidavit with 16 attached

---

46. 497 F.2d 1190 (2d Cir.), *cert. denied*, 419 U.S. 998 (1974).
47. Id. at 1194-1195.

exhibits—the court concluded that his action was the "most effective way for him to substantiate his story."[48]

While Goldberg acted properly in revealing information to the plaintiffs' counsel in an effort to obtain dismissal of the suit filed against him, his earlier actions are questionable. Goldberg apparently informed the SEC and filed an affidavit with the agency before any allegations were made against him. While the self-defense exception does not require lawyers to wait until formal proceedings are instituted against them, it does require an assertion of complicity be made against the lawyer. See Model Rule 1.6, cmt. 10. Goldberg may have acted improperly by making a preemptive disclosure before any allegations were made against him.[49]

Reporting out under the self-defense exception protects the interests of the lawyer over the interests of the client. Model Rule 1.6 also authorizes reporting out to protect third parties from serious harm caused by their clients. We have already considered Model Rule 1.6(b)(1), which gives lawyers discretion to reveal confidential information to prevent reasonably certain death or substantial bodily harm. In the business context, most criminal or fraudulent conduct involves financial harm to which Rule 1.6(b)(1) would not apply. However, if a client planned on continuing to market a product that was defective and dangerous to consumers in violation of applicable law, the lawyer would be authorized to reveal the information under Rule 1.6(b)(1). Model Rules 1.6(b)(2) and (b)(3), which were added by the ABA in 2003, expand the scope of reporting out. These rules authorize lawyers to disclose confidential information to prevent or to rectify substantial financial harm resulting from a crime or fraud that the client is planning or has committed, but only if the lawyer's services are being or have been used in the commission of the crime or fraud. Thus, under Rules 1.6 a lawyer could not reveal confidential information to prevent or to rectify a financial fraud when the lawyer knows about the fraud but the lawyer's services are not involved in the fraud. While Rule 1.6(b)(1) is based completely on the policy of preventing serious harm to others, rules 1.6(b)(2) and (3) reflect this policy only in part because of the requirement that the lawyer's services be used in the commission of the crime or fraud. Comment 7 indicates that the rationale for these exceptions is that the client has forfeited the protections of confidentiality by a serious abuse of the client-attorney relationship.

Reporting out is also permissible under Model Rule 1.13(c), added by the ABA in 2003. This section applies when the lawyer has reported up to the highest authority that can act on behalf of the organization, that authority has refused to act, and the lawyer reasonably believes that the matter involves a clear violation of law that is reasonably certain to result in substantial injury to the organization. Reporting out is permitted in this situation but only to the extent reasonably necessary to prevent substantial injury to the organization.

48. Id. at 1195.
49. See 1 Hazard & Hodes, The Law of Lawyering §§9.23 & 9.27 (discussing whether preemptive disclosure is permissible under the Model Rules).

Comment 6 discusses the relationship between Rule 1.13(c) and the exceptions to confidentiality under Rule 1.6. The comment states that Rule 1.13(c) supplements Rule 1.6(b) providing an additional ground for disclosure. Rules 1.6(b) and 1.13(c) differ in two significant ways. Under Rule 1.13(c) a lawyer may report out even though the lawyer's services were not used in the crime or fraud. See comment 6. In this sense Rule 1.13(c) expands on Rule 1.6(b). However, Rule 1.13(c) is narrower in that disclosure under this rule is only allowed to prevent reasonably certain substantial injury to the organization not to prevent or rectify harm to others. When would Rule 1.13(c) apply? The clearest example is a case in which the lawyer has informed the board of criminal or fraudulent conduct by a constituent of the organization, but the board refuses to act because of self-interest or personal involvement of board members.[50] To whom should the lawyer report if Rule 1.13(c) applies? The rule and comments give no guidance, but the natural answer is to some group of shareholders who are being harmed by the wrongdoing and who are not disabled from acting because of personal involvement in the misconduct or loyalty to the wrongdoer. If the entity were a nonprofit organization without shareholders, the lawyer could report to some authority authorized to regulate the entity. Rule 1.13(c) indicates that the disclosure should be limited to the extent the lawyer reasonably believes necessary to prevent substantial harm to the organization. This limitation implies that in most instances, unlike Rule 1.6(b), disclosure to the victims would be inappropriate. However, disclosure to the victims should not be precluded under Rule 1.13(c) if that is the best way to prevent harm to the organization by stopping the misconduct.

New Rule 1.13(d) limits the authority of a lawyer to report out under Rule 1.13(c). Under Rule 1.13(d) if the lawyer has been retained either to investigate allegations of violation of the law by the organization or to defend the organization or a person associated with the organization against charges of criminal or fraudulent conduct, then Rule 1.13(c) does not apply. Comment 7 indicates that this limitation is necessary to enable the client to receive the full benefit of counsel in conducting an investigation or defending a claim. The ABA Task Force Report states that full and frank communication is essential when the lawyer is conducting an investigation or defending a claim and in this case confidentiality outweighs any interest in disclosure.[51] Application of this new section should be reasonably clear if the corporation retains outside counsel not formerly associated with the organization to investigate the matter or to defend the organization or the wrongdoer in legal proceedings. Involvement of in-house counsel, however, can make the application of the section unclear. Suppose in-house counsel who has received information about potential criminal or fraudulent conduct is then appointed by management to conduct the investigation. Does section (d) apply? If it does not apply because of the lawyer's preexisting information, then the goal of having full and frank commu-

---

50. ABA Task Force on Corporate Responsibility, Report at 58 (2003) (available online, see note 38 above.
51. Id. at 59-60.

nication of information during an investigation is undermined. If it does apply, then it would be possible to cut off a lawyer's disclosure obligations simply by appointing the lawyer to conduct an investigation. Suppose outside counsel is appointed to conduct the investigation and outside counsel reports information to in-house counsel. Section (d) applies to outside counsel, but what about the information received by in-house counsel who is not conducting the investigation?

The preceding discussion assumes that the entity is fairly large. The lawyer's obligations are likely to be different if the entity is closely held. Unless the lawyer's engagement clearly specifies otherwise, in closely held entities it is likely that the attorney has a client-lawyer relationship with all the principals.[52] If such a relationship with the principals does exist, two courses of action seem available to the attorney. One is to make full disclosure to all clients; disclosure would be justified on the ground that there is no expectation of confidentiality nor does the attorney-client privilege apply to joint clients. See Model Rule 1.7, cmts. 30 and 31. The other option is to withdraw from the matter, based on the principle that an irreconcilable conflict of interest exists between multiple clients. See Model Rule 1.16(a)(1).

Reporting Up and Reporting Out under the SEC's attorney conduct regulations adopted pursuant to the Sarbanes-Oxley Act[53]

Introduction.   Congress enacted the Sarbanes-Oxley Act of 2002 in response to widespread corporate accounting scandals involving major corporations, particularly Enron and WorldCom. The Act contains 11 titles, dealing with topics such as establishing a Public Accounting Oversight Board, improving auditor independence, enhancing financial disclosures, strengthening the powers of the SEC, and increasing criminal penalties. Only one provision focuses directly on lawyers. Section 307 of the Act[54] (Rules of Professional Responsibility for Attorneys) states:

> Not later than 180 days after the date of enactment of this Act, the Commission shall issue rules, in the public interest and for the protection of investors, setting forth minimum standards of professional conduct for attorneys appearing and practicing before the Commission in any way in the representation of issuers, including a rule—
> (1) requiring an attorney to report evidence of a material violation of securities law or breach of fiduciary duty or similar violation by the company

---

52. *Compare* Rosman v. Shapiro, 653 F. Supp. 1441 (S.D.N.Y. 1987) (in two-person corporation, it is reasonable for each shareholder to view corporate counsel as his individual attorney), *with* Bovee v. Gravel, 811 A.2d 137 (Vt. 2002) (finding no duty to shareholders).

53. For insight into the drafting of the regulations and criticism of the final product, see Susan P. Koniak, When the Hurlyburly's Done: The Bar's Struggle with the SEC, 103 Colum. L. Rev. 1236, 1269-1278 (2003).

54. 15 U.S.C. §7245.

or any agent thereof, to the chief legal counsel or the chief executive officer of the company (or the equivalent thereof); and

(2) if the counsel or officer does not appropriately respond to the evidence (adopting, as necessary, appropriate remedial measures or sanctions with respect to the violation), requiring the attorney to report the evidence to the audit committee of the board of directors of the issuer or to another committee of the board of directors comprised solely of directors not employed directly or indirectly by the issuer, or to the board of directors.

After receiving extensive comments, in January 2003, the Commission promulgated final regulations, effective August 5, 2003, implementing the statute's mandate to impose a reporting up requirement.[55]

Relationship between the Sarbanes-Oxley regulations and state rules of professional conduct. The regulations provide that they supplement standards of conduct in jurisdictions where the attorney is admitted to practice.[56] Thus, if a state imposes more demanding requirements than the regulations, state rules govern. The regulations preempt state rules, however, to the extent that they conflict with the regulations and impose lesser obligations.[57] Therefore, to determine their obligations, attorneys who are covered by the regulations must consult both the regulations and state rules of professional conduct.

Covered attorneys. The regulations apply to "attorneys appearing and practicing before the Commission in the representation of an issuer."[58] The definitional section broadly defines "appearing and practicing before the Commission."[59] The term includes lawyers who transact business with the Commission or who represent issuers in connection with Commission proceedings. In addition, lawyers who give advice with regard to U.S. securities issues will be covered by the definition if their advice relates to documents filed with the Commission or if they advise about exemptions from filing or other regulatory requirements. Lawyers retained by issuers to investigate reports required by the regulation are also treated as appearing and practicing before the Commission, although they have limited obligations under the regulations.[60] The rule excludes "non-appearing foreign attorneys."[61]

Standard for reporting. The obligations of attorneys covered by the regulations attach when an attorney "becomes aware of evidence of a material violation

---

55. *See* SEC Release 33-8185 (Jan. 29, 2003).
56. 17 C.F.R. §205.1 (2003).
57. Id.
58. Id.
59. Id. §205.2(a).
60. Id. §205.3(b)(5),(6),(7).
61. Id. §§205.2(a)(2)(ii) and 205.2(j).

by the issuer or by any officer, director, employee, or agent of the issuer."[62]
The regulations adopt the following definition:

> *Evidence of a material violation* means credible evidence, based upon which it
> would be unreasonable, under the circumstances, for a prudent and competent
> attorney not to conclude that it is reasonably likely that a material violation has
> occurred, is ongoing, or is about to occur.[63]

This definition represents a compromise among the differing views presented
to the Commission. The final standard is objective, but it also recognizes the
possibility of a range of reasonable professional behavior.[64] The combination
of negatives ("unreasonable" and "not"), however, is likely to be confusing.
The easiest way to understand the definition is by focusing on the concept of
"reasonably likely that a material violation has occurred." The comments to
the definition explain:

> To be "reasonably likely" a material violation must be more than a mere possibility,
> but it need not be "more likely than not." If a material violation is reasonably
> likely, an attorney must report evidence of this violation.[65]

Several other points about the triggering standard are worth noting. It is clear
that a lawyer cannot refuse to report evidence of a material violation on the
ground that the lawyer does not know that a violation has occurred.[66] Under
revised ABA Model Rule 1.13(b) a lawyer must know of a crime of fraud
before having a duty to report up, but as discussed above, the regulations
preempt less demanding state standards. Similarly, a lawyer cannot refrain from
reporting on the ground that nonfrivolous arguments can be made that a
material violation has not occurred.[67] Thus, a lawyer could properly refuse to
report evidence of a material violation only if a competent and prudent lawyer,
under the circumstances, would conclude based on the evidence that a finding
of a material violation is not reasonably likely. How will lawyers make this
determination? The commentary indicates the circumstances that lawyers
should take into account:

> The "circumstances" are the circumstances at the time the attorney decides
> whether he or she is obligated to report the information. These circumstances

---

62. Id. §205.3(b)(1) and §205(c)(1). The former section applies to issuers that have
not established Qualified Legal Compliance Committees (QLCC); the latter to issuers that
have created such committees. The triggering language is the same for both. QLCCs are
discussed below.

63. Id. §205.2(e).

64. *See* SEC Release 33-8185 (Jan. 29, 2003) at n.46 (discussing comments on the
proposed rule in Section-by-Section Discussion of Final Rule).

65. Id. at n.50.

66. Id. at n.48.

67. Id. at n.49.

may include, among others, the attorney's professional skills, background and experience, the time constraints under which the attorney is acting, the attorney's previous experience and familiarity with the client, and the availability of other lawyers with whom the lawyer may consult. Under the revised definition, an attorney is not required (or expected) to report "gossip, hearsay, [or] innuendo." Nor is the rule's reporting obligation triggered by "a combination of circumstances from which the attorney, in retrospect, should have drawn an inference." . . .[68]

While these factors are useful, they do not provide the kind of clear guidance that attorneys facing these difficult decisions will want. How a lawyer should proceed will depend on whether the lawyer is a supervisory[69] or subordinate attorney.[70]

Obligations of subordinate attorneys.   If the attorney is a subordinate attorney, the attorney should normally report the matter to the attorney's supervisor. This would be the prudent course of action even if the subordinate did not believe that a material violation was reasonably likely. Under the regulations subordinate attorneys comply with their obligations if they report the matter to their supervisory attorneys:

> A subordinate attorney complies with §205.3 if the subordinate attorney reports to his or her supervising attorney under §205.3(b) evidence of a material violation of which the subordinate attorney has become aware in appearing and practicing before the Commission.[71]

It should be noted that the obligations of subordinate attorneys under the regulations are quite different from their obligations under rules of professional conduct applicable in most states. Under ABA Model Rule 5.2(b) a subordinate attorney "does not violate the Rules of Professional Conduct if that lawyer acts in accordance with a supervisory lawyer's reasonable resolution of an arguable question of professional duty." Thus, under ABA rules a subordinate attorney is not relieved of responsibility simply by reporting a matter to a supervisory attorney. Under the regulations, however, subordinates enjoy greater protection. Once a subordinate reports a matter to a supervisory lawyer, the subordinate need not take any further action.[72] The comments to the regulations explain why subordinate attorneys should *not* be exempted from compliance with the regulations:

---

68. Id. at n.47.
69. 17 C.F.R. §205.4 (responsibilities of supervisory attorneys).
70. Id. §205.5.
71. Id. §205.5(c).
72. Id. Subordinate attorneys are authorized, but not required, to take further action if they reasonably believe that their supervisors have failed to comply with the reporting obligations under the regulations. Id. §205.5(d).

We believe that creation of such an exemption would seriously undermine Congress' intent to provide for the reporting of evidence of material violations to issuers. Indeed, because subordinate attorneys frequently perform a significant amount of work on behalf of issuers, we believe that subordinate attorneys are at least as likely (indeed, potentially more likely) to learn about evidence of material violations as supervisory attorneys.[73]

But the comments fail to explain why the regulations deviate from the ABA Model Rules and exempt subordinate attorneys from compliance with the regulations once they have reported matters to their supervisory attorneys. The comments simply state that this provision received relatively little comment and those comments typically supported allowing subordinate attorneys to satisfy their obligations by reporting to supervisory attorneys.[74] One possible justification is that the determination of whether evidence of a material violation exists can often be a complex question. Many subordinate attorneys will lack the experience to make this decision. Fearful of their reputations and of personal liability, subordinates may be inclined to overreport. In addition, by shifting responsibility to the supervisory attorney, the regulations are likely to diminish difficult confrontations between supervisory and subordinate lawyers.

Obligations of supervisory attorneys.   Once a matter is brought to the attention of a supervisory lawyer, either directly or by report of a subordinate attorney, the supervisory attorney must then make the decision whether the evidence is sufficient to require reporting under the regulations:

> A supervisory attorney is responsible for complying with the reporting requirements in §205.3 when a subordinate attorney has reported to the supervisory attorney evidence of a material violation.[75]

How should a supervisory attorney make this determination? One way to proceed is to err on the side of caution and report the matter, particularly if the matter involves potentially serious wrongdoing. A supervisory attorney who is contemplating not reporting a matter should consider obtaining advice of independent counsel on the issue. If the supervisory lawyer receives an opinion stating that a material violation was reasonably likely, then the lawyer would be required to report as set forth in the regulations. An opinion from a qualified independent counsel stating that a material violation is not reasonably likely should be sufficient to justify that attorney taking no further action.

If a lawyer concludes that he or she possesses evidence of a material violation, then the lawyer is required to report the matter as set forth in the regulations. The regulations envision two ways in which the lawyer can report, depending on whether or not the client has established a Qualified Legal

---

73. *See* SEC Release 33-8185 (Jan. 29, 2003) at n.120.
74. Id.
75. 17 C.F.R. §205.4(c).

Compliance Committee (QLCC).[76] If the client has not established a QLCC, the attorney is required to act as follows:

> If an attorney, appearing and practicing before the Commission in the representation of an issuer, becomes aware of evidence of a material violation by the issuer or by any officer, director, employee, or agent of the issuer, the attorney shall report such evidence to the issuer's chief legal officer (or the equivalent thereof) or to both the issuer's chief legal officer and its chief executive officer (or the equivalents thereof) forthwith.[77]

The chief legal officer (CLO) (or the equivalent) is then required to investigate the matter.[78] As a result of the investigation, the CLO may conclude that no material violation is involved. In that case the CLO shall inform the reporting attorney and explain the basis for that determination.[79] Unless the CLO reasonably believes that a material violation is not involved, the CLO "shall take all reasonable steps to cause the issuer to adopt an appropriate response, and shall advise the reporting attorney thereof."[80] What amounts to an "appropriate response" is discussed in more detail below. If the issuer has established a QLCC, the CLO, rather than conducting an investigation, may turn the matter over to the QLCC.[81]

If the reporting attorney does not reasonably believe that the CLO has made an appropriate response within a reasonable period of time, the attorney must then report the evidence of a material violation to either the audit committee of the issuer, another committee of the issuer that consists solely of independent directors, or to the issuer's board of directors.[82]

An attorney who reasonably believes that he or she has received an appropriate response to a report "need do nothing more under this section."[83] On the other hand, if a reporting attorney does not reasonably believe that he or she has received an appropriate response to a report required by the regulations, then the attorney "shall explain his or her reasons therefor to the chief legal officer (or the equivalent thereof), the chief executive officer (or the equivalent thereof), and directors to whom the attorney reported the evidence of a material violation."[84]

Qualified Legal Compliance Committees. The regulations provide for an alternative reporting regime if the issuer has established a QLCC.[85] The regula-

---

76. *Compare* id. §205.3(b)(1), *with* id. §205.3(c)(1).
77. Id. §205.3(b)(1).
78. Id. §205.3(b)(2).
79. Id.
80. Id.
81. Id. §205.3(b)(2).
82. Id. §205.3(b)(3).
83. Id. §205.3(b)(8).
84. Id. §205.3(b)(9).
85. Id. §205.3(c).

tions define specifically the requirements for a QLCC in order to assure its independence.[86] The regulations allow reporting to a QLCC only if the committee was established before the matter arises.[87] Thus, an issuer cannot create a QLCC to deal with a matter that has already arisen.

Rather than reporting evidence of a material violation to an issuer's CLO, an attorney may report the matter to a QLCC.[88] An attorney who reports a matter to a QLCC is not required to take any further action: "An attorney who reports evidence of a material violation to such a qualified legal compliance committee has satisfied his or her obligation to report such evidence and is not required to assess the issuer's response to the reported evidence of a material violation."[89] Similarly, a CLO may turn the matter over to a QLCC, which then has full responsibility for the matter.[90]

Appropriate response to a report.   Crucial to the application of the regulations is the concept of an "appropriate response." As discussed previously reporting attorneys need not take any further action if they receive an appropriate response.[91] A CLO to whom a matter is reported and who determines that a material violation is reasonably likely must take reasonable steps to cause an issuer to make an appropriate response.[92] A QLCC to which a matter has been referred has the power to recommend that the issuer make an appropriate response.[93] Under the regulations there are three types of appropriate responses:

- a response that the reporting attorney reasonably believes that no material violation is involved.[94]
- a response that the reporting attorney reasonably believes that the issuer has adopted appropriate remedial measures, "including appropriate steps or sanctions to stop any material violations that are ongoing, to prevent any material violation that has yet to occur, and to remedy or otherwise appropriately address any material violation that has already occurred and to minimize the likelihood of its recurrence."[95]
- a response that the issuer, with the consent of the board of directors, a QLCC, or a committee to which a report could be made under the regulations,[96] has retained an attorney to investigate the material violation and either (1) the issuer has reasonably implemented the

86. Id. §205.2(k).
87. Id. §205.3(c)(1) ("if the issuer has previously formed such a committee"). Id. §205.3(c)(2) ("previously established qualified legal compliance committee").
88. Id. §205.3(c)(1).
89. Id.
90. Id. §205.3(c)(2).
91. Id. §205.3(b)(8).
92. Id. §205.3(b)(2).
93. Id. §205.2(k)(3)(iii).
94. Id. §205.2(b)(1).
95. Id. §205.3(b)(2).
96. Id. §205.3(b)(3).

> remedial measures recommended by the attorney after a reasonable investigation or (2) the issuer has been advised by the attorney that "such attorney may, consistent with his or her professional obligations, assert a colorable defense . . . in any investigation or judicial or administrative proceeding relating to the reported evidence of a violation.[97]

Probably the most striking aspect of the definition of an appropriate response is the last part. Under this section, if an issuer, with the consent of either the board of directors or one of the listed independent committees, has retained an attorney to review the matter, and if the attorney "consistent with his or her professional obligations" concludes that a "colorable defense" exists, that conclusion amounts to an appropriate response. The comments explain that a "colorable defense" is essentially a defense that is not frivolous.[98] This standard is exceedingly weak. The investigating attorney need not even be outside counsel. The comments refer to an attorney "whether employed or retained by it."[99] While there is an element of independence in the process through the requirement that the attorney be selected with the consent of one of the independent committees, that protection is not great. Even if counsel that is chosen is truly independent and makes an objective inquiry, it is very likely that counsel will find that a colorable defense exists.

Reporting out. As discussed previously, the Model Rules have several provisions that allow lawyers to report out if reporting up has not produced a successful resolution of the wrongdoing. The SEC's regulations also include reporting out provisions, but they are somewhat different from the reporting out sections of the Model Rules. The regulations provide:

> (d) *Issuer confidences.*
> (1) Any report under this section (or the contemporaneous record thereof) or any response thereto (or the contemporaneous record thereof) may be used by an attorney in connection with any investigation, proceeding, or litigation in which the attorney's compliance with this part is in issue.
> (2) An attorney appearing and practicing before the Commission in the representation of an issuer may reveal to the Commission, without the issuer's consent, confidential information related to the representation to the extent the attorney reasonably believes necessary:
> > (i) To prevent the issuer from committing a material violation that is likely to cause substantial injury to the financial interest or property of the issuer or investors;
> > (ii) To prevent the issuer, in a Commission investigation or administrative proceeding from committing perjury, proscribed in 18 U.S.C. §1621; sub-

---

97. Id. §205.2(b)(3)(ii).
98. *See* SEC Release 33-8185 (Jan. 29, 2003), cmt. to §205.2(b) (definition of "appropriate response").
99. Id.

orning perjury, proscribed in 18 U.S.C. §1622; or committing any act proscribed in 18 U.S.C. §1001 that is likely to perpetrate a fraud upon the Commission; or

(iii) To rectify the consequences of a material violation by the issuer that caused, or may cause, substantial injury to the financial interest or property of the issuer or investors in the furtherance of which the attorney's services were used.[100]

Section (d)(1) is similar to the self-defense exception of Model Rule 1.6(b)(5). Section (d)(2)(i) is similar to Model Rule 1.6(b)(2) but with significant differences. It does not require that the lawyer's services be used; it focuses on prevention of harm to the issuer or investors, while Model Rule 1.6(b)(2) applies to financial harm to any person; it authorizes the lawyer to report to the Commission. Section (d)(2)(ii) is broadly similar to Model Rule 3.3, which imposes obligations on lawyers with regard to false testimony. Section (d)(ii) is directed at prevention rather than rectification of false testimony, but perhaps rectification is implicit in the rule. Section (d)(2)(iii) is similar to Model Rule 1.6(b)(3), but this section, unlike (d)(2)(i), includes a requirement that the lawyer's services be used in furtherance of the material violation.

The reporting out provisions discussed above are discretionary with attorneys. In addition, the SEC has proposed a mandatory noisy notice of withdrawal requirement if the reporting attorney does not receive an appropriate response to a report of a material violation. The SEC has received comments but has not yet acted on the proposal.[101]

Civil liability of attorneys with regard to illegal or fraudulent conduct by their clients

To what extent are lawyers legally liable for damages to third persons because of their involvement in transactions in which a client committed a crime or engaged in fraud? The question cannot be answered simply because of the wide variety of legal theories, both statutory and common law, that can form the basis of lawyer liability to third parties.[102] This section surveys some of the most significant theories.

Aiding and abetting liability under the federal securities laws.   Beginning in the 1970s a number of courts ruled that lawyers could be held legally liable for "aiding and abetting" violations of the federal securities laws. Probably the

---

100. 17 C.F.R. §205(3)(d).
101. See SEC Release 33-8186 (Jan. 29, 2003).
102. See Chem-Age Industries, Inc. v. Glover, 652 N.W.2d 756 (S.D. 2002) (discussing theories of fraud, conversion, legal malpractice, breach of fiduciary duty, and aiding and abetting breach of fiduciary duty); Marc I. Steinberg, Corporate/Securities Attorneys: Ethical and Legal Concerns, 1374 PLI/Corp 497 (2003) (on Westlaw).

best known of these cases is SEC v. National Student Marketing Corp.,[103] in which the court found that a prominent New York law firm was liable as an aider and abetter when it participated in the closing of a merger even though it knew that management had solicited proxies based on false financial statements. After *National Student Marketing*, many courts held lawyers civilly liable for aiding and abetting securities law violations. Another highly publicized situation in which lawyers were accused of aiding or abetting client fraud was the OPM leasing scandal. In that matter a law firm continued to close leasing transactions even after it had learned that its client was using phony leases as collateral for loans.[104]

In 1994 the Supreme Court, in Central Bank of Denver, N.A. v. First Interstate Bank of Denver, N.A.,[105] surprised many members of the securities bar. The Court overturned more than 20 years of case law and repudiated the decisions of all 11 circuit courts of appeal, holding in a 5-4 decision that "aider and abetter" liability did not exist under the federal securities laws. Reasoning from the plain text of the statute and from the scope of the statute's express causes of action, the Court concluded that Congress did not intend to create aider and abetter liability. The Court rejected arguments that Congress had adopted or acquiesced in judicial creation of aider and abetter liability.

While *Central Bank* appears to insulate lawyers and other professionals from secondary liability under the federal securities laws, this protection is not unlimited.[106] In 1995 Congress passed the Private Securities Litigation Reform Act. The act provides that the SEC (as opposed to a private civil litigant) may bring an enforcement action against any person who knowingly provides substantial assistance to another person in the violation of the antifraud provisions of the securities laws.[107] Regardless of legal liability, lawyers still have an ethical obligation not to counsel or assist illegal or fraudulent conduct. Model Rule 1.2(d).

Primary liability under the federal securities laws. Central Bank recognized that if the professional's conduct went beyond aiding or abetting to the level of a primary securities violation, the professional could still be held legally liable. Relying on this principle, in 2002 the District Court for the Southern District of Texas held that investors stated causes of action against the firm of

---

103. 457 F. Supp. 682 (D.D.C. 1978).

104. For a complete discussion of the OPM case, see Philip B. Heymann & Lance Liebman, The Social Responsibilities of Lawyers 184-197 (1988).

105. 511 U.S. 164 (1994).

106. For articles analyzing the implications of the *Central Bank* decision, see Symposium on the *Central Bank* Decision: The Demise of Aiding and Abetting?, 49 Bus. Law. 1429 (1994). See also Gareth T. Evans & Daniel S. Floyd, Secondary Liability Under Rule 10b-5: Still Alive and Well After *Central Bank*?, 52 Bus. Law. 13 (1996); Ann Maxey, Competing Duties? Securities Lawyers' Liability After *Central Bank*, 64 Fordham L. Rev. 2185 (1996).

107. Private Securities Litigation Reform Act of 1995, Pub. L. No. 104-67, §104, 109 Stat. 737.

Vinson & Elkins for primary violations of the federal securities laws in connection with the firm's representation of the Enron Corporation. The court stated:

> [T]he complaint goes into great detail to demonstrate that Vinson & Elkins did not remain silent, but chose not once, but frequently, to make statements to the public about Enron's business and financial situation. . . . Moreover in light of its alleged voluntary, essential, material, and deep involvement as a primary violator in the ongoing Ponzi scheme, Vinson & Elkins was not merely a drafter, but essentially a co-author of the documents it created for public consumption concealing its own and other participants' actions. Vinson & Elkins made the alleged fraudulent misrepresentations to potential investors, credit agencies, and banks, whose support was essential to the Ponzi scheme, and Vinson & Elkins deliberately or with severe recklessness directed those public statements toward them in order to influence those investors to purchase more securities, credit agencies to keep Enron's credit high, and banks to continue providing loans to keep the Ponzi scheme afloat. Therefore Vinson & Elkins had a duty to be accurate and truthful. Lead Plaintiff has alleged numerous inadequate disclosures by Vinson & Elkins that breached that duty.[108]

Common law liability for fraud, negligent misrepresentation, or aiding and abetting. Lawyers who have actively participated in fraudulent transactions through issuance of legal opinions or otherwise have been subject to common law liability to third parties, usually for fraud or negligent misrepresentation.[109] Problem 5-5 examines legal and ethical obligations that apply to lawyers issuing opinions in tax matters and other transactions. Many jurisdictions recognize common law aider and abetter liability when a person knowingly provides substantial assistance or encouragement to another person's primary wrong.[110] As noted above, the Supreme Court in *Central Bank* held that the federal securities laws should not be interpreted to provide for aider and abetter liability.

Liability for nondisclosure. If a lawyer does not actively participate in a fraudulent transaction, it is unlikely that the lawyer would be held liable to a third party simply for nondisclosure of the client's wrongdoing. For example,

---

108. In re Enron Corp. Securities, Derivative & ERISA Litigation, 235 F. Supp. 2d 549, 705 (S.D.Tex. 2002). The court dismissed allegations against another prominent law firm, Kirkland & Ellis, because it found that Kirkland & Ellis did not make public representations or prepare documents for public solicitation of funds. Id. at 706. For discussion of the legal and ethical responsibility of attorneys in connection with the Enron scandal, see Roger C. Cramton, Enron and the Corporate Lawyer: A Primer on Legal and Ethical Issues, 58 Bus. Law. 143 (Nov. 2002).

109. See McCamish, Martin, Brown & Loeffler v. F.E. Appling Interests, 991 S.W.2d 787 (Tex. 1999) (borrower states cause of action against lender's attorney for negligent misrepresentation under Restatement (Second) of Torts §552).

110. See Restatement (Second) of Torts §876(b) (actor liable for tort of another if actor knows that other's conduct is breach of duty to third person and provides substantial assistance or encouragement); Granewich v. Harding, 985 P.2d 788 (Or. 1999) (complaint alleging that law firm assisted corporate directors in breach of fiduciary duty to minority shareholders stated cause of action under §876).

in Tew v. Arky, Freed, Stearns, Watson, Greer, Weaver & Harris, P.A.[111] the district court dismissed a legal malpractice complaint against a law firm alleging that the firm had failed to disclose its knowledge of the client's insolvency to its auditors. The firm had not issued an opinion letter or otherwise taken part in the transaction.

In 1992 the Office of Thrift Supervision (OTS) created quite a stir in the legal profession when it brought an administrative complaint against Kaye, Scholer, Fierman, Hays & Handler,[112] a prominent New York law firm, for its representation of Lincoln Savings & Loan. The complaint contained ten charges against Kaye, Scholer, a number of which alleged that the firm had failed to disclose material facts to the Federal Home Loan Bank Board. The OTS claimed that in acting as Lincoln's agent under the governing statutory laws, Kaye, Scholer had a duty not to omit material facts. The OTS's action was controversial in another sense because it accompanied its complaint with an "asset protection order" that limited the firm's ability to transfer assets and required sequestration of 25 percent of the earnings of all partners with a higher percentage for certain named defendants. Under the pressure of the order, Kaye, Scholer promptly settled the case, paying $41 million in restitution—so the issue of whether the firm had a duty of disclosure as contended by the OTS was not resolved. Professor Hazard argues that the case should be understood not as a third-party liability case but rather as a case involving the scope of a law firm's obligations to a regulatory agency that has jurisdiction over the lawyer's client.[113] Other commentators, however, see much broader implications in the case.[114]

B. Specialized Areas of Office Practice

─────────────────── **Problem 5-3** ───────────────────

Real Estate Practice

a. Your firm has a substantial residential real estate practice. The typical transaction proceeds as follows: The purchaser signs a standard form contract completed by the broker who has been assisting the purchaser in finding a residence. The broker then submits the contract to

---

111. 655 F. Supp. 1571 (S.D. Fla. 1987), *aff'd*, 846 F.2d 753 (11th Cir.), *cert. denied*, 488 U.S. 854 (1988).

112. Reported as In re Fishbein, OTS AP-92-19, 1992 WL 560939 (Mar. 1, 1992).

113. Geoffrey C. Hazard, Jr., Lawyer Liability in Third Party Situations: The Meaning of the *Kaye Scholer* Case, 26 Akron L. Rev. 395 (1993).

114. See Symposium, From the Trenches and Towers: The *Kaye Scholer* Affair, 23 L. & Soc. Inquiry 237 (1998); Symposium, In the Matter of Kaye, Scholer, Fierman, Hays & Handler: A Symposium on Government Regulation, Lawyers' Ethics, and the Rule of Law, 66 S. Cal. L. Rev. 977 (1993); Symposium, The Attorney-Client Relationship in a Regulated Society, 35 S. Tex. L. Rev. 571 (1994).

the "listing" broker, the one who listed the seller's home for sale. If the parties are able to negotiate a final contract, the financing process then begins. Most contracts are subject to a "financing contingency." The purchaser, usually with the assistance of the broker, takes the contract and applies to one or more financial institutions for a mortgage loan. In connection with the loan application, the lender will ask the purchaser to identify the attorney who will be representing the purchaser in the transaction. Since many lenders require title insurance as a condition of their loans, the attorney selected by the buyer must be approved by a title insurance company to issue opinions on which it can rely. Your firm is an agent for a major title insurance company and receives a commission from the sale of title insurance. The terms of the loan require the purchaser to pay the legal fees of the closing attorney. After the lender completes its credit examination and approves the loan, the lender sends to the attorney its standard package of closing documents for the transaction. Residential real estate transactions occur in high volume under time pressure. Lenders normally provide real estate attorneys with closing packages only a few days before the closing is to occur.

Your firm does the following in the typical transaction: (1) prepares the note, mortgage, and various disclosure documents using forms supplied by the lending institution; (2) arranges for title examination, usually by employing a title abstract company that examines the title and then gives the firm a report that it uses to prepare your title opinion; (3) obtains a title insurance policy for the lender, and for the owner if the owner desires to pay the additional premium required for an owner's policy, with a commission payable to your firm for selling the insurance; (4) prepares a general warranty deed for the seller to sign if the seller does not have an attorney at closing, which is often the case; (5) completes the closing statement showing the source and disbursement of all funds; (6) handles the closing, answering any questions that the parties may have; disburses funds, and records various documents; (7) institutes foreclosure actions on behalf of the lender in those cases in which borrowers default. The lender often asks the closing attorney to handle any foreclosure action because the attorney already has the file and is familiar with the transaction. To reduce the expense of real estate closings, your firm has several experienced paralegals who handle all aspects of the typical transaction, including the closing, although a lawyer is always available should any problems arise.

For the next firm meeting, you have been asked to review and comment on the ethical and malpractice issues involved in your firm's handling of the typical residential real estate transaction.

  b. Pending before your state supreme court is a petition by the Unauthorized Practice Committee (UPC) of the bar seeking a ruling by the court that the following activities constitute the unauthorized practice of law unless conducted under the supervision of an independent lawyer not employed by any of the following entities:

(1) completion of real estate contracts and advice about the legal aspects of real estate transactions by real estate brokers,

(2) preparation of title abstracts and title opinions by abstractors, title insurance companies, or similar entities,

(3) handling of real estate closings by nonlawyer employees of title companies or lending institutions,

(4) filing of deeds, mortgages, and other legal documents by nonlawyer employees of title companies or lending institutions. The Committee relies on decisions of the South Carolina Supreme Court in State v. Buyers Service Co., 357 S.E.2d 15 (S.C. 1987) and Doe v. McMaster, 585 S.E.2d 773 (S.C. 2003).

A number of parties have intervened in the proceeding. The State Association of Real Estate Brokers (SAREB) argues that the court should hold that the preparation by licensed brokers of real estate contracts and advice given to their clients incident to their business should not be treated as the unauthorized practice of law. The association relies on the decision of the New Jersey Supreme Court in In re Opinion No. 26 of the Commission on the Unauthorized Practice of Law, 654 A.2d 1344 (N.J. 1995).

The State Bankers Association (SBA) argues that the court should rule that it does not constitute the unauthorized practice of law for employees of banks that make mortgage loans to prepare documents incident to such transactions, to conduct closings, and to file deeds, mortgages, and other documents. The Association of Title Companies (ATC) supports the SBA with regard to closings and filing of documents. In addition, it argues that the court should rule that title examinations incident to the business of issuing title policies do not constitute the unauthorized practice of law. The SBA and the ATC rely on the New Jersey decision cited above and on the decision of the Kentucky Supreme Court in Countrywide Home Loans, Inc. v. Kentucky Bar Assn., 113 S.W.3d 105 (Ky. 2003).

Finally, the United States Department of Justice (DOJ) and the Federal Trade Commission (FTC) are appearing as amicus curiae in support of the positions of SAREB, SBA, and ATC. See Letter from the DOJ and the FTC to the Ethics Committee of the North Carolina Bar regarding restrictions on nonlawyer involvement in real estate closings and refinancings, see http://www.ftc.gov/opa/2001/12/ncstatebar.htm (visited Sept. 17, 2003).

Your professor will appoint members of the class to represent the parties involved in this proceeding and to present arguments to the court on behalf of their clients.

Read Model Rules 1.7, 1.8(a), 1.15, 4.3, 5.3, 5.4, 5.5, and comments.

The role of attorneys and conflicts of interest in real estate transactions

Real estate transactions vary considerably in their form and complexity, from large commercial transactions, in which all or almost all of the interested parties will be independently represented by counsel, to relatively routine residential sales, in which one attorney handles the closing on behalf of all the parties. Indeed, in most jurisdictions lawyers are becoming marginalized in residential real estate transactions, largely because of the development of title insurance.[115]

When all the parties in a real estate transaction are represented by counsel, uncertainties about the lawyer's role are largely eliminated, but problems of role can surface when a single lawyer handles the transaction. Unfortunately, lawyers often fail to reach a clear agreement about whom they represent with the parties to real estate transactions. Lawyers who allow such uncertainties to occur face an increased risk of disciplinary action or malpractice liability.[116] In addition, as discussed below, lawyers who fail to clarify their role in real estate transactions are likely to encounter conflict-of-interest problems if they represent one of the parties to the transaction in a subsequent dispute arising out of the transaction.

How can lawyers avoid confusion about whom they represent in real estate transactions? In large commercial transactions, the possibility of confusion is reduced because each party is typically represented by counsel. Even in commercial transactions, however, if a lawyer is preparing documents that will be executed by other parties, it would be prudent for the lawyer to have the other parties sign statements acknowledging that the attorney does not represent them and that they will look to their own counsel for advice in the transaction. In fairly routine residential real estate transactions, the expense of separate counsel often renders this option infeasible.

If the parties to a real estate transaction are not separately represented, real estate attorneys have two models available to clarify their roles: the multiple-representation model and the single-client model. In the multiple-representation model, the lawyer has multiple clients: buyer and seller; buyer and lender; buyer, seller, and lender; or perhaps even buyer, seller, lender, and title company. As discussed in Problem 5-1, Model Rule 1.7 authorizes lawyers to represent multiple clients in business transactions under some circumstances. To do so, lawyers must conclude that they can reasonably undertake the representation without adverse impact on any of the clients, and each client must give informed consent confirmed in writing.

Is a real estate transaction the type of matter in which a lawyer can reasonably undertake multiple representation without adverse impact on the representation of any of the clients? In some cases, courts have found that lawyers have acted improperly by representing multiple clients in real estate

---

115. Michael Braunstein, Structural Change and Inter-professional Competitive Advantage: An Example Drawn from Residential Real Estate Conveyancing, 62 Mo. L. Rev. 241 (1997).

116. E.g., Iowa Supreme Court Bd. of Prof. Ethics & Conduct v. Wagner, 599 N.W. 2d 721 (Iowa 1999) (lawyer suspended for misconduct arising from representation of buyer and seller in sale of commercial property); Stinson v. Brand, 738 S.W.2d 186 (Tenn. 1987) (question of fact whether attorney who handled real estate closing had client-lawyer relationship with sellers, exposing attorney to malpractice liability).

transactions. These cases, however, typically involved attorneys who failed to obtain the informed consent of their clients or who neglected to carry out their duties to one of the clients.[117] While such cases highlight the dangers of multiple representation, they do not go so far as to establish a per se bar to multiple representation in real estate transactions.[118] Attorneys should recognize, however, that multiple representation, even in fairly routine residential real estate transactions, has risks. Further, the climate of professional opinion may be shifting against the practice. For example, the leading treatise on legal malpractice states:

> Historically, the practice of an attorney representing both parties to a transaction in the transfer of a property interest was common and, seemingly, approved. Today such representation is doubtful, at best, and usually is improper.[119]

If a lawyer concludes that he can adequately represent multiple parties, the lawyer must also obtain the informed consent of the parties confirmed in writing. Informed consent requires more than a statement that the lawyer does not have a conflict of interest.[120] On the requirements for informed consent to represent multiple parties in business transactions, see Model Rule 1.0(e) and cmt. 6 and Model Rule 1.7, cmt. 18.

If an attorney decides to undertake multiple representation, the fundamental problem facing the attorney is how to advise and counsel the clients on solutions to issues that may benefit one party at the expense of another. The problem is especially acute if the attorney is employed before the buyer and seller have executed a binding contract. Real estate contracts, like other agreements, can be drafted to favor either of the parties. Even if the attorney is not employed until after the parties sign a contract, as is usually the case in residential transactions, issues may still arise. For example, suppose the contract fails to specify which party bears the cost of a certain item, such as repairs resulting from a termite inspection. Or suppose at closing a question arises whether certain fixtures are included with the sale to the purchaser or may be taken by the seller. One way in which an attorney could respond to such issues

---

117. E.g., Florida Bar v. Teitelman, 261 So. 2d 140 (Fla. 1972) (failure to obtain informed consent to multiple representation); Attorney Grievance Comm. v. Lockhart, 403 A.2d 1241 (Md. 1979) (improper certification of title and release of funds). See generally Annotation, Attorney and Client: Conflict of Interest in Real Estate Closing Situations, 68 A.L.R.3d 967 (1976).

118. See Westport Bank & Trust Co. v. Corcoran, Mallin & Aresco, 605 A.2d 862 (Conn. 1992) (potential for conflict of interest does not preclude such representation). But see Baldasarre v. Butler, 625 A.2d 458 (N.J. 1993) (because of high likelihood of actual conflict of interest in complex commercial real estate transactions, multiple representation is improper even with consent of parties).

119. 4 Mallen & Smith, Legal Malpractice §31.6, at 664.

120. See In re Lanza, 322 A.2d 445 (N.J. 1974) (lawyer disciplined for representing buyer and seller without informed consent and for continuing representation of both once actual conflict developed over payment of portion of purchase price).

is to act in essence as an arbitrator. The attorney informs the parties how the issue should be resolved, either based on the lawyer's opinion or based on what the lawyer believes is customarily done. While it is possible for the clients to agree for the lawyer to act as arbitrator of any disputes they may have, absent such an agreement the arbitration approach seems inconsistent with the lawyer's obligations as a representative of both parties.

How can lawyers act consistently with their obligations as representatives of both parties? Consider the possibility of acting as a "neutral information source." In this role, the lawyer identifies any issue that is likely to be of concern to either of the parties, whether raised by them or not. The lawyer provides information to the clients about how they could resolve the issue. This information includes the lawyer's understanding of how such matters are customarily resolved in the locality, but the method of presenting this information differs from the approach when the lawyer assumes the role of arbitrator. In the capacity of "neutral information source," the lawyer supplies this information but also advises the parties that the custom is not necessarily binding on them and that they can agree to a different resolution of the issue. The lawyer should also inform the parties that if the issue is significant to them, and if they are unable to reach agreement, the lawyer cannot proceed with the closing. See Model Rule 1.7, cmt. 29.

Instead of undertaking multiple representation, lawyers handling real estate transactions could decide to adopt a single-client representation model. Under this approach, the lawyer represents only one party to the transaction. Whom does the lawyer represent? The natural answer is either the buyer or the lender, since they are the principal parties in the transaction. As between the buyer and the lender, the buyer is obviously more in need of legal advice and protection than a sophisticated lender. Further, statutes in some jurisdictions grant borrowers in residential real estate financing transactions the right to select counsel.[121] Some lenders may insist, however, that lawyers represent their interests at closing. Lawyers who want to do business with such lenders must accept a client-lawyer relationship with the lender as well as with the buyer. The following discussion assumes that single-client representation is a feasible alternative for the lawyer.

If the lawyer represents only the buyer, the lawyer must comply with the requirements of Rule 4.3 when communicating with other parties to the transaction. In dealing with an unrepresented seller, a prudent lawyer who represents the buyer will have the seller sign a statement acknowledging that the lawyer represents the buyer, not the seller, that the attorney has informed the seller to retain independent counsel for advice about the seller's legal rights and obligations, and that the seller should understand that any communications made by the attorney are in the attorney's capacity as lawyer for the buyer. Notification of the lawyer's role should be given to the seller in writing in advance of the closing so that the seller has sufficient time to retain counsel.

121. E.g., S.C. Code Ann. §37-10-102(a).

This may not be easy given the time pressures under which many real estate closings occur. The fact that the attorney is representing the buyer does not prevent the attorney from drafting documents to be executed by the seller, such as the deed, nor does it preclude the attorney from telling the seller the attorney's view of the meaning of a document or the legal obligations that a document entails. See Model Rule 4.3, cmt. 2.[122] Although the lender may be a sophisticated commercial party, a prudent closing attorney will also clarify in writing that the attorney is handling the closing as the attorney for the buyer, not the lender.

How are the lender's legal interests protected if the lawyer represents only the buyer? Lenders' commitment letters will attach various conditions to the closing of the loan to protect the lender. These conditions typically include use of the lender's closing documents and issuance of a title insurance policy to protect the lender. Many lenders have their own general or in-house counsel who review the lender's standard form closing package and advise them should any problems arise. The use of the lender's closing package generally precludes the possibility of the lawyer negotiating changes in the forms on behalf of the buyer. Since the forms are fairly standard in most jurisdictions, rarely would there be much to negotiate in any event. The attorney would, of course, have an obligation to advise the buyer generally as to the nature of the documents the buyer is signing and to point out any unusual provisions of which the buyer should be aware. Although the lender requires the buyer's attorney to use its forms, this should not be considered to be improper third-party interference with the lawyer's relationship with the buyer. See Model Rule 5.4(c). The use of the lender's forms is simply a condition to the loan, similar to other conditions, such as the buyer's creditworthiness.

Even if a real estate attorney makes it clear that she represents only one party in the transaction, in many jurisdictions the attorney may still be held liable to one of the other parties to the transaction, typically on a theory of negligent misrepresentation.[123]

May a lawyer who has handled the closing of a real estate transaction represent one of the parties in a subsequent legal dispute arising from the transaction, such as litigation between the buyer and seller or a mortgage foreclosure action brought by the lender? The answer depends largely on whom the attorney represented in the original transaction. If the lawyer represented only one client, the lawyer could generally handle a matter on behalf of that

---

122. Restatement (Third) of the Law Governing Lawyers §163, cmt. *d*. See also, Dolan v. Hickey, 431 N.E.2d 229 (Mass. 1982) (drafting and presentation of documents does not amount to legal advice).

123. See First Nat. Bank of Durant v. Trans Terra Corp. Intl., 142 F.3d 802 (5th Cir. 1998) (no client-lawyer relationship between lender and borrower's attorney, but lender may recover from attorney under theory of negligent misrepresentation for inaccurate title opinion); Petrillo v. Bachenberg, 655 A.2d 1354 (N.J. 1995) (attorney for seller of real estate owed duty of care to buyer to avoid misleading buyer concerning suitability of land for septic system). But see MacMillan v. Scheffy, 787 A.2d 867 (N.H. 2001) (attorney who represented seller and drafted deed did not owe duty of due care to purchasers).

client against any of the other parties to the transaction. Thus, a lawyer who represented the buyer at the closing could represent the buyer in subsequent litigation with the seller or lender.

If the lawyer represented multiple clients, the lawyer generally may not represent any of these clients in a subsequent dispute arising from the transaction. This conclusion follows from a standard application of the subsequent representation rule. See Model Rules 1.7 cmt. 33 and 1.9(a). Some courts, however, have recognized a "scrivener's" exception to the rule that prohibits a lawyer from undertaking representation against a former client in the same or a substantially related matter. Under this exception, if the lawyer does nothing more than prepare a document, typically using a standard form, without receiving any confidential information from the party for whom the document is prepared, the lawyer is not precluded from undertaking representation against that former party in the same or a substantially related matter. Thus, a lawyer who prepared a deed using a statutory form to transfer property to the buyer could represent the seller in a subsequent related matter that was adverse to the buyer.[124] Similarly, a lawyer who prepared a standard form mortgage for the buyer's signature could represent the lender in a subsequent mortgage foreclosure action.[125]

Regardless of whether the lawyer represented one client or multiple clients in the original transaction, the lawyer could not represent a party in a subsequent proceeding if the current representation would involve an attack on the lawyer's own work.[126] Thus, a lawyer could not represent a party in attacking a deed or mortgage that the lawyer prepared for another party to the transaction. In some situations, the advocate-witness rule might also preclude the lawyer from handling a subsequent matter. See Model Rule 3.7.

In residential real estate transactions, lawyers often have a financial interest in the transaction arising from their relationship with title insurance companies. Lawyers frequently act as agents for title insurance companies, receiving a commission from the sale of title insurance to owners and lenders. Further, some lawyers have an ownership interest in title insurance companies. In Formal Opinions 304 (1962) and 331 (1972), the ABA Committee on Ethics and Professional Responsibility decided that lawyers could properly advise their clients about the availability of title insurance even though they received a commission or had a financial interest in a title insurance company, but such financial relationships should be fully disclosed and consented to by the client.[127]

---

124. Griffith v. Taylor, 937 P.2d 297 (Alaska 1997) (recognizing "scrivener's exception" to representation against former client, when attorney merely drafted statutory form of deed or performed clerical or ministerial tasks).

125. In re Anonymous Member of the S.C. Bar, 378 S.E.2d 821, 821 n.1 (S.C. 1989).

126. See Restatement (Third) of the Law Governing Lawyers §132(1) and cmt. d(ii).

127. But see N.J. Adv. Comm. on Prof. Ethics, Op. No. 682 (1996), 1996 WL 74060 (inherent, nonwaivable conflict for lawyers to refer clients to title company for

Model Rule 1.8(a) now applies to these transactions. See comment 1.[128] In addition, the Real Estate Settlement Procedures Act (RESPA)[129] requires lawyers to disclose to buyers commissions received from selling title insurance.

In some commercial real estate transactions, lawyers may have a financial interest in the transaction or in one of the parties to the transaction. A lawyer who has a financial interest also has a duty to comply with Model Rule 1.8(a) regarding the transaction. Lawyers have been disciplined and held liable for damages to their clients for failing to disclose their financial interest in real estate transactions.[130] If the lawyer's financial interest in the transaction is substantial, prudence dictates that the lawyer decline representation in the matter.

Unauthorized practice of law issues in real estate transactions

Lawyers involved in real estate practice frequently deal with nonlawyers: real estate brokers, title insurance companies, title examiners or abstractors, and paralegals. Rules of professional conduct prohibit lawyers from assisting nonlawyers in the unauthorized practice of law. Model Rule 5.5(a). The definition of what constitutes the practice of law varies among the jurisdictions.[131] Traditionally, courts have broadly defined the practice of law to include not only appearances in court but also advice to clients about legal matters and preparation of documents having legal consequences.[132] Over the years, tensions and disputes have developed between lawyers and nonlawyers when nonlawyers have attempted to provide services in real estate transactions that lawyers have considered to be the practice of law.[133] Areas of controversy have revolved around completion of real estate forms, title examinations, and real estate closings.[134] In some states, real estate brokers or title companies have been able to convince state legislatures to enact statutes authorizing their activities, but courts have often invalidated such legislation on separation of powers

---

examination and insurance when they retain portion of premium as compensation, because lawyer's financial interest interferes with independent professional judgment).

128. See also Restatement (Third) of the Law Governing Lawyers §126, cmt. c.

129. 12 U.S.C. §2607(c).

130. See Iowa Supreme Court Board of Prof. Ethics & Conduct v. Wagner, 599 N.W. 2d 721 (Iowa 1999) (lawyer failed to disclose to buyer percentage commission to be paid by seller).

131. See Model Rule 5.5, cmt. 2, and Restatement (Third) of the Law Governing Lawyers §4, cmt. c.

132. E.g., State v. Buyers Serv. Co., 357 S.E.2d 15 (S.C. 1987).

133. For a review of these developments, see Joyce Palomar, The War Between Attorneys and Lay Conveyancers—Empirical Evidence Says "Cease Fire!" 31 Conn. L. Rev. 423 (1999).

134. See, e.g., Perkins v. CTX Mortgage Co., 969 P.2d 93 (Wash. 1999) (en banc) (mortgage company did not engage in unauthorized practice when its lay employees filled in blanks in mortgage forms without exercising discretion).

grounds. The courts have reasoned that these statutes invade the province of the courts to regulate the practice of law.[135] In Arizona an association of realtors was able to obtain a constitutional amendment overturning a supreme court decision prohibiting them from completing real estate contracts and related documents.[136]

Some state supreme courts have adopted rules allowing exceptions to the traditional restrictions on the unauthorized practice of law. In 1983 Washington became the first state to provide for licensing of nonlawyers, but on an extremely limited basis. By rule the state supreme court created a Limited Practice Board, which has the authority to certify "closing officers." Closing officers must pass an examination, demonstrate financial responsibility, and meet continuing education requirements. The rule allows closing officers to do the following:

> select, prepare and complete documents in a form previously approved by the Board for use in closing a loan, extension of credit, sale or other transfer of real or personal property. Such documents shall be limited to deeds, promissory notes, guaranties, deeds of trust, reconveyances, mortgages, satisfactions, security agreements, releases, Uniform Commercial Code documents, assignments, contracts, real estate excise tax affidavits, and bills of sale. Other documents may be from time to time approved by the Board.[137]

Closing officers cannot give legal advice and all parties to the transaction must consent to their participation.[138]

New Jersey has adopted an even more open approach than Washington in real estate transactions. The New Jersey Supreme Court has held that activities of real estate brokers and title officers in preparing contracts and in closing real estate transactions constitute the practice of law, but that the public interest justifies allowing such practices provided the broker or title officer notifies the vendor and purchaser of their conflicting interest in such transactions and of the general risk involved in not being represented by an attorney.[139]

Virginia has taken a quite different approach to the issue of the unauthorized practice of law. That state's supreme court has adopted a set of rules defining what constitutes the unauthorized practice of law in the following areas: practice before tribunals, lay adjusters, collection agencies, estate planning and settlement, tax practice, real estate practice, title insurance, trade

135. E.g., Bennion, Van Camp, Hagen & Ruhl v. Kassler Escrow, Inc., 635 P.2d 730 (Wash. 1981) (en banc).
136. See Palomar, The War Between Attorneys and Lay Conveyancers, 31 Conn. L. Rev. at 470.
137. Wash. Ct. Rules, Admission to Practice Rule 12(d).
138. Id. Rule 12(e).
139. In re Opinion No. 26 of the Comm. on the Unauthorized Practice of Law, 654 A.2d 1344 (N.J. 1995). See also Countrywide Home Loans, Inc. v. Kentucky Bar Assn., 113 S.W.3d 105 (Ky. 2003) (allowing nonlawyers to handle real estate closings because closings do not constitute the practice of law when handled without legal advice, but not considering other aspects of real estate transactions).

associations, and administrative agency practice.[140] Rather than providing for licensing, the Virginia rules attempt to define fairly precisely the kinds of activities that nonlawyers may perform incident to their business activities. While the Virginia rules allow nonlawyers to perform certain legal services, they also operate as a restriction on nonlawyer practice by prohibiting those activities that they do not specifically allow. For example, Rule 6-103 deals with preparation of legal instruments incident to real estate transactions:

UPR 6-103. Preparation of Legal Instruments

(A) Unless a party to the transaction, a non-lawyer shall not, with or without compensation, prepare for another legal instruments of any character affecting the title to or use of real estate. . . .

(3) A real estate agent, or his regular employee, involved in the negotiation of a transaction and incident to the regular course of conducting his licensed business, may prepare a contract of sale, exchange, option or lease with respect to such transaction, for which no separate charge shall be made.

(4) A lending institution may in the regular course of conducting its business prepare a deed of trust or mortgage on real estate securing the payment of its loan, for which no separate charge shall be made. . . .

In 1997 the Virginia legislature enacted the Consumer Real Estate Settlement Protection Act (CRESPA)[141] and the Real Estate Settlement Agent Registration Act (RESARA),[142] allowing nonlawyers to provide closing, escrow, and various settlement services. The Virginia Supreme Court amended its unauthorized practice rules to incorporate this legislation.

Lawyers' use of paralegals in real estate transactions also involves unauthorized practice questions. Comment 2 to Model Rule 5.5 provides that lawyers may properly delegate to nonlawyers a variety of legal tasks: "This Rule does not prohibit a lawyer from employing the services of paraprofessionals and delegating functions to them, so long as the lawyer supervises the delegated work and retains responsibility for their work." (See also Model Rule 5.3 on the supervisory responsibilities of lawyers for nonlawyers.) Under Model Rule 5.5, lawyers could delegate a wide variety of tasks to paralegals, including title examination, preparation of closing documents, and recording of instruments. How far may lawyers go in using paralegals? May lawyers allow paralegals to deal personally with clients? May paralegals sign opinion letters? May they sign other correspondence that does not amount to a formal legal opinion? May paralegals handle closings without lawyers being present if lawyers are available should problems arise? May lawyers use independent paralegal firms or must paralegals be their employees? All of these questions stem from the general issue of the adequacy of supervision. Occasionally, a court decision addresses

---

140. Va. Sup. Ct., Unauthorized Practice Rules and Considerations.
141. Va. Code §§6.1-2.19, et seq.
142. Id. §§6.1-2.30.

the issue of supervision of paralegals.[143] Some states have adopted rules dealing with the use of paralegals.[144] Ethics advisory opinions may provide some guidance on these issues, but most of these questions are left to the judgment of lawyers about what constitutes proper supervision of their nonlawyer employees. We will consider the issue of supervision of paralegals and nonlawyer personnel in Problem 7-1.

Trust account management and disbursement of funds at real estate closings

Real estate transactions, even relatively routine matters, involve substantial sums of money. Rules of professional conduct require lawyers to use trust or escrow accounts for depositing of client funds. See Model Rule 1.15. Recall Problem 2-2. Typically, lawyers have real estate escrow accounts that are separate from their firms' general trust accounts.

A major issue that has troubled real estate attorneys deals with disbursement of funds at closing. The parties who receive money from the transaction, usually the seller and any real estate brokers, want to take their checks with them from the closing. The closing attorney typically receives funds at closing from the lender and the buyer. But even if the lawyer deposits these funds immediately, the lawyer's bank has not yet collected these funds. If the lawyer issues checks to the seller and broker at closing and later either the buyer's or the lender's check is not honored for some reason, then the lawyer has an escrow account problem. If the escrow account contains the funds of other clients, which is normally the case, the lawyer will have disbursed funds belonging to other clients. The lawyer could try to stop payment on checks issued to the seller or brokers, but it may be too late to do so.[145]

Various ways exist for lawyers to avoid the problem of disbursement against uncollected funds. In Advisory Opinion 454 (1980), the New Jersey Supreme Court Advisory Committee on Professional Ethics suggested three possibilities:

(1)   escrow closings in which no funds are disbursed and no closing completed until all funds have cleared;

(2)   pre-arrangement by the attorneys involved so that the necessary closing figures are known far enough in advance for the parties to provide funds in such a manner as to obviate the necessity of using the trust account (undoubtedly this would require cooperation of the bank-mortgagee which may be asked to provide mortgage funds in several checks);

---

143. See In re Lester, 578 S.E.2d 7 (S.C. 2003) (finding lawyer guilty of misconduct for allowing paralegal to handle real estate closings without lawyer's presence).

144. See Ky. Sup. Ct. R. Practice 3.700.

145. See Legacy Homes, Inc. v. Cole, 421 S.E.2d 127 (Ga. Ct. App. 1992).

(3) establishment of an account by the attorney of his own funds which can be used to accommodate a client when there is no other solution.[146]

The committee understood, however, that these solutions might not be practical. It then addressed the question of whether it was ever proper for an attorney to disburse funds at a real estate closing from uncollected funds. Recognizing the practical reasons and customary practice of doing so among many attorneys, the committee ruled that an attorney could properly disburse at closing from uncollected funds if the funds consisted of a certified or cashier's check issued by a bank. The committee concluded that such disbursements involved almost nonexistent risk because the checks were the obligations of the bank rather than a private party. Later the committee extended this rule to cashier's and certified checks issued by savings and loan institutions but it refused to do so for "official checks" issued by certain financial institutions.[147] The committee went on to make clear that disbursement against the personal check of the buyer was improper.[148]

While receptive to the practicalities of real estate practice, the approach authorized by the New Jersey committee does expose attorneys and clients who have funds in escrow accounts to some degree of risk. Indeed, given the debacle in the savings and loan industry, the committee's assumption that checks issued by financial institutions bear almost no risk can be questioned. Most states do not follow the New Jersey approach and prohibit lawyers from making disbursements against uncollected funds.

Problem 5-4

Estate Planning and Probate Practice

a. John and Ellen Bryson have come to you seeking advice regarding an estate plan. The couple has two minor children and total assets, including insurance, of approximately $3 million. Almost all of the assets are in John's name, although they own their home as tenants in common. Ellen's father is deceased and her mother is in poor health. On her mother's death, Ellen expects to inherit approximately $300,000. You have discussed with them a fairly typical estate plan for their situation. Under the plan each spouse would execute a will with two parts: a "credit shelter trust" (sometimes called a "bypass trust") and a "marital deduction" bequest.

The credit shelter portion is an amount equal to the maximum credit allowed for federal estate tax purposes; this figure is gradually rising from

---

146. 105 N.J.L.J. 441 (1980).
147. New Jersey Supreme Court Adv. Comm. on Prof. Ethics, Op. 687, 159 N.J.L.J. 454 (2000).
148. See In re Moras, 619 A.2d 1007, 1011 (N.J. 1993).

$1.5 million to $3.5 million over the next few years. The credit shelter share goes into trust for the benefit of the surviving spouse for life, with remainder to their children. Use of the bypass trust avoids taxation of the credit shelter amount on the death of both spouses. On the death of the first spouse, the credit shelter amount is not taxed in that spouse's estate because of the application of the federal estate tax credit. On the death of the second spouse, the credit shelter amount still escapes tax because the second spouse only has a life interest in the trust. The income and principal of the credit shelter trust are available for the surviving spouse if needed, although it is typically anticipated that the surviving spouse will have sufficient assets from the marital portion to avoid encroaching on the principal of the credit shelter trust.

The marital deduction bequest consists of the remainder of the first spouse's estate. On the death of the first spouse, this portion passes free of estate tax as a result of the marital deduction. On the second spouse's death, the marital deduction portion will be subject to tax. The marital deduction portion can be left to the surviving spouse outright, or it can be placed in what is called a QTIP (Qualified Terminable Interest Property) trust. The major difference between an outright bequest and the QTIP trust deals with the degree of control that the first spouse can exercise over the principal of the bequest. With an outright bequest, the surviving spouse enjoys the unfettered right to use the income and principal of the marital bequest. With a QTIP trust, the first spouse can limit the surviving spouse to an income interest in the bequest and can control the ultimate disposition of the trust when the surviving spouse dies.

After you met with John and Ellen, they decided that they wanted to think about your suggested plan for a few days. About a week later, you receive a call from John. He tells you that he and Ellen have decided to go ahead with the plan. For his will, he says that he wants Ellen's marital portion held in a QTIP trust. John says that Ellen is a very attractive woman, and he knows that she will remarry if something happens to him. He wants to make sure that his estate goes to their children, and not to a second husband. John says that in Ellen's will the marital portion should go to him outright rather than in trust; because she does not have a large estate, a trust is unnecessary and too much paperwork for him. John also asks you about an executor and trustee for his will. He wants to know if you would be willing to serve because he really doesn't trust a bank to handle his estate. Be prepared to continue the conversation with John from that point.

b. Suppose John and Ellen have executed wills following the general structure that you outlined. About a year later, John calls and asks for an appointment. At the meeting John tells you that when he was in college a coed that he was dating became pregnant with John's child. John offered to pay for an abortion, but Lizzie, the young woman, refused and insisted that she wanted to have the baby. John asked Lizzie to marry him, but she declined. The child, whose name is Cloe, was born. John has kept in touch with Lizzie and has met Cloe, but neither John nor Lizzie has told Cloe that John is her father. Cloe is now eight years old. Because Lizzie is not well off financially, John has decided that he would like to put aside some money in a trust for Cloe to pay for her education if she decides to go to college, or to give her a nest egg if she doesn't. He is considering setting up a trust to which he would contribute around $10,000 per year. He would like your advice about this arrangement and wants to know if you would be willing to serve as trustee. What would you do?

    c. You are attorney for the estate of Horace Bellrod. Bellrod died recently, leaving an estate of approximately $10 million. He is survived by his wife, Nancy, age 77, and three adult children. Bellrod's will leaves half of his estate outright to his children and half in trust for his wife, remainder to the children. Bellrod appointed his three children as personal representatives of his estate and as cotrustees of a marital deduction trust created under his will. Under the law of your jurisdiction, a surviving spouse can elect to receive a statutory share of one-third of the estate instead of taking under the will. You have advised the children of this. They have asked you whether it is necessary for their mother to take this amount because they question her ability to manage the money. They also say that her memory appears to be failing, and they are concerned that she may be suffering from early stages of Alzheimer's disease. They believe that the trust arrangement is much better for her and that this arrangement is what their father wanted. You have advised them that Nancy has the right to elect a forced share, but that she does not have to exercise this right. The children tell you that they do not plan to inform their mother of her statutory right and simply hope that it lapses. Under local law the statutory right expires unless it is exercised within eight months after the date of death. A few days after meeting with the children to discuss the statutory forced share matter, you receive a telephone call from Nancy Bellrod. She says that she is calling to see what she needs to do about the estate. Be prepared to continue the conversation from that point.

Read Model Rules 1.4, 1.6, 1.7, 1.8(c), 1.14, 2.1, 5.3, and comments.

The Model Rules and ethical issues facing lawyers engaged in estate planning and administration

The trust and estate bar has criticized the Model Rules for failing to provide adequate guidance regarding common ethical problems in this area of practice. A study by a committee of the Real Property, Probate, and Trust Law Section of the ABA concluded that "the Model Rules do not deal effectively with some of the most important and most difficult problems of professional conduct in the practice of estate planning."[149]

As a result of this criticism, the ABA Real Property, Probate, and Trust Law Section appointed a special committee to study ethical issues confronting trust and estate lawyers. In 1993 the special committee issued three reports that were approved by the council of the section:

- Comments and Recommendations on the Lawyer's Duties in Representing Husband and Wife (hereinafter Special Report—Representing Husband and Wife);
- Preparation of Wills and Trusts that Name Drafting Lawyer as Fiduciary (hereinafter Special Report—Drafting Lawyer as Fiduciary); and
- Counseling the Fiduciary (hereinafter Special Report—Counseling the Fiduciary).[150]

In addition, the American College of Trust and Estate Counsel has adopted Commentaries on the Model Rules of Professional Conduct.[151] The material that follows focuses on several of the most important ethical problems facing lawyers in trust and estate practice.

Conflicts of interest and confidentiality in estate planning

Model Rule 1.7 deals with conflicts of interest when a lawyer is asked to represent multiple clients in a single matter. We have explored the application of this rule in a number of areas of practice: criminal defense (Problem 2-7), joint representation of plaintiffs in tort matters (Problem 3-8), insurance defense practice (Problem 3-9), family practice (Problem 3-10), and business practice (Problem 5-1). How does Rule 1.7 apply to representation of spouses in estate planning?[152] Rule 1.7(a)(2) provides that a concurrent conflict exists

---

149. Committee on Significant New Developments in Probate and Trust Law Practice, Developments Regarding the Professional Responsibility of the Estate Planning Lawyer: The Effect of the Model Rules of Professional Conduct, 22 Real Prop. Prob. & Tr. J. 1, 1-2 (1987). See also American College of Trust and Estate Counsel, Commentaries on the Model Rules of Professional Conduct, Preface (3d ed. 1999) (hereinafter referred to as the ACTEC Commentaries, http://www.actcc.org/pubInfoArk/comm/toc.html (visited Sept. 19, 2003). For discussion of the Commentaries see Bruce S. Ross, Ethical Guidelines for the Estates and Trusts Lawyer: The ACTEC Commentaries on the Model Rules of Professional Conduct and Note on Ethics 2002, SH005 ALI-ABA 393 (2002) (on Westlaw).

150. All three reports are published in 28 Real Prop. Prob. & Tr. J. 765, 803, 825 (1994).

151. See note 149.

152. For a different approach, see Russell G. Pearce, Family Values and Legal Ethics: Competing Approaches to Conflicts in Representing Spouses, 62 Fordham L. Rev. 1253 (1994) (proposing modification of rules of ethics to allow lawyers to represent families as communities rather than collection of individuals). See generally Symposium, Should the Family Be Represented as an Entity? 22 Seattle U. L. Rev. 1 (1998).

if there is a "significant risk that the representation of one or more clients will be materially limited by the lawyer's responsibilities to another client." If a concurrent conflict exists, the lawyer may proceed with joint representation if the lawyer "reasonably believes" that the lawyer can competently and diligently represent each client and each client gives informed consent, confirmed in writing. Model Rule 1.7(b)(1), (4). In the context of estate planning for spouses, Rule 1.7 raises a number of issues: Is it always necessary for a lawyer to obtain informed consent before handling estate planning for spouses? Is joint representation ever improper, even with informed consent? May a lawyer undertake separate representation of the spouses rather than joint representation? What are a lawyer's ethical obligations if the lawyer receives confidential information from one spouse that is material to the other spouse's estate plan?

The authorities are divided on whether a lawyer must always obtain informed consent before providing estate planning services. Some authorities take the position that in many cases there is no conflict and the lawyer may proceed without consent. The Restatement of the Law Governing Lawyers offers the following illustration:

> Husband and Wife consult Lawyer for estate-planning advice about a will for each of them. Lawyer has had professional dealings with the spouses, both separately and together, on several prior occasions. Lawyer knows them to be knowledgeable about their respective rights and interests, competent to make independent decisions if called for, and in accord on their common and individual objectives. Lawyer may represent both clients in the matter without obtaining consent (see §121). While each spouse theoretically could make a distribution different from the other's, including a less generous bequest to each other, those possibilities do not create a conflict of interest, and none reasonably appears to exist in the circumstances.[153]

The Restatement reasons that a lawyer is "not required to suggest or assume discord where none exists."[154] The Special Report—Representing Husband and Wife also adopts the view that a lawyer may ethically proceed with the representation of both spouses in estate planning without complying with the requirements of Rule 1.7(b) when the lawyer has no reason to believe that a potential conflict exists between the spouses. The report goes on to state that the mere fact of marriage is not in itself sufficient to trigger the requirements of Rule 1.7(b).[155]

The Model Rules are unclear on the necessity for disclosure and consent, although they seem to indicate that the lawyer should at least disclose the lawyer's role. Comment 27 to Rule 1.7 provides:

> For example, conflict questions may arise in estate planning and estate administration. A lawyer may be called upon to prepare wills for several family

153. Restatement (Third) of the Law Governing Lawyers §130, illus. 1.
154. Id. cmt. c.
155. 28 Real Prop. Prob. & Tr. J. at 779.

members, such as husband and wife, and, depending upon the circumstances, a conflict of interest may be present. . . . In order to comply with conflict of interest rules, the lawyer should make clear the lawyer's relationship to the parties involved.

Professor Jeffrey Pennell disagrees with the view that a lawyer may proceed with joint representation without disclosure and consent of the spouses, even when the lawyer has no reason to believe that a conflict of interest exists between the spouses. He argues that if there is no real conflict, consent should be easy to obtain. If one of the spouses is reluctant or unwilling to consent, then a conflict may well be present and the lawyer should be wary about beginning the representation.[156]

Is joint representation of spouses in estate planning ever improper even if the spouses are willing to consent? Some cases will arise in which the lawyer could not represent both spouses, even with their informed consent,[157] but they are likely to be rare.[158] For example, the Restatement would allow a lawyer to proceed with multiple representation with informed consent even if the differences between the spouses seem significant:

> The same facts as in Illustration 1, except that Lawyer has not previously met the spouses. Spouse A does most of the talking in the initial discussions with Lawyer. Spouse B, who owns significantly more property than Spouse A, appears to disagree with important positions of Spouse A but to be uncomfortable in expressing that disagreement and does not pursue them when Spouse A appears impatient and peremptory. Representation of both spouses would involve a conflict of interest. Lawyer may proceed to provide the requested legal assistance only with consent given under the limitations and conditions provided in §122.[159]

Of course, if the estates are large and the differences between the spouses appear to be great, a prudent lawyer would refuse a joint engagement.

In the estate planning field some practitioners have adopted an approach of "separate representation." Both the ACTEC Commentaries[160] and The Special Report—Representing Husband and Wife approve of separate representation. The Special Report discusses the differences between separate and joint representation in some detail.

In separate representation, the lawyer represents each spouse separately as to that spouse's rights and interests.[161] Further, in separate representation

---

156. Jeffrey N. Pennell, Ethics, Professionalism, and Malpractice Issues in Estate Planning and Administration, SH092 ALI-ABA 1063, 1075 (2003) (on Westlaw).

157. ACTEC Commentaries, commentary to Model Rule 1.7, *Conflicts of Interest May Preclude Multiple Representation*.

158. For example, it is generally improper for a lawyer to represent both parties to a prenuptial agreement. Id.

159. Restatement (Third) of the Law Governing Lawyers §130, illus. 2.

160. ACTEC Commentaries, commentary to Model Rule 1.7, *Joint or Separate Representation*.

161. 28 Real Prop. Prob. & Tr. J. at 772.

the lawyer must maintain the confidentiality of information received from either spouse, even if the information might affect the estate plan of the other spouse.[162] The lawyer, however, may have a duty to withdraw if the receipt of confidential information means that an actual conflict of interest exists between the spouses.[163] By contrast, in joint representation the lawyer represents both spouses "joined to accomplish a mutual goal."[164] If a lawyer who is engaged in joint representation receives confidential information from one spouse that has an impact on the estate plan of the other spouse, the lawyer must act as a fiduciary to both spouses and must choose to disclose, to maintain confidentiality, or to withdraw based on the lawyer's determination of which action does the least harm.[165]

The report also considers two methods by which a lawyer may undertake representation: either with or without an agreement regarding the nature of the lawyer's representation. As discussed above, the report concludes that a lawyer may ethically represent both spouses in estate planning without the need for consent if no apparent conflict exists.[166] If the lawyer proceeds in this manner, that is, without discussion of the lawyer's role, the report concludes that the representation should be deemed joint rather than separate.[167]

Alternatively, a lawyer could choose to undertake representation after full discussion with the clients about the differences between joint and separate representation. The report provides that a lawyer who does so has flexibility to set the terms of the engagement: "The lawyer may confirm the implicit disclosure rules discussed above; may define his or her duty to require immediate disclosure and withdrawal; or may agree to neither disclosure nor withdrawal."[168] Even with an engagement agreement, however, the report recognizes limits on the lawyer's conduct. For example, a lawyer could not participate in active deception of the other spouse.[169]

While the report concludes that engagement agreements are not required, it advises that discussion and agreement are the "better practice."[170] If the lawyer does use an engagement agreement, how does the lawyer choose between separate or joint representation?

> The lawyer may determine to use consistently either mode, or to adopt different modes of representation for different fact patterns. Some practitioners may offer both modes and allow the couple to choose, although this should be offered only by the lawyer who is confident he or she can perform competently in either mode. However, the method of representation must be constantly recon-

162. Id. at 796.
163. Id. at 794-795.
164. Id. at 771.
165. Id. at 787.
166. Id. at 779.
167. Id. at 778.
168. Id. at 793-794.
169. Id. at 794-795.
170. Id. at 801-802.

sidered by the lawyer as new facts and situations arise. The lawyer also must make a personal choice, individually developed, based on his or her perspective of the couple's planning needs, their sophistication, their responsibilities to each other, and his or her ability to remain independent and loyal as competing goals emerge.[171]

Professor Geoffrey Hazard has criticized probate and estate lawyers for claiming that their practice should be subject to special rules. He argues that while joint representation is consistent with the Model Rules, separate representation is "incorrect as a matter of law and therefore a legally dangerous mode of practice."[172] The Restatement of the Law Governing Lawyers, while not rejecting the concept of separate representation outright, refers to it as "novel" and cautions lawyers about the substantial risks involved in undertaking this form of representation.[173]

If a lawyer has undertaken either separate or joint representation, the lawyer may encounter a situation in which the lawyer receives confidential information from one spouse that may be material to the estate plan of the other spouse, but the spouse who revealed the information refuses to allow the lawyer to disclose the information to the other spouse. The following case examines the lawyer's obligations in this difficult situation.

A. v. B.

Supreme Court of New Jersey 726 A.2d 924 (N.J. 1999)

POLLOCK, J.

This appeal presents the issue whether a law firm may disclose confidential information of one co-client to another co-client. Specifically, in this paternity action, the mother's former law firm, which contemporaneously represented the father and his wife in planning their estates, seeks to disclose to the wife the existence of the father's illegitimate child.

A law firm, Hill Wallack (described variously as "the law firm" or "the firm"), jointly represented the husband and wife in drafting wills in which they devised their respective estates to each other. The devises created the possibility that the other spouse's issue, whether legitimate or illegitimate, ultimately would acquire the decedent's property.

Unbeknown to Hill Wallack and the wife, the husband recently had fathered an illegitimate child. Before the execution of the wills, the child's mother

---

171. Id. at 796-797. For examples of engagement agreements for joint and separate representation, see ACTEC Foundation, Engagement Letters: A Guide for Practitioners (1999), http://www.actec.org/pubInfoArk/comm/engltrtoc.htm (visited Sept. 19, 2003).

172. Geoffrey C. Hazard, Jr., Conflict of Interest in Estate Planning for Husband and Wife, 20 Prob. Law. 1, 6 (1994) (published by the Am. Coll. of Tr. & Estate Counsel).

173. Restatement (Third) of the Law Governing Lawyers §130, Reporter's Note to cmt. *c.*

retained Hill Wallack to institute this paternity action against the husband. Because of a clerical error, the firm's computer check did not reveal the conflict of interest inherent in its representation of the mother against the husband. On learning of the conflict, the firm withdrew from representation of the mother in the paternity action. Now, the firm wishes to disclose to the wife the fact that the husband has an illegitimate child. To prevent Hill Wallack from making that disclosure, the husband joined the firm as a third-party defendant in the paternity action. . . .

I.

Although the record is both informal and attenuated, the parties agree substantially on the relevant facts. Because the Family Part has sealed the record, we refer to the parties without identifying them by their proper names. So viewed, the record supports the following factual statement.

In October 1997, the husband and wife retained Hill Wallack, a firm of approximately sixty lawyers, to assist them with planning their estates. On the commencement of the joint representation, the husband and wife each signed a letter captioned "Waiver of Conflict of Interest." In explaining the possible conflicts of interest, the letter recited that the effect of a testamentary transfer by one spouse to the other would permit the transferee to dispose of the property as he or she desired. The firm's letter also explained that information provided by one spouse could become available to the other. Although the letter did not contain an express waiver of the confidentiality of any such information, each spouse consented to and waived any conflicts arising from the firm's joint representation.

Unfortunately, the clerk who opened the firm's estate planning file misspelled the clients' surname. The misspelled name was entered in the computer program that the firm uses to discover possible conflicts of interest. The firm then prepared reciprocal wills and related documents with the names of the husband and wife correctly spelled.

In January 1998, before the husband and wife executed the estate planning documents, the mother coincidentally retained Hill Wallack to pursue a paternity claim against the husband. This time, when making its computer search for conflicts of interest, Hill Wallack spelled the husband's name correctly. Accordingly, the computer search did not reveal the existence of the firm's joint representation of the husband and wife. As a result, the estate planning department did not know that the family law department had instituted a paternity action for the mother. Similarly, the family law department did not know that the estate planning department was preparing estate plans for the husband and wife.

A lawyer from the firm's family law department wrote to the husband about the mother's paternity claim. The husband neither objected to the firm's representation of the mother nor alerted the firm to the conflict of interest. Instead, he retained Fox Rothschild to represent him in the paternity action.

After initially denying paternity, he agreed to voluntary DNA testing, which revealed that he is the father. Negotiations over child support failed, and the mother instituted the present action.

After the mother filed the paternity action, the husband and wife executed their wills at the Hill Wallack office. The parties agree that in their wills, the husband and wife leave their respective residuary estates to each other. If the other spouse does not survive, the contingent beneficiaries are the testator's issue. The wife's will leaves her residuary estate to her husband, creating the possibility that her property ultimately may pass to his issue. Under N.J.S.A. 3B:1-2; :3-48, the term "issue" includes both legitimate and illegitimate children. When the wife executed her will, therefore, she did not know that the husband's illegitimate child ultimately may inherit her property.

The conflict of interest surfaced when Fox Rothschild, in response to Hill Wallack's request for disclosure of the husband's assets, informed the firm that it already possessed the requested information. Hill Wallack promptly informed the mother that it unknowingly was representing both the husband and the wife in an unrelated matter.

Hill Wallack immediately withdrew from representing the mother in the paternity action. It also instructed the estate planning department not to disclose any information about the husband's assets to the member of the firm who had been representing the mother. The firm then wrote to the husband stating that it believed it had an ethical obligation to disclose to the wife the existence, but not the identity, of his illegitimate child. Additionally, the firm stated that it was obligated to inform the wife "that her current estate plan may devise a portion of her assets through her spouse to that child." The firm suggested that the husband so inform his wife and stated that if he did not do so, it would. Because of the restraints imposed by the Appellate Division, however, the firm has not disclosed the information to the wife.

II.

This appeal concerns the conflict between two fundamental obligations of lawyers: the duty of confidentiality, Rules of Professional Conduct (RPC) 1.6(a), and the duty to inform clients of material facts, RPC 1.4(b). The conflict arises from a law firm's joint representation of two clients whose interests initially were, but no longer are, compatible.

Crucial to the attorney-client relationship is the attorney's obligation not to reveal confidential information learned in the course of representation. Thus, RPC 1.6(a) states that "[a] lawyer shall not reveal information relating to representation of a client unless the client consents after consultation, except for disclosures that are impliedly authorized in order to carry out the representation." Generally, "the principle of attorney-client confidentiality imposes a sacred trust on the attorney not to disclose the client's confidential communication." State v. Land, 73 N.J. 24, 30, 372 A.2d 297 (1977).

A lawyer's obligation to communicate to one client all information needed to make an informed decision qualifies the firm's duty to maintain the confidentiality of a co-client's information. RPC 1.4(b), which reflects a lawyer's duty to keep clients informed, requires that "[a] lawyer shall explain a matter to the extent reasonably necessary to permit the client to make informed decisions regarding the representation." . . . In limited situations, moreover, an attorney is permitted or required to disclose confidential information. Hill Wallack argues that RPC 1.6 mandates, or at least permits, the firm to disclose to the wife the existence of the husband's illegitimate child. RPC 1.6(b) requires that a lawyer disclose "information relating to representation of a client" to the proper authorities if the lawyer "reasonably believes" that such disclosure is necessary to prevent the client "from committing a criminal, illegal or fraudulent act that the lawyer reasonably believes is likely to result in death or substantial bodily harm or substantial injury to the financial interest or property of another." RPC 1.6(b)(1). Despite Hill Wallack's claim that RPC 1.6(b) applies, the facts do not justify mandatory disclosure. The possible inheritance of the wife's estate by the husband's illegitimate child is too remote to constitute "substantial injury to the financial interest or property of another" within the meaning of RPC 1.6(b).

By comparison, in limited circumstances RPC 1.6(c) permits a lawyer to disclose a confidential communication. RPC 1.6(c) permits, but does not require, a lawyer to reveal confidential information to the extent the lawyer reasonably believes necessary "to rectify the consequences of a client's criminal, illegal or fraudulent act in furtherance of which the lawyer's services had been used." RPC 1.6(c)(1). Although RPC 1.6(c) does not define a "fraudulent act," the term takes on meaning from our construction of the word "fraud," found in the analogous "crime or fraud" exception to the attorney-client privilege. See N.J.R.E. 504(2)(a) (excepting from attorney-client privilege "a communication in the course of legal service sought or obtained in the aid of the commission of a crime or fraud"). . . . When construing the "crime or fraud" exception to the attorney-client privilege, "our courts have generally given the term 'fraud' an expansive reading." Fellerman v. Bradley, 99 N.J. 493, 503-04, 493 A.2d 1239 (1985).

We likewise construe broadly the term "fraudulent act" within the meaning of RPC 1.6(c). So construed, the husband's deliberate omission of the existence of his illegitimate child constitutes a fraud on his wife. When discussing their respective estates with the firm, the husband and wife reasonably could expect that each would disclose information material to the distribution of their estates, including the existence of children who are contingent residuary beneficiaries. The husband breached that duty. Under the reciprocal wills, the existence of the husband's illegitimate child could affect the distribution of the wife's estate, if she predeceased him. Additionally, the husband's child support payments and other financial responsibilities owed to the illegitimate child could deplete that part of his estate that otherwise would pass to his wife.

From another perspective, it would be "fundamentally unfair" for the husband to reap the "joint planning advantages of access to information and certainty of outcome," while denying those same advantages to his wife. Teresa

S. Collett, Disclosure, Discretion, or Deception: The Estate Planner's Ethical Dilemma from a Unilateral Confidence, 28 Real Prop. Prob. Tr. J. 683, 743 (1994). In effect, the husband has used the law firm's services to defraud his wife in the preparation of her estate.

[The court then discussed the history of New Jersey Rule 1.6, which contains much more extensive exceptions to confidentiality than found in the ABA Model Rules as they existed in 1999.] Described as an "openly-radical experiment," Geoffrey C. Hazard, Jr. & W. William Hodes, 2 The Law of Lawyering §AP4:104 (1998), RPC 1.6 "contained the most far-reaching disclosure requirements of any attorney code of conduct in the country," Leslie C. Levin, Testing the Radical Experiment: A Study of Lawyer Response to Clients Who Intend to Harm Others, 47 Rutgers L. Rev. 81, 92 (1994).

Under RPC 1.6, the facts support disclosure to the wife. The law firm did not learn of the husband's illegitimate child in a confidential communication from him. Indeed, he concealed that information from both his wife and the firm. The law firm learned about the husband's child through its representation of the mother in her paternity action against the husband. Accordingly, the husband's expectation of nondisclosure of the information may be less than if he had communicated the information to the firm in confidence.

In addition, the husband and wife signed letters captioned "Waiver of Conflict of Interest." These letters acknowledge that information provided by one client could become available to the other. The letters, however, stop short of explicitly authorizing the firm to disclose one spouse's confidential information to the other. Even in the absence of any such explicit authorization, the spirit of the letters supports the firm's decision to disclose to the wife the existence of the husband's illegitimate child.

Neither our research nor that of counsel has revealed a dispositive judicial decision from this or any other jurisdiction on the issue of disclosure of confidential information about one client to a co-client. Persuasive secondary authority, however, supports the conclusion that the firm may disclose to the wife the existence of the husband's child.

The forthcoming Restatement (Third) of The Law Governing Lawyers §112 comment 1 (Proposed Final Draft No. 1, 1996) ("the Restatement") [Now §60] suggests, for example, that if the attorney and the co-clients have reached a prior, explicit agreement concerning the sharing of confidential information, that agreement controls whether the attorney should disclose the confidential information of one co-client to another. Ibid. ("Co-clients . . . may explicitly agree to share information" and "can also explicitly agree that the lawyer is not to share certain information . . . with one or more other co-clients. A lawyer must honor such agreements."); see also Report of the ABA Special Study Committee on Professional Responsibility: Comments and Recommendations on the Lawyer's Duties in Representing Husband and Wife, 28 Real Prop. Prob. Tr. J. 765, 787 (1994) ("Although legally and ethically there is no need for a prior discussion and agreement with the couple about the mode of representation, discussion and agreement are the better practice. The agreement may cover . . . the duty to keep or disclose confidences.");

American College of Trust and Estate Counsel, ACTEC Commentaries on the Model Rules of Professional Conduct 65-66 (2d ed. 1995) ("When the lawyer is first consulted by the multiple potential clients the lawyer should review with them the terms upon which the lawyer will undertake the representation, including the extent to which information will be shared among them.").

As the preceding authorities suggest, an attorney, on commencing joint representation of co-clients, should agree explicitly with the clients on the sharing of confidential information. In such a "disclosure agreement," the co-clients can agree that any confidential information concerning one co-client, whether obtained from a co-client himself or herself or from another source, will be shared with the other co-client. Similarly, the co-clients can agree that unilateral confidences or other confidential information will be kept confidential by the attorney. Such a prior agreement will clarify the expectations of the clients and the lawyer and diminish the need for future litigation.

In the absence of an agreement to share confidential information with co-clients, the Restatement reposes the resolution of the lawyer's competing duties within the lawyer's discretion:

> [T]he lawyer, after consideration of all relevant circumstances, has the . . . discretion to inform the affected co-client of the specific communication if, in the lawyer's reasonable judgment, the immediacy and magnitude of the risk to the affected co-client outweigh the interest of the communicating client in continued secrecy. Restatement (Third) of The Law Governing Lawyers, supra, §112 [Now §60] comment l.

Additionally, the Restatement advises that the lawyer, when withdrawing from representation of the co-clients, may inform the affected co-client that the attorney has learned of information adversely affecting that client's interests that the communicating co-client refuses to permit the lawyer to disclose. Ibid.

In the context of estate planning, the Restatement also suggests that a lawyer's disclosure of confidential information communicated by one spouse is appropriate only if the other spouse's failure to learn of the information would be materially detrimental to that other spouse or frustrate the spouse's intended testamentary arrangement. Id. §112 [Now §60] comment l, illustrations 2, 3. The Restatement provides two analogous illustrations in which a lawyer has been jointly retained by a husband and wife to prepare reciprocal wills. The first illustration states:

> Lawyer has been retained by Husband and Wife to prepare wills pursuant to an arrangement under which each spouse agrees to leave most of their property to the other. Shortly after the wills are executed, Husband (unknown to Wife) asks Lawyer to prepare an inter vivos trust for an illegitimate child whose existence Husband has kept secret from Wife for many years and about whom Husband had not previously informed Lawyer. Husband states that Wife would be distraught at learning of Husband's infidelity and of Husband's years of silence and that disclosure of the information could destroy their marriage. Husband directs Lawyer not to inform Wife. The inter vivos trust that Husband proposes to create would

not materially affect Wife's own estate plan or her expected receipt of property under Husband's will, because Husband proposes to use property designated in Husband's will for a personally favored charity. In view of the lack of material effect on Wife, Lawyer may assist Husband to establish and fund the inter vivos trust and refrain from disclosing Husband's information to Wife. Id. §112 [Now §60] comment l, illustration 2.

In authorizing non-disclosure, the Restatement explains that an attorney should refrain from disclosing the existence of the illegitimate child to the wife because the trust "would not materially affect Wife's own estate plan or her expected receipt of property under Husband's will." Ibid.

The other illustration states:

Same facts as [the prior Illustration], except that Husband's proposed inter vivos trust would significantly deplete Husband's estate, to Wife's material detriment and in frustration of the Spouses' intended testamentary arrangements. If Husband will neither inform Wife nor permit Lawyer to do so, Lawyer must withdraw from representing both Husband and Wife. In the light of all relevant circumstances, Lawyer may exercise discretion whether to inform Wife either that circumstances, which Lawyer has been asked not to reveal, indicate that she should revoke her recent will or to inform Wife of some or all the details of the information that Husband has recently provided so that Wife may protect her interests. Alternatively, Lawyer may inform Wife only that Lawyer is withdrawing because Husband will not permit disclosure of information that Lawyer has learned from Husband. Id. §112 [Now §60] comment l, illustration 3.

Because the money placed in the trust would be deducted from the portion of the husband's estate left to his wife, the Restatement concludes that the lawyer may exercise discretion to inform the wife of the husband's plans. Ibid.

An earlier draft of the Restatement described the attorney's obligation to disclose the confidential information to the co-client as mandatory. Id. (Council Draft No. 11, 1995); cf. Collett, supra, at 743 (arguing that nature of joint representation of husband and wife supports mandatory disclosure rule). When reviewing the draft, however, the governing body of the American Law Institute, the Council, modified the obligation to leave disclosure within the attorney's discretion.

Similarly, the American College of Trust and Estate Counsel (ACTEC) also favors a discretionary rule. It recommends that the "lawyer should have a reasonable degree of discretion in determining how to respond to any particular case." American College of Trust and Estate Counsel, supra, at 68. The ACTEC suggests that the lawyer first attempt to convince the client to inform the co-client. Ibid. When urging the client to disclose the information, the lawyer should remind the client of the implicit understanding that all information will be shared by both clients. The lawyer also should explain to the client the potential legal consequences of non-disclosure, including invalidation of the wills. Ibid. Furthermore, the lawyer may mention that failure to communicate the information could subject the lawyer to a malpractice claim or disciplinary action. Ibid.

The ACTEC reasons that if unsuccessful in persuading the client to disclose the information, the lawyer should consider several factors in deciding whether to reveal the confidential information to the co-client, including: (1) duties of impartiality and loyalty to the clients; (2) any express or implied agreement among the lawyer and the joint clients that information communicated by either client to the lawyer regarding the subject of the representation would be shared with the other client; (3) the reasonable expectations of the clients; and (4) the nature of the confidence and the harm that may result if the confidence is, or is not, disclosed. Id. at 68-69.

The Section of Real Property, Probate and Trust Law of the American Bar Association, in a report prepared by its Special Study Committee on Professional Responsibility, reached a similar conclusion:

> Faced with any adverse confidence, the lawyer must act as a fiduciary toward joint clients. The lawyer must balance the potential for material harm to the confiding spouse caused by disclosure against the potential for material harm to the other spouse caused by a failure to disclose. Report of the Special Study Committee on Professional Responsibility: Comments and Recommendations on the Lawyer's Duties in Representing Husband and Wife, supra, 28 Real Prop. Prob. Tr. J. at 787.

The report stresses that the resolution of the balancing test should center on the expectations of the clients. Id. at 784. In general, "the available ruling authority . . . points toward the conclusion that a lawyer is not required to disclose an adverse confidence to the other spouse." Id. at 788. At the same time, the report acknowledges, as did the Restatement, that the available ruling authority is "scant and offers little analytical guidance." Id. at 788 n.27.

The Professional Ethics Committees of New York and Florida, however, have concluded that disclosure to a co-client is prohibited. New York State Bar Ass'n Comm. on Professional Ethics, Op. 555 (1984); Florida State Bar Ass'n Comm. on Professional Ethics, Op. 95-4 (1997).

The New York opinion addressed the following situation:

> A and B formed a partnership and employed Lawyer L to represent them in connection with the partnership affairs. Subsequently, B, in a conversation with Lawyer L, advised Lawyer L that he was actively breaching the partnership agreement. B preceded this statement to Lawyer L with the statement that he proposed to tell Lawyer L something "in confidence." Lawyer L did not respond to that statement and did not understand that B intended to make a statement that would be of importance to A but that was to be kept confidential from A. Lawyer L had not, prior thereto, advised A or B that he could not receive from one communications regarding the subject of the joint representation that would be confidential from the other. B has subsequently declined to tell A what he has told Lawyer L. New York State Bar Ass'n Comm. on Professional Ethics, Op. 555, supra.

In that situation, the New York Ethics Committee concluded that the lawyer may not disclose to the co-client the communicating client's statement. The Committee based its conclusion on the absence of prior consent by the clients to the sharing of all confidential communications and the fact that the client "specifically in advance designated his communication as confidential, and the lawyer did not demur." Ibid.

The Florida Ethics Committee addressed a similar situation:

> Lawyer has represented Husband and Wife for many years in a range of personal matters, including estate planning. Husband and Wife have substantial individual assets, and they also own substantial jointly-held property. Recently, Lawyer prepared new updated wills that Husband and Wife signed. Like their previous wills, their new wills primarily benefit the survivor of them for his or her life, with beneficial disposition at the death of the survivor being made equally to their children. . . .
>
> Several months after the execution of the new wills, Husband confers separately with Lawyer. Husband reveals to Lawyer that he has just executed a codicil (prepared by another law firm) that makes substantial beneficial disposition to a woman with whom Husband has been having an extra-marital relationship. Florida State Bar Ass'n Comm. on Professional Ethics, Op. 95-4, supra.

Reasoning that the lawyer's duty of confidentiality takes precedence over the duty to communicate all relevant information to a client, the Florida Ethics Committee concluded that the lawyer did not have discretion to reveal the information. In support of that conclusion, the Florida committee reasoned that joint clients do not necessarily expect that everything relating to the joint representation communicated by one co-client will be shared with the other co-client.

In several material respects, however, the present appeal differs from the hypothetical cases considered by the New York and Florida committees. Most significantly, the New York and Florida disciplinary rules, unlike RPC 1.6, do not except disclosure needed "to rectify the consequences of a client's . . . fraudulent act in the furtherance of which the lawyer's services had been used." RPC 1.6(c). But see New York Code of Professional Responsibility DR 4-101; Florida Rules of Professional Conduct 4-1.6. Second, Hill Wallack learned of the husband's paternity from a third party, not from the husband himself. Thus, the husband did not communicate anything to the law firm with the expectation that the communication would be kept confidential. Finally, the husband and wife, unlike the co-clients considered by the New York and Florida Committees, signed an agreement suggesting their intent to share all information with each other.

Because Hill Wallack wishes to make the disclosure, we need not reach the issue whether the lawyer's obligation to disclose is discretionary or mandatory. In conclusion, Hill Wallack may inform the wife of the existence of the husband's illegitimate child. . . .

Notes and Questions

1. The Restatement, the ACTEC Commentaries, and the Probate and Trust Report, provide that even if the harm to the other spouse is material, disclosure is still discretionary with the lawyer. Professor Teresa Collett in an article cited by the court argues for mandatory disclosure to the other spouse in such a situation. She contends that, absent a clear agreement providing for confidentiality, a lawyer should make "disclosure of unilateral confidences when the information contained within that confidence is relevant to the estate planning process, is unknown to the nonconfiding client, and is adverse to the interests of the nonconfiding client." Teresa S. Collett, Disclosure, Discretion, or Deception: The Estate Planner's Ethical Dilemma from a Unilateral Confidence, 28 Real Prop. Prob. & Tr. J. 683, 762 (1994). Collett justifies this approach because (1) spouses reasonably expect that information will be shared; (2) the spouse who claims confidentiality is acting unfairly, seeking the benefit of complete information from the other spouse, while refusing to accept the burden of full disclosure; and (3) the lawyer is at fault in not obtaining a clear agreement with the clients at the inception of the relationship regarding confidentiality. By contrast, the Florida and New York opinions direct lawyers to maintain confidentiality even in the absence of a specific agreement requiring them to do so. Which approach—discretionary disclosure, mandatory disclosure, or mandatory confidentiality—do you favor? Why?

2. The court states that the waiver document was unclear on whether the firm was required to disclose confidential information received from one spouse to the other. Suppose the agreement had clearly stated that any information received in confidence from one spouse would not be disclosed to the other without the consent of the disclosing spouse. What should the lawyers have done then? Should a lawyer draft a consent form with such a provision? What provision would you suggest putting in an engagement agreement regarding confidentiality?

3. As the case illustrates, even the best designed conflict of interest systems can fail due to misspellings or other errors. Because conflicts of interest arise so frequently in the practice of law, proper training of staff that operate such systems is essential. See Model Rule 5.3.

Bequests to lawyers and wills that name the drafting lawyer as fiduciary

Occasions may arise in which a client would like to make a gift or bequest to a lawyer. The lawyer and client may be related or may have developed a close, personal relationship. Although the Code of Professional Responsibility did not contain a disciplinary rule making it improper for a lawyer to draft an instrument in which the lawyer was also a beneficiary, some courts disciplined lawyers who did so.[174]

---

174. See Committee on Professional Ethics & Conduct v. Behnke, 276 N.W.2d 838 (Iowa), *appeal dismissed*, 444 U.S. 805 (1979).

Model Rule 1.8(c) now deals with this problem:

> A lawyer shall not solicit any substantial gift from a client, including a testamentary gift, or prepare on behalf of a client an instrument giving the lawyer or a person related to the lawyer any substantial gift unless the lawyer or other recipient of the gift is related to the client. For purposes of this paragraph, related persons include a spouse, child, grandchild, parent, grandparent or other relative or individual with whom the lawyer or the client maintains a close, familial relationship.[175]

Note that the rule does not preclude a lawyer from preparing a will for the lawyer's spouse or other relative when the lawyer will be receiving a bequest under the will. If a client wishes to leave a bequest to a lawyer to whom the client is not related, the lawyer must advise the client that the lawyer cannot prepare the will and that the will must be drafted by independent counsel. Another lawyer in the lawyer-beneficiary's firm could not prepare the will because disqualification would be imputed to the other lawyer under Model Rule 1.8(k).[176]

Some states have statutory provisions invalidating gifts and bequests to the person who drafted the instrument. For example, California law invalidates certain donative transfers, including a transfer to any person who drafted the instrument.[177] An exception applies if an independent attorney counsels the transferor about the instrument, and completes and delivers to the drafter and to the transferor a statutory form stating that the instrument has not been the product of undue influence or other misconduct.[178]

The Restatement goes somewhat beyond the Model Rules with regard to client gifts. Under the Restatement, a lawyer may not draft an instrument making a gift or bequest to the lawyer even when the lawyer is related to the donor if the amount of the transfer is significantly disproportionate to those made to other similarly situated donees.[179] This prohibition would not prevent a lawyer from preparing a will in which the lawyer's spouse left the spouse's entire estate to the lawyer because it would not run afoul of the disproportionality rule, but it could apply if a lawyer drafted an instrument for a parent that gave the lawyer a greater share of the estate than other children.[180] The Restatement also prohibits lawyers from receiving substantial gifts from clients to whom they are not related, even if the lawyer does not prepare a document effectuating

---

175. See In re Polevoy, 980 P.2d 985 (Colo. 1999) (en banc) (suspension for drafting will in which lawyer named as beneficiary).

176. Cf. People v. Berge, 620 P.2d 23 (Colo. 1980) (en banc) (lawyer-beneficiary who received bequest from client under will drafted by attorney who shared office space with lawyer-beneficiary was suspended for 90 days).

177. Cal. Prob. Code §21350(a)(1).

178. Id. §21351.

179. Restatement (Third) of the Law Governing Lawyers §127(1).

180. Id. illus. 1.

the gift, when the client has not had the opportunity to receive independent advice before making the gift.[181]

A more common situation in which a lawyer has a financial interest in the will occurs when a client asks if the lawyer would be willing to serve as a fiduciary under the will.[182] Clients may make this request because of reasons such as trust in the lawyer, distrust of corporate fiduciaries, and a desire to save fees that would otherwise be payable to a corporate fiduciary. May a lawyer draft a will in which the lawyer will be named as a fiduciary? Lawyers are not prohibited from serving as fiduciaries on behalf of their clients and drafting instruments in which they are so named. Model Rule 1.8(c) does not apply to this situation because the lawyer is not receiving a gift from the client.[183]

Nonetheless, if a client wishes to name the drafting lawyer as a fiduciary, the lawyer must comply with other ethical obligations.[184] First, and probably most importantly, the lawyer must counsel the client about the advantages, disadvantages, and alternatives to the lawyer serving as fiduciary.[185] Second, if the lawyer's representation may be materially limited by the interest of other clients, third parties, or the lawyer himself, then the lawyer must obtain the client's informed consent in writing as required by Rule 1.7(b).[186]

The Special Report—Drafting Lawyer as Fiduciary provides specifics regarding counseling, disclosure, and consent:

> [B]efore the lawyer prepares a document in which he or she is designated as fiduciary, the client should be counseled, with disclosures by the lawyer, regarding: (1) the nature of the fiduciary office (the role and function of the fiduciary); (2) those persons and institutions available and suitable for appointment; (3) any potential conflicts of interest with other fiduciary relationships or with other clients, including the client's family members, which the fiduciary appointment might trigger; (4) compensation issues; and (5) the additional factors discussed . . . below.[187]

Statutes in some states may require lawyers to make certain disclosures before the testator executes a will that names the drafting lawyer as the executor.[188]

---

181. Id §127(2).

182. See generally Edward D. Spurgeon & Mary Jane Ciccarello, The Lawyer in Other Fiduciary Roles: Policy and Ethical Considerations, 62 Fordham L. Rev. 1357 (1994).

183. ABA Formal Op. 02-426, n.7.

184. See Special Report—Drafting Lawyer as Fiduciary, 28 Real Prop. Prob. & Tr. J. at 805. See also ACTEC Commentaries, commentary to Model Rule 1.7, *Appointment of Scrivener as Fiduciary.*

185. ABA Formal Op. 02-426.

186. Id.

187. See Special Report—Drafting Lawyer as Fiduciary, 28 Real Prop. Prob. & Tr. J. at 818.

188. N.Y. Surr. Ct. Proc. Act §2307-a (requiring disclosures before testator executes will in which drafting attorney or an affiliated attorney will be named as executor).

As to compensation issues, the Special Report outlined the following disclosures:

> (1) whether the lawyer or his or her firm may be retained by the fiduciary to provide legal services and the fees to which the lawyer would be entitled as lawyer and as fiduciary; (2) any understanding or practice the attorney has with the named fiduciary regarding hiring the drafting attorney; (3) the extent, if any, to which dual compensation for legal services and fiduciary services is allowed; (4) a comparison of fees if a fiduciary other than the lawyer is appointed; and (5) a comparison with other options, including any local practice that is common in the community of professional fiduciaries retaining the drafting lawyer for representation of the fiduciary.[189]

In Formal Opinion 02-426, the ABA Committee on Ethics and Professional Responsibility advised that a lawyer could receive compensation for serving as a fiduciary and could also hire his law firm to provide legal services to the estate or trust, although it pointed out that issues could arise regarding the reasonableness of the compensation for legal services under Rule 1.5(a). The Committee also noted that some jurisdictions may impose limitations on "dual compensation." For example, California law imposes limitations on an attorney's ability to receive compensation for serving as both attorney for an estate or trust and as the fiduciary.[190]

Finally, the Special Report indicated additional factors that the drafting lawyer should consider and discuss with the client before preparing a will in which the lawyer is named as a fiduciary, including the following: (1) increased risk of challenge to the will resulting from the drafting lawyer's being named as a fiduciary, (2) the lawyer's competency to perform the duties of fiduciary, (3) possible conflicts with other clients, and (4) whether the will may contain a provision exonerating the attorney from liability for negligence as a fiduciary in light of Model Rule 1.8(h).[191]

Ethical problems in estate administration: conflicts of interest, confidentiality, fees, and supervision of nonlawyers

The administration of many estates proceeds routinely without serious controversy regarding the estate or its distribution.[192] Depending on the number of individuals involved, their personalities, and the complexity and size of the

---

189. See Special Report—Drafting Lawyer as Fiduciary, 28 Real Prop. Prob. & Tr. J. at 819-820.

190. Cal. Prob. Code §§10804 (personal representative) and 15687 (trustee).

191. See Special Report—Drafting Lawyer as Fiduciary, 28 Real Prop. Prob. & Tr. J. at 820-822.

192. See ACTEC Commentaries, commentary to Model Rule 1.7, *General Nonadversary Character of Estates and Trusts Practice; Representation of Multiple Clients*.

estate, however, disputes may arise among the parties, creating the possibility that the lawyer may face conflict-of-interest issues.[193]

An initial step for lawyers in recognizing and handling conflicts of interest in estate administration is identification of whom the lawyer represents when the lawyer is retained to handle the legal work for the estate. This situation should be distinguished from one in which a beneficiary retains a lawyer to advise the beneficiary regarding the estate, or a situation in which the fiduciary hires the lawyer personally rather than to represent the estate. In these cases the identity of the client is clear.[194]

Three possible answers to the question "Who is the client?" are apparent: the beneficiaries, the estate, or the fiduciary.[195] Since the estate is being administered in the interest of the beneficiaries, it is plausible to conclude that a lawyer handling the legal work involved in administering an estate represents the beneficiaries. This answer, however, presents some difficulties. First, the fiduciary rather than the beneficiaries has the legal authority to make a number of decisions regarding the estate. It seems odd to place the lawyer in the position of representing a group of individuals who do not have authority to act, while not representing the one person who legally has the power to act. Second, although it is true that the estate is being administered in the interest of the beneficiaries, that does not mean that the beneficiaries' desires or decisions should control. The testator appointed the fiduciary for the purpose of making decisions, in some cases because the testator did not fully trust the beneficiaries to make such decisions. The fiduciary should be entitled to retain independent counsel to receive advice about these matters.

The second possible answer to the client identification question is that the lawyer represents the "estate" rather than either the beneficiaries or the fiduciary.[196] This approach treats the estate as an entity, like a corporation. Under Model Rule 1.13(a) a lawyer retained by an organization is treated as representing the entity rather than any of its "constituents." Under the entity representation approach, a lawyer is generally required to follow the decisions of a duly appointed representative of the entity, even if the lawyer does not agree with the decision or thinks it to be unwise. Model Rule 1.13, cmt. 3. Model Rule 1.13(b) recognizes, however, that in some cases a lawyer must take steps to protect the entity from misconduct by a representative.

Thus, under the entity theory, if the fiduciary engaged in misappropriation of funds, the lawyer would be required to act "in the best interest" of the estate. In serious cases Rule 1.13(b) would require the lawyer to refer the matter "to the highest authority that can act on behalf of the organization as determined by

---

193. See Special Report—Counseling the Fiduciary, 28 Real Prop. Prob. & Tr. J. 825 (1994).

194. See id. at 840-842 (duties when representing beneficiary) and 854-855 (fiduciary hiring separate counsel to protect its personal or corporate interests).

195. See generally Jeffrey N. Pennell, Representations Involving Fiduciary Entities: Who Is the Client? 62 Fordham L. Rev. 1319 (1994).

196. See id. (arguing for adoption of entity theory).

applicable law." In the case of an estate, who or what is the "highest authority"? Because an estate, unlike a corporation, does not have a board of directors, the highest authority would probably be the court that supervises the estate.

The third approach to defining the client of the lawyer handling estate matters is that the lawyer represents the fiduciary rather than either the beneficiaries or the estate as an entity. A possible objection to this approach is that it seems to ignore the fact that the fiduciary has duties to the beneficiaries for whom the estate is being administered. While this argument would have force if an estate lawyer had no obligations to the beneficiaries, it loses some of its power when it is recognized that lawyers have some duties to third parties, even if they are not treated as clients of the lawyer. These duties are discussed more fully below.

Despite scholarly arguments for the entity theory, scant authority supports it.[197] Most courts have reached the conclusion that a lawyer represents the fiduciary, not the estate or its beneficiaries.[198] In a number of jurisdictions, however, courts have found that an attorney for the fiduciary nonetheless owes duties to the beneficiaries, and this trends seems to be growing.[199] The Special Report—Counseling the Fiduciary adopts the view that a lawyer retained to handle estate matters represents the fiduciary rather than the estate or its beneficiaries, although it does note that the entity theory "offers some interesting solutions where the fiduciary has engaged or is engaged in misconduct."[200] Given this uncertainty, Comment 27 to Model Rule 1.7 provides good advice:

> In estate administration the identity of the client may be unclear under the law of a particular jurisdiction. Under one view, the client is the fiduciary; under another view the client is the estate or trust, including its beneficiaries. In order to comply with conflict of interest rules, the lawyer should make clear the lawyer's relationship to the parties involved.[201]

197. See Steinway v. Bolden, 460 N.W.2d 306 (Mich. Ct. App. 1990).

198. See, e.g., Goldberg v. Frye, 266 Cal. Rptr. 483 (Ct. App. 1990) (no cause of action by beneficiaries against lawyer for administrator of estate because attorney does not owe duty to beneficiaries); Ferguson v. Cramer, 709 A.2d 1279 (Md. 1998) (same); Spinner v. Nutt, 631 N.E.2d 542 (Mass. 1994) (attorney for testamentary trustee does not owe duty to beneficiaries because recognition of such a duty would create conflicting loyalties). See also S.C. Code Ann. §62-1-109 (lawyer retained by fiduciary represents fiduciary rather than beneficiaries).

199. See Fickett v. Superior Court, 558 P.2d 988 (Ariz. Ct. App. 1976) (upholding cause of action on behalf of ward against lawyer for former guardian based on allegations that lawyer knew or should have known that guardian was misappropriating funds and engaging in other misconduct); A. Frank Johns, *Fickett*'s Thicket: The Lawyer's Expanding Fiduciary and Ethical Boundaries When Serving Older Americans of Moderate Wealth, 32 Wake Forest L. Rev. 445 (1997). See also Restatement (Third) of the Law Governing Lawyers §51(4) and cmt. *h* (treating beneficiary as nonclient but recognizing duty of lawyer in some situations).

200. 28 Real Prop. Prob. & Tr. J. at 827. See also ACTEC Commentaries to Model Rule 1.2 (normally fiduciary is the client).

201. See also 28 Real Prop. Prob. & Tr. J. at 860-863 (defining duties of lawyer by written agreement).

Reaching the conclusion that the lawyer represents the fiduciary rather than the estate or its beneficiaries, does not, however, mean that the lawyer owes no duties to the beneficiaries. Lawyers for fiduciaries must take into account a number of duties to beneficiaries. First, beneficiaries may well misunderstand the role of the lawyer and may view the lawyer as protecting or representing their interests. Such misunderstanding is especially likely to occur when the lawyer has represented the beneficiary in the past or is currently handling an unrelated matter on behalf of the beneficiary. We have already studied on several occasions the application of Model Rule 4.3, which deals with communications with unrepresented parties. Recall Problem 2-4 (dealing with tangible criminal material) and Problem 3-10 (family practice). Under Rule 4.3, when a lawyer "knows or reasonably should know that the unrepresented person misunderstands the lawyer's role in the matter, the lawyer shall make reasonable efforts to correct the misunderstanding."[202]

Second, a lawyer for a fiduciary may not counsel or assist the fiduciary in criminal or fraudulent conduct. See Model Rule 1.2(d). This prohibition would include participation in the preparation or filing of fraudulent tax returns or assisting the fiduciary in self-dealing.[203]

Third, under some circumstances a lawyer may have discretion or a duty to inform either the beneficiaries or the court of wrongdoing by a fiduciary. Whether a lawyer has the right or obligation to disclose wrongdoing by a fiduciary will depend on the rules of ethics in the jurisdiction in which the lawyer practices. For example, Rule 1.6(c) of the Washington Rules of Professional Conduct provides that "a lawyer may reveal to the tribunal confidences or secrets which disclose any breach of fiduciary responsibility by a client who is a guardian, personal representative, receiver, or other court appointed fiduciary." See also the New Jersey rules quoted in A. v. B. earlier in this problem. Under revisions to Model Rule 1.6 adopted by the ABA in 2003, a lawyer may disclose confidential information to prevent or to rectify substantial harm to the financial interest of a person that is reasonably certain to result from a crime or fraud committed by a client in which the lawyer's services are or were being used. Thus, if the lawyer prepared incorrect tax returns or fiduciary reports and then learned about the fiduciary's fraud, the lawyer would have discretion to reveal the fraud under the revised ABA Rule 1.6. In fact, the lawyer might well have a duty to disclose the false information to correct prior representations that the lawyer now knows are false. See Model Rules 3.3(a)(1) and 4.1 cmt. 3. If the lawyer's services were not involved in the fraud, the lawyer would not have discretion to disclose under the ABA rule, but in many cases the lawyer would probably be required to withdraw to prevent the lawyer's continued representation from being viewed as assistance of the fraud.

Lawyers who fail to disclose a crime or fraud committed by a fiduciary

---

202. See also id. at 837-839; ACTEC Commentaries to Model Rule 4.3.
203. Special Report—Counseling the Fiduciary, 28 Real Prop. Prob. & Tr. J. at 836-837. See Pierce v. Lyman, 3 Cal. Rptr. 2d 236 (Ct. App. 1991) (beneficiaries state cause of action against trustee's lawyer for participation in trustee's breach of fiduciary duty).

when they are permitted or required to do so under the rules of ethics are likely to be subject to civil liability to beneficiaries. The Restatement provides that a lawyer owes a duty of due care to a nonclient in certain circumstances, including the following:

> (4) to a nonclient when and to the extent that:
>   (a) the lawyer's client is a trustee, guardian, executor, or fiduciary acting primarily to perform similar functions for the nonclient;
>   (b) the lawyer knows that appropriate action by the lawyer is necessary with respect to a matter within the scope of the representation to prevent or rectify the breach of a fiduciary duty owed by the client to the nonclient, where (i) the breach is a crime or fraud or (ii) the lawyer has assisted or is assisting the breach;
>   (c) the nonclient is not reasonably able to protect its rights; and
>   (d) such a duty would not significantly impair the performance of the lawyer's obligations to the client.[204]

If a lawyer has either the duty or discretion to reveal a fraud or crime by the fiduciary, disclosure should not significantly impair the performance of the lawyer's obligations to the fiduciary.

The previous discussion has focused on the issue of who is the client. In some estates a lawyer may be asked to undertake multiple representation: for example, a beneficiary and a fiduciary, or multiple beneficiaries, or multiple fiduciaries. The Special Report—Counseling the Fiduciary advises that lawyers are generally permitted to engage in multiple representation of a beneficiary and the fiduciary because in the typical case a harmony of interests exists between the beneficiary and the fiduciary.[205] The lawyer must, however, be alert to potential conflicts of interest, and if they exist, the lawyer should proceed only after informed consent by both the clients, as required by Model Rule 1.7(b).[206] If an actual conflict develops between clients, the lawyer should not continue the multiple representation.[207] The lawyer will be required to withdraw from representation of both clients unless one of the clients is willing to consent under Model Rule 1.9.[208]

For some time in many jurisdictions, based either on custom or on statute, lawyers charged fees for estate administration based on a percentage of the estate. In a number of jurisdictions, however, fees based on a percentage of the estate have been declared improper either by legislation or court decision

---

204. See Restatement (Third) of the Law Governing Lawyers §51(4) and cmt. *h*.

205. See Special Report—Counseling the Fiduciary, 28 Real Prop. Prob. & Tr. J. at 855-858. See also ACTEC Commentaries to Model Rule 1.7, example 1.7-3 (permissible for lawyer to represent both bank and wife with full disclosure and consent).

206. Special Report—Counseling the Fiduciary, 28 Real Prop. Prob. & Tr. J. at 842-846.

207. Id. at 847.

208. Id. at 848.

on the ground that a fee based on a percentage of the estate, regardless of the difficulty of the work, is unreasonable.[209]

Estate administration is an area in which lawyers often make extensive use of paralegals and other nonlawyers. Lawyers must be aware of and careful to adhere to the obligations regarding supervision of nonlawyers. See Model Rule 5.3. Problem 7-1 examines lawyers' supervisory obligations in more detail. In Office of Disciplinary Counsel v. Ball[210] the attorney's long-time secretary and paralegal became delinquent in filing various documents and papers in probate proceedings, and she misappropriated more than $200,000 from estate and guardianship accounts. This misconduct had taken place over a 10-year period. The attorney learned about his secretary's misconduct when he was contacted about a delinquent probate matter. He immediately reviewed his accounts, discovered what had taken place, fired the secretary, and paid all misappropriated funds with interest. The attorney denied any knowledge of his secretary's actions, and his secretary fully exonerated him from any participation in her wrongdoing. Nonetheless, the Ohio Supreme Court found the attorney guilty of misconduct because of his failure to supervise his secretary, and the court administered a six-month suspension. The court rejected the attorney's argument that he was not responsible for his secretary's actions under Model Rule 5.3(c) unless he had knowledge of her misconduct. The court ruled that an attorney has a duty under Rule 5.3(a) to adopt proper supervisory practices.

Problem 5-5

Tax Practice

a. You represent Johnson Supply Company, a privately held corporation that provides plumbing materials to contractors for commercial and residential construction.[211] The company has elected Subchapter S status under the Internal Revenue Code.[212] Subchapter S status means that a corporation is taxed like a partnership. Generally, a Subchapter S

---

209. See, e.g., In re Estate of Painter, 567 P.2d 820 (Colo. Ct. App. 1977) (Colorado legislature has repealed authorization for percentage fees and adopted reasonable fee standard); Estate of Davis, 509 A.2d 1175 (Me. 1986) (abuse of discretion for probate court to rely on local custom of using percentage method in setting attorney fee); In re Estate of Rolfe, 615 A.2d 625 (N.H. 1992) (disapproval of fee guidelines based on size of estate). But see Fla. Stat. Ann. §733.6171 (attorneys are entitled to compensation at flat rate for estates under $100,000 and on percentage basis for larger estates for ordinary services; attorneys may seek additional compensation for extraordinary services).

210. 618 N.E.2d 159 (Ohio 1993). See also Restatement (Third) of the Law Governing Lawyers §11.

211. This hypothetical, and *b* below, are based on the article by Deborah H. Schenk, Conflicts Between the Tax Lawyer and the Client: Vignettes in the Law Office, 20 Cap. U. L. Rev. 387 (1991).

212. I.R.C. §§1361, 1362.

corporation pays no tax at the corporate level.[213] Instead, the shareholders report their pro rata share of income and losses of the company on their individual returns.[214] A Subchapter S election thus avoids "double taxation": taxation to the corporation on its income and taxation to the shareholders of distributions received from the corporation. To qualify as a Subchapter S corporation, the corporation must meet various requirements, one of which is that the corporation cannot have more than one class of stock.[215]

You have just received a call from Johnson Supply's accountant. He explains to you that the corporation has substantial income for the current calendar year. He also informs you that one of the shareholders made a substantial working capital loan to the corporation. The loan is in writing and bears interest, but is convertible into common stock. The shareholder also has certain additional voting rights if the loan is not repaid within a certain time period. The accountant is concerned that the convertible loan constitutes a second class of stock, invalidating the Subchapter S election. He has asked you to provide him with an opinion that this loan does not amount to a second class of stock and does not disqualify the corporation from Subchapter S status.

You have researched the matter. Under IRS regulations, "straight debt" is not treated as a second class of stock, but this loan does not qualify as straight debt because of its convertibility feature.[216] When a loan does not qualify as straight debt, it will be treated as a second class of stock when the loan amounts to "equity" rather than "debt" for tax purposes.[217] Whether a loan amounts to debt or equity is a question of fact. Section 385 of the Internal Revenue Code and relevant case law set out a variety of factors to determine whether a loan amounts to debt or equity. Based on your analysis of section 385 and the case law, you have concluded that only a weak argument could be made that the loan qualifies as debt rather than equity. How would you respond to the accountant's request? What obligations, if any, do you have regarding tax returns that were filed for prior years when the loan was also outstanding?

b.   Repayment of Johnson Supply's loan to its shareholder would not eliminate the Subchapter S problem because the existence of the loan has already jeopardized Subchapter S status. However, repayment of the loan might make it less likely that the IRS would discover the problem if the corporation were audited. For example, repayment of the loan would remove the loan from the corporation's year-end balance sheet. Would it

213. I.R.C. §1363(a).
214. I.R.C. §1366(a).
215. I.R.C. §1361(b)(1)(D).
216. Treas. Reg. §1.1361-1(*l*)(5).
217. Treas. Reg. §1.1361-1(*l*)(4)(ii)(A)(1),(iv).

be proper for you to advise Johnson to consider repaying the loan for this reason?

Suppose Johnson does repay the loan. Subsequently, the IRS audits Johnson for the year in which the loan was repaid. During the audit, the agent asks: "Did the corporation have any other classes of stock outstanding during the year?" How would you respond?

    c. Johnson Supply has negotiated a loan from Central Bank & Trust Company. In connection with the loan, the bank has asked Johnson to supply an opinion of counsel stating that Johnson is in compliance with all applicable laws and is not in breach or default of any agreements to which it is a party and the firm is unaware of any pending or threatened litigation that would have a material affect on Johnson's operations.

    Your firm has a committee on opinion letters. Any opinion by the firm must have the approval of the committee before it can be issued. You have discussed the opinion request with the committee, which has told you that the Bank's request for a comprehensive opinion is too broad. In making this determination the committee relied on customary practice with regard to legal opinions as reflected in the work of the Committee on Legal Opinions of the ABA Section of Business Law. Section 4.3 of the Committee's Guidelines provides:

§4.3 Comprehensive Legal or Contractual Compliance

An opinion giver should not be asked for an opinion that its client possesses all necessary licenses and permits or has obtained all approvals and made all filings required for the conduct of the client's business. Similarly, an opinion giver should not be asked for an opinion that its client is not in violation of any applicable laws or regulations or that its client is not in default under any of the client's contractual obligations. Neither a materiality exception nor a knowledge limitation makes these opinions appropriate.[218]

Instead of the comprehensive opinion requested by the bank, the committee has advised you to issue an opinion stating that (1) the proposed loan agreement is enforceable against Johnson, (2) execution, delivery, and performance of the loan agreement will not result in a default under any other agreements or obligations to which Johnson is a party, (3) execution, delivery, and performance of the loan agreement will not violate any applicable provisions of statutory law or regulations, and (4) no actions or proceedings against Johnson are pending or overtly threatened in writing before any court, governmental agency, or arbitrator, which would affect the enforceability of the agreement or would be material to Johnson's

---

218. See Committee on Legal Opinions, Guidelines for the Preparation of Closing Opinions, 57 Bus. Law. 875, 880 (2002).

operations. In addition, the opinion would state that the opinion is being provided by your firm to Johnson Supply and may not be used or relied on by any third person without your firm's written consent. In reviewing the ABA Committee's Guidelines, you notice section 1.5, which provides as follows:

1.5 Misleading Opinions

An opinion giver should not render an opinion that the opinion giver recognizes will mislead the recipient with regard to the matters addressed by the opinions given. [FN . . . This Guideline does not preclude limiting the matters addressed by an opinion through the use of specific language if the limitation itself will not mislead the recipient. . . .][219]

Would it be proper for the firm to issue this limited opinion? Would it make any difference if the IRS had formally notified the corporation that it was denying Subchapter S status and assessing taxes, penalties, and interest against the corporation for current and prior years?

Read Model Rules 1.2(d), 2.3, 3.1, and comments.

Advising clients with regard to tax return positions

One of the most significant responsibilities of tax lawyers is providing advice to clients regarding issues involved in filing tax returns. While lawyers may also prepare returns for clients, it is probably more common for accountants to prepare the returns, with lawyers providing advice about significant issues.

What are tax lawyers' ethical and legal responsibilities in providing advice to clients in connection with their tax returns? In Formal Opinion 85-352 the ABA Committee on Ethics and Professional Responsibility noted that in matters before the IRS an attorney was acting as both an advocate and an advisor.[220] As an advocate, under Model Rules 1.2(d) and 3.1, a lawyer could assert any position so long as the lawyer had a good faith belief that the position was not frivolous and so long as the lawyer was not counseling or assisting the client in fraud. While a lawyer could have a good faith belief that the client's position was not frivolous even though the attorney believed that the client would lose, there must be "some realistic possibility of success if the matter is litigated."[221] If a realistic possibility of success existed, the lawyer was not ethically required

---

219. Id. at 876.

220. For an earlier statement of the lawyer's ethical obligations in tax practice, see Formal Opinion 314 (1965). For a critique of this view of the lawyer's role, see Loren D. Prescott, Jr., Challenging the Adversarial Approach to Taxpayer Representation, 30 Loy. L.A. L. Rev. 693 (1997).

221. ABA Comm. on Ethics and Prof. Resp., Formal Op. 85-352, at 3.

to insist that the client attach a rider to the return fully disclosing the client's position.[222] In discussing the "realistic possibility" standard, the committee noted that it was possible for a client's position to meet this standard, even though no "substantial authority" in support of the client's position existed. The lawyer's role as advisor meant that the lawyer should discuss with the client the likelihood of success of the client's proposed position, the penalties that would apply if the position was not sustained, and the advantages and disadvantages of disclosing the position by rider.[223] The committee warned tax lawyers not to deliberately mislead the IRS "either by misstatements or by silence or by permitting the client to mislead."[224] The committee summarized the lawyer's obligations as follows:

> [A] lawyer may advise reporting a position on a return even where the lawyer believes the position probably will not prevail, there is no "substantial authority" in support of the position, and there will be no disclosure of the position in the return. However, the position to be asserted must be one which the lawyer in good faith believes is warranted in existing law or can be supported by good faith argument for an extension, modification or reversal of existing law. This requires that there is some realistic possibility of success if the matter is litigated. In addition, in his role as advisor, the lawyer should refer to potential penalties and other legal consequences should the client take the position advised.[225]

The IRS, like most federal agencies, has published standards of conduct for lawyers and other practitioners admitted to practice before the agency. These standards are commonly referred to as "Treasury Circular 230" and are codified in the Code of Federal Regulations.[226] Two of the important standards applicable to tax return advice and preparation are the following:

§10.21 Knowledge of client's omission

A practitioner who, having been retained by a client with respect to a matter administered by the Internal Revenue Service, knows that the client has not complied with the revenue laws of the United States or has made an error in or omission from any return, document, affidavit, or other paper which the client submitted or executed under the revenue laws of the United States, must advise the client promptly of the fact of such noncompliance, error, or omission. The

---

222. Id.
223. Id. at 4.
224. Id.
225. Id. For elaboration of the duties set forth in the opinion see ABA Committee on Standards of Tax Practice, Report of the Special Task Force on Formal Opinion 85-352, reprinted in 39 Tax Lawyer 635 (1986). For criticisms of the ABA's position in Formal Opinion 85-352, see Theodore C. Falk, Tax Ethics, Legal Ethics, and Real Ethics: A Critique of ABA Formal Opinion 85-352, 39 Tax Law. 643 (1986). For defense of the opinion see Camilla E. Watson, Tax Lawyers, Ethical Obligations, and the Duty to the System, 47 U. Kan. L. Rev. 847 (1999).
226. 31 C.F.R. §§10.0 et seq.

practitioner must advise the client of the consequences as provided under the Code and regulations of such noncompliance, error, or omission.[227]

§10.34.   Standards for advising with respect to tax return positions and for preparing or signing returns

(a) Realistic possibility standard. A practitioner may not sign a tax return as a preparer if the practitioner determines that the tax return contains a position that does not have a realistic possibility of being sustained on its merits (the realistic possibility standard) unless the position is not frivolous and is adequately disclosed to the Internal Revenue Service. A practitioner may not advise a client to take a position on a tax return, or prepare the portion of a tax return on which a position is taken, unless—

(1) The practitioner determines that the position satisfies the realistic possibility standard; or

(2) The position is not frivolous and the practitioner advises the client of any opportunity to avoid the accuracy-related penalty in section 6662 of the Internal Revenue Code by adequately disclosing the position and of the requirements for adequate disclosure.

(b) Advising clients on potential penalties. A practitioner advising a client to take a position on a tax return, or preparing or signing a tax return as a preparer, must inform the client of the penalties reasonably likely to apply to the client with respect to the position advised, prepared, or reported. The practitioner also must inform the client of any opportunity to avoid any such penalty by disclosure, if relevant, and of the requirements for adequate disclosure. This paragraph (b) applies even if the practitioner is not subject to a penalty with respect to the position.

(c) Relying on information furnished by clients. A practitioner advising a client to take a position on a tax return, or preparing or signing a tax return as a preparer, generally may rely in good faith without verification upon information furnished by the client. The practitioner may not, however, ignore the implications of information furnished to, or actually known by, the practitioner, and must make reasonable inquiries if the information as furnished appears to be incorrect, inconsistent with an important fact or another factual assumption, or incomplete.

(d) Definitions. For purposes of this section—

(1) Realistic possibility. A position is considered to have a realistic possibility of being sustained on its merits if a reasonable and well informed analysis of the law and the facts by a person knowledgeable in the tax law would lead such a person to conclude that the position has approximately a one in three, or greater, likelihood of being sustained on its merits. The authorities described in 26 CFR 1.6662-4(d)(3)(iii), or any successor provision, of the substantial understatement penalty regulations may be taken into account for purposes of this analysis. [This regulation lists various authorities that can be taken into account in determining whether a position has a realistic possibility of success. It includes proposed regulations but excludes treatises, law review articles, and opinions of tax experts.—Ed.] The possibil-

---

227. 31 C.F.R. §10.21.

ity that a tax return will not be audited, that an issue will not be raised on audit, or that an issue will be settled may not be taken into account.

(2) Frivolous. A position is frivolous if it is patently improper.[228]

Several points about the IRS standards of conduct in comparison to the position of the ABA committee in Formal Opinion 85-352 are worth noting. First, unlike the ABA opinion, which is merely persuasive, IRS standards have the force of law; violation of these standards could result in proceedings to disbar a lawyer from appearing before the IRS, although the standard for discipline is quite high.[229] Second, in Opinion 85-352 the committee defined frivolous to mean not having a "realistic possibility of success." The IRS standards draw a sharper distinction between the realistic possibility of success standard and frivolousness. A position is frivolous if it is "patently improper," while a realistic possibility of success requires a one in three chance of success. Thus, the IRS standard is substantially tougher than the standard set forth in Opinion 85-352. Third, the IRS standards apply not only to return preparers but also to practitioners who "advise a client to take a position on a tax return," even if the practitioner will not be signing the return. This is the most common role for tax lawyers.

The IRS standards for practitioners regarding advising and preparing tax returns provide that a practitioner must advise the client of "the penalties reasonably likely to apply to the client with respect to the position advised, prepared, or reported" and also must "inform the client of any opportunity to avoid any such penalty by disclosure, if relevant, and of the requirements for adequate disclosure."[230] What are these penalties?[231]

Section 6662 of the Internal Revenue Code provides a penalty in the amount of 20 percent of the portion of any underpayment of tax under certain circumstances, which include the following: (1) negligence or disregard of rules or regulations or (2) any substantial understatement of income tax. The section provides the following definition:

> [T]he term "negligence" includes any failure to make a reasonable attempt to comply with the provisions of this title, and the term "disregard" includes any careless, reckless, or intentional disregard.[232]

---

228. 31 C.F.R. §10.34.
229.   *§10.52 Violation of regulations*

    A practitioner may be censured, suspended or disbarred from practice before the Internal Revenue Service for any of the following:

      (a) Willfully violating any of the regulations contained in this part.

      (b) Recklessly or through gross incompetence (within the meaning of §10.51(l)) violating §10.33 or 10.34.

230. 31 C.F.R. §10.34(b).
231. See Gersham Goldstein & Christopher K. Heuer, Ethical Disclosure Requirements in Corporate Tax Representation, 557 PLI/Tax 703 (2002) (on Westlaw) (discussing various penalty provisions).
232. I.R.C. §6662(c).

The section provides that a taxpayer makes a substantial understatement if the amount of the understated tax exceeds the greater of 10 percent of the tax due or $5,000 ($10,000 in the case of a corporation).[233] In determining whether a substantial understatement occurs, however, the amount of any understatement is excluded if there is or was "substantial authority" for the taxpayer's position, or if "the relevant facts affecting the item's tax treatment are adequately disclosed in the return or in a statement attached to the return, and there is a reasonable basis for the tax treatment of such item by the taxpayer."[234] The section goes on to provide that the Secretary of the Treasury is required to publish annually in the Federal Register a list of positions for which "the Secretary believes there is not substantial authority."[235] Section 6662, however, must be read in light of section 6664(c), which provides that the IRS may not impose a penalty "with respect to any portion of an underpayment if it is shown that there was a reasonable cause for such portion and the taxpayer acted in good faith with respect to such portion." Thus, a taxpayer is liable for a penalty only if the IRS establishes "fault" by the taxpayer. In addition to the negligence and substantial understatement penalties of section 6662, section 6663 provides for a penalty of 75 percent of the amount of any understatement of tax due to fraud.

The penalties set forth in sections 6662 and 6663 apply to taxpayers. Section 6694 of the Code imposes a penalty in the amount of $250 per return on a tax return preparer who prepares a return with understated tax liability if (1) the understatement results from a position "for which there was not a realistic possibility of being sustained on its merits," (2) the preparer knew or should have known of the position, and (3) the position was not fully disclosed on the return or was frivolous. If the understatement results from a willful attempt to understate tax liability or a reckless or intentional disregard of rules or regulations, the penalty is $1,000 per return. In addition, section 6701 provides a penalty of $1,000 in the case of individual returns and $10,000 in the case of corporate returns against any person who aids and abets an understatement of tax liability by another person. Since aiding and abetting includes providing advice about the preparation of a return, it clearly covers lawyers in their normal role as tax counselors. The Internal Revenue Code also has some penalties specially applicable to "abusive tax shelters."[236]

Third-party opinions regarding tax matters and other issues

Another major activity for tax lawyers is providing opinions in connection with transactions in which their clients seek financing of their business operations

233. I.R.C. §6662(d).

234. I.R.C. §6662(d)(2)(B). More demanding standards apply for reporting of items attributable to tax shelters. See I.R.C. §6662(d)(2)(C).

235. I.R.C. §6662(d)(2)(D).

236. See I.R.C. §6700.

or investments from third parties. The Model Rules of Professional Conduct do not specifically address the standards applicable to lawyers in preparing opinions that involve third parties.[237] The rules, however, do consider circumstances under which a lawyer may not undertake such an evaluation. Under Model Rule 2.3(a) a lawyer may prepare an evaluation for a third party at the request of the client provided the lawyer reasonably believes that "making the evaluation is compatible with other aspects of the lawyer's relationship with the client." Comment 3 elaborates on this standard:

> The lawyer must be satisfied as a matter of professional judgment that making the evaluation is compatible with other functions undertaken in behalf of the client. For example, if the lawyer is acting as advocate in defending the client against charges of fraud, it would normally be incompatible with that responsibility for the lawyer to perform an evaluation for others concerning the same or a related transaction.

If the lawyer knows or reasonably should know that providing the evaluation is likely to have a material, adverse effect on the client's interests, the lawyer must obtain the client's informed consent to provide the evaluation. Model Rule 2.3(b). In connection with such an evaluation the lawyer may disclose confidential information to the extent authorized by the client. Model Rule 2.3(c).

While the Model Rules do not establish standards for issuance of third-party opinions, the IRS and the ABA Committee on Ethics and Professional Responsibility have developed guidelines for such opinions. During the 1970s the IRS began investigating abusive tax shelters and the role of lawyers and accountants in connection with such offerings. The IRS found that some tax shelters were being marketed based on opinions from lawyers that, among other defects, ignored material facts or failed to address material issues. Such partial or incomplete opinions had the potential to mislead investors. As a result the Treasury Department published standards for lawyers to follow when issuing opinions in connection with tax shelters.[238] The regulation requires lawyers to comply with specific requirements in the following areas:

(1) factual matters
(2) the relation of law to facts
(3) identification of material issues
(4) opinion on each material issue
(5) overall evaluation
(6) description of opinion

---

237. The Restatement also does not establish specific standards for issuance of tax and other legal opinions. See Restatement (Third) of the Law Governing Lawyers §96, cmt. *g.*

238. See 31 C.F.R. §10.33.

The IRS's regulation on tax shelter opinions applies to lawyers practicing before the IRS. The ABA Committee on Ethics and Professional Responsibility has issued Formal Opinion 346 (1982) setting forth ethical obligations for lawyers in connection with tax shelter opinions. Opinion 346 is similar in most important respects to the IRS's regulation. The committee summarized the ethical obligations of lawyers regarding tax shelter opinions as follows:

1. Establish in the beginning the lawyer's relationship with the offeror-client, making clear that in order to issue the opinion, the lawyer requires from that client a full disclosure of the structure and intended operations of the venture and complete access to all relevant information.
2. Make inquiry as to the relevant facts and, consistent with the standards developed in ABA Formal Opinion 335, be satisfied that the material facts are accurately and completely stated in the offering materials, and that the representations as to intended future activities are clearly identified, reasonable and complete.
3. Relate the law to the actual facts to the extent ascertainable and, when addressing issues based on future activities, clearly identify what facts are assumed.
4. Make inquiries to ascertain that a good faith effort has been made to address legal issues other than those to be addressed in the tax shelter opinion.
5. Take reasonable steps to assure that all material federal income and excise tax issues have been considered and that all of those issues which involve the reasonable possibility of a challenge by the Internal Revenue Service have been fully and fairly addressed in the offering materials.
6. Where possible, provide an opinion as to the likely outcome on the merits of the material tax issues addressed in the offering materials.
7. Where possible, provide an overall evaluation of the extent to which the tax benefits in the aggregate are likely to be realized.
8. Assure that the offering materials correctly represent the nature and extent of the tax shelter opinion.[239]

In 2002 the Treasury Department announced a major initiative to deal with what it considers to be a worsening problem of abusive tax shelters.[240] Lax standards for issuance of opinions by lawyers and others continue to be a significant reason why abusive tax shelter transactions proceed.[241] One aspect of the Treasury's initiative deals with revisions to the sections of Circular 230 dealing with tax shelter opinions. In January 2001 the Treasury had issued

239. ABA Comm. on Ethics and Prof. Resp., Formal Op. 346, at 9 (1982).
240. Treasury's Plan to Combat Abusive Tax Avoidance Transactions, http://www.treas.gov/press/releases/po2018.htm (visited Sept. 22, 2003).
241. For articles discussing the role of lawyers in abusive tax shelters see Anthony C. Infanti, Eyes Wide Shut: Surveying Erosion in the Professionalism of the Tax Bar, 22 Va. Tax Rev. 589 (2003) (using examples of tax shelters to show decline in professionalism); Richard Lavoie, Deputizing The Gunslingers: Co-Opting the Tax Bar into Dissuading Corporate Tax Shelters, 21 Va. Tax Rev. 43 (2001) (discussing the deficiencies in tax shelter opinions and steps that can be taken to deal with the problem).

proposed amendments to Circular 230.[242] The proposed regulations impose significant new obligations on lawyers and others who issue opinions in connection with tax shelter transactions. For example, the proposed regulations require that opinions address the application of various anti-abuse doctrines:

> The opinion would be required to state that the practitioner has considered the possible application to the facts of all potentially relevant judicial doctrines, including the step transaction, business purpose, economic substance, substance over form, and sham transaction doctrines, as well as potentially relevant statutory and regulatory anti-abuse rules, and the opinion must analyze whether the tax shelter item or items is (are) vulnerable to challenge under all such potentially relevant doctrines and anti-abuse rules.[243]

In July 2002, the Treasury Department adopted final regulations on a number of amendments to Circular 230, but the tax shelter opinion regulations remain in proposed form as of September 2003.[244]

Tax shelter opinions are not the only form of opinions that lawyers issue. In Formal Opinion 335 the ABA committee addressed the lawyer's ethical obligations in connection with opinions in securities offerings. The committee focused in particular on whether lawyers had an obligation to inquire into facts provided by their clients or could instead accept those facts as given. The committee rejected the notion that lawyers had a general obligation to audit or to investigate their clients' affairs, but it also ruled that under some circumstances lawyers were ethically and legally required to make further inquiry regarding the facts on which their opinions are based:

> [T]he lawyer should, in the first instance, make inquiry of his client as to the relevant facts and receive answers. If any of the alleged facts, or the alleged facts taken as a whole, are incomplete in a material respect; or are suspect; or are inconsistent; or either on their face or on the basis of other known facts are open to question, the lawyer should make further inquiry. The extent of this inquiry will depend in each case upon the circumstances; for example, it would be less where the lawyer's past relationship with the client is sufficient to give him a basis for trusting the client's probity than where the client has recently engaged the lawyer, and less where the lawyer's inquiries are answered fully than when there appears a reluctance to disclose information.
>
>   Where the lawyer concludes that further inquiry of a reasonable nature would not give him sufficient confidence as to all the relevant facts, or for any other reason he does not make the appropriate further inquiries, he should refuse to give an opinion. However, assuming that the alleged facts are not incomplete in a material respect, or suspect, or in any way inherently inconsistent, or on their face or on the basis of other known facts open to question, the lawyer may

---

242. See 66 FR 3276-01 (Jan. 12, 2001).

243. Proposed Regulation 31 C.F.R. 10.33(3) and 10.35(3), 66 FR 3276-01 (Jan. 12, 2001).

244. See 67 FR 48760-01 (July 26, 2002).

properly assume that the facts as related to him by his client, and checked by him by reviewing such appropriate documents as are available, are* accurate.[245]

Another form of opinion that lawyers are often asked to render involves responses to accountants' requests for information about clients' loss contingencies. Accountants use this information in preparing clients' financial statements. For many years such requests were a source of tension between lawyers and accountants. Accountants naturally wanted to receive complete information from lawyers because they were concerned about their legal liability for preparing misleading financial statements. Lawyers were wary about revealing confidential information that could generate claims that otherwise might not have been brought. In 1975 the ABA and the American Institute of Certified Public Accountants reached an accord to resolve the question how lawyers could respond to auditors' requests for information consistently with their ethical obligations.[246] See also Model Rule 2.3 and cmt. 6.

As Problem 5-5 mentions, the Committee on Legal Opinions of the ABA Section of Business Law has issued guidelines for lawyers in issuing general third-party opinions as opposed to specialized opinions relating to tax or securities matters.[247] Other bar association committees have issued reports dealing with legal opinions.[248]

In addition to these standards, lawyers who issue opinions in transactions involving third parties also face the possibility of legal liability to third parties. The traditional rule has been that lawyers are liable only to their clients and not to third parties with whom there is no privity of contract.[249] In a number of jurisdictions, however, the privity barrier has been eroded. Depending on the jurisdiction, lawyers who fraudulently or negligently issue false opinions can be held liable to third parties.[250] Opinion letters typically state that they

---

245. ABA Comm. on Ethics and Prof. Resp., Formal Op. 335, at 3 (1974).

246. See ABA Statement of Policy Regarding Lawyers' Responses to Auditors' Requests for Information, 31 Bus. Law. 1709 (1976).

247. 57 Bus. Law. 875 (2002).

248. See citation to reports and bibliography included in Association of the Bar of the City of New York et al., Mortgage Loan Opinion Report, 54-Nov Bus. Law. 119, 132 (1998).

249. Savings Bank v. Ward, 100 U.S. 195 (1879).

250. See Greycas, Inc. v. Pound, 826 F.2d 1560 (7th Cir. 1987) (attorney who represented borrower may be liable to lender for negligent misrepresentation in stating no prior liens on farm machinery); Roberts v. Ball, Hunt, Hart, Brown & Baerwitz, 128 Cal. Rptr. 901 (Ct. App. 1976) (law firm may be liable for negligent misrepresentation in issuing opinion letters under California law); Mehaffy, Rider, Windholz & Wilson v. Central Bank Denver, N.A., 892 P.2d 230 (Colo. 1995) (en banc) (law firm retained by borrower may be liable for negligent misrepresentation to lender); Prudential Ins. Co. v. Dewey, Ballantine, Bushby, Palmer & Wood, 605 N.E.2d 318 (N.Y. 1992) (recognizing cause of action under New York law against law firm for negligent misrepresentation). See also Restatement (Second) of Torts §552(1) (1977) (liability for information negligently supplied for guidance of others in business transaction). But see Krawczyk v. Bank of Sun Prairie, 496 N.W.2d 218 (Wis. Ct. App.), *review denied*, 501 N.W.2d 458 (Wis. 1993) (lawyers subject to liability to third parties only for fraud, not for negligent misrepresentation).

are intended for the use of the client only and should not be relied on by third parties. Such statements, however, will not necessarily protect a law firm from liability if it is aware that its opinion letter is being used to obtain investors.[251] If the claim against the lawyer is for failure to disclose information rather than fraudulent or negligent misrepresentation, liability of the lawyer to third parties, especially under the federal securities laws, may be difficult to establish.[252]

Other ethical obligations in tax practice

The preceding discussion has focused on some of the most important legal and ethical obligations of lawyers in connection with tax matters. Internal Revenue Service regulations establishing standards of conduct for practitioners cover a number of other topics, including conflicts of interest, contingent fees, and solicitation of business.[253]

Lawyers who engage in tax practice are, of course, subject to malpractice liability.[254] In addition, it is likely that general practitioners who undertake to handle tax matters will be held to the standard of conduct expected of a specialist in tax law.[255]

---

251. See Kline v. First W. Govt. Sec., Inc., 24 F.3d 480 (3d Cir.), *cert. denied*, 513 U.S. 1092 (1994).

252. See Central Bank of Denver, N.A. v. First Interstate Bank of Denver, N.A., 511 U.S. 164 (1994), discussed in connection with Problem 5-2 above (no aider and abetter liability under federal securities laws); Fortson v. Winstead, McGuire, Sechrest & Minick, 961 F.2d 469 (4th Cir. 1992) (law firm not liable under federal securities laws for failure to disclose material information in connection with real estate limited partnership offering; duty to disclose under securities laws is determined by state law, and Texas law does not recognize exceptions to requirement of privity; no cause of action for violation of ABA opinions and IRS regulations governing issuance of tax shelter opinions). But see Rubin v. Schottenstein, Zox & Dunn, 143 F.3d 263 (6th Cir. 1998) (lawyer assumes duty to provide complete and nonmisleading information with respect to subjects on which lawyer undertakes to speak).

253. Practice before the Internal Revenue Service, 31 C.F.R. pt. 10. For a general discussion of the ethical obligations of tax practitioners, see Bernard Wolfman et al., James P. Holden, Ethical Problems in Federal Tax Practice (3d ed. 1995).

254. See Jacob L. Todres, Malpractice and the Tax Practitioner: An Analysis of the Areas in Which Malpractice Occurs, 48 Emory L.J. 547 (1999).

255. See Horne v. Peckham, 158 Cal. Rptr. 714 (Ct. App. 1979).

Chapter 6

Lawyers in Public Service: Judges, Government Attorneys, and Public Interest Lawyers

The preceding four chapters have examined ethical problems facing lawyers in private practice: criminal defense and prosecution, civil litigation, and business practice. The Statistical Abstract of the United States reports 805,872 lawyers practiced in the United States in 1991. Of this number, 87,763, or approximately 10.9 percent, were engaged in some form of public legal service rather than private practice. This number consisted of the following:

Federal government	27,985
State government	38,242
Federal judicial	3,119
State and county judicial	18,417[1]

Lawyers engaged in public rather than private practice face special ethical problems because their roles and the governing standards differ from those of private counsel. Federal and state judges perform their duties subject to the Code of Judicial Conduct and to various special statutory provisions. Federal and state prosecutors act pursuant to a wide range of statutory provisions, and they are required to adhere to ethical standards that differ from those applicable to private counsel.

1. United States Bureau of the Census, Statistical Abstract of the United States 210, chart no. 327 (1994).

547

This chapter examines the ethical issues facing lawyers in public service. Section A considers issues of judicial ethics, focusing principally on two questions: When are judges disqualified from hearing cases? What are the limitations on judges' extrajudicial activities? Section A touches on other topics: ex parte communications between lawyers and judges, methods of judicial selection, and restrictions on campaign activities of judges.[2] Section B examines the ethical obligations of government lawyers, and considers a phenomenon that straddles the public/private distinction: the development of the public interest law movement.

A. Judicial Ethics

───────────────────────── **Problem 6-1** ─────────────────────────

Judges in Their Official Capacities

a.   You are a clerk for a newly appointed state supreme court justice. The justice and her husband have substantial investments in common stock and real estate. The real estate investments are principally limited partnerships in which she or her husband or both are limited partners. In every case the property is subject to a mortgage to a financial institution, typically a bank. She asks you whether their present investments will cause any disqualification problems for her, and if so, how her investments could be restructured to avoid those problems.

b.   You are federal district judge appointed to the bench 18 months ago. A group of related securities class actions has been assigned to you to coordinate pretrial discovery. Your wife is a partner in a law firm that is representing one of the defendants in one of the class actions. The law firm where you practiced before your appointment to the bench represents another defendant. You are the personal representative of the estate of your father, who died six months ago. Your father's estate is relatively modest, less than $500,000, but it does include some common stocks, including 100 shares in one of the defendant corporations. Do any of these circumstances require your recusal? What steps would you take?

c.   A class action claiming that conditions in the state's prisons violate the prisoners' constitutional rights is pending in federal court. You are counsel for the plaintiffs. In several conferences about the case, the judge has expressed hostility to your position. At one conference he re-

─────────────

2. On judicial ethics generally, see The Responsible Judge: Readings in Judicial Ethics (John T. Noonan, Jr. & Kenneth I. Winston eds. 1993). See also Cynthia Gray, Key Issues in Judicial Ethics (series of background papers available from the American Judicature Society, ⟨http://www.ajs.org⟩).

ferred to you as "one of those liberal lawyers who doesn't care anything about cleaning up crime, only making a reputation in big cases." The judge initially denied the state's motion to dismiss, but otherwise has consistently ruled against you on discovery motions. In particular, the judge has granted numerous requests and motions of the defense to delay discovery. You have also learned that the judge has made telephone calls to both prison officials and expert witnesses in the case asking them various questions. How would you evaluate the likelihood of success of a disqualification motion?

Read Canon 3 of the Code of Judicial Conduct and 28 U.S.C. §455.

Regulation of judicial conduct: standards and procedure

Regulation of the behavior of judges both in their official and in their unofficial capacities rests on important policies. First, the adversarial system is founded on a principle of judicial impartiality. As a matter of fairness, litigants are entitled to have judges who are not swayed by bias, prejudice, or favoritism. Second, the primary function of our judicial system is to provide a mechanism for resolving disputes nonviolently. Public use of and acceptance of the results of the judicial system depend in part on the public's respect for judicial integrity.

The ABA has been active in establishing standards of conduct for judges, just as it has been for lawyers. The ABA first adopted Canons of Judicial Ethics in 1924. In 1972 the ABA approved the Code of Judicial Conduct to replace the Canons of Ethics. Almost every state adopted the Code or used it as the model for standards of judicial conduct.[3]

In 1990 the ABA issued a major revision of the Code of Judicial Conduct. The 1990 Code is divided into five articles. Canons 1 and 2 are relatively short. Canon 1 provides that judges "shall uphold the integrity and independence of the judiciary." Canon 2 directs judges to "avoid impropriety and the appearance of impropriety in all of the judge's activities." An important addition to the 1990 Code, not found in the 1972 Code, is Canon 2(C), which prohibits judges from holding membership in any organization that practices invidious discrimination on the basis of race, sex, religion, or national origin. Canons 3, 4, and 5 contain the bulk of the substantive provisions of the Code. Canon 3 deals with a judge's adjudicative responsibilities, while Canon 4 regulates nonjudicial conduct. Canon 5 controls a judge's political activities. The 1990 Code also requires judges not to manifest bias or prejudice in the performance of judicial duties, to prevent such conduct by court personnel, and to require lawyers appearing before them to refrain from such conduct. Canon 3(B)(5), (6). The discussion that follows is based on the 1990 Code unless otherwise indicated.

---

3. Jeffrey M. Shaman et al., Judicial Conduct and Ethics §1.02 (3d ed. 2000).

All states and the District of Columbia have judicial conduct commissions or organizations that have the power to investigate, prosecute, and adjudicate allegations of judicial misconduct. The structure and method of appointment of these organizations vary from state to state.[4] In August 1994 the ABA adopted Model Rules for Judicial Disciplinary Enforcement.[5] The ABA rules call for the creation of a 12-member Commission on Judicial Conduct, consisting of four judges of the intermediate or appellate courts of the state, appointed by the highest court in the state; four lawyers appointed by the bar association; and four members of the public appointed by the governor. Rule 2(C). The commission has responsibility for investigating charges of misconduct against judges, conducting hearings into such charges, and making recommendations to the highest court of the state. The ABA rules provide that the highest court of the state has the power to discipline judges found guilty of misconduct, including the power to remove a judge from office. Rule 6(B)(1).

The Judicial Conference of the United States adopted the Code of Judicial Conduct to apply to federal judges in 1973.[6] The Code of Conduct for federal judges has been amended to include some of the provisions from the ABA's 1990 Code, but it is still based largely on the 1972 Code.[7] The Committee on Codes of Conduct of the Judicial Conference of the United States issues formal advisory opinions that are available at the Web site of the Judicial Conference.[8]

Federal judges serve for life tenure and may be removed from office only through the impeachment process.[9] Congress has enacted legislation establishing a process for discipline of federal judges short of removal by federal judicial councils and for referral of serious matters to the House of Representatives for possible impeachment proceedings.[10]

Disqualification of judges because of personal involvement or interest in matters

One of the most important aspects of judicial conduct involves disqualification of judges from hearing cases.[11] Canon 3(E) of the Code of Judicial Conduct deals with disqualification of judges. The Code begins with a general principle of disqualification: whenever the judge's "impartiality might reasonably be

---

4. For a directory of these organizations, see the Web site of the American Judicature Society, ⟨http://www.ajs.org⟩.

5. See http://www.abanet.org/cpr/juddis/contents.html (visited Sept. 23, 2003).

6. Judicial Conf. of United States, Rep. of Proc. at 9-11 (1973).

7. For the current text of the Code of Judicial Conduct applicable to United States judges, see the website of the Judicial Conference of the United States, http://www.uscourts .gov/guide/vol2/ch1.html#N_1_ (visited Sept. 24, 2003).

8. See http://www.uscourts.gov/guide/vol2/ch4.html (visited Sept. 24, 2003).

9. U.S. Const. art. II, §4.

10. See Judicial Improvements Act of 2002, codified in 28 U.S.C. §§351 et seq.

11. See Richard E. Flamm, Judicial Disqualification (1996).

questioned."[12] The Code contains, however, a number of specific rules of disqualification, and because of the vagueness of the general standard, it is useful to begin with the specific rules. The disqualification rules distinguish circumstances affecting the judge personally from situations in which a judge is disqualified because of a relationship with another person who has an interest in the matter.

Four situations requiring disqualification of judges based on personal involvement in the matter are fairly straightforward. A judge is disqualified when the judge

(1) has personal knowledge of disputed evidentiary facts, Canon 3(E)(1)(a)
(2) served as a lawyer in the matter in controversy before assuming the bench, Canon 3(E)(1)(b)
(3) has been a material witness to the matter in controversy, Canon 3(E)(1)(b)
(4) is a party to the proceeding, or an officer, director, or trustee of a party, Canon 3(E)(1)(d)(i)

While these disqualification rules are relatively easy to apply, two further disqualification provisions are more difficult. The Code of Judicial Conduct requires disqualification when a judge has "personal bias or prejudice concerning a party." Canon 3(E)(1)(a). The meaning of this provision and its interrelationship with the general standard that requires disqualification when a judge's "impartiality might reasonably be questioned" has been the subject of several Supreme Court decisions. These cases are discussed in the section below that examines disqualification of federal judges.

Under the 1990 Code, a judge is subject to disqualification when the judge either personally or as a fiduciary has an economic interest in the subject matter in controversy or in a party to the proceeding. Canon 3(E)(1)(c). The 1990 Code of Judicial Conduct made a substantial change from the 1972 Code regarding disqualification because of economic interest. (The 1972 Code used the term "financial interest.") Under the 1972 Code, a judge's financial interest in a party or in the subject matter of a proceeding, *no matter how small*, required disqualification. Thus, under the 1972 Code, if a judge held one share of stock in a party, the judge was disqualified. By contrast to the 1972 Code, the 1990 Code provides that "economic interest" means "ownership of a more than de minimis legal or equitable interest, or a relationship as officer, director, advisor or other active participant in the affairs of a party," subject to certain exceptions. (See Terminology section of 1990 Code, definition of "economic interest.") The Code goes on to define a de minimis interest as "an insignificant interest that could not raise reasonable question as to a judge's impartiality." (See Terminology section of 1990 Code, definition of "De minimis.")

12. See Leslie W. Abramson, Appearance of Impropriety: Deciding When a Judge's Impartiality "Might Reasonably Be Questioned," 14 Geo. J. Legal Ethics 55 (2000).

The Code of Judicial Conduct lists certain exceptions to what constitutes an economic interest:

(1)   ownership of a mutual fund does not amount to ownership of securities owned by the fund unless the judge participates in the management of the fund or unless the case could substantially affect the value of the fund shares

(2)   service by the judge or a member of the judge's family in an active role in a charitable or similar organization does not create an economic interest in securities owned by the organization

(3)   deposits in financial institutions, ownership of insurance policies, and similar propriety interests do not constitute economic interests in those institutions unless the proceeding could substantially affect the value of the judge's interest

(4)   ownership of government securities is not an economic interest in the issuer unless the proceeding could substantially affect the value of the judge's interest

(See Terminology section, definition of "Economic interest.") These exceptions are sensibly designed to allow judges to continue to have routine financial interests without forcing their disqualification.

In 2003, the ABA added Canon 3(E)(1)(f), providing that a judge should disqualify himself or herself if the judge while a judge or candidate for office made a public statement that commits or appears to commit the judge to an issue in a proceeding or the controversy in the proceeding. The amendment responded to the Supreme Court's decision in Republican Party of Minnesota v. White,[13] which declared the "Announce Clause" of the Minnesota's version of the Code of Judicial Conduct, Canon 5(A)(3)(d)(i) unconstitutional under the First Amendment. Problem 6-2 examines *White* and the 2003 amendments to the Code.

Disqualification of judges based on relationships with persons interested in the matter

Judges are subject to disqualification not only because of personal involvement or interest in a matter but also because of certain relationships with persons interested in a matter. Canon 3(E)(1)(b) provides that a judge is disqualified if "a lawyer with whom the judge previously practiced law served during such association as a lawyer concerning the matter." Note that the mere fact that the judge's former law partner appears in a case is not disqualifying under this rule; the case must be one that was "in the office" when the judge was practicing. Should judges recuse themselves from cases involving their former firms on the ground that the judge's "impartiality might reasonably be questioned"? In

---

13. 536 U.S. 765 (2002).

Informal Opinion 87-1524, the ABA Committee on Ethics and Professional Responsibility ruled that a judge was not required to disqualify himself simply because the judge had been associated with counsel for one of the parties two years earlier. The committee indicated that a period of one or two years after termination of professional association was appropriate, depending on factors such as the closeness of the relationship and the amount of continued contact.[14]

As noted earlier, a judge is disqualified if the judge personally has an economic interest in the subject matter in controversy or in a party to the proceeding. The judge is also disqualified if close family members—the judge's spouse, the judge's parent or child wherever residing, or any other member of the judge's family residing in the judge's household—have an economic interest in the subject matter or a party to the proceeding. Canon 3(E)(1)(c). Thus, if the judge's grandchild residing in the judge's house has more than a de minimis financial interest in a party to a proceeding, the judge is disqualified.

Finally, Canon 3(E)(1)(d) requires disqualification when the judge's spouse or a person within the third degree of relationship to either of them, or the spouse of such a person,

(1) is a party to the proceeding, or an officer, director, or trustee of a party
(2) is acting as a lawyer in the proceeding
(3) is known by the judge to have a more than de minimis interest that could be substantially affected by the proceeding
(4) is to the judge's knowledge likely to be a material witness in the proceeding

The following relatives are included within the third degree of relationship: great-grandparent, grandparent, parent, uncle, aunt, brother, sister, child, grandchild, great-grandchild, nephew, or niece. (See Terminology section of 1990 Code, definition of "third degree of relationship.") Cousins are not included. Under this rule, a judge is disqualified if one of the listed relatives is a lawyer in the proceeding, but would not be disqualified simply because the relative is a member of a firm that is handling a case, unless the relative has an interest that could be substantially affected by the case. (See the commentary to Canon 3(E)(1)(d).) This could occur, for example, if the firm was handling a major class action and the relative's potential compensation from the case was substantial.

---

14. See Kinard v. Kinard, 986 S.W.2d 220 (Tenn. Ct. App. 1998, *appeal denied*) (trial judge's two-year office-sharing arrangement with husband's attorney eight years before filing of divorce suit did not require recusal). See generally Anne M. Payne, Annotation, Judge's Previous Legal Association with Attorney Connected to Current Case as Warranting Disqualification, 85 A.L.R.4th 700 (1991).

Disqualification of federal judges

Two statutes, 28 U.S.C. §§144 and 455, govern disqualification of federal judges.[15] Section 455 is the broader of the two statutes. It applies to all federal judges, whether trial or appellate, and specifies numerous grounds for disqualification. Section 144, enacted much earlier, deals only with disqualification of district court judges because of bias or prejudice. Most cases will be governed by section 455 because of its broader scope. The only aspect of section 144 that is not covered by section 455 is the requirement of filing a timely affidavit of disqualification.

Section 455 was based on the ABA's 1972 Code of Judicial Conduct. Because the ABA's 1990 Code incorporates many principles from the 1972 Code, the 1990 Code and section 455 remain very similar in many respects. Section 455, like the Code of Judicial Conduct, has two broad disqualification provisions. Section 455(a) provides that a judge is disqualified if the judge's "impartiality might reasonably be questioned." See also Canon 3(E)(1). Section 455(b)(1) provides that a judge is disqualified if the judge "has a personal bias or prejudice concerning a party." See also Canon 3(E)(1)(a) (which adds "or a party's lawyer").

Disqualification based on "personal bias or prejudice" is the older of the provisions. In United States v. Grinnell Corp.[16] the Court considered a motion by the defendants to disqualify the district judge in an antitrust case under 28 U.S.C. §144 on the ground that the judge had expressed views regarding the merits of the government's case. Ironically, it was the defendants who had sought the judge's expression of his position on the government's case. In affirming the denial of the disqualification motion, the Court stated: "The alleged bias and prejudice to be disqualifying must stem from an extrajudicial source and result in an opinion on the merits on some basis other than what the judge learned from his participation in the case."[17] Over the years, *Grinnell* came to stand for an "extrajudicial source doctrine." Under this doctrine, disqualification was not appropriate unless the basis for disqualification arose from an extrajudicial source. Thus, anger or irritation expressed by a judge during a case,[18] consistent rulings by the judge against a party,[19] and participation in previous proceedings involving a party[20] were all insufficient to warrant disqualification.

---

15. See Debra Lyn Bassett, Judicial Disqualification in the Federal Appellate Courts, 87 Iowa L. Rev. 1213 (2002) (criticizing present rules and calling for a modified peremptory challenge procedure).

16. 384 U.S. 563 (1966).

17. Id. at 583.

18. E.g., Souder v. Owens-Corning Fiberglas Corp., 939 F.2d 647 (8th Cir. 1991).

19. E.g., Nilsson, Robbins, Dalgarn, Berliner, Carson & Wurst v. Louisiana Hydrolec, 854 F.2d 1538 (9th Cir. 1988).

20. E.g., United States v. Bond, 847 F.2d 1233 (7th Cir. 1988).

In Liteky v. United States[21] the Court again addressed the application of the extrajudicial source doctrine. *Liteky* was a criminal prosecution for a political protest at a military installation. The judge hearing the case had presided over a prior case involving one of the defendants. During the case, the judge admonished and limited defense counsel's representation in several respects. The Court in *Liteky* decided that the extrajudicial source doctrine should not be used as a litmus test to decide disqualification based on bias or prejudice. Instead, extrajudicial source was only a factor in deciding whether bias or prejudice existed. Nonetheless, the Court reaffirmed the results of decisions that had used the extrajudicial source doctrine:

> As we have described it, however, there is not much doctrine to the doctrine. The fact that an opinion held by a judge derives from a source outside judicial proceedings is not a *necessary* condition for "bias or prejudice" recusal, since predispositions developed during the course of a trial will sometimes (albeit rarely) suffice. Nor is it a *sufficient* condition for "bias or prejudice" recusal, since *some* opinions acquired outside the context of judicial proceedings (for example, the judge's view of the law acquired in scholarly reading) will *not* suffice. Since neither the presence of an extrajudicial source necessarily establishes bias, nor the absence of an extrajudicial source necessarily precludes bias, it would be better to speak of the existence of a significant (and often determinative) "extrajudicial source" *factor*, than of an "extrajudicial source" *doctrine*, in recusal jurisprudence.
>
> The facts of the present case do not require us to describe the consequences of that factor in complete detail. It is enough for present purposes to say the following: First, judicial rulings alone almost never constitute a valid basis for a bias or partiality motion. See United States v. Grinnell Corp., 384 U.S. at 583. In and of themselves (i.e., apart from surrounding comments or accompanying opinion), they cannot possibly show reliance upon an extrajudicial source; and can only in the rarest circumstances evidence the degree of favoritism or antagonism required (as discussed below) when no extrajudicial source is involved. Almost invariably, they are proper grounds for appeal, not for recusal. Second, opinions formed by the judge on the basis of facts introduced or events occurring in the course of the current proceedings, or of prior proceedings, do not constitute a basis for a bias or partiality motion unless they display a deep-seated favoritism or antagonism that would make fair judgment impossible. Thus, judicial remarks during the course of a trial that are critical or disapproving of, or even hostile to, counsel, the parties, or their cases, ordinarily do not support a bias or partiality challenge. They *may* do so if they reveal an opinion that derives from an extrajudicial source; and they *will* do so if they reveal such a high degree of favoritism or antagonism as to make fair judgment impossible. An example of the latter (and perhaps of the former as well) is the statement that was alleged to have been

---

21. 510 U.S. 540 (1994). *Liteky* actually involved the scope and meaning of §455(a), which deals with disqualification because a judge's impartiality might reasonably be questioned. The Court considered the meaning of §455(b)(1), which deals with disqualification because of bias or prejudice, because it was examining the relationship between §455(a) and 455(b)(1).

made by the District Judge in Berger v. United States, 255 U.S. 22 (1921), a World War I espionage case against German-American defendants:

> "One must have a very judicial mind, indeed, not [to be] prejudiced against the German Americans" because their "hearts are reeking with disloyalty." Id., at 28.

Not establishing bias or partiality, however, are expressions of impatience, dissatisfaction, annoyance, and even anger, that are within the bounds of what imperfect men and women, even after having been confirmed as federal judges, sometimes display. A judge's ordinary efforts at courtroom administration—even a stern and short-tempered judge's ordinary efforts at courtroom administration—remain immune.[22]

As the Court indicated in *Liteky,* extrajudicial source is no longer a requirement for disqualification, but it remains an important factor.[23] A judge's race, religion, gender, and political affiliation are, of course, extrajudicial but do not constitute a basis for disqualification.[24]

Disqualification because a judge's impartiality might reasonably be questioned under section 455(a) was added to the statute in 1974. The Court first addressed the meaning of this provision in Liljeberg v. Health Services Acquisition Corp.,[25] an action by Health Services seeking a declaration of ownership of a hospital corporation. The district court found for Liljeberg. Ten months after the decision, Health Services learned that at the time the district judge rendered his decision he was a member of the board of trustees of Loyola University and that Liljeberg had been negotiating with Loyola to purchase a parcel of land on which to construct a hospital. The success and benefit of these negotiations turned in part on Liljeberg's prevailing in the litigation with Health Services.

Health Services moved to vacate the judgment under Federal Rule of Civil Procedure 60(b)(6) on the ground that the judge was disqualified under 28 U.S.C. §455. Section 455(b)(4) provides that a judge shall disqualify himself when he "knows that he, individually or as a fiduciary, . . . has . . . any other interest that could be substantially affected by the outcome of the proceeding." The Supreme Court found that the judge was not disqualified under that section because the evidence showed that the judge did not "know" of Loyola's interest when he decided the case. Nonetheless, the Court held that the judge was disqualified under section 455(a) because a reasonable person would conclude that the judge's impartiality might be questioned. The Court reasoned that knowledge was irrelevant to determining whether a violation of section

---

22. 510 U.S. at 554-556.

23. See Hathcock v. Navistar Int. Transp. Corp., 53 F.3d 36 (4th Cir. 1995) (district judge disqualified in part for remarks made about defense counsel at continuing legal education program). But see Andrade v. Chojnacki, 338 F.3d 448 (5th Cir. 2003) (rejecting 15 grounds for disqualification, both intrajudicial and extrajudicial).

24. See MacDraw, Inc. v. CIT Group Equip. Fin., Inc., 138 F.3d 33 (2d Cir.), *cert. denied*, 525 U.S. 874 (1998).

25. 486 U.S. 847 (1988).

455(a) had occurred because the purpose of the section was "to promote public confidence in the integrity of the judicial process."[26] The Court recognized that it was absurd to require judges to disqualify themselves based on facts of which they are unaware, but when the matter was brought to the judge's attention, the judge could then have taken appropriate action to recuse himself.[27]

The Court also discussed the relationship between the specific disqualification provisions of section 455(b) and section 455(a). Liljeberg contended that section 455(a) was limited by section 455(b)(4), and accordingly the judge was not disqualified absent actual knowledge of the disqualifying circumstances. The Court rejected this argument. Noting several differences between section 455(b) and section 455(a), the Court found that the sections were independent, that is, a judge is disqualified if any of the provisions of section 455(b) apply, but in addition the judge's participation in the case is also subject to the general standard of whether the judge's impartiality might reasonably be questioned.[28]

The Court also addressed the remedy appropriate for violation of section 455(a). The statute itself does not specify a remedy, and the Court declined to adopt a per se rule that required vacating the judgment simply because the judge was disqualified from hearing the case. Instead, the Court stated:

> We conclude that in determining whether a judgment should be vacated for a violation of §455(a), it is appropriate to consider the risk of injustice to the parties in the particular case, the risk that the denial of relief will produce injustice in other cases, and the risk of undermining the public's confidence in the judicial process.[29]

On the facts of the case, the Court found the "violation is neither insubstantial nor excusable," and agreed with the court of appeals that the judgment should be vacated and a new trial ordered.[30]

Three dissenting Justices argued that an actual rather than a constructive knowledge standard should apply under section 455(a) as well as under section 455(b). Given the trial judge's lack of knowledge, they also questioned the propriety of the remedy of vacating the judgment.

The Court's opinion in *Liteky,* however, decided six years after *Liljeberg,* raises questions about the standard that applies in cases governed by section 455(a). In *Liljeberg* the Court held that a judge was disqualified under section 455(a) if a reasonable person would conclude that the judge should be disqualified. The Court also reasoned that section 455(a) established a standard for disqualification that was separate from and not limited by section 455(b). By contrast, in *Liteky* the Court held that under section 455(a) the standard for

---

26. Id. at 860.
27. Id. at 861.
28. Id. at 860 n.8.
29. Id. at 864.
30. Id. at 867.

disqualification was whether "fair judgment was impossible" and that section 455(a) was limited by the specific standards of section 455(b).

One important difference between the ABA's 1990 Code and the federal disqualification statute deals with disqualification because of financial interest. Under the Code a judge is not disqualified if the judge or a close relative has a de minimis financial interest, while the statute disqualifies a judge for "ownership of a legal or equitable interest, however small." Compare Canon 3(E)(1)(c) with 28 U.S.C. §455(b)(4), (d)(4).[31] Thus, if a federal judge owns one share of stock in a party to the proceeding, the judge is disqualified from hearing the matter. Note that federal judges are also disqualified if their spouses or minor children residing in their household have even a small financial interest in a party.[32] In In re Cement Antitrust Litigation[33] a federal judge who had been handling a class action antitrust case for more than five years was required to disqualify himself because his wife owned stock worth less than $30 in seven of the 210,235 members of the plaintiff class. The Court of Appeals for the Ninth Circuit bemoaned the strictness of the statute and called for legislative evaluation of the reasonableness and consequences of the per se rule.[34]

In 1988 Congress took action to ameliorate the harshness of the "however small" rule, adding 28 U.S.C. §455(f), which allows judges to avoid disqualification by divestiture of financial interests in a party when the disqualifying interest appears or is discovered after substantial judicial time has been devoted to the matter. The divestiture rule also applies to financial interests held by a judge's spouse and minor children. The section does not apply, however, if the interest could be substantially affected by the outcome of the case. The Code of Judicial Conduct does not have a rule on divestiture equivalent to the federal statute.

In re Cement dealt with a situation in which the judge learned of the disqualifying interest after the judge had issued numerous substantive rulings and had devoted substantial time to the case. Suppose the judge becomes aware of the disqualifying interest at the beginning of the case before the judge has made any substantive rulings, is the judge automatically disqualified or can the judge avoid disqualification by taking steps to remove the disqualifying interest? For example, if the judge or a close family member owns stock in a party, the judge or the relative could sell the stock. Similarly, if the judge or a close family member is a member of a putative class, the judge or the family member could opt out of the class. The courts are divided. On the one hand, it has been argued that section (f) is clear and that the disqualification can only be removed if the judge has devoted substantial time to the case.[35] On the other hand, the legislative history indicates that §455(f) was added to deal

---

31. For the legislative history behind the statutory per se rule see In re Initial Public Offering Securities Litigation, 174 F. Supp. 2d 70, 81-86 (S.D.N.Y. 2001).

32. 28 U.S.C. §455(b)(4).

33. 688 F.2d 1297 (9th Cir. 1982), aff'd by absence of a quorum, 459 U.S. 1191 (1983).

34. 688 F.2d at 1315.

35. Tramonte v. Chrysler Corp., 136 F.3d 1025, 1031-1032 (5th Cir. 1998).

with the particular problem presented by *In re Cement* where the grounds for disqualification do not come to the judge's attention until well into the case after the judge has issued substantive rulings. The amendment was not intended to disturb prior case law and long-standing practice under which judges could avoid disqualification by taking steps to remove the disqualifying interest at the beginning of the case before they had issued any substantive rulings.[36]

If the judge has an interest other than a financial interest, the impact on the interest must be substantial to warrant disqualification.[37] For example, in In re New Mexico Natural Gas Antitrust Litigation,[38] the Tenth Circuit held that the district judge was not disqualified from handling an antitrust case against various oil companies alleging price fixing when the judge was a member of the class of plaintiffs involved in one of the consolidated cases. The court found that the possible future effect on the judge's utility bills was too remote and contingent to amount to a financial interest that would require per se disqualification. Any impact on the judge's utility bills was too insubstantial to warrant recusal.[39]

Waiver or remittal of disqualification

Both the Code of Judicial Conduct and the federal statute provide for *remittal* (the term used by the Code) or *waiver* (the term used by the federal statute) of disqualification, but they differ dramatically in the situations in which waiver is allowed. Under the Code, disqualification may be remitted in all cases except ones in which the judge is disqualified because of personal bias or prejudice concerning a party. The Code allows remittal in situations in which the judge was disqualified because of economic interest. Canon 3(F). The procedure for remittal is as follows: The judge discloses the basis for disqualification on the record and asks the parties and their lawyers to consider, out of the presence of the judge, whether to waive disqualification. If all parties and the judge agree to waive disqualification, the judge may continue in the case. The agreement waiving disqualification should be made part of the record in the case. Canon 3(F).

Under the federal statute, waiver of disqualification is allowed only in cases involving the general standard of when the judge's impartiality might reasonably be questioned. Waiver is not allowed for any cases in which rules

36. See In re Initial Public Offering Securities Litigation, 174 F. Supp. 2d 70, 87-90 (S.D.N.Y. 2001).

37. 28 U.S.C. §455(b)(4) ("or any other interest that could be substantially affected by the outcome of the proceeding").

38. 620 F.2d 794 (10th Cir. 1980).

39. But see Gordon v. Reliant Energy, Inc., 141 F. Supp. 2d 1041 (S.D. Cal. 2001) (holding that interest of judge as a rate payer in utility class actions was a financial interest requiring application of per se rule; disqualification was not cured by amendment to plaintiffs' complaint excluding judge and close family members from class).

specifically provide for disqualification, including cases of disqualification be-cause of financial interest.[40]

Ex parte contacts

Another important provision of the Code of Judicial Conduct dealing with judges' official functions is the rule prohibiting judges from initiating, permit-ting, or considering ex parte communications. Canon 3(B)(7). Model Rule 3.5(b) prohibits lawyers from engaging in ex parte communications during proceedings except when authorized by law or court order. The Restatement of the Law Governing Lawyers contains similar restrictions.[41] An ex parte communication is any communication between the judge, juror, or official and any other person regarding the case except a communication in the course of official proceedings. The prohibition applies to parties, their lawyers, witnesses, and even third persons unconnected with the litigation. The purpose of the rule is to protect the integrity of the adversarial process, which assumes that each party has the opportunity to respond to contentions and facts presented by an adversary.

The Code of Judicial Conduct provides several practical exceptions to the prohibition on ex parte communications to judges. See Canon 3(B)(7)(a)-(e). For example, the Code allows ex parte communications "for scheduling, administrative purposes or emergencies that do not deal with substantive mat-ters or issues on the merits." Canon 3(B)(7)(a).[42] Even in these situations, however, the judge must reasonably believe that no party will gain a procedural or tactical advantage because of the ex parte communication, and the judge must promptly notify all parties of the ex parte communication and give them an opportunity to respond. Canon 3(B)(7)(a)(i), (ii). In some cases ex parte communications are permissible, for example, when a party is seeking a tempo-rary restraining order to prevent irreparable harm.[43] Ex parte communications are permitted in this situation because the communication is "authorized by law." Canon 3(B)(7)(e). See also Model Rule 3.3(d), which requires lawyers in an ex parte proceeding to inform the tribunal of all material facts to enable the tribunal to make an informed decision, even when the facts are adverse.

The rule prohibiting judges from engaging in ex parte communications is long standing. Canon 3 of the ABA's 1908 Canons of Ethics prohibited ex parte communications. Nonetheless, it is surprising how many judges seem to freely seek advice and information about cases in violation of the rule against ex parte communication. Such ex parte initiatives by judges can put lawyers

---

40. 28 U.S.C. §455(e).

41. Restatement (Third) of the Law Governing Lawyers §113(1) (prohibition on ex parte communication with judge or official before whom case is pending). See also id. §115(1), (2) (prohibition on communication with prospective and sitting jurors).

42. See also id. §113, cmt. c.

43. See Fed. R. Civ. P. 65(b).

in very awkward situations. Most courts have held, however, that ex parte communications do not warrant reversal of a case absent a showing of prejudice.[44]

─────────────────────── **Problem 6-2** ───────────────────────

Extrajudicial Conduct and Judicial Selection

a. You are a law clerk for Justice Gates, an associate justice on your state supreme court. Before appointment to the bench Justice Gates had a distinguished legal career. She served as president of the state bar association, had an active litigation practice, and was a member of the state legislature for a number of years. Justice Gates was also very involved in civic and charitable organizations and often spoke before legal and nonlegal groups. Justice Gates has asked you to give her advice about the propriety of the following situations now that she has been appointed to the bench:

(1) Justice Gates is a member of a task force appointed by the state legislature to study and make recommendations regarding control of violence in the public schools. Justice Gates believes that she will receive invitations to serve on similar task forces and commissions in the future.

(2) Justice Gates is a member of the board of visitors of the state university where she attended both undergraduate and law school. The board comes to the university annually, meets with the president and the various deans, discusses problems facing the university, and makes recommendations for the administration to consider.

(3) While in practice Justice Gates handled a number of employment discrimination cases. She has been asked to write an introductory essay to a symposium on "Emerging Issues in Employment Discrimination Litigation."

(4) Justice Gates has been asked to deliver a speech to the Defense Lawyers Association at its annual meeting. She will not receive a fee for her speech, but the association will pay all expenses for her and her husband for the weekend.

(5) Justice Gates and her husband are close friends with Tom and Eleanor Landing, both attorneys who were in the same class with Justice Gates in law school. Eleanor is a trial attorney and from time to time has cases in the supreme court. The Gates and the Landings frequently have dinner together, and Justice Gates and Ms. Landing have a regular once-a-month golf game. In addition, they jointly own a beach house.

───

44. *Compare* Bakala v. Bakala, 576 S.E.2d 156 (S.C. 2003) (reversal not warranted because no showing of prejudice), *with* Strothers v. Strothers, 567 N.E.2d 222 (Mass. Ct. App. 1991) (reversal warranted when ex parte communication had effect on judge's decision in divorce case). See Leslie W. Abramson, The Judicial Ethics of Ex Parte and Other Communications, 37 Hous. L. Rev. 1343 (2000).

b.   You have been asked to speak to a meeting of a statewide organization devoted to political reform. Your topic is "Judicial Selection." The organization has asked you to address the following questions, as well as others that you consider important: What is the method of judicial selection in your state for judges of trial courts of general jurisdiction and for state supreme court justices? What are the advantages and disadvantages of this method compared to selection methods used in other states? What suggestions for reform or improvement of the current system do you have?

Read Canons 4 and 5 of the Code of Judicial Conduct.

Limitations on judges' extrajudicial activities

Canon 4 of the Code of Judicial Conduct deals with limitations on judges' nonjudicial activities. The Canon reflects a balance between contending policies. On one hand, judges should avoid any conduct that casts doubt on their impartiality, demeans their office, or interferes with their judicial duties. Canon 4(A). On the other hand, judges should not be isolated from the people and activities of the communities in which they live. See commentary to Canon 4(A).

The Code prohibits extrajudicial activities that clearly violate one or more of the policies expressed in Canon 4(A). Thus, judges may not practice law (except that they may act pro se, and they may draft or review legal documents and give legal advice to family members without compensation). Canon 4(G). Similarly, judges may not appear as private arbitrators or mediators unless authorized by law. Canon 4(F). The Code also prohibits judges from serving in a fiduciary capacity (for example, as a personal representative, a trustee, or a guardian), except for family members, and even then the judge cannot appear if it is likely that the judge as fiduciary would handle a matter that would come before the judge. Canon 4(E). Note that some provisions of the Code (including the prohibitions against practicing law, serving as arbitrators or mediators, and acting as fiduciaries) do not apply to part-time judges. See Application of the Code of Judicial Conduct sections C, D, and E.

By contrast to these prohibited activities, the Code broadly authorizes judges to "speak, write, lecture, teach and participate in other extrajudicial activities concerning the law, the legal system, the administration of justice and non-legal subjects, subject to the requirements of this Code." Canon 4(B). Under this section, a judge may speak or write on controversial topics of policy as well as ones that involve technical improvements of the legal system, and may advocate change in the law. The limitation expressed in Canon 4(B)— "subject to the requirements of this Code"—is intended to remind judges that even in connection with educational activities, judges are still subject to other Canons of the Code. For example, a judge should not "while a proceeding is pending or impending in any court, make any public comment that might reasonably be expected to affect its outcome or impair its fairness or make any nonpublic comment that might substantially interfere with a fair trial or hearing." Canon 3(B)(9).[45] Judges are always subject to the dictates of Canon 1, which requires them to maintain high standards of integrity and independence.

The Code allows judges to receive compensation and expense reimbursement for speaking and writing, subject to the financial reporting requirements of Canon 4(II). Thus, within the guidelines of Canon 4(H)(1), a judge could receive a salary for teaching part time at a law school and could accept an honorarium and expense reimbursement for delivering a speech. Canon 4(H)(1) provides that compensation and expense reimbursement must be reasonable and the source of payments must not "give the appearance of influencing the judge's performance of judicial duties or otherwise give the appearance of impropriety."

The difficulty of striking a balance between social involvement and regulation of nonjudicial conduct appears quite clearly in connection with governmental, civic, and charitable activities. Canon 4(C). The Canon provides that judges may not appear at public hearings or consult with legislative or executive bodies or officials except on matters concerning "the law, the legal system or the administration of justice," or except when the judge appears pro se in a matter affecting the judge's own interest. Although the Canon is written as a prohibition, it could be construed as a rather broad authorization for judicial participation in governmental and civic activities, because such participation will often involve issues of law. Indeed, even some of the most controversial political topics of our day—abortion, health care reform, government spending—arguably involve "the law, the legal system or the administration of justice." But perhaps a fair reading of the intent of the Canon is that judges should not become involved with other branches of government in issues of public policy or politics. Viewed in that light, an appearance by a judge at a legislative hearing on health care reform would probably be improper. This distinction finds support in the wording of Canon 4(C)(2), which states that a "judge shall not accept appointment to a governmental committee or commission or other governmental position that is concerned with issues of fact or policy on matters other than the improvement of the law, the legal system or the administration of justice [subject to exceptions for ceremonial occasions]." It should be noted that this provision prohibiting judges from serving on governmental committees and commissions constitutes a departure from the historical practice of many respected judges. Probably the most famous example of judicial service that

---

45. The rule has been applied to comments about cases in any court, not just the one where the judge sits. See In re Broadbelt, 683 A.2d 543 (N.J. 1996) (improper for New Jersey municipal court judge to appear on Court TV and Geraldo Live to comment about cases in other jurisdictions). For discussion of the rule see Ronald D. Rotunda, Judicial Comments on Pending Cases: The Ethical Restrictions and the Sanctions—A Case Study of the Microsoft Litigation, 2001 U. Ill. L. Rev. 611. The Rule may be vulnerable to First Amendment attack in light of the Supreme Court's decision in Republican Party of Minnesota v. White, discussed later in this problem.

would now be a violation of this canon was Chief Justice Earl Warren's acceptance of an appointment to serve as chair of the commission investigating the assassination of President John F. Kennedy.

Canon 4 allows a judge to serve as an official (officer, director, trustee) or nonlegal advisor of an organization or governmental agency devoted to the improvement of law, the legal system, or the administration of justice or of "an educational, religious, charitable, fraternal or civic organization not conducted for profit," subject to "other requirements of this Code." Canon 4(C)(3). A judge may not engage in such service if the organization is likely to be involved in proceedings before the judge or in any court subject to the appellate jurisdiction of the court of which the judge is a member. Canon 4(C)(3)(a).

The Code limits judges' involvement in fund-raising activities and membership solicitation on behalf of such organizations. A judge may help in planning fund raising and may give advice regarding fund raising and investments, but may not participate personally in fund raising (except that a judge may solicit contributions from other judges over whom the judge does not have appellate jurisdiction or supervisory authority), nor may a judge lend the prestige of the judge's office to fund raising or membership solicitation (for example, by permitting a quotation or statement that the judge endorses the activities of the organization). Canon 4(C)(3)(b). The commentary to Canon 4(C)(3)(b) draws some precise distinctions. For example, a judge may attend but may not speak at a fund-raising dinner. A judge may be listed on the letterhead of an organization's fund-raising letter, provided comparable listings are made for other persons. Note also that under the 1990 Code, a judge may not hold membership (much less serve in a leadership capacity) in any organization that practices "invidious discrimination" on the basis of race, sex, religion, or national origin. Canon 2(C).

Business and financial activities by judges pose two potential problems. First, judges can exploit their public position for private gain. Second, judges can be placed in a position where they must disqualify themselves because of financial interest in a party or proceeding. See Canon 4(D)(1). Recall the discussion in Problem 6-1. The Code generally allows judges to hold and manage their own investments and those of their family members and to engage in remunerative activity, but this authorization is subject to other provisions of the Code. Canon 4(D)(2). The Code requires judges to manage their investments "to minimize the number of cases in which the judge is disqualified," and judges are directed to divest themselves of financial interests that might require frequent disqualification. Canon 4(D)(4). Judges may not serve in a managerial capacity in a business, with two exceptions: a business closely held by the judge or members of the judge's family and a business entity operated primarily to manage the investments of the judge or members of the judge's family. Participation in even these entities would still be improper if the entity were to regularly appear before the judge. Commentary to Canon 4(D)(3).

Acceptance by judges of gifts, bequests, loans, and favors poses obvious problems of improper influence. Canon 4(D)(5) states a broad general rule prohibiting judges from accepting a gift, bequest, favor, or loan from anyone, subject to certain exceptions. The canon requires judges to urge family members residing in the judge's household to comply with the rule. The broadest exception is found in Canon 4(D)(5)(h), which allows the judge to accept a gift, bequest, favor, or loan from any person so long as the transaction does not involve a person or interest that has appeared or is likely to appear before the judge and provided the judge reports any such transaction that exceeds $150.

A number of the other exceptions to the general prohibition on gifts, loans, bequests, and favors recognize that judges should not be required to act as hermits and are allowed to engage in many activities in which other citizens can engage. Thus, Canon 4(D)(5)(f) permits judges to receive loans from lending institutions in the regular course of business of the institution on the same general terms available to others. Similarly, Canon 4(D)(5)(g) permits the receipt of scholarships or fellowships awarded on the same general terms and criteria applied to other applicants. Canon 4(D)(5)(d) permits gifts from relatives or friends on special occasions (weddings and birthdays), provided the gift is commensurate with the occasion and the relationship. Canon 4(D)(5)(e) allows judges to receive gifts, bequests, and loans from a relative or close friend "whose appearance or interest in a case would in any event require disqualification under Section 3E." Canon 4(D)(5)(b) allows the spouse of a judge or a family member residing in the judge's household to accept gifts, awards, or other benefits "incident to the business, profession or other separate activity" of such person, even if the judge receives an incidental benefit, provided the transaction "could not reasonably be perceived as intended to influence the judge in the performance of judicial duties."

One potentially troublesome exception is Canon 4(D)(5)(c), which permits judges to accept "ordinary social hospitality." The section allows judges to have social contacts with anyone, including lawyers who regularly appear before them. The Reporter's Notes to the 1972 Code of Judicial Conduct, which also included a "social hospitality" exception to the prohibition on gifts, stated that a "judge should not be excluded from all social relationships with lawyers or persons who are likely to be litigants in his court."[46] The Code does not, however, define what is meant by "ordinary social hospitality." De minimis matters such as infrequent lunch or dinner engagements with lawyers or others should clearly be proper under the exception. Suppose, however, the judge has regular and substantial contacts with either a lawyer or another person who may appear regularly before the judge. The Reporter's Notes give the following example of conduct that exceeds the ordinary social hospitality exception:

> The Committee felt that there are common sense limits and that the standard is understandable and defensible; for example, the offer to a judge of a month at the mountain cabin of a lawyer friend who practices in the judge's court is clearly not ordinary social hospitality, and acceptance is prohibited.[47]

46. E. Wayne Thode, Reporter's Notes to Code of Judicial Conduct 84 (1973).
47. Id. at 84-85.

Canon 4(D)(5)(a) allows judges to accept gifts incident to public testimonials and to accept materials from publishers on a complimentary basis for official use. That canon also allows judges to accept gifts (expense payments, for example) incident to bar-related functions or to activities devoted to the improvement of the law, the legal system, or the administration of justice.[48] The comment to that section states, however, that the canon does not allow such gifts from individual lawyers or groups of lawyers. Such gifts would be subject to Canon 4(D)(5)(h), which prohibits judges from accepting gifts from any person whose interests have or are likely to come before the judge. Thus, it appears to be improper for a judge to receive an expense-paid weekend at a convention sponsored by a specialized bar group, for example, one representing either the plaintiffs' bar or the defense bar, but it would be proper for a judge to receive an expense-paid weekend at a convention sponsored by the bar association representing the entire bar membership of the state. Could a judge make a speech before a specialized bar group and receive as compensation for the speech (rather than a gift) an honorarium plus expenses? As discussed above, Canon 4(H) allows judges to receive compensation and expense reimbursement for activities permitted by the Code (note that Canon 4(B) authorizes judges to speak, write, or lecture on legal topics), provided the compensation and expense reimbursement are reasonable and provided that the source of payment "does not give the appearance of influencing the judge's performance of judicial duties or otherwise give the appearance of impropriety." Canon 4(H)(1). Expense reimbursement may include that of the judge's spouse or guest, "where appropriate to the occasion." Canon 4(H)(1)(b).

Methods of judicial selection and the problem of judicial independence

The choice of method of judicial selection involves a tension between the goals of independence and accountability. The rule of law, one of the core principles of our society, requires an independent judiciary in which judges render decisions based on the law rather than on political considerations or favoritism to one of the litigants. Yet at the same time, the rule of law demands that judges, like other public officials, be accountable for their conduct.

The Constitution adopts a system of judicial selection that emphasizes independence over accountability. Federal judges are nominated by the president, subject to confirmation by the Senate.[49] Once appointed, federal judges

---

48. Bruce A. Green, Should Judicial Education Be Privatized?: Questions of Judicial Ethics and Policy, 29 Fordham Urb. L.J. 941 (2002) (concluding that judicial attendance at expense-paid educational programs sponsored by private organizations devoted to law and economics principles is permissible under current rules but that such programs raise broader policy questions that should be addressed by the judiciary institutionally).

49. U.S. Const. art. II, §2, cl. 2 ("[The President] shall nominate, and by and with the Advice and Consent of the Senate, shall appoint Ambassadors, other public Ministers and Consuls, Judges of the Supreme Court, and all other Officers of the United States, whose Appointments are not herein otherwise provided for, and which shall be established by Law. . . .").

serve for life tenure and may be removed from office only through the impeachment process.[50]

During the past 75 years, the federal judiciary has come to exercise significant power over important social issues both through constitutional decisions
and cases involving statutory interpretation. As a result of this expansion of
judicial power, the accountability of federal judges has become an increasingly
important issue. In Problem 6-1 we discussed the creation of judicial councils
in each federal circuit to take disciplinary action against federal judges, short
of removal from office. The Senate has been active in seeking to increase the
accountability of federal judges. Beginning with the confirmation hearings of
Robert Bork in 1987, the Senate Judiciary Committee has conducted searching
inquiries into the constitutional and judicial philosophies of nominees.[51] The
Senate has also streamlined the impeachment process.[52]

Most states originally struck the balance between independence and accountability more toward the accountability side than was the case at the federal
level, but the general trend among the states has been toward greater judicial
independence. During the colonial era, judges were appointed by the king.
After the Revolution, distaste for the arbitrary exercise of royal power led many
states to place the authority to appoint judges with one or both houses of the
legislature. In the "democratic period" in American history, the vast majority
of states moved to popular elections to select judges. Dissatisfaction with
some of the political excesses resulting from popular elections (particularly
control of judges by political machines) produced a late nineteenth-century
movement for reform of judicial selection. Some states changed to "nonpartisan" elections, but this system also had its critics because it failed to take
politics out of the election process and because it deprived voters of information
about the party affiliation of candidates.[53] During the early twentieth century,
reformers presented various proposals for judicial nominating commissions.
In 1940 Missouri became the first state to adopt a nominating commission.
(Today, a plan to use a judicial nominating commission, regardless of form,
to select judges is often referred to as a "Missouri Plan.")[54]

A study of methods of judicial selection currently used throughout the
country comments on the lack of uniformity among the states:

50. U.S. Const. art. II, §4.
51. Stephen J. Wermiel, Confirming the Constitution. The Role of the Senate Judiciary Committee, 56 Law & Contemp. Probs. 121 (autumn 1993) (part of Symposium:
Elected Branch Influences in Constitutional Decisionmaking).
52. See Nixon v. United States, 506 U.S. 224 (1993) (constitutionality of Senate
rule allowing committee rather than full Senate to hear testimony and gather evidence
presents nonjusticiable political question).
53. For a criticism of the legitimacy of an elective judiciary, see Steven P. Croley,
The Majoritarian Difficulty: Elective Judiciaries and the Rule of Law, 62 U. Chi. L. Rev.
689 (1995).
54. On the history of judicial selection, see Republican Party of Minnesota v. White,
536 U.S. 765, 790-792 (2002) (O'Connor J., concurring); Larry C. Berkson (updated
by Seth Anderson), Judicial Selection in the United States, http://www.ajs.org/selection/
berkson.pdf (visited Oct. 7, 2003).

One of the first things to strike one who looks at judicial selection in the states is the amazing variability not only between states, but within the individual states. Almost no two states choose all their judges the same way. Very few states use the same selection method for all levels of court.[55]

States generally follow, however, one of four models of judicial selection,[56] although a state may choose to use different methods for different courts:

Appointive systems—the governor or the legislature appoints and/or reappoints judges;

Partisan elective systems—voters select and/or retain judges from among competing candidates identified by political party label;

Nonpartisan elective systems—voters select and/or retain judges through elections where competing candidates are not identified by party label; and

"Merit selection" systems—the governor initially appoints judges from a short list of candidates evaluated and recommended by a nominating committee and voters decide periodically whether to keep judges in office by voting "yes" or "no" on their retention.[57]

The details of nominating commissions vary from state to state, but some features are common to commission plans. Typically, the legislature creates a permanent nominating commission consisting of both lawyers and nonlawyers. Various public and private officials (as set forth in the enabling legislation) appoint members of the commission. The commission has the task of identifying, investigating, and evaluating candidates for judicial office. Typically, it will hold public hearings on candidates. When a judicial vacancy occurs, the commission, after investigation and deliberation, forwards to the governor a list of nominees (three to five is a common number). The governor appoints judges from the list for a probationary period of one to three years. At the end of the probationary period, the judge runs unopposed on the question of whether the judge should be retained in office for a full term. Periodically, the judge must stand for unopposed reelection in which the public votes whether to retain or to remove the judge from office. While many states use nominating commissions, nonetheless more than 80 percent of state trial and appellate judges are still subject to some form of election.[58]

Recent developments have raised questions about the appropriate balance between judicial independence and accountability at both the state and federal level. Retention elections for state judges were low profile until 1986, when a

55. American Judicature Socy., Judicial Selection in the United States: A Compendium of Provisions, at v (Lyle Warrick ed., 2nd ed. 1993).

56. For a detailed discussion of the various methods of selection and retention of judges in each state, see id.

57. Sara Mathias, Electing Justice: A Handbook of Judicial Election Reforms 5 (1990). See Elizabeth A. Larkin, Judicial Selection Methods: Judicial Independence and Popular Democracy, 79 Denver U. L. Rev. 65 (2001).

58. Larkin, supra n.57, at 76 n.126.

coalition of groups defeated the reelection of Chief Justice Rose Bird and two associate justices of the California Supreme Court.[59] Later in Texas, a coalition of medical, business, and insurance interests ousted a number of state supreme court justices who were viewed as proplaintiff.[60] In the 1996 election, grass roots political campaigns removed a number of judges from state appellate courts.[61]

At the federal level, during the 1996 presidential election, Republican candidate Robert Dole criticized federal district judge Harold Baer for issuing a ruling suppressing evidence of seizure of cocaine and heroin by New York City police officers. Dole called for Judge Baer's impeachment. In response to Dole's charge, the White House suggested that President Clinton would ask for Judge Baer's resignation unless he changed his decision. Judge Baer did in fact reverse his ruling.[62] In Bush v. Gore,[63] the United States Supreme Court effectively decided the 2000 presidential election. Many commentators raised questions about whether the decisions of the Florida Supreme Court, the United States Supreme Court, or both were politically motivated.[64]

The topic of judicial independence continues to be debated in academic symposia.[65] The ABA established a standing committee on judicial independence and has created several commissions that have issued reports on various aspects of judicial selection and independence.[66] The American Judicature Society also publishes extensive material on these subjects.[67]

Judges and political activity

The relationship between judging and political activity poses both interesting questions about legal theory as well as practical questions regarding permissible nonjudicial activities. A widely accepted ideal for judges is one of political

59. Paul D. Carrington, Judicial Independence and Democratic Accountability in Highest State Courts, 61 Law & Contemp. Probs. 79, 81-87 (summer 1998).

60. See Rogers v. Bradley, 909 S.W.2d 872 (Tex. 1995) (with appendix containing "Court Wars" report from the television show *60 Minutes*).

61. West Legal News, 1996 WL 652140, 652141 (Nov. 12, 1996). For other examples, see Charles G. Geyh, Why Judicial Elections Stink, 64 Ohio St. L.J. 43, 50-51 (2003). On the increasing importance of money in state judicial elections, see Mark Hansen, Run for the Bench, 84-Oct A.B.A. J. 68 (1998).

62. Stephen B. Bright, Casualties of the War on Crime: Fairness, Reliability and the Credibility of Criminal Justice Systems, 51 U. Miami L. Rev. 413, 415-416 (1997).

63. 531 U.S. 98 (2000).

64. See articles on the issue in Symposium, Perspectives on Judicial Independence, 64 Ohio St. L.J. 1 (2003).

65. See Symposium, Judicial Elections: Selecting Judges in the 21st Century, 30 Cap. U.L. Rev. 437 (2002); Symposium, National Summit on Improving Judicial Selection, 34 Loy. L.A. L. Rev. 1353 (2001); Symposium, Perspectives on Judicial Independence, 64 Ohio St. L.J. 1 (2003).

66. http://www.abanet.org/judind/jud_selection.html (visited Oct. 7, 2003).

67. http://www.ajs.org (visited Oct. 8, 2003).

neutrality. Under this view, law and politics are separate activities. Judges should decide cases in accordance with the law; issues of politics should be left to the legislative and executive branches. A substantial body of scholarly literature challenges the view that judges can be politically neutral. Under this view, all law is to some extent vague or "open textured." Because law has this characteristic, judges must develop approaches or theories to a wide range of legal questions, many of which involve controversial questions of morals, values, and politics.[68]

Even if one accepts the view that the judicial process inherently involves questions of politics or values, it does not follow that judges should participate in other political activities, particularly the work of political parties and organizations. Such participation undermines public confidence in the independence of judges and exposes them to situations in which they may be forced to disqualify themselves. The Code of Judicial Conduct establishes some restrictions on political activity by judges. Canon 5(A)(1) imposes broad restrictions on participation in political activities by all judges and candidates for judicial office, including prohibitions on participation in political gatherings and fundraising activities. Canon 5(A)(3) directs candidates for judicial office to "maintain the dignity appropriate to judicial office." The Code then defines this limitation more specifically to include, among other restrictions, prohibitions on campaign pledges on matters that are likely to come before the court. Canon 5(A)(3)(d). Canon 5(B) sets forth restrictions on political activity applicable to judges seeking judicial appointments; Canon 5(C) limits political activity by judges subject to public election. These canons reflect obvious differences between these selection methods. For example, when judges are appointed to the bench, candidates can engage in only very limited political activity, but when judges are selected or retained by public election, candidates are permitted greater political participation. Thus, a candidate for an appointive position may not solicit campaign funds, Canon 5(B)(1), while a candidate for an elected position may solicit funds through a campaign committee, Canon 5(C)(2). Model Rule 8.2(b) requires lawyers who are candidates for judicial office to comply with the applicable provisions of the Code of Judicial Conduct. In addition, Model Rule 8.2(a) prohibits lawyers from making statements that the lawyer knows to be false or with reckless disregard of the truth or falsity of the statement about the qualifications or integrity of judges, candidates for judicial office, or other public legal officers. Section 114 of the Restatement of the Law Governing Lawyers adopts similar standards.

The constitutionality of restrictions on political activity by judges has been called into question by the Supreme Court's decision in Republican Party of Minnesota v. White.[69] Gregory Wersal, a candidate for associate justice on the Minnesota Supreme Court, brought suit in federal court alleging that a provision of the Minnesota Code of Judicial Conduct, known as the "Announce

---

68. See generally Ronald M. Dworkin, Taking Rights Seriously (1977).
69. 536 U.S. 765 (2002).

Clause," violated his First Amendment rights. The Announce Clause provided that a candidate for judicial office shall not "announce his or her views on disputed legal or political issues."[70] The Announce Clause was found in the 1972 version of the ABA's Code of Judicial Conduct, but is not part of the 1990 Code.[71] In *White*, the Court was careful to distinguish the Announce Clause from the Pledge Clause, under which a candidate is prohibited from making pledges or promises regarding conduct in office other than the faithful and impartial performance of duties in office. The Court stated that the Pledge Clause "is not challenged here and on which we express no view."[72]

In a 5-4 decision the Court held that the Announce Clause violated Wersal's First Amendment rights. After discussing the meaning of the Announce Clause, the Court concluded that the clause was subject to strict scrutiny because it dealt with the content of speech and with a category of speech that was at the core of the First Amendment—speech about qualifications of candidates for elective office. Under this test the state must show that a restriction is (1) narrowly tailored to serve (2) a compelling state interest.[73] The state contended that the clause served compelling state interests in impartiality and in the appearance of impartiality of the state judiciary. The Court then proceeded to analyze whether the clause could be sustained on these grounds. This analysis required the Court to determine the meaning of impartiality. One meaning, which the Court considered to be the core meaning, was lack of bias or partiality for or against a party to a proceeding.[74] The Court found that the clause was not narrowly tailored to achieve impartiality in this sense because it was directed at issues rather than parties.[75] The Court then considered another meaning of impartiality: lack of a preconceived legal view. The Court found that this state interest was not a compelling one because it would be almost impossible to find judges who did not have preconceptions about the law.[76] Finally the Court considered a third meaning of impartiality—open-mindedness. The Court found that the clause was not tailored to protect this interest because it was "woefully underinclusive."[77] Statements in election campaigns are only a small part of the many ways in which a judge could commit himself or herself on a legal issue. For example, a judge might author a book on a legal subject. The Announce Clause would not prohibit this activity even though it would be far more likely to commit the judge than would statements made during a political campaign. In its opinion the Court indicated that underlying the Announce Clause was antagonism to election of judges. The Court stated that such "opposition may be well taken (it certainly had

---

70. Id. at 768.
71. Id.
72. Id. at 770.
73. Id. at 774-775.
74. Id. at 775-776.
75. Id. at 776.
76. Id. at 777-778.
77. Id. at 778-781.

the support of the Founders of the Federal Government), but the First Amendment does not permit it to achieve its goal by leaving the principle of elections in place while preventing candidates from discussing what the elections are about."[78]

The dissenting justices (Stevens, Souter, Ginsburg, and Breyer) argued that the work of judges is fundamentally different from that of other elected officials. Accordingly, the state had a compelling state interest in appropriate restrictions on candidates for judicial office.[79] They found that the Announce Clause served the state's interest in impartiality of judges in all of the senses discussed by the majority. To the dissenters, campaign statements about the judge's views on disputed legal questions were very different than other statements and were inconsistent with judicial open-mindedness.[80] In addition, the dissenters contended that it would violate the due process rights of a litigant if a judge sat on the case when the judge had announced his or her views on a disputed issue in the case during a campaign for office.[81] The dissenters also argued that the Announce Clause complemented the Pledge Clause and prevented statements that were in form not pledges but which amounted to the same thing.[82]

As noted above, the ABA Code of Judicial Conduct does not have an Announce Clause, so the constitutionality of the ABA Code was not directly before the Court in *White*. The 1990 version of the Code did have another clause, the Commit Clause, which provided that a judge shall not "make statements that commit or appear to commit the candidate with respect to cases, controversies or issues that are likely to come before the court." Canon 5A(3)(d)(ii) (1990 version). The Commit Clause is narrower than the Announce Clause but broader than the Pledge Clause, so its constitutionality is uncertain. Indeed, the Court in *White* did not even pass on the constitutionality of the Pledge Clause, although it seemed to indicate that the clause was constitutional. In any event, at its August 2003 meeting, the ABA amended Canon 5A(3)(d) to narrow its scope and increase the likelihood that it would be upheld against constitutional attack. Canon 5A(3)(d) now provides that a candidate for judicial office shall not:

> with respect to cases, controversies, or issues that are likely to come before the court, make pledges, promises or commitments that are inconsistent with the impartial* performance of the adjudicative duties of the office;

The 2003 amendments include a number of other related provisions: The terminology section adds a definition of impartiality:

---

78. Id. at 787-788.
79. Id. at 797-798.
80. Id. at 801-802.
81. Id. at 814-817.
82. Id. at 819-821.

"Impartiality" or "impartial" denotes absence of bias or prejudice in favor of, or against, particular parties or classes of parties, as well as maintaining an open mind in considering issues that may come before the judge.

New Canon 3(B)(10) parallels revised Canon 5 by stating that a sitting judge shall not "with respect to cases, controversies or issues that are likely to come before the court, make pledges, promises or commitments that are inconsistent with the impartial* performance of the adjudicative duties of the office." Finally, revised Canon 3(E)(1)(f) requires disqualification of a judge when the judge while either a judge or candidate for judicial office has made a public statement that "commits, or appears to commit, the judge with respect to (i) an issue in the proceeding; or (ii) the controversy in the proceeding."

It appears certain, however, that a number of provisions of the Code of Judicial Conduct limiting the speech of judges both in connection with political activities and otherwise will now be subject to constitutional attack. In February 2003 a federal district court in New York held that a number of provisions of the state's Code of Judicial Conduct were unconstitutional, although the Second Circuit later vacated the judgment holding that the district court should have abstained.[83] In June 2003, the New York Court of Appeals in two cases upheld the constitutionality of both the Pledge Clause[84] and of restrictions on political contributions by judges.[85]

B. Representation of the Public Interest

─────────── **Problem 6-3** ───────────

Government Attorneys[86]

You are an assistant state attorney general. Your boss, the deputy attorney general, has been asked to speak to a convention of attorneys employed by the federal and state governments; the lecture is titled "The Ethical

83. Spargo v. New York State Commn. on Judicial Conduct, 351 F.3d 65 (2nd Cir. 2003).

84. In re Watson, 794 N.E.2d 1 (N.Y. 2003).

85. In re Raab, 793 N.E.2d 1287 (N.Y. 2003).

86. Federal and state governments employ attorneys in a wide variety of capacities: for example, as prosecutors, agency counsel, members of legislative staffs, judges, and law clerks. See generally Symposium, Government Lawyering, 61 Law & Contemp. Probs. Nos. 1 & 2 (1998); Symposium: Legal Ethics for Government Lawyers: Straight Talk for Tough Times, 9 Widener J. Pub. L. 199 (2000). The duties and ethical obligations of these attorneys are obviously not the same. Problems 6-1 and 6-2 dealt with the ethical obligations of judges. The material that follows deals principally with the ethical issues facing executive or legislative branch attorneys, such as attorneys employed by the Justice Department, by the office of a state attorney general, by a federal or state regulatory agency or department, by a member of Congress, or by a state legislator. Prosecutors face some additional special ethical problems; see Problem 2-10.

Obligations of Lawyers Employed by the Federal and State Governments."
Several lawyers who will be attending the lecture have written to your
boss with questions that they would like her to address. These questions
include the following:

(1) "To preserve confidentiality. I am asking this question generally
and omitting reference to my state. I am an assistant attorney general in
my state defending a class action against the Department of Juvenile
Justice (DJJ), which claims that facilities maintained by the department
are grossly understaffed and in dangerous condition (inadequate medical
care, violent assaults, etc.). In my judgment, the allegations of the lawsuit
are largely meritorious. The director of the department, who is appointed
by the Governor, wants to defend the lawsuit vigorously, delaying as long
as possible making changes in the department's facilities. In my judgment
this is the wrong approach. Defending this lawsuit is a waste of money
that could be better spent on improving conditions. Juveniles are exposed
to a substantial risk of physical harm unless the department improves its
facilities quickly. The state is exposed to civil liability if a juvenile is hurt
or killed because of dangerous conditions that the department knew about
but failed to correct. I think the director should be marshalling evidence
and political support to convince the Governor and the legislature that
additional funding is essential to remedy dangerous conditions at DJJ.
What advice can you give me?"

(2) "What should an attorney who works for a state agency do if the
attorney becomes aware of serious improprieties by agency officials? I'm
talking about use of agency equipment and personnel for personal purposes."

(3) "Suppose a lawyer with a federal agency has been involved in
the agency's investigation into the health hazards associated with a certain
product. The attorney is planning on leaving the agency and has made
overtures to a number of firms about the possibility of joining those firms.
One of the firms that the lawyer has contacted represents a company that
markets the product that the lawyer's agency is investigating. What ethical
and legal restrictions apply to the lawyer's possible employment by the
firm?"

Read Model Rules 1.11, 1.12, 1.13, and comments.

The role of the government lawyer and the duty to seek justice

The prevailing ethic of the profession is that lawyers representing private clients
do not have a professional obligation to strive for a fair outcome or to seek
justice in cases they handle. Thus, a private lawyer may assert a defense such
as the statute of limitations even if the defense would bar a claim that the
lawyer knows to be otherwise valid. This position flows from the role of lawyers

in an adversarial system. The adversarial system is process oriented rather than substantively based. The system assumes that so long as the process is fair, the outcome that occurs is fair. Indeed, for lawyers to undertake obligations to produce substantively fair outcomes would itself be procedurally unfair since it would undermine the adversarial process.[87]

To say that lawyers in private practice do not have a professional obligation to seek a fair outcome in cases they handle does not mean that lawyers should be indifferent to fairness. Under the current model of lawyers' professional obligations, lawyers should counsel their clients regarding both legal and nonlegal aspects of their cases, including the fairness of any action that the client intends to take. Model Rule 2.1.[88] The client retains, however, the right to reject the advice of the lawyer, and the lawyer does not bear any responsibility if the client chooses to act in a way that is unfair. Model Rule 1.2(b). Some commentators have questioned this view of lawyers' ethical obligations and have argued that lawyers should, at least in some circumstances, have obligations regarding the fairness of the outcomes of matters in which they are involved.[89]

Do government lawyers have different obligations from lawyers in private practice regarding the fairness of the outcomes of cases they handle?

> The conventional wisdom . . . suggests that zealous representation of clients is inappropriate for government lawyers. Most lawyers and judges who have considered the ethical responsibilities of the government lawyer have assumed that government counsel should temper their advocacy in the interests of "justice." This notion has been expressed by judges both on and off the bench, by the American Bar Association, by former government attorneys, by scholars, and by other commentators generally.[90]

Various justifications have been offered for the view that the government lawyer has an ethical obligation to seek justice. It has been argued that government lawyers represent the public interest rather than particular individuals or agencies. Since the public interest favors just resolution of cases, imposing an obligation on government lawyers to seek just outcomes does nothing more than require government lawyers to carry out the goals of their "clients." Further, since the government usually has substantially greater resources than private litigants, imposing an obligation of fairness on government lawyers helps prevent governmental oppression of private citizens.[91]

---

87. See, e.g., Catherine J. Lanctot, The Duty of Zealous Advocacy and the Ethics of the Federal Government Lawyer: The Three Hardest Questions, 64 S. Cal. L. Rev. 951, 958-964 (1991).

88. See also Restatement (Third) of the Law Governing Lawyers §94(3).

89. See the materials in connection with Problem 1-1.

90. Lanctot, The Duty of Zealous Advocacy and the Ethics of the Federal Government Lawyer, 64 S. Cal. L. Rev. at 955-957.

91. See generally id. at 981-982; Jack B. Weinstein & Gay A. Crosthwait, Some Reflections on Conflicts Between Government Attorneys and Clients, 1 Touro L. Rev. 1, 11-12 (1985).

As noted above, one of the principal arguments in support of imposing a duty to seek fairness or justice on government lawyers is that the government lawyer's client is the public interest rather than an agency or official of the government. Professor Geoffrey Miller has vigorously attacked this view:

> Despite its surface plausibility, the notion that government attorneys represent some transcendental "public interest" is, I believe, incoherent. It is commonplace that there are as many ideas of the "public interest" as there are people who think about the subject. . . . If attorneys could freely sabotage the actions of their agencies out of a subjective sense of the public interest, the result would be a disorganized, inefficient bureaucracy, and a public distrustful of its own government. More fundamentally, the idea that government attorneys serve some higher purpose fails to place the attorney within a structure of democratic government. Although the public interest as a reified concept may not be ascertainable, the Constitution establishes procedures for approximating that ideal through election, appointment, confirmation, and legislation. Nothing systemic empowers government lawyers to substitute their individual conceptions of the good for the priorities and objectives established through these governmental processes. Accordingly, the initial intuition, which suggested that sabotage might be justified as a means of combating a bad policy, seems seriously misguided.[92]

Professor Miller goes on to argue that because an agency lawyer operates within a constitutional system, the agency lawyer's client is the executive branch. This means that the attorney's duties run to the official who has legal authority to decide a matter. Normally, that will be an official within the agency, although circumstances may exist in which the president has delegated authority to decide a matter to a person outside the agency.[93]

What is the position of the Model Rules on the issue? By way of background, Ethical Consideration 7-14 of the Code of Professional Responsibility seemed to accept the position that government lawyers have special responsibilities to justice:

> A government lawyer who has discretionary power relative to litigation should refrain from instituting or continuing litigation that is obviously unfair.

---

92. Geoffrey P. Miller, Government Lawyers' Ethics in a System of Checks and Balances, 54 U. Chi. L. Rev. 1293, 1294-1295 (1987).

93. Id. at 1298. See also Lanctot, The Duty of Zealous Advocacy and the Ethics of the Federal Government Lawyer, 64 S. Cal. L. Rev. at 1012-1017 (also rejecting view that government lawyers have obligation to do justice or to produce fair outcomes, resting conclusion on benefits of adversarial system in addition to constitutional principles). But see Steven K. Berenson, Public Lawyers, Private Values: Can, Should, and Will Government Lawyers Serve the Public Interest?, 41 B.C. L. Rev. 789 (2001) and Bruce A Green, Must Government Lawyers "Seek Justice" in Civil Litigation?, 9 Widener J. Pub. L. 235 (2000) (defending view that government lawyers should serve the public interest or do justice). See also Note, Rethinking the Professional Responsibilities of Federal Agency Lawyers, 115 Harv. L. Rev. 1170 (2002) (developing a new model of professional responsibility for agency lawyers based on critical lawyering theory).

A government lawyer not having such discretionary power who believes there is lack of merit in a controversy submitted to him should so advise his superiors and recommend the avoidance of unfair litigation. A government lawyer in a civil action or administrative proceeding has the responsibility to seek justice and to develop a full and fair record, and he should not use his position or the economic power of the government to harass parties or to bring about unjust settlements or results.

The Model Rules do not include a provision similar to EC 7-14. In Formal Opinion 94-387, the ABA Committee on Ethics and Professional Responsibility concluded that the Model Rules impose no greater obligation on government attorneys than on private lawyers to achieve just outcomes. Comment 18 of the Scope section of the Model Rules does recognize the possibility that "other law" may grant government lawyers greater authority than private counsel over the outcome of litigation:

> Under various legal provisions, including constitutional, statutory and common law, *the responsibilities of government lawyers may include authority concerning legal matters that ordinarily reposes in the client in private client-lawyer relationships.* For example, a lawyer for a government agency may have authority on behalf of the government to decide upon settlement or whether to appeal from an adverse judgment. Such authority in various respects is generally vested in the attorney general and the state's attorney in state government, and their federal counterparts, and the same may be true of other government law officers. Also, lawyers under the supervision of these officers may be authorized to represent several government agencies in intragovernmental legal controversies in circumstances where a private lawyer could not represent multiple private clients. These Rules do not abrogate any such authority. [Emphasis added.]

Unlike EC 7-14, however, comment 18 does not direct government lawyers how to exercise authority that "ordinarily reposes in the client," nor does it include any mention of justice or the public interest. In fact, the 2002 revision of the Model Rules deleted the following sentence from the comment: "They also may have authority to represent the 'public interest' in circumstances where a private lawyer would not be authorized to do so." Nonetheless, a government lawyer possessing such authority presumably could exercise this power in the interests of justice or fairness. As the Model Rules indicate, when this authority exists, it is based on constitutional, statutory, and common law principles.[94]

The Restatement of the Law Governing Lawyers largely agrees with the approach of the Model Rules.[95] Under the Restatement, government lawyers, like private attorneys, do not have a general obligation to represent the public

---

94. Agencies could also develop their own policies to guide lawyers in making decisions that promote justice. For example, as discussed in Problem 2-11 the Department of Justice has developed numerous policies on the exercise of prosecutorial discretion.

95. Restatement (Third) of the Law Governing Lawyers §97.

interest or to promote justice. Instead, government lawyers are required to
follow the directions of their clients, which are normally the agencies by which
they are employed.[96] The Restatement, like the Model Rules, recognizes that
applicable law sometimes grants governmental lawyers (prosecutors, for example) discretionary authority, which they should exercise to advance the governmental and public objectives of the lawyer's client as defined by law.[97]

When do constitutional, statutory, or common law principles provide a
government attorney with "client authority" over a matter? Suppose, for example, that the Justice Department is representing a federal agency in litigation.
Who has the authority to decide what the government's position will be if the
Justice Department and the agency have different views on the issue?[98] The
highest legal official in the federal government is the attorney general. Federal
law provides that the attorney general has the power to control litigation in
which the United States is involved:

> Except as otherwise authorized by law, the conduct of litigation in which
> the United States, an agency, or officer thereof is a party, or is interested, and
> securing evidence therefor, is reserved to officers of the Department of Justice,
> under the direction of the Attorney General.[99]

This authority is exclusive and plenary, so long as the attorney general acts
within the law.[100] Thus, the attorney general has the authority to determine
the legal position of the United States and to authorize settlement, subject
to legal restrictions.[101] If an agency disagrees with the position the Justice
Department plans to take in litigation, the agency can attempt to convince the
Justice Department to change its position. If this is unsuccessful, the agency's
only resort would be to the president, who has authority over the executive
branch, including the attorney general. If the president agrees with the position
of the agency rather than the attorney general, the president can order the
attorney general to adopt the agency's view as the official position of the United
States in litigation. Since the attorney general serves at the pleasure of the
president, the president could discharge an attorney general who refused to
follow the president's policy.[102] In summary, in the federal system, Justice

---

96. Id. cmts. *c, f.*
97. Id. cmt. *g.*
98. See generally James R. Harvey III, Note, Loyalty in Government Litigation:
Department of Justice Representation of Agency Clients, 37 Wm. & Mary L. Rev. 1569
(1996) (discussing various models of Justice Department representation).
99. 28 U.S.C. §516. See also 28 U.S.C. §§518, 519 (argument of cases and supervision
of litigation); 5 U.S.C. §3106 (prohibiting heads of departments from employing counsel
to handle litigation and requiring matters to be referred to the DOJ, unless authorized by
law).
100. See, e.g., Executive Business Media, Inc. v. United States Dept. of Defense, 3
F.3d 759 (4th Cir. 1993).
101. See United States v. Hercules, Inc., 961 F.2d 796 (8th Cir. 1992).
102. See 28 U.S.C. §503.

Department lawyers, acting pursuant to the authority of the attorney general, rather than agency officials, have the right to control litigation, unless authority is specifically given by statute to the agency rather than to the attorney general.[103]

The authority of the attorneys general in the states depends on the particular constitutional, statutory, and common law framework of each state. Some states are much like the federal system, with the attorney general having the power to control litigation involving the state, subject to the authority of the governor. For example, in People ex rel. Deukmejian v. Brown[104] the California Supreme Court held that the attorney general of California did not have authority to seek a writ of mandamus to stop the governor from enforcing an allegedly unconstitutional statute because the authority of the attorney general was subject to that of the governor, who was entrusted with executive power of state. In other states, the attorney general may be the final legal authority. In Feeney v. Commonwealth[105] the Supreme Judicial Court of Massachusetts decided that the attorney general had authority to seek judicial review of a lower court decision holding that a civil service preference for veterans unconstitutionally discriminated against women, despite objections of the agency and the governor. In still other jurisdictions the attorney general is treated much like private counsel whose client is the agency that the attorney general represents pursuant to statute. Thus, in Chun v. Board of Trustees of the Employees' Retirement System[106] the Hawaii Supreme Court held that the state attorney general did not have authority to file an appeal that the attorney general believed was in the state's interest in a class action involving computation of retirement benefits when the retirement system in a divided vote had refused to authorize the appeal.

Suppose an attorney employed by the DOJ, the office of the attorney general of a state, or a federal or state regulatory agency disagrees with the policy position taken by that attorney's superiors. The attorney can, and should, argue for the position that the attorney believes is correct. If the attorney's superiors reject those arguments, the attorney is bound to follow the decision of the superiors since they have the legal authority to make the decision. If the attorney in good conscience cannot accept the decision, the attorney should ask to be relieved from participation in the matter or resign. To the extent that the decision of the superior involves ethical rather than policy issues, the subordinate lawyer may still follow the senior attorney's decision if it is a

---

103. Congress has, however, authorized agencies to handle litigation on their own in a number of situations. See, e.g., FDIC v. Irwin, 727 F. Supp. 1073 (N.D. Tex. 1989), aff'd, 916 F.2d 1051 (5th Cir. 1990) (FDIC has statutory authority under "sue and be sued" clause to litigate without approval of attorney general). See also Neal Devins & Michael Herz, The Uneasy Case for Department of Justice Control of Federal Litigation, 5 U. Pa. J. Const. L. 558 (2003) (supporting the general principle of control by the DOJ but arguing in favor of shifting responsibility for some aspects of litigation away from the DOJ to agency lawyers).

104. 624 P.2d 1206 (Cal. 1981) (en banc).
105. 366 N.E.2d 1262 (Mass. 1977).
106. 952 P.2d 1215 (Haw. 1998).

"reasonable resolution of an arguable question of professional duty." See Model Rule 5.2(b). In some cases, agency attorneys may be justified in taking a matter higher in the government. See Model Rule 1.13 and cmt. 9. In situations that involve illegal conduct by officials, agency attorneys may be justified in revealing the matter beyond the agency. The next section discusses the scope of the government attorney's duty of confidentiality.

Confidentiality of information: government attorneys and wrongdoing by government officials

Earlier we considered the issue of the scope of the lawyer's duty of confidentiality when the client has engaged or intends to engage in wrongdoing. Recall Problem 2-5 (perjury in criminal cases) and Problem 5-2 (fraud by clients in business transactions). As we saw in these problems, lawyers in private practice may not counsel or assist their clients in conduct that is illegal or fraudulent. Lawyers must generally maintain the confidentiality of information that they receive regarding client wrongdoing, but in some situations they have either a duty or discretion to reveal confidential information to prevent or to rectify wrongdoing by their clients. Lawyers employed by organizations have a duty to protect the organization from harm caused to the organization by its constituents. In fulfilling this duty, lawyers generally must reveal information about wrongdoing by constituents to higher authority in the organization. See Model Rule 1.13(b). In addition, in some situations lawyers for organizations have discretion to "report out" confidential information.

Do government lawyers have any special legal or ethical obligations when they learn of wrongdoing by employees of an agency that they represent? The Model Rules do not contain any specific provisions regarding the scope of the duty of confidentiality as applied to government lawyers. Comment 9 to Model Rule 1.13, which deals with an organization as client, states that the rule also applies to governmental organizations. The comment goes on to refer to the complexity of the matter when the client is a governmental entity and to the possible applicability of statutes and regulations. The Restatement takes the position that a government lawyer should follow the principles applicable to entity clients when dealing with wrongdoing by a constituent, unless applicable law provides otherwise.[107]

Statutory or regulatory provisions at the federal, state, or local level, however, regulate the disclosure or release of government information and the scope of the government lawyer's duty of confidentiality.[108] Federal law provides that in most cases the head of an agency or department shall report violations

---

107. Restatement (Third) of the Law Governing Lawyers §97(2) and cmt. *j*.

108. Roger C. Cramton, The Lawyer as Whistleblower: Confidentiality and the Government Lawyer, 5 Geo. J. Legal Ethics 291, 294-295 (1991).

of federal criminal law to the attorney general.[109] In In re Lindsey (Grand Jury Testimony),[110] one of the legal proceedings in connection with the investigation by the Office of Independent Counsel of the Monica Lewinsky matter, the independent counsel subpoenaed Deputy White House Counsel Bruce Lindsey to testify before a federal grand jury. While the court recognized that the attorney-client privilege applies to government entities, the court held that the privilege must yield in the context of criminal investigations:

> The public interest in honest government and in exposing wrongdoing by government officials, as well as the tradition and practice, acknowledged by the Office of the President and by former White House Counsel, of government lawyers reporting evidence of federal criminal offenses whenever such evidence comes to them, lead to the conclusion that a government attorney may not invoke the attorney-client privilege in response to grand jury questions seeking information relating to the possible commission of a federal crime.[111]

In its opinion the court stated that tradition and practice show government lawyers, including White House counsel, have an obligation to report criminal conduct.[112] Initially, the government lawyer should report the matter to the head of the lawyer's agency or department. If the head officer is involved, the attorney may report directly to the attorney general or other appropriate Justice Department official.[113] Such disclosure does not involve a breach of confidentiality if the client of the government attorney is considered to be the executive branch of the government since the agency head and the attorney general are both part of that branch.[114]

Congress has also enacted "whistleblower" legislation to protect government employees who disclose information from retaliation for their disclosures, particularly from losing their jobs. The act makes it unlawful for the government to take a personnel action against a governmental employee who discloses information that the employee "reasonably believes evidences" either (1) "a violation of any law, rule, or regulation" or (2) "gross mismanagement, a gross waste of funds, an abuse of authority, or a substantial and specific danger to public health or safety."[115] The act allows an employee to make disclosure within the government either to a designated official in the agency or to the

---

109. 28 U.S.C. §535(b).

110. 158 F.3d 1263 (D.C. Cir.), cert. denied, 525 U.S. 996 (1998).

111. Id. at 1266.

112. Id. at 1274-1276. See also In re Witness Before Special Grand Jury 2000-2, 288 F.3d 289 (7th Cir. 2002) (in context of federal criminal investigation, attorney-client privilege does not apply to communication between state officer holder and state attorney).

113. See Fed. Bar Assn. Op. 73-1, 32 Fed. Bar J. 71, 73-74 (1973) (cited with approval in Lindsey; federal government lawyer may report "corrupt conduct and other illegal conduct of a criminal character, that is, the willful or knowing disregard of or breach of law, in either the legislative or executive branch" to head of department or agency).

114. Cramton, The Lawyer as Whistleblower, 5 Geo. J. Legal Ethics at 303.

115. Civil Service Reform Act of 1978, as amended by the Whistleblower Protection Act of 1989, 5 U.S.C. §2302(b)(8), (b)(9).

Office of Special Counsel of the Merit Systems Protection Board.[116] Further, the act authorizes employees to disclose information outside the government provided "such disclosure is not specifically prohibited by law and if such information is not specifically required by Executive order to be kept secret in the interest of national defense or the conduct of foreign affairs."[117] Disclosure outside the government could be made to a reporter, congressional staffer, or interest-group representative.[118]

The whistleblower provision does not expressly apply to government attorneys, nor does it expressly exclude government attorneys from its application. While it is possible that courts would construe the act not to override an attorney's duty of confidentiality, given the strong public policies behind the act and the absence of any specific exclusion for attorneys, it is unlikely that they will do so.[119] In an analysis of the act, Professor Roger Cramton argues that the general professional obligation of confidentiality is "overridden by the more specific permission of disclosure afforded by the whistleblower enactments."[120] Professor Cramton finds this to be a desirable result to the extent that a lawyer is reporting government corruption, but he questions the wisdom of the act to the extent it would give protection to lawyers for reporting what are in essence policy disagreements.[121] Note, however, that the whistleblower act does not require government attorneys to disclose confidential information. Assuming the legislation applies to attorneys, the act would simply protect them from various personnel actions, including discharge, if they did blow the whistle.

In Crandon v. State[122] the general counsel for the office of the Kansas banking commissioner was discharged after she reported alleged misconduct by the deputy commissioner to the Federal Deposit Insurance Corporation. She sued, claiming that her discharge violated the Kansas whistleblower statute. The Kansas Supreme Court affirmed summary judgment for the state, however, finding that the general counsel had acted improperly by failing to present the matter to the banking commissioner before reporting it outside the agency.[123] The court also found that the attorney acted recklessly in reporting the matter because she relied on secondhand information without conducting an adequate investigation to verify the allegations of misconduct.[124]

---

116. 5 U.S.C. §2302(b)(8)(B).
117. 5 U.S.C. §2302(b)(8)(A).
118. Cramton, The Lawyer as Whistleblower, 5 Geo. J. Legal Ethics at 308.
119. See Jacobs v. Schiffer, 47 F. Supp. 2d 16 (D.D.C. 1999) (Justice Department attorney allowed to reveal confidential government information to his privately retained counsel to determine whether attorney may have claim under whistleblower statute).
120. Cramton, The Lawyer as Whistleblower, 5 Geo. J. Legal Ethics at 313.
121. Id.
122. 897 P.2d 92 (Kan. 1995), *cert. denied*, 516 U.S. 1113 (1996).
123. Id. at 103.
124. Id. at 103-104.

The "revolving door": movement of lawyers into and out of government practice

The "revolving door" refers to "the phenomenon of individuals who move between government and the private sector and who are often regulators one day, regulated the next, and regulators again the day after."[125] While the term is often used in a derogatory manner, the revolving door offers both public benefits as well as problems. A Harvard Developments Note identifies the following benefits and problems:

Benefits of the Revolving Door

The first and most fundamental benefit of the revolving door is avoidance of the likely alternative: a permanent legal bureaucracy. . . . [The] professionalism of government service is in direct conflict with the model of citizen participation in government. . . .

The revolving door also enhances the quality of official decisionmaking. Policymakers must always strike a careful balance between independence and accountability, and an official will be better able to maintain his independence if he is relatively free to leave the government. . . .

Finally, the revolving door is an important aid to government recruitment of attorneys with talent and imagination. The main advantages that government agencies have to offer young attorneys are training and experience, both of which can be turned into financial gain when and if the attorney chooses to leave the government. . . .

Problems of the Revolving Door

Perhaps the most frequently voiced fear concerning the revolving door is that the government attorney might abuse his position to benefit his future career in the private sector. . . .

A second danger of the revolving door involves one of the principal bases for conflict of interest regulation in all types of legal practice: protection of client confidences. . . . This danger is real, but its significance should not be exaggerated [because of the presence of various statutes that make a wide variety of government information public].

A third problem with the revolving door is the unfair advantage that it might give private parties who are able to hire former agency attorneys having special contacts and expertise. . . .

A fourth abuse attributed to the revolving door is that it encourages favoritism to former government attorneys by their former colleagues in the agency or department in which they worked. . . .

Finally, there is a basic objection to the fact that the revolving door continually permits the fundamental impropriety of "switching sides."[126]

---

125. Developments in the Law—Conflicts of Interest in the Legal Profession, 94 Harv. L. Rev. 1244, 1428 (1981).
126. Id. at 1428-1433.

Regulation of the revolving door occurs through a complex array of rules of ethics, statutes, and regulations. Model Rule 1.11 deals with ethical limitations on successive governmental and private employment. (See also Model Rule 1.12 dealing with former judges and third party neutrals.) Rules 1.11(a), (b), and (c) apply to movement from government service into private practice, while Rule 1.11(d) applies to movement from private practice to government service. Rule 1.11(d) also applies when a lawyer moves from one government agency to another. See comment 5.

Rule 1.11(a) imposes two limitations on former government lawyers. First, a former government lawyer may not use confidential information to the disadvantage of the former government client or reveal such information unless permitted by the rules of professional conduct. Model Rules 1.11(a)(1) and 1.9(c). Rule 1.11(a)(1) protects the government against misuse of information by former government lawyers. In addition, Rule 1.11(c) protects other people from having former government lawyers use confidential government information against them when the lawyer leaves government service. Second, a former government lawyer may not "represent a client in connection with a matter in which the lawyer participated personally and substantially as a public officer or employee, unless the appropriate government agency gives its informed consent, confirmed in writing, to the representation." Model Rule 1.11(a)(2). An example of the application of Rule 1.11(a) is In re Sofaer,[127] where the respondent received an informal admonition for undertaking representation of the government of Libya in connection with various legal matters arising from the 1988 bombing of Pan American Flight 103 over Lockerbie, Scotland, after the respondent, while serving as legal advisor to the State Department, took part personally and substantially in the government's investigation of the bombing and in related diplomatic and legal activities.

Several aspects of the scope and limitations of Rule 1.11 are particularly significant. First, the rule bars representation by former government lawyers of any clients as to matters in which the attorney was personally and substantially involved while in government employment. It is not necessary that the former government client be involved in the matter or have an adverse interest to the lawyer's private client. While the rule protects the government from disloyalty and misuse of confidential information, it has a broader goal. The rule prevents former government lawyers from "exploiting public office for the advantage of another client." Model Rule 1.11, cmt. 3.[128]

Second, Rule 1.11(a)(2) restricts the activities of a former government lawyer only as to a "matter" in which the lawyer participated personally and substantially. Under Rule 1.11(e), a matter generally is limited to a proceeding involving specific parties, as distinguished from rulemaking and issues of general policy, although conflict-of-interest rules of an agency may define a matter

127. 728 A.2d 625 (D.C. 1999), *cert. denied*, 529 U.S. 1053 (2000).
128. For a discussion of the policies behind the rule, see ABA Comm. on Ethics and Prof. Resp., Formal Op. 97-409.

more broadly.[129] Thus, a former agency lawyer who was directly involved in drafting regulations for a governmental agency is not precluded from advising a private client about those regulations after leaving government service, unless the agency's conflict-of-interest rules provide otherwise.[130]

Third, Rule 1.11(a)(2) provides that with the informed consent of the agency confirmed in writing, a former government lawyer may handle a matter in which the lawyer was personally and substantially involved. If the agency refuses to consent, the lawyer is personally disqualified from handling the matter, but other members of the lawyer's new firm are not disqualified from handling the matter if the disqualified lawyer is timely screened from any participation in the matter, receives no part of the fee from the matter, and the agency receives notice so that it can monitor compliance with the rule. Model Rule 1.11(b).[131] Note that the Model Rules have different provisions on screening of former government lawyers and screening when private lawyers switch firms. See Problem 3-6. Comment 4 to Model Rule 1.11 explains that the rules allow screening in the government context "to prevent the disqualification rule from imposing too severe a deterrent against entering public service." Section 133 of the Restatement follows Rule 1.11 in most material respects.

Professor Monroe Freedman has criticized the screening and waiver provisions of Rule 1.11(a) on three grounds. First, "no workable standards for the screening have ever been suggested." Second, "it is virtually impossible to police violations of screening once a waiver has been given." Third, "waiver by a government agency compounds the initial conflict of interest. Agency lawyers who are called upon to grant or deny a waiver on behalf of a former colleague's law firm have a substantial personal incentive to be generous in granting the waiver, because they will themselves be making similar requests within a short time when they leave government service." Freedman also argues that the rationale for the provision—the government's need to be able to attract competent lawyers—is totally speculative.[132]

Rule 1.11 applies to all government lawyers, whether federal, state, or local. The rule must be read, however, in conjunction with federal and state statutory and regulatory provisions. This body of law imposes restrictions on former government lawyers in addition to those found in Rule 1.11. Unlike

129. At one time rules of the Environmental Protection Agency defined "matter" to include participation in rulemaking, but that restriction has been repealed. See 50 Fed. Reg 39,622-01 (1985).

130. See ABA Comm. on Ethics and Prof. Resp., Formal Op. 97-409 (former agency attorney may represent private party in challenge to agency rules even though lawyer was personally involved in development and implementation of those rules, unless lawyer has confidential information under Rule 1.9(c); even if lawyer is personally disqualified because of possession of confidential information, firm is not if it implements appropriate screening procedures pursuant to Rule 1.11).

131. See Armstrong v. McAlpin, 625 F.2d 433 (2d Cir. 1980) (en banc), (denying motion to disqualify firm when former government lawyer who joined firm had been screened from participation in matter) *vacated on other grounds,* 449 U.S. 1106 (1981).

132. Monroe H. Freedman, Understanding Lawyers' Ethics 208-209 (1990).

Rule 1.11, the statutory provisions are not limited to lawyers but apply to other government officials and employees. Moreover, violation of these statutory provisions may subject government officials to criminal penalties. State statutes and regulations dealing with former governmental employees vary considerably, so attorneys leaving state governmental employment must consult these provisions. For federal governmental employees, the most important provision is 18 U.S.C. §207. That statute contains two provisions somewhat similar to Rule 1.11, although these provisions are narrower in scope than the rule. Section (a)(1) provides as follows:

> (a) Restrictions on all officers and employees of the executive branch and certain other agencies.—
> (1) Permanent restrictions on representation on particular matters.—Any person who is an officer or employee (including any special Government employee) of the executive branch of the United States (including any independent agency of the United States), or of the District of Columbia, and who, after the termination of his or her service or employment with the United States or the District of Columbia, knowingly makes, with the intent to influence, any communication to or appearance before any officer or employee of any department, agency, court, or court-martial of the United States or the District of Columbia, on behalf of any other person (except the United States or the District of Columbia) in connection with a particular matter—
> (A) in which the United States or the District of Columbia is a party or has a direct and substantial interest,
> (B) in which the person participated personally and substantially as such officer or employee, and
> (C) which involved a specific party or specific parties at the time of such participation, shall be punished as provided in section 216 of this title.

The section is narrower than Rule 1.11(a) in at least two respects. First, it applies only to communications or appearances before the federal government or the District of Columbia, while Rule 1.11 applies to any private representation. Second, the statute applies only if the United States or the District of Columbia is a party or has a direct or substantial interest; Rule 1.11 applies even if the government is not directly involved.

Federal statute 18 U.S.C. §207(a)(2) is similar to section (a)(1) except that it applies only to matters that the former employee reasonably should know were "under his or her official responsibility" during the one-year period before termination of employment. In this case, the restriction is effective for two years rather than permanently.

Remaining subsections of 18 U.S.C. §207 are quite different in scope from Rule 1.11. These sections establish one-year "cooling off" periods for certain executive and legislative officials and employees, prohibiting various appearances or contacts. For example, certain former employees of the executive branch and of independent federal agencies are prohibited for one year from making any appearances or communications with employees of their former departments or agencies with an intention to influence a decision.[133] Similarly, any employee of a senator or representative is prohibited for one year after termination of employment from communicating with the senator or representative for whom the former employee worked or with any employee of that senator or representative with the intent to influence an official decision.[134]

Model Rule 1.11(d) deals with lawyers currently serving as government employees. The rule provides that government lawyers are subject to the concurrent and former conflict rules, Model Rules 1.7 and 1.9. Model Rule 1.11(d)(1). The rule prohibits a government lawyer from participating "in a matter in which the lawyer participated personally and substantially while in private practice or nongovernmental employment, unless the appropriate government agency gives its informed consent, confirmed in writing." Model Rule 1.11(d)(2)(i). This rule is the converse of Rule 1.11(a)(2), which deals with departure from government service. Finally, the rule imposes limitations on a government lawyer negotiating for private employment. Model Rule 1.11(d)(2)(ii). Comment 2 provides that disqualification under Rule 1.11(d) is personal to the lawyer and is not imputed to other government employees, even if the agency does not screen the disqualified government lawyer. The comment explains that it may pose special problems to a government agency to institute screening measures but warns that "ordinarily it will be prudent to screen such lawyers."

In addition to Model Rule 1.11, lawyers who come to work for the federal government are subject to a number of statutory provisions and regulations governing their conduct.[135] Each state will have its own statutory and regulatory scheme for government attorneys.[136]

The preceding material has focused on ethical problems facing lawyers employed by the government. A related area involves ethical issues facing lawyers who are elected to serve in state legislatures. In most states, service in the state legislature is a part-time job. As a result lawyer-legislators must deal with a variety of conflicts of interest between their official duties and their private interests.[137]

---

133. 18 U.S.C. §207(c).

134. 18 U.S.C. §207(e)(2).

135. See generally 5 C.F.R. pt. 2600, subch. B et seq. (Government Ethics). See Crandon v. United States, 494 U.S. 152 (1990) (separation payment by company to official leaving company to accept government position did not violate statutory provision prohibiting dual compensation for government employees). For a critical discussion see Kathleen Clark, Do We Have Enough Ethics in Government Yet?: An Answer from Fiduciary Theory, 1996 U. Ill. L. Rev. 57.

136. For a critical evaluation of such restrictions, see W. J. Michael Cody & Richardson R. Lynn, Honest Government: An Ethics Guide for Public Service (1992).

137. See George F. Carpinello, Should Practicing Lawyers Be Legislators? 41 Hastings L.J. 87 (1989); Dennis M. Henry, Commentary, Lawyer-Legislator Conflicts of Interest, 17 J. Legal Prof. 261 (1992); Thomas M. Kellenberg, When Lawyers Become Legislators: An Essay and a Proposal, 76 Marq. L. Rev. 343 (1993).

——————————————— **Problem 6-4** ———————————————

Public Interest Practice

a.   You are an attorney for a public interest law firm, Protecting the Environment Public Interest Law Firm, Inc. (PEPILF). Your firm has agreed to represent Norton Eckstein, Nancy Knowles, and Juan Hernandez in a lawsuit against the Tomkins Leather Co., alleging that Tomkins violated federal and state law by releasing toxic material into the water system that serves the plaintiffs' neighborhood. You filed the case as a class action with Eckstein, Knowles, and Hernandez as the named plaintiffs, but you have not yet filed a motion for class certification. Before undertaking representation you explained the nature of a class action to the named plaintiffs and their responsibilities as class representatives. You also explained to them that any settlement of a class action is subject to court approval. Before undertaking representation, you gave the plaintiffs a copy of the policies of your law firm, one of which is as follows: "It is the general policy of PEPILF to recommend rejection of any settlement proposal that does not include substantial reduction of the environmental hazard that is the subject of the lawsuit. In particular, PEPILF will generally recommend rejection and oppose in fairness hearings any settlement that provides for monetary compensation without substantial relief of the environmental hazard at issue."

Before answering the complaint, lawyers for Tomkins Leather have asked to meet with you and have offered to settle the case on very generous terms. Tomkins will pay each of the named plaintiffs an amount equal to the decline in the fair market value of their property based on expert appraisals. Tomkins is willing to allow you to select the expert so long as it retains the right to veto any expert that it thinks may not be qualified or that has a conflict of interest. In addition, Tomkins will pay each of the named plaintiffs an amount to reflect their loss of enjoyment of their property. Tomkins asks you to come up with a figure for this amount. Finally, Tomkins will pay the plaintiffs' expenses including your legal fees. In exchange, Tomkins wants an agreement by the plaintiffs not to seek class certification, to dismiss the lawsuit with prejudice, and to enter into confidentiality agreements.

What are your ethical obligations in responding to this settlement offer?

b.   You are a member of a public interest law firm dealing with gay and lesbian issues. The firm has decided that it would like to include in its engagement agreement provisions that protect the firm to the maximum extent possible in dealing with conflicts between desires of individual clients and the goals of the firm. What provisions would you suggest including?

———

Read Model Rules 1.2, 2.1, and comments.

The history and meaning of public interest law

Oliver A. Houck, With Charity for All
93 Yale L.J. 1415, 1439-1443 (1984)

The concept of providing disadvantaged people with legal representation—as opposed to hot meals, hospital care, and a variety of other charitable services—arose in this country at least as early as 1876, when the German Society of New York established a legal aid office in New York City to assist newly arrived immigrants. By 1917, forty-one cities had established legal aid programs for the poor, and the numbers have risen and fallen since then with the revenue available from local governments, community drives, and the private bar. In the early 1960s, the Federal Office of Economic Opportunity began funding independent legal services; the funding grew to over $71 million in the next five years, and in 1974, Congress created the independent Legal Services Corporation. The original legal aid programs dealt with arbitrary landlords, impounded property, and the day-to-day problems of the poor, as they walked in the door, in the after-the-injury manner of a traditional law practice. The legal services programs, representing the same poverty-level clients, began to draw some conclusions about the causes of these problems from their recurring problems and began to seek larger remedies: They not only asked for the apartment back, they wanted to change the rules for eviction. In arriving at this law reform approach, which came to be known as "impact litigation," they were not alone.

A second root of public interest practice grew from the American Civil Liberties Union (ACLU), created in 1916 as the American Union Against Militarism to protect the rights of pacifists when much of America was calling for war. Led from this beginning into the defense of labor organizers and deportees, the organization broadened its name and scope to include the rights of agnostics, Nazis, and an almost unlimited spectrum of political and social minorities. With this growth came a change in style. A handful of prestigious, volunteer attorneys in the early years, filing selective briefs of amicus curiae, became by 1974 an organization of 275,000 members with 34 full-time lawyers in local offices and another 18 staff attorneys at national headquarters. These numbers were multiplied through volunteer counsel in every state, enlisted for specific cases on a low-fee and even no-fee basis. With this growth came a shift in tactics, from amicus to direct representation, and to the offense. Of the eighteen attorneys at ACLU headquarters in 1974, fourteen were addressing not the problems of individual clients but rather, in more general actions, the rights of juveniles, treatment of prisoners, and military justice. The ACLU was catching the same "impact litigation" breeze.

The National Association for the Advancement of Colored People (NAACP), founded in 1909, entered litigation on behalf of black Americans as early as 1914 and has been involved in suits against individual acts of discrimination ever since. In 1930, however, having received a major foundation grant, the NAACP launched a long-term litigation strategy to eliminate discrimination in housing, education, and employment. Its 1934 Annual Report described the strategy as follows: "It should be made clear that the campaign is a carefully planned one to secure decisions, rulings, and public opinion on the broad principle instead of being devoted to merely miscellaneous cases." In 1939, this campaign was assumed by the newly-created NAACP Legal Defense and Educational Fund (NAACP/LDF) which ran a string of successes through *Brown v. Board of Education* in 1954. By 1975, NAACP/LDF maintained a staff of twenty-five attorneys and a network of volunteer cooperating lawyers in every state. The caseload was enormous, and bottomed heavily on the defense of individuals as demonstrators, draft resistors, freedom riders, and a dozen similar postures, defending the accused. Concurrently, however, the NAACP/LDF was mounting initiatives to eliminate the death penalty, de facto segregation, voting inequalities, and discrimination in the real estate market. It, too, was in the business of law reform.

These three large movements in poverty, civil liberties, and civil rights practice changed more than the law of their respective fields. As they evolved, particularly into the 1960s, these organizations changed the way lawyers approached the law. Their lawyers had clients and the clients were injured, but so also was a larger sense of justice which is as difficult to define precisely as it would be to deny. Most importantly, they did not simply seek compensation for their clients; increasingly they sought to change the law.

There are no "three sources" of anything, neither the Fall of the Roman Empire nor the rise of public interest law. The strategy and success of these three organizations were propelled by other movements of the times, each contributing to the character of public interest law. Prominent among them was the attitude of the organized bar. As recently as 1951, the President of the American Bar Association was writing that the greatest threat to America, apart from Communism, was "the propaganda campaign for a federal subsidy to finance a nation-wide plan for legal aid and low-cost legal service." Within the next twenty years, the Bar came to full support not only of federal assistance to legal aid programs, but also to Bar involvement in a far broader range of unrepresented or underrepresented interests. The Lawyer's Committee for Civil Rights Under Law was formed, and sent hundreds of lawyers into the South to come up against "the system" and to come away dedicated to changing the system through the use of law.

At the same time, thousands of middle-class urban residents, solid citizens who led lives no closer to protest than the headlines of their evening newspapers, were suddenly confronting intractable government programs like the federal Interstate Highway System and the destruction, as they saw it, of downtown Chicago, Boston, Baltimore, New York, Atlanta, San Francisco, San Antonio, New Orleans, Nashville, Memphis, Washington . . . and were taking their cases to court. Moreover, for the first time, under the impetus of the Administrative Procedure Act, the courts were overcoming their traditional difficulties with sovereign immunity, standing, law to apply, ripeness, mootness and private rights of action . . . and listening. . . . Scientist Rachel Carson published

Silent Spring. Consumer advocate Ralph Nader published *Unsafe at Any Speed.* Americans read them. Foundations read them, and increased their funding not only for the ACLU and NAACP's law programs but for new ones directed to consumer protection and the environment. The Environmental Defense Fund was formed in 1968. The Center for Law and Social Policy, a catalyst for public interest law in Washington, D.C., began in 1969.[138]

What is *public interest law?* The term is not easy to define, but some distinctions may be helpful in clarifying the concept. First, public interest law is not the same as *pro bono* representation. Pro bono cases normally involve the representation of individuals in typical legal problems, such as divorce or landlord/tenant. Such cases usually do not involve broad issues of public interest, other than the public interest in the fair and just resolution of all disputes. This is not to say that pro bono cases cannot involve public interest issues, only that the terms *pro bono* and *public interest law* are not coextensive. Pro bono and public interest representation differ in another respect. Lawyers typically provide pro bono representation without compensation. Indeed, the term *pro bono* has come to mean without charge, although the Latin phrase *pro bono publico* means for the public good. In public interest cases, lawyers usually seek payment of their fees from the opposing party pursuant to a fee-shifting statute.

Public interest law is not linked to any particular area of substantive law, to any specific form of litigation, or with any political movement. For example, public interest law is not limited to consumer cases; public interest issues range across the entire spectrum of law, from voting rights to employment discrimination. While it is certainly true that many public interest cases involve class actions or other "big" litigation, that is not always the case. A lawsuit on behalf of an individual that seeks to establish important principles of law qualifies as a public interest case. While the public interest law movement originally had strong liberal leanings, conservatives responded in the 1970s by establishing their own public interest law organizations. Today it would be inaccurate to characterize public interest law as either liberal or conservative.[139]

Professor Robert Rabin argues that the key factor in distinguishing public interest practice from ordinary private practice is the criteria lawyers use to select cases. In public interest practice, lawyers select cases because they are "socially desirable." By contrast, in traditional private practice, cases are chosen on the basis of the market—the demand for legal services and the availability of lawyers to provide those services.[140]

138. On the history of public interest law, see also Robert L. Rabin, Lawyers for Social Change: Perspectives on Public Interest Law, 28 Stan. L. Rev. 207 (1976).

139. See Houck, With Charity for All, 93 Yale L.J. at 1454-1514.

140. Rabin, Lawyers for Social Change, 28 Stan. L. Rev. at 209 n.8. For a description of the realities of public interest practice, see Anita P. Arriola & Sidney M. Wolinsky, Public Interest Practice in Practice: The Law and Reality, 34 Hastings L.J. 1207 (1983); Debra S. Katz & Lynne Bernabei, Practicing Public Interest Law in a Private Public Interest Law Firm: The Ideal Setting to Challenge the Power, 96 W. Va. L. Rev. 293 (1993/1994);

A more detailed definition of public interest law comes from the Internal Revenue Service, which has issued a Revenue Procedure that defines when a public interest law firm qualifies for tax-exempt treatment.[141] The Revenue Procedure outlines general requirements that a public interest law firm must satisfy (section 3) and then establishes specific requirements regarding attorney fees (sections 4, 5). Under IRS rules, the basic requirement that a public interest law firm must meet to qualify for tax-exempt status is that the firm must engage in "representation of a broad public interest rather than a private interest."

> Litigation will be considered to be in representation of a broad public interest if it is designed to present a position on behalf of the public at large on matters of public interest. Typical of such litigation may be class actions in which the resolution of the dispute is in the public interest; suits for injunction against action by government or private interests broadly affecting the public; similar representation before administrative boards and agencies; test suits where the private interest is small; and the like.[142]

By contrast, the IRS's guidelines characterize private representation as "actions between private persons where the financial interests at stake would warrant representation from private legal sources."[143] (A public interest law firm may, however, participate as amicus curiae in private litigation even though it would be precluded from direct representation because of the financial interests at stake.)[144]

To ensure that public interest law firms are operated in the public interest, the guidelines establish the following requirement for organizational policies:

> The policies and programs of the organization (including compensation arrangements) are the responsibility of a board or committee representative of the public interest, which is not controlled by employees or persons who litigate on behalf of the organization nor by any organization that is not itself an organization described in section 501(c)(3) of the Code.[145]

Patricia M. Wald, Whose Public Interest Is It Anyway? Advice for Altruistic Young Lawyers, 47 Me. L. Rev. 3 (1995). See also Nan Aron, Liberty and Justice for All: Public Interest Law in the 1980s and Beyond (1989). For a discussion of the current state of public interest law, see David R. Esquivel, Note, The Identity Crisis in Public Interest Law, 46 Duke L.J. 327 (1996). For a defense on moral grounds against various criticisms of public interest practice, see David Luban, Lawyers and Justice 293-391 (1988).

141. Rev. Proc. 92-59, 1992-2 C.B. 411.
142. Id. §3.01.
143. Id. §3.02.
144. Id.
145. Id. §3.05.

The IRS rules also provide that a public interest law firm may not engage in political campaigns and "no substantial part of its activities may consist of carrying on propaganda or otherwise attempting to influence legislation."[146]

Under IRS rules a public interest law firm may accept reimbursement from clients or opposing parties for direct out-of-pocket expenses incurred in litigation.[147] Public interest law firms may charge fees to their clients (although they rarely do so) only if the fee does not exceed the "actual cost" incurred in such case, including salaries, overhead, and other costs fairly attributable to the case.[148] Public interest law firms may also receive fees awarded or approved by a court or administrative body, provided such fees do not exceed 50 percent of the total operating cost of the organization's legal functions.[149]

Ethical problems facing public interest lawyers

The most difficult ethical problems facing public interest lawyers involve conflicts of interest. Public interest representation takes several forms: representation of an individual whose claim reflects a broader public interest, representation of a group of individuals who are not formally organized but who have a common interest in pursuing a public interest claim, representation of an entity that wishes to pursue a public interest claim, or representation of a class of plaintiffs.[150] Each of these forms of representation poses conflict-of-interest issues.[151]

For example, if a public interest law firm is representing an individual plaintiff, a conflict between the policies of the public interest firm and the desires of the client can develop. Such conflicts could arise at any stage of the case, but they become particularly acute when the opposing party offers a settlement. A defendant may find it advantageous to settle an individual claim to avoid adverse publicity, to reduce the possibility of being subject to an avalanche of similar suits, or to avoid an adverse precedent. Because of such factors, defendants are often willing to pay a premium to settle an individual case. In addition, in connection with such settlements, defendants typically demand confidentiality agreements. Confidentiality agreements take various forms, from private agreements to court orders sealing discovery and other

---

146. Id. §3.09.

147. Id. §3.10.

148. Id. §5.01.

149. Id. §§4.01, 4.05. See generally Nicole T. Chapin, Note, Regulation of Public Interest Law Firms by the IRS and the Bar: Making It Hard to Serve the Public Good, 7 Geo. J. Legal Ethics 437 (1993).

150. See Stephen Ellmann, Client-Centeredness Multiplied: Individual Autonomy and Collective Mobilization in Public Interest Lawyers' Representation of Groups, 78 Va. L. Rev. 1103 (1992).

151. See Ann Southworth, Collective Representation for the Disadvantaged: Variations in Problems of Accountability, 67 Fordham L. Rev. 2449 (1999) (based on interviews with public interest lawyers, conflicts of interest are less difficult when lawyers represent organizations with established decisionmaking procedures).

records in a case.[152] A client may be willing to settle a public interest case for a payment that seems advantageous to the client, subject to confidentiality provisions, but the public interest lawyer may believe that the settlement, particularly its confidentiality provisions, is not in the public interest. We have discussed some of the legal and ethical restrictions on confidentiality agreements and court orders sealing records in connection with Problem 4-5 on negotiation.

How should public interest lawyers deal with such conflicts? Under a traditional client-lawyer model, the lawyer could advise the client of the advantages and disadvantages of the settlement, including any moral, economic, social, or political factors. See Model Rule 2.1. The right to accept or reject the settlement, however, rests with the client. Model Rule 1.2(a). If the client decides to accept a settlement offer against the lawyer's advice, the lawyer has a choice: carry out the client's wishes or move to withdraw. Under the Model Rules a lawyer may withdraw if "withdrawal can be accomplished without material adverse effect on the interests of the client," Model Rule 1.16(b)(1), or if "the client insists upon taking action that the lawyer considers repugnant or with which the lawyer has a fundamental disagreement," Model Rule 1.16(b)(4). Neither option is attractive to the public interest lawyer. If the lawyer carries out the client's wishes, the lawyer is acting contrary to the policies of his firm and to his own strongly held views. Further, the lawyer's actions could conceivably jeopardize the tax-exempt status of the organization. Withdrawal is not a satisfactory solution, either. First, a court will often deny a motion to withdraw either because of the stage of the case, because substitute counsel is not available, or because the client has the right to decide whether to accept or reject a settlement. Second, withdrawal means that the firm has devoted its limited resources to the case without producing results that advance its goals.[153]

One technique that public interest law firms can consider to deal with such potential conflicts is the use of *limited engagement agreements*. Under such an engagement the client agrees to be bound by the policies of the organization in the conduct and settlement of the litigation, in exchange for the organization's agreement to provide legal representation without charge to the client. A limited engagement agreement could specify that the client agrees not to accept any settlement with confidentiality provisions that would keep from disclosure evidence of danger of substantial physical harm to members of the public.[154] The Model Rules authorize the use of limited engagement agreements as long as the agreement is "reasonable under the circumstances and the client gives informed consent." Model Rule 1.2(c). Comment 6 approves engagement agreements that limit the means used to carry out the representation: "[T]he terms upon which representation is undertaken may exclude specific means

152. See generally Richard Zitrin & Carol M. Langford, The Moral Compass of the American Lawyer ch. 9 (1999).

153. See Chapin, Note, Regulation of Public Interest Law Firms by the IRS and the Bar, 7 Geo. J. Legal Ethics at 459-460.

154. See Zitrin & Langford, The Moral Compass of the American Lawyer at 207 (suggesting such a provision).

that might otherwise be used to accomplish the client's objectives. Such limitations may exclude actions that the client thinks are too costly or that the lawyer regards as repugnant or imprudent."[155]

The Restatement of the Law Governing Lawyers also generally approves limited engagement agreements.[156] One commentator has argued that the rules of ethics do not provide adequate guidance for public interest lawyers and has called on the bar to draft a specific rule dealing with their problems.[157]

When a public interest case is brought as a class action, conflicts of interest can become even more difficult, particularly if the class involves minors or individuals with disabilities.[158] In class actions, conflicts can develop not only between the wishes of the clients and the policies of the public interest firm, but between groups of clients. David Luban gives the following example:

> In one of its class-action suits . . . Public Interest Law Center attempted to force the construction of a housing project in a racially mixed neighborhood that already had one project. The residents of that development opposed the action because they feared (correctly) that the second project would "tip" the neighborhood and turn it into a ghetto. The center purported to be representing the interests of public housing residents, but in formulating its strategy it chose to disregard the preferences of some of these residents. What gave the lawyers the right to act in opposition to the wishes of some of the very people whose interests they claim to represent? What if those people had been in the majority? This is the problem of class conflicts in class actions. It arises often.[159]

How class counsel should deal with class conflicts is controversial. Professor Luban rejects the claim that lawyers should simply attempt to determine the wishes of the class members because it is often impractical to identify their desires and because class members may not fully represent the interests of the entire class, particularly when the case can affect future generations. Instead, he argues that lawyers should be as "responsibly representative of the client class as a whole" as it is possible to be.[160] Other scholars argue that public

---

155. See Marshall J. Breger, Accountability and the Adjudication of the Public Interest, 8 Harv. J.L. & Pub. Poly. 349, 350-351 (1985) (questioning validity of limited engagement agreements). But see Joel S. Newman, Gagging on the Public Interest, 4 Geo. J. Legal Ethics 371 (1990) (arguing that provisions in engagement agreements in which clients of public interest lawyers agree not to settle cases subject to confidentiality agreements should be valid).

156. See Restatement (Third) of the Law Governing Lawyers §19, cmt. c (quoted in Problem 3-2).

157. Chapin, Note, Regulation of Public Interest Law Firms by the IRS and the Bar, 7 Geo. J. Legal Ethics at 467-471.

158. See, e.g., Martha Matthews, Ten Thousand Tiny Clients: The Ethical Duty of Representation in Children's Class-Action Cases, 64 Fordham L. Rev. 1435 (1996).

159. Luban, Lawyers and Justice at 341.

160. Id. at 356. For further treatment of the ethical and legal problems facing lawyers in class actions, see Deborah L. Rhode, Class Conflicts in Class Actions, 34 Stan. L. Rev. 1183 (1982). See also William B. Rubenstein, Divided We Litigate: Addressing Disputes Among Group Members and Lawyers in Civil Rights Campaigns, 106 Yale L.J. 1623

interest lawyers have gone too far in asserting their views of the public interest in opposition to their clients' interests.[161] Scholars developing *critical lawyering theory* and ideas of *progressive lawyering* have called on lawyers to help to empower rather than to control their clients.[162] Problems of lawyer control of clients are not unique to public interest practice.[163]

Recovery of legal fees can also pose ethical problems in public interest representation. In Evans v. Jeff D.[164] the Supreme Court ruled that statutes providing for recovery of attorney fees did not confer any rights on attorneys; clients, therefore, had the right to waive recovery of legal fees without the consent of their attorneys. As a result of this decision, a potential conflict exists between public interest lawyers and their clients when defendants make settlement proposals that seek waiver of fees. A carefully drafted engagement agreement that addresses the client's obligation to pay the fees of the public interest lawyer out of any settlement that the plaintiff receives is one way of dealing with this problem. (*Evans* held that the plaintiff could agree to waive its claim to fees against the defendant, but the plaintiff's obligation to pay fees to the plaintiff's lawyer is a matter of contract between them.)[165] Such a provision would not be helpful, however, when the plaintiff seeks injunctive rather than monetary relief.

In some situations, public interest lawyers may conclude that it is necessary for them to reach out to educate and even to enlist clients to bring litigation. The Supreme Court has given a measure of constitutional protection to such efforts. Recall In re Primus, discussed in connection with Problem 4-7. The precise contours of that protection, however, are uncertain.

(1997) (examining individualist, democratic, and expertise models of decision making in litigation affecting groups).

161. See Derrick A. Bell, Jr., Serving Two Masters: Integration Ideals and Client Interests in School Desegregation Litigation, 85 Yale L.J. 470 (1976) (questioning propriety of civil rights lawyers' commitment to integration when many of their clients favored educational improvement). See also William B. Rubenstein, Divided We Litigate: Addressing Disputes Among Group Members and Lawyers in Civil Rights Campaigns, 106 Yale L.J. 1623 (1997) (considering ways in which traditional individualistic method of litigation could be modified to take into account democratic values and to provide greater emphasis on expertise).

162. See, e.g, Gerald P. Lopez, Rebellious Lawyering: One Chicano's Vision of Progressive Law Practice (1992); Lucie E. White, To Learn and Teach: Lessons from Driefontein on Lawyering and Power, 1988 Wis. L. Rev. 699. For a criticism of this approach, see Ann Southworth, Taking the Lawyer out of Progressive Lawyering, 46 Stan. L. Rev. 213 (1993) (reviewing Lopez, above).

163. See Douglas E. Rosenthal, Lawyer and Client: Who's in Charge? (1974).

164. 475 U.S. 717 (1986).

165. For a discussion of these fee issues, see Stephen Yelenosky & Charles Silver, A Model Retainer Agreement for Legal Services Programs: Mandatory Attorney Fee Provisions, 28 Clearinghouse Rev. 114 (1994).

Finding public interest jobs

Many law students would love to have the opportunity to confront ethical problems in public interest practice, but have found it difficult to obtain information about such opportunities. A Web site started by two Harvard Law students in 2002 provides information about opportunities for public interest practice in the private sector.[166]

---

166. www.just-advocates.com (visited Oct. 1, 2003).

Chapter 7

Special Ethical Problems of Law Firms

In previous chapters we have focused on ethical problems lawyers face in specific areas of practice. Regardless of the type of practice, most lawyers work in private law firms. The law firm method of organization, however, creates a number of ethical problems. In this chapter we examine issues involving supervision of lawyers and nonlawyers, departures of lawyers from firms, expansion of law firms beyond legal services into ancillary businesses, and quality of life for lawyers practicing in firms.

A. Regulation Within Firms

Problem 7-1

The Duty to Supervise

a. At a recent partnership retreat, members of your firm attended a continuing legal education program in which the presenter warned members of the firm of their obligation to supervise paralegals, office personnel, investigators, associates, and even other partners. The presentation included citations to cases in which lawyers had been disciplined or sanctioned for failure to supervise.[1] With regard to nonlawyers, the presenter recommended that at a minimum the firm prepare a memorandum that all nonlawyers are required to read and sign when they are hired, providing them with information about their obligations as nonlawyers working in a law firm. You have been asked to prepare a draft of this memorandum. The presenter also advised the firm to have in place proce-

---

1. See In re Anonymous Member of the S.C. Bar, 552 S.E.2d 10 (S.C. 2001) (discussing responsibilities of supervisory lawyers regarding discovery).

dures for supervision of lawyers, including both senior partners as well as associates. You have been asked to make recommendations for the types of procedures that would be appropriate for supervision of lawyers, including senior lawyers.

b.   Another issue that the firm is considering is whether to adopt a policy on romantic relationships between members of the firm and individual clients, representatives of entity clients, other members of the firm, and nonlawyer members of the firm. What policy if any would you recommend? Why?

Read Model Rules 5.1, 5.2, 5.3, and comments.

Supervisory principles

The Model Rules set forth three principles that apply to supervision of partners, associates, and nonlawyers. First, partners in a firm (or those with "comparable managerial authority") have a duty to make reasonable efforts to ensure that the firm has in place "measures giving reasonable assurance" that the conduct of other partners, associates, and nonlawyers employed or retained by the firm conforms to the rules of professional conduct. See Model Rules 5.1(a), 5.3(a). Second, a lawyer having direct supervisory responsibility over another lawyer or a nonlawyer has a duty to use reasonable efforts to ensure that the conduct of the other lawyer or nonlawyer conforms to the rules of professional conduct. Model Rules 5.1(b), 5.3(b). Finally, a lawyer is subject to discipline for the conduct of another lawyer or a nonlawyer if the lawyer (1) orders the lawyer or nonlawyer to engage in conduct that violates the rules of professional conduct or with knowledge ratifies such conduct, or (2) is a partner, a lawyer with comparable managerial authority, or a supervising lawyer who knows of misconduct by the other lawyer or nonlawyer and fails to take corrective action when the consequences of misconduct could be avoided or mitigated. Model Rules 5.1(c), 5.3(c).

Rule 5.2 governs the duties of subordinate lawyers. Under Rule 5.2(a) a subordinate lawyer is personally responsible for complying with the rules of professional conduct even if the lawyer is acting at the direction of a senior lawyer. However, Rule 5.2(b) recognizes that subordinate lawyers will often lack the judgment and experience of senior lawyers; this rule provides that a subordinate lawyer may rely on a senior lawyer's reasonable resolution of an arguable question of professional duty.[2] The Restatement contains similar principles.[3]

---

2. See Douglas R. Richmond, Subordinate Lawyers and Insubordinate Duties, 105 W. Va. L. Rev. 449 (2003).

3. Restatement (Third) of the Law Governing Lawyers §§11, 12.

There are, of course, differences between supervision of lawyers and non-lawyers. As the Restatement states:

> Supervision of a non-lawyer must often be more extensive and detailed than of a supervised lawyer because of the presumed lack of training of many non-lawyers on legal matters generally and on such important duties as those on dealing properly with confidential client information . . . and with client funds and other property . . . , which may be different from duties generally imposed in non-law practices and businesses.[4]

Supervision of nonlawyers generally requires at least an informal program of instruction in which nonlawyers are educated about basic ethical principles.[5] In addition, lawyers must monitor the activities of nonlawyers working under their supervision to assure compliance with standards of professional conduct.[6]

While lawyers may generally delegate legal work to nonlawyers provided the nonlawyers are properly supervised, nonlawyers may not perform certain legal activities. Court rules or state ethics advisory opinions often provide guidance on these prohibited activities. For example, the ABA Standing Committee on Paralegals has established Model Guidelines for the Utilization of Paralegals (1991).[7] The ABA guidelines provide that a lawyer may not delegate to a nonlawyer responsibility for establishing a client-lawyer relationship, the amount of a fee to be charged for legal services, or a legal opinion for a client. The ABA guidelines do not mention, but probably assume, that nonlawyers cannot appear in court on behalf of clients.[8]

The duty to supervise nonlawyers also applies to independent contractors, such as investigators employed by a firm. See Comment 1 to Model Rule 5.3, which specifically refers to investigators and independent contractors. In Formal Opinion 95-396, the ABA Committee on Ethics and Professional Responsibility addressed the applicability of Rule 4.2, which prohibits lawyers from communicating with represented parties, to the conduct of investigators employed by lawyers. The committee stated that lawyers have ethical responsibility for the conduct of investigators they employ both under Rule 5.3 and

4. Id. §11 cmt. *f.*
5. Id cmt. *c.*
6. See Spencer v. Steinman, 179 F.R.D. 484 (E.D. Pa. 1998) (lawyer sanctioned for failure to supervise paralegal who issued subpoena to nonparty without notice to parties); Mays v. Neal, 938 S.W.2d 830 (Ark. 1997) (lawyer disciplined for improper delegation and supervision of nonlawyers).
7. See http://www.abanet.org/legalservices/legalassistants/resource.html (visited Oct. 1, 2003). See also the Code of Ethics, Model Standards, and Guidelines published by the National Association of Legal Assistants http://www.nala.org/stand.htm#NALA %20Code%20of%20Ethics%20and%20Professional%20Responsibility (visited Oct. 1, 2003) and ABA, The Legal Assistant's Practical Guide to Professional Responsibility (1998).
8. See Pa. Bar Assn. Comm. on Legal Ethics and Prof. Resp., Ethical Considerations in the Use of Nonlawyer Assistants, Formal Op. 98-75 (nonlawyer assistants may not appear in court, conduct depositions, conduct real estate closings, or impersonate lawyers).

under Model Rule 8.4(a), which prohibits lawyers from knowingly violating a rule of professional conduct "through the acts of another":

> Since a lawyer is barred under Rule 4.2 from communicating with a repre-
> sented party about the subject matter of the representation, she may not circum-
> vent the Rule by sending an investigator to do on her behalf that which she is
> herself forbidden to do. Whether in a civil or a criminal matter, if the investigator
> acts as the lawyer's "alter-ego," the lawyer is ethically responsible for the investiga-
> tor's conduct.

Similarly, in Upjohn Co. v. Aetna Casualty & Surety Co.[9] Aetna's lawyers hired an investigation firm to interview former employees of Upjohn about the environmental damages that were the subject matter of the litigation. The investigators did not determine whether the former employees were represented by counsel, did not identify themselves as working for attorneys representing a client in litigation, and did not state the purpose of the interview. The court found that the investigators had misled Upjohn's former employees and had violated Rule 4.3. The court's order included suppression of evidence obtained through improper interviews.[10]

Supervision of lawyers is both easier and more difficult than supervision of nonlawyers. Supervision of lawyers is easier because they have received instruction in the rules of professional conduct while in law school. But supervision of lawyers, particularly senior attorneys, is difficult because of the status and power they possess. Nonetheless, partners in a firm must establish methods of supervision of all lawyers, including the most senior lawyers in the firm, both because it is an ethical obligation to have such procedures and because of the risks that members of the firm face if senior lawyers are allowed to practice without any degree of supervision.[11] For example, in Home Insurance Co. v. Dunn[12] the senior partner in a firm applied for renewal of the firm's malpractice coverage. The senior partner had embezzled client funds. His failure to reveal this information to the insurer entitled the insurer to void the entire malpractice policy, even against innocent members of the firm. Similarly, in Weeks v. Baker & McKenzie[13] the firm was held liable for $3.5 million in punitive damages in a sexual harassment case because the managing agents of

9. 768 F. Supp. 1186 (W.D. Mich. 1990).

10. Id. at 1212-1217. However, it appears that most courts will allow investigators employed by lawyers to pose as customers engaged in ordinary business transactions to obtain evidence necessary to support their client's claims. See, e.g., Gidatex, S.r.L. v. Campaniello Imports, Ltd., 82 F. Supp. 2d 119 (S.D.N.Y. 1999) (trademark infringement action).

11. See Susan Saab Fortney, Are Law Firm Partners Islands unto Themselves? An Empirical Study of Law Firm Peer Review and Culture, 10 Geo. J. Legal Ethics 271 (1997). See also Elizabeth Chambliss & David B. Wilkins, A New Framework for Law Firm Discipline, 16 Geo. J. Legal Ethics 335 (2003) (calling for an "alternative framework for law firm discipline based on the emerging role of in-house compliance specialists").

12. 963 F.2d 1023 (7th Cir. 1992).

13. 74 Cal. Rptr. 2d 510 (Ct. App. 1998, *review denied*).

the firm ignored for more than four years evidence that the partner had a propensity to engage in sexual harassment.[14] The court stated that when such conduct becomes known the firm may not continue to "employ the abusive employee without taking reasonable steps to prevent him or her from being or continuing to be abusive."[15]

While partners in a firm have an obligation to make sure that the firm has in place measures designed to give reasonable assurance that the conduct of lawyers and nonlawyers complies with the rules of professional conduct, partners may delegate aspects of this duty to other members of the firm, such as a managing partner or an executive committee.[16] However, a delegating partner remains responsible to take corrective action if the partner reasonably should know that the person or body to whom delegation has been made is not providing or implementing proper supervisory practices.[17]

Regulation of sexual relationships between lawyers and clients, other lawyers, and nonlawyers

Weeks v. Baker & McKenzie holds that a law firm has an obligation to take steps to prevent a partner from continuing to engage in sexual harassment of a secretary. Sexual relationships can develop between lawyers and clients and between lawyers and other lawyers. In addition, unlike *Weeks*, such relationships can be voluntary rather than coercive, although the possibility exists that a relationship that was at one time voluntary can become coercive. Should the bar or law firms attempt to regulate this broad range of possible sexual relationships in whole or in part? If so, how?

In 1992 the ABA Committee on Ethics and Professional Responsibility made the following observation about sexual relationships between lawyers and clients: "Although no detailed statistics are presently available to document the incidence of sexual relations between clients and their lawyers, there is information enough to substantiate both the existence and the seriousness of problems in this area."[18] While no specific Model Rule prohibited sexual relations between lawyers and clients at that time, the committee warned lawyers about the serious dangers such relationships posed.[19]

Model Rule 1.8(j), added in 2002, now provides: "A lawyer shall not have sexual relations with a client unless a consensual sexual relationship existed between them when the client-lawyer relationship commenced." The comments point out that sexual relations with clients present risks of exploitation, impairment of independent judgment, and loss of confidentiality. Because of these

14. Id. at 529.
15. Id. at 528.
16. Restatement (Third) of the Law Governing Lawyers §11, cmt. *d.*
17. Id.
18. ABA Comm. on Ethics and Prof. Resp., Formal Op. 92-364, at 1-2.
19. Id. at 9.

serious dangers, the rules prohibit such relationships even if the client consents. Comment 17. Sexual relationships that predate the formation of the attorney-client relationship are not improper because the risk of exploitation is reduced, but a lawyer involved in such a relationship must determine whether representation of the client would materially impair the lawyer's ability to represent the client under Rule 1.7(a)(2). Comment 18. If the lawyer represents an organization, the rule prohibits sexual relations with constituents of the organization who supervise, direct, or regularly consult with "that lawyer" concerning the organization's legal matters. Comment 19. Thus, if the general counsel of a corporation were to develop a relationship with a law firm partner who does not handle the corporation's legal work, no violation occurs.

A California statute provides that an attorney engages in misconduct if the attorney (1) expressly or impliedly conditions performance of legal services on the client's willingness to engage in sexual relations, (2) employs coercion or undue influence in entering into sexual relations, or (3) continues representation of the client if the sexual relationship would cause the lawyer to act incompetently or to otherwise prejudice the client's case.[20] The statute provides several exceptions, one of which is for sexual relationships that predate the formation of the client-lawyer relationship.[21]

B. Organizational Form, Departing Lawyers, and Sale of a Practice

1. Legal Structures

Traditionally, law firms have been organized as general partnerships. It was considered improper for lawyers to practice in corporations because law was a profession rather than a business. In addition, the corporate form of organization interfered with the personal nature of the client-lawyer relationship and improperly limited lawyers' liability to their clients.

Beginning in the 1960s state legislatures passed statutes making new forms of business organization available to professionals. The first wave of legislation involved adoption of professional corporation or association statutes, which were designed to give professionals the same tax benefits of corporate organization as were available to ordinary businesses. Many of the tax advantages of corporate organization for professionals, however, no longer exist.[22]

In the 1980s and 1990s, many state legislatures passed limited liability company (LLC) and limited liability partnership (LLP) statutes. Both LLCs and LLPs are taxed as partnerships rather than corporations, so their owners

---

20. Cal. Bus. & Prof. Code §6106.9(a).
21. Cal. Bus. & Prof. Code §6106.9(b).
22. Robert W. Hillman, The Impact of Partnership Law on the Legal Profession, 67 Fordham L. Rev. 393, 393 n.1 (1998).

avoid double taxation of income.[23] LLP statutes allow existing general partnerships to convert into LLPs. LLC statutes require the creation of a new legal entity. LLCs can have centralized management like a corporation, but most LLCs involving professionals will have decentralized management, like a general partnership.[24]

The most controversial aspect of LLCs and LLPs when used by lawyers is limitation of liability. State statutes vary in the degree to which they provide for limited liability. In assessing the scope of protection provided by a statute, it is useful to distinguish four forms of liability that lawyers may face: (1) personal liability for professional malpractice or for failure to supervise; (2) vicarious liability for malpractice or other wrongful acts committed by lawyers or nonlawyers with whom the lawyer practices; (3) personal liability for general business debts of the firm, such as leases or other contractual obligations; and (4) personal liability for torts unrelated to the practice of law.[25]

State supreme courts have the inherent power to regulate the practice of law.[26] They could refuse to allow lawyers to practice as LLCs or LLPs, although it appears unlikely that many courts will take this extreme step. Instead, courts could restrict the degree to which lawyers are entitled to limited liability or perhaps require lawyers to have adequate malpractice insurance coverage.[27] In all states lawyers remain liable for their personal malpractice, regardless of the form in which they practice.[28] A lawyer's attempt to limit liability for personal malpractice is unethical. See Model Rule 1.8(h)(1). Jurisdictions vary on the extent to which lawyers may receive the protections of limited liability for vicarious malpractice liability, for nonmalpractice torts, and for business debts.[29]

While not binding on state supreme courts, the ABA Committee on Ethics and Professional Responsibility has supported the use of limited liability forms of business organization by lawyers. In Formal Opinion 303 (1961), the committee ruled that lawyers could ethically practice in professional corporations or associations so long as (1) the lawyers rendering legal services to the client remained personally responsible to the client, (2) limitations on liability of

---

23. See 26 C.F.R. §301.7701-3, superseding Rev. Rul. 88-76, 1988-2 C.B. 360 (taxation of LLCs).

24. See Jennifer J. Johnson, Limited Liability for Lawyers: General Partners Need Not Apply, 51 Bus. Law. 85 (1995).

25. Id. at 91.

26. See Charles W. Wolfram, Inherent Powers in the Crucible of Lawyer Self-Protection: Reflections on the LLP Campaign, 39 S. Tex. L. Rev. 359 (1998).

27. Id. at 397-398.

28. Johnson, Limited Liability for Lawyers, 51 Bus. Law. at 104, 107.

29. See Henderson v. HSI Financial Servs., Inc., 471 S.E.2d 885 (Ga. 1996) (while court reserves right to regulate practice of law, lawyers may practice in professional corporations and receive same statutory benefits as other professionals, including limited liability for misconduct committed by other lawyers in firm in which lawyer was not personally involved), *overruling* First Bank & Trust Co. v. Zagoria, 302 S.E.2d 674 (Ga. 1983) (attorneys may practice in professional corporations, but they remain vicariously liable for misconduct of other lawyers practicing in firm).

other lawyers in the firm were made apparent to the client, and (3) prohibitions on the financial or managerial involvement of nonlawyers were maintained. In Formal Opinion 96-401, the committee extended the same analysis to LLPs. The committee advised that lawyers may ethically practice in LLPs provided the lawyer who renders services is personally responsible to the client and any restrictions on liability of other lawyers in LLPs are made apparent to clients. A majority of the committee decided that the use of the initials "LLP" is sufficient to put clients on notice of limitations of liability. The committee noted that while lawyers practicing in LLPs may take advantage of statutory provisions limiting their liability for conduct of others, they continue to have an ethical duty to supervise.[30] Despite support from the ABA and many courts of the use of limited liability forms of organization, a number of scholars have questioned the wisdom of the trend.[31]

2.   *Covenants Not to Compete and Other Restrictions on Departures from Firms*

Problem 7-2

Law Firm Organization and Breakups

a.   You and two other classmates have decided to form a limited liability company (LLC) when you leave law school. You have been discussing various provisions to include in the operating agreement. One issue deals with compensation if one of you decides to withdraw from the firm. What provision would you recommend to deal with this issue? Why? Be prepared to participate in a meeting in which you discuss the issue with your classmates.

b.   A lawyer who is a partner in a local firm has sought your advice about her plans to leave the firm and open her own practice. What issues would you raise with her and what advice would you give?

Read Model Rule 5.6 and comments.

In recent years the legal profession has witnessed a growth in lawyer turnover. Lawyers leave their old firms, join new firms, and open their own practices.[32]

---

30. For a criticism of Formal Opinion 96-401, see Susan Saab Fortney, Professional Responsibility and Liability Issues Related to Limited Liability Law Partnerships, 39 S. Tex. L. Rev. 399 (1998).

31. See generally Symposium, Ethical Obligations and Liabilities Arising from Lawyers' Professional Associations, 39 S. Tex. L. Rev. 205 (1998). See also Susan Saab Fortney, Seeking Shelter in the Minefield of Unintended Consequences—The Traps of Limited Liability Law Firms, 54 Wash. & Lee L. Rev. 717 (1997); Martin C. McWilliams, Jr., Limited Liability Law Practice, 49 S.C. L. Rev. 359 (1998).

32. See generally Robert W. Hillman, Hillman on Lawyer Mobility (2d ed. 1998).

Departures of lawyers from their firms[33] raise some difficult legal and ethical issues. Three issues have been of particular significance: First, to what extent may departing lawyers notify firm clients of their departure? Second, for those clients who decide to employ the departing lawyers, how are fees received in those cases allocated between the departing lawyers and the old firm? Finally, may firms impose restrictions through covenants not to compete or other agreements on the practice of departing lawyers?

First, with regard to the issue of notification of clients, both the departing lawyer and the firm must recognize that clients do not "belong" to either of them. Clients have the right to choose to have either the departing lawyer or the firm represent their interests.[34] Thus, both the firm and the departing lawyers have the right and the obligation to notify clients of their departure so that clients can decide whether the firm, the departing lawyer, or some other attorney will handle the case.[35] In Formal Opinion 99-414 the ABA committee advised that joint notification by the departing lawyer and the firm was the preferred approach. Recognizing that joint notice was infeasible if the departure was not amicable,[36] the committee concluded that departing lawyers could properly provide either in-person or written notice to their current clients—those clients for whom the lawyer was responsible or for whom the lawyer played a principal role in the firm's delivery of legal services—but not clients with whom the lawyer had little or no personal involvement.[37] The committee advised that the initial notice of the lawyer's anticipated departure to clients should conform to the following requirements:

1.   The notice should be limited to current clients.
2.   The departing lawyer should not ask the client to end its relationship with the firm but the notice could state the departing lawyer's availability to provide services.
3.   The notice must make clear that the client has the ultimate right to decide who will handle the client's matter.
4.   The departing lawyer must not disparage the former firm.[38]

The committee stated that the departing lawyer could provide the client with additional information, including a statement of whether the lawyer will be

---

33. The discussion that follows focuses on partners withdrawing from partnerships, but similar rules should apply to withdrawals by associates, see In re Smith, 843 P.2d 449 (Or. 1992) (en banc) (associate disciplined for breach of fiduciary duty in connection with departure from firm), and to withdrawals from PCs, LLCs, or LLPs, see Fox v. Abrams, 210 Cal. Rptr. 260 (Ct. App. 1985) (partnership principles apply to dissolution of professional corporation).

34. See ABA Comm. on Ethics and Prof. Resp., Formal Op. 99-414.

35. Id.

36. Id. at 6-7.

37. Id. at 2-4.

38. Id. at 5.

able to continue to represent the client at her new firm.[39] A departing lawyer may also ethically respond to requests for information from clients to assist them in making informed decisions about the handling of their cases.[40] Notification to clients, while important, is only one of many issues that arise when lawyers depart from their firms. Professor Robert Hillman, the leading authority on lawyer mobility, has offered a set of principles, drawn from decided cases and ethics opinions, to guide departing lawyers and their firms on these issues.[41]

While departing lawyers have a right and duty to inform current clients of their departure, these lawyers owe fiduciary duties to their former firms. A wide range of conduct can constitute a breach of fiduciary duty or violate other legal standards, such as unfair competition. Breach of fiduciary duty can lead to disciplinary action or civil liability. For example, in In re Smith,[42] during the two and one-half months prior to his departure from his firm Smith met secretly with 31 clients and had them sign individual retainer agreements. He did not open firm files for these cases while he was planning his departure. When he left the firm, he took with him the information relating to these cases as well as the files in other cases that he was handling. Smith immediately wrote to these clients informing them that they should contact his new office regarding their cases. The Oregon Supreme Court imposed a four-month suspension on the attorney for misconduct. The court pointed out that his conduct involved potential harm to clients because of his failure to open files. In addition, the court found that the attorney's conduct violated his fiduciary duties to his firm:

> Although there is no explicit rule requiring lawyers to be candid and fair with their partners or employers, such an obligation is implicit in the prohibition of DR 1-102(A)(3) [see Model Rule 8.4(c)] against dishonesty, fraud, deceit, or misrepresentation. Moreover, such conduct is a violation of the duty of loyalty owed by a lawyer to his or her firm based on their contractual or agency relationship.[43]

Departing lawyers who violate fiduciary obligations to their former firms can also be subject to civil liability to their firms.[44] In the leading case of

---

39. Id. at 6.

40. Id. See also Restatement (Third) of the Law Governing Lawyers §9(3) and cmt. *i*.

41. See Robert W. Hillman, Loyalty in the Firm: A Statement of General Principles on the Duties of Partners Withdrawing from Law Firms, 55 Wash. & Lee L. Rev. 997 (1998).

42. 843 P.2d 449 (Or. 1992) (en banc).

43. Id. at 452. See also In re Cupples, 952 S.W.2d 226 (Mo. 1997) (en banc) (attorney secreted client files prior to his withdrawal, removed files without appropriate consent from clients, and concealed from clients change in nature of representation).

44. Conversely, law firms can also be liable to partners for wrongful expulsion. See, e.g., Cadwalader, Wickersham & Taft v. Beasley, 728 So. 2d 253 (Fla. Dist. Ct. App. 1998).

Meehan v. Shaughnessy[45] the Supreme Judicial Court of Massachusetts held that departing partners owed fiduciary obligations to their remaining partners and that they could be held civilly liable for breach of those obligations. The court decided that the withdrawing partners did not breach their fiduciary obligations by making "logistical arrangements" (executing a lease, preparing a list of clients they expected to retain after their departure, and arranging for financing based on their expected clientele) for their new firm because fiduciaries may "plan to compete with the entity to which they owe allegiance," provided that they do not otherwise breach their fiduciary obligations.[46] The court found, however, that the withdrawing partners did breach their fiduciary duties by seeking and obtaining prior to their departure secret consents from clients to retain their services after they left the firm.[47] The court remanded for a determination of whether there was a causal connection between the departing lawyers' breach of fiduciary duty and damage to the partnership. It imposed the burden of proving lack of causation on the departing lawyers because of their breach of duty.[48]

Second, for those clients who decide to retain the services of the departing lawyer rather than the old firm, how are the fees from these cases allocated between the departing lawyer and her old firm? Traditionally, the withdrawal of a partner constituted a dissolution of the partnership.[49] Further, during the period in which a partnership's affairs were being wound up following a partner's withdrawal, the *no-additional-compensation rule* applied. This rule of partnership law meant that withdrawing partners were not entitled to additional compensation for services rendered in winding up partnership business.[50] Thus, under the no-additional-compensation rule, if a lawyer leaves a firm and a client that

---

45. 535 N.E.2d 1255 (Mass. 1989).

46. Id. at 1264.

47. Id. See Dowd & Dowd, Ltd. v. Gleason, 693 N.E.2d 358 (Ill. 1998) (firm states causes of action against departing lawyers for breach of fiduciary duty, tortious interference with prospective economic advantage, and civil conspiracy for allegedly soliciting clients prior to departure); Graubard Mollen Dannett & Horowitz v. Moskovitz, 653 N.E.2d 1179 (N.Y. 1995) (summary judgment denied in breach of fiduciary duty claim against departing lawyer who sought and received assurances from long-term client that client would continue to retain lawyer after lawyer left firm; court outlines poles of permitted and improper conduct).

48. 535 N.E.2d at 1267.

49. Under the Uniform Partnership Act, the withdrawal of a partner amounts to a dissolution of the partnership. Unif. Partnership Act §29 (1914). The partnership continues, however, during the period necessary to wind up partnership business. Id. §30. The Revised Uniform Partnership Act makes some fundamental changes in partnership law, one of which is that the "dissociation" of a partner does not necessarily result in the dissolution of a partnership. Unif. Partnership Act §801 and comment 1 (1997).

50. Unif. Partnership Act §18(f) (1914); Jewel v. Boxer, 203 Cal. Rptr. 13 (Ct. App. 1984) (postdissolution fees should be allocated to partners based on their respective partnership interests without any additional compensation for work done to complete cases); Fox v. Abrams, 210 Cal. Rptr. 260 (Ct. App. 1985) (rule of Jewel v. Boxer applies to professional corporations). The Revised Uniform Partnership Act reverses this rule, §401(h) (1997).

the lawyer was representing while a member of the firm elects to have the lawyer complete the client's case, the lawyer is *not* entitled to the full fee from that matter. Under partnership law, the fee would be paid to the old firm, and the lawyer would receive the lawyer's share pursuant to the partnership agreement or pro rata based on the lawyer's interest in the partnership in the absence of an agreement.[51] Note that departing partners also receive benefits from the no-additional-compensation rule because they are paid their partnership percentage in any cases that remain with the firm, even though they will not be performing any services on those cases.

Lawyers practicing in partnerships, LLCs, or LLPs are free to modify the no-additional-compensation rule by agreement.[52] Provided the agreement is reasonable and does not amount to an indirect attempt to restrict the departing lawyer's ability to practice law, the agreement should be enforceable.[53] In the absence of an agreement, a court has a choice on how to allocate fees between the departing lawyer and the old firm. The court could apply the no-additional-compensation rule[54] or it could allocate the fees between the departing lawyer and the old firm on a quantum meruit basis.[55]

Third, to what extent may firms impose restrictions on the practice of law by departing lawyers? In the business world, covenants not to compete are quite common and are legally enforceable provided the covenant protects a legitimate interest of the covenantee and provided the covenant is reasonable in its restrictions. Thus, a reasonable covenant by a seller of a business not to compete with the purchaser, or by an employee not to compete with his employer, is valid.[56]

By contrast to the "rule of reason" that governs covenants in general,

---

51. For a case that follows a different approach, awarding the firm from which the lawyers departed compensation on a quantum meruit basis, see In re L-Tryptophan Cases, 518 N.W.2d 616 (Minn. Ct. App. 1994).

52. Unif. Partnership Act §18 (1914) (rules are subject to any agreement between parties); Unif. Partnership Act §103 (1997). See Kelly v. Smith, 611 N.E.2d 118 (Ind. 1993) (recognizing no-additional-compensation rule but interpreting partnership agreement to provide that firm would be paid on quantum meruit basis for work done on cases where clients elected to retain departing lawyer).

53. See Barna, Guzy & Steffen, Ltd. v. Beens, 541 N.W.2d 354 (Minn. Ct. App. 1995), *review denied* (1996) (shareholder agreement requiring departing lawyer to turn over 50 percent of contingent fees received upheld). See also Miller v. Jacobs & Goodman, P.A., 699 So. 2d 729 (Fla. Dist. Ct. App. 1997), *review denied*, 717 So. 2d 533 (Fla. 1998) (employment agreement with associates that required them to pay 75 percent of fees that they receive after their departure not against public policy, but particular clause held to be invalid because it allowed firm to recover additional damages above 75 percent of fees).

54. See Hurwitz v. Padden, 581 N.W.2d 359 (Minn. Ct. App. 1998) (in absence of agreement, no-additional-compensation rule should be applied to LLC).

55. See Miller v. Jacobs & Goodman, P.A., 820 So. 2d 438 (Fla. Dist. Ct. App. 2002), *review denied*, 842 So. 2d 845 (Fla. 2003) (in subsequent proceedings to earlier decision cited in note 53, upholding trial court's allocation of 46 percent of fees received by departing associates to former firm using quantum meruit principles).

56. See Restatement (Second) of Contracts §188 (1979).

covenants by lawyers not to compete are per se invalid. See Model Rule 5.6(a). The rationale for this prohibition rests on the interests of clients. The client-lawyer relationship is personal and fiduciary in character. It is against public policy to deprive a client of the right to employ the lawyer of the client's choosing.[57] The rule also protects young lawyers from bargaining away their future employment prospects.[58] See Model Rule 5.6, cmt. 1.

The rule applies not only to direct restrictions on a lawyer's right to practice law but also to indirect restrictions as well. Partnership agreements typically provide for payments to a departing partner of that partner's share of the capital of the partnership and of any earned but uncollected fees. If a partnership agreement provides that a departing lawyer forfeits that partner's share of termination payments when the partner continues practice in competition with the partner's former firm, courts are likely to find such a provision invalid as an indirect restriction on the departing lawyer's right to practice law. In Cohen v. Lord, Day & Lord[59] the New York Court of Appeals ruled that a partnership agreement that conditioned payment of a departing partner's share of earned but uncollected revenues on noncompetition by the departing partner was unenforceable because of the ethical prohibition on restriction of practice by lawyers.[60] Other courts have agreed with this approach.[61]

In cases like *Cohen* the departing lawyers forfeited all payments from their former firms if they continued to practice law. Less restrictive provisions may be upheld. For example, clauses may be valid if they reasonably reduce the amount that a departing lawyer receives to reflect the financial impact on the firm of the lawyer's departure, or if they attempt to measure compensation due the firm for its quantum meruit contribution to cases in which clients elect

57. See Dwyer v. Jung, 336 A.2d 498 (N.J. Super. Ct. Ch. Div.) *aff'd*, 348 A.2d 208 (N.J. Super. Ct. App. Div. 1975). Note that in contrast to covenants not to compete between lawyers, covenants not to compete by other professionals are enforceable provided that they satisfy the reasonableness requirement. See, e.g., Karlin v. Weinberg, 390 A.2d 1161 (N.J. 1978).

58. See Robert M. Wilcox, Enforcing Lawyers' Noncompetition Agreements While Maintaining the Profession: The Role of Conflict of Interest Principles, 84 Minn. L. Rev. 915 (2000) (arguing for the need to address the tensions between the economic interests of the contracting lawyers and the professional obligations they owe to their clients).

59. 550 N.E.2d 410 (N.Y. 1989).

60. See also Denburg v. Parker Chapin Flattau & Klimpl, 624 N.E.2d 995 (N.Y. 1993) (financial disincentives objectionable on public policy grounds because they interfere with client's choice of counsel). But see Hackett v. Milbank, Tweed, Hadley & McCloy, 654 N.E.2d 95 (N.Y. 1995) (arbitrator's determination that clause requiring reduction of departing partner's payments to extent compensation from other sources exceeds $100,000 does not violate public policy because clause was "competition neutral").

61. See Jacob v. Norris, McLaughlin & Marcus, Inc., 607 A.2d 142 (N.J. 1992) (service termination agreement providing that departing partners could receive compensation only if they did not render services to clients of firm during one year following termination was unenforceable); Spiegel v. Thomas, Mann & Smith, P.C., 811 S.W.2d 528 (Tenn. 1991) (agreement that denied deferred compensation to withdrawing stockholder who continued to practice law was void as against public policy set forth in rules governing attorney ethics).

to retain the departing lawyer rather than continue to have the firm represent them.[62]

In Howard v. Babcock[63] the California Supreme Court rejected decisions from other states and held that a contractual provision imposing a reasonable cost on departing partners to compensate their former firm for their loss was enforceable. The court noted the change in economic climate in which law firms now operate. It expressed the view that such provisions could benefit clients by reducing the "culture of mistrust" among partners that can damage law firm stability.[64]

Model Rule 5.6 does contain an exception to the general prohibition against covenants not to compete among lawyers: Covenants not to compete are permissible when the lawyer is receiving "benefits upon retirement." The exception is not limited to full retirement by a lawyer because it would be unnecessary in such a situation. However, the exception applies only to bona fide retirement plans, not to disguised attempts to restrict competition on departure from a firm.[65] Comment 3 to Rule 5.6 states that the prohibition against covenants not to compete does not apply to the sale of a practice under Rule 1.17. One of the conditions of Rule 1.17 is that the selling lawyer must cease to engage in the practice of law (either in the geographical area or in the jurisdiction, as elected by the jurisdiction). See Model Rule 1.17(a).

3. Sale of a Law Practice

Traditionally, the profession has viewed the sale of "good will" of a law practice as unethical. ("Good will" refers to the value of the list of clients as opposed to the tangible assets of the practice.) In Formal Opinion 266 (1945), the ABA Committee on Professional Ethics and Grievances dealt with the issue as follows:

> A law firm has asked the opinion of the committee as to the ethical propriety of the purchase from the heirs or personal representatives of a deceased lawyer who had no partner, of his good will and practice, whether by payment of a lump sum or by an agreement to pay a stated percentage of the future receipts, gross or net, from his clients. . . .
>
> The good will of the practice of a lawyer is not, however, of itself an asset,

---

62. See Groen, Laveson, Goldberg & Rubenstone v. Kancher, 827 A.2d 1163 (N.J. Super. A.D. 2003) (distinguishing *Jacob*, note 61 above, and upholding provision of partnership agreement requiring departing partner to remit 50 percent of fees received to former firm).

63. 863 P.2d 150 (Cal. 1993).

64. Id. at 159.

65. See Donnelly v. Brown, Winick, Graves, Gross, Baskerville, Schoenebaum & Walker, P.L.C., 599 N.W.2d 677 (Iowa 1999). For other cases dealing with the retirement exception see Schoonmaker v. Cummings & Lockwood, 747 A.2d 1017 (Conn. 2000) and Neuman v. Akman, 715 A.2d 127 (D.C. 1998).

which either he or his estate can sell. As said by the Committee on Professional Ethics of the New York County Lawyers' Association in its Opinion 109 (October 6, 1943):

> Clients are not merchandise. Lawyers are not tradesmen. They have nothing to sell but personal service. An attempt, therefore, to barter in clients, would appear to be inconsistent with the best concepts of our professional status.

Aside from professionalism concerns, sale of good will of a practice raises various ethical problems. Professor Leslie Minkus summarizes these as follows:

(1) To turn over the selling lawyer's files to the purchasing lawyer would, in virtually all cases, constitute a violation of the selling lawyer's duty of confidentiality.

(2) To the extent that the purchase price is a function of fees earned by the purchasing lawyer, the agreement violates the proscription of sharing fees without sharing the effort and/or responsibility.

(3) To the extent that some or all of the purchase price is paid, not to the selling lawyer, but to his estate, the agreement violates the proscription against sharing of fees with laypersons.

(4) The fact that the value of the lawyer's practice will depend largely on the number of clients who follow his recommendation and retain the purchasing lawyer puts the selling lawyer in a position of direct conflict with his clients.

(5) The sale would almost inevitably involve the recommendation of employment of the purchaser in violation of the prohibition against the payment of money by a lawyer for the recommendation of him by another. Such recommendation might also be considered improper solicitation.

(6) Because most sales will include a covenant not to compete with the purchasing lawyer, the agreement arguably violates the prohibition against such covenants except as a condition to payment of retirement benefits by a lawyer's former firm.[66]

Some commentators argued, however, that the ethical concerns outlined above did not justify a total ban on the sale of the good will of law practices.[67] In addition, proponents of allowing sales of law practices made two arguments in favor of their position. First, they made a "consumer protection" case for permitting sales of practices. By allowing such sales, sole practitioners would have a financial incentive to provide for the orderly transition of their cases in the event of their illness, retirement, or death. The present prohibition on sales

---

66. Leslie A. Minkus, The Sale of a Law Practice: Toward a Professionally Responsible Approach, 12 Golden Gate U. L. Rev. 353, 356-357 (1982).

67. See Stephen E. Kalish, The Sale of a Law Practice: The Model Rules of Professional Conduct Point in a New Direction, 39 U. Miami L. Rev. 471 (1985); Minkus, The Sale of a Law Practice, 12 Golden Gate U. L. Rev. at 357-377.

removes that incentive. Second, proponents made a fairness case for allowing sales. They argued that the rules of ethics discriminated in favor of partners over sole practitioners.[68] Under the Code of Professional Responsibility and the original Model Rules of Professional Conduct, partners and their beneficiaries could receive retirement payments that included compensation for the good will value of their partnerships interests. See DR 2-107(B), 3-102(A), and Model Rule 5.4(a). Sole practitioners, however, could not capitalize on their good will by selling their interests.[69]

Note, however, that the traditional prohibition on the sale of a law practice did not actually prevent many sole practitioners from receiving compensation for their good will. Sole practitioners could ethically provide for the orderly transition of their practices after their retirement or death by entering into a partnership agreement in which the new partner could continue the practice while paying death or retirement benefits to the former partner.

In 1989 the California Supreme Court amended its Rules of Professional Conduct to allow lawyers to sell their practices, including good will, provided certain conditions for the protection of clients were met.[70] Following the lead of the California Supreme Court, the ABA amended the Model Rules of Professional Conduct at its February 1990 meeting to include Model Rule 1.17, permitting the sale of law practices.[71]

A number of states have adopted rules like ABA Model Rule 1.17 providing for sale of law practices.[72] In states that have not adopted such a rule, sale of the good will of a law practice is still unethical. Further, any resulting contract may be unenforceable because it violates public policy. For example, in O'Hara v. Ahlgren, Blumenfeld & Kempster[73] the Illinois Supreme Court held that the widow of a deceased attorney could not enforce a contract for the sale of her husband's law practice because the agreement violated the ethical prohibition on fee splitting.

---

68. But see James K. Sterrett II, The Sale of a Law Practice, 121 U. Pa. L. Rev. 306 (1972) (arguing that different treatment for sole practitioners, who were prohibited from selling their practices, and partners, who were permitted to receive retirement payments based on their partnership interests, was justified because the quality of legal service that clients may expect to receive from partners is higher than the quality that they can expect to receive from purchasers of practices). See also ABA Comm. on Prof. Ethics and Grievances, Formal Op. 266 (1945) (permissible to make arrangements for handling cases in event of emergency).

69. See generally Laurel S. Terry, Law Firms for Sale . . . The Rules Are Changing, 12 Pa. Law. 7 (June 1990) (on Westlaw).

70. Cal. R. Prof. Conduct 2-300.

71. For criticism of various aspects of Model Rule 1.17, see Scott M. Schoenwald, Model Rule 1.17 and the Ethical Sale of Law Practices: A Critical Analysis, 7 Geo. J. Legal Ethics 395 (1993).

72. See, e.g., N.Y. Code Prof. Resp. DR 2-111.

73. 537 N.E.2d 730 (Ill. 1989).

C.   Ancillary Businesses and Multidisciplinary Practice

1.   Ancillary Businesses

Rules of ethics have traditionally prevented lawyers from entering into partnerships (or corporations) with nonlawyers, including other professionals, when the activities of the entity will involve the practice of law. Canon 33 of ABA's 1908 Canons of Ethics provided as follows: "Partnerships between lawyers and members of other professions or nonprofessional persons should not be formed or permitted where any part of the partnership's employment consists of the practice of law." This prohibition was carried forward in DR 3-103(A) (partnerships) and DR 5-107(C) (corporations or associations) of the Code of Professional Responsibility and in Model Rules 5.4(b), (d). This restriction rested on two rationales: prevention of interference by nonlawyers with lawyers' independent professional judgment on behalf of their clients and concern about the unauthorized practice of law. See EC 3-8, EC 5-24, and Model Rule 5.4(b), cmt.[74]

In the 1980s some prominent law firms began offering to their clients a variety of nonlegal services. A 1991 survey[75] identified the following "ancillary business" activities by law firms:

15 engaged in lobbying, legislative services, or government relations
13 tax, investment, and financial consulting
13 international trade
4 environmental consulting
4 real estate brokerage and development
4 labor relations
3 economic research
3 public affairs
2 media relations

Some law firms provided these services directly by lawyers or nonlawyer employees of the firm. For example, many law firms have lawyers who engage in lobbying or other legislative activities. More typically, however, a firm creates a corporate or partnership subsidiary or affiliate to furnish ancillary services. The subsidiary form was particularly appealing when other professionals would be providing the ancillary services. Such professionals often demanded an ownership interest in any ventures in which they engaged. The rules of ethics, however, prohibited nonlawyers from owning an interest in a partnership or professional corporation that involved the practice of law. Thus, nonlawyer

---

74. See Wolfram, Modern Legal Ethics §16.2.1 at 879. See also Restatement (Third) of the Law Governing Lawyers §10.

75. Stephanie B. Goldberg, More Than the Law: Ancillary Business Growth Continues, 78-Mar A.B.A. J. 54 (1992) (citing a study done by Phyllis W. Haserot).

professionals could not own an interest in the law firm itself. The subsidiary form avoided this ethical problem because the subsidiary engaged only in nonlegal services.

Spurred by concerns expressed by Chief Justice Warren Burger about trends in the profession, in 1984 the ABA created a Commission on Professionalism (the Stanley Commission). The commission issued a report in 1986 finding the development of ancillary businesses by law firms "disturbing" and calling for further study of the trend.[76] Over the next eight years the ABA debated and oscillated on the regulation of ancillary business services by law firms. In 1991 the ABA House of Delegates in a narrow vote of 197 to 186 adopted a proposal from the ABA Section of Litigation's Task Force on Ancillary Business Activities. The proposal would have eliminated many of the nonlegal service activities that law firms had developed during the 1980s, even ones conducted through subsidiaries or affiliates, because of professionalism concerns.[77] In 1992 and then in 1994, the House of Delegates reversed itself and adopted Rule 5.7, which permits lawyers to participate in the delivery of "law-related services" and defines when lawyers are subject to the rules of professional conduct with regard to such services.[78]

Despite the adoption of Rule 5.7, the rules of professional conduct, as presently structured, create questionable distinctions with regard to business relationships between lawyers and nonlawyers.[79] Lawyers cannot participate in an entity in which nonlawyers have ownership interests or serve as officers or directors, if any of the activities of the organization constitute the practice of law. Model Rule 5.4. Lawyers may, however, employ nonlawyers to provide various law-related services. Lawyers cannot share legal fees with nonlawyers, but lawyers may pay nonlawyer employees salaries or bonuses, even though such payments come from legal fees. In addition, lawyers may participate with nonlawyers in business entities that provide law-related services. Nonlawyers may have ownership interests, even controlling interests, in such organizations. Whether the lawyer is subject to the rules of professional conduct with regard

76. ABA Commission on Professionalism, ". . . In the Spirit of Public Service": A Blueprint for the Rekindling of Lawyer Professionalism, 112 F.R.D. 243, 281 (1986).

77. See Dennis J. Block et al., Model Rule of Professional Conduct 5.7: Its Origin and Interpretation, 5 Geo. J. Legal Ethics 739, 764-777, 816 (1992) (Block was chair of the Litigation Section's task force).

78. Laws. Man. on Prof. Conduct (ABA/BNA), 10 Current Rep. 13 (1994). For a review and criticism of the ABA's original decision to prohibit ancillary business activities, see Ted Schneyer, Policymaking and the Perils of Professionalism: The ABA's Ancillary Business Debate as a Case Study, 35 Ariz. L. Rev. 363 (1993). Professor Gary Munneke offers a different perspective on the issue. He argues that rules of ethics prohibiting law firm diversification impede the ability of lawyers to compete in the market for professional services. Professor Munneke also claims that the rules may not withstand antitrust and First Amendment scrutiny. See Gary A. Munneke, Dances with Nonlawyers: A New Perspective on Law Firm Diversification, 61 Fordham L. Rev. 559 (1992). For a contrary view on the constitutionality of restrictions on ancillary business activities, see Block et al., Model Rule of Professional Conduct 5.7, 5 Geo. J. Legal Ethics at 811-814.

79. See 2 Hazard & Hodes, The Law of Lawyering ch. 45.

to such services is governed by Rule 5.7. This patchwork of inconsistent rules is unlikely to continue.

State supreme courts are, of course, free to adopt their own rules on the issue of ancillary businesses. (If a court does nothing, ancillary business activities would be largely unregulated when conducted through subsidiaries or affiliates. The Rules of Professional Conduct prohibit partnerships and fee splitting involving the practice of law with nonlawyers, but these have little impact on ancillary business activities conducted through related entities.)

2. Multidisciplinary Practice

Multidisciplinary practice (MDP) refers to a partnership, corporation, or other legal entity that includes lawyers and has as one of its purposes the providing of legal services to clients other than the MDP itself.[80] While lawyers cannot practice in MDPs in the United States under current rules of ethics, major accounting firms and other entities have formed MDPs in other countries where the rules are not as strict or as strictly enforced.[81]

In 1998 the president of the ABA created the Commission on Multidisciplinary Practice to make recommendations to the ABA on whether to relax the rules of professional conduct dealing with practice and fee splitting with nonlawyers so as to permit MDPs to develop in the United States. In 1999 the commission issued its report in which it recommended "a limited relaxation of the prohibitions against sharing legal fees and forming a partnership or other association with a nonlawyer when one of the activities is the practice of law."[82] Central to its recommendations was a proposed rule of professional conduct in which an MDP would be required to provide assurances that it would respect the professional obligations of lawyers.[83] At it July 2000 meeting, however, the

---

80. ABA Commn. on Multidisciplinary Practice, Report to House of Delegates app. A (1999).

81. Id. app. C, notes 8, 9. However, in 2002 the European Court of Justice held that PriceWaterhouseCoopers and Arthur Andersen could not incorporate two Dutch law practices as part of their efforts to form an MDP because of incompatibility between accounting and legal services. Case C-309/99, Wouters v. Algemene Raad van de Nederlandse Orde van Advocaten, 2002 E.C.R. I-01577. See also Laura Noroski, Note, New York's Controversial Ethics Code Changes: An Attempt to Fit Multidisciplinary Practice Within Existing Ethical Boundaries, 76 S. Cal. L. Rev. 483, 488-490 (2003) (discussing the international status of MDPs).

82. ABA Commn. on Multidisciplinary Practice, Report at app. C.

83. The literature on MDPs is vast. See Mary C. Daly, Choosing Wise Men Wisely: The Risks and Rewards of Purchasing Legal Services from Lawyers in a Multidisciplinary Partnership, 13 Geo. J. Legal Ethics 217 (2000); Daniel R. Fischel, Multidisciplinary Practice, 55 Bus. Law. 951 (2000) responded to by Lawrence J. Fox, Dan's World: A Free Enterprise Dream; An Ethics Nightmare, 55 Bus. Law. 1533 (2000); Business Law Symposium: Multidisciplinary Practice, 36 Wake Forest L. Rev. 1 (2001); Jonathan M. Ault Symposium: Professional Responsibility and Multi-Disciplinary Practice, 52 Case W. Res. L. Rev. 861 (2002); The Future of the Profession: A Symposium on Multidisciplinary Practice, 84 Minn. L. Rev. 1083 (2000).

ABA House of Delegates overwhelmingly rejected the Commission's proposal and adopted a sweeping resolution condemning the development of MDPs as inconsistent with the "core values" of the legal profession.[84]

Despite the ABA's repudiation of MDPs, development of economic relationships between lawyers and nonlawyers who provide law-related services is certain to continue.[85] Movement now seems to be in the direction of allowing contractual relationships between lawyers and nonlawyers by which both legal and law-related services can be offered to clients. In 2001 the Appellate Divisions of the New York Supreme Court adopted new rules on "cooperative business arrangements" allowing a lawyer or a law firm to "enter into and maintain a contractual relationship with a non-legal professional or non-legal professional service firm for the purpose of offering to the public, on a systematic and continuing basis, legal services performed by the lawyer or law firm, as well as other non-legal professional services."[86] Following New York's lead, in 2002 the ABA adopted amendments to Model Rule 7.2(b), which authorize lawyers to enter into nonexclusive reciprocal referral agreements provided clients are informed of the existence and nature of the agreement.[87]

━━━━━━━━━━━━━━━━━━━━ **Problem 7-3** ━━━━━━━━━━━━━━━━━━━━

Practicing with Nonlawyers

a. Helen Slater is a lawyer practicing in a relatively small but growing retirement community. For a number of years she had a general practice, but she has gradually come to specialize in legal problems of the elderly. In fact, she now refers to herself on her letterhead and business cards as an ElderLaw Attorney. As Helen has learned, senior citizens face a wide range of legal and nonlegal issues: estate planning, health care, financial advice, tax advice, and tax return preparation to name a few. Helen is considering expanding her practice so that she could offer a full range of services both legal and nonlegal to the elderly. What advice would you give her about the ethical issues involved in providing such services?

b. You practice in a state that has adopted Model Rule 7.2(b)(4). You limit your practice to commercial real estate matters. You are considering entering into referral arrangements with commercial real estate brokers and bankers. If you enter into such arrangements, what will you need to

---

84. See John Gibeaut, "It's a Done Deal": House of Delegates vote crushes chances for MDP, 86-SEP A.B.A. J. 92 (2000) (314-106 vote). For a history of the MDP debate, see Robert R. Keatinge, Multidimensional Practice in a World of Invincible Ignorance: MDP, MJP, and Ancillary Business after Enron, 44 Ariz. L. Rev. 717 (2002).

85. See John Gibeaut, Cash Boughs, 87-FEB A.B.A. J. 50 (2001) (discussing the development of law-related businesses since the ABA voted down MDPs).

86. See N.Y. Code of Prof. Resp. DR 1-107 [22 NYCRR §1200.5-c].

87. See Keatinge, Multidimensional Practice, 44 Ariz. L. Rev. at 748-750.

tell your clients to comply with the rule? Draft a provision for inclusion in your engagement agreement.

Read Model Rules 5.4, 5.7, 7.2, and comments.

D. Quality of Life in Law Firms

In a 1999 article, Professor Patrick Schiltz presented a disturbing portrait of the quality of life in American law firms.[88] Lawyers suffer from depression, anxiety, alcoholism, drug abuse, divorce, and suicide at rates significantly greater than the population as a whole.[89] Job dissatisfaction among lawyers is substantial and growing worse.[90] A RAND study of California lawyers found that only half of the members of the bar would become lawyers if they had to do it over again.[91] ABA surveys of lawyers conducted in 1984 and 1990 showed significant declines in job satisfaction:

> In the past six years, the extent of lawyer dissatisfaction has increased throughout the profession. It is now reported in significant numbers by lawyers in all positions—partners as well as junior associates. It is now present in significant numbers in firms of all sizes, not just the largest and the smallest firms.[92]

Job dissatisfaction varies depending on practice setting and is particularly acute in large firms.[93]

Professor Schiltz argues that overwork is the major cause of these problems. Various studies show substantial increases in the number of billable hours expected of attorneys. Thirty years ago associates typically billed 1,400 to 1,600 hours per year. In the mid-1980s, the norm for New York firms had increased to 1,800 hours per year. Today, most associates are expected to bill a minimum of 2,000 hours per year.[94] Professor Schiltz attributes the increase in the amount of work that lawyers do to the pervasive influence of money on the practice of law. Clients, senior partners, junior partners, and senior associates all have

---

88. Patrick J. Schiltz, On Being a Happy, Healthy, and Ethical Member of an Unhappy, Unhealthy, and Unethical Profession, 52 Vand. L. Rev. 871 (1999). See also Deborah L. Rhode, The Profession and Its Discontents, 61 Ohio St. L.J. 1335 (2000).

89. 52 Vand. L. Rev. at 874-881.

90. Id. at 881 n. 68. For a study showing different results, at least among Chicago lawyers, see John P. Heinz et al., Lawyers and Their Discontents: Findings from a Survey of the Chicago Bar, 74 Ind. L.J. 735 (1999).

91. 52 Vand. L. Rev. at 881 n. 69.

92. Id. at 883-884, quoting ABA, Young Lawyers Div., The State of the Legal Profession 1990 at 81 (1991).

93. 52 Vand. L. Rev. at 886.

94. Id. at 891.

financial interests in seeing that those below them work "inhumane hours, year after year."[95]

The impact of excessive work loads has a disproportionately negative effect on women. At a time in their lives when many women wish to consider starting a family, they are also faced with career demands of increasingly high levels of work and responsibility.[96]

African-Americans, Latinos, gays and lesbians continue to face discrimination.[97] The ABA has not adopted a Model Rule prohibiting discrimination in employment. Comment 3 to Model Rule 8.4, however, does condemn discrimination in representation of clients when such conduct is prejudicial to the administration of justice. Some states have gone further. For example, Rule 2-400 of the California Rules of Professional Conduct provides that

> In the management or operation of a law practice, a member shall not unlawfully discriminate or knowingly permit unlawful discrimination on the basis of race, national origin, sex, sexual orientation, religion, age or disability in:
>
> (1) hiring, promoting, discharging or otherwise determining the conditions of employment of any person; or
> (2) accepting or terminating representation of any client.

DR 1-102(A)(6) of the New York Code of Professional Responsibility is similar.[98]

Note that attorneys are entitled to legal protection against some forms of discrimination in employment. In Hishon v. King & Spalding[99] the Supreme Court held that a female associate who had been passed over for partnership stated a cause of action for sex discrimination against her firm under Title VII of the Civil Rights Act of 1964.

Possible solutions to quality of life issues facing law firms have come from several sources. Professor Deborah Rhode has outlined a bold program for institutional reform to deal with these issues.[100] Scholars working in other

---

95. Id. at 902. See also Susan Saab Fortney, Soul for Sale: An Empirical Study of Associate Satisfaction, Law Firm Culture, and the Effects of Billable Hour Requirements, 69 UMKC L. Rev. 239 (2000). For criticism of Schiltz's views, see Kathleen E. Hull, Cross-Examining the Myth of Lawyers' Misery, 52 Vand. L. Rev. 971 (1999); Mary A. McLaughlin, Beyond the Caricature: The Benefits and Challenges of Large-Firm Practice, 52 Vand. L. Rev. 1003 (1999).

96. 52 Vand. L. Rev. 915-916, n. 267.

97. David B. Wilkins & G. Mitu Gulati, Why Are There So Few Black Lawyers in Corporate Law Firms? An Institutional Analysis, 84 Cal. L. Rev. 493 (1996).

98. For discussions of the issue of discrimination in the profession, see American Bar Association, Miles to Go (2000) and American Bar Association, The Unfinished Agenda: Women and the Legal Profession (2001).

99. 467 U.S. 69 (1984).

100. See Deborah L. Rhode, Balanced Lives for Lawyers, 70 Fordham L. Rev. 2207 (2002). Professor Rhode's article represents part of her larger vision for the legal profession. See In the Interests of Justice: Reforming the Legal Profession (2000).

disciplines have provided insights for dealing with such problems.[101] In addition, market pressures from corporate clients are forcing many law firms to diversity.[102] While law firm diversity programs offer many potential benefits, some scholars have suggested that they may also extract a high price from the attorneys they are intended to assist, unless the initiatives are instilled with a real commitment to diversity.[103]

Problem 7-4

Discrimination and Related Issues

Your instructor will show a videotape or lead a panel discussion of a group of lawyers who practice in various types of law firms. The tape or the panel will focus on issues involving the quality of life in firms. Prepare a list of questions that you have about the quality of life in law firms.

Read Model Rule 8.4 and comments.

101. See Martin E.P. Seligman et al., Why Lawyers Are Unhappy, 23 Cardozo L. Rev. 33 (2001) (identifying causes of lawyer unhappiness and suggesting remedies based on field of "positive psychology").

102. See Jeffrey Ghannam, Making Diversity Work, 87-MAR A.B.A. J. 58 (2001) (innovative law firm programs to enhance diversity).

103. See J. Cunyon Gordon, Painting by Numbers: "And, Um, Let's Have a Black Lawyer Sit at Our Table," 71 Fordham L. Rev. 1257 (2003).

Table of Cases

Table of Model Rules, Restatements, and Other Standards

Table of Articles, Books, and Reports

Index